COMPLETE BOOK OF
LAW
SCHOOLS

The Princeton Review

COMPLETE BOOK OF
LAW SCHOOLS

2003 EDITION

ERIC OWENS

Random House, Inc.
New York
www.PrincetonReview.com

Princeton Review Publishing, L.L.C.
2315 Broadway
New York, NY 10024
E-mail: bookeditor@review.com

© 2002 by Princeton Review Publishing, L.L.C.

All rights reserved under International and Pan-American Copyright Conventions. Published in the United States by Random House, Inc., New York, and simultaneously in Canada by Random House of Canada Limited, Toronto.

ISBN: 0-375-76271-X

Editorial Director: Robert Franek
Production Editor: Julieanna Lambert
Production Coordinator: Scott Harris
Account Manager: Kevin McDonough
Editor: Erik Olson

Manufactured in the United States of America on partially recycled paper.

9 8 7 6 5 4 3 2 1

2003 Edition

ACKNOWLEDGMENTS

Eric Owens would like to say, "Thank you, John Katzman, for pretty much everything."

Thanks also to Bob Spruill for his LSAT expertise.

In addition, much thanks should go to Kevin McDonough for his focus, accountability, and inherent ability to stay in character to meet the fickle tastes of our office. High-fives to Michelene Rhymer and Jennifer Fallon for all of their help. Thanks also to Yojaira Cordero, Thacher Goodwin, Jose Guillermo, and Eric Ansler for their dedication to proper data collection and input.

As usual, to Chris Wujciak, what would we do without you? Thanks to Chris for his ever-present guidance and patience throughout the book pouring process.

A special thanks must go to our entire production team, Scott Harris, Vanessa Wanderlingh, and Julieanna Lambert. Your commitment, flexibility, and attention to detail are always appreciated in both perfect and crunch times.

CONTENTS

Preface	ix
All About Law School	1
Chapter 1 So You Want to Go to Law School...	3
Chapter 2 Applying to Law School	13
Chapter 3 The LSAT	21
Chapter 4 Writing a Great Personal Statement	33
Chapter 5 Recommendations	41
Chapter 6 Real Life Work Experience and Community Service	47
Chapter 7 Interviews	51
Chapter 8 Choosing a Law School	53
Chapter 9 Money Matters	59
Chapter 10 Career Matters	67
Chapter 11 Law School 101	71
Chapter 12 How to Excel at Any Law School	79
Chapter 13 How to Use This Book	87
Law School Profiles	97
Indexes	307
Alphabetical List of Schools	309
Law Program Name	311
Location	313
Cost	317
Enrollment of Law School	319
Average LSAT	321
Average Undergrad GPA	323
Average Starting Salary	325
Pass Rate for First-Time Bar	327
About the Author	329

PREFACE

Welcome to the *Complete Book of Law Schools*, The Princeton Review's truly indispensable guide for anyone thinking about entering the law school fray. This is not simply a reprint of the garden-variety fluff from each law school's admissions booklet. What we have attempted to do is provide a significant amount of essential information from a vast array of sources to give you a complete, accurate, and easily digestible snapshot of each and every law school in the country. Here you'll find a wealth of practical advice on admissions, taking and acing the Law School Admissions Test (LSAT), choosing the right school, and doing well once you're there. You'll also find all the information you need on schools' bar exam pass rates, ethnic and gender percentages, tuition, average starting salaries of graduates, and much more. Indeed, with this handy reference, you should be able to narrow your choices from the few hundred law schools in North America to a handful in no time at all.

Never trust any single source too much, though—not even us. Take advantage of all the resources available to you, including friends, family members, the Internet, and your local library. Obviously, the more you explore all the options available to you, the better decision you'll make. We hope you are happy wherever you end up and that we were helpful in your search for the best law school for you.

Best of luck!

ALL ABOUT LAW SCHOOL

CHAPTER 1
So You Want to Go to Law School . . .

Congrats! Law school is a tremendous intellectual challenge and an amazing experience. It can be confusing and occasionally traumatic—especially during the crucial first year—but the cryptic ritual of legal education will make you a significantly better thinker, a consummate reader, and a far more mature person over the course of three years.

The application process is rigorous, but it's not brutal. Here's our advice.

WHAT MAKES A COMPETITIVE APPLICANT?

It depends. One of the great things about law schools in the United States is that there are a lot of them and standards for admission run the gamut from appallingly difficult to not very hard at all.

Let's just say, for example, you have your heart set on Yale Law School, arguably the finest law school in all the land. Let's also say you have stellar academic credentials: a 3.45 GPA and an LSAT score in the 99th percentile of everyone who takes it. With these heady numbers, you've got a whopping 2 percent chance of getting into Yale, at best. On the other hand, with this same 3.45 GPA and LSAT score in the 99th percentile, you are pretty much a lock at legal powerhouses like Duke University School of Law and Boston College Law School. With significantly lower numbers—say, a 3.02 GPA and an LSAT score in the 81st percentile—you stand a mediocre chance of getting into top-flight law schools like Case Western or Indiana. But with a little bit of luck, these numbers might land you at George Washington or UCLA.

This is good news. The even better news is that there are several totally respectable law schools out there that will let you in with a 2.5 GPA and an LSAT of 148 (which is about the 36th percentile). If you end up in the top 10 percent of your class at one of these schools and have even a shred of interviewing skills, you'll get a job that is just as prestigious and pays just as much money as the jobs garnered by Yale grads. Honest to Christmas. Notice the important catch here, though: You *must* graduate in the top 10 percent of your class at so-called "lesser" schools. Almost every Yale Law grad who wants a high-paying job can land one.

Fascinating Acronyms
LSAC: Law School Admission Council, headquartered in beautiful Newtown, Pennsylvania
LSAT: Law School Admissions Test
LSDAS: Law School Data Assembly Service
ABA: American Bar Association

Ultimately, there's a law school out there, somewhere, for you. If you want to get into a "top-flight" or "pretty good" school, though, you're in for some pretty stiff competition. Unfortunately, it doesn't help that the law school admissions process is somewhat formulaic; your LSAT score and your GPA are vastly more important to the process than anything else about you. But if your application ends up in the "maybe" pile, your recommendations, your major, the reputation of your college alma mater, a well-written and nongeneric essay, and various other factors will play a larger role in determining your fate.

THE ADMISSIONS INDEX
The first thing most law schools will look at when evaluating your application is your "index." It's a number (which varies from school to school) that is made up of a weighted combination of your undergraduate GPA and LSAT score. In virtually every case, the LSAT is weighted more heavily than the GPA.

While the process differs from school to school, it is generally the case that your index will put you into one of three piles:

(Probably) Accepted. A select few applicants with high LSAT scores and stellar GPAs are admitted pretty much automatically. If your index is very, very strong compared to the school's median or target number, you're as good as in, unless you are a convicted felon or you wrote your personal statement in crayon.

(Probably) Rejected. If your index is very weak compared to the school's median or target number, you are probably going to be rejected without much ado. When admissions officers read weaker applications (yes, at almost every school every application is read) they will be looking for something so outstanding or unique that it makes them willing to take a chance. Factors that can help here include ethnic background, where you are from, or very impressive work or life experience. That said, don't hold your breath, because not many people in this category are going to make the cut.

Admission Decision Criteria
According to the Law School Admission Council (LSAC), there are no less than 20 factors that law schools might consider in deciding to admit or reject applicants. They are:
- *LSAT score*
- *Undergraduate grade point average (UGPA)*
- *Undergraduate course of study*
- *College attended*
- *Graduate work*
- *Improvement in grades and grade distribution*
- *Extracurricular activities in college*
- *Ethnic background*
- *Character and personality*
- *Letters of recommendation*
- *Writing skills*
- *Personal statement/essay*
- *Work experience and other relevant experience*
- *Community activities*
- *Motivation and reasons for studying law*
- *State of residency*
- *Difficulties overcome*
- *Pre-college preparation*
- *Past accomplishments and leadership*
- *That old catchall: anything else about you*

Well . . . Maybe. The majority of applicants fall in the middle; their index number is right around the median or target index number. Folks in this category have decent enough LSAT scores and GPAs for the school, just not high enough for automatic admission. Why do most people fall into this category? Because for the most part, people apply to schools they think they have at least a shot of getting into based on their grades and LSAT scores; Yale doesn't see very many applicants who got a 140 on the LSAT. What will determine the fate of those whose applications hang in the balance? One thing law schools often look at is the competitiveness of your undergraduate program. Someone with a 3.3 GPA in an easy major from a school where everybody graduates with a 3.3 or higher will face an uphill battle. On the other hand, someone with the same GPA in a difficult major from a school that has a reputation for being stingy with A's is in better shape. Admissions officers will also pore over the rest of your application—personal statement, letters of recommendation, resume, etc.—for reasons to admit you, reject you, or put you on their waiting list.

ARE YOU MORE THAN YOUR LSAT SCORE?

Aside from LSAT scores and GPAs, what do law schools consider when deciding who's in and who's out? It's the eternal question. On the one hand, we should disabuse you hidebound cynics of the notion that they care about nothing else. On the other hand, if you harbor fantasies that a stunning application can overcome truly substandard scores and grades, you should realize that such hopes are unrealistic.

Nonquantitative factors are particularly important at law schools that receive applications from thousands of numerically qualified applicants. A "Top Ten" law school that receives ten or fifteen applications for every spot in its first-year class has no choice but to "look beyond the numbers," as admissions folks are fond of saying. Such a school will almost surely have to turn away hundreds of applicants with near-perfect LSAT scores and college grades, and those applicants who get past the initial cut will be subjected to real scrutiny.

Waiting Lists
If a law school puts you on its waiting list, it means you may be admitted depending on how many of the applicants they've already admitted decide to go to another school. Most schools rank students on their waiting list; they'll probably tell you where you stand if you give them a call. Also, note that schools routinely admit students from their waiting lists in late August. If you are on a school's waiting list and you really, really want to go there, keep your options at least partially open. You just might be admitted in the middle of first-year orientation.

Less competitive schools are just as concerned, in their own way, with "human criteria" as are the Harvards and Stanfords of the world. They are on the lookout for capable people who have relatively unimpressive GPAs and LSAT scores. The importance of the application is greatly magnified for these students, who must demonstrate their probable success in law school in other ways.

CAN PHYSICS MAJORS GO TO LAW SCHOOL?

"What about my major?" is one of the more popular questions we hear when it comes to law school admissions. The conventional answer to this question goes something like "There is no prescribed, pre-law curriculum, but you should seek a broad and challenging liberal arts education, and yadda, yadda, yadda."

Here's the truth: It really doesn't matter what you major in. Obviously, a major in aviation or hotel and restaurant management is not exactly ideal, but please—we beg you!—don't feel restricted to a few majors simply because you want to attend law school. This is especially true if those particular majors do not interest you. Comparative literature? Fine. American studies? Go to town. Physics? No problem whatsoever. You get the idea.

Think about it. Because most would-be law students end up majoring in the *same* few fields (e.g., political science and philosophy), their applications all look the *same* to the folks in law school admissions offices. You want to stand out, which is why it is a good idea to major in something *different*. Ultimately, you should major in whatever appeals to you. By the way, of course, if you want to major in political science or philosophy (or you already have), well, that's fine too.

DOES GRAD SCHOOL COUNT?

Your grades in graduate school will not be included in the calculation of your GPA (only the UGPA, the undergraduate grade point average, is reported to the schools) but will be taken into account separately by an admissions committee if you make them available. Reporting grad school grades would be to your advantage, particularly if they are better than your college grades. Admissions committees are likely to take this as a sign of improvement with maturation.

Engineering and Math Majors Make Great Law Students
A disproportionate number of law students with backgrounds in the so-called "hard sciences" (math, physics, engineering, etc.) make very high grades in law school, probably because they are trained to think methodically and efficiently about isolated problems (which is what law students are supposed to do on exams).

ADVICE FOR THE "NONTRADITIONAL" APPLICANT

The term "nontraditional" is, of course, used to describe applicants who are a few years or many years older than run-of-the-mill law school applicants.

In a nutshell, there's no time like the present to start law school. It's true that most law students are in their early to mid-twenties, but if you aren't, don't think for a minute that your age will keep you from getting in and having a great experience. It won't. Applicants for full-time and part-time slots at all manner of law schools all over the fruited plain range in age from twenty-one to seventy-one and include every age in between. Some of these older applicants always intended to go to law school and simply postponed it to work, travel, or start a family. Other older applicants never seriously considered law school until after they were immersed in another occupation.

Part-time attendance is especially worth checking into if you've been out of college for a few years. Also, dozens of law schools offer evening programs—particularly in urban centers.

MINORITY LAW SCHOOL APPLICANTS

Things are definitely looking up. Back in 1978, according to figures published by the American Bar Association's Committee on Legal Education, over 90 percent of the law students in the ABA's 167 schools were white. In recent years, though, the number of nonwhites enrolled in law school has nearly doubled, from about 10 percent to approximately 19 percent. Taking an even longer view, figures have tripled since 1972, when minority enrollment was only 6.6 percent. These days, the American Bar Association and the legal profession in general seem pretty committed to seeking and admitting applicants who are members of historically under-represented minority groups.

Pre-Law Advisors Are Your Pals
It really pays to cozy up to them. Love them. Shower them with gifts. They are an invaluable source of insight and information before, during, and even after the law school admission process. If you are thinking about law school, do yourself a favor and introduce yourself to a pre-law advisor at your undergraduate institution just as soon as possible.

Already graduated? Don't be bashful about calling a pre-law advisor at the old alma mater. The odds are, they'll still be more than happy to help you out.

MINORITY REPRESENTATION
Here is a sampling of law schools around the United States that boast notably high minority representation among students.

School Name	% Minority
Arizona State University	28
City University of New York	43
Columbia University	36
George Washington University	31
Loyola Marymount University	37
New College of California	43
North Carolina Central University	63
Northwestern University	30
Santa Clara University	30
Southwestern University	34
St. Mary's University	46
St. Thomas University	46
Stanford University	32
Texas Southern University	77
University of California, Davis	32
University of California, Hastings	33
University of California, Los Angeles	28
University of Florida	28
University of Miami	30
University of New Mexico	36
University of Pennsylvania	31
University of San Francisco	32
University of Southern California	40
University of the District of Columbia	74
University of West Los Angeles	32
Western State University	31
Yale University	30

WOMEN IN LAW SCHOOL

During the past decade, the number of women lawyers has escalated rapidly, and women undeniably have become more visible in the uppermost echelons of the field. Two women sit on the United States Supreme Court, for instance. Also, according to statistics compiled by the American Bar Association (ABA), about 12 percent of all law firm partners are women and women have comprised about 30 percent of all federal judicial appointments over the last eight years.

More and more women are going to law school as well. At a solid majority of the ABA-approved law schools in the United States, the percentage of women in the student population is 45 percent or higher, and women make up well over half of the students at a handful of schools.

Gender discrimination certainly lingers here and there, though. You might want to check certain statistics on the law schools you are interested in, such as the percentage of women on law review and the percentage of female professors who are tenured or on track to be tenured. (Nationally, 19 percent of all full law school professors are women.) Also, go to each law school and talk with female students and female professors about how women are treated at that particular school. Finally, see if the school has published any gender studies about itself. If it has, you obviously ought to check them out, too.

__Making Law Review__
Every law school has something called a law review, which is an academic periodical produced and edited by law students. It contains articles about various aspects of law—mostly written by professors. While some schools sponsor more than one law review, there is generally one that is more prestigious than all the others. In order to "make" law review, you will have to finish the all-important first year at (or very, very near) the top of your class or write an article that will be judged by the existing members of the law review. You might have to do both. Making law review is probably the easiest way to guarantee yourself a job at a blue-chip firm, working for a judge, or in academia. In all honesty, it is a credential you will proudly carry for the rest of your life.

PROPORTION OF FEMALE STUDENTS

Here is a sampling of law schools around the United States and Canada that boast notably high percentages of female students.

School Name	% Female
Boston University	53
California Western	55
City University of New York	60
Emory University	54
Golden Gate University	61
Hamline University	56
Loyola University New Orleans	57
New College of California	55
North Carolina Central University	61
Northeastern University	60
Pace University	60
Seattle University	57
Southwestern University	54
Stetson University	55
Suffolk University	54
Union University	53
University of British Columbia	54
University of California, Davis	57
University of California, Hastings	53
University of Colorado	54
University of Maryland	55
University of New Mexico	59
University of San Francisco	58
University of the District of Columbia	64
University of Victoria	58
University of Windsor	57

Required Reading
These two law review articles plus one study discuss the difficulties women face in law school and the legal profession. Check them out.

Lani Guinier, "Becoming Gentlemen: Women's Experiences at One Ivy League Law School," University of Pennsylvania Law Review, November 1994.

Catherine Weiss and Louise Melling, "The Legal Education of Twenty Women," Stanford Law Review, May 1988.

Deborah L. Rhode, "The Unfinished Agenda: Women and the Legal Profession," ABA Commission on Women in the Profession, 2001.

CHAPTER 2
APPLYING TO LAW SCHOOL

Our advice: Start early. The LSAT alone can easily consume 80 or more hours of prep time, and a single application form might take as much as 30 hours if you take great care with the essay questions. Don't sabotage your efforts through last-minute sloppiness or let this already-annoying process become a gigantic burden.

WHEN TO APPLY

Yale Law School's absolute final due date is February 15, but Loyola University Chicago's School of Law will receive your application up to April 1. There is no pattern. However, the longer you wait to apply to a school, regardless of its deadline, the worse your chances of getting into that school may be. No efficient admissions staff is going to wait for all the applications before starting to make their selections.

If you're reading this in December and hope to get into a law school for the fall but haven't done anything about it, you're in big trouble. If you've got an LSAT score you are happy with, you're in less trouble. However, your applications will get to the law schools after the optimum time and, let's face it, they may appear a bit rushed. The best way to think about applying is to start early in the year, methodically take care of one thing at a time, and *finish by December*.

Early Admissions Options. A few schools have "early admissions" options, so you may know by December if you've been accepted (for instance, New York University's early admission deadline is on or about October 15). Early admission is a good idea for a few reasons. It can give you an indication of what your chances are at other schools. It can relieve the stress of waiting until April to see where you'll be spending the next three years of your life. Also, it's better to get waitlisted in December than April (or whenever you would be notified for regular admission); if there is a "tie" among applicants on the waiting list, they'll probably admit whoever applied first. Of course, not every school's early admission option is the same (and many schools don't even have one).

Rolling Admissions. Many law schools evaluate applications and notify applicants of admission decisions continuously over the course of several months (ordinarily from late fall to midsummer). Obviously, if you apply to one of these schools, it is vital that you apply as early as possible because there will be more places available at the beginning of the process.

Applying on Computer. More and more law schools are allowing applicants to submit applications via the Internet, though you will still find some that want their applications typed. While typing is not exactly rocket science, it is a pain in the neck. A few services can make the process easier. The Princeton Review's very own PrincetonReview.com will allow you to fill out law school applications electronically for free on its site. The LSACD, a CD-ROM/online service (215-968-1001 or www.lsac.org; $59/$54 respectively), has a searchable database and applications to ABA-approved schools.

> *Looking for a Typewriter?*
> *Most libraries will have one you can use for free. Almost all law libraries have typewriters available if you ask nicely.*

LAW SCHOOL ADMISSIONS COUNCIL: THE LAW SCHOOL APPLICATION MAFIA

In addition to single-handedly creating and administering the LSAT, an organization called the Law School Admissions Council (LSAC) maintains a stranglehold on communication between you and virtually every law school in the United States. It runs the Law School Data Assembly Service (LSDAS), which provides information (in a standard format) on applicants to the law schools. They—not you—send your grades, your LSAT score, and plenty of other information about you to the schools. You'll send only your actual applications directly to the law schools themselves. Oh, by the way, the fee for this service is almost $100 of your hard-earned money plus $9 (or more) every time you want LSDAS to send a report about you to an additional law school.

THE BIG HURDLES IN THE APPLICATION PROCESS: A BRIEF OVERVIEW

Take the LSAT. The Law School Admission Test is a roughly three-and-a-half-hour multiple-choice test used by law schools to help them select candidates. The LSAT is given in February, June, October (or, occasionally, late

September), and December of each year. It's divided into five multiple-choice sections and one (completely useless) writing sample. All ABA-approved and most non-ABA-approved law schools in the United States and Canada require an LSAT score from each and every applicant.

Register for LSDAS. You can register for the Law School Data Assembly Service at the same time you register to take the LSAT; all necessary forms are contained in the *LSAT and LSDAS Registration Information Book* (hence the name).

Get applications from six or seven schools. Why so many? Better safe than sorry. Fairly early—like in July—select a couple "reach" schools, a couple schools to which you've got a good shot at being accepted, and a couple "safety" schools where you are virtually assured of acceptance. Your safety school—if you were being realistic—will probably accept you pretty quickly. It may take a while to get a final decision from the other schools, but you won't be totally panicked because you'll know your safety school is there for you. If, for whatever reason, your grades or LSAT score are extremely low, you should apply to several safety schools.

Write your personal statement. With any luck, you'll only have to write one personal statement. Many, many schools will simply ask you the same question: basically, "Why do you want to obtain a law degree?" However, you may need to write several personal statements and essays—which is one more reason you need to select your schools fairly early.

Obtain two or three recommendations. Some schools will ask for two recommendations, both of which must be academic. Others want more than two recommendations and want at least one to be from someone who knows you outside traditional academic circles. As part of your LSDAS file, the LSAC will accept up to three letters of recommendation on your behalf, and they will send them to all the schools to which you apply. This is one of the few redeeming qualities of the LSAC. The last thing the writers of your recommendations are going to want to do is sign, package, and send copies of their letters all over the continent.

LSDAS Fees

LSDAS Subscription Fee: $99 (This buys you an LSDAS "subscription" for 12 months and a single, solitary report to one law school.)

LSDAS Law School Reports: $10 (when you initially subscribe)

Additional LSDAS Law School Reports: $12 (after you subscribe)

A Legal Education: Priceless

Update/create your resume. Most law school applicants ask that you submit a resume. Make sure yours is up-to-date and suitable for submission to an academic institution. Put your academic credentials and experience first—no matter what they are. This is just a supplement to the rest of the material; it's probably the simplest part of the application process.

Get your academic transcripts sent to LSDAS. When you subscribe to LSDAS, you must request that the registrar at every undergraduate, graduate, and professional school you ever attended send an official transcript to Law Services. Don't even think about sending your own transcripts anywhere; these people don't trust you any farther than they can throw you. *Make these requests in August.* If you're applying for early decision, start sending for transcripts as early as May. Law schools require complete files before making their decisions, and LSDAS won't send your information to the law schools without your transcripts. Undergraduate institutions can and will screw up and delay the transcript process—even when you go there personally and pay them to provide your records. Give yourself some time to fix problems should they arise.

Write any necessary addenda. An addendum is a brief explanatory letter written to explain or support a "deficient" portion of your application. If your personal and academic life has been fairly smooth, you won't need to include any addenda with your application. If, however, you were ever on academic probation, arrested, or if you have a low GPA, you may need to write one. Other legitimate addenda topics are a low/discrepant LSAT score, DUI/DWI suspensions, or any "time gap" in your academic or professional career.

An addendum is absolutely not the place to go off on polemics about the fundamental unfairness of the LSAT or how that evil campus security officer was only out to get you when you got arrested. If, for example, you have taken the LSAT two or three times and simply did not do very well, even after spending time and money preparing with a test prep company or a private tutor, merely tell the admissions committee that you worked diligently to achieve

---

Fee Waivers
Taking the LSAT, subscribing to LSDAS, and applying to law schools at $50 a pop will cost you an arm and a leg (though these costs are but a drop in the bucket compared to the amount of money you are about to spend on your law school education). The LSAC and most law schools offer fee waiver programs. If you are financially strapped and are accepted into the LSAC program, you get to take the LSAT and subscribe to LSDAS for free. You also get three LSDAS law school reports and a complimentary book of three previously administered LSATs.

You can request a fee waiver packet from Law Services at 215-968-1001, or write to them at:
Law Services
Attn: Fee Waiver Packet
Box 2000
661 Penn Street
Newtown, PA 18940-0998

a high score. Say you explored all possibilities to help you achieve that goal. Whatever the case, lay out the facts, but let them draw their own conclusions. Be brief and balanced. Be fair. Do not go into detailed descriptions of things. Explain the problem and state what you did about it. This is no time to whine.

Send in your seat deposit. Once you are accepted at a particular school, that school will ask you to put at least some of your money where your mouth is. A typical fee runs $200 or more. This amount will be credited to your first-term tuition once you actually register for classes.

Do any other stuff. You may find that there are other steps you must take during the law school application process. You may request a fee waiver, for example. Make extra-special sure to get a copy of the LSAC's *LSAT/LSDAS Registration and Information Book*, which is unquestionably the most useful tool in applying to law school. It has the forms you'll need, a sample LSAT, admissions information, the current Law Forum schedule, and sample application schedules.

The Princeton Review — LAW SCHOOL APPLICATION CHECKLIST
(suitable for framing)

January	• **Take a practice LSAT.** Do it at a library or some place where you won't be interrupted. Also, take it all at once.
February	• **Investigate LSAT prep courses.** If you don't take one with The Princeton Review, do *something*. Just as with any test, you'll get a higher score on this one if you prepare for it first.
March	• **Obtain an *LSAT/LSDAS Registration and Information Book*.** The books are generally published in March of each year. You can get one at any law school, by calling the LSAC at 215-968-1001, or by stopping by The Princeton Review office nearest you.
April	• **Register for the June LSAT.** • **Begin an LSAT prep course.** At the very, very least, use some books or software.
May	• **Continue your LSAT prep.**
June	• **Take the LSAT.** If you take the test twice, most law schools will consider just your highest LSAT score. Some, however, will average them. Your best bet is to take it once, do exceedingly well, and get it out of your hair forever.
July	• **Register for LSDAS.** • **Research law schools.**
August	• **Obtain law school applications.** You can call or write, but the easiest and cheapest way to get applications sent to you is via the Internet. • **Get your undergraduate transcripts sent to LSDAS.** Make sure to contact the registrar at each undergraduate institution you attended.
September	• **Write your personal statements.** Proofread them. Edit them. Edit them again. Have someone else look them over for all the mistakes you missed. • **Update your resume.** Or create a resume if you don't have one. • **Get your recommendations in order.** You want your recommenders to submit recommendations exactly when you send your applications (in October and November).
October	• **Complete and send early decision applications.**
November	• **Complete and send all regular applications.**
December	• **Chill.** • **Buy holiday gifts.** • **Make plans for New Year's.**

CHAPTER 3
THE LSAT

Celebrity Lawyers
John Grisham, writer
Geraldo Rivera, talk-show host
Paul Tagliabue, NFL commissioner
Richard Nixon, U.S. president
Cole Porter, musician

As you may know, we at The Princeton Review are pretty much disgusted with most of the standardized tests out there. They make us a lot of money, of course, and we like that, but they are hideously poor indicators of anything besides how well you do on that particular standardized test. They are certainly not intelligence tests. The LSAT is no exception. It is designed to keep you out of law school, not facilitate your entrance into it. For no good reason we can think of, this 101-question test is *the single most important factor in all of law school admissions*, and, at least for the foreseeable future, we're all stuck with it.

Unfortunately, with the possible exception of the MCAT (for medical school), the LSAT is the toughest of all the standardized tests. Only 23–24 of the 101 questions have a "correct" answer (Logic Games), as opposed to Arguments and Reading Comprehension, where you must choose the elusive "best" answer. As ridiculous as they are, the GMAT, GRE, SAT, MCAT, and ACT at least have large chunks of math or science on them. There are verifiably correct answers on these tests, and occasionally you even have to know something to get to them. *Only the LSAT requires almost no specific knowledge of anything whatsoever, which is precisely what makes it so difficult.* The only infallible way to study for the LSAT is to study the LSAT itself. The good news is that *anybody* can get significantly better at the LSAT by working diligently at it. In fact, your score will increase exponentially in relation to the amount of time and work you put into preparing for it.

HOW IMPORTANT IS THE LSAT?

The LSAT figures very prominently in your law school application, especially if you've been out of school for a few years. Some law schools won't even look at your application unless you achieve a certain score on your LSAT. By the way, each score you receive is valid for five years after you take the test.

LSAT STRUCTURE

Section Type	Sections	Questions Per Section	Time
Logical Reasoning (Arguments)	2	24-26	35 minutes
Analytical Reasoning (Games)	1	23-24	35 minutes
Reading Comprehension	1	26-28	35 minutes
Experimental	1	????	35 minutes
Writing Sample	1	1	30 minutes

Each test has 101 questions. Neither the experimental section nor the writing sample counts toward your score. The multiple-choice sections may be given in any order, but the writing sample is always administered last. The experimental section can be any of the three types of multiple-choice sections and is used by the test writers to test out new questions on your time and at your expense.

Not only is the writing sample not scored, but it is also unlikely that anyone other than you will ever read it. However, the law schools to which you apply will receive a copy of your writing sample, so you should definitely do it. A blank page would stand out like a sore thumb, and you wouldn't want the folks in the admissions office to think you were some kind of revolutionary.

WHAT'S ON THE LSAT, EXACTLY?

We asked the experts in the LSAT Course Division of The Princeton Review for the lowdown on the various sections of the LSAT. Here's what they had to say:

Analytical Reasoning: If you've ever worked logic problems in puzzle books, then you're already somewhat familiar with the Analytical Reasoning section of the LSAT. The situations behind these problems—often called "games" or "logic games"—are common ones: deciding in what order to interview candidates, or assigning employees to teams, or arranging dinner guests around a table. The arrangement of "players" in these games is governed by a set of rules you must follow in answering the questions. Each Analytical Reasoning section is made up of four games, with five to seven questions each. Questions may ask you to find out what must be true under the rules or what could be true under the rules, they may add a new condition that applies to just that question, they may ask you to count the number of possible arrangements under the stated conditions. These questions are difficult mostly because of the time constraints under which they must be worked; very few test-takers find themselves able to complete the twenty-three or twenty-four questions on this section in the time allotted.

Logical Reasoning: Because there are two scored sections of them, Logical Reasoning questions on the LSAT are the most important to your score. Each Logical Reasoning—sometimes called "arguments"—question is made up of a short paragraph, often written to make a persuasive point. These small arguments are usually written to contain a flaw—some error of reasoning or unwarranted assumption that you must identify in order to answer the question successfully. Questions may ask you to draw conclusions from the stated information, to weaken or strengthen the argument, to identify its underlying assumptions, or to identify its logical structure or method. There are most often a total of fifty or fifty-one argument questions between the two sections—roughly half of the scored questions on the LSAT.

Registering for the LSAT
You can register for the LSAT by mail, over the phone, or on the Internet. To register by mail, you will need a copy of the Registration and Information Bulletin, which you may either request from Law Services or pick up from your pre-law advisor. You may also register for the LSAT online at www.lasc.org. The LSAT fee is currently a whopping $103; if you're late, it's an extra $54. To avoid late fees, mail your registration form at least six weeks—six weeks—before the test. Also, by registering early, you are more likely to be assigned your first choice of test center.
You can reach the Law School Admissions Council at:
   Phone: 215-968-1001
   www.lsac.org
   lsacinfo@lsac.org

Reading Comprehension: Reading Comprehension is familiar to anyone who's taken the SAT or virtually any other standardized test. The Reading Comprehension section is made up of four passages, each roughly 500 words in length, with six to eight associated questions. The material of these reading passages is often obscure or esoteric, but answering the questions correctly doesn't depend on any specialized knowledge. Questions may ask you to identify the passage's main idea, to identify descriptions of its structure or purpose, to evaluate the purpose of specific examples or contentions, or to understand its argumentation. Although the form of this section is familiar, the language and length of passages, questions, and answer choices make it challenging; like the Analytical Reasoning section, the Reading Comprehension section is for many test-takers simply too long to finish in the time allotted.

You really ought to prep for this test. You certainly don't have to take The Princeton Review's course (or buy our book, *Cracking the LSAT*, or sign up for our awesome distance learning course), as much as we'd obviously like it. There are plenty of books, software products, courses, and tutors out there. The evil minions who make the LSAT will gleefully sell you plenty of practice tests as well. The key is to find the best program for you. Whatever your course of action, though, make sure you remain committed to it so you can be as prepared as possible when you take the actual test.

WHEN SHOULD YOU TAKE THE LSAT?
Here is a quick summary of test dates along with some factors to consider for each.

JUNE
The June administration is the only time the test is given on a Monday afternoon. If you have trouble functioning at the ordinary 8 A.M. start-time, June may be a good option. Furthermore, taking the LSAT in June frees up your summer and fall to research schools and complete applications. On the other hand, if you are still in college, you'll have to balance LSAT preparation with academic course work and, in some cases, final exams. Check your exam schedules before deciding on a June LSAT test date.

OCTOBER/SEPTEMBER

The October test date (which is sometimes in late September) will allow you to prepare for the LSAT during the summer. This is an attractive option if you are a college student with some free time on your hands. Once you've taken the LSAT, you can spend the remainder of your fall completing applications.

DECEMBER

December is the last LSAT administration that most competitive law schools will accept. If disaster strikes and you get a flat tire on test day, you may end up waiting another year to begin law school. December testers also must balance their time between preparing for the LSAT and completing law school applications. Doing so can make for a hectic fall, especially if you're still in college. You should also remember that, while a law school may accept December LSAT scores, taking the test in December could affect your chances of admission. Many law schools use a rolling admissions system, which means that they begin making admissions decisions as early as mid-October and continue to do so until the application deadline. Applying late in this cycle could mean that fewer spots are available. Check with your potential law schools to find out their specific policies.

FEBRUARY

If you want to begin law school in the following fall, the February LSAT will be too late for most law schools. However, if you don't plan to begin law school until the *next* academic year, you can give yourself a head start on the entire admissions process by taking the LSAT in February, then spending your summer researching schools and your fall completing applications.

| UPCOMING LSAT TEST DATES ||||
TEST DATE	Registration Deadline	Late Registration Periods by Mail	Registration by Phone/Online
December 7, 2002	November 6	November 7–13	November 7–13
February 8, 2003	January 8	January 9–15	January 7–13

HOW IS THE LSAT SCORED?

LSAT scores currently range from 120 to 180. Why that range? We have no idea. The following table indicates the percentile rating of the corresponding LSAT scores between 141 and 180. This varies slightly from test to test.

This is the case because your raw score (the number of questions you answer correctly) doesn't always produce the same scaled score as previous LSATs. What actually happens is that your raw score is compared to that of everyone else who took the test on the same date you did. The LSAC looks at the scales from every other LSAT given in the past three years and "normalizes" the current scale so that it doesn't deviate widely from those scaled scores in the past.

LSAT Score	Percent Below	LSAT Score	Percent Below
180	99.9	160	83.1
179	99.9	159	80.6
178	99.9	158	77.4
177	99.9	157	74.2
176	99.8	156	70.7
175	99.7	155	67.1
174	99.5	154	63.3
173	99.3	153	59.3
172	99.1	152	55.2
171	98.7	151	51.5
170	98.2	150	47.3
169	97.5	149	43.2
168	97.0	148	39.3
167	95.9	147	35.6
166	94.8	146	32.2
165	93.5	145	28.4
164	91.9	144	25.5
163	90.0	143	22.2
162	88.2	142	19.6
161	85.7	141	16.9

Most law schools will consider just your highest LSAT score, rather than average them, which is what they used to do.

A GOOD LSAT SCORE
A good score on the LSAT is the score that gets you into the law school you want to attend. Remember that a large part of the admissions game is the formula of your UGPA (undergraduate grade point average) multiplied by your LSAT score. Chances are, you are at a point in life where your UGPA is pretty much fixed (if you're reading this early in your college career, start getting very good grades pronto), so the only piece of the formula you can have an impact on is your LSAT score.

A LITTLE IMPROVEMENT GOES A LONG WAY
A student who scores a 154 is in the 63rd percentile of all LSAT-takers. If that student's score were 161, however, that same student would jump to the 86th percentile. Depending upon your score, a 7-point improvement can increase your ranking by over 30 percentile points.

COMPETITIVE LSAT SCORES AROUND THE UNITED STATES
The range of LSAT scores from the 25th to 75th percentile of incoming full-time students at U.S. law schools is pretty broad. Here is a sampling.

Law School	Score
Widener University, School of Law	145–151
The John Marshall Law School	145–152
Gonzaga University, School of Law	148–155
University of North Dakota, School of Law	146–153
University of Pittsburgh, School of Law	153–159
Temple University, James E. Beasley School of Law	154–160
Northeastern University, School of Law	152–160
Rutgers University—Newark, Rutgers School of Law at Newark	151–159
University of Florida, Levin College of Law	152–161
University of Missouri–Columbia, School of Law	153–158
University of Tennessee, College of Law	154–159
Case Western Reserve University, School of Law	154–160
University of Alabama, School of Law	157–161
Southern Methodist University, School of Law	156–161
Loyola University Chicago, School of Law	156–160
Brigham Young University, J. Reuben Clark Law School	158–164
Boston University, School of Law	161–165
Emory University, School of Law	158–162
University of Southern California the Law School	160–165
George Washington University, Law School	160–164
Duke University, School of Law	162–168
University of Michigan, Law School	164–168
Stanford University, School of Law	165–170
New York University, School of Law	167–171
University of Chicago, Law School	165–172
Yale University, Yale Law School	168–174

PREPARING FOR THE LSAT

No matter who you are—whether you graduated *magna cum laude* from Cornell University or you're on academic probation at Cornell College—the first thing you need to do is order a recent LSAT. One comes free with every *Official LSAT Registration Booklet*. Once you get the test, take it, but not casually over the course of two weeks. Bribe someone to be your proctor. Have them administer the test to you under strict time conditions. Follow the test booklet instructions exactly and do it right. Your goal is to simulate an actual testing experience as much as possible. When you finish, score the test honestly. Don't give yourself a few extra points because "you'll do better on test day." The score on this practice test will provide a baseline for mapping your test preparation strategy.

If your practice LSAT score is already at a point where you've got a very high-percentage shot of getting accepted to the law school of your choice, chances are you don't need much preparation. Order a half dozen or so of the most recent LSATs from LSAC and work through them over the course of a few months, making sure you understand why you are making specific mistakes. If your college or university offers a free or very cheap prep course, consider taking it to get more tips on the test. Many of these courses are taught by pre-law advisors who will speak very intelligently about the test and are committed to helping you get the best score you can.

If, after you take a practice LSAT, your score is not what you want or need it to be, you are definitely not alone. Many academically strong candidates go into the LSAT cold because they assume that the LSAT is no more difficult than or about the same as their college courses. Frankly, many students are surprised at how poorly they do the first time they take a dry run. Think about it this way: It's better to be surprised sitting at home with a practice test than while taking the test for real.

If you've taken a practice LSAT under exam conditions and it's, say, 10 or 15 points below where you want it to be, you should probably consult an expert. Test preparation companies spend quite a lot of money and time poring over the tests and measuring the improvements of their students. We sure do. Ask around. Assess your financial situation.

Talk to other people who have improved their LSAT scores and duplicate their strategies.

Whatever you decide to do, make sure you are practicing on real LSAT questions—again and again and again.

SOME ESSENTIAL, DOWN-AND-DIRTY LSAT TIPS

Slow down. Way down. The slower you go, the better you'll do. It's that simple. Any function you perform, from basic motor skills to complex intellectual problems, will be affected by the rate at which you perform that function. This goes for everything from cleaning fish to taking the LSAT. You can get twenty-five questions wrong and still get a scaled score of 160, which is a very good score (it's in the 84th percentile). You can get at least six questions wrong per section or, even better, you can ignore the two or three most convoluted questions per section, *still* get a few *more* questions wrong, and you'll get an excellent overall score. Your best strategy is to find the particular working speed at which you will get the most questions correct.

There is no guessing penalty. If you don't have time to finish the exam, it's imperative that you leave yourself at least 30 seconds at the end of each section in which to grab free points by bubbling in some answer to every question before time is called. Pick a letter of the day—like B—don't bubble in randomly. If you guess totally randomly, you might get every single guess right. Of course, you may also get struck by lightning in the middle of the test. The odds are about the same. *You are far more likely to miss every question if you guess without a plan.* On the other hand, if you stick with the same letter each time you guess, you will definitely be right once in a while. It's a conservative approach, but it is also your best bet for guaranteed points, which is what you want. By guessing the same letter pretty much every time as time runs out, you can pick up anywhere from two to four raw points per section. Be careful about waiting until the very last second to start filling in randomly, though, because proctors occasionally cheat students out of the last few seconds of a section.

Use process of elimination all the time. This is absolutely huge. On 75 percent of the LSAT (all the Logical Reasoning and the Reading Comprehension questions), you are *not*

The Princeton Review's Online LSAT Resources
The Princeton Review combines cutting-edge technology with its standardized-testing expertise to accommodate the needs of LSAT-takers everywhere.

Visit www.PrincetonReview.com for fantastic resources, free practice material, and information on The Princeton Review's classroom and online courses.

Law School Trivia
The last president to argue a case before the United States Supreme Court was Richard Nixon (a Duke alumnus). He argued the case between his tenure as vice president and his presidency. The case was Time, Inc. v. Hill (1967), a rather complicated First Amendment case.

looking for the *right* answer, only the *best* answer. It says so right there in the instructions. Eliminating even one answer choice increases your chances of getting the question right by 20 to 25 percent. If you can cross off two or three answer choices, you are really in business. Also, very rarely will you find an answer choice that is flawless on the LSAT. Instead, you'll find four answer choices that are definitely wrong and one that is the least of five evils. You should constantly look for reasons to get rid of answer choices so you can eliminate them. This strategy will increase your odds of getting the question right, and you'll be a happier and more successful standardized test-taker. We swear.

Attack! Attack! Attack! Read the test with an antagonistic, critical eye. Read it like it's a contract you are about to sign with the devil; look for holes and gaps in the reasoning of arguments and in the answer choices. Many LSAT questions revolve around what is wrong with a particular line of reasoning. The more you can identify what is wrong with a problem before going to the answer choices, the more successful you'll be.

Write all over your test booklet. Actively engage the exam and put your thoughts on paper. Circle words. *Physically cross out wrong answer choices you have eliminated.* Draw complete and exact diagrams for the logic games. Use the diagrams you draw.

Do the questions in whatever order you wish. Just because a logic game question is first doesn't mean you should do it first. There is *no order of difficulty* on the LSAT—unlike some other standardized tests—so you should hunt down and destroy those questions at which you are personally best. If you are doing a Reading Comprehension question, for example, or tackling an argument, and you don't know what the hell is going on, then cross off whatever you can, guess, and move on. If you have no idea what is going on in a particular logic game, don't focus your energy there. Find a game you can do and milk it for points. Your mission is to gain points wherever you can. By the way, if a particular section is really throwing you, it's probably because it is the dastardly experimental section (which is often kind of sloppy and, thankfully, does not count toward your score).

CHAPTER 4
WRITING A GREAT PERSONAL STATEMENT

There is no way to avoid writing the dreaded personal statement. You'll probably need to write only one personal statement, and it will probably address the most commonly asked question: "Why do you want to obtain a law degree?" This question, in one form or another, appears on virtually every law school application and often represents your only opportunity to string more than two sentences together. Besides your grades and your LSAT score, it is the most important part of your law school application. Your answer should be about two pages long, and it should amount to something significantly more profound than "A six-figure salary really appeals to me," or "Because I watch *Law & Order* every night."

Unlike your application to undergraduate programs, the personal statement on a law school application is not the time to discuss what your trip to Europe meant to you, describe your wacky chemistry teacher, or try your hand at verse. It's a fine line. While you want to stand out, you definitely don't want to be *overly* creative here. You want to be unique, but you don't want to come across as a weirdo or a loose cannon. You want to present yourself as intelligent, professional, mature, persuasive, and concise because these are the qualities law schools seek in applicants.

THE BASICS

Here are the essentials of writing essays and personal statements.

Find your own unique angle. The admissions people read tons of really boring essays about "how great I am" and how "I think there should be justice for everyone." If you must explain why you want to obtain a law degree, strive to find an angle that is interesting and unique to you. If what you write *isn't* interesting to you, we promise that it won't be remotely interesting to an admissions officer. Also, in addition to being more effective, a unique and interesting essay will be far more enjoyable to write.

In general, avoid generalities. Again, admissions officers have to read an unbelievable number of boring essays. You will find it harder to be boring if you write about particulars. It's the details that stick in a reader's mind.

Good writing is writing that is easily understood. You want to get your point across, not bury it in words. Don't talk in circles. Your prose should be clear and direct. If an admissions officer has to struggle to figure out what you are trying to say, you'll be in trouble. Also, legal writing courses make up a significant part of most law school curriculums; if you can show that you have good writing skills, you have a serious edge.

Buy and read *The Elements of Style*, by William Strunk, Jr. and E. B. White. We can't recommend it highly enough. In fact, we're surprised you don't have it already. This little book is a required investment for any writer (and, believe us, you'll be doing plenty of writing as a law student and a practicing attorney). You will refer to it forever, and if you do what it says, your writing will definitely improve.

Have three or four people read your personal statement and critique it. If your personal statement contains misspellings and grammatical errors, admissions officers will conclude not only that you don't know how to write but also that you aren't shrewd enough to get help. What's worse, the more time you spend with a piece of your own writing, the less likely you are to spot any errors. You get tunnel vision. Ask friends, boyfriends, girlfriends, professors, brothers, sisters—somebody—to read your essay and comment on it. Use a computer with a spellchecker. *Be especially careful about punctuation!* Another tip: Read your personal statement aloud to yourself or someone else. You will catch mistakes and awkward phrases that would have gotten past you otherwise because it sounded fine in your head.

Don't repeat information from other parts of your application. It's a waste of time and space.

Stick to the length that is requested. It's only common courtesy.

Maintain the proper tone. Your essay should be memorable without being outrageous and easy to read without being too formal or sloppy. When in doubt, err on the formal side.

Being funny is a lot harder than you think. An applicant who can make an admissions officer laugh never gets lost

---

Law School Trivia
Four law schools that can claim both a United States president and a United States supreme court justice as either alumni or one-time students:
Harvard University: *Rutherford B. Hayes and Harry Blackmun (among many, many others)*
Yale University: *William Jefferson Clinton and Clarence Thomas (also among many, many others)*
University of Missouri—Kansas City: *Harry S Truman (took night classes but did not graduate) and Charles Evans Whittaker*
University of Cincinnati: *William Howard Taft (who served both as president and as a member of the Supreme Court)*

Websites about Getting into Law School
www.PrincetonReview.com
You can access tons of information about law school and the LSAT at our site.
www.lsac.org
This site is home to the people who bring you the LSAT and the LSDAS application processing service.
www.pre-law.com
This is a confidential service designed to answer your questions about how best to prepare for and successfully apply to law school. Once registered, you become eligible for up to a full year of unlimited, personalized, high-quality, pre-law advising for one flat fee.

in the shuffle. The clever part of the personal statement is passed around and read aloud. Everyone smiles and the admissions staff can't bear to toss your app into the "reject" pile. But beware! Most people think they're funny, but only a few are able to pull it off in this context. Obviously, stay away from one liners, limericks, and anything remotely off-color.

WHY DO YOU WANT TO GO TO LAW SCHOOL?

Writing about yourself often proves to be surprisingly difficult. It's certainly no cakewalk explaining who you are and why you want to go to law school, and presenting your lifetime of experiences in a mere two pages is nearly impossible. On the bright side, though, the personal statement is the only element of your application over which you have total control. It's a tremendous opportunity to introduce yourself, if you avoid the urge to communicate your entire genetic blueprint. Your goal should be much more modest.

DON'T GET CARRIED AWAY

Although some law schools set no limit on the length of the personal statement, you shouldn't take their bait. You can be certain that your statement will be at least glanced at in its entirety, but admissions officers are human, and their massive workload at admissions time has an understandable impact on their attention spans. You should limit yourself to two or three typed, double-spaced pages. Does this make your job any easier? Not at all. In fact, practical constraints on the length of your essay demand a higher degree of efficiency and precision. Your essay needs to convey what kind of thinking, feeling human being you are, and a two-page limit allows for absolutely no fat.

MAKE YOURSELF STAND OUT

We know you know this, but you will be competing against thousands of well-qualified applicants for admission to just about any law school. Consequently, your primary task in writing your application is to separate yourself from the crowd. Particularly if you are applying directly from college or if you have been out of school for a very short time, you must do your best to see that the admissions committee cannot categorize you too broadly. Admissions committees will see innumerable applications from bright twenty-two-year-olds with good grades. Your essay presents an opportunity to put those grades in context, to define and differentiate yourself.

WHAT MAKES A GOOD PERSONAL STATEMENT?

Like any good writing, your law school application should tend towards clarity, conciseness, and candor. The first two of these qualities, clarity and conciseness, are usually the products of a lot of reading, rereading, and rewriting. Without question, repeated critical revision by yourself and others is the surest way to trim and tune your prose. The third quality, candor, is the product of proper motivation. Honesty cannot be superimposed after the fact; your writing must be candid from the outset.

In writing your personal statement for law school applications, pay particularly close attention to the way it is structured and the fundamental message it communicates. Admissions committees will read your essay two ways: as a product of your handiwork and as a product of your mind. Don't underestimate the importance of either perspective. A well-crafted essay will impress any admissions officer, but if it does not illuminate, you will not be remembered. You will not stand out. This is bad. Conversely, a thoughtful essay that offers true insight will stand out unmistakably, but if it is not readable, it will not receive serious consideration.

WHAT, PARTICULARLY, TO WRITE ABOUT

Given the most popular topic—"Why do you want to obtain a law degree?"—this one is pretty obvious. If you are having serious writer's block, try to express in a compelling manner some moment in your life, some experience you've had, or some intellectual slant of personal interest that is directing you to law school.

THINGS TO AVOID IN YOUR PERSONAL STATEMENT

"MY LSAT SCORE ISN'T GREAT, BUT I'M JUST NOT A GOOD TEST TAKER."

If you have a low LSAT score, avoid directly discussing it in your personal statement like the plague. Law school is a test-rich environment. In fact, grades in most law-school courses are determined by a single exam at the semester's end, and as a law student, you'll spend your Novembers and Aprils in a study carrel, completely removed from society. Saying that you are not good at tests will do little to convince an admissions committee that you've got the ability to succeed in law school once accepted.

Consider also that a low LSAT score speaks for itself—all too eloquently. It doesn't need you to speak for it, too. The LSAT may be a flawed test but don't go arguing the merits of the test to admissions officers because ordinarily it is the primary factor they use to make admissions decisions. We feel for you, but you'd be barking up the wrong tree here. The attitude of most law school admissions departments is that while the LSAT may be imperfect, it is equally imperfect for all applicants. Apart from extraordinary claims of serious illness on test day, few explanations for poor performance on the LSAT will mean much to the people who read your application.

About the only situation in which a discussion of your LSAT score is necessary is if you have two (or more) LSAT scores and one is significantly better than another. If you did much better in your second sitting than in your first, or vice versa, a brief explanation couldn't hurt. However, your explanation may mean little to the committee, which may have its own hard-and-fast rules for interpreting multiple LSAT scores. Even in this scenario, however, you should avoid bringing up the LSAT in the personal statement. *Save it for an addendum.*

The obvious and preferable alternative to an explicit discussion of a weak LSAT score would be to focus on what you *are* good at. If you really are bad at standardized tests, you must be better at something else, or you wouldn't have gotten as far as you have. If you think you are a marvelous researcher, say so. If you are a wonderful writer, show it.

Let your essay implicitly draw attention away from your weak points by focusing on your strengths. There is no way to convince an admissions committee that they should overlook your LSAT score. You may, however, present compelling reasons for them to look beyond it.

"MY COLLEGE GRADES WEREN'T THAT HIGH, BUT . . ."

This issue is a bit more complicated than the low LSAT score. Law school admissions committees will be more willing to listen to your interpretation of your college performance, but only within limits. Keep in mind that law schools require official transcripts for a reason. Members of the admissions committee will be aware of your academic credentials before ever getting to your essay. Just like with low LSAT scores, your safest course of action is to *save low grades for an addendum*.

Make no mistake: if your grades are unimpressive, you should offer the admissions committee something else by which to judge your abilities. Again, the best argument for looking past your college grades is evidence of achievement in another area, whether in your LSAT score, your extracurricular activities, your economic hardship as an undergraduate, or your career accomplishments.

"I'VE ALWAYS WANTED TO BE A LAWYER."

Sure you have. Many applicants seem to feel the need to point out that they really, really want to become attorneys. You will do yourself a great service by avoiding such throwaway lines. They'll do nothing for your essay but water it down. Do not convince yourself in a moment of desperation that claiming to have known that the law was your calling since age six (when—let's be honest—you really wanted to be a firefighter) will somehow move your application to the top of the pile. The admissions committee is not interested in how much you want to practice law. They want to know *why*.

"I WANT TO BECOME A LAWYER TO FIGHT INJUSTICE."

No matter how deeply you feel about battling social inequity, between us, writing it down makes you sound like a superhero on a soapbox. Moreover, though some people really do want to fight injustice, way down in the cockles

---

Law School Trivia
Supreme Court justices William Rehnquist and Sandra O'Connor were classmates at Stanford Law School.

More Celebrity Lawyers
Tony La Russa, manager of the St. Louis Cardinals and Oakland A's
Larry Rosenfeld and Rick Flax, founders of California Pizza Kitchen
Paul Cézanne, artist
Honoré de Balzac, writer
Igor Stravinsky, musician

of their hearts, most applicants are motivated to attend law school by less altruistic desires. Among the nearly one million practicing lawyers in the United States, there are relatively few who actually earn a living defending the indigent or protecting civil rights. Tremendously dedicated attorneys who work for peanuts and take charity cases are few and far between. We're not saying you don't want to be one of them; we're merely saying that folks in law school admissions won't *believe* you want to be one of them. They'll take your professed altruistic ambitions (and those of the hundreds of other personal statements identical to yours) with a chunk of salt.

If you can in good conscience say that you are committed to a career in the public interest, show the committee something tangible on your application and in your essay that will allow them to see your statements as more than mere assertions. However, if you cannot show that you are already a veteran in the Good Fight, don't claim to be. Law school admissions committees certainly do not regard the legal profession as a Saints vs. Sinners proposition, and neither should you. Do not be afraid of appearing morally moderate. If the truth is that you want the guarantee of the relatively good jobs a law degree practically ensures, be forthright. Nothing is as impressive to the reader of a personal statement as the ring of truth. And what's wrong with a good job, anyhow?

CHAPTER 5
RECOMMENDATIONS

The law schools to which you apply will require two or three letters of recommendation in support of your application. Some schools will allow you to submit as many letters as you like. Others make it clear that any more than the minimum number of letters of recommendation is unwelcome. If you've ever applied to a private school (or perhaps a small public school) then you know the drill.

Unlike the evaluation forms for some colleges and graduate programs, however, law school recommendation forms tend toward absolute minimalism. All but a few recommendation forms for law school applications ask a single, open-ended question. It usually goes something like, "What information about this applicant is relevant that is not to be found in other sources?" The generic quality of the forms from various law schools may be both a blessing and a curse. On the one hand, it makes it possible for those writing your recommendations to write a single letter that will suffice for all the applications you submit. This convenience will make everybody a lot happier. On the other hand, if a free-form recommendation is to make a positive impression on an admissions committee, it must convey real knowledge about you.

WHOM TO ASK

Your letters of recommendation should come from people who know you well enough to offer a truly informed assessment of your abilities. Think carefully before choosing whom to ask to do this favor for you, but, as a general rule, pick respectable people you've known for a long time. The better the writers of your recommendations know you and understand the broader experience that has brought you to your decision to attend law school, the more likely they will be able to write a letter that is specific enough to do you some good. You also want people who can and are willing to contribute to an integrated, cohesive application.

The application materials from most law schools suggest that your letters should come, whenever possible, from people in an academic setting. Some schools want at least two recommendations, both of which must be academic. Others explicitly request that the letters come from someone who has known you in a professional setting, especially if you've been out of school for a while.

HELP YOUR RECOMMENDATION WRITERS HELP YOU

Here, in essence, is the simple secret to great recommendations: Make sure the writers of your recommendations know you, your academic and professional goals, and the overall message you are trying to convey in your application. The best recommendations will fit neatly with the picture you present of yourself in your own essay, even when they make no specific reference to the issues your essay addresses. An effective law school application will present to the admissions committee a cohesive picture, not a pastiche. A great way to point your recommendation writers in the right direction and maximize their ability to contribute to your overall cause is to provide them with copies of your personal statement. Don't be bashful about amiably communicating a few "talking points" that don't appear in your personal statement, as well.

ACADEMIC REFERENCES

Most applicants will (and should) seek recommendations from current or former professors. The academic environment in law school is extremely rigorous. Admissions committees will be looking for assurance that you will be able not just to survive, but to excel. A strong recommendation from a college professor is a valuable corroboration of your ability to succeed in law school.

You want nothing less than stellar academic recommendations. While a perfunctory, lukewarm recommendation is unlikely to damage your overall application, it will obviously do nothing to bolster it. Your best bet is to choose at least one professor from your major field. An enthusiastic endorsement from such a professor will be taken as a sign that you are an excellent student. Second—and we hope that this goes without saying—you should choose professors who do not immediately associate your name with the letter C.

Specifics are of particular interest to admissions officers when they evaluate your recommendations. If a professor can make *specific* reference to a particular project you completed, or at least make substantive reference to your work in a particular course, the recommendation will be strengthened considerably. Make it your responsibility to

---

Helpful Websites
www.findlaw.com
Findlaw has the mother lode of free information about law, law schools, and legal careers.
www.ilrg.com
Mother lode honorable mention.
www.hg.org/students.html
Another honorable mention.
www.canadalawschools.org
Pretty much everything you ever wanted to know about Canadian law schools, eh.
www.jurist.law.pitt.edu
The University of Pittsburgh School of Law's splendid "Legal Education Network" offers a wealth of useful information.

Even More Celebrity Lawyers
Henry James, writer
Howard Cosell, sportscaster
David Stern, NBA commissioner
Abraham Lincoln, U.S. president
Tim and Nina Zagat, the people who bring you Zagat's restaurant and hotel guides

enable your professors to provide specifics. Drop hints, or just lay it out for them. You might, for example, make available a paper you wrote for them of which you are particularly proud. Or you might just chat with the professor for a while to jog those dormant memories. You might feel uncomfortable tooting your own horn, but it's for the best. Unless your professors are well enough acquainted with you to be able to offer a very personal assessment of your potential, they will greatly appreciate a tangible reminder of your abilities on which to base their recommendation.

ESCAPING THE WOODWORK

If you managed to get through college without any professors noticing you, it's not the end of the world. Professors are quite talented at writing recommendations for students they barely know. Most consider it part of their job. Even seemingly unapproachable academic titans will usually be happy to dash off a quick letter for a mere student. However, these same obliging professors are masters of a sort of opaque prose style that screams to an admissions officer, "I really have no idea what to say about this kid who is, in fact, a near-total stranger to me!" Although an admissions committee will not dismiss out of hand such a recommendation, it's really not going to help you much.

REELING IN THE YEARS

Obviously, the longer it has been since you graduated, the tougher it is to obtain academic recommendations. However, if you've held on to your old papers, you may still be able to rekindle an old professor's memory of your genius by sending a decent paper or two along with your request for a recommendation (and, of course, a copy of your personal statement). You want to provide specifics any way you can.

NONACADEMIC REFERENCES

Getting the mayor, a senator, or the CEO of your company to write a recommendation helps only if you have a personal and professional connection with that person. Remember, you want the writers of your recommendations to provide specifics about your actual accomplishments. If you're having trouble finding academic recommendations, choose people from your workplace, from the community, or from any other area of your life that is important to you. If at all possible, talk to your boss or a supervisor from a previous job who knows you well (and, of course, likes you).

SEND A THANK-YOU NOTE

Always a good idea. It should be short and handwritten. Use a blue pen so the recipient knows for sure that your note is no cheap copy. As with any good thank-you note (and any good recommendation), mention a specific. (Send a thank-you note if you have an interview at a law school, too.)

CHAPTER 6
REAL LIFE WORK EXPERIENCE AND COMMUNITY SERVICE

WORK EXPERIENCE IN COLLEGE

Most law school applications will ask you to list any part-time jobs you held while you were in college and how many hours per week you worked. If you had to (or chose to) work your way through your undergraduate years, this should come as good news. A great number of law schools make it clear that they take your work commitments as a college student into consideration when evaluating your undergraduate GPA.

WORK EXPERIENCE IN REAL LIFE

All law school applications will ask you about your work experience beyond college. They will give you three or four lines on which to list such experience. Some schools will invite you to submit a resume. If you have a very good one, you should really milk this opportunity for all it's worth. Even if you don't have a marvelous resume, these few lines on the application and your resume are the only opportunities you'll have to discuss your post-college experience meaningfully—unless you choose to discuss professional experience in your personal statement as well.

The kind of job you've had is not as important as you might think. What interests the admissions committee is what you've made of that job and what it's made of you. Whatever your job was or is, you want to offer credible evidence of your competence. For example, mention in your personal statement your job advancement or any increase in your responsibility. Most importantly, though, remember your overriding goal of cohesive presentation: you want to show off your professional experience within the context of your decision to attend law school. This does not mean that you need to offer a geometric proof of how your experience in the workplace has led you inexorably to a career in the law. You need only explain truthfully how this experience influenced you and how it fits nicely into your thinking about law school.

Would You Believe? . . . Still More Celebrity Lawyers
Steve Young, retired NFL quarterback
Wallace Stevens, poet
Otto Preminger, filmmaker
Mahatma Ghandi, Indian political leader
Franz Kafka, writer

COMMUNITY SERVICE

An overwhelming majority of law schools single out community involvement as one of several influential factors in their admissions decisions. Law schools would like to admit applicants who show a long-standing commitment to something other than their own advancement.

It is certainly understandable that law schools would wish to determine the level of such commitment before admitting an applicant, particularly since so few law students go on to practice public interest law. Be forewarned, however, that nothing—*nothing*—is so obviously bogus as an insincere statement of a commitment to public interest issues. It just reeks. Admissions committees are well aware that very few people take the time out of their lives to become involved significantly in their communities. If you aren't one of them, trying to fake it can only hurt you.

CHAPTER 7
INTERVIEWS

> **Law School Trivia**
> You probably know about John Marshall, Thurgood Marshall, Oliver Wendell Holmes, and other significant Supreme Court justices, but we bet you can't name the justice appointed by Grover Cleveland whom one newspaper described as "the most obscure man ever appointed Chief Justice."
>
> If you said Melvin Fuller, you really should get out more.

The odds are very good that you won't ever encounter an interview in the law school admissions process. Admissions staffs just aren't very keen on them. They do happen occasionally, though, and if you are faced with one, here are a few tips.

Be prepared. Interviews do make impressions. Some students are admitted simply because they had great interviews; less often, students are rejected because they bombed. Being prepared is the smartest thing you can do.

Don't ask questions that are answered in the brochures you got in the mail. This means you have to read those brochures. At breakfast before the interview is an ideal time.

If there is a popular conception of the school (e.g., Harvard is overly competitive), don't ask about it. Your interviewer will have been through the same song and dance too many times. You don't want to seem off the wall by asking bizarre questions; but even more, you don't want to sound exactly like every other boring applicant before you.

Look good, feel good. Wear nice clothes. If you aren't sure what to wear, *ask the admissions staff*. Say these words: "What should I wear?" Get a respectable haircut. Don't chew gum. Clean your fingernails. Brush your teeth. Wash behind your ears. You can go back to being a slob just as soon as they let you in.

Don't worry about time. Students sometimes are told that the sign of a good interview is that it lasts longer than the time allowed for it. Forget about this. Don't worry if your interview lasts exactly as long as the secretary said it would. And don't try to stretch out the end of your interview by suddenly becoming long-winded or asking a lot of questions you don't care about.

CHAPTER 8
Choosing a Law School

Attend a Law School Forum
These "college fairs" for law schools from all around the United States are held between July and November at different sites around the country. Law School Forums are a terrific way to get a broad overview of the whole field of schools; more than 150 programs send admissions officers to these forums, affording you a chance to gather information from representatives of almost every law school in the country—all in one place. Contact the LSAC or visit their website for more information.

There are some key things you should consider before randomly selecting schools from around the country or just submitting your application to somebody else's list of the Top 10 law schools.

GEOGRAPHY

It's a big deal. If you were born and raised in the state of New Mexico, care deeply about the "Land of Enchantment," wish to practice law there, and want to be the governor someday, then your best bet is to go to the University of New Mexico. A school's reputation is usually greater on its home turf than anywhere else (except for some of the larger-than-life schools, like Harvard and Yale). Also, most law schools tend to teach law that is specific to the states in which they are located. Knowledge of the eccentricities of state law will help you immensely three years down the road when it comes time to pass the bar exam. Even further, the career services office at your school will be strongly connected to the local legal industry. And, as a purely practical matter, it will be much easier to find a job and get to interviews in Boston, for example, if you live there. Still another reason to consider geography is the simple fact that you'll put down professional and social roots and get to know a lot of really great people throughout your law school career. Leaving them won't be any fun. Finally, starting with geographic limitations is the easiest way to dramatically reduce your number of potential schools.

SPECIALIZATION

Word has it that specialization is the trend of the future. General practitioners in law are becoming less common, so it makes sense to let future lawyers begin to specialize in school. At certain schools, you may receive your JD with an official emphasis in, say, taxation. Specialization is a particularly big deal at smaller or newer schools whose graduates cannot simply get by on their school's established reputation of excellence. Just between us, though, it's kind of hard to specialize in anything in most law schools because every graduate has to take this huge exam—the bar—that tests about a dozen topics. Most of your course selections will (and should) be geared toward passing the bar, which leaves precious few hours for specialization.

You'll almost certainly specialize, but it's not something to worry about until you actually look for a job. All of that said, if you already know what kind of law you want to specialize in, you're in good shape. Many schools offer certain specialties because of their location. If you are very interested in environmental law, you'd be better off going to Vermont Law School or Lewis and Clark's Northwestern School of Law than to Brooklyn Law School. Similarly, if you want to work with children as an attorney, check out Loyola University Chicago's Child Law Center. So look at what you want to do in addition to where you want to do it.

JOINT DEGREE PROGRAMS

In addition to offering specialized areas of study, many law schools have instituted formal dual-degree programs. These schools, nearly all of which are directly affiliated with a parent institution, offer students the opportunity to pursue a JD while also working toward some other degree. Although the JD/MBA combination is the most popular joint degree sought, many universities offer a JD program combined with degrees in everything from public policy to public administration to social work. Amidst a perpetually competitive legal market, dual degrees may make some students more marketable for certain positions come job time. However, don't sign up for a dual-degree program on a whim—they require a serious amount of work and often, a serious amount of tuition. (See page 95 for a list of joint degree programs available at some of the schools in this book.)

YOUR CHANCE OF ACCEPTANCE

Who knows how law schools end up with their reputations, but everything else being equal, you really do want to go a to a well-respected school. It will enhance your employment opportunities tremendously. Remember, whoever you are and whatever your background, your best bet is to select a couple "reach" schools, a couple schools at which you've got a good shot at being accepted, and a couple "safety" schools where you are virtually assured of acceptance. Remember also that being realistic about your chances will save you from unnecessary emotional letdowns. Getting in mostly boils down to numbers. Look at the acceptance rates and the average LSATs and GPAs of incoming classes at various schools to assess how you stack up.

Dean's List
According to a letter signed by just about every dean of every ABA-approved law school in the country, here are the factors you should consider when choosing a law school:

- Breadth and support of alumni network
- Breadth of curriculum
- Clinical programs
- Collaborative research opportunities with faculty
- Commitment to innovative technology
- Cost
- Externship options
- Faculty accessibility
- Intensity of writing instruction
- Interdisciplinary programs
- International programming
- Law library strengths and services
- Loan repayment assistance for low-income lawyers
- Location
- Part-time enrollment options
- Public interest programs
- Quality of teaching
- Racial and gender diversity within the faculty and student body
- Religious affiliation
- Size of first-year classes
- Skills instruction
- Specialized areas of faculty expertise

The Dreaded Bar Exam
Once you graduate, most states require you to take a bar exam before you can practice law. Some state bar exams are really, really hard. New York and California are examples. If you don't want to take a bar exam, consider a law school in beautiful Wisconsin. Anyone who graduates from a state-certified Wisconsin law school does not need to take the state bar exam to practice law in the Badger State, as long as they are approved by the Board of Bar Examiners.

PERSONAL APPEAL
A student at a prominent law school in the Pacific Northwest once described his law school to us as "a combination wood-grain bomb shelter and Ewok village." Another student at a northeastern law school told us her law school was fine except for its "ski-slope classrooms" and "East German Functionalist" architecture. While the curricula at various law schools are pretty much the same, the weather, the surrounding neighborhoods, the nightlife, and the character of the student populations are startlingly different. An important part of any graduate program is enjoying those moments in life when you're not studying. If you aren't comfortable in the environment you choose, it's likely to be reflected in the quality of work you do and your attitude. Before you make a $10,000 to $80,000 investment in any law school, you really ought to check it out in person. While you are there, talk to students and faculty. Walk around. Kick the tires. *Then* make a decision.

EMPLOYMENT PROSPECTS
Where do alumni work? How much money do they make? What percentage of graduates is employed within six months of graduation? How many major law firms interview on campus? These are massively important questions, and you owe it to yourself to look into the answers before choosing a school.

YOUR VALUES
It is important that you define honestly the criteria for judging law schools. What do you want out of a law school? Clout? A high salary? A hopping social life? To live in a certain city? To avoid being in debt up to your eyeballs? A noncompetitive atmosphere? Think about it.

MAKE A LIST
Using these criteria (and others you find relevant), develop a list of prospective schools. Ideally, you'll find this book useful in creating the list. Assign a level to each new school you add (something like "reach," "good shot," and "safety").

At your "reach" schools, the average LSAT scores and GPAs of incoming students should be higher than yours are. These are law schools that will probably not accept you based on your numbers alone. In order to get in, you'll need to wow them with everything else (personal statement, stellar recommendations, work experience, etc.).

Your "good shot" schools should be the schools you like that accept students with about the same LSAT scores and GPA as yours. Combined with a strong and *cohesive* application, you've got a decent shot at getting into these schools.

At your "safety" schools, the average LSAT scores and GPAs of their current students should be below yours. These schools should accept you pretty painlessly if there are no major blemishes on your application (e.g., a serious run-in with the law) and you don't just phone in the application. They hate that.

Did You Know?
According to the people who make the LSAT, the average applicant applies to between 4 and 5 law schools.

CHAPTER 9
Money Matters

Law school is a cash cow for colleges and universities everywhere and, especially at a private school, you are going to be gouged for a pretty obscene wad of cash over the next three years. Take New York University School of Law, where tuition is just over $30,000. If you are planning to eat, live somewhere, buy books, and (maybe) maintain health insurance, you are looking at about $47,000 per year. Multiply that by three years of law school. You should get $141,000. Now faint. Correct for inflation (NYU certainly will), add things like computers and other miscellany, and you can easily spend $150,000 to earn a degree. Assume that you have to borrow every penny of that $150,000. Multiply it by 8 percent over 10 years (a common assumption of law school applicants is that they will be able to pay all their debt back in 10 years or less). Your monthly payments will be around $1,825.

Tuition at ABA-accredited schools has increased 127 percent in the last decade or so. Over the past 20 years the increase has been a whopping 570 percent.

On the bright side, while law school is certainly an expensive proposition, the financial rewards of practicing can be immensely lucrative. You won't be forced into bankruptcy if you finance it properly. There are tried-and-true ways to reduce your initial costs, finance the costs on the horizon, and manage the debt you'll leave school with—all without ever asking "Have you been in a serious accident recently?" in a television commercial.

LAW SCHOOL ON THE CHEAP

Private schools aren't the only law schools and you don't have to come out of law school saddled with tens of thousands of dollars of debt. Many state schools have reputations that equal or surpass some of the top privates. It might be worth your while to spend a year establishing residency in a state with one or more good public law schools. Here's an idea: Pack up your belongings and move to a cool place like Minneapolis or Seattle or Berkeley or Austin or Boulder. Spend a year living there. Wait tables, hang out, listen to music, walk the earth, write the Great American Novel, and *then* study law.

COMPARISON SHOPPING

Here are the full-time tuition costs at law schools around the country. They are randomly paired schools in the same region (one public and one private) and are provided to help you get a feel of what law school costs are going to run you. Those schools that have the same tuition in both columns are private law schools.

Law School	In State	Out of State
Florida State University, College of Law	$4,414	$11,713
University of Miami, School of Law	$24,876	$24,876
Indiana University—Bloomington, School of Law	$7,989	$20,491
Notre Dame Law School	$24,920	$24,920
University of Tennessee, College of Law	$6,118	$17,580
Vanderbilt University, Law School	$26,960	$26,960
University of Iowa, College of Law	$8,152	$20,274
Drake University, Law School	$19,450	$19,450
Louisiana State University, Law Center	$6,711	$12,552
Tulane University, School of Law	$23,500	$23,500
University of California, Hastings College of Law	$10,175	$19,661
Golden Gate University, School of Law	$22,910	$22,910
University of Texas, School of Law	$6,060	$15,060
Baylor University, School of Law	$14,719	$14,719
University of Illinois, College of Law	$9,872	$21,770
Northwestern University, School of Law	$30,226	$30,226
University of Pittsburgh, School of Law	$13,980	$21,845
University of Pennsylvania, Law School	$27,960	$27,960
University of Oregon, School of Law	$11,500	$15,600
Lewis and Clark College, Northwestern School of Law	$22,090	$23,090

LOAN REPAYMENT ASSISTANCE PROGRAMS

If you are burdened with loans, we've got more bad news. The National Association of Law Placement (NALP) shows that while salaries for law school graduates who land jobs at the big, glamorous firms have skyrocketed in the past few years, salaries of $35,000–$40,000 are just as common as salaries of $70,000–$130,000 for the general run of law school grads. There are, however, a growing number of law schools and other sources willing to pay your loans for you (it's called loan forgiveness—as if you've sinned by taking out loans) in return for your commitment to employment in public interest law.

While doing a tour of duty in public service law will put off dreams of working in a big firm or becoming the next Johnnie Cochran, the benefits of these programs are undeniable. Here's how just about all of them work. You commit to working for a qualified public service or public interest job. As long as your gross income does not exceed the prevailing public service salary, the programs will pay off a good percentage of your debt. Eligible loans are typically any educational debt financed through your law school, which really excludes only loan sharks and credit-card debts.

MAXIMIZE YOUR AID

A simple but oft-forgotten piece of wisdom: if you don't ask, you usually don't get. Be firm when trying to get merit money from your school. Some schools have reserves of cash that go unused. Try simply asking for more financial aid. The better your grades, of course, the more likely they are to crack open their safe of financial goodies for you. Unfortunately, grants aren't as prevalent for law students as for undergrads. Scholarships are not nearly as widely available, either. To get a general idea of availability of aid at a law school, contact the financial aid office.

PARENTAL CONTRIBUTION?!

If you are operating under the assumption that, as a taxpaying grownup who has been out of school for a number of years, you will be recognized as the self-supporting adult you are, well, you could be in for a surprise. Veterans of financial aid battles will not be surprised to hear that even law school financial aid offices have a difficult time recognizing when apron strings have legitimately been cut. Schools may try to take into account your parents'

The Skinny on Loan Repayment Assistance Programs
For a comprehensive listing of assistance programs and for other loan-forgiveness information, call Equal Justice Works at 202-466-3686, or look them up on the Web at www.napil.org.

income in determining your eligibility for financial aid, regardless of your age or tax status. Policies vary widely. Be sure to ask the schools you are considering exactly what their policy is regarding financial independence for the purposes of financial aid.

BORROWING MONEY

It's an amusingly simple process and several companies are in the business of lending large chunks of cash specifically to law students. Your law school financial aid office can tell you how to reach them. You should explore more than one option and shop around for the lowest fees and rates.

WHO'S ELIGIBLE?

Anyone with reasonably good credit, regardless of financial need, can borrow enough money to finance law school. If you have financial need, you will probably be eligible for some types of financial aid if you meet the following basic qualifications:

- You are a United States citizen or a permanent U.S. resident.

- You are registered for Selective Service if you are a male, or you have the documentation to prove that you are exempt.

- You are not in default on student loans already.

- You don't have a horrendous credit history.

- You haven't been busted for certain drug-related crimes, including possession.

WHAT TYPES OF LOANS ARE AVAILABLE?

There are four basic types of loans: federal, state, private, and institutional.

Federal

The federal government funds federal loan programs. Federal loans, particularly the Stafford Loan, are usually the "first resort" for borrowers. Most federal loans are need-based, but some higher-interest loans are available regardless of financial circumstances.

Let the Law School Pick Up the Tab for Phone Calls Whenever Possible
A lot of schools have free telephone numbers that they don't like to publish in books like this one. If the number we have listed for a particular law school is not an 800-number, it doesn't necessarily mean that you have to pay every time you call the school. Check out the school's Internet site, or ask for the 800-number when you call the first time.

TABLE OF LOANS

NAME OF LOAN	SOURCE	ELIGIBILITY	MAXIMUM ALLOCATION
Subsidized Federal Stafford Student Loan (SSL, formerly GSL)	Federal, administered by participating lender	Demonstrated financial need; selective service registration; not in default on any previous student loan	$8,500/year with maximum aggregate of $65,500; aggregate includes undergraduate subsidized loans made under the same program
Unsubsidized Stafford Student Loan	Federal, administered by participating lender	Not need-based; selective service registration; not in default on any previous student loan.	$18,500/year with maximum aggregate of $138,500; aggregate includes undergraduate loans made under the same program and undergraduate and graduate loans made under the Unsubsidized and Subsidized Stafford Student Loan program
Perkins Loan (formerly NDSL)	Federal, administered by school	Demonstrated financial need; selective service registration; not in default on student loans.	Aggregate of $30,000; aggregate amount includes undergraduate loans
Law Access Loan (LAL)	Access Group	Not need-based	$120,000 for most schools (up to amount certified by your school)

Private

Private loans are funded by banks, foundations, corporations, and other associations. A number of private loans are targeted to aid particular segments of the population. You may have to do some investigating to identify private loans for which you might qualify. Like always, contact your law school's financial aid office to learn more.

Institutional

The amount of loan money available and the method by which it is disbursed vary greatly from one school to another. Private schools, especially those that are older and more established, tend to have larger endowments and can offer more assistance. To find out about the resources available at a particular school, refer to its catalogue or contact—you guessed it—the financial aid office.

TABLE OF LOANS

REPAYMENT AND DEFERRAL OPTIONS	INTEREST RATE	PROS	CONS
10 years to repay; begin repayment 6 months after graduation; forbearance possible.	Variable, doesn't exceed 8.25%	Most common law school loan; interest is subsidized by the feds during school; once you get a loan, any subsequent loans are made at the same rate	None
10 years to repay; principal is deferred while in school, but interest accrues immediately; begin repayment six months after graduation; forbearance possible	Variable, doesn't exceed 8.25%	Not need based; same interest rates as Federal Stafford; once you get a loan, any subsequent loans are made at the same rate	Interest accrues immediately and is capitalized if deferred.
10 years to repay; begin repayment 9 months after graduation	Fixed, 5%	Low interest rate	Low maximum allocation; primarily restricted to first- and second-year students
20 years to repay; principal repayment begins nine months after graduation.	Varies quarterly; 91-day T-bill rate plus 3.25% with no cap; average rate has recently hovered around 11%	High maximum allocation, not need based	High interest rate

CHAPTER 10
CAREER MATTERS

A Few Good Books
If you are thinking about law school, here are a few books you might find interesting:

Boykin Curry, Essays That Worked for Law School: 35 Essays from Successful Applications to the Nation's Top Law Schools
Looking for a little inspiration? Perhaps you'll find it among this cornucopia of knockouts.

Jeff Deaver, The Complete Law School Companion: How to Excel at America's Most Demanding Post-Graduate Curriculum
This straightforward law school survival guide has much to commend it.

Paul M. Lisnek, Law School Companion: The Ultimate Guide to Excelling in Law School and Launching Your Career
We'd be remiss if we did not recommend our own modest contribution to the pile of books about succeeding in law school. It's worth a look, in our humble opinion.

Okay, it's a long time away, but you really ought to be thinking about your professional career beyond law school from Day One, especially if your goal is to practice with a major law firm. What stands between you and a job as an "associate," the entry-level position at one of these firms, is a three-stage evaluation: first, a review of your resume, including your grades and work experience; second, an on-campus interview; and last, one or more "call-back" interviews at the firm's offices. It's a fairly intimidating ordeal, but there are a few ways to reduce the anxiety and enhance your chances of landing a great job.

YOUR RESUME

The first thing recruiters tend to notice after your name is the name of the law school you attend. Tacky, but true. Perhaps the greatest misconception among law students, however, is that hiring decisions turn largely upon your school's prestige. All those rankings perpetuate this myth. To be sure, there are a handful of schools with reputations above all others, and students who excel at these schools are in great demand. But you are equally well, if not better, situated applying from the top of your class at a strong, less prestigious law school class than from the bottom half of a "Top 10" law school class.

FIRST-YEAR GRADES ARE THE WHOLE ENCHILADA

Fair or not, the first year of law school will unduly influence your legal future. It's vital that you hit the ground running because law school grades are *the* critical factor in recruitment. An even harsher reality is that *first-year grades are by far the most critical in the hiring process*. Decisions about who gets which fat summer jobs are generally handed down before students take a single second-year exam. Consequently, you're left with exactly no time to adjust to law-school life and little chance to improve your transcript if you don't come out on top as a first-year student.

WORK EXPERIENCE

If you're applying to law school right out of college, chances are your most significant work experience has been a summer job. Recruiters don't expect you to have spent these months writing Supreme Court decisions. They are generally satisfied if you have shown evidence that you worked diligently and seriously at each opportunity. Students who took a year or more off after college obviously have more opportunities to impress, but also more of a burden to demonstrate diligence and seriousness.

Work experience in the legal industry—clerkships and paralegal jobs, just for instance—can be excellent sources of professional development. They are fairly common positions among job applicants, though, so don't feel you have to pursue one of these routes just to show your commitment to the law. You'll make a better impression, really, by working in an industry in which you'd like to specialize (e.g., a prospective securities lawyer summering with an investment bank).

THE INTERVIEWS

There are as many "right approaches" to an interview as there are interviewers. That observation provides little comfort, of course, especially if you're counting on a good interview to make up for whatever deficiencies there are on your resume. Think about the purpose of the initial 30-minute interview you are likely to have: it provides a rough sketch not only of your future office personality but also your demeanor under stress. The characteristics you demonstrate and the *impression* you give are more important than anything you say. Composure, confidence, maturity, articulation, an ability to develop rapport—these are characteristics recruiters are looking for. Give them what they want.

CHAPTER 11
LAW SCHOOL 101

An Old Law School Adage
First year they scare you to death.
Second year they work you to death.
Third year they bore you to death.

IS IT REALLY THAT BAD?

The first semester of law school has the well-deserved reputation of being among the greatest challenges to the intellect and stamina that you'll ever face. It is tons and tons of work and, in many ways, it's an exercise in intellectual survival. Just as the gung-ho army recruit must survive boot camp, so too must the bright-eyed law student endure the homogenizing effects of that first year.

Though complex and difficult, the subject matter in first-year law-school courses is probably no more inherently difficult than what is taught in other graduate or professional schools. The particular, private terror that is shared by roughly 40,000 1Ls every year stems more from law school's peculiar *style*. The method of instruction here unapologetically punishes students who would prefer to learn passively.

THE FIRST-YEAR CURRICULUM

The first-year curriculum in the law school you attend will almost certainly be composed of a combination of the following courses:

TORTS

The word comes from the Middle French for "injury." The Latin root of the word means "twisted." Torts are wrongful acts, excluding breaches of contract, over which you can sue people. They include battery, assault, false imprisonment, and intentional infliction of emotional distress. Torts can range from the predictable to the bizarre, from "Dog Bites Man" to "Man Bites Dog" and everything in between. The study of torts mostly involves reading cases in order to discern the legal rationale behind decisions pertaining to the extent of, and limits on, the civil liability of one party for harm done to another.

CONTRACTS

They may seem fairly self-explanatory but contractual relationships are varied and complicated, as two semesters of contracts will teach you. Again, through the study of past court cases, you will follow the largely unwritten law governing the system of conditions and obligations a contract represents, as well as the legal remedies available when contracts are breached.

CIVIL PROCEDURE

Civil procedure is the study of how you get things done in civil (as opposed to criminal) court. "Civ Pro" is the study of the often dizzyingly complex rules that govern not only who can sue whom, but also how, when, and where they can do it. This is not merely a study of legal protocol, for issues of process have a significant indirect effect on the substance of the law. Rules of civil procedure govern the conduct of both the courtroom trial and the steps that might precede it: obtaining information (discovery), making your case (pleading), pretrial motions, etc.

PROPERTY

You may never own a piece of land, but your life will inevitably and constantly be affected by property laws. Anyone interested in achieving an understanding of broader policy issues will appreciate the significance of this material. Many property courses will emphasize the transfer of property and, to varying degrees, economic analysis of property law.

CRIMINAL LAW

Even if you become a criminal prosecutor or defender, you will probably never run into most of the crimes you will be exposed to in this course. Can someone who shoots the dead body of a person he believes to be alive be charged with attempted murder? What if they were both on drugs or had really rough childhoods? Also, you'll love the convoluted exam questions, in which someone will invariably go on a nutty crime spree.

CONSTITUTIONAL LAW

"Con Law" is the closest thing to a normal class you will take in your first year. It emphasizes issues of government structure (e.g., federal power versus state power) and individual rights (e.g., personal liberties, freedom of expression, property protection). You'll spend a great deal of time studying the limits on the lawmaking power of Congress as well.

Good Law School Joke
In contracts class, the professor asked a student, "If you were to give someone an orange, how would you go about it?"
The student replied, "Here's an orange."
The professor was outraged. "No! No!" she exclaimed. "Think like a lawyer!"
The student then replied, "Okay. I'd say, 'I hereby give and convey to you all and singular, my estate and interests, rights, claim, title, and claim of and in, said orange, together with all its rind, juices, pulp, and seeds, and all rights and advantages contained therein, with full power to bite, cut, freeze, and otherwise eat, or give, bequeath, or devise with and without aforementioned rind, juices, pulp, and seeds. Anything herein before or hereinafter or in any deed, or deeds, instruments of whatever nature or kind whatsoever to the contrary in anywise notwithstanding . . .'"

Tips for Classroom Success

Be alert. Review material immediately before class so that it is fresh in your memory. Then review your notes from class later the same day and the week's worth of notes at the end of each week.

Remember that there are few correct answers. The goal of a law school class is generally to analyze, understand, and attempt to resolve issues or problems.

Learn to state and explain legal rules and principles with accuracy.

You don't want to focus on minutiae from cases or class discussions; always be trying to figure out what the law is.

Accept the ambiguity in legal analysis and class discussion; classes are intended to be thought-provoking, perplexing, and difficult.

No one class session will make or break you. Keep in mind how each class fits within the course overall.

Don't write down what other students say. Write down the law. Concentrate your notes on the professor's hypotheticals and emphasis in class.

A simple but effective way of keeping yourself in touch with where the class is at any given time is to review the table of contents in the casebook.

If you don't use a laptop, don't sit next to someone who does. The constant tapping on the keys will drive you crazy, and you may get a sense that they are writing down more than you (which is probably not true).

If you attend class, you don't need to tape record it. There are better uses of your time than to spend hours listening to the comments of students who were just as confused as you were when you first dealt with the material in class.

LEGAL METHODS

One of the few 20th-century improvements on the traditional first-year curriculum that has taken hold nearly everywhere, this course travels under various aliases, such as Legal Research and Writing, or Elements of the Law. In recent years, increased recognition of the importance of legal writing skills has led over half of the U.S. law schools to require or offer a writing course after the first year. This class will be your smallest, and possibly your only, refuge from the Socratic Method. Methods courses are often taught by junior faculty and attorneys in need of extra cash, and are designed to help you acquire fundamental skills in legal research, analysis, and writing. The Methods course may be the least frightening you face, but it can easily consume an enormous amount of time. This is a common lament, particularly at schools where very few credits are awarded for it.

In addition to these course requirements, many law schools require 1Ls to participate in a moot-court exercise. As part of this exercise, students—sometimes working in pairs or even small groups—must prepare briefs and oral arguments for a mock trial (usually appellate). This requirement is often tied in with the methods course so that those briefs and oral arguments will be well researched—and graded.

THE CASE METHOD

In the majority of your law school courses, and probably in all of your first-year courses, your only texts will be things called casebooks. The case method eschews explanation and encourages exploration. In a course that relies entirely on the casebook, you will never come across a printed list of "laws." Instead, you will learn that in many areas of law there is no such thing as a static set of rules, but only a constantly evolving system of principles. You are expected to understand the principles of law—in all of its layers and ambiguity—through a critical examination of a series of cases that were decided according to such principles. You will often feel utterly lost, groping for answers to unarticulated questions. This is not merely normal; it is intended.

In practical terms, the case method works like this: For every class meeting, you will be assigned a number of cases to read from your casebook, which is a collection of (extremely edited) written judicial decisions in actual court cases. The names won't even have been changed to protect the innocent. The cases are the written judicial opinions rendered in court cases that were decided at the appeals or Supreme Court level. (Written opinions are not generally rendered in lower courts.)

Your casebook will contain no instructions and little to no explanation. Your assignments simply will be to read the cases and be in a position to answer questions based on them. There will be no written homework assignments, just cases, cases, and more cases.

You will write, for your own benefit, summaries—or briefs—of these cases. Briefs are your attempts to summarize the issues and laws around which a particular case revolves *By briefing, you figure out what the law is*. The idea is that, over the course of a semester, you will try to integrate the content of your case briefs and your notes from in-class lectures, discussions, or dialogues into some kind of cohesive whole.

THE SOCRATIC METHOD

As unfamiliar as the case method will be to most 1Ls, the real source of anxiety is the way the professor presents it. Socratic instruction entails directed questioning and limited lecturing. Generally, the Socratic professor invites a student to attempt a cogent summary of a case assigned for that day's class. Hopefully, it won't be you (but someday it will be). Regardless of the accuracy and thoroughness of your initial response, the professor then grills you on details overlooked or issues unresolved. Then, the professor will change the facts of the actual case at hand into a hypothetical case that may or may not have demanded a different decision by the court.

The overall goal of the Socratic Method is to forcibly improve your critical reasoning skills. If you are reasonably well prepared, thinking about all these questions will force you beyond the immediately apparent issues in a given case to consider its broader implications. The dia-

> **Watch The Paper Chase. *Twice.***
> This movie is the only one ever produced about law school that comes close to depicting the real thing. Watch it before you go to orientation. Watch it again on Thanksgiving break and laugh when you can identify your classmates.

logue between the effective Socratic instructor and the victim-of-the-moment will also force nonparticipating students to question their underlying assumptions of the case under discussion.

WHAT IS CLINICAL LEGAL EDUCATION?

The latest so-called innovation in legal education is ironic in that it's a return to the old emphasis on practical experience. Hands-on training in the practical skills of lawyering now travels under the name "Clinical Legal Education."

HOW IT WORKS

Generally, a clinical course focuses on developing practical lawyering skills. "Clinic" means exactly what you would expect: a working law office where second- and third-year law students counsel clients and serve human beings. (A very limited number of law schools allow first-year students to participate in legal clinics.)

In states that grant upper-level law students a limited right to represent clients in court, students in a law school's clinic might actually follow cases through to their resolution. Some schools have a single on-site clinic that operates something like a general law practice, dealing with cases ranging from petty crime to landlord-tenant disputes. At schools that have dedicated the most resources to their clinical programs, numerous specialized clinics deal with narrowly defined areas of law, such as employment discrimination. The opportunities to participate in such live-action programs, however, are limited.

OTHER OPTIONS
Clinical legal education is a lot more expensive than traditional instruction, which means that few law schools can accommodate more than a small percentage of their students in clinical programs. If that's the case, check out external clinical placements and simulated clinical courses. In a clinical externship, you might work with a real firm or public agency several hours a week and meet with a faculty advisor only occasionally. Though students who participate in these programs are unpaid, they will ordinarily receive academic credit. Also, placements are chosen quite carefully to ensure that you don't become a gopher.

There are also simulated clinical courses. In one of these, you'll perform all of the duties that a student in a live-action clinic would, but your clients are imaginary.

CHAPTER 12
How to Excel at Any Law School

Contact Law Preview
Law Preview
255 North Bedford Road
Mount Kisco, NY 10549
Phone: 800-PREP-YOU
E-mail: admin@lawpreview.com
Website: www.lawpreview.com

Preparation for law school is something you should take very seriously. Law school will be one of the most interesting and rewarding experiences of your life, but it's also an important and costly investment. Your academic performance in law school will influence your career for years to come. Consider the following facts when thinking about how important it is to prepare for law school:

- The average full-time law student spends more than $125,000 to attend law school.

- The average law student graduates with over $80,000 of debt.

- The median income for law school graduates is only about $59,000.

As you can see, most law students cannot afford to be mediocre. Money isn't everything, but when you're strapped with close to six figures of debt, money concerns will weigh heavily on your career choices. Even if money is not a concern for you, your academic performance in law school will profoundly affect your employment options after graduation and, ultimately, your legal career. Consider these additional facts:

- Students who excel in law school often have opportunities to earn up to $160,000 right out of law school.

- Only law students who excel academically have opportunities to obtain prestigious judicial clerkships, teaching positions, and distinguished government jobs.

As you can see, law students who achieve academic success enjoy better career options and have a greater ability to escape the crushing debt of law school. The point here is obvious: Your chances of achieving your goals—no matter what you want to do with your career—are far better if you succeed academically.

Now comes the hard part: How do you achieve academic success? You are going to get plenty of advice about how to excel in law school—much of it unsolicited. You certainly don't need any from us. We strongly advise, however, that you pay extra-special attention to what Don Macaulay, the president of Law Preview, has to say about surviving, and thriving, as a law student. Macaulay, like all the founders of Law Preview, graduated at the top of his law school class and worked at a top law firm before he began developing and administering Law Preview's law school prep course in 1998.

While there are many resources that claim to provide a recipe for success in law school, Law Preview is the best of the lot. They have retained some of the most talented legal scholars in the country to lecture during their week-long sessions, and they deliver what they promise—a methodology for attacking and conquering the law school experience.

We asked Macaulay a few questions we thought prospective law students might like to know the answers to:

Q: **It is often said that the "first year" of law school is the most important year. Is this true and, if so, why?**

A: It is true. Academic success during the first year of law school can advance a successful legal career unlike success in any other year, because many of the top legal employers start recruiting so early that your first-year grades are all they will see. Most prestigious law firms hire their permanent attorneys from among the ranks of the firm's "summer associates"—usually second-year law students who work for the firm during the summer between the second and third years of law school. Summer associates are generally hired during the fall semester of the second year, a time when only the first year grades are available. A student who does well during the first year, lands a desirable summer associate position, and then impresses her employer, is well on her way to a secure legal job regardless of her academic performance after the first year.

In addition, first-year grades often bear heavily upon a student's eligibility for law review and other prestigious scholastic activities, including other law journals and moot court. These credentials are considered the most significant signs of law school achievement, often even more than a high grade point average. Many of the top legal employers in the private and the public sectors seek out young lawyers with these credentials, and some employers will not even interview candidates who lack these honors, even after a few years of experience. As a result, a solid performance during the first year of law school can have a serious impact upon your professional opportunities available after graduation.

All B+s put you in the top quarter at most schools, in the top fifth at many.

Websites About Doing Well in Law School

www.lawpreview.com
Law Preview is an intensive week-long seminar designed to help you conquer law school. Learn why hundreds of students have made Law Preview their first step to law review. The site also offers free features such as law school news and a daily advice column written by Atticus Falcon, author of Planet Law School.

www.barristerbooks.com
BarristerBooks.com is the best place to purchase legal study aids, cheap!

Q: How does law school differ from what students experienced as undergraduates?

A: Many students, especially those who enjoyed academic success in college, presume that law school will be a mere continuation of their undergraduate experience, and that, by implementing those skills that brought them success in college, they will enjoy similar success in law school. This couldn't be farther from the truth. Once law school begins, students often find themselves thrown into deep water. They are handed an anchor in the form of a casebook (and they are told it's a life preserver), and they are expected to sink or swim. While almost nobody sinks in law school anymore, most spend all of first year just trying to keep their heads above water. In reality, virtually every student who is admitted into law school possesses the intelligence and work ethic needed to graduate. But in spite of having the tools needed to survive the experience, very few possess the know-how to truly excel and make law review at their schools.

What makes the law school experience unique is its method of instruction and its system of grading. Most professors rely on the case method as a means for illustrating legal rules and doctrines encountered in a particular area of the law. With the case method, students are asked to read a particular case or, in some instances, several cases, that the professor will use to lead a classroom discussion illustrating a particular rule of law. The assigned readings come from casebooks, which are compilations of cases for each area of law. The cases are usually edited to illustrate distinct legal rules, often with very little commentary or enlightenment by the casebook editor. The casebooks often lack anything more than a general structure, and law professors often contribute little to the limited structure. Students are asked to read and analyze hundreds of cases in a vacuum. Since each assigned case typically builds upon a legal rule illustrated in a previous case, it isn't until the end of the semester or, for some classes, the end of the year, that students begin to form an understanding of how these rules interrelate.

One of the objectives of Law Preview's law school prep course is to help students to understand the "big picture" before they begin their classes. We hire some of the most talented law professors from around the country to provide "previews" of the core first-year law school courses:

Civil Procedure, Constitutional Law, Contracts, Criminal Law, Property, and Torts. During their lectures, our professors provide students with a roadmap for each subject by discussing the law's development, legal doctrines, and recurring themes and policies that students will encounter throughout the course. By providing entering law students with a conceptual framework for the material they will study, Law Preview eliminates the frustration that most of them will encounter when reading and analyzing case law in a vacuum.

Q: What is the best way to prepare for law school, and when should you start?

A: When preparing for law school, students should focus on two interrelated tasks: 1) developing a strategy for academic success, and 2) getting mentally prepared for the awesome task ahead. The primary objective for most law students is to achieve the highest grades possible, and a well-defined strategy for success will help you direct your efforts most efficiently and effectively toward that goal. You must not begin law school equipped solely with some vague notion of hard work. Success requires a concrete plan that includes developing a reliable routine for classroom preparation, a proficient method of outlining, and a calculated strategy for exam-taking. The further you progress in law school without such a plan, the more time and energy you will waste struggling through your immense work load without moving discernibly closer toward achieving academic success.

You must also become mentally prepared to handle the rigors of law school. Law school can be extremely discouraging because students receive very little feedback during the school year. Classes are usually graded solely based on final exam scores. Mid-term exams and graded papers are uncommon, and classroom participation is often the only way for students to ascertain if they understand the material and are employing effective study methods. As a result, a winning attitude is critical to success in law school. Faith in yourself will help you continue to make the personal sacrifices during the first year that you need to make to succeed in law school, even when the rewards are not immediately apparent.

Books About Doing Well in Law School

Professors Jeremy Paul and Michael Fischl, Getting To Maybe: How To Excel on Law School Exams
This book is excellent! While many books and professors may preach "IRAC" as a way of structuring exam answers, Getting to Maybe correctly points out that such advice does not help students first correctly identify legal issues and, more importantly, master the intricacies of legal analysis.

Atticus Falcon, Planet Law School: What You Need to Know (Before You Go) . . . But Didn't Know to Ask
This is what everyone is reading before going to law school. Pseudonymned author Atticus Falcon gives a critical appraisal of the state of law school education. The author's assessments are usually directed and well-reasoned. This book tells you what the real "rules of the game" are, so you'll know exactly what you are facing. It's also the only book that gives you detailed information—including recommendations of "primers" and other aids—that you can you use to get a head start before you go to law school.

Incoming law students should begin preparing for law school during the summertime prior to first year, and preparation exercises should be aimed at gaining a general understanding of what law school is all about. A solid understanding of what you are expected to learn during the first year will give you the information you need to develop both your strategy for success and the confidence you need to succeed. There are several books on the market that can help in this regard, but those students who are best prepared often attend Law Preview's one-week intensive preparatory course specifically designed to teach beginning law students the strategies for academic success.

Q: What factors contribute to academic success in law school?

A: Academic success means one thing in law school—exam success. The grades that you receive, particularly during the first year, will be determined almost exclusively by the scores you receive on your final exams. Occasionally, a professor may add a few points for class participation, but that is rare. In most classes, your final exam will consist of a three- or four-hour written examination at the end of the semester or—if the course is two semesters long—at the end of the year. The amount of material you must master for each final exam will simply dwarf that of any undergraduate exam you have ever taken. The hope that you can "cram" a semester's worth of information into a one-week reading period is pure fantasy and one that will surely lead to disappointing grades. The focus of your efforts from day one should be success on your final exams. Don't get bogged down in class preparation or in perfecting a course outline if it will not result in some discernible improvement in your exam performance. All of your efforts should be directed at improving your exam performance in some way. It's as simple as that.

Q: What skills are typically tested on law school exams?

A: Law school exams usually test three different skills: 1) the ability to accurately identify legal issues, 2) the ability to recall the relevant law with speed, and 3) the ability to apply the law to the facts efficiently and skillfully. The proper approach for developing these skills differs, depending on the substantive area of law in question and whether your exam is open-book or closed-book.

Identifying legal issues is commonly known as issue-spotting. On most of your exams, you will be given complex, hypothetical fact patterns. From the facts you are given, you must identify the particular legal issues that need to be addressed. This is a difficult skill to perfect and can only be developed through practice. The best way to develop issue-spotting skills is by taking practice exams. For each of your classes, during the first half of the semester you should collect all of the available exams that were given by your professor in the past. Take all of these exams under simulated exam conditions—find an open classroom, get some blue books, time yourself, and take the exams with friends so that you can review them afterwards. It is also helpful for you to practice any legal problems you were given during the semester. Issue-spotting is an important skill for all lawyers to develop. Lawyers utilize this skill on a daily basis when they listen to their clients' stories and are asked to point out places where legal issues might arise.

The ability to recall the law with speed is also very important and frequently tested. On all of your exams, you will be given a series of legal problems, and for each problem you will usually be required to provide the relevant substantive law and apply it to the facts of the problem. Your ability to recall the law with speed is critical, because in most classes, you will be under time constraints to answer all of the problems. The faster you recall the law, the more problems you will complete and the more time you will have to spend on demonstrating your analytical skills. For courses with closed-book exams, this means straight memorization or the use of memory recall devices, such as mnemonics. Do not be passive about learning the law—repeatedly reviewing your outline is not enough. You must actively learn the law by studying definitions and using memory-assistance devices like flash cards. When you have become exceedingly familiar with your flash cards, rewrite them so as to test your memory in different words. This is particularly critical for courses such as Torts and Criminal Law where you must learn a series of definitions with multiple elements. For courses with open-book exams, this means developing an index for your outline that will enable you to locate the relevant law quickly. Create a cover page for your outline that lists the page number for each substantive sub-topic. This will help you get there without any undue delay.

More Books About Doing Well in Law School

Professor Jay Feinman, Law 101: Everything You Need to Know About the American Justice System
This is another excellent book! Professor Feinman has provided an easy-to-understand introduction to the American legal system using simple language and intriguing cases.

Robert H. Miller, Esq, Law School Confidential: A Complete Guide to the Law School Experience
The author—a graduate of Penn Law, member of the law review, and former federal judicial clerk—and his team of "mentors" from law schools across the country pull no punches in providing revealing and honest chronological advice for all three years of the law school experience, from picking the law school that's right for you and funding your legal education, to how to study efficiently and how to make the law review, get judicial clerkships, and properly assess job opportunities. This critically acclaimed book also features the much-discussed interview with Penn Law's dean of admissions, which provides a shockingly candid look into the admissions process at one of the nation's finest law schools.

The final skill you need to develop is the ability to apply the law to the facts efficiently and skillfully. On your exams, once you have correctly identified the relevant issue and stated the relevant law, you must engage in a discussion of how the law applies to the facts that have been given. The ability to engage in such a discussion is best developed by taking practice exams. When you are practicing this skill, you should focus on efficiency. Try to focus on the essential facts, and do not to engage in irrelevant discussions that will waste your energy and your professor's time.

Q: **Any final comments for our audience of aspiring law students?**

A: The study of law is a wonderful and noble pursuit, one that I thoroughly enjoyed. Law school is not easy, however, and proper preparation can give you a firm foundation for success. I invite you to visit our website (www.lawpreview.com) and contact us with any questions (888-PREP-YOU).

CHAPTER 13
How to Use This Book

It's pretty simple.

The first part of this book provides a wealth of indispensable information covering everything you need to know about selecting and getting into the law school of your choice. There is also a great deal here about what to expect from law school and how to do well. You name it—taking the LSAT, choosing the best school for you, writing a great personal statement, interviewing, paying for it—it's all here.

The second part is the real meat and potatoes of the *Complete Book of Law Schools*. It comprises portraits of more than 200 schools across the United States and Canada. Each school has a directory entry that contains the same basic information and follows the same basic format. Unless noted in the descriptions below, The Princeton Review collected all of the data presented in these directory entries. As is customary with college guides, all data reflects the figures for the academic year prior to publication, unless otherwise indicated. Since law school offerings and demographics vary significantly from one institution to another and some schools report data more thoroughly than others, some entries will not include all the individual data described below.

Some schools have also opted to include a "School Says..." profile, giving extended descriptions of their admissions process, curriculum, internship opportunities, and much more. This is your chance to get in-depth information on programs that interest you. These schools have paid us a small fee for the chance to tell you more about themselves, and the editorial responsibility is solely that of the law school. We think you'll find these profiles add lots to your picture of a school.

WHAT'S IN THE PROFILES

The Heading: The first thing you will see for each profile is (obviously) the school's name. Just below the name, you'll find the school's snail mail address, telephone number, fax number, e-mail address, and Internet site. You can find the name of the admissions office contact person in the heading, too.

INSTITUTIONAL INFORMATION

Public/Private: Indicates whether a school is state-supported or funded by private means.

Affiliation: If the school is affiliated with a particular religion, you'll find that information here.

Environment: Urban, suburban, or rural. Pretty self-explanatory.

Academic Calendar: The schedule of academic terms. Semester—two long terms. Trimester—three terms. Quarter—three terms plus an optional summer term.

Schedule: Whether only full-time or both full- and part-time programs are available.

Student/Faculty Ratio: The ratio of law students to full-time faculty.

Total Faculty: The number of faculty members at the law school.

% Part Time: The percentage of faculty who are part time.

% Female: The percentage of faculty who are women.

% Minority: You guessed it! The percentage of people who teach at the law school who are also members of minority groups.

PROGRAMS

Academic Specialties: Different areas of law and academic programs in which the school prides itself.

Advanced Degrees Offered: Degrees available through the law school, and the length of the program.

Combined Degrees Offered: Programs at this school involving the law school and some other college or degree program within the larger university, and how long it will take you to complete the joint program.

Grading System: Scoring system used by the law school.

Clinical Program Required? Indicates whether clinical programs are required to complete the core curriculum.

Clinical Program Description: Programs designed to give students hands-on training and experience in the practice of some area of law.

Even More Good Books
    Law Services, **Thinking About Law School: A Minority Guide**
This free publication, which offers pointers on finding and getting into the right school for minority applicants, is worth checking out.

    Scott Turow, **One L: The Turbulent True Story of a First Year at Harvard Law School**
This law school primer is equal parts illuminating and harrowing.

Law School Trivia
The least litigated amendment in the Bill of Rights is the Third Amendment, which prohibits the quartering of soldiers in private homes without consent of the owner.

Legal Writing/Methods Course Requirements: The components of the curriculum included to develop the research, analysis, and writing skills vital to the practice of law.

Legal Writing Course Requirement? Tells you whether there is a required course in legal writing.

Legal Writing Description: A description of any course work, required or optional, designed specifically to develop legal writing skills vital to the practice of law.

Legal Method Course Requirements? Indicates whether there is a mandatory curriculum component to cover legal methods.

Legal Methods Description: A description of any course work, required or optional, designed specifically to develop the skills vital to legal analysis.

Legal Research Course Requirements? If a school requires course work specifically to develop legal research skills, this field will tell you.

Legal Research Description: A description of any course work, required or optional, designed specifically to develop legal research skills vital to the practice of law.

Moot Court Requirement? Indicates whether participation in a moot court program is mandatory.

Moot Court Description: Surprise! This will describe any moot court program, mandatory or optional, designed to develop skills in legal research, writing, and oral argument.

Public Interest Law Requirement? If a school requires participation on a public interest law project, we'll let you know here.

Public Interest Law Description: Programs designed to expose students to the public interest law field through clinical work, volunteer opportunities, or specialized course work.

Academic Journals: This field will list any academic journals offered at the school.

STUDENT INFORMATION

Enrollment of Law School: The total number of students enrolled in the law school.

% Out of State: The percentage of full-time students who are from out of state. This field only applies to state schools.

% Male/Female: The percentage of students with an X and a Y chromosome and the percentage of students with two X chromosomes, respectively.

% Full Time: The percentage of students who attend the school on a full-time basis.

% Full Time That Are International: The percentage of students that hails from foreign soil.

% Minority: The percentage of students who represent minority groups.

Average Age of Entering Class: On the whole, how old the 1Ls are.

RESEARCH FACILITIES

Research Resources Available: Online retrieval resources, subscription services, libraries, databases, etc. available for legal research.

% of JD Classrooms Wired: You got it—the percentage of dedicated law school classrooms wired for laptops and Internet access.

Computers/Workstations Available: The number of computers on campus.

Computer Labs: The number of rooms full of computers that you can use for free.

Campuswide Network? Indicates whether the campus is wired.

School-Supported Research Centers: Indicates whether the school has on-campus, internally supported research centers.

EXPENSES/FINANCIAL AID

Annual Tuition (Residents/Nonresidents): What it costs to go to school there for an academic year. For state schools, both in-state and out-of-state tuition is listed.

Room and Board (On/Off campus): This is the school's estimate of what it costs to buy meals and to pay for decent living quarters for the academic year. Where available, on- and off-campus rates are listed.

Books and Supplies: Indicates how much students can expect to shell out for textbooks and other assorted supplies during the academic year.

Financial Aid Application Deadline: The last day on which students can turn in their applications for monetary assistance.

Average Grant: Average amount awarded to students that does not have to be paid back. This figure can include scholarships as well.

Average Loan: Average amount of loan dollars accrued by students for the year.

% of Aid That Is Merit-Based: The percentage of aid not based on financial need

% Receiving Some Sort of Aid: The percentage of the students here presently accumulating a staggering debt.

Average Total Aid Package: How much aid each student here receives on average for the year.

Average Debt: The amount of debt—or, in legal lingo, arrears—you'll likely be saddled with by the time you graduate.

Tuition Per Credit (Residents/Nonresidents): Dollar amount charged per credit hour. For state schools, both in-state and out-of-state amounts are listed when they differ.

Fees Per Credit (Residents/Nonresidents): That mysterious extra money you are required to pay the law school in addition to tuition and everything else, on a per-credit basis. If in-state and out-of-state students are charged differently, both amounts are listed.

ADMISSIONS INFORMATION

Application Fee: The fee is how much it costs to apply to the school.

Regular Application Deadline and "Rolling" Decision: Many law schools evaluate applications and notify applicants of admission decisions on a continuous, "rolling" basis over the course of several months (ordinarily from late fall to midsummer). Obviously, if you apply to one of these schools, you want to apply early because there will be more places available at the beginning of the process.

Regular Notification: The official date on which a law school will release a decision for an applicant who applied using the "regular admission" route.

LSDAS Accepted? A "Yes" here indicates that the school utilizes the Law School Data Assembly Service.

Average GPA/Range of GPA: It's usually on a 4.0 scale.

Average LSAT/Range of LSAT: Indicates the average LSAT score of incoming 1Ls, as reported by the school.

Transfer Students Accepted? Whether transfer students from other schools are considered for admission.

Other Schools to Which Students Applied: The law schools to which applicants to this school also apply. It's important. It's a reliable indicator of the overall academic quality of the applicant pool.

Other Admissions Factors Considered: Additional criteria the law schools considers when admitting applicants.

Number of Applications Received: The number of people who applied to the law school.

Number of Applicants Accepted: The number of people who were admitted to the school's class.

Number of Applicants Enrolled: The number of those admitted who chose to attend that particular institution.

INTERNATIONAL STUDENTS

TOEFL Required of International Students? Indicates whether or not international students must take the TOEFL, or Test of English as a Foreign Language, in order to be admitted to the school.

Minimum TOEFL: Minimum score an international student must earn on the TOEFL in order to be admitted.

Law School Trivia
The guarantee that each state must have an equal number of votes in the United States Senate is the only provision in the Constitution of 1787 that cannot be amended.

EMPLOYMENT INFORMATION

The **bar graph** will let you know in which fields a law school's grads are working. The fields are as follows:

Public Interest: The percentage of (mostly) altruistic graduates who got jobs providing legal assistance to folks who couldn't afford it otherwise and fighting the power in general.

Private Practice: The percentage of graduates who got jobs in traditional law firms of various sizes, or "put out a shingle" for themselves as sole practitioners.

Military: The percentage of lawyers who work to represent the Armed Forces in all kinds of legal matters. Like Tom Cruise in *A Few Good Men*. We knew you could handle the truth.

Judicial Clerkships: The number of graduates who got jobs doing research for judges.

Government: Uncle Sam needs lawyers like you wouldn't even believe.

Business/Industry: The number of graduates who got jobs working in business, in corporations, in consulting, etc. These jobs are sometimes law-related and sometimes not.

Academic: The number of graduates who got jobs at law schools, universities, and think tanks.

Rate of Placement: Placement rate into the job market upon completion of the Juris Doctor.

Average Starting Salary: The amount of money the average graduate of this law school makes the first year out of school.

Employers Who Frequently Hire Grads: Firms where past grads have had success finding jobs.

Prominent Alumni: Those who made it.

State for Bar Exam: The state for which most students from the school will take the bar exam.

Number Taking Bar Exam: Number of students taking the bar.

Pass Rate for First-Time Bar: After three years, the percentage of students who passed the bar exam the first time they took it. It's a crucial statistic. You *don't* want to fail your state's bar.

DECODING DEGREES

Many law schools offer joint or combined degree programs with other departments (or sometimes even with other schools) that you can earn along with your Juris Doctor. You'll find the abbreviations for these degrees in the individual school profiles, but we thought we'd give you a little help in figuring out exactly what they are.

AMBA	Accounting Master of Business
BCL	Bachelor of Civil Law
DJUR	Doctor of Jurisprudence
DL	Doctor of Law
DLaw	Doctor of Law
EdD	Doctor of Education
HRIR	Human Resources and Industrial Relations
IMBA	International Master of Business Administration
JD	Juris Doctor
JSD	Doctor of Juridical Science
JSM	Master of the Science of Law
LLB	Bachelor of Law
LLCM	Master of Comparative Law (for international students)
LLM	Master of Law
MA	Master of Arts
MAcc	Master of Accounting
MALD	Masters of Arts in Law and Diplomacy
MAM	Master of Arts Management
MM	Master of Management
MANM	Master of Nonprofit Management
MAPA	Master of Public Administration
MAUA	Masters of Arts in Urban Affairs
MBA	Master of Business Administration
MCJ	Master of Criminal Justice
MCL	Master of Comparative Law
MCP	Master of Community Planning
MCRP	Master of City and Regional Planning

MDiv	Master of Divinity	MSI	Master of Science in Information
ME	Master of Engineering OR Master of Education	MSIA	Master of Industrial Administration
MEd	Master of Education	MSIE	Master of Science in International Economics
MED	Master of Environmental Design	MSJ	Master of Science in Journalism
MEM	Master of Environmental Management	MSPH	Master of Science in Public Health
MFA	Master of Fine Arts	MSW	Master of Social Welfare OR Master of Social Work
MHA	Master of Health Administration	MT	Master of Taxation
MHSA	Master of Health Services Administration	MTS	Master of Theological Studies
MIA	Master of International Affairs	MUP	Master of Urban Planning
MIB	Master of International Business	MUPD	Master of Urban Planning and Development
MIP	Master of Intellectual Property	MURP	Master of Urban and Regional Planning
MIR	Masters in Industrial Relations	PharmD	Doctor of Pharmacy
MIRL	Masters Industrial and Labor Relations	PhD	Doctor of Philosophy
MJ	Master of Jurisprudence	REES	Russian and Eastern European Studies Certificate
MJS	Master of Juridical Study (not a JD)	SJD	Doctor of Juridcial Science
MLIR	Master of Labor and Industrial Relations	DVM	Doctor of Veterinary Medicine
MLIS	Master of Library and Information Sciences	MALIR	Master of Arts in Labor and Industrial Relations
MLS	Master of Library Science		
MMA	Masters Marine Affairs		
MOB	Master of Organizational Behavior		
MPA	Master of Public Administration		
MPAFF	Master of Public Affairs		
MPH	Master of Public Health		
MPP	Master of Public Planning OR Master of Public Policy		
MPPA	Master of Public Policy		
MPPS	Master of Public Policy Sciences		
MPS	Master of Professional Studies in Law		
MRP	Master of Regional Planning		
MS	Master of Science		
MSEL	Master of Studies in Environmental Law		
MSES	Master of Science in Environmental Science		
MSF	Master of Science in Finance		
MSFS	Master of Science in Foreign Service		

LAW SCHOOL PROFILES

ALBANY LAW SCHOOL
Union University

Admissions Contact: Assistant Dean of Admissions and Financial Aid, Dawn Chamberlaine
80 New Scotland Avenue, Albany, NY 12208
Admissions Phone: 518-445-2326 • Admissions Fax: 518-445-2369
Admissions E-mail: admissions@mail.als.edu • Web Address: www.als.edu

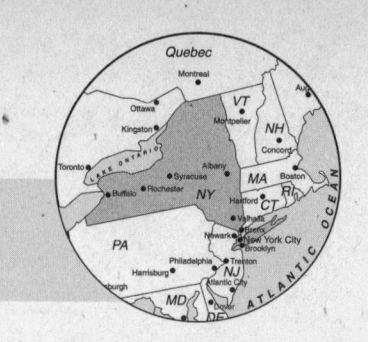

INSTITUTIONAL INFORMATION
Public/Private: Private
Student/Faculty Ratio: 17:1
Total Faculty: 73
% Part Time: 37
% Female: 36
% Minority: 7

PROGRAMS
Academic Specialties: Health Law, Intellectual Property Law, Criminal Law, International Law, Civil Procedure, Constitutional Law, Environmental Law, Government Services, Labor Law, Taxation, Business Law, Estate Planning, Family and Elder Law
Advanced Degrees Offered: JD (3 years)
Combined Degrees Offered: JD/MBA (3.5 to 4 years), JD/MPA (3.5 to 4 years), JD/MSW (3.5 to 4 years), JD/MRP (3.5 to 4 years)
Grading System: A+ (4.3), A (4.0), A– (3.7), B+ (3.3), B (3.0), B– (2.7), C+ (2.3), C (2.0), C– (1.7), D+ (1.3), D (1.0), D– (0.7), F (0.0)
Clinical Program Required? No
Clinical Programs Description: AIDS Law Project, Disabilities Law Project, Domestic Violence Law Project, Litigation Project, various placements and externships, semester in government programs
Legal Writing Course Requirements? Yes
Legal Writing Description: Introduction to Lawyering gives students an opportunity to begin developing their professional skills in a year-long case simulation that combines legal writing and clinical methodology.
Legal Methods Course Requirements? Yes
Legal Methods Description: 1 week prior to start of classes
Legal Research Course Requirements? Yes
Legal Research Description: See Legal Writing.
Moot Court Requirement? No
Public Interest Law Requirement? No
Academic Journals: Law Review, Journal of Science and Technology, Environmental Outlook, Literary Review

STUDENT INFORMATION
Enrollment of Law School: 771
% Out of State: 11
% Male/Female: 47/53
% Full Time: 92
% Full Time That Are International: 3
% Minority: 20
Average Age of Entering Class: 27

RESEARCH FACILITIES
Research Resources Available: Because of Albany Law School's location in the capital of New York State students have access to the agencies of state government, the legislature, executive offices, and the state's highest court, the Court of Appeals.
School-Supported Research Centers: Government Law Center, Schaffer Law Library, Science and Technology Law Center

EXPENSES/FINANCIAL AID
Annual Tuition: $22,250
Room and Board (Off Campus): $6,100
Books and Supplies: $595
Average Grant: $7,100
Average Loan: $22,600
% of Aid That Is Merit-Based: 29
% Receiving Some Sort of Aid: 93
Average Total Aid Package: $29,640
Average Debt: $60,000
Tuition Per Credit: $765

ADMISSIONS INFORMATION
Application Fee: $50
Regular Application Deadline: 3/15
Regular Notification: Rolling
LSDAS Accepted? Yes
Average GPA: 3.2
Range of GPA: 3.0–3.5
Average LSAT: 150
Range of LSAT: 146–153
Transfer Students Accepted? Yes
Other Schools to Which Students Applied: New York Law School, New England School of Law, Pace University, Syracuse University, University at Buffalo, The State University of NY
Other Admissions Factors Considered: Academic strength of undergraduate institution, rigor of the undergraduate program, uniqueness of life experience and background, employment experience
Number of Applications Received: 1,468
Number of Applicants Accepted: 877
Number of Applicants Enrolled: 279

EMPLOYMENT INFORMATION

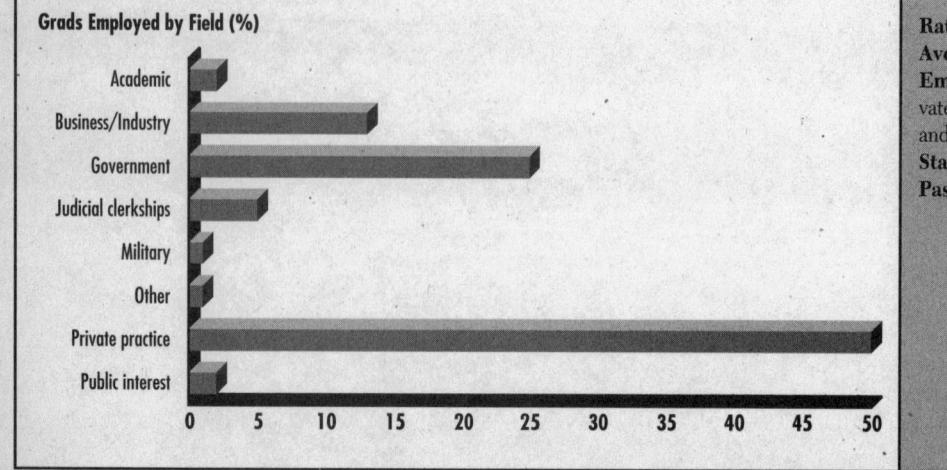

Grads Employed by Field (%)
- Academic
- Business/Industry
- Government
- Judicial clerkships
- Military
- Other
- Private practice
- Public interest

Rate of Placement: 94%
Average Starting Salary: $53,469
Employers Who Frequently Hire Grads: Private law firms, government agencies, business and industry
State for Bar Exam: NY
Pass Rate for First-Time Bar: 77%

AMERICAN UNIVERSITY
Washington College of Law

Admissions Contact: Director of Admissions, Sandra Oakman
4801 Massachusetts Avenue NW, Washington, DC 20016
Admissions Phone: 202-274-4101 • Admissions Fax: 202-274-4107
Admissions E-mail: admissions@wcl.american.edu • Web Address: www.wcl.american.edu

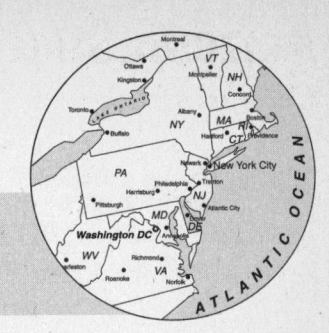

INSTITUTIONAL INFORMATION
Public/Private: Private
Environment: Urban
Academic Calendar: Semester
Schedule: Full time or part time
Student/Faculty Ratio: 18:1
Total Faculty: 193
% Part Time: 68
% Female: 34
% Minority: 16

PROGRAMS
Academic Specialties: International Law (Human Rights, International Business, International Organizations, Gender), Clinical Education, externships and experiential learning in General Law and Government, Legal Theory (especially History, Jurisprudence)
Advanced Degrees Offered: LLM International Legal Studies (12–18 months), LLM Law and Government (12 months), SJD program newly approved during 1999–2000 academic year (no estimate of program length available)
Combined Degrees Offered: JD/MBA, JD/MBA Health Care Management, JD/MA International Relations, JD/MS Mass Communication, JD/MA Preservation Studies, JD/MPH Public Health, JD/MA Philosophy, JD/LLM Taxation (all 3.5–4 years)
Grading System: A, A–, B+, B–, C+, C, D, F, with no mandatory curve
Clinical Program Required? No
Clinical Program Description: Criminal Justice, D.C. Civil Litigation, Civil Clinic, Domestic Violence, International Human Rights, Tax, Women and the Law, Community and Economic Development
Legal Writing/Methods Course Requirements: 26 small sections; 1-year program on legal research, writing, skills

STUDENT INFORMATION
Enrollment of Law School: 1,321
% Male/Female: 37/63
% Full Time: 66
% Full Time That Are International: 4
% Minority: 21
Average Age of Entering Class: 24

RESEARCH FACILITIES
Computers/Workstations Available: 100
School-Supported Research Centers: Assistance for students with laptop configuration for access to the network; high-capacity printer access in the library and labs; every student with a laptop can access the WCL network and internet in each and every classroom; 32 Pentium class and 8 PowerPC class computers, which run Microsoft Windows 95 and Mac OS 8.1 respectively; Lexis-Nexis and Westlaw research software; for students in the Clinic Program, WCL offers a lab of 16 workstations including 10 on which Amicus case management software is installed and a dedicated and secure Novell file server; several online databases support an Externship program, a Clinic program, a Clerkship program and jobs and mentoring opportunities for current students and alumni

EXPENSES/FINANCIAL AID
Annual Tuition: $23,696
Room and Board: $9,126
Books and Supplies: $830
Financial Aid Application Deadline: 3/1
Average Grant: $8,063
Average Loan: $16,926
% of Aid That Is Merit-Based: 2
% Receiving Some Sort of Aid: 80
Average Total Aid Package: $25,042
Average Debt: $53,310
Tuition Per Credit: $382
Fees Per Credit: $837

ADMISSIONS INFORMATION
Application Fee: $55
Regular Application Deadline: 3/1
Regular Notification: Rolling
LSDAS Accepted? Yes
Average GPA: 3.3
Range of GPA: 3.0–3.5
Average LSAT: 156
Range of LSAT: 153–159
Transfer Students Accepted? Yes
Other Schools to Which Students Applied: George Washington University, Georgetown University, Catholic University of America, Boston College, Boston University, University of Maryland, George Mason University, College of William and Mary
Other Admissions Factors Considered: All of the above criteria may be important.
Number of Applications Received: 5,021
Number of Applicants Accepted: 2,117
Number of Applicants Enrolled: 524

INTERNATIONAL STUDENTS
TOEFL Required of International Students? Yes
Minimum TOEFL: 600

EMPLOYMENT INFORMATION

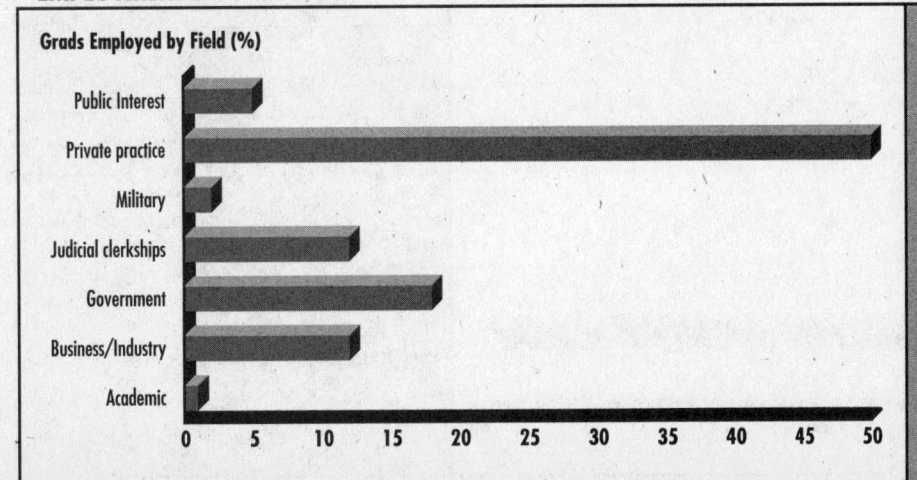

Grads Employed by Field (%)
- Public Interest
- Private practice
- Military
- Judicial clerkships
- Government
- Business/Industry
- Academic

Rate of Placement: 96%
Average Starting Salary: $49,340
Employers Who Frequently Hire Grads: Akin, Gump, Strauss, Hauer and Feld, LLP; Jones, Day, Reavis and Pogue; Manhattan District Attorney; Department of Justice; Shearman and Sterling; Dickstein, Shapiro and Morin, LLP
Prominent Alumni: Robert Byrd, U.S. senator (D-WV); Enrico Lazio, congressman (R-NY); Carol Crawford, comissioner, International Trade Comission; Joseph Hartaler, chief prosecutor, Oklahoma City bombing case—Timothy McVeigh, Department of Justice
State for Bar Exam: MD
Number Taking Bar Exam: 89
Pass Rate for First-Time Bar: 68%

Arizona State University
College of Law

Admissions Contact: Assistant Dean for Admissions, Brenda Brock
PO Box 877906, Tempe, AZ 85287-7906
Admissions Phone: 602-965-1474 • Admissions Fax: 602-965-5550
Admissions E-mail: law.admissions@asu.edu • Web Address: www.law.asu.edu

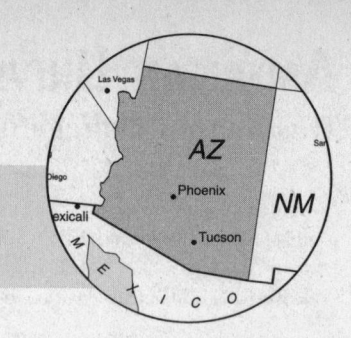

INSTITUTIONAL INFORMATION
Public/Private: Public
Student/Faculty Ratio: 14:1
Total Faculty: 51
% Part Time: 0
% Female: 25
% Minority: 10

PROGRAMS
Academic Specialties: Clinical program; Indian Legal Program/Certificate in Indian Law; Certificate in Law, Science, and Technology (Intellectual Property, Environment, or Health); Constitutional Law; Philosophy of Law
Advanced Degrees Offered: JD (3 years)
Combined Degrees Offered: JD/MBA (4 years), JD/PhD Justice Studies (varies)
Grading System: Distinguished (99–90), Excellent (89–85), Very Good (84–80), Good (79–75), Satisfactory (74–70), Deficient (69–65), Failing (64). Some Pass/Fail courses are offered.
Clinical Program Required? No
Clinical Programs Description: 4 "hands-on" clinics supplemented by innovative simulation courses in trial advocacy, pre-trial discovery practice, negotiation and mediation, and alternative dispute resolution. Students enrolled in the Criminal Practice Clinic or Public Defender Clinic represent either the State of Arizona or individual clients in misdemeanor cases. Students in the Civil Practice Clinic handle civil cases in local courts and represent criminal clients in contested administrative hearings. In the Mediation Clinic, students explore the problem-solving dimension of lawyering, as they work on nonlitigation solutions to a broad range of disputes.
Legal Writing Course Requirements? Yes
Legal Writing Description: Required as part of the first-year Legal Method and Writing Program; 2-semester course, which includes writing legal memoranda, motions, letters, and other assignments.
Legal Methods Course Requirements? Yes
Legal Methods Description: Required as part of the first-year Legal Method and Writing Program; 2-semester course, which covers legal analysis, including case analysis, statutory analysis, synthesis, etc.
Legal Research Course Requirements? Yes
Legal Research Description: Required as part of the first-year Legal Method and Writing Program; 2-semester course, which covers manual legal research, and electronic legal research.
Moot Court Requirement? Yes
Moot Court Description: Numerous moot court competitions.
Public Interest Law Requirement? No
Academic Journals: *Arizona State Law Journal, Jurimetrics Journal of Law, Science and Technology*

STUDENT INFORMATION
Enrollment of Law School: 534
% Out of State: 25
% Male/Female: 50/50
% Full Time: 100
% Full Time That Are International: 1
% Minority: 28
Average Age of Entering Class: 28

RESEARCH FACILITIES
Research Resources Available: Lexis/Nexis, Westlaw
School-Supported Research Centers: Center for the Study of Law, Science, and Technology; Indian Legal Program

EXPENSES/FINANCIAL AID
Annual Tuition (Residents/Nonresidents): $5,162/$13,028
Room and Board (Off Campus): $7,026
Books and Supplies: $726
Financial Aid Application Deadline: 3/2
Average Grant: $4,988
Average Loan: $14,407
% Receiving Some Sort of Aid: 86
Average Total Aid Package: $15,260
Average Debt: $39,759

ADMISSIONS INFORMATION
Application Fee: $45
Regular Application Deadline: 2/15
Regular Notification: Rolling
LSDAS Accepted? Yes
Average GPA: 3.3
Average LSAT: 156
Other Schools to Which Students Applied: University of Arizona
Number of Applications Received: 2,003
Number of Applicants Accepted: 490
Number of Applicants Enrolled: 176

INTERNATIONAL STUDENTS
TOEFL Required of International Students? Yes

EMPLOYMENT INFORMATION

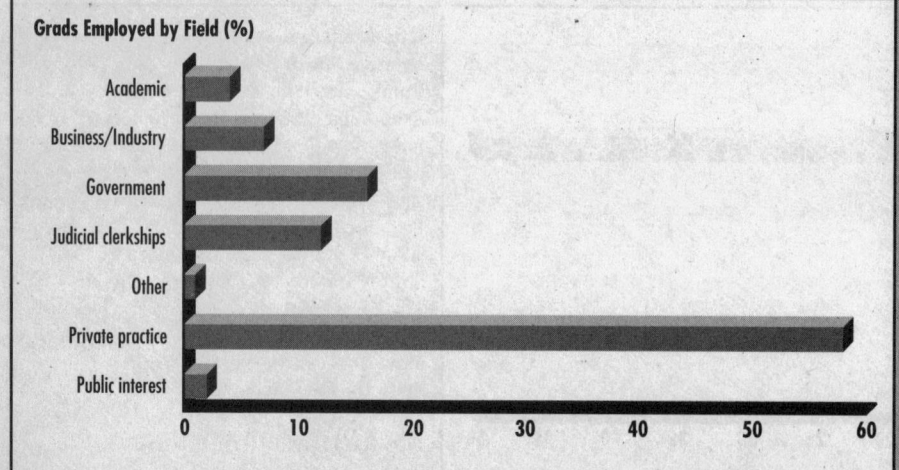

Grads Employed by Field (%)

Field	%
Academic	~2
Business/Industry	~12
Government	~17
Judicial clerkships	~12
Other	~1
Private practice	~57
Public interest	~2

Rate of Placement: 97%
Average Starting Salary: $72,910
Employers Who Frequently Hire Grads: Snell & Wilmer; Brown & Bain; Gammage & Birnham; Lewis and Roca; Fennemore Craig; Jennings, Strouss & Salmon; Gallagher & Kennedy; Quarles & Brady, Streich, Lang; Ryley, Carlock & Applewhite; Steptoe Johnson; Morrison Hecker; Mariscal Weeks; Meyer Hendricks; Osborn Maledon; Bryan Cave; Squires, Sanders & Dempsey
State for Bar Exam: AZ
Pass Rate for First-Time Bar: 86%

BAYLOR UNIVERSITY
School of Law

Admissions Contact: Admission Director, Becky Beck
PO Box 97288, Waco, TX 76798
Admissions Phone: 254-710-1911 • Admissions Fax: 254-710-2316
Admissions E-mail: becky_becky@baylor.edu • Web Address: law.baylor.edu

INSTITUTIONAL INFORMATION
Public/Private: Private
Affiliation: Southern Baptist
Student/Faculty Ratio: 20:1
Total Faculty: 56
% Part Time: 61
% Female: 20
% Minority: 4

PROGRAMS
Academic Specialties: General Civil Litigation, Business Litigation, Estate Planning, Criminal Practice, Business Transaction, Administrative Practice, Civil Procedure, Criminal Law
Combined Degrees Offered: JD/MBA, JD/M Taxation, JD/MPPA (all 3.5 to 4 years)
Grading System: Letter and numerical system, 4.0 scale: A (4.0), A– (3.5), B (3.0), B– (2.5), C (2.0), D (1.0), F (0.0)
Clinical Program Required? Yes
Clinical Program Description: All students are required to participate in our 2-quarter, 12-credit-hour Practice Court Program with a minimum of 4 trials plus other advocacy training exercises.
Legal Writing Course Requirements? Yes
Legal Writing Description: In the students' third quarter, they take a required 2-credit-hour Legal Analysis, Research and Communications III course. The students are required to write and rewrite an appellate brief.
Legal Methods Course Requirements? Yes
Legal Methods Description: Legal Analysis, Research and Communications. 3-part course for 4 quarter hours taught over 3 quarters. LARC I focuses on legal analysis and memo writing. LARC II concentrates on research skills. For LARC III, students continue with writing exercises and write and argue an appellate brief.
Legal Research Course Requirements? Yes
Legal Research Description: Our 1-credit-hour LARC II course is taken in the students' second quarter of law school. The course concentrates on research skills, both using technology and without the assistance of technology.
Moot Court Requirement? Yes
Moot Court Description: As part of our third-quarter required LARC III course, students are required to write a competition brief and participate in a class moot court round. Students then complete a minimum of 3 rounds as part of the fall or spring intraschool moot court competitions.
Public Interest Law Requirement? No
Academic Journals: *Baylor Law Review*

STUDENT INFORMATION
Enrollment of Law School: 389
% Out of State: 21
% Male/Female: 61/39
% Full Time: 100
% Full Time That Are International: 1
% Minority: 11
Average Age of Entering Class: 27

EXPENSES/FINANCIAL AID
Annual Tuition: $14,719
Room and Board (On/Off Campus): $9,051/$13,194
Books and Supplies: $600
Financial Aid Application Deadline: 5/1
Average Grant: $4,860
Average Loan: $21,170
% of Aid That Is Merit-Based: 32
% Receiving Some Sort of Aid: 98
Average Total Aid Package: $19,512
Average Debt: $46,457
Tuition Per Credit: $359
Fees Per Credit: $20

ADMISSIONS INFORMATION
Application Fee: $40
Regular Application Deadline: 3/1
Regular Notification: Rolling
LSDAS Accepted? Yes
Average GPA: 3.6
Range of GPA: 3.3–3.8
Average LSAT: 161
Range of LSAT: 159–163
Transfer Students Accepted? Yes
Other Schools to Which Students Applied: University of Texas at Austin, University of Houston, Texas Tech University, Southern Methodist University
Other Admissions Factors Considered: Achievements, work and life experiences, evidence of maturity, strong work ethic
Number of Applications Received: 1,259
Number of Applicants Accepted: 461
Number of Applicants Enrolled: 63

EMPLOYMENT INFORMATION

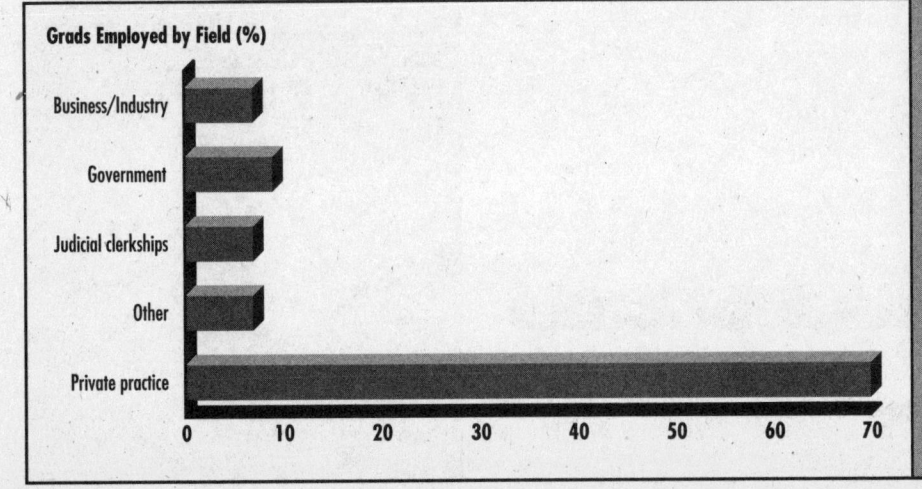

Grads Employed by Field (%)

Field	%
Business/Industry	~7
Government	~8
Judicial clerkships	~8
Other	~7
Private practice	~70

Rate of Placement: 96%
Average Starting Salary: $57,000
Employers Who Frequently Hire Grads: Akin Gump, Jenkins & Gilcrest, Thompson & Knight, Strasburger & Price, Baker & Botts, Haynes & Boone, Bracewell & Patterson, Jackson Walker, Fulbright & Jaworski, Andrews & Kurth, Winstead Sechrest, Liddell Sapp
State for Bar Exam: TX
Pass Rate for First-Time Bar: 89%

Boston College
Law School

Admissions Contact: Director of Admissions
885 Centre Street, Newton, MA 02459
Admissions Phone: 617-552-4351 • Admissions Fax: 617-552-2917
Admissions E-mail: bclawadmis@bc.edu • Web Address: www.bc.edu/lawschool

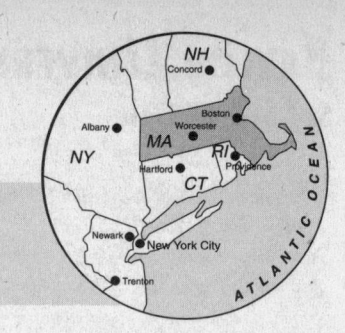

INSTITUTIONAL INFORMATION
Public/Private: Private
Affiliation: Roman Catholic
Student/Faculty Ratio: 13:1
Total Faculty: 78
% Part Time: 35
% Female: 27
% Minority: 11

PROGRAMS
Academic Specialties: Civil Procedure, Commercial Law, Constitutional Law, Corporation Securities Law, Criminal Law, Environmental Law, Human Rights Law, International Law, Labor Law, Legal History, Legal Philosophy, Property, Taxation
Advanced Degrees Offered: JD (3 years)
Combined Degrees Offered: JD/MBA (4 years), JD/MSW (4 years), JD/MEd (3 years)
Grading System: Standard A, B, C, D system on a 4.0 scale
Clinical Program Required? No
Clinical Program Description: Legal Assistance Bureau, Criminal Process, Attorney General Clinical Program, Judicial Process, Urban Legal Laboratory, Juvenile Rights Advocacy, and Immigration Law Clinic
Legal Writing Course Requirements? Yes
Legal Writing Description: First year, 2 semesters, 5 credits total (see below)
Legal Methods Course Requirements? Yes
Legal Methods Description: 5 credits, 2 semesters
Legal Research Course Requirements? Yes
Moot Court Requirement? No
Public Interest Law Requirement? No
Academic Journals: Boston College Law Review, International and Comparative Law Journal, Environmental Law Journal, Third World Law Journal, Uniform Commercial Code Digest

STUDENT INFORMATION
Enrollment of Law School: 805
% Out of State: 63
% Male/Female: 49/51
% Full Time: 100
% Full Time That Are International: 2
% Minority: 19
Average Age of Entering Class: 25

RESEARCH FACILITIES
% of JD Classrooms Wired: 98

EXPENSES/FINANCIAL AID
Annual Tuition: $27,080
Room and Board (Off Campus): $12,985
Books and Supplies: $840
Financial Aid Application Deadline: 3/15
Average Grant: $10,063
Average Loan: $26,017
% Receiving Some Sort of Aid: 85
Average Debt: $63,500

ADMISSIONS INFORMATION
Application Fee: $65
Regular Application Deadline: 3/1
Regular Notification: Rolling
LSDAS Accepted? Yes
Average GPA: 3.5
Range of GPA: 3.3–3.7
Average LSAT: 162
Range of LSAT: 159–164
Transfer Students Accepted? Yes
Other Schools to Which Students Applied: Fordham University, Boston University, George Washington University, Georgetown University
Number of Applications Received: 5,363
Number of Applicants Accepted: 1,263
Number of Applicants Enrolled: 276

EMPLOYMENT INFORMATION

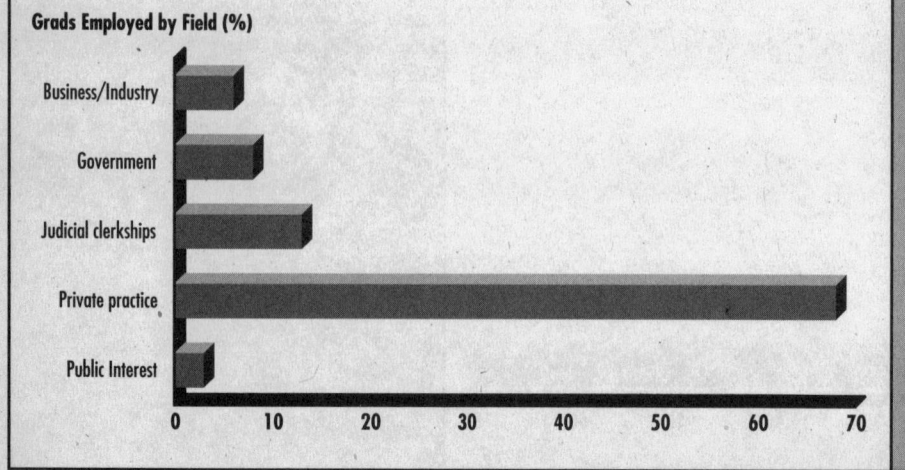

Grads Employed by Field (%)
- Business/Industry
- Government
- Judicial clerkships
- Private practice
- Public Interest

Rate of Placement: 98%
State for Bar Exam: MA
Pass Rate for First-Time Bar: 92%

Boston University
School of Law

Admissions Contact: Director of Admissions and Financial Aid, Joan Horgan
765 Commonwealth Avenue, Boston, MA 02215
Admissions Phone: 617-353-3100 • Admissions Fax: 617-353-0578
Admissions E-mail: bulawadm@bu.edu • Web Address: www.bu.edu/law

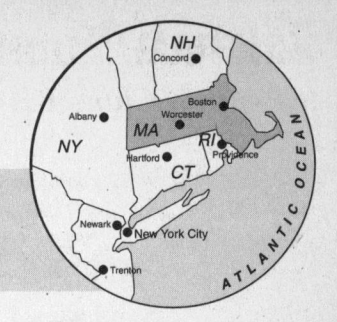

INSTITUTIONAL INFORMATION
Public/Private: Private
Student/Faculty Ratio: 11:1
Total Faculty: 142
% Part Time: 47
% Female: 26
% Minority: 6

PROGRAMS
Academic Specialties: Academic specialties of faculty are very broad ranging; special strengths of curriculum include Antitrust, Law and Economics, Constitutional Law, Administrative Law, Health Law, Labor Law, Intellectual Property Law, International Law, Civil Procedure, Corporate Law, Legal Philosophy, Civil and Criminal clinical programs, Corporation Securities Law, Taxation, Litigation and Dispute Resolution
Advanced Degrees Offered: LLM Taxation (1 year full time, up to 6 years part time); LLM Banking and Financial Law (1 year full time, up to 5 years part time); LLM American Law (1 year full time)
Combined Degrees Offered: JD/MBA, JD/MBA Health Care Management, JD/MA International Relations, JD/MS Mass Communication, JD/MA Preservation Studies, JD/MPH, JD/MSW, JD/MA Philosophy, JD/LLM Taxation, JD/LLM Banking (all 3.5 to 4 years)
Grading System: Letter and numerical system on a 4.3 scale
Clinical Program Required? No
Clinical Programs Description: Legislative Services (Health Law, Intellectual Property Law), Legislative Externship Program, Criminal Trial Advocacy (Prosecution and Criminal Defense), Judicial Internship, Legal Externship, Civil Litigation Program (Disability Law, Employment Law, Housing Law, Family Law, Immigration/Human Rights Law)
Legal Writing Course Requirements? Yes
Legal Writing Description: Full-year, small-group program for first-year students
Legal Methods Course Requirements? No
Legal Research Course Requirements? Yes
Legal Research Description: Full-year, small-group program for first-year students
Moot Court Requirement? No
Public Interest Law Requirement? No
Academic Journals: American Journal of Law and Medicine, Annual Review of Banking Law, Boston University Law Review, International Law Journal, Public Interest Law Journal, Journal of Science and Technology Law

STUDENT INFORMATION
Enrollment of Law School: 837
% Out of State: 62
% Male/Female: 47/53
% Full Time: 100
% Full Time That Are International: 3
% Minority: 22
Average Age of Entering Class: 23

EXPENSES/FINANCIAL AID
Annual Tuition: $25,872
Room and Board: $9,795
Books and Supplies: $1,056
Financial Aid Application Deadline: 3/1
Average Grant: $14,680
Average Loan: $26,163
% of Aid That Is Merit-Based: 5
% Receiving Some Sort of Aid: 83
Average Total Aid Package: $25,428
Average Debt: $72,953

ADMISSIONS INFORMATION
Application Fee: $60
Regular Application Deadline: 3/1
Regular Notification: Rolling
LSDAS Accepted? Yes
Average GPA: 3.4
Range of GPA: 3.1–3.6
Average LSAT: 163
Range of LSAT: 161–165
Transfer Students Accepted? Yes
Other Schools to Which Students Applied: American University, Boston College, Fordham University, George Washington University, Georgetown University, New York University
Other Admissions Factors Considered: Grade trends, quality and difficulty of courses taken, leadership ability, motivation for study of law, economic or social obstacles overcome by an applicant, outstanding nonacademic achievements
Number of Applications Received: 5,171
Number of Applicants Accepted: 1,310
Number of Applicants Enrolled: 246

INTERNATIONAL STUDENTS
TOEFL Required of International Students? Yes
Minimum TOEFL: 250

EMPLOYMENT INFORMATION

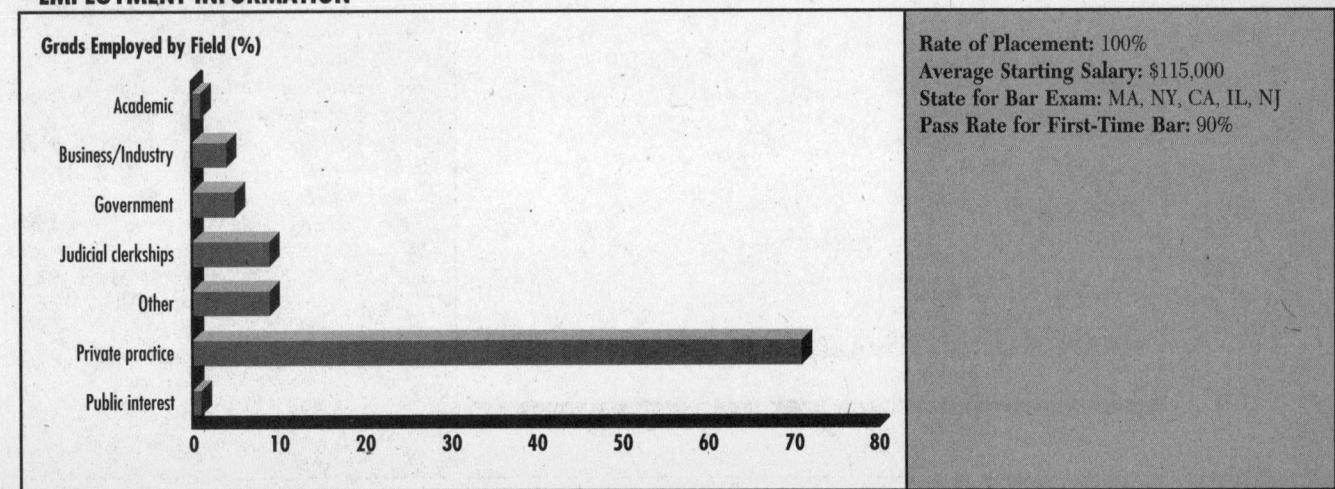

Grads Employed by Field (%)
- Academic
- Business/Industry
- Government
- Judicial clerkships
- Other
- Private practice
- Public interest

Rate of Placement: 100%
Average Starting Salary: $115,000
State for Bar Exam: MA, NY, CA, IL, NJ
Pass Rate for First-Time Bar: 90%

BRIGHAM YOUNG UNIVERSITY
J. Reuben Clark Law School

Admissions Contact: Director of Admissions, Lola Wilcock
340 JRCB, Brigham Young University Law School, Provo, UT 84602
Admissions Phone: 801-378-4277 • Admissions Fax: 801-378-5897
Admissions E-mail: wilcockl@lawgate.byu.edu • Web Address: www.law2.byu.edu

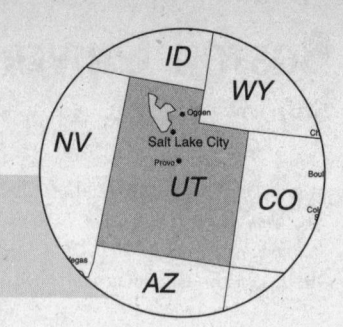

INSTITUTIONAL INFORMATION
Public/Private: Private
Affiliation: Church of Jesus Christ of Latter-day Saints
Student/Faculty Ratio: 17:1
Total Faculty: 70
% Part Time: 46
% Female: 26
% Minority: 7

PROGRAMS
Academic Specialties: The faculty and curriculum are strong across the board, but particular curricular strengths include Intellectual Property, International and Comparative Law, Federal Taxation, Commercial Law, Constitutional Law, and skills training.
Advanced Degrees Offered: Comparative Law (1 school year)
Combined Degrees Offered: JD/MBA, JD/MPA, JD/MAcc, JD/MOB, JD/MEd (each 4 years); JD/EdD (5 years)
Grading System: 4.0 scale with a set median of 3.2 and no credit for grades under 2.2
Clinical Program Required? No
Legal Writing Course Requirements? Yes
Legal Writing Description: Advocacy 1 and 2 are required first-year courses focusing on legal writing, research, analysis, and appellate oral advocacy. Students prepare 3 predictive memoranda in the fall semester and prepare an appellate brief and orally argue a case during the winter semester.
Legal Methods Course Requirements? No
Legal Research Course Requirements? Yes

Legal Research Description: As part of first-year Advocacy, students develop skills using both manual and electronic legal research sources. They also acquire and exercise research strategy skills as they work with fact situations and prepare memoranda and briefs. An upper division Advanced Legal Research course is also required during the second or third year.
Moot Court Requirement? Yes
Moot Court Description: All first-year students participate in a moot court competition as part of their Advocacy course.
Public Interest Law Requirement? No
Academic Journals: *Law Review, Journal of Public Law, Education and Law Journal*

STUDENT INFORMATION
Enrollment of Law School: 480
% Out of State: 57
% Male/Female: 69/31
% Full Time: 100
% Full Time That Are International: 2
% Minority: 18
Average Age of Entering Class: 26

RESEARCH FACILITIES
Research Resources Available: Central European University (Budapest, Hungary); T.C. Beirne School of Law at the University of Queensland (Brisbane, Australia)
School-Supported Research Centers: World Family Policy Center, Center for Law and Religion Studies, Rex E. Lee Advocacy Program

EXPENSES/FINANCIAL AID
Annual Tuition: $6,140
Room and Board (On/Off Campus): $6,100/$7,375
Books and Supplies: $1,230
Financial Aid Application Deadline: 6/1
Average Grant: $2,500
Average Loan: $12,000
% of Aid That Is Merit-Based: 33
% Receiving Some Sort of Aid: 89
Average Total Aid Package: $10,000
Average Debt: $24,000
Tuition Per Credit: $342

ADMISSIONS INFORMATION
Application Fee: $50
Regular Application Deadline: 2/1
Regular Notification: Rolling
LSDAS Accepted? Yes
Average GPA: 3.7
Average LSAT: 161
Transfer Students Accepted? Yes
Other Schools to Which Students Applied: Georgetown, Loyola Marymount, U. of Nevada Las Vegas, U. of Southern California, U. of Utah, UT Austin
Number of Applications Received: 677
Number of Applicants Accepted: 240
Number of Applicants Enrolled: 153

INTERNATIONAL STUDENTS
TOEFL Required of International Students? Yes
Minimum TOEFL: 242

EMPLOYMENT INFORMATION

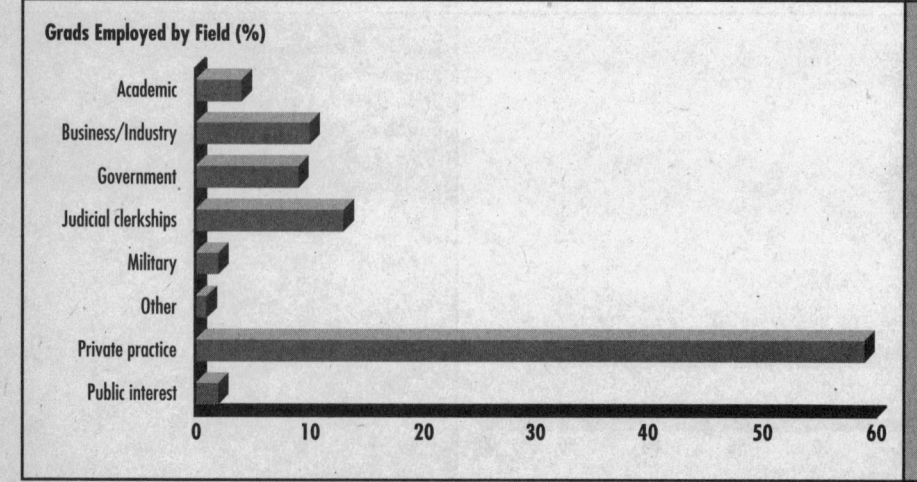

Grads Employed by Field (%)

Field	%
Academic	~3
Business/Industry	~10
Government	~8
Judicial clerkships	~14
Military	~1
Other	~2
Private practice	~60
Public interest	~2

Rate of Placement: 100%
Average Starting Salary: $76,453
Employers Who Frequently Hire Grads: Alston & Bird; Alverson Taylor; Baker & McKenzie; Blakely, Sokoloff, Taylor & Zafman; Covington & Burling; Dechert; federal and state courts; Fennemore Craig; Gallagher & Kennedy; Gibson, Dunn & Crutcher; Hughes & Luce; U.S. JAG Corps; Knobbe, Martens, Olson & Bear; Latham & Watkins; Milbank Tweed; Morrison & Foerster; Nixon Peabody; Ray, Quinney & Nebeker; Stoel

BROOKLYN LAW SCHOOL

Admissions Contact: Dean of Admissions and Financial Aid, Henry W. Haverstick III
250 Joralemon Street, Brooklyn, NY 11201
Admissions Phone: 718-780-7906 • Admissions Fax: 718-780-0395
Admissions E-mail: admitq@brooklaw.edu • Web Address: www.brooklaw.edu

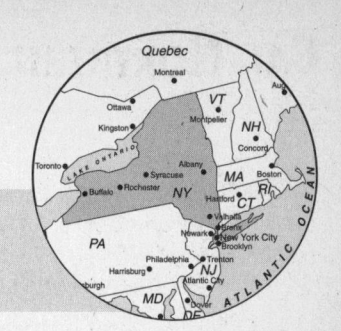

INSTITUTIONAL INFORMATION
Public/Private: Private
Student/Faculty Ratio: 20:1
Total Faculty: 152
% Female: 39
% Minority: 6

PROGRAMS
Academic Specialties: Criminal Law, Advocacy, International Business Law, International Human Rights, Liability, Intellectual Property, Public Interest, Litigation, Civil Procedure, Commercial Law, Constitutional Law, Corporation Securities Law, Government Services, International Law, Legal History, Legal Philosophy, Property, Taxation, Law and Cognition
Combined Degrees Offered: JD/MA Political Science, JD/MS Planning, JD/MBA, JD/MLIS, JD/MUP, JD/MPA
Grading System: Letter system
Clinical Program Required? No
Clinical Programs Description: Capital Defender Clinic, Bankruptcy Clinic, Corporate and Real Estate Clinic, Criminal Appeals Clinic-Manhattan District Attorney's Office, Elderlaw Clinic, Federal Litigation Clinic, Immigration and Asylum (Safe Harbor Project), Legislation and Law Reform Clinic, Mediation Clinic, Prosecutor's Clinic, Civil Practice Internship, Criminal Practice Internship, Judicial Clerkship Internship. Simulation courses offered include Alternative Dispute Resolution, Appellate Advocacy, Civil Practice Workshop: Class and Derivative Action, Discovery Workshop, Evidence Workshop, Family Law Workshop

Legal Writing Course Requirements? Yes
Legal Writing Description: Year-long Legal Writing course, plus one upper-division writing elective; 1 semester of Legal Process
Legal Methods Course Requirements? Yes
Legal Methods Description: See Legal Writing.
Legal Research Course Requirements? Yes
Legal Research Description: Part of the Legal Writing course
Moot Court Requirement? Yes
Moot Court Description: First-year Moot Court Competition as part of Legal Writing course
Public Interest Law Requirement? No
Academic Journals: Brooklyn Law Review, Brooklyn Journal of International Law, Journal of Law and Policy

STUDENT INFORMATION
Enrollment of Law School: 1,515
% Out of State: 31
% Male/Female: 48/52
% Full Time: 71
% Full Time That Are International: 1
% Minority: 19
Average Age of Entering Class: 25

RESEARCH FACILITIES
School-Supported Research Centers: Center for the Study of International Business Law; Edward Sparer Public Interest Fellowship Program; Center for Law, Language, and Cognition

EXPENSES/FINANCIAL AID
Annual Tuition: $26,570
Room and Board (Off Campus): $12,024

Books and Supplies: $1,200
Financial Aid Application Deadline: 3/15
Average Grant: $5,439
Average Loan: $24,923
% of Aid That Is Merit-Based: 63
% Receiving Some Sort of Aid: 43
Average Total Aid Package: $26,141
Average Debt: $70,938
Tuition Per Credit: $19,995
Fees Per Credit: $155

ADMISSIONS INFORMATION
Application Fee: $60
Regular Application Deadline: Rolling
Regular Notification: Rolling
LSDAS Accepted? Yes
Average GPA: 3.4
Range of GPA: 3.1–3.6
Average LSAT: 158
Range of LSAT: 155–160
Transfer Students Accepted? Yes
Other Schools to Which Students Applied: Fordham University, University of Miami, Yeshiva University
Other Admissions Factors Considered: Quality of undergraduate institution; major; GPA trends; grade inflation; advanced degree; maturity; moral character; geographic diversity; economic, racial/ethnic, cultural backgrounds; alumni/ae relationship; honors
Number of Applications Received: 2,812
Number of Applicants Accepted: 1,104
Number of Applicants Enrolled: 307

EMPLOYMENT INFORMATION

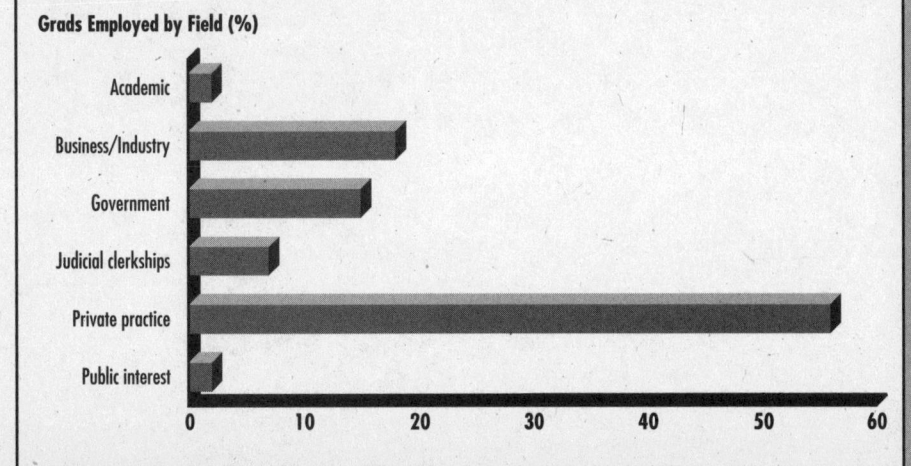

Grads Employed by Field (%)
- Academic: ~2
- Business/Industry: ~18
- Government: ~15
- Judicial clerkships: ~7
- Private practice: ~57
- Public interest: ~2

Rate of Placement: 98%
Average Starting Salary: $94,174
Employers Who Frequently Hire Grads: Fried, Frank, Harris, Shriver & Jacobson; Pillsbury, Winthrop; Proskauer Rose; Kings County District Attorney's Office; New York City Law Department; Skadden, Arps, Slate, Meagher & Flom; Stroock & Stroock & Lavan; Administration for Children's Services; Davis, Polk & Wardwell
State for Bar Exam: NY, NJ
Pass Rate for First-Time Bar: 82%

CAL NORTHERN SCHOOL OF LAW

Admissions Contact: Dean, Sandra L. Brooks
1395 Ridgewood Drive, Chico, CA 95973
Admissions Phone: 530-891-6900 • Admissions Fax: 530-891-3429
Admissions E-mail: info@calnorthern.edu • Web Address: www.calnorthern.edu

INSTITUTIONAL INFORMATION
Public/Private: Private
Student/Faculty Ratio: 4:1
Total Faculty: 18
% Part Time: 100
% Female: 17

PROGRAMS
Academic Specialties: All faculty are practicing attorneys or sitting judges.
Advanced Degrees Offered: JD (4 years)
Clinical Program Required? No
Legal Writing Course Requirements? Yes
Legal Writing Description: Legal Writing required in the first year. Advanced Legal Writing required in the fourth year.
Legal Methods Course Requirements? Yes
Legal Methods Description: See Legal Writing.
Legal Research Course Requirements? Yes
Legal Research Description: Legal Research required in the first year.
Moot Court Requirement? Yes
Moot Court Description: Fourth-Year Trial Advocacy (15 weeks)
Public Interest Law Requirement? No

STUDENT INFORMATION
Enrollment of Law School: 75
% Male/Female: 100/0
% Minority: 0
Average Age of Entering Class: 36

RESEARCH FACILITIES
Research Resources Available: California State University, Chico and Butte County Law Library

EXPENSES/FINANCIAL AID
Annual Tuition: $5,312
Books and Supplies: $300
Average Grant: $250
Average Loan: $5,000
% Receiving Some Sort of Aid: 5
Tuition Per Credit: $275

ADMISSIONS INFORMATION
Application Fee: $50
Regular Application Deadline: 6/2
Regular Notification: 7/2
LSDAS Accepted? No
Average GPA: 3.1
Average LSAT: 145
Transfer Students Accepted? Yes
Number of Applications Received: 32
Number of Applicants Accepted: 32
Number of Applicants Enrolled: 32

CALIFORNIA WESTERN
School of Law

Admissions Contact: Director of Admissions, Traci Howard
225 Cedar Street, San Diego, CA 92101
Admissions Phone: 619-525-1401 • Admissions Fax: 619-615-1403
Admissions E-mail: admissions@cwsl.edu • Web Address: www.californiawestern.edu

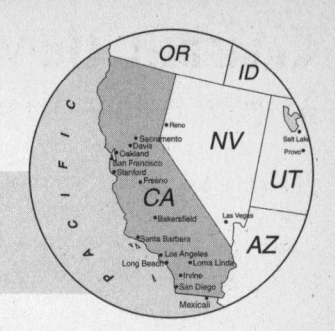

INSTITUTIONAL INFORMATION
Public/Private: Private
Student/Faculty Ratio: 21:1
Total Faculty: 58
% Part Time: 43
% Female: 38
% Minority: 1

PROGRAMS
Academic Specialties: Constitutional Law, Criminal Law, Environmental Law, International Law, Labor Law, Taxation, Child/Family/Elder Law, Creative Problem Solving, Biotechnology Law, Telecommunications Law
Advanced Degrees Offered: JD (2 to 3 years), MCL/LLM (9 months), LLM Trial Advocacy (1 year)
Combined Degrees Offered: JD/MSW (4 years), JD/MBA (4 years), JD/PhD Political Science or History (5 years)
Grading System: 95–50 numerical scale with mandatory curve
Clinical Program Required? No
Legal Writing Course Requirements? Yes
Legal Writing Description: 3-course series required first, second, third, or fourth trimester
Legal Methods Course Requirements? Yes
Legal Methods Description: See Legal Writing.
Legal Research Course Requirements? Yes
Legal Research Description: See Legal Writing.
Moot Court Requirement? No
Public Interest Law Requirement? No
Academic Journals: California Western Law Review, California Western International Law Journal

STUDENT INFORMATION
Enrollment of Law School: 763
% Out of State: 43
% Male/Female: 45/55
% Full Time: 86
% Full Time That Are International: 2
% Minority: 24
Average Age of Entering Class: 27

EXPENSES/FINANCIAL AID
Annual Tuition: $24,750
Room and Board (Off Campus): $13,196
Books and Supplies: $780
Financial Aid Application Deadline: 3/16
Average Grant: $10,000
Average Loan: $30,000
% of Aid That Is Merit-Based: 10
% Receiving Some Sort of Aid: 87
Average Total Aid Package: $27,000
Average Debt: $84,347
Tuition Per Credit: $870
Fees Per Credit: $70

ADMISSIONS INFORMATION
Application Fee: $45
Regular Application Deadline: 4/2
Regular Notification: Rolling
LSDAS Accepted? Yes
Average GPA: 3.1
Range of GPA: 2.8–3.4
Average LSAT: 151
Range of LSAT: 148–154
Transfer Students Accepted? Yes
Other Schools to Which Students Applied: University of San Diego
Other Admissions Factors Considered: Work experience, volunteer and extracurricular activities, diversity (ethnic, cultural, age)
Number of Applications Received: 1,527
Number of Applicants Accepted: 1,000
Number of Applicants Enrolled: 272

INTERNATIONAL STUDENTS
TOEFL Required of International Students? Yes

EMPLOYMENT INFORMATION

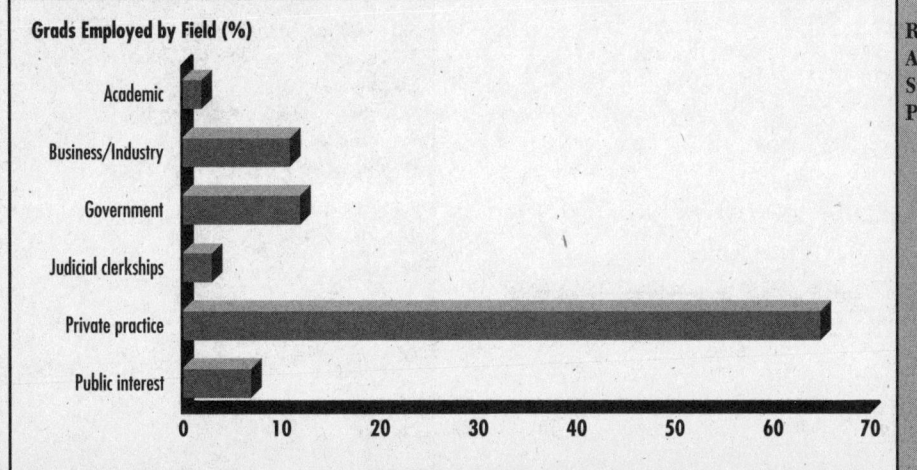

Grads Employed by Field (%)
- Academic
- Business/Industry
- Government
- Judicial clerkships
- Private practice
- Public interest

Rate of Placement: 88%
Average Starting Salary: $60,827
State for Bar Exam: CA, NV, AZ, NY, HI
Pass Rate for First-Time Bar: 82%

CAMPBELL UNIVERSITY
Norman Adrian Wiggins School of Law

Admissions Contact: Associate Dean for Admissions, Alan D. Woodlief, Jr.
Box 158, Buies Creek, NC 27506
Admissions Phone: 910-893-1754 • Admissions Fax: 910-893-1780
Admissions E-mail: culaw@webster.campbell.edu • Web Address: www.law.campbell.edu

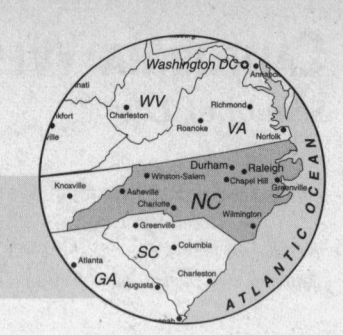

INSTITUTIONAL INFORMATION
Public/Private: Private
Affiliation: Baptist
Student/Faculty Ratio: 15:1
Total Faculty: 31
% Part Time: 42
% Female: 13
% Minority: 3

PROGRAMS
Academic Specialties: Our Trial and Appellate Advocacy Program is a special strength of our curriculum.
Advanced Degrees Offered: JD (3 years/90 semester hours)
Combined Degrees Offered: JD/MBA
Grading System: Graded courses: Superior (93–99), Above Average (84–92), Satisfactory (75–83), Unsatisfactory but Passing (68–74), Failing (60–67). Elective courses: H (honors), S (satisfactory), UP (unsatisfactory pass), UF (unsatisfactory fail).
Clinical Program Required? No
Legal Writing Course Requirements? Yes
Legal Writing Description: Legal writing is a component of our Legal Methods course.
Legal Methods Course Requirements? Yes
Legal Methods Description: 3-semester course. The first fall semester focuses on legal research. The spring semester focuses on an introduction to legal writing, with students preparing various legal documents including complaints, motions, and legal memoranda. The second fall semester focuses on appellate advocacy, with students preparing an appellate brief and presenting an oral argument before a panel of alumni and judges.
Legal Research Course Requirements? Yes
Legal Research Description: Legal research is a component of our Legal Methods course.
Moot Court Requirement? No
Public Interest Law Requirement? No
Academic Journals: *Campbell Law Review*, *Campbell Law Observer*

STUDENT INFORMATION
Enrollment of Law School: 311
% Male/Female: 53/47
% Full Time: 100
% Minority: 7
Average Age of Entering Class: 26

EXPENSES/FINANCIAL AID
Annual Tuition: $19,750
Room and Board (On/Off Campus): $8,608/$11,010
Books and Supplies: $750
Financial Aid Application Deadline: 4/15
Average Grant: $4,600
Average Loan: $28,000
% Receiving Some Sort of Aid: 84

ADMISSIONS INFORMATION
Application Fee: $50
Regular Application Deadline: Rolling
Regular Notification: Rolling
LSDAS Accepted? Yes
Average GPA: 3.3
Range of GPA: 2.9–3.5
Average LSAT: 154
Range of LSAT: 150–156
Transfer Students Accepted? Yes
Other Schools to Which Students Applied: Mercer University, University of North Carolina at Chapel Hill, University of Richmond, University of South Carolina, Wake Forest University
Number of Applications Received: 672
Number of Applicants Accepted: 225
Number of Applicants Enrolled: 113

EMPLOYMENT INFORMATION

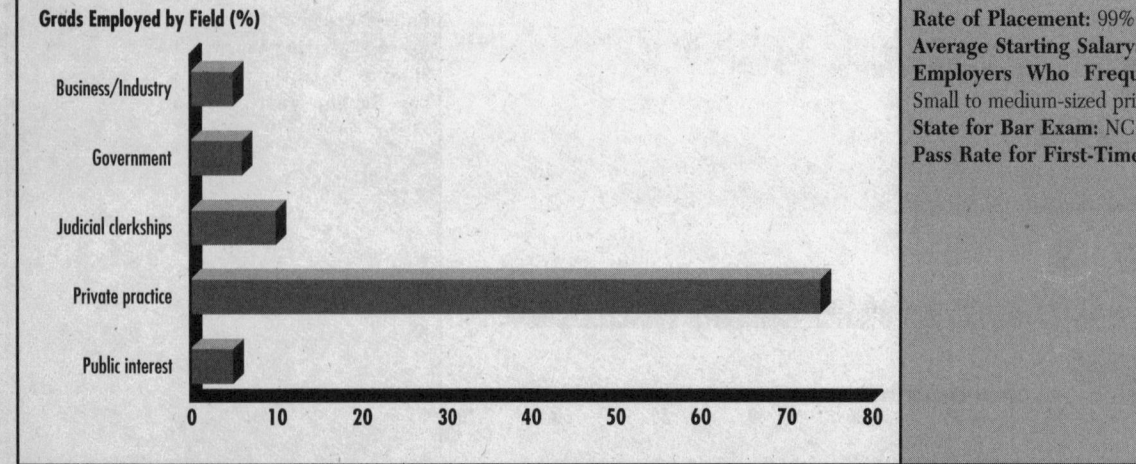

Grads Employed by Field (%)
- Business/Industry: ~5
- Government: ~5
- Judicial clerkships: ~10
- Private practice: ~75
- Public interest: ~5

Rate of Placement: 99%
Average Starting Salary: $40,000
Employers Who Frequently Hire Grads: Small to medium-sized private firms
State for Bar Exam: NC
Pass Rate for First-Time Bar: 93%

CAPITAL UNIVERSITY
Law School

Admissions Contact: Assistant Dean of Admissions and Financial Aid, Linda J. Mihely
303 E. Broad Street, Columbus, OH 43215-3200
Admissions Phone: 614-236-6310 • Admissions Fax: 614-236-6972
Admissions E-mail: admissions@law.capital.edu • Web Address: www.law.capital.edu

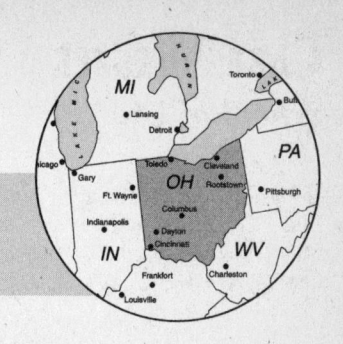

INSTITUTIONAL INFORMATION
Public/Private: Private
Affiliation: Lutheran
Student/Faculty Ratio: 23:1
Total Faculty: 29
% Part Time: 36
% Female: 21
% Minority: 14

PROGRAMS
Academic Specialties: Dispute Resolution, Business Law, Corporate Securities Law, Environmental Law, Children and Family Law, Taxation, Labor Law, International Law, and Government Law are among the faculty's specialties. Strengths include commitment to teaching, innovative centers and institutes, positive relationships with students, open access to students.
Advanced Degrees Offered: LLM in Taxation (1 to 6 years), LLM in Business (1 to 6 years), LLM in Business and Taxation (1 to 6 years), MT (1 to 6 years)
Combined Degrees Offered: JD/MBA (3.5 to 6 years), JD/MSN (3.5 to 6 years), JD/MSA (3.5 to 4 years), JD/MTS (4 to 6 years)
Grading System: 4.0 scale: A, A–, B+, B, B–, C+, C, C–, D, E
Clinical Program Required? No
Clinical Programs Description: General Civil Litigation Clinic, Mediation Clinic, General Criminal Litigation Clinic, Domestic Violence Clinic
Legal Writing Course Requirements? Yes
Legal Writing Description: Year-long course covering research, writing, and methods
Legal Methods Course Requirements? Yes
Legal Methods Description: See Legal Writing.
Legal Research Course Requirements? Yes
Legal Research Description: See Legal Writing.
Moot Court Requirement? No
Moot Court Description: The law school has an active intercollegiate moot court program as well as a first-year student moot court competition.
Public Interest Law Requirement? No
Public Interest Law Description: Students may receive a certificate for participation in the Pro Bono Program.
Academic Journals: *Capital University Law Review*

STUDENT INFORMATION
Enrollment of Law School: 726
% Out of State: 27
% Male/Female: 50/50
% Full Time: 56
% Full Time That Are International: 0
% Minority: 13
Average Age of Entering Class: 25

RESEARCH FACILITIES
Research Resources Available: Supreme Court Law Library, Columbus Law Library Association, Computer Lab, Clinic and Recreation Center
School-Supported Research Centers: Center for Dispute Resolution, Institute for International Legal Education, Institute for Citizen Education, Institute for Adoption Law

EXPENSES/FINANCIAL AID
Annual Tuition: $18,009
Room and Board (Off Campus): $9,471
Books and Supplies: $887
Financial Aid Application Deadline: 4/1
Average Grant: $6,000
Average Loan: $20,400
% of Aid That Is Merit-Based: 40
% Receiving Some Sort of Aid: 93
Average Total Aid Package: $28,737
Average Debt: $53,485
Tuition Per Credit: $621
Fees Per Credit: $621

ADMISSIONS INFORMATION
Application Fee: $35
Regular Application Deadline: Rolling
Regular Notification: Rolling
LSDAS Accepted? Yes
Average GPA: 3.1
Average LSAT: 150
Transfer Students Accepted? Yes
Other Schools to Which Students Applied: Ohio State, University of Dayton, University of Akron, University of Toledo, Cleveland State, Ohio Northern, University of Cincinnati
Other Admissions Factors Considered: Writing skills, employment history, graduate coursework, socio-economic status, demonstrated ability to overcome hardship, diversity, leadership ability, commitment to justice
Number of Applications Received: 1,034
Number of Applicants Accepted: 599
Number of Applicants Enrolled: 276

EMPLOYMENT INFORMATION

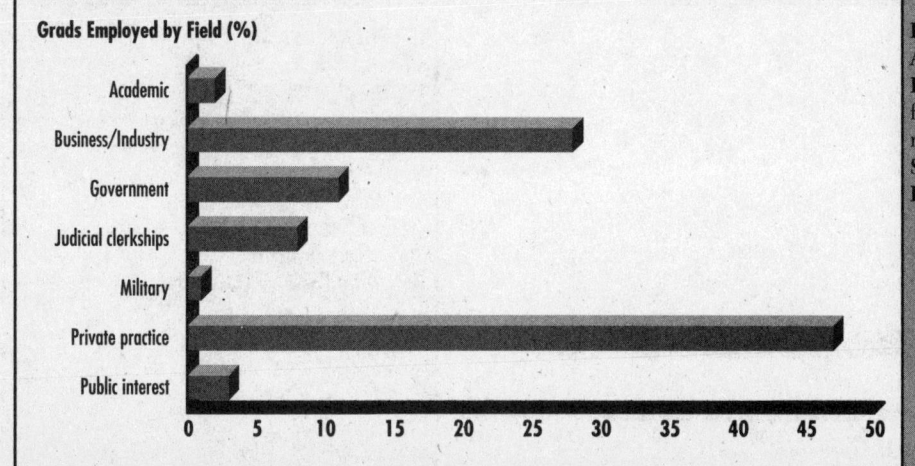

Grads Employed by Field (%)
- Academic: ~1
- Business/Industry: ~28
- Government: ~12
- Judicial clerkships: ~3
- Military: ~1
- Private practice: ~48
- Public interest: ~2

Rate of Placement: 95%
Average Starting Salary: $55,069
Employers Who Frequently Hire Grads: Law firms, government agencies, business and corporate employers
State for Bar Exam: OH
Pass Rate for First-Time Bar: 62%

CASE WESTERN RESERVE UNIVERSITY
School of Law

Admissions Contact: Director of Admissions, Christopher Lucak
11075 East Boulevard, Cleveland, OH 44106
Admissions Phone: 800-756-0036 • Admissions Fax: 216-368-1042
Admissions E-mail: lawadmissions@po.cwru.edu • Web Address: www.law.cwru.edu

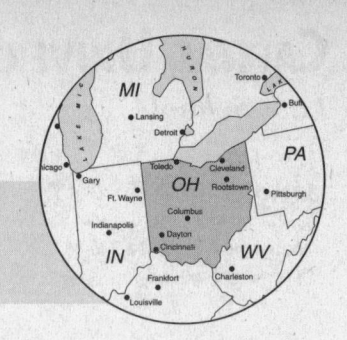

INSTITUTIONAL INFORMATION
Public/Private: Private
Student/Faculty Ratio: 14:1
Total Faculty: 83
% Female: 19
% Minority: 7

PROGRAMS
Academic Specialties: The curriculum is distinguished for both its breadth and depth, with courses offered in virtually every area of the law. Students may pursue concentrations in Law, Technology, and the Arts; Health Law; International Law; Criminal Law; Business Organizations; Public Law; Litigation; Commercial Law; Constitutional Law; Corporation Securities Law; Government Services; Human Rights Law; Intellectual Property Law; or Taxation.
Advanced Degrees Offered: LLM Taxation (1 year), LLM U.S. Legal Studies (1 year),
Combined Degrees Offered: JD/MBA Management (4 years), JD/MNM (4 years), JD/CNM (3 years), JD/MSSA Social Work (4 years), JD/MA Legal History (4 years), JD/MA Bioethics (4 years), JD/MD (7 years), JD/MPH (4 years)
Grading System: A, A–, B+, B, B–, C+, C, C–, D+, D, D–, P, F, WF, W, N (No A+)
Clinical Program Required? No
Clinical Programs Description: Civil Law, Criminal Law, Immigration Law, Community Development Law, Health Law
Legal Writing Course Requirements? Yes
Legal Writing Description: The first-year writing program, known as "RAW" (Research, Analysis, and Writing), is a 2-semester course taught solely by full-time instructors, each of whom is an experienced attorney. Each RAW section meets in a small group of 20–25 students. During the course of the year, students undertake a rigorous program of research and legal writing, ranging from legal memoranda to contracts to trial briefs to appellate briefs.
Legal Methods Course Requirements? No
Legal Research Course Requirements? No
Moot Court Requirement? No
Moot Court Description: The Moot Court Board sponsors both intramural and interschool competitions. Students refine their brief-writing and oral advocacy skills through second-year competition; the most outstanding candidates represent the school in national competition during their third year.
Public Interest Law Requirement? No
Academic Journals: Law Review, Health Matrix, The Journal of Law and Medicine, The Journal of International Law

STUDENT INFORMATION
Enrollment of Law School: 630
% Out of State: 57
% Male/Female: 55/45
% Full Time: 98
% Minority: 15
Average Age of Entering Class: 24

RESEARCH FACILITIES
School-Supported Research Centers: Law-Medicine Center International Law Center, The Milton A. Kramer Law Clinic Center, The Center for Professional Ethics, Center for Law, Technology, and the Arts

EXPENSES/FINANCIAL AID
Annual Tuition: $23,300
Room and Board: $12,005
Books and Supplies: $1,000
Financial Aid Application Deadline: 5/1
Average Grant: $12,800
Average Loan: $23,400
% of Aid That Is Merit-Based: 100
% Receiving Some Sort of Aid: 80
Average Total Aid Package: $28,200
Average Debt: $54,000
Tuition Per Credit: $971

ADMISSIONS INFORMATION
Application Fee: $40
Regular Application Deadline: 4/1
Regular Notification: Rolling
LSDAS Accepted? Yes
Average GPA: 3.2
Range of GPA: 3.0–3.5
Average LSAT: 157
Range of LSAT: 154–160
Transfer Students Accepted? Yes
Other Admissions Factors Considered: Looking at each applicant's file in its entirety, we assess whether we believe the applicant has the intellectual ability to succeed in our program.
Number of Applications Received: 1,554
Number of Applicants Accepted: 861
Number of Applicants Enrolled: 221

EMPLOYMENT INFORMATION

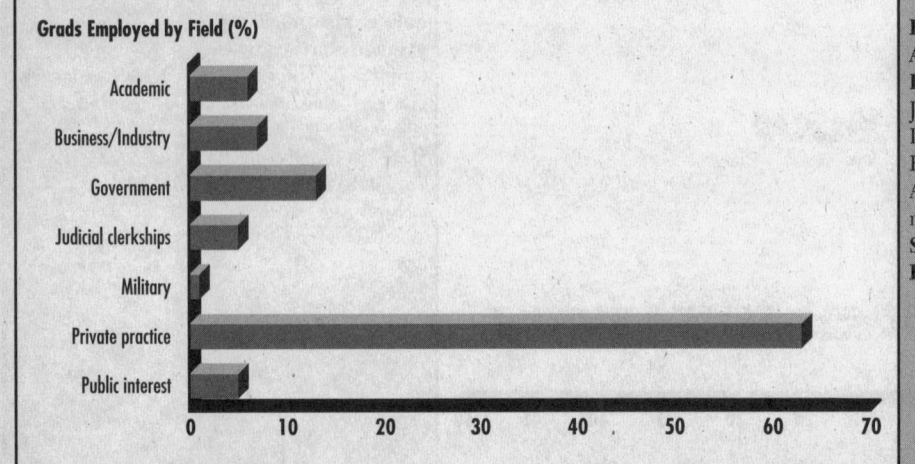

Grads Employed by Field (%)

Field	%
Academic	~2
Business/Industry	~5
Government	~13
Judicial clerkships	~3
Military	~1
Private practice	~63
Public interest	~5

Rate of Placement: 97%
Average Starting Salary: $75,728
Employers Who Frequently Hire Grads: Jones, Day, Reavis & Pogue; Squire, Sanders and Dempsey; Baker & Hostetler; Jenner & Block; Ernst & Young; PricewaterhouseCoopers; Altheimer & Gray; federal government; Department of Justice; state and federal judiciaries
State for Bar Exam: OH
Pass Rate for First-Time Bar: 85%

CATHOLIC UNIVERSITY OF AMERICA
Columbus School of Law

Admissions Contact: Director of Admissions, George Braxton
Office of Admissions, Washington, DC 20064
Admissions Phone: 202-319-5151 • Admissions Fax: 202-319-6285
Admissions E-mail: braxton@law.edu • Web Address: www.law.edu

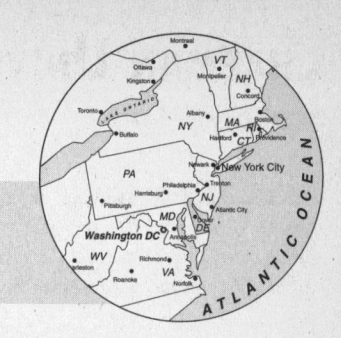

INSTITUTIONAL INFORMATION
Public/Private: Private
Affiliation: Roman Catholic
Environment: Urban
Academic Calendar: Semester
Schedule: Full time or part time
Student/Faculty Ratio: 21:1
Total Faculty: 93
% Part Time: 53
% Female: 34
% Minority: 13

PROGRAMS
Academic Specialties: 3 Institutes/Certificate Programs, Institute for Communications Law Studies, Comparative and International Law Institute, Law and Public Policy
Advanced Degrees Offered: JD (3 years full time, 4 years part time)
Combined Degrees Offered: JD/MA programs in Accounting, Canon Law, History, Philosophy, Psychology, Politics, Library Science, Economics, and Social Work (all 3–4 years)
Grading System: Numerical system on 50–100 scale. A letter-based system will be instituted with the entering class of 1999
Clinical Program Required? No
Clinical Program Description: General Clinic, Families and the Law Clinic, Advocacy for the Elderly, Advocacy for Victims of Gun Violence, Criminal Prosecution Clinic, D.C. Law Students in Court, legal externships, SEC Training Program

STUDENT INFORMATION
Enrollment of Law School: 925
% Male/Female: 48/52
% Full Time: 71
% Full Time That Are International: 1
% Minority: 25
Average Age of Entering Class: 24

RESEARCH FACILITIES
Computers/Workstations Available: 300

EXPENSES/FINANCIAL AID
Annual Tuition: $25,360
Room and Board (On/Off Campus): $6,772/$6,620
Books and Supplies: $780
Financial Aid Application Deadline: 3/15
Average Grant: $7,000
Average Loan: $27,000
% of Aid That Is Merit-Based: 25
% Receiving Some Sort of Aid: 84
Average Total Aid Package: $34,500
Average Debt: $68,000
Fees Per Credit: $880

ADMISSIONS INFORMATION
Application Fee: $55
Regular Application Deadline: 3/1
Regular Notification: Rolling
Average GPA: 3.2
Range of GPA: 3.1–3.3
Average LSAT: 156
Range of LSAT: 153–158
Transfer Students Accepted? Yes
Other Schools to Which Students Applied: George Washington University, American University, Georgetown University, University of Maryland, Boston College, University of Baltimore, George Mason University, Syracuse University
Number of Applications Received: 2,110
Number of Applicants Accepted: 840
Number of Applicants Enrolled: 300

INTERNATIONAL STUDENTS
TOEFL Required of International Students? Yes
Minimum TOEFL: 600

EMPLOYMENT INFORMATION

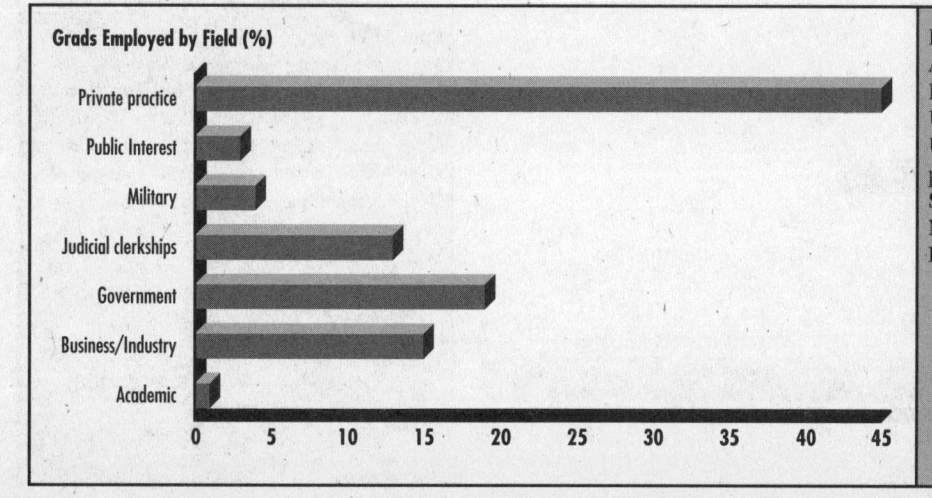

Grads Employed by Field (%)
- Private practice: ~45
- Public Interest: ~3
- Military: ~3
- Judicial clerkships: ~13
- Government: ~20
- Business/Industry: ~15
- Academic: ~1

Rate of Placement: 98%
Average Starting Salary: $50,521
Prominent Alumni: Charlene Barshefsky, JD, U.S. trade representative; Thomas Harkin, JD, U.S. senator; Karen Hastie Williams, JD, senior partner, Crowell and Moring
State for Bar Exam: MD
Number Taking Bar Exam: 104
Pass Rate for First-Time Bar: 70%

CHAPMAN UNIVERSITY
School of Law

Admissions Contact: Assistant Director of Admissions, Diann Heyer
One University Drive, Orange, CA 92866
Admissions Phone: 714-628-2515 • Admissions Fax: 714-628-2501
Admissions E-mail: lawadm@chapman.edu • Web Address: www.chapman.edu/law

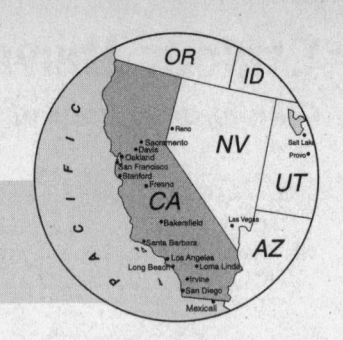

INSTITUTIONAL INFORMATION
Public/Private: Private
Affiliation: Disciples of Christ
Student/Faculty Ratio: 13:1
Total Faculty: 21
% Female: 40
% Minority: 15

PROGRAMS
Academic Specialties: Business/Commercial Law, Taxation, Constitutional Law, Land Use/Environment/Property Law, Elder Law, Criminal Law
Advanced Degrees Offered: JD (3 years full time, 4 years part time),
Combined Degrees Offered: JD/MBA (4 years full time)
Grading System: Letter system on a 4.0 scale using plus and minus grades; 2.0 required for good academic standing and graduation
Clinical Program Required? No
Clinical Programs Description: Live client clinics in Taxation, Bankruptcy, and Elder Law; numerous simulation courses in Advocacy, Dispute Resolution, and Trial Practice
Legal Writing Course Requirements? Yes
Legal Writing Description: 2 semesters (first year) for a total of 5 credits, plus a paper of publishable quality in the second or third year.
Legal Methods Course Requirements? Yes
Legal Methods Description: Incorporated into first-year Legal Writing requirement
Legal Research Course Requirements? Yes
Legal Research Description: Incorporated into first-year Legal Writing requirement
Moot Court Requirement? No
Public Interest Law Requirement? No
Academic Journals: *Chapman Law Review*, *Nexus: A Journal of Opinion*

STUDENT INFORMATION
Enrollment of Law School: 311
% Out of State: 18
% Male/Female: 50/50
% Full Time: 66
% Full Time That Are International: 2
% Minority: 26
Average Age of Entering Class: 26

RESEARCH FACILITIES
Research Resources Available: New state-of-the-art building with computerized classrooms, labs, and the newest technology in courtrooms

EXPENSES/FINANCIAL AID
Annual Tuition: $23,200
Room and Board (Off Campus): $11,000
Books and Supplies: $1,600
Financial Aid Application Deadline: 6/2
Average Grant: $9,800
Average Loan: $16,000
% of Aid That Is Merit-Based: 45
% Receiving Some Sort of Aid: 85
Average Debt: $51,000
Tuition Per Credit: $15,950

ADMISSIONS INFORMATION
Application Fee: $50
Regular Application Deadline: Rolling
Regular Notification: Rolling
LSDAS Accepted? Yes
Average GPA: 3.1
Range of GPA: 2.8–3.3
Average LSAT: 154
Range of LSAT: 150–158
Transfer Students Accepted? Yes
Other Schools to Which Students Applied: Loyola Marymount University, University of San Diego, Pepperdine University, Southwestern University School of Law, Whittier College
Other Admissions Factors Considered: Writing ability, community service
Number of Applications Received: 962
Number of Applicants Accepted: 401
Number of Applicants Enrolled: 131

INTERNATIONAL STUDENTS
TOEFL Required of International Students? Yes
Minimum TOEFL: 250

EMPLOYMENT INFORMATION

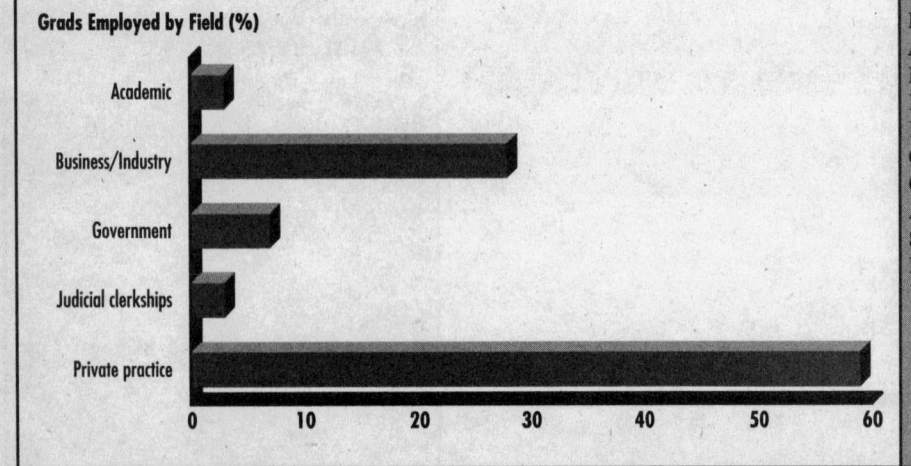

Grads Employed by Field (%)
- Academic: ~1
- Business/Industry: ~28
- Government: ~5
- Judicial clerkships: ~3
- Private practice: ~60

Rate of Placement: 88%
Average Starting Salary: $68,000
Employers Who Frequently Hire Grads: Rutan & Tucker, Kirkland Ellis, O'Melveny & Myers, Orange County District Attorney, Orange County Public Defender, Public Interest Law Center, California courts, Los Angeles District Attorney, Knobbe Martens, Berger Khan
State for Bar Exam: CA, CO
Pass Rate for First-Time Bar: 73%

CITY UNIVERSITY OF NEW YORK
School of Law at Queens College

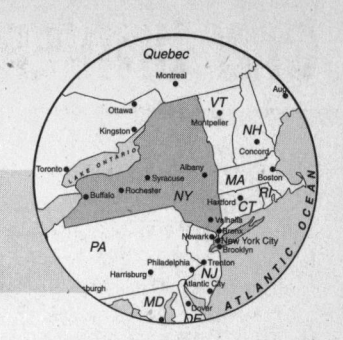

Admissions Contact: Assistant Dean for Enrollment Management & Director of Admissions: Yvonne Cherena Pacheco
65-21 Main Street, Flushing, NY 11367-1358
Admissions Phone: 718-340-4210 • Admissions Fax: 718-340-4435
Admissions E-mail: admissions@mail.law.cuny.edu • Web Address: www.law.cuny.edu

INSTITUTIONAL INFORMATION
Public/Private: Public
Student/Faculty Ratio: 12:1
Total Faculty: 50
% Part Time: 20
% Female: 60
% Minority: 36

PROGRAMS
Academic Specialties: International Human Rights, International Law, Criminal Law, Civil Rights, Women's Rights, Health Law, Labor and Workers Law, Environmental Law, Community Lawyering
Advanced Degrees Offered: JD (3 years)
Grading System: A, A–, B+, B, B–, C+, C, C–, D, F. Some courses have credit/no credit option.
Clinical Program Required? Yes
Clinical Programs Description: Battered Women's Rights Clinic, Defender Clinic, Elder Law Clinic, Immigrant and Refugee Rights Clinic, International Women's Human Rights Clinic, Mediation Clinic, Equality Concentration, Health Law Concentration
Legal Writing Course Requirements? Yes
Legal Writing Description: In Lawyering Seminar, an 8-credit, 2-semester, first-year required course, the central focus is on legal analysis and legal writing
Legal Methods Course Requirements? Yes
Legal Methods Description: Lawyering Seminar (see Legal Writing Description), also teaches lawyering skills (including interviewing, negotiation, and oral advocacy), usually taught via participatory simulation.
Legal Research Course Requirements? Yes
Legal Research Description: Legal Research is the third core component of the Lawyering Seminar program (see Legal Writing Description).
Moot Court Requirement? Yes
Moot Court Description: Any student may participate in the competitive selection process for Moot Court, a student-run organization that operates as a student club. Additionally, any student may apply for acceptance in a 2-credit Moot Court "credit/no credit" course.
Public Interest Law Requirement? Yes
Public Interest Law Description: Minimum of 12 credits of live-client clinical experience required. Six "in-house clinics" and two concentrations are available to satisfy this requirement.
Academic Journals: *NY City Law Review*—not an official publication of the Law School

STUDENT INFORMATION
Enrollment of Law School: 442
% Out of State: 31
% Male/Female: 40/60
% Full Time: 100
% Full Time That Are International: 3
% Minority: 45
Average Age of Entering Class: 29

RESEARCH FACILITIES
School-Supported Research Centers: Immigrants' Initiatives is an institute that is developing innovative ways of incorporating immigrants' perspectives across the curriculum and providing access to immigrant communities resulting in both curricular and volunteer opportunities for law students.

EXPENSES/FINANCIAL AID
Annual Tuition (Residents/Nonresidents): $5,700/$8,930
Financial Aid Application Deadline: 5/15
Average Grant: $2,652
Average Loan: $9,250
% Receiving Some Sort of Aid: 83
Average Total Aid Package: $18,416
Average Debt: $40,630

ADMISSIONS INFORMATION
Application Fee: $40
Regular Application Deadline: 3/15
Regular Notification: 4/15
LSDAS Accepted? Yes
Average GPA: 3.0
Average LSAT: 148
Transfer Students Accepted? Yes
Other Schools to Which Students Applied: Brooklyn Law School, Fordham, New York Law School, Rutgers Newark, St. John's University
Number of Applications Received: 1,267
Number of Applicants Accepted: 529
Number of Applicants Enrolled: 165

EMPLOYMENT INFORMATION
Rate of Placement: 77%
Average Starting Salary: $45,000
Employers Who Frequently Hire Grads: Legal Aid Society (NYC); District Attorneys' Offices (NYC); U.S. Court of Appeals; U.S. Magistrate Judges; U.S. Department of Justice Honors Program
State for Bar Exam: NY
Pass Rate for First-Time Bar: 74%

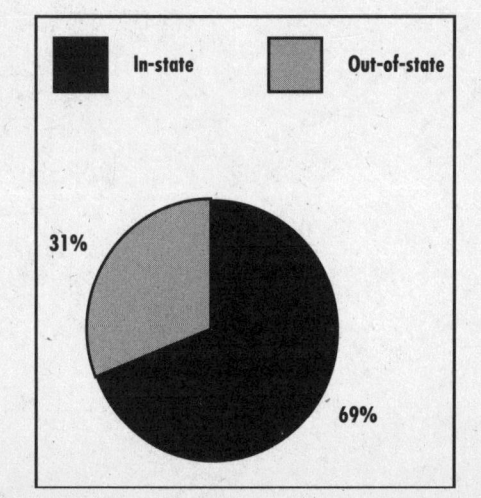

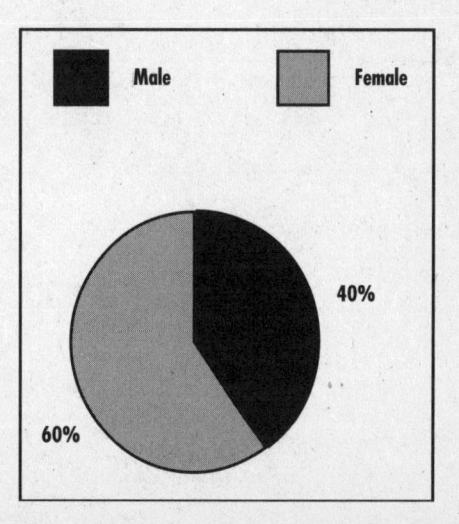

CITY UNIVERSITY OF NEW YORK

THE SCHOOL AT A GLANCE
Opened in 1983, the City University of New York (CUNY) School of Law at Queens College is the only law school which, from its inception, has defined its mission as training law students for public service—teaching students to be excellent lawyers who will use their skills to serve the public interest and who want to embody the School's motto, "Law in the Service of Human Needs." The National Association for Public Interest Law, the Student Division of the American Bar Association, and the Society of American Law Teachers have all commended CUNY's program. CUNY graduates have won the 2001 ABA Pro Bono Award and the 2002 Legal Services Award, and CUNY students have won the 2002 New York State Bar Association's Pro Bono Award.

CURRICULUM
CUNY's curriculum is a unique integration of traditional doctrinal law with all the lawyering skills that have been identified by the profession as critical to successful practice, like client counseling, oral and written advocacy, negotiation, alternative dispute resolution, and legal ethics. The curriculum leads to the Juris Doctor (JD) degree, and with a student/faculty ratio of 12:1, combines traditional classroom instruction with innovative lawyering seminars, interactive learning, simulations, and an extensive choice of clinical training opportunities. CUNY faculty members are outstanding scholars and public interest practitioners who care deeply about the success of every student. A unique atmosphere of collegiality exists, with faculty and students alike on a first-name basis.

CUNY'S CLINICAL PROGRAM
For 11 years, CUNY's clinical program has been recognized by a national survey of legal educators as one of the best in the country. Our clinic teachers are celebrated as innovators and leaders in the field, and teach through, supervised, live-client representation, which also provides critical legal services to poor people and underserved communities. Clinics (in-house client representation) and Concentrations (highly supervised external placements) are available to every third-year student and include Battered Women's Rights, Criminal Defense, Immigrant and Refugee Rights, International Women's Human Rights, Elder Law, Mediation, Health Law, and Equality Law. As a result of their clinical training, CUNY students are fully competent to practice law immediately upon graduation.

EMPLOYMENT SUCCESSES
CUNY places more graduates in traditional public interest jobs (like Legal Aid and Legal Services, the American Civil Liberties Union, the Center for Constitutional Rights, Gay Men's Health Crisis, Sanctuary for Families, Asian-American Legal Defense Fund, and Lawyers for Children) than virtually any law school in the country. Many graduates also work in government agencies—including local District Attorneys' offices, the Department of Justice, city and state legislatures, and the U.S. Congress—and in the court system as judicial clerks in the federal and state courts in New York and across the country. Because of CUNY's exceptional commitment to international human rights, graduates also work in international organizations and nongovernmental organizations (NGOs) in places like The Hague, Rwanda, and the UN. An increasing number of graduates are teaching at law schools around the country. Those graduates who choose community-based practices that increase access to justice are supported by the Law School's innovative Community Legal Resource Network.

School of Law at Queens College

SPECIAL PROGRAMS

Community Legal Resource Network (CLRN) provides mentoring, professional and technical assistance, resources, and networking for CUNY graduates in community-based solo and small firms, expanding the definition of public interest law by helping them sustain viable practices as they supply legal assistance to underserved and underrepresented communities. Worker, Employment, Labor Program (WELP) creates curricular and extracurricular opportunities for students whose interests lie in representing workers in unionized and nonunionized settings, and in the larger contexts of globalization and human rights. CUNY Immigrant Initiatives brings together students, faculty, and graduates to furnish legal services and citizenship assistance to immigrant communities, offering invaluable training for those who aspire to a career in immigration law and immigrants' law. An on-site childcare program—one of the very few in the country—provides reasonably priced, high-quality recreational and educational opportunities for students' children aged two-and-a-half to six.

AFFORDABLE TUITION

An excellent legal education at CUNY School of Law costs less than half of what most private schools charge. In 2002–2003, in-state residents will pay a tuition of $2,850 per semester, out-of-state residents $4,465 per semester. Student fees, covering all books, materials, technology assistance, and student activities, will run $600 per semester. CUNY's low tuition makes it possible for graduates to fulfill their career aspirations without being burdened by enormous student debt.

STUDENTS

CUNY is the most diverse law school in the country. Students come from all racial and ethnic groups, more than half of them women and nearly half people of color. CUNY is a comfortable place for older students; a majority are returning second-career students, bringing unparalleled experience and richness to the classroom and beyond. At CUNY, students participate in some 30 active student groups, including the Children's Rights Association, the International Law Students Association, CUNY OUTLaws (gay, lesbian, bisexual, transgender, and allies association), Moot Court, Labor Coalition, BLSA, APALSA, and La SED (the Latino student organization), to mention just a few.

ADMISSIONS

Students admitted to the School are recognized for their cultural, ethnic, and economic diversity; their strong academic ability; and possession of the less tangible qualities that make outstanding lawyers: judgment, initiative, empathy, and the ability to work collaboratively as well as independently. The School's program allows its students to fulfill their aspirations for a legal career that will express their commitment to justice, fairness, and equality. Prior experience in public interest and a commitment to CUNY's program are valued when considering admission; prospective students are encouraged to submit an extensive personal statement to describe their background, experience, and achievements.

For more information, contact:

Assistant Dean for Enrollment Management and Director of Admissions
Yvonne Cherena-Pacheco
CUNY School of Law
65-21 Main Street
Flushing NY 11367
Telephone: 718-340-4200
Fax: 718-340-4435
E-mail: admissions@mail.law.cuny.edu
Internet: www.law.cuny.edu

CLEVELAND STATE UNIVERSITY
Cleveland-Marshall College of Law

Admissions Contact: Assistant Dean for Admissions, Margaret McNally
1801 Euclid Avenue, Cleveland, OH 44115
Admissions Phone: 216-687-2304 • Admissions Fax: 216-687-6881
Admissions E-mail: admissions@law.csuohio.edu • Web Address: www.law.csuohio.edu

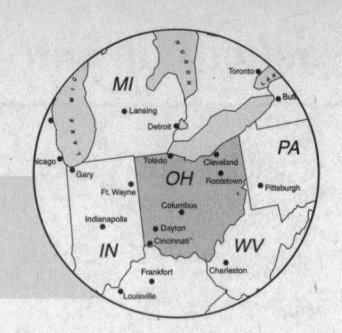

INSTITUTIONAL INFORMATION
Public/Private: Public
Student/Faculty Ratio: 20:1
Total Faculty: 72
% Part Time: 37
% Female: 42
% Minority: 6

PROGRAMS
Academic Specialties: Advocacy, Health Law, Business and Tax Law, Commercial Law, Corporation Securities Law, Criminal Law, Environmental Law, International Law, Labor Law, Taxation
Advanced Degrees Offered: LLM (20 to 24 credits, may be completed in 1 to 4 years)
Combined Degrees Offered: JD/MPA, JD/MUPDD, JD/MA Environmental Studies, JD/MBA (all 4 years, full time)
Grading System: 4.0 scale: A, B+, B, C+, C, D+, D, F; limited Pass/D+/D/F option
Clinical Program Required? No
Clinical Programs Description: Community Advocacy, Employment Law, Environmental Law, Fair Housing Law, Judicial Externship, U.S. Attorney Externship, Public Service Externship
Legal Writing Course Requirements? Yes
Legal Writing Description: First-year legal writing course (5 credit hours). Students must also take a third semester of legal writing and complete an upper-level writing project.
Legal Methods Course Requirements? Yes
Legal Methods Description: Research, writing and advocacy are included in first-year legal writing course.
Legal Research Course Requirements? Yes
Legal Research Description: Included in first-year legal writing course; an upper level elective in Advanced Legal Research is offered occasionally.
Moot Court Requirement? No
Moot Court Description: Second-year (and second or third-year part-time) students who have taken Advanced Brief Writing may participate in spring Moot Court competition. Up to 18 students are selected for interscholastic competition the following year. Up to 6 first-year students are selected for interscholastic competition in their second year on the basis of a special competition.
Public Interest Law Requirement? No
Public Interest Law Description: The law school recognizes students who serve 50 hours per more in a variety of pro bono and community service projects and has a number of awards and scholarships for students who distinguish themselves in public service activities.
Academic Journals: *Cleveland State Law Review, Journal of Law and Health*

STUDENT INFORMATION
Enrollment of Law School: 827
% Male/Female: 55/45
% Full Time: 63
% Full Time That Are International: 1
% Minority: 9

RESEARCH FACILITIES
Research Resources Available: General purpose computer labs

EXPENSES/FINANCIAL AID
Annual Tuition (Residents/Nonresidents): $8,535/$17,435
Room and Board: $7,950
Books and Supplies: $700
Financial Aid Application Deadline: 4/1
Average Grant: $4,080
Average Loan: $15,271
% of Aid That Is Merit-Based: 90
% Receiving Some Sort of Aid: 87
Average Total Aid Package: $13,400
Average Debt: $46,849
Tuition Per Credit (Residents/Nonresidents): $328/$670
Fees Per Credit: $20

ADMISSIONS INFORMATION
Application Fee: $35
Regular Application Deadline: 4/1
Regular Notification: 5/1
LSDAS Accepted? Yes
Average GPA: 3.1
Range of GPA: 2.8–3.4
Average LSAT: 151
Range of LSAT: 147–154
Transfer Students Accepted? Yes
Other Schools to Which Students Applied: Case Western Reserve, University of Akron
Other Admissions Factors Considered: Work experience, other personal experience and information, graduate degree, letters of recommendation, resume, personal statement
Number of Applications Received: 1,158
Number of Applicants Accepted: 636
Number of Applicants Enrolled: 278

EMPLOYMENT INFORMATION

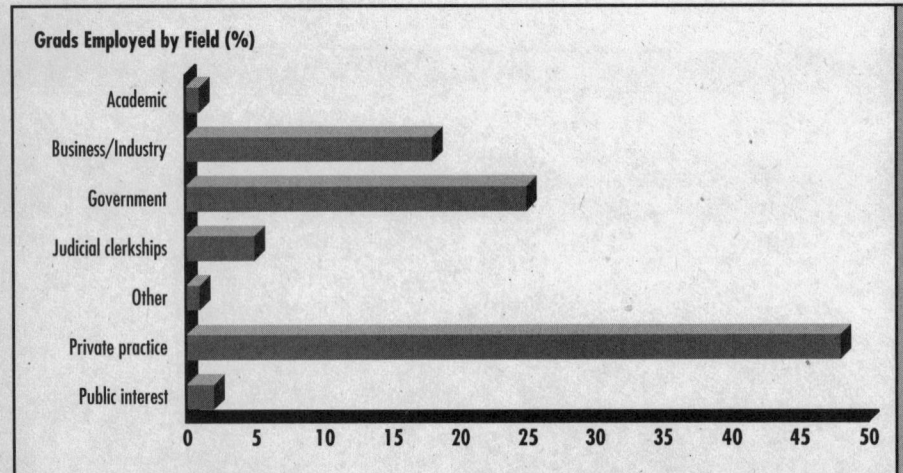

Grads Employed by Field (%)
- Academic: ~1
- Business/Industry: ~18
- Government: ~25
- Judicial clerkships: ~5
- Other: ~2
- Private practice: ~48
- Public interest: ~2

Rate of Placement: 90%
Average Starting Salary: $47,297
Employers Who Frequently Hire Grads: Jones, Day, Reavis & Pogue; Thompson, Hine; Squire, Sanders & Dempsey; Calfee, Halter & Griswold; Arter & Hadden; Ernst & Young; Benesch, Friedlander, Coplan & Arnold; Hahn, Loeser & Parks, LLP; Fay, Sharpe, Fagan, Minnich & McKee LLP are among the many employers who hire our students. A broad range of employers representing small, medium, and large firms as well as business and government agencies employ our graduates.
State for Bar Exam: OH, NY, CA, FL, IL
Pass Rate for First-Time Bar: 68%

COLLEGE OF WILLIAM AND MARY
Law School

Admissions Contact: Associate Dean, Faye Shealy
Office of Admission, PO Box 8795, Williamsburg, VA 23187-8795
Admissions Phone: 757-221-3785 • Admissions Fax: 757-221-3261
Admissions E-mail: lawadm@wm.edu • Web Address: www.wm.edu/law/

INSTITUTIONAL INFORMATION
Public/Private: Public
Student/Faculty Ratio: 17:1
Total Faculty: 82
% Part Time: 49
% Female: 31
% Minority: 4

PROGRAMS
Academic Specialties: Bill of Rights Law, Civil Procedure, Commercial Law, Constitutional Law, Corporation Securities Law, Criminal Law, Environmental Law, Government Services, Human Rights Law, Intellectual Property Law, International Law, Labor Law, Legal History, Legal Philosophy Property, Taxation.
Advanced Degrees Offered: LLM in American Legal System (1 year)
Combined Degrees Offered: JD/MPP (4 years), JD/MBA (4 years), JD/MA American Studies (4 years)
Grading System: 4.0 scale: A, B+, B, B–, C+, C, C–, D, F
Clinical Program Required? No
Clinical Programs Description: Attorney General, Legal Aid, International Law, Court of Appeals, Environmental Law, Employee Relations
Legal Writing Course Requirements? Yes
Legal Writing Description: Incorporated in required 2-year Legal Skills Program covering professional skills and ethics development
Legal Methods Course Requirements? Yes
Legal Methods Description: Incorporated in mandatory 2-year Legal Skills Program

Legal Research Course Requirements? No
Moot Court Requirement? No
Moot Court Description: Governed by a student-run board. Students participate in an intra-school competition in fall of second year. Winners are placed on inter-school teams in their third year.
Public Interest Law Requirement? No
Academic Journals: *William and Mary Bill of Rights Journal, William and Mary Environmental Law and Policy Review, William and Mary Journal of Women and the Law, William and Mary Law Review*

STUDENT INFORMATION
Enrollment of Law School: 556
% Out of State: 42
% Male/Female: 58/42
% Full Time: 100
% Full Time That Are International: 2
% Minority: 16
Average Age of Entering Class: 25

RESEARCH FACILITIES
Research Resources Available: National Center for State Courts, William and Mary Environmental Science and Policy Cluster, Virginia Institute for Marine Science
School-Supported Research Centers: Courtroom 21 Project, Institute of Bill of Rights Law

EXPENSES/FINANCIAL AID
Annual Tuition (Residents/Nonresidents): $10,400/$19,750
Room and Board (Off Campus): $6,300
Books and Supplies: $1,000
Financial Aid Application Deadline: 2/15

Average Grant: $3,500
Average Loan: $21,322
% of Aid That Is Merit-Based: 75
% Receiving Some Sort of Aid: 85
Average Total Aid Package: $22,585
Average Debt: $59,304
Tuition Per Credit (Residents/Nonresidents): $327/$640

ADMISSIONS INFORMATION
Application Fee: $40
Regular Application Deadline: 3/1
Regular Notification: 4/1
LSDAS Accepted? Yes
Average GPA: 3.4
Range of GPA: 3.2–3.7
Average LSAT: 163
Range of LSAT: 160–165
Transfer Students Accepted? Yes
Other Schools to Which Students Applied: American University, Boston College, Boston University, George Washington University, Georgetown University, University of Virginia, Washington and Lee University
Other Admissions Factors Considered: Quality of school(s) attended, difficulty of the major or department in which the degree was earned, hours spent on outside employment or other time-consuming extracurricular activities
Number of Applications Received: 2,641
Number of Applicants Accepted: 718
Number of Applicants Enrolled: 205

INTERNATIONAL STUDENTS
TOEFL Required of International Students? Yes

EMPLOYMENT INFORMATION

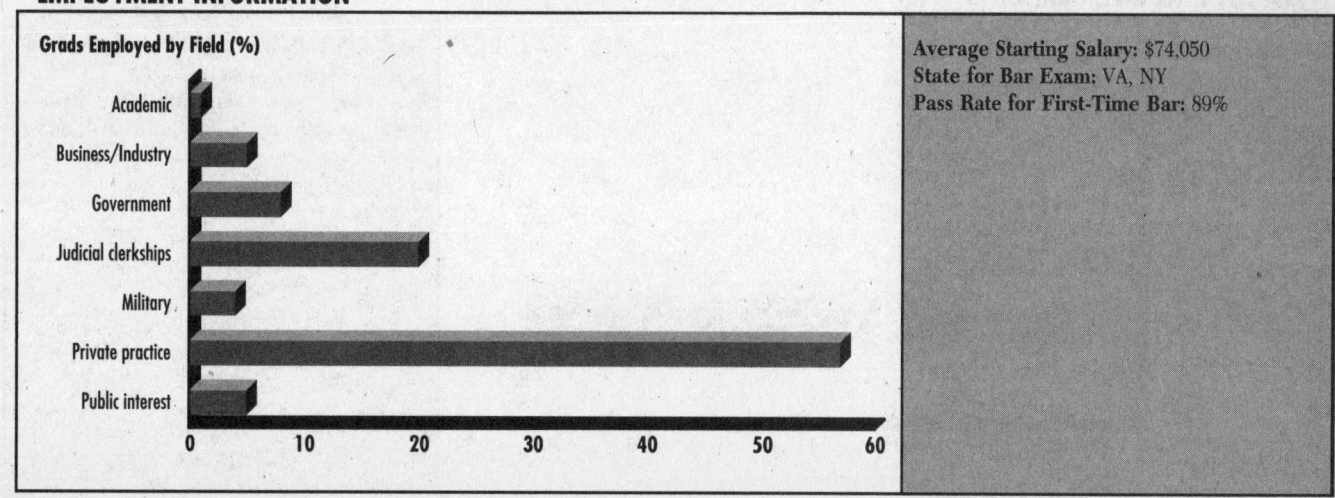

Grads Employed by Field (%)

Field	%
Academic	~1
Business/Industry	~5
Government	~10
Judicial clerkships	~20
Military	~1
Private practice	~57
Public interest	~3

Average Starting Salary: $74,050
State for Bar Exam: VA, NY
Pass Rate for First-Time Bar: 89%

COLUMBIA UNIVERSITY
School of Law

Admissions Contact: Dean of Admissions, James Milligan
435 West 116th Street, New York, NY 10027
Admissions Phone: 212-854-2674 • Admissions Fax: 212-854-1109
Admissions E-mail: admissions@law.columbia.edu • Web Address: www.law.columbia.edu

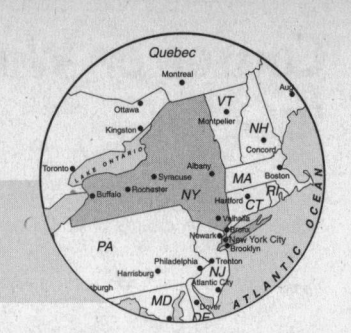

INSTITUTIONAL INFORMATION
Public/Private: Private
Student/Faculty Ratio: 16:1
Total Faculty: 150
% Part Time: 50
% Female: 27
% Minority: 12

PROGRAMS
Academic Specialties: Corporate Law, Criminal Law, Environmental Law, Human Rights, Intellectual Property, International and Comparative Law, Profession of Law (professional responsibility), Constitutional Law, Critical Race Theory and Feminist Jurisprudence, Civil Procedure, Commercial Law, Corporation Securities Law, Government Services, Labor Law, Legal History, Legal Philosophy Property, Taxation
Advanced Degrees Offered: LLM (1 year), JSD (2 semesters in residence and a dissertation)
Combined Degrees Offered: JD/PhD in History, Philosophy, Anthropology, Economics, Political Science, Psychology, Sociology (7 years); JD/MBA (3 to 4 years); JD/MFA Arts Administration (4 years); JD/MSW (4 years); JD/MUP (4 years); JD/MSJ (3.5 years); JD/MIA (4 years); JD/MPA with Columbia (4 years); JD/MPAFF with Woodrow Wilson School at Princeton (4 years)
Grading System: A+, A, A–, B+, B, B–, C, F. Some CR or F.
Clinical Program Required? No
Clinical Programs Description: Child Advocacy, Human Rights, Mediation, Nonprofit Organizations/Small Business, Prisoners and Families, Law and the Arts, Fair Housing
Legal Writing Course Requirements? Yes
Legal Writing Description: Intensive training in the analysis of legal problems and the use of legal materials.
Legal Methods Course Requirements? Yes
Legal Methods Description: An introduction to legal institutions and processes.
Legal Research Course Requirements? Yes
Legal Research Description: Students must write 2 research papers.
Moot Court Requirement? Yes
Moot Court Description: Spring semester of the first year. Specialized opportunities for upper-class students.
Public Interest Law Requirement? Yes
Public Interest Law Description: Must devote 40 hours of uncompensated time to public interest field work.
Academic Journals: *American Journal of International Arbitration, Columbia Business Law Review, Columbia Human Rights Law Review,* and more.

STUDENT INFORMATION
Enrollment of Law School: 1,129
% Out of State: 71
% Male/Female: 52/48
% Full Time: 100
% Full Time That Are International: 7
% Minority: 36
Average Age of Entering Class: 24

RESEARCH FACILITIES
Research Resources Available: Personal home pages, lifetime e-mail account forwarding, free Internet access from home via a 56K modem pool, a Unix account, web kiosks throughout campus, specialized technology teaching and learning consultation by the Center for New Media, and more.
School-Supported Research Centers: Variety of research programs and enrichment projects.

EXPENSES/FINANCIAL AID
Annual Tuition: $29,396
Room and Board: $14,360
Books and Supplies: $885
Financial Aid Application Deadline: 3/1
Average Grant: $14,076
Average Loan: $31,550
% of Aid That Is Merit-Based: 75
% Receiving Some Sort of Aid: 80
Average Total Aid Package: $35,076
Average Debt: $83,204
Fees Per Credit: $1,470

ADMISSIONS INFORMATION
Application Fee: $65
Regular Application Deadline: 2/15
Regular Notification: Rolling
LSDAS Accepted? Yes
Average GPA: 3.6
Average LSAT: 169
Transfer Students Accepted? Yes
Other Schools to Which Students Applied: Harvard, NYU, Stanford, Yale
Other Admissions Factors Considered: Applicant's personal statement, letters of recommendation, course selection, extracurricular involvement, community service
Number of Applications Received: 6,743
Number of Applicants Enrolled: 367

EMPLOYMENT INFORMATION

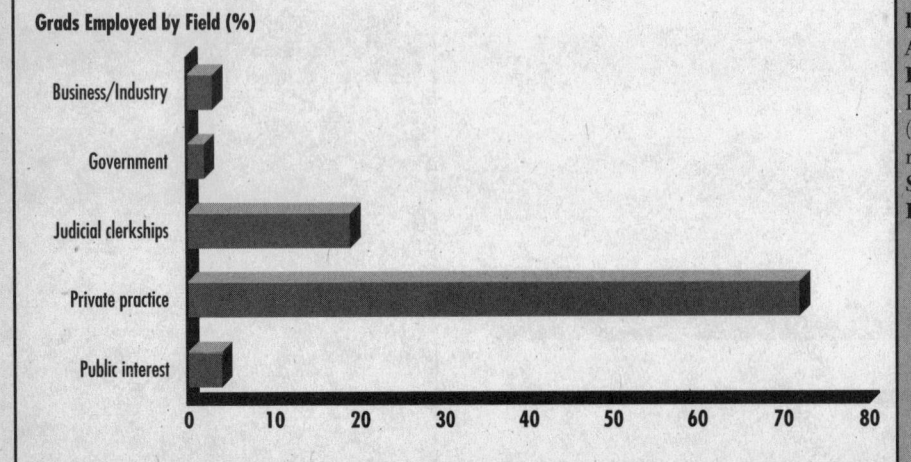

Grads Employed by Field (%)
- Business/Industry
- Government
- Judicial clerkships: ~20
- Private practice: ~72
- Public interest

Rate of Placement: 100%
Average Starting Salary: $125,000
Employers Who Frequently Hire Grads: Large corporate law firms and federal judges. (Columbia has one of the 4 or 5 highest clerkship rates in the country.)
State for Bar Exam: NY, NJ, CA, FL, TX
Pass Rate for First-Time Bar: 92%

CORNELL UNIVERSITY
Cornell Law School

Admissions Contact: Dean of Admissions, Richard Geiger
Myron Taylor Hall, Ithaca, NY 14853-4901
Admissions Phone: 607-255-5141 • Admissions Fax: 607-255-7193
Admissions E-mail: lawadmit@law.mail.cornell.edu • Web Address: www.lawschool.cornell.edu

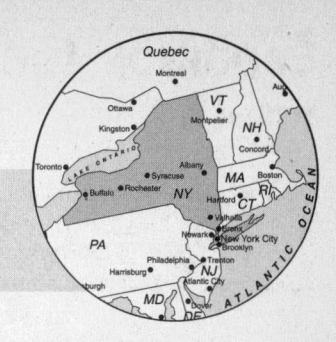

INSTITUTIONAL INFORMATION
Public/Private: Private
Student/Faculty Ratio: 12:1
Total Faculty: 43
% Female: 26
% Minority: 10

PROGRAMS
Academic Specialties: International Law
Advanced Degrees Offered: JD (3 years), LLM (1 year), JSD (2 years)
Combined Degrees Offered: JD/MBA, JD/MPA, JD/MA, JD/PhD, JD/MIRL, JD/MRP, JD/MILR, JD/LLM in International and Comparative Law (3 years), JD/Maitrise en Driot French Law degree (4 years), JD/MLL Master of German and European Law and Legal Practice (4 years)
Grading System: Letter system
Clinical Program Required? No
Clinical Programs Description: Legal Aid, Capital Punishment, Appellate Advocacy, Civil Liberties, Government Benefits, Women and the Law, Judicial Externship, Legislative Externship, Neighborhood Legal Services Externship, Public International Law Clinic, Law Guardian Externship, Religious Liberty Clinic
Legal Writing Course Requirements? No
Legal Methods Course Requirements? Yes
Legal Methods Description: Full-year skills course designed to introduce first-year students to the techniques of research, analysis, and writing that are necessary in legal practice. Instruction occurs in small sections of approximately 30 students and in individual conferences. Each student receives extensive editorial and evaluative feedback on each written assignment.
Legal Research Course Requirements? No
Moot Court Requirement? No
Public Interest Law Requirement? No
Academic Journals: *Law Review, International Law Journal, Journal of Law and Public Policy, LII Bulletin*

STUDENT INFORMATION
Enrollment of Law School: 551
% Out of State: 75
% Male/Female: 51/49
% Full Time: 100
% Full Time That Are International: 2
% Minority: 25
Average Age of Entering Class: 25

RESEARCH FACILITIES
Research Resources Available: Vast resources of Cornell University; law students can take 12 credits in another graduate program at Cornell University for law school credit.
School-Supported Research Centers: Legal Information Institute (Law School's legal research website), Keck Program on Legal Ethics, Empirical Studies on Federal and State Court Cases, Olin Program in Law and Economics, Death Penalty Project, Religious Liberty Institute, Feminism Legal Theory Project, and Gender, Sexuality, and Family Project

EXPENSES/FINANCIAL AID
Annual Tuition: $29,200
Room and Board (Off Campus): $7,870
Books and Supplies: $760
Financial Aid Application Deadline: 3/15
Average Grant: $9,000

ADMISSIONS INFORMATION
Application Fee: $65
Regular Application Deadline: 2/1
Regular Notification: Rolling
LSDAS Accepted? Yes
Average GPA: 3.6
Range of GPA: 3.3–3.7
Average LSAT: 165
Range of LSAT: 163–166
Transfer Students Accepted? Yes
Other Admissions Factors Considered: Undergraduate and graduate coursework, work experience, extracurricular activities, community involvement, and leadership
Number of Applications Received: 3,717
Number of Applicants Accepted: 801
Number of Applicants Enrolled: 189

EMPLOYMENT INFORMATION

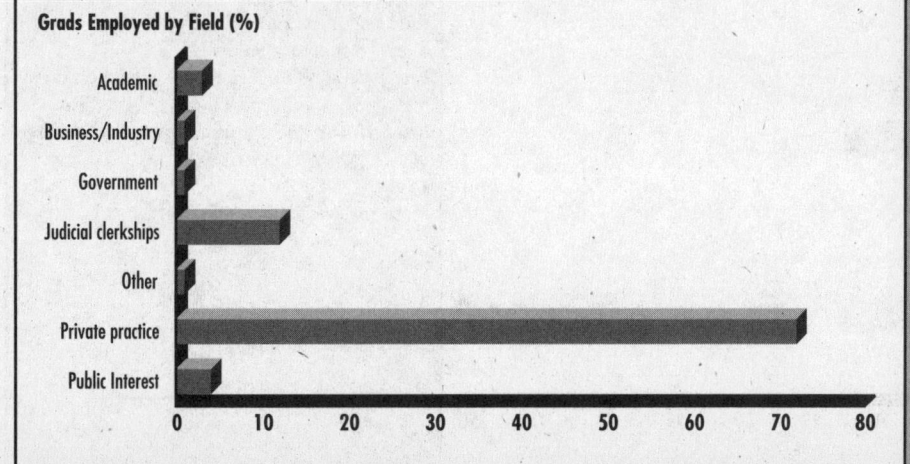

Grads Employed by Field (%):
- Academic: ~2
- Business/Industry: ~2
- Government: ~3
- Judicial clerkships: ~13
- Other: ~1
- Private practice: ~72
- Public Interest: ~3

Rate of Placement: 100%
Average Starting Salary: $106,021
State for Bar Exam: NY
Pass Rate for First-Time Bar: 97%

CREIGHTON UNIVERSITY
School of Law

Admissions Contact: Assistant Dean, Andrea D. Bashara
2500 California Plaza, Omaha, NE 68178
Admissions Phone: 402-280-2872 • Admissions Fax: 402-280-3161
Admissions E-mail: admit@creighton.edu • Web Address: culaw.creighton.edu

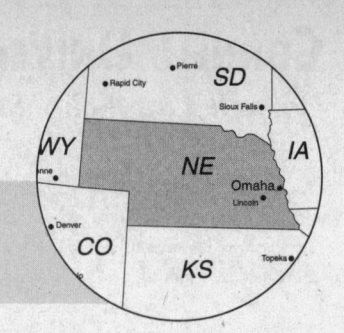

INSTITUTIONAL INFORMATION
Public/Private: Private
Affiliation: Roman Catholic
Student/Faculty Ratio: 16:1
Total Faculty: 73
% Part Time: 60
% Female: 29
% Minority: 5

PROGRAMS
Academic Specialties: Corporate/Commercial/Tax, Constitutional Law, Evidence/Litigation and Alternate Dispute Resolution, Civil Procedure/Federal Courts/Conflict of Laws, International Law, Commercial Law, Corporation Securities Law, Criminal Law, Taxation. Strengths include small classes in first year, strong skills programs in trial practice, negotiations, and client counseling.
Combined Degrees Offered: JD/MBA (3 years), JD/MS Electronic Commerce (3 years)
Grading System: A (100–86), B (85–75), C (74–65), D (64–57), F (56–50)
Clinical Program Required? No
Clinical Programs Description: Milton R. Abrahams Legal Clinic, clinical and judicial internships with government and legal aid offices
Legal Writing Course Requirements? Yes
Legal Writing Description: 2-semester Legal Writing program required
Legal Methods Course Requirements? No
Legal Research Course Requirements? Yes
Legal Research Description: 1 semester of Legal Research required

Moot Court Requirement? Yes
Moot Court Description: Part of Legal Writing II required course; includes brief writing and oral argument, elimination rounds
Public Interest Law Requirement? No
Academic Journals: Creighton Law Review

STUDENT INFORMATION
Enrollment of Law School: 467
% Male/Female: 58/42
% Full Time: 95
% Full Time That Are International: 2
% Minority: 12
Average Age of Entering Class: 26

RESEARCH FACILITIES
Research Resources Available: The Klutznick Law Library has over 275,000 volumes and access to a wide range of online research products.

EXPENSES/FINANCIAL AID
Annual Tuition $18,506
Room and Board: $10,350
Books and Supplies: $1,120
Financial Aid Application Deadline: 3/1
Average Grant: $8,500
Average Loan: $18,500
% of Aid That Is Merit-Based: 33
% Receiving Some Sort of Aid: 92
Average Total Aid Package: $20,000
Average Debt: $66,578
Tuition Per Credit: $620

ADMISSIONS INFORMATION
Application Fee: $45
Regular Application Deadline: 5/1
Regular Notification: Rolling
LSDAS Accepted? Yes
Average GPA: 3.2
Range of GPA: 2.9–3.5
Average LSAT: 151
Range of LSAT: 148–154
Transfer Students Accepted? Yes
Other Schools to Which Students Applied: Drake University, Gonzaga University, University of Nebraska—Lincoln
Other Admissions Factors Considered: Type of courses completed, grade patterns, military achievements, graduate studies, adjustment to individual hardship
Number of Applications Received: 662
Number of Applicants Accepted: 417
Number of Applicants Enrolled: 162

EMPLOYMENT INFORMATION

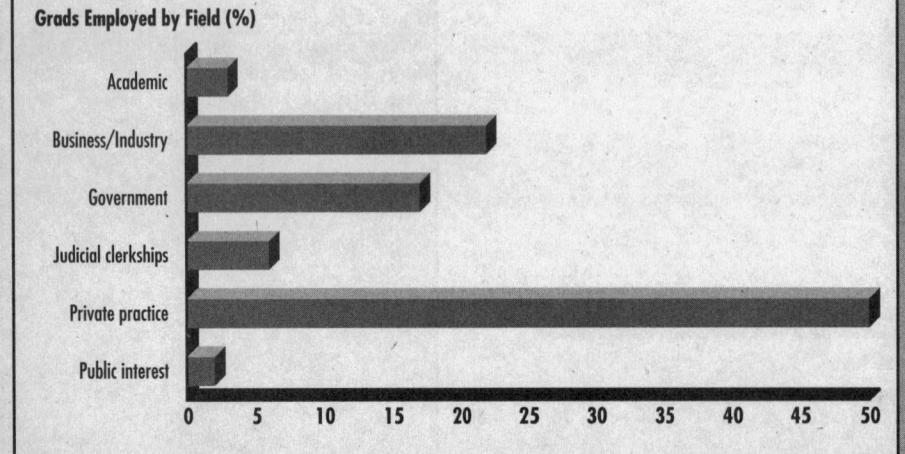

Grads Employed by Field (%):
- Academic: ~2
- Business/Industry: ~17
- Government: ~17
- Judicial clerkships: ~7
- Private practice: ~50
- Public interest: ~2

Rate of Placement: 97%
Average Starting Salary: $43,013
Employers Who Frequently Hire Grads: McGrath North; Kutak Rock; Fraser Stryker; Baird Holm; Koley Jessen; Blackwell Sanders; Stinson Mag; Erickson Sederstrom; Fitzgerald Schorr
State for Bar Exam: NE
Pass Rate for First-Time Bar: 84%

DALHOUSIE UNIVERSITY
Law School

Admissions Contact: Director of Admissions and Placement, Rose Godfrey
Dalhousie Law School, Halifax, NS B3P 1P8 Canada
Admissions Phone: 902-494-1018 • Admissions Fax: 902-494-1316
Admissions E-mail: rose.godfrey@dal.ca • Web Address: www.dal.ca/law/admission.html

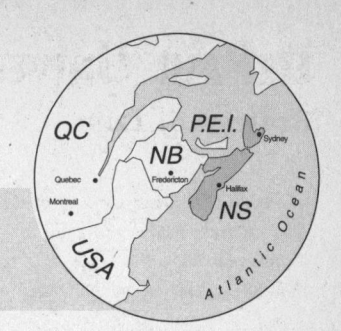

INSTITUTIONAL INFORMATION
Public/Private: Public
Student/Faculty Ratio: 13:1
Total Faculty: 35
% Female: 45
% Minority: 6

PROGRAMS
Academic Specialties: Environmental Law, International Law, Marine Law, Maritime Law
Advanced Degrees Offered: LLM, JSD
Combined Degrees Offered: LLB/MBA, LLB/MLIS, LLB/MPA, LLB/MHSA (4 years)
Grading System: Pass/Fail
Clinical Program Required? No
Clinical Program Description: Legal Aid Clinic, Criminal Clinic
Legal Writing/Methods Course Requirements: Full year

STUDENT INFORMATION
Enrollment of Law School: 458
% Male/Female: 50/50
% Part Time: 4
% Full Time: 96
% Minority: 12
Average Age of Entering Class: 25

RESEARCH FACILITIES
Computers/Workstations Available: 60

EXPENSES/FINANCIAL AID
Annual Tuition: $5,900
Room and Board (On Campus): $3,500
Books and Supplies: $1,200
Average Grant: $4,212
% of Aid That Is Merit-Based: 43
% Receiving Some Sort of Aid: 57%
Average Total Aid Package: $1,257

ADMISSIONS INFORMATION
Application Fee: $65
Regular Application Deadline: 2/8
Regular Notification: 4/1
Average GPA: 3.7
Average LSAT: 158
Transfer Students Accepted? Yes
Other Schools to Which Students Applied: University of British Columbia, University of New Brunswick, Western University, McGill University, University of Toronto, Queens University, Winsor University, Osgoode University
Number of Applications Received: 1,077
Number of Applicants Accepted: 317
Number of Applicants Enrolled: 161

INTERNATIONAL STUDENTS
TOEFL Required of International Students? Yes
Minimum TOEFL: 600

EMPLOYMENT INFORMATION

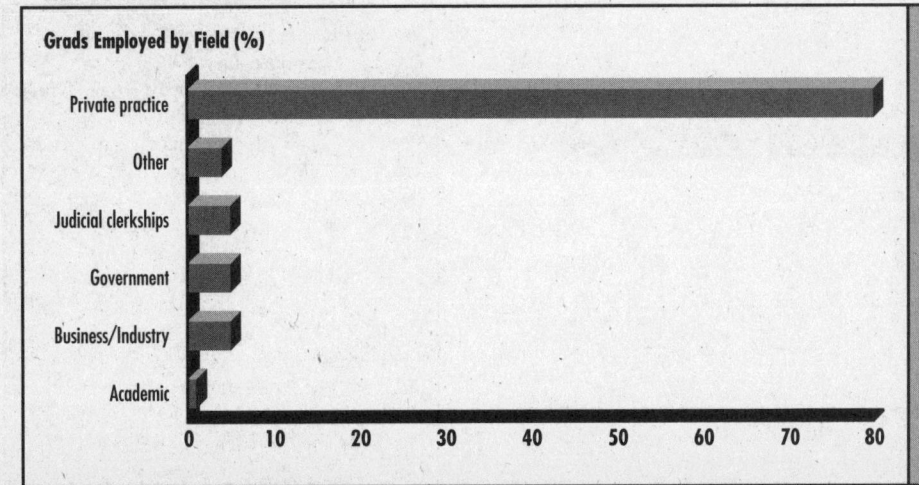

Grads Employed by Field (%)

Field	%
Private practice	~80
Other	~5
Judicial clerkships	~5
Government	~5
Business/Industry	~5
Academic	~1

Rate of Placement: 90%
Employers Who Frequently Hire Grads: Law firms, government, courts
Prominent Alumni: Sir Graham Day, chancellor, Dalhousie University; Purdy A. Crawford, chairman, Imasco Limited; The Honourable Anne MacLellan, justice minister, Canada

DePaul University
College of Law

Admissions Contact: Director of Admission, Dennis Shea
25 East Jackon Boulevard, Chicago, IL 60604
Admissions Phone: 312-362-6831 • Admissions Fax: 312-362-5280
Admissions E-mail: lawinfo@wppost.depaul.edu • Web Address: www.law.depaul.edu

INSTITUTIONAL INFORMATION
Public/Private: Private
Affiliation: Roman Catholic
Environment: Urban
Academic Calendar: Semester
Schedule: Full time or part time
Student/Faculty Ratio: 21:1
Total Faculty: 110
% Part Time: 55
% Female: 37
% Minority: 7

PROGRAMS
Academic Specialties: Intellectual Property, Health Law, Tax Law, Human Rights Law, Litigation Skills, special IP/Legal Writing integrated program during first year
Advanced Degrees Offered: LLM Health Law (2 years), LLM Tax Law (2 years),
Combined Degrees Offered: JD/MBA (3–4 years)
Grading System: A, B+, B, C+, C, D, F with a curve in all years
Clinical Program Required? No
Clinical Program Description: Asylum Law, Criminal Appellate, Mediation, Community Development, Family Law, externships
Legal Writing/Methods Course Requirements: 1 year required (2 courses); multiple electives

STUDENT INFORMATION
Enrollment of Law School: 1,108
% Male/Female: 47/53
% Full Time: 70
% Full Time That Are International: 1
% Minority: 20
Average Age of Entering Class: 25

RESEARCH FACILITIES
Computers/Workstations Available: 250
School-Supported Research Centers: Numerous state, local, and federal libraries as well as Chicago and Illinois Bar Associations and Libraries

EXPENSES/FINANCIAL AID
Annual Tuition: $20,700
Room and Board (Off Campus): $12,500
Books and Supplies: $750
Average Grant: $1,776
Average Loan: $18,500
% of Aid That Is Merit-Based: 20
% Receiving Some Sort of Aid: 80
Average Total Aid Package: $21,000
Average Debt: $60,000
Tuition Per Credit: $725
Fees Per Credit: $725

ADMISSIONS INFORMATION
Application Fee: $40
Regular Application Deadline: 4/1
Regular Notification: 3/1
LSDAS Accepted? Yes
Average GPA: 3.2
Range of GPA: 2.9–3.4
Average LSAT: 153
Range of LSAT: 150–155
Transfer Students Accepted? Yes
Other Schools to Which Students Applied: Loyola University Chicago, Illinois Institute of Technology, John Marshall Law School, Northwestern University, University of Illinois, University of Chicago, University of Notre Dame, Wayne State University
Number of Applications Received: 2,033
Number of Applicants Accepted: 1,274
Number of Applicants Enrolled: 363

INTERNATIONAL STUDENTS
TOEFL Required of International Students? Yes
Minimum TOEFL: 550

EMPLOYMENT INFORMATION

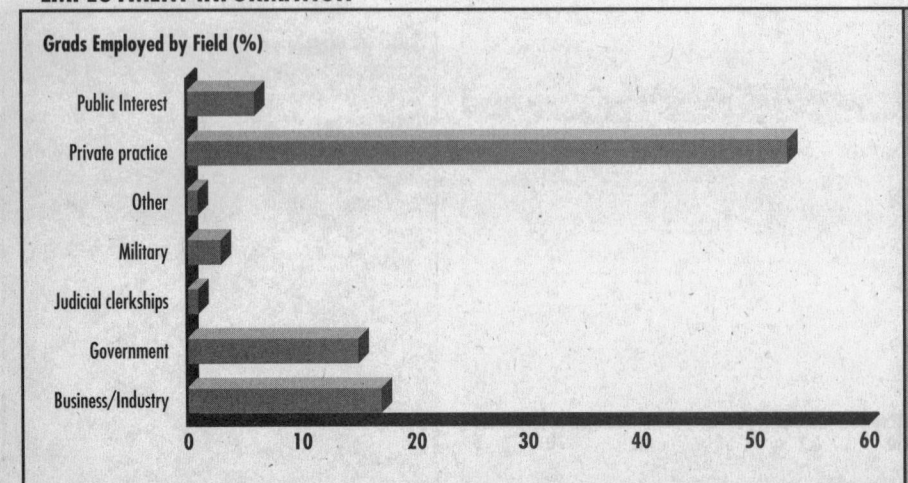

Grads Employed by Field (%)
- Public Interest
- Private practice
- Other
- Military
- Judicial clerkships
- Government
- Business/Industry

Rate of Placement: 91%
Average Starting Salary: $50,900
Employers Who Frequently Hire Grads: Cook County State's Attorney's Office; Seyfarth Shaw; City of Chicago, Department of Law; Katten, Muchin & Zavis; Mayer, Brown & Platt; Cook County Public Guardian; DeLoitte and Touche; Arthur Andersen; Ernst and Young; Lake County State's Attorney's Office
Prominent Alumni: Richard M. Daley, mayor, City of Chicago; Jack M. Greenburg, CEO, McDonald's Corporation; Benjamin Hooks, former executive director, NAACP
State for Bar Exam: IL
Number Taking Bar Exam: 238
Pass Rate for First-Time Bar: 89%

DRAKE UNIVERSITY
Law School

Admissions Contact: Director of Admissions and Financial Aid, Kara Blanchard
2507 University Avenue, Des Moines, IA 50311
Admissions Phone: 515-271-2782 • Admissions Fax: 515-271-1990
Admissions E-mail: lawadmit@drake.edu • Web Address: www.law.drake.edu

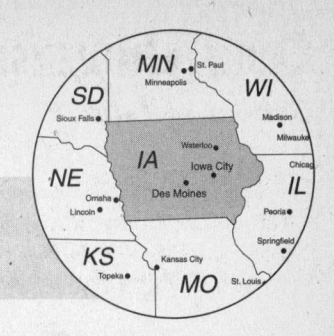

INSTITUTIONAL INFORMATION
Public/Private: Private
Student/Faculty Ratio: 13:1
Total Faculty: 47
% Part Time: 67
% Female: 28
% Minority: 3

PROGRAMS
Academic Specialties: Very strong in Corporate/Commercial offerings and Trial Practice/Litigation offerings; other specialties include Constitutional Law, Environmental Law, Agricultural Law, Legislative Practice, clinics and internships
Advanced Degrees Offered: JD (3 years)
Combined Degrees Offered: JD/MBA (6 semesters, 2 summers), JD/MPA (6 semesters, 2 summers), JD/MA Mass Communication (6 semesters, 1summer), JD/PharmD, JD/MA Political Science (6 semesters, 1 summer), JD/MS Agricultural Economics (6 semesters, 1 summer)
Grading System: 4.0/A; CR (credit), I (incomplete), IP (in progress)
Clinical Program Required? No
Legal Writing Course Requirements? Yes
Legal Writing Description: First-semester course that must be taken concurrently with Legal Research
Legal Methods Course Requirements? Yes
Legal Methods Description: See Legal Writing and Research.
Legal Research Course Requirements? Yes

Legal Research Description: Required first-semester course that must be taken concurrently with Legal Writing; Legal Research, Writing and Appellate Practice required second semester
Moot Court Requirement? No
Public Interest Law Requirement? No
Academic Journals: *Drake Law Review, Drake Agricultural Law Review*

STUDENT INFORMATION
Enrollment of Law School: 398
% Out of State: 43
% Male/Female: 50/50
% Full Time: 97
% Full Time That Are International: 2
% Minority: 11
Average Age of Entering Class: 25

RESEARCH FACILITIES
Research Resources Available: Iowa State Law Library
School-Supported Research Centers: Agricultural Law Center, Constitutional Law Center, Legal Clinic, Jaon and Lyle Middleton Center for Children's Rights, Center for Legislative Practice

EXPENSES/FINANCIAL AID
Annual Tuition $19,450
Room and Board: $7,100
Books and Supplies: $1,100
Financial Aid Application Deadline: 3/1
Average Grant: $9,714
Average Loan: $23,450

% of Aid That Is Merit-Based: 71
% Receiving Some Sort of Aid: 93
Average Total Aid Package: $30,640
Average Debt: $60,000
Tuition Per Credit: $660

ADMISSIONS INFORMATION
Application Fee: $40
Regular Application Deadline: Rolling
Regular Notification: Rolling
LSDAS Accepted? Yes
Average GPA: 3.2
Range of GPA: 2.9–3.5
Average LSAT: 152
Range of LSAT: 149–156
Transfer Students Accepted? Yes
Other Schools to Which Students Applied: Creighton University, Hamline University, University of Iowa
Other Admissions Factors Considered: The admission committee, consisting of 5 faculty, thoroughly reviews each file. All materials and information contained in the application for admission are considered in the decision-making process.
Number of Applications Received: 734
Number of Applicants Accepted: 466
Number of Applicants Enrolled: 139

INTERNATIONAL STUDENTS
TOEFL Required of International Students? Yes

EMPLOYMENT INFORMATION

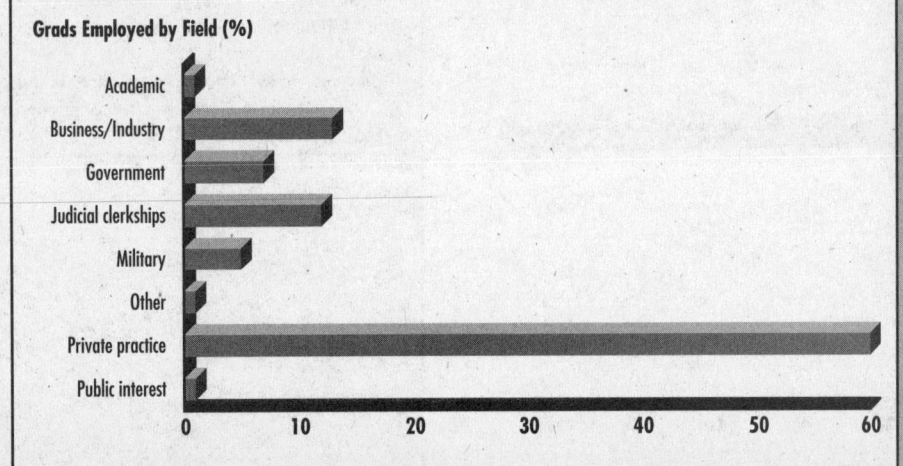

Grads Employed by Field (%)

Field	%
Academic	~1
Business/Industry	~13
Government	~5
Judicial clerkships	~13
Military	~3
Other	~2
Private practice	~60
Public interest	~1

Rate of Placement: 92%
Average Starting Salary: $50,718
Employers Who Frequently Hire Grads: Davis, Brown (Des Moines); Nyemaster, Goode (Des Moines); Department of Justice; JAG Corps; Blackwell Sanders (Kansas City); Shughart Thompson (Kansas City); Bryan Cave (Kansas City)
State for Bar Exam: IA, MN, MO, IL
Pass Rate for First-Time Bar: 89%

DUKE UNIVERSITY
School of Law

Admissions Contact: Associate Dean for Admissions and Financial Aid, Dennis Shields
PO Box 90393, Durham, NC 27708-0393
Admissions Phone: 919-613-7020 • Admissions Fax: 919-613-7257
Admissions E-mail: admissions@law.duke.edu • Web Address: admissions.law.duke.edu

INSTITUTIONAL INFORMATION
Public/Private: Private
Student/Faculty Ratio: 16:1
Total Faculty: 72
% Part Time: 50
% Female: 32
% Minority: 10

PROGRAMS
Academic Specialties: International and Comparative Law, Intellectual Property, Gender Law, Corporate Law, Environmental Law, Constitutional Law and Civil Rights, Alternative Dispute Resolution
Advanced Degrees Offered: JD (3 years), LLM (1 year), SJD (1 year, international students only)
Combined Degrees Offered: JD/MA in 11 Fields: English, History, Humanities, Philosophy, Romance Studies, Cultural Anthropology, Economics, Political Science, Psychology, Forestry and Environmental Studies, Public Policy Studies; JD/MS Mechanical Engineering; JD/MBA; JD/MPP; JD/MEM; JD/MTS (4 years); JD/MD (6 years); JD/PhD (7 years); JD/LLM International and Comparative Law (3 years)
Grading System: 4.0 scale
Clinical Program Required? Yes
Clinical Programs Description: Aids Law Clinic, Death Penalty Clinic, Pro Bono Project, Children's Law Clinic
Legal Writing Course Requirements? Yes
Legal Writing Description: Legal Analysis, Research, and Writing is a required 2-semester course taken in the first year.
Legal Methods Course Requirements? Yes
Legal Methods Description: See Legal Writing.
Legal Research Course Requirements? Yes
Legal Research Description: See Legal Writing.
Moot Court Requirement? Yes
Moot Court Description: All first-year students participate in moot court competition as part of their Legal Analysis, Research, and Writing Class.
Public Interest Law Requirement? No
Academic Journals: *Duke Law Journal, Law and Contemporary Problems, Duke Environmental Law and Policy Forum, Alaska Law Review, Duke Journal of Comparative and International Law, Duke Law and Technology Review*

STUDENT INFORMATION
Enrollment of Law School: 668
% Male/Female: 50/50
% Full Time: 100
% Minority: 25

EXPENSES/FINANCIAL AID
Annual Tuition $28,250
Room and Board (Off Campus): $8,700
Books and Supplies: $1,200
Financial Aid Application Deadline: 3/15
Average Grant: $8,000
Average Loan: $22,649
Average Debt: $61,000

ADMISSIONS INFORMATION
Application Fee: $65
Regular Application Deadline: 1/1
Regular Notification: Rolling
LSDAS Accepted? Yes
Average GPA: 3.6
Range of GPA: 3.4–3.7
Average LSAT: 166
Range of LSAT: 162–168
Transfer Students Accepted? Yes
Other Admissions Factors Considered: Demonstrated leadership, dedication to community service, excellence in a field, graduate study in another discipline, work experience, other information indicating academic or professional potential
Number of Applications Received: 3,348
Number of Applicants Accepted: 831
Number of Applicants Enrolled: 203

INTERNATIONAL STUDENTS
TOEFL Required of International Students? Yes

EMPLOYMENT INFORMATION

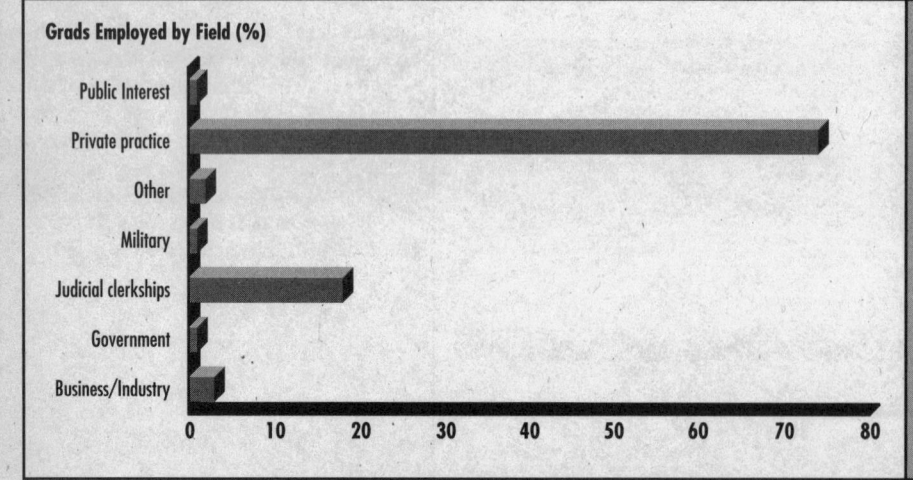

Grads Employed by Field (%)

Field	%
Public Interest	~1
Private practice	~75
Other	~3
Military	~1
Judicial clerkships	~20
Government	~2
Business/Industry	~1

Rate of Placement: 100%
Average Starting Salary: $86,000
Employers Who Frequently Hire Grads: Over 400 law firms annually offer positions to Duke Law students.
State for Bar Exam: NY, NC, CA, MD, VA
Pass Rate for First-Time Bar: 92%

Duquesne University
School of Law

Admissions Contact: Dean of Admissions, Joseph Campion
900 Locust Street, Pittsburgh, PA 15282
Admissions Phone: 412-396-6296 • Admissions Fax: 412-396-6283
Admissions E-mail: campion@eduq.edu • Web Address: www.duq.edu

INSTITUTIONAL INFORMATION
Public/Private: Private
Affiliation: Roman Catholic
Environment: Urban
Academic Calendar: Semester
Schedule: Full time or part time
Student/Faculty Ratio: 23:1
Total Faculty: 24
% Female: 21
% Minority: 20

PROGRAMS
Academic Specialties: Strong teaching faculty
Combined Degrees Offered: JD/MBA (4 years), JD/MDiv (4 years), JD/Master of Environmental Science and Management (4 years)
Grading System: Numerical system on 4.0 scale; minimum 3.0 cumulative GPA required to graduate
Clinical Program Required? No
Clinical Program Description: Development Law Clinic, Criminal Justice Clinic, Family and Poverty Law Clinic

STUDENT INFORMATION
Enrollment of Law School: 691
% Male/Female: 55/45
% Full Time: 55
% Full Time That Are International: 0
% Minority: 6
Average Age of Entering Class: 23

EXPENSES/FINANCIAL AID
Annual Tuition: $14,942
Room and Board (On/Off Campus): $6,984/$8,000
Average Grant: $4,500
Average Loan: $12,000
% of Aid That Is Merit-Based: 50
% Receiving Some Sort of Aid: 35
Average Total Aid Package: $11,000
Average Debt: $35,000

ADMISSIONS INFORMATION
Application Fee: $50
Regular Application Deadline: 4/1
Regular Notification: Rolling
Average GPA: 3.3
Average LSAT: 154
Transfer Students Accepted? Yes
Other Schools to Which Students Applied: University of Pittsburgh, Pennsylvania State University, Temple University, University of Dayton, University of Akron, Villanova University, University of Baltimore, Case Western Reserve University

INTERNATIONAL STUDENTS
TOEFL Required of International Students? Yes

EMPLOYMENT INFORMATION

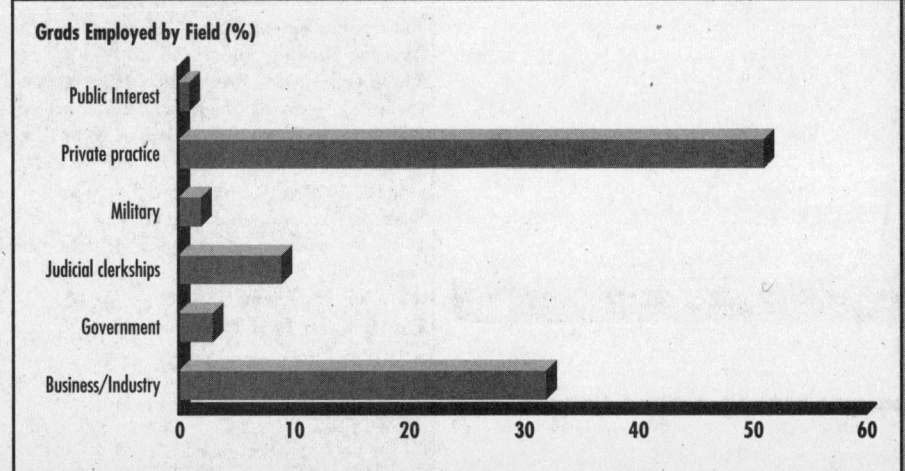

Grads Employed by Field (%)

Field	%
Public Interest	~1
Private practice	~52
Military	~2
Judicial clerkships	~5
Government	~3
Business/Industry	~32

Rate of Placement: 92%
Average Starting Salary: $46,100
Employers Who Frequently Hire Grads: Reed, Smith, Shaw & McClay, Kirkpatrick & Lockhart, Buchanon Ingersoll
Prominent Alumni: Alan Braverman, general counsel, ABC; William Kostopolous, criminal trial attorney; Carol Los Mansmann, judge, 3rd Circuit Court of Appeals
Number Taking Bar Exam: 147
Pass Rate for First-Time Bar: 73%

EMORY UNIVERSITY
School of Law

Admissions Contact: Assistant Dean for Admission, Lynell A. Cadray
1301 Clifton Road, Atlanta, GA 30322-2770
Admissions Phone: 404-727-6802 • Admissions Fax: 404-727-2477
Admissions E-mail: lawinfo@law.emory.edu • Web Address: www.law.emory.edu

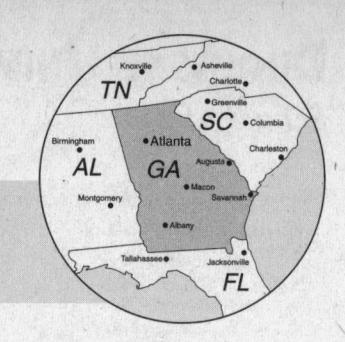

INSTITUTIONAL INFORMATION
Public/Private: Private
Affiliation: Methodist
Student/Faculty Ratio: 12:1
Total Faculty: 55
% Part Time: 4
% Female: 27
% Minority: 6

PROGRAMS
Academic Specialties: Criminal Law, Constitutional Law, Law and Religion, Commercial Law, Human Rights Law, International Law, Taxation, Corporate Law, Environmental Law, Labor Law
Advanced Degrees Offered: LLM (1 year)
Combined Degrees Offered: JD/MBA (4 years), JD/MTS (4 years), JD/MDiv (5 years), JD/MPH (3.5 years), JD/LLM (4 years), JD/REES (3 years), JD/PhD Religion, JD/MA Judaic Studies (4 years)
Grading System: A+ (4.3), A (4.0), A– (3.7), B+ (3.3), B (3.0), B– (2.7), C+ (2.3), C (2.0), C– (1.7), D+ (1.3), D (1.0), D– (0.7), F (0/failing). A cumulative average of 2.25 is required for good standing and for graduation.
Clinical Program Required? No
Clinical Programs Description: Turner Environmental Law Clinic, Barton Child Law and Policy Clinic; more than 27 companies and organizations offer field placement opportunities.
Legal Writing Course Requirements? Yes
Legal Writing Description: The Legal Writing, Research, and Appellate Advocacy (LWRAP) course is a 2-credit class required in both semesters of the first year. The course covers an introduction to law and sources of law, legal bibliography and research techniques and strategies, the analysis of problems in legal terms, the writing of an office memorandum of law and an appellate brief, and the presentation of a case in appellate oral argument.
Legal Methods Course Requirements? Yes
Legal Methods Description: The Legal Methods class is a 3-credit class taken in the first year. This course explores the essential sources, institutions, process, and traditions of modern American law. The emphasis is on the role of judges and legislatures in making law in our society. In addition, a variety of perspectives on the jurisprudence of lawmaking will be examined.
Legal Research Course Requirements? Yes
Legal Research Description: Part of the Legal Writing, Research and Appellate Advocacy (LWRAP) course that is required in the first year.
Moot Court Requirement? No
Public Interest Law Requirement? No
Academic Journals: *Emory Law Journal, Emory International Law Review, Emory Bankruptcy Developments Journal*

STUDENT INFORMATION
Enrollment of Law School: 638
% Out of State: 85
% Male/Female: 46/54
% Full Time: 100
% Full Time That Are International: 1
% Minority: 22
Average Age of Entering Class: 23

EXPENSES/FINANCIAL AID
Annual Tuition: $26,318
Room and Board: $11,704
Books and Supplies: $1,100
Average Grant: $14,173
Average Loan: $29,990
% of Aid That Is Merit-Based: 2
% Receiving Some Sort of Aid: 84
Average Total Aid Package: $31,616
Tuition Per Credit: $1,097

ADMISSIONS INFORMATION
Application Fee: $65
Regular Application Deadline: 3/1
Regular Notification: Rolling
LSDAS Accepted? Yes
Average GPA: 3.5
Range of GPA: 3.3–3.7
Average LSAT: 161
Range of LSAT: 158–162
Transfer Students Accepted? Yes
Other Admissions Factors Considered: Letters of recommendation, significant obstacles overcome, personal essays, community service, leadership ability, quality and level of difficulty of undergraduate work, work experience
Number of Applications Received: 2,983
Number of Applicants Accepted: 1,037
Number of Applicants Enrolled: 227

INTERNATIONAL STUDENTS
TOEFL Required of International Students? Yes
Minimum TOEFL: 250

EMPLOYMENT INFORMATION

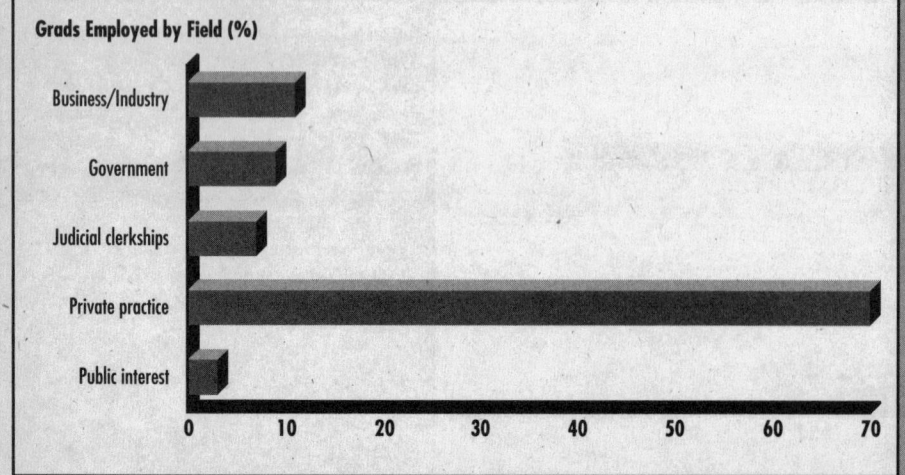

Grads Employed by Field (%)
- Business/Industry: ~12
- Government: ~8
- Judicial clerkships: ~5
- Private practice: ~70
- Public interest: ~3

Rate of Placement: 95%
Average Starting Salary: $76,954
Employers Who Frequently Hire Grads: Cadwalader, Wickersham & Taft; Dewey Ballantine; Milbank, Tweed, Hadley & McCloy; Skadden, Arps, Slate, Meaghert & Flom; Akin, Gump; Arent Fox; Alston & Bird; King & Spalding; McDermott, Will & Emery; Paul, Hastings; Wiley, Rein & Fielding; Troutman Sanders
State for Bar Exam: GA, NY
Pass Rate for First-Time Bar: 90%

EMPIRE COLLEGE
School of Law

Admissions Contact: Admissions Officer, Aimee M. Lute
3035 Cleveland Avenue, Santa Rosa, CA 95403
Admissions Phone: 707-546-4000 • Admissions Fax: 707-546-4058
Admissions E-mail: alute@empirecollege.com • Web Address: www.empcol.com

INSTITUTIONAL INFORMATION
Public/Private: Private
Student/Faculty Ratio: 40:1
Total Faculty: 45
% Part Time: 100
% Female: 22

PROGRAMS
Academic Specialties: All faculty are practicing attorneys or judges; small class ratio; wide variety of elective courses offered
Grading System: A (100–90), B (89–80), C (79–70), D (69–65), F (below 65)
Clinical Program Required? No
Clinical Programs Description: Students may clerk in law offices, the Public Defender's office, or the District Attorney's office.
Legal Writing Course Requirements? Yes
Legal Writing Description: 1 year
Legal Methods Course Requirements? No
Legal Research Course Requirements? Yes
Legal Research Description: 1 semester
Moot Court Requirement? Yes
Moot Court Description: 1 semester
Public Interest Law Requirement? No

STUDENT INFORMATION
Enrollment of Law School: 142
% Out of State: 0
% Male/Female: 100/0
% Full Time That Are International: 0
% Minority: 2
Average Age of Entering Class: 43

EXPENSES/FINANCIAL AID
Annual Tuition: $5,400
Books and Supplies: $600
Tuition Per Credit: $270
Fees Per Credit: $195

ADMISSIONS INFORMATION
Application Fee: $95
Regular Application Deadline: Rolling
Regular Notification: Rolling
LSDAS Accepted? No
Average GPA: 3.1
Range of GPA: 2.3–3.8
Average LSAT: 147
Transfer Students Accepted? Yes
Number of Applications Received: 56
Number of Applicants Accepted: 52

EMPLOYMENT INFORMATION
Employers Who Frequently Hire Grads: Office of the District Attorney, Public Defender's office
State for Bar Exam: CA
Pass Rate for First-Time Bar: 75%

Florida Coastal School of Law

Admissions Contact: Director of Admissions, Steve Jones
7555 Beach Blvd., Jacksonville, FL 32216
Admissions Phone: 904-680-7710 • Admissions Fax: 904-680-7777
Admissions E-mail: admissions@fcsl.edu • Web Address: www.fcsl.edu

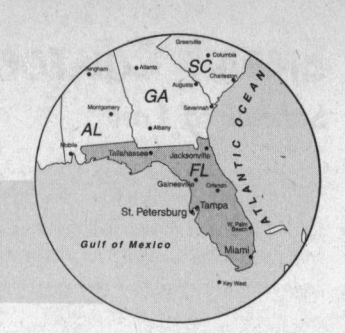

INSTITUTIONAL INFORMATION
Public/Private: Private
Student/Faculty Ratio: 15:1
Total Faculty: 48
% Part Time: 66
% Female: 44
% Minority: 25

PROGRAMS
Academic Specialties: FCSL's program is student-centered, responsive to concerns about the focus of legal education, attentive to technology, premised upon humanistic values, appreciative of multiculturalism, and grounded in real-world experience. FCSL's program provides a thorough grounding in doctrine, essential skills such as interviewing, counseling, negotiation, trial advocacy, and various methods of dispute resolution. Specialties include Civil Procedure, Commercial Law, Constitutional Law, Corporation Securities Law, Criminal Law, Environmental Law, Government Services, Human Rights Law, International Law, Labor Law, Legal History, Legal Philosophy, Property, and Taxation.
Advanced Degrees Offered: JD (2.5 to 3 years full time, 3.5 to 4 years part time)
Grading System: 4.0 scale
Clinical Program Required? Yes
Clinical Programs Description: All students are required to take a skills course or participate in one of the following clinics: Criminal Law Clinic, Civil Practice Clinic, Domestic Violence Clinic, Municipal Law Clinic, International Law Clinic.
Legal Writing Course Requirements? Yes
Legal Writing Description: All students take Legal Writing in their first full year and are also required to take an advanced legal writing course in their second or third year.
Legal Methods Course Requirements? Yes
Legal Methods Description: First-year students are required to develop legal problem-solving, research and writing skills and focus upon development and enhancement of lawyering skills in rule-related and professional responsibility contexts.
Legal Research Course Requirements? Yes
Legal Research Description: All students take Legal Research in their first full year and can elect to take an advanced legal research course in their second or third year.
Moot Court Requirement? No
Moot Court Description: The Moot Court program is voluntary.
Public Interest Law Requirement? No
Academic Journals: *Florida Coastal Law Journal*

STUDENT INFORMATION
Enrollment of Law School: 452
% Out of State: 56
% Male/Female: 54/46
% Full Time: 55
% Full Time That Are International: 2
% Minority: 19
Average Age of Entering Class: 26

RESEARCH FACILITIES
Research Resources Available: University of North Florida, Jacksonville University, CALI (Computer Assisted Learning Center), Lexis/Nexis, Westlaw, Microsoft Campus Agreement Program

EXPENSES/FINANCIAL AID
Annual Tuition: $18,420
Room and Board (Off Campus): $12,168
Books and Supplies: $800
Average Grant: $6,200
Average Loan: $18,500
% of Aid That Is Merit-Based: 11
% Receiving Some Sort of Aid: 71
Average Total Aid Package: $18,500
Average Debt: $28,883
Fees Per Credit: $840

ADMISSIONS INFORMATION
Application Fee: $50
Regular Application Deadline: Rolling
Regular Notification: Rolling
LSDAS Accepted? Yes
Average GPA: 3.0
Average LSAT: 151
Transfer Students Accepted? Yes
Other Schools to Which Students Applied: Florida State, Mercer, Nova Southeastern, St. Thomas, Stetson, U. of Florida, U. of Miami
Other Admissions Factors Considered: Leadership ability, maturity, organizational skills, a history of overcoming disadvantage, extraordinary accomplishment, or success in a previous career. Our goal is to create an intellectually stimulating student body comprised of persons with diverse backgrounds who share a desire for academic excellence and accomplishment in the practice of law.
Number of Applications Received: 2,156
Number of Applicants Accepted: 585
Number of Applicants Enrolled: 165

EMPLOYMENT INFORMATION

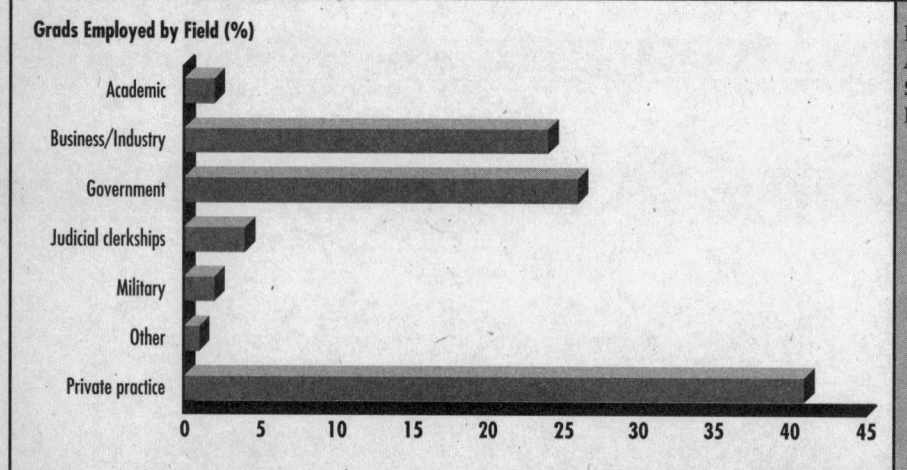

Grads Employed by Field (%)
- Academic: ~1
- Business/Industry: ~25
- Government: ~26
- Judicial clerkships: ~2
- Military: ~1
- Other: ~1
- Private practice: ~42

Rate of Placement: 82%
Average Starting Salary: $47,654
State for Bar Exam: FL, GA, TX, TN, SC
Pass Rate for First-Time Bar: 80%

128 • COMPLETE BOOK OF LAW SCHOOLS

Florida State University
College of Law

Admissions Contact: Director of Admissions and Records, Sharon J. Booker
425 West Jefferson Street, Tallahassee, FL 32306-1601
Admissions Phone: 850-644-3787 • Admissions Fax: 805-644-7284
Admissions E-mail: admissions@law.fsu.edu • Web Address: www.law.fsu.edu

INSTITUTIONAL INFORMATION
Public/Private: Public
Student/Faculty Ratio: 22:1
Total Faculty: 40
% Female: 33
% Minority: 13

PROGRAMS
Academic Specialties: International Law, Environmental Law, Administrative Law, Cyber Law, Intellectual Property Law
Advanced Degrees Offered: JD
Combined Degrees Offered: JD/MBA, JD/MURP, JD/MIA, JD/MS Economics, JD/MPA, JD/MSW, JD/MLIS. Most programs take 4 years to complete.
Grading System: 100–60 numerical range with corresponding letter grades of A+ to F
Clinical Program Required? No.
Clinical Programs Description: Students can earn academic credit while learning to assume the role of attorney or judicial clerk at one of more than 60 placement sites.
Legal Writing Course Requirements? Yes
Legal Writing Description: First-year Legal Writing and Research is required, plus upper-level writing requirement (course, seminar, or Directed Individual Study)
Legal Methods Course Requirements? Yes
Legal Methods Description: See Legal Writing.
Legal Research Course Requirements? Yes
Legal Research Description: See Legal Writing.
Moot Court Requirement? No.
Moot Court Description: Legal issues addressed include the First Amendment, Criminal Law, Intellectual Property, Sports Law, International Law, Environmental Law, Evidence, Workers' Compensation, Cyber Law, Corporate Law, Securities, Labor & Employment, and Entertainment/Communications Law. All first-year students are eligible to try out.
Public Interest Law Requirement? Yes
Public Interest Law Requirement: Students must do a minimum of 20 hours of civil pro bono legal work during their second or third year of law school.
Academic Journals: Law Review, Journal of Land Use & Environmental Law, Journal of Transnational Law and Policy

STUDENT INFORMATION
Enrollment of Law School: 714
% Out of State: 10
% Male/Female: 54/46
% Full Time: 100
% Minority: 22
Average Age of Entering Class: 25

RESEARCH FACILITIES
Research Resources Available: University Library of the Florida State University and its branches, as well as to all the libraries of the state universities of Florida.
School-Supported Research Centers: The FSU College of Law Library is open to law students 24 hours per day.

EXPENSES/FINANCIAL AID
Annual Tuition (Residents/Nonresidents): $4,414/$11,713
Room and Board: $14,000
Books and Supplies: $1,000
Financial Aid Application Deadline: 2/15
Average Grant: $1,040
Average Loan: $18,500
% Receiving Some Sort of Aid: 98
Average Total Aid Package: $18,500
Average Debt: $44,650

ADMISSIONS INFORMATION
Application Fee: $20
Regular Application Deadline: 2/15
Regular Notification: Rolling
LSDAS Accepted? Yes
Average GPA: 3.3
Range of GPA: 3.0–3.6
Average LSAT: 155
Range of LSAT: 153–158
Transfer Students Accepted? Yes
Other Schools to Which Students Applied: American University, Emory, Stetson, Tulane, U. of Florida, U. of Georgia, U. of Miami
Other Admissions Factors Considered: Exceptional personal talents, interesting or demanding work experience, service experience, leadership potential, academic rigor, graduate study, maturity, history of overcoming economic or other social hardships
Number of Applications Received: 2,209
Number of Applicants Accepted: 765
Number of Applicants Enrolled: 215

INTERNATIONAL STUDENTS
TOEFL Required of International Students? Yes
Minimum TOEFL: 213

EMPLOYMENT INFORMATION

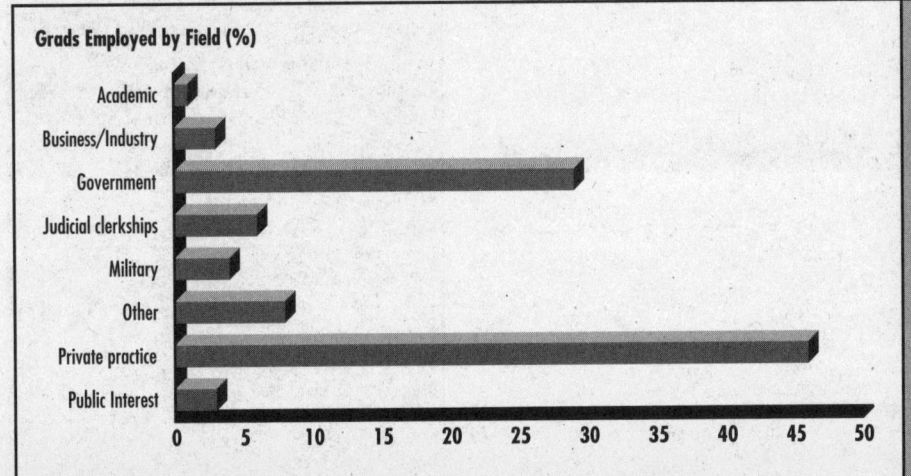

Grads Employed by Field (%):
- Academic: ~1
- Business/Industry: ~3
- Government: ~30
- Judicial clerkships: ~7
- Military: ~1
- Other: ~5
- Private practice: ~47
- Public Interest: ~3

Rate of Placement: 96%
Average Starting Salary: $48,000
Employers Who Frequently Hire Grads: Law firms, state agencies
State for Bar Exam: FL
Pass Rate for First-Time Bar: 86%

FORDHAM UNIVERSITY
School of Law

Admissions Contact: Associate Director of Admissions, John Chalmers
Admissions Office, 140 West 62nd Street, New York, NY 10023
Admissions Phone: 212-636-6810
Admissions E-mail: lawadmissions@mail.lawnet.fordham.edu • Web Address: www.fordham.edu/law

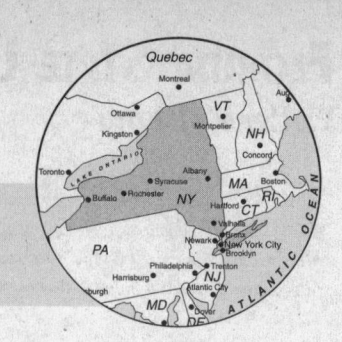

INSTITUTIONAL INFORMATION
Public/Private: Private
Affiliation: Roman Catholic
Environment: Urban
Academic Calendar: Semester
Schedule: Full time or part time
Student/Faculty Ratio: 17:1
Total Faculty: 214
% Part Time: 71
% Female: 28
% Minority: 8

PROGRAMS
Academic Specialties: Constitutional Law, Professional Responsibility and Ethics, Business and Financial Law, Evidence
Advanced Degrees Offered: JD (3 years full time, 4 years part time), LLM (1 year full time)
Combined Degrees Offered: JD/MBA with Fordham Graduate School of Business (4 years full time), JD/MSW with Fordham Graduate School of Social Work (4 years full time)
Grading System: Letter grades; mandatory grading curve for first-year courses, grading guidelines for other courses
Clinical Program Required? No
Clinical Program Description: Separate clinics for Employment Discrimination, Welfare Rights, Criminal Defense, Battered Women's Rights, Mediation, Civil Rights, etc.
Legal Writing/Methods Course Requirements: Writing and Research (first year)

STUDENT INFORMATION
Enrollment of Law School: 1,437
% Male/Female: 56/44
% Full Time: 75
% Full Time That Are International: 2
% Minority: 24
Average Age of Entering Class: 24

RESEARCH FACILITIES
Computers/Workstations Available: 200
School-Supported Research Centers: The libraries at Fordham, Columbia, NYU, Penn, and Yale are affiliated so that the students may use any of the 5 libraries.

EXPENSES/FINANCIAL AID
Annual Tuition: $25,035
Room and Board: $17,350
Books and Supplies: $725
Average Grant: $4,865
Average Loan: $3,467
% of Aid That Is Merit-Based: 10
% Receiving Some Sort of Aid: 44
Average Total Aid Package: $7,691
Average Debt: $72,674

ADMISSIONS INFORMATION
Application Fee: $60
Regular Application Deadline: 3/1
Regular Notification: Rolling
LSDAS Accepted? Yes
Average GPA: 3.4
Range of GPA: 3.1–3.6
Average LSAT: 164
Range of LSAT: 161–165
Transfer Students Accepted? Yes
Other Schools to Which Students Applied: New York University, Columbia University, Brooklyn Law School, Boston University, Georgetown University, George Washington University, Yeshiva University, New York Law School
Other Admissions Factors Considered: Prior employment, student activities, service to the community, leadership ability, propensity for public service, communication skills, grade trend, course selection, grades in the major, choice of major, undergraduate institution
Number of Applications Received: 5,030
Number of Applicants Accepted: 1,384
Number of Applicants Enrolled: 454

INTERNATIONAL STUDENTS
TOEFL Required of International Students? Yes
Minimum TOEFL: 600

EMPLOYMENT INFORMATION

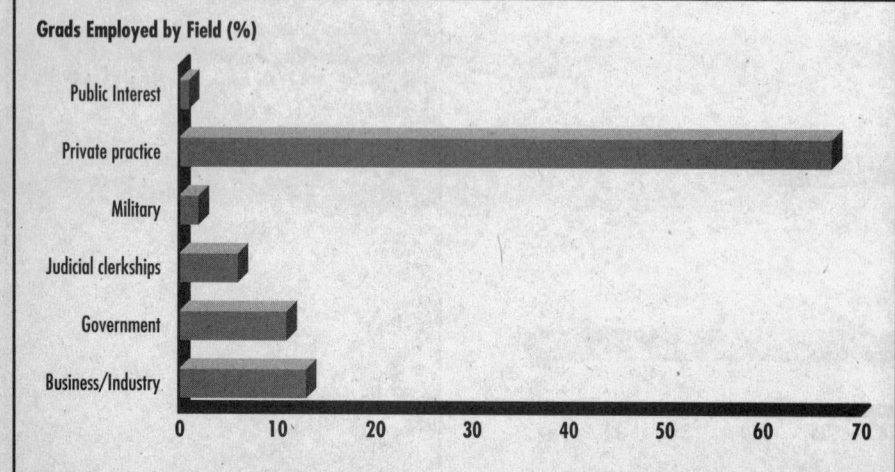

Grads Employed by Field (%)
- Public Interest
- Private practice
- Military
- Judicial clerkships
- Government
- Business/Industry

Rate of Placement: 97%
Average Starting Salary: $79,429
Employers Who Frequently Hire Grads: Cahill, Gordon & Reindel; Department of Justice; Simpson, Thatcher & Bartlett; NY Legal Aid; Skadden, Arps, Slate, Meagher & Flom; AT&T; Merrill Lynch; U.S. Courts
Prominent Alumni: Geraldine Ferraro, former democratic vice presidential candidate; Jack Ford, anchor, NBC *Weekend Today* Show; Joseph M. McGlauglin, judge, U.S. Court of Appeals for the 2nd Circuit
State for Bar Exam: NY
Number Taking Bar Exam: 482
Pass Rate for First-Time Bar: 86%

FRANKLIN PIERCE LAW CENTER

Admissions Contact: Director of Admissions, Lory Attacca
2 White Street, Concord, NH 03301
Admissions Phone: 603-228-9217 • Admissions Fax: 603-228-1074
Admissions E-mail: admissions@fplc.edu • Web Address: www.fplc.edu

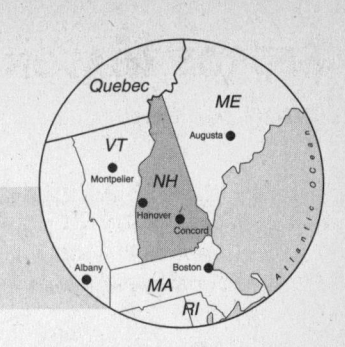

INSTITUTIONAL INFORMATION
Public/Private: Private
Student/Faculty Ratio: 20:1
Total Faculty: 81
% Part Time: 58
% Female: 24
% Minority: 1

PROGRAMS
Academic Specialties: Intellectual Property, Patents, Trademarks, Licensing, Management, Information Law, Entertainment Law, Public Interest and Community Lawyering, Children's Law, Education Law, Health Law, Criminal Law, Nonprofit Organization Law, Civil Procedure, Commercial Law, International Law
Advanced Degrees Offered: LLM (1 year), MIP (1 year), Master of Education Law (MEL) degree pending ABA acquiesence, Certificate of Advanced Graduate Study in Education Law (CAGS in Law) degree pending ABA acquiescence
Combined Degrees Offered: JD/MIP (3 years)
Grading System: Anonymous grading using A+ to F. Students may take electives Pass/Fail. In all classes with more than 15 students, the mean grade in the class will be no higher than B. Waivers of this policy may be sought through the Teaching Effectiveness Committee.
Clinical Program Required? No
Clinical Program Description: Children's Advocacy Clinic, Civil Practice Clinic, Administrative Law and Advocacy, Advanced Civil Practice Clinic, Appellate Defender Clinic, Criminal Practice Clinic, Dispute Resolution in Action, Innovation Clinic, Juvenile Corrections, Small Claims Mediation Program, Nonprofit Organizations Clinic
Legal Writing Course Requirements? No
Legal Methods Course Requirements? Yes
Legal Research Course Requirements? No
Moot Court Requirement? No
Public Interest Law Requirement? No

STUDENT INFORMATION
Enrollment of Law School: 370
% Out of State: 73
% Male/Female: 56/44
% Full Time: 100
% Full Time That Are International: 6
% Minority: 14
Average Age of Entering Class: 28

EXPENSES/FINANCIAL AID
Annual Tuition: $19,962
Room and Board (Off Campus): $10,491
Books and Supplies: $600
Average Grant: $2,000
Average Loan: $21,700
% of Aid That Is Merit-Based: 57
% Receiving Some Sort of Aid: 85
Average Total Aid Package: $25,200
Average Debt: $72,100
Tuition Per Credit: $681

ADMISSIONS INFORMATION
Application Fee: $55
Regular Application Deadline: 5/1
Regular Notification: Rolling
LSDAS Accepted? Yes
Average GPA: 3.0
Range of GPA: 2.0–3.9
Average LSAT: 150
Range of LSAT: 138–166
Transfer Students Accepted? Yes
Other Admissions Factors Considered: Personal or academic achievement
Number of Applications Received: 768
Number of Applicants Enrolled: 134

EMPLOYMENT INFORMATION

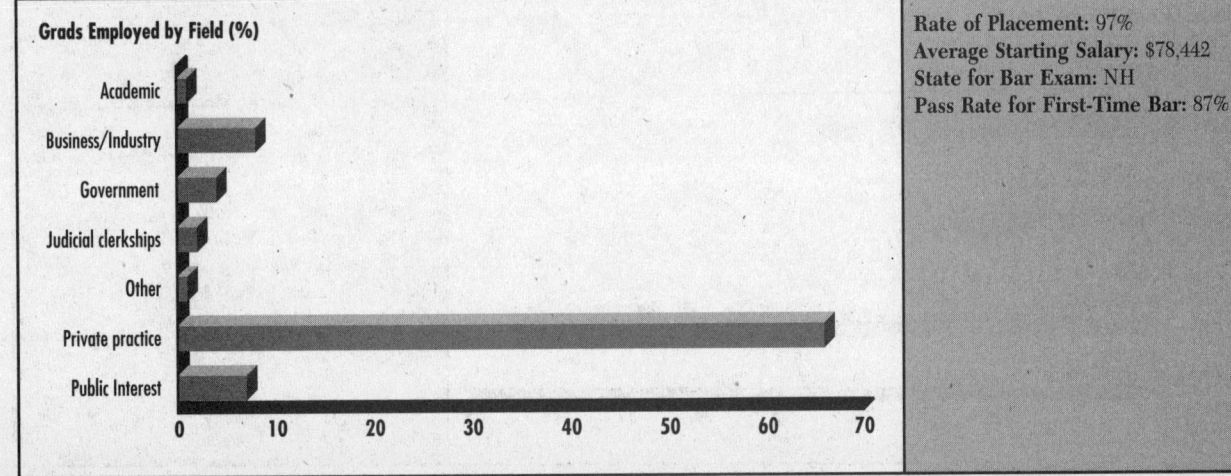

Grads Employed by Field (%)

Field	%
Academic	~0
Business/Industry	~7
Government	~3
Judicial clerkships	~3
Other	~2
Private practice	~67
Public Interest	~7

Rate of Placement: 97%
Average Starting Salary: $78,442
State for Bar Exam: NH
Pass Rate for First-Time Bar: 87%

GEORGE MASON UNIVERSITY
School of Law

Admissions Contact: Assistant Dean and Director of Admissions, Anne M. Richard
3301 North Fairfax Drive, Arlington, VA 22201
Admissions Phone: 703-993-8010 • Admissions Fax: 703-993-8260
Admissions E-mail: arichar5@gmu.edu • Web Address: www.law.gmu.edu

INSTITUTIONAL INFORMATION
Public/Private: Public
Student/Faculty Ratio: 16:1
Total Faculty: 126
% Part Time: 70
% Female: 21
% Minority: 6

PROGRAMS
Academic Specialties: Law and Economics is a focus of many faculty members and is integrated with the curriculum to provide students with knowledge of legal methods along with economic and quantitative tools. Other specialties include Civil Procedure, Corporation Securities Law, Criminal Law, Government Services, International Law, Intellectual Property Law, and Technology Law.
Advanced Degrees Offered: Juris Master Policy Analysis (2 years, part-time evening program)
Grading System: Numerical system, 4.33 scale
Clinical Program Required? No
Clinical Programs Description: Legal Clinic, Law and Mental Illness Clinic, Public Interest Clinic, Board of Immigration Appeals Clinic, supervised externships
Legal Writing Course Requirements? Yes
Legal Writing Description: 3-year program requires 4 semesters of Legal Research, Writing, and Analysis (LRWA) classes, plus at least 2 additional writing courses beyond the first 2 years
Legal Methods Course Requirements? No
Legal Research Course Requirements? Yes
Legal Research Description: Incorporated into the Legal Research, Writing, and Analysis (LRWA) program courses
Moot Court Requirement? Yes
Moot Court Description: Required first-year moot court competition. Upper-class students may participate in moot court activities internally or externally.
Public Interest Law Requirement? No
Public Interest Law Description: Public Interest Law Clinic, student-run Association for Public Interest Law.
Academic Journals: *Civil Rights Law Journal, Federal Circuit Bar Journal, George Mason Law Review*

STUDENT INFORMATION
Enrollment of Law School: 732
% Out of State: 17
% Male/Female: 54/46
% Full Time: 51
% Full Time That Are International: 1
% Minority: 8
Average Age of Entering Class: 27

RESEARCH FACILITIES
Research Resources Available: There are a total of 50 Pentium computers providing access to all databases and online services offered via the university libraries. In addition to a core reference collection, Arlington Campus Libraries is a depository for European Union documents.
School-Supported Research Centers: National Center for Technology and Law established at the law school in 1999

EXPENSES/FINANCIAL AID
Annual Tuition (Residents/Nonresidents): $8,092/$18,704
Room and Board (Off Campus): $14,965
Books and Supplies: $750
Financial Aid Application Deadline: 3/1
Average Grant: $3,530
Average Loan: $15,102
% of Aid That Is Merit-Based: 2
% Receiving Some Sort of Aid: 68
Average Total Aid Package: $15,100
Average Debt: $34,266
Tuition Per Credit (Residents/Nonresidents): $6,358/$14,696

ADMISSIONS INFORMATION
Application Fee: $35
Regular Application Deadline: 3/15
Regular Notification: 4/15
LSDAS Accepted? Yes
Average GPA: 3.3
Average LSAT: 159
Transfer Students Accepted? Yes
Other Schools to Which Students Applied: Georgetown, U. of Maryland, U. of Virginia, College of William and Mary, American U., U. of Richmond
Other Admissions Factors Considered: Writing ability as illustrated in LSAT writing sample and personal statement, difficulty of undergraduate curriculum, quality of undergraduate institution, graduate degrees earned, demonstrated commitment to public and community service
Number of Applications Received: 2,667
Number of Applicants Accepted: 615
Number of Applicants Enrolled: 246

EMPLOYMENT INFORMATION

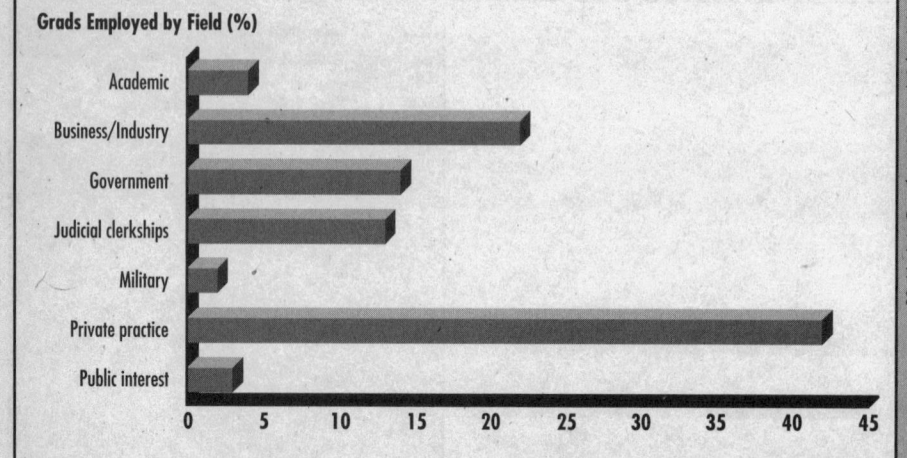

Grads Employed by Field (%)

Field	%
Academic	~1
Business/Industry	~22
Government	~14
Judicial clerkships	~13
Military	~2
Private practice	~43
Public interest	~3

Rate of Placement: 98%
Average Starting Salary: $74,400
Employers Who Frequently Hire Grads: Hunton & Williams; McGuire Woods LLP; Finnegan, Henderson, Farabow, Garret & Dunner, LLP; U.S. Government; Shaw Pittman; Wiley, Rein, and Fielding; Sterne, Kessler, Goldstein, and Fox; Sutherland, Asbill, and Brennan; Crowell & Moring; Fried, Frank, Harris, Shriver & Jacobsen
State for Bar Exam: VA, MD, DC, CA, NY

GEORGE WASHINGTON UNIVERSITY
Law School

Admissions Contact: Associate Dean for Admissions and Financial Aid, Robert V. Stanek
700 20th Street, NW, Washington, DC 20052
Admissions Phone: 202-994-7230 • Admissions Fax: 202-994-3597
Admissions E-mail: jdadmit@law.gwu.edu • Web Address: www.law.gwu.edu

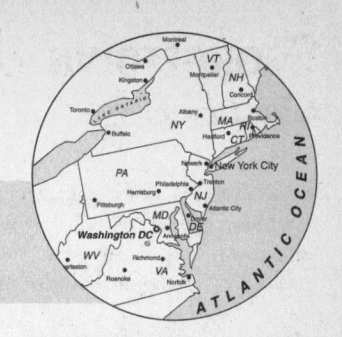

INSTITUTIONAL INFORMATION
Public/Private: Private
Student/Faculty Ratio: 19:1
Total Faculty: 301
% Part Time: 70
% Female: 30
% Minority: 9

PROGRAMS
Academic Specialties: The JD curriculum is very diverse with over 200 elective courses. Specialized areas of the curriculum include Intellectual Property Law, Environmental Law, International and Comparative Law, Government Procurement Law, Civil Procedure, Commercial Law, Constitutional Law, Corporation Securities Law, Criminal Law, Government Services, Human Rights Law, Labor Law, Legal History, Legal Philosophy, Property, and Taxation.
Advanced Degrees Offered: JD (3 years full time, 4 years part time), LLM (1 to 2 years), SJD (3 years)
Combined Degrees Offered: JD/MBA, JD/MPA, JD/MAIA, JD/MA History, JD/MA Women's Studies, JD/MPH (all can be completed in 4 years with full-time and summer attendance)
Grading System: A+ to F (4.33–0.00)
Clinical Program Required? No
Legal Writing Course Requirements? No
Legal Methods Course Requirements? Yes
Legal Methods Description: In the first year, students take Legal Research and Writing in the fall and Introduction to Advocacy in the spring. Both courses are taught in small sections.

Legal Research Course Requirements? No
Moot Court Requirement? No
Public Interest Law Requirement? No
Academic Journals: *The George Washington Law Review, The George Washington International Law Review, The Environmental Lawyer, The American Intellectual Property Law Association Quarterly Journal, The Public Contract Law Journal*

STUDENT INFORMATION
Enrollment of Law School: 1,489
% Out of State: 94
% Male/Female: 53/47
% Full Time: 83
% Full Time That Are International: 5
% Minority: 31
Average Age of Entering Class: 24

RESEARCH FACILITIES
Research Resources Available: An information portal dedicated to JDs only

EXPENSES/FINANCIAL AID
Annual Tuition $28,045
Room and Board: $9,600
Books and Supplies: $840
Average Grant: $12,000
Average Loan: $23,000
% of Aid That Is Merit-Based: 5
% Receiving Some Sort of Aid: 72
Average Total Aid Package: $35,000
Average Debt: $67,000
Tuition Per Credit: $987

ADMISSIONS INFORMATION
Application Fee: $65
Regular Application Deadline: 3/1
Regular Notification: Rolling
LSDAS Accepted? Yes
Average GPA: 3.5
Range of GPA: 3.3–3.6
Average LSAT: 163
Range of LSAT: 160–164
Transfer Students Accepted? Yes
Other Schools to Which Students Applied: American University, Boston College, Boston University, Columbia University, Fordham University, Georgetown University, North Carolina Central University
Number of Applications Received: 8,447
Number of Applicants Accepted: 1,996
Number of Applicants Enrolled: 367

EMPLOYMENT INFORMATION

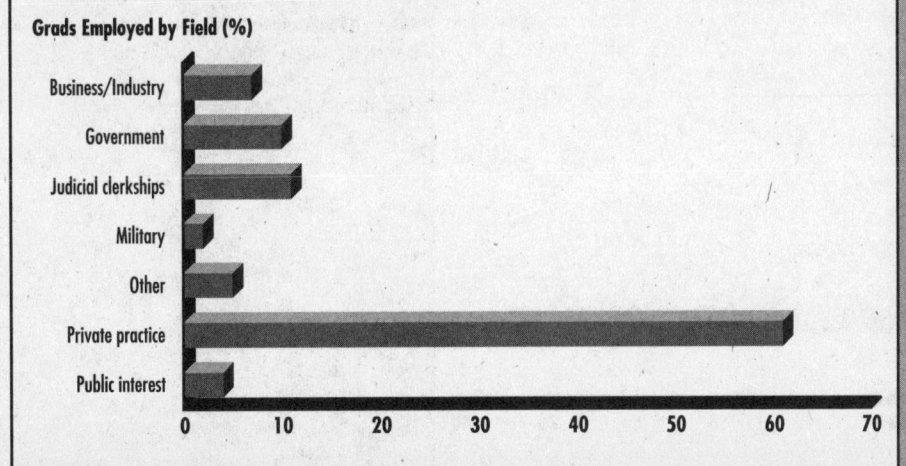

Grads Employed by Field (%)

Field	%
Business/Industry	~3
Government	~10
Judicial clerkships	~12
Military	~1
Other	~2
Private practice	~62
Public interest	~3

Rate of Placement: 97%
Average Starting Salary: $97,298
Employers Who Frequently Hire Grads: Department of Justice; Howrey & Simon; Finnegan, Henderson et al.; Akin, Gump, et al.; Shearman & Sterling; Arnold & Porter; Wiley, Rein & Fielding; Arent Fox; various government agencies
State for Bar Exam: NY
Pass Rate for First-Time Bar: 92%

GEORGETOWN UNIVERSITY
Law Center

Admissions Contact: Assistant Dean of Admissions, Andrew P. Cornblatt
600 New Jersey Avenue, NW, Washington, DC 20001
Admissions Phone: 202-662-9010 • Admissions Fax: 202-662-9439
Admissions E-mail: admis@law.georgetown.edu • Web Address: www.law.georgetown.edu

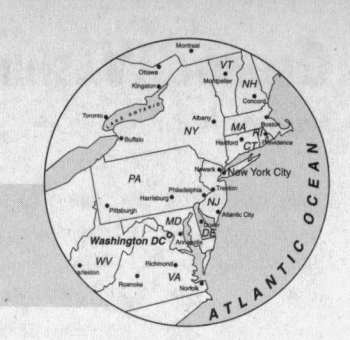

INSTITUTIONAL INFORMATION
Public/Private: Private
Affiliation: Roman Catholic
Student/Faculty Ratio: 15:1
Total Faculty: 210
% Female: 35
% Minority: 11

PROGRAMS
Academic Specialties: Administrative Law, Alternate Dispute Resolution, Constitutional Law, Corporate and Securities Law, Criminal Law, Environmental Law, Health Law and Policy, Immigration and Refugee Law, Intellectual Property Law, International and Comparative Law, Legal Ethics, Legal History, Legal Philosophy, Litigation and Judicial Process, Public Interest Law, Taxation, Civil Procedure, Commercial Law, Government Services, Human Rights Law, and Labor Law
Advanced Degrees Offered: JD (3 years full time, 4 years part time); SJD (2 to 5 years); LLM Taxation, LLM Securities and Financial Regulation, LLM International and Comparative Law, LLM Individualized (all 1 to 3 years); LLM General Studies, LLM International Legal Studies (both for foreign students only, 1 year); Certificate in Employee Benefits (10 credits, 1 to 3 years part time only)
Combined Degrees Offered: JD/MBA (4 years), JD/MPH (4 years), JD/MPP (4 years), JD/MSFS (4 years), JD/Government (4+ years), JD/Philosophy (4+ years)
Grading System: 4.0 system: A, A–, B+, B, B–, C+, C, C–, D, F
Clinical Program Required? No

Clinical Programs Description: Appellate Litigation Clinic, Center for Applied Legal Studies, Criminal Justice Clinic, D.C. Law Students in Court, Domestic Violence Clinic, Family Advocacy Clinic Federal Legislation Clinic, Harrison Institute Housing and Community Development Clinic, Harrison Institute Policy Clinic, Institute for Public Representation, International Women's Human Rights Clinic, Juvenile Justice Clinic, Street Law in High Schools, and Street Law in the Community.
Legal Writing Course Requirements? Yes
Legal Writing Description: A year-long program in the first year introduces students to legal discourse through problem analysis, legal research, writing, oral skills, and legal citation, through a combination of large classes and workshops.
Legal Methods Course Requirements? Yes
Legal Methods Description: See Legal Writing.
Legal Research Course Requirements? Yes
Legal Research Description: See Legal Writing.
Moot Court Requirement? No
Moot Court Description: The Barrister's Council is the student governing body of the Moot Court and Mock Trial programs.
Public Interest Law Requirement? No
Public Interest Law Description: The voluntary Pro Bono Pledge encourages every Georgetown law student to perform 75 hours of law-related pro bono work prior to graduation.
Academic Journals: *Georgetown Law Journal, American Criminal Law Review, Georgetown Journal on Poverty Law and Policy,* and more

STUDENT INFORMATION
Enrollment of Law School: 1,954
% Male/Female: 50/50
% Full Time: 78
% Full Time That Are International: 3
% Minority: 24
Average Age of Entering Class: 24

RESEARCH FACILITIES
Research Resources Available: Library of Congress, National Library of Medicine, Edward Bennett William Law Library, Joseph Mark Lauinger Library, John Vinton Dahlgren Library

EXPENSES/FINANCIAL AID
Annual Tuition: $29,440
Room and Board: $14,325
Books and Supplies: $740
Financial Aid Application Deadline: 3/1
Average Grant: $9,250
Average Loan: $27,800
% of Aid That Is Merit-Based: 0
% Receiving Some Sort of Aid: 85
Average Total Aid Package: $31,105
Average Debt: $83,500
Tuition Per Credit: $1,060

ADMISSIONS INFORMATION
Application Fee: $65
Regular Application Deadline: 2/1
Regular Notification: Rolling
LSDAS Accepted? Yes
Average GPA: 3.6
Average LSAT: 167
Transfer Students Accepted? Yes
Number of Applications Received: 9,006
Number of Applicants Accepted: 1,998
Number of Applicants Enrolled: 496

EMPLOYMENT INFORMATION

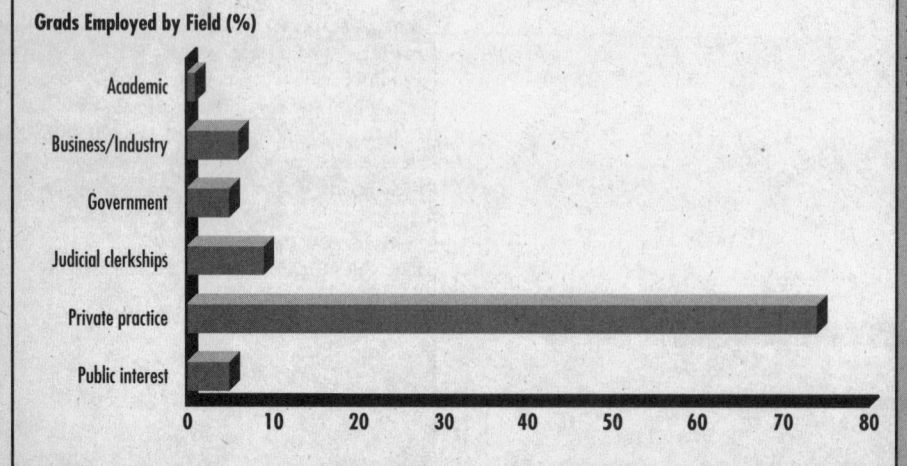

Grads Employed by Field (%)
- Academic
- Business/Industry
- Government
- Judicial clerkships
- Private practice
- Public interest

Rate of Placement: 99%
Average Starting Salary: $105,000
State for Bar Exam: NY
Pass Rate for First-Time Bar: 93%

GEORGIA STATE UNIVERSITY
College of Law

Admissions Contact: Director of Admissions, Dr. Cheryl Jester Jeckson
PO Box 4049, Atlanta, GA 30302-4049
Admissions Phone: 404-651-2048 • Admissions Fax: 404-651-1244
Admissions E-mail: admissions@gsulaw.gsu.edu • Web Address: law.gsu.edu

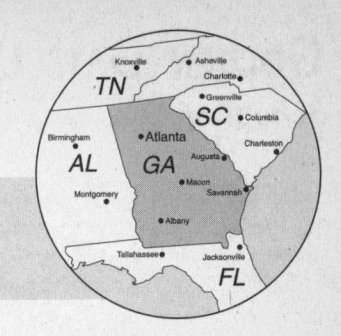

INSTITUTIONAL INFORMATION
Public/Private: Public
Student/Faculty Ratio: 16:1
Total Faculty: 72
% Part Time: 30
% Female: 38
% Minority: 17

PROGRAMS
Academic Specialties: Tax, Commercial Law, Constitutional Law, Alternative Dispute Resolution, Law and Technology, Civil Procedure, Corporation Securities Law, Criminal Law, Environmental Law, Human Rights Law, International Law
Combined Degrees Offered: JD/MBA (4 years), JD/MPA (4 years), JD/MA Philosophy (4 years)
Grading System: A (100–90), B (89–80), C (79–70), D (69–60), F (59–55)
Clinical Program Required? No
Clinical Programs Description: Tax Clinic, Externship Program
Legal Writing Course Requirements? Yes
Legal Methods Course Requirements? No
Legal Methods Description: Tax Clinic, Externship Program
Legal Research Course Requirements? Yes
Moot Court Requirement? No
Public Interest Law Requirement? No
Academic Journals: *Law Review*

STUDENT INFORMATION
Enrollment of Law School: 646
% Out of State: 12
% Male/Female: 49/51
% Full Time: 68
% Full Time That Are International: 3
% Minority: 15
Average Age of Entering Class: 27

RESEARCH FACILITIES
Research Resources Available: University computer centers

EXPENSES/FINANCIAL AID
Annual Tuition (Residents/Nonresidents): $3,696/$14,784
Room and Board (On/Off Campus): $4,680/$8,190
Books and Supplies: $690
Financial Aid Application Deadline: 4/1
Average Grant: $3,542
Average Loan: $10,000
% Receiving Some Sort of Aid: 62
Average Total Aid Package: $12,983
Average Debt: $37,811
Tuition Per Credit (Residents/Nonresidents): $154/$616
Fees Per Credit: $377

ADMISSIONS INFORMATION
Application Fee: $30
Regular Application Deadline: 3/5
Regular Notification: Rolling
LSDAS Accepted? Yes
Average GPA: 3.2
Range of GPA: 2.9–3.9
Average LSAT: 156
Range of LSAT: 154–158
Transfer Students Accepted? Yes
Other Schools to Which Students Applied: Emory University, Mercer University, University of Florida, University of Georgia
Other Admissions Factors Considered: LSDAS report, letters of recommendation, personal statement, school and community activities, employment experience, advanced study or degrees
Number of Applications Received: 2,009
Number of Applicants Accepted: 558
Number of Applicants Enrolled: 237

EMPLOYMENT INFORMATION

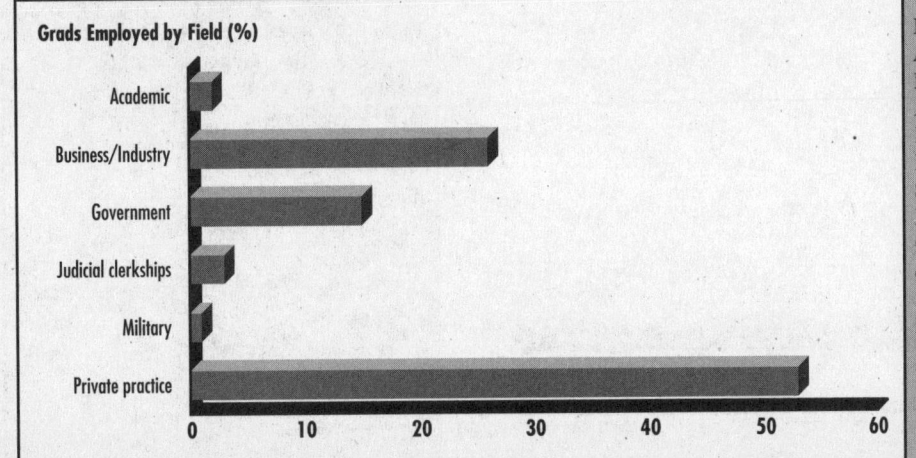

Grads Employed by Field (%):
- Academic: ~2
- Business/Industry: ~27
- Government: ~16
- Judicial clerkships: ~3
- Military: ~1
- Private practice: ~53

Rate of Placement: 95%
Average Starting Salary: $69,677
Employers Who Frequently Hire Grads: Alston & Burd; Arnall, Golden & Gregory; Drew Eckl; Greenberg, Traurig, Kilpatrick & Stockton; Holland & Knight; Hunton and Williams; King & Spalding; Long, Aldridge & Norman; Paul, Hastings, Janofosky, and Walker; Powell, Goldstein, Frazer & Murphy; Troutman & Sanders; Fisher & Phillips
State for Bar Exam: GA
Pass Rate for First-Time Bar: 93%

GOLDEN GATE UNIVERSITY
School of Law

Admissions Contact: Assistant Dean, Tracy Simmons
536 Mission Street, San Francisco, CA 94105
Admissions Phone: 415-442-6630 • Admissions Fax: 415-442-6631
Admissions E-mail: lawadmit@ggu.edu • Web Address: www.ggu.edu/law/

INSTITUTIONAL INFORMATION
Public/Private: Private
Student/Faculty Ratio: 18:1
Total Faculty: 160
% Part Time: 75
% Female: 41
% Minority: 10

PROGRAMS
Academic Specialties: Intellectual Property Law, Real Estate Law, Environmental Law, Litigation, International Law, Immigration Law, Civil Rights Law (includes Affirmative Action, Homeless Rights, Minority, Women, and Gay and Lesbian Issues), Criminal Law, Labor Law, Business Law, Litigation, Public Interest Law
Advanced Degrees Offered: JD (3 years full time, 4 years part time), LLM (1 year)
Combined Degrees Offered: JD/MBA (3 to 4 years), JD/PhD (7 years)
Grading System: Letter and numerical system on a 4.0 scale
Clinical Program Required? No
Clinical Programs Description: More than half of the students at Golden Gate participate in either in-house clinics or field placement clinics.
Legal Writing Course Requirements? Yes
Legal Writing Description: 2 semesters of Writing and Research in first year; Appellate Advocacy required in second year.
Legal Methods Course Requirements? No
Legal Research Course Requirements? Yes
Legal Research Description: See Legal Writing.
Moot Court Requirement? No
Moot Court Description: Teams attend various national and international contests.
Public Interest Law Requirement? No
Academic Journals: *Golden Gate University Law Review*

STUDENT INFORMATION
Enrollment of Law School: 543
% Out of State: 9
% Male/Female: 39/61
% Full Time: 70
% Full Time That Are International: 6
% Minority: 26
Average Age of Entering Class: 28

RESEARCH FACILITIES
Research Resources Available: CALI, Dialog, Dow-Jones, InfoTrac, Legal-Trac, Lexis/Nexis, LOIS, Mathew Bender, Westlaw; law building has recently undergone renovation to wire almost all law classrooms

EXPENSES/FINANCIAL AID
Annual Tuition: $22,910
Room and Board (Off Campus): $7,875
Books and Supplies: $870
Financial Aid Application Deadline: 4/15
Average Grant: $6,000
Average Loan: $21,600
% of Aid That Is Merit-Based: 95
% Receiving Some Sort of Aid: 75
Average Total Aid Package: $30,000
Average Debt: $60,000
Tuition Per Credit: $790
Fees Per Credit: $790

ADMISSIONS INFORMATION
Application Fee: $40
Regular Application Deadline: 4/15
Regular Notification: Rolling
LSDAS Accepted? Yes
Average GPA: 3.1
Range of GPA: 2.7–3.4
Average LSAT: 147
Range of LSAT: 145–151
Transfer Students Accepted? Yes
Other Admissions Factors Considered: Strength of undergraduate program, work experience that engages/develops writing and research skills
Number of Applications Received: 1,433
Number of Applicants Accepted: 937
Number of Applicants Enrolled: 204

EMPLOYMENT INFORMATION

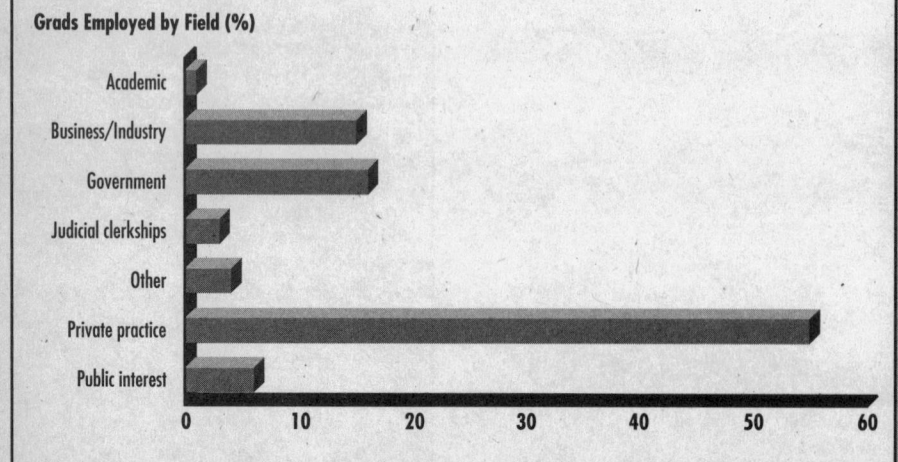

Grads Employed by Field (%)

Field	%
Academic	~1
Business/Industry	~15
Government	~15
Judicial clerkships	~4
Other	~4
Private practice	~55
Public interest	~5

Rate of Placement: 84%
Average Starting Salary: $60,330
Employers Who Frequently Hire Grads: Small, medium, and large firms; government agencies; public interest organizations; and businesses and corporations
State for Bar Exam: CA
Pass Rate for First-Time Bar: 53%

GONZAGA UNIVERSITY
School of Law

Admissions Contact: Assistant Dean and Director of Admissions, Tamara Martinez-Anderson
PO Box 3528, Spokane, WA 99220
Admissions Phone: 800-793-1710 • Admissions Fax: 509-323-3697
Admissions E-mail: admissions@lawschool.gonzaga.edu • Web Address: law.gonzaga.edu

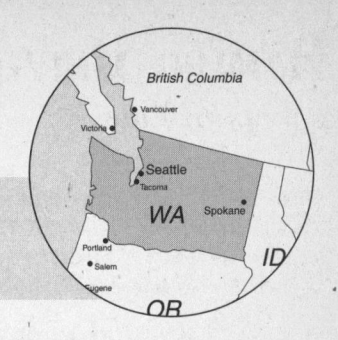

INSTITUTIONAL INFORMATION
Public/Private: Private
Affiliation: Roman Catholic
Student/Faculty Ratio: 21:1
Total Faculty: 101
% Part Time: 47
% Female: 31
% Minority: 1

PROGRAMS
Academic Specialties: Integrated curriculum emphasizes skills training and professional ethics and values. Award-winning clinic has 3 options: university legal assistance (15 credits over 2 semesters), mini-clinics (3 to 5 credits), and externship placements. Other specialties include Environmental Law and Taxation.
Combined Degrees Offered: JD/MBA, JD/MAcc (both 3.5 to 4 years)
Grading System: Letter and numerical system on a 4.0 scale; students must maintain a cumulative 2.2 GPA
Clinical Program Required? No
Clinical Programs Description: Full-service clinic and externship program
Legal Writing Course Requirements? Yes
Legal Writing Description: 2 credits per semester first year, 1 credit per semester second year
Legal Methods Course Requirements? No
Legal Research Course Requirements? Yes
Legal Research Description: 2 credits per semester first year, 1 credit per semester second year
Moot Court Requirement? No
Moot Court Description: Intra- and inter-mural teams.
Public Interest Law Requirement? Yes
Public Interest Law Description: 30 hours of public service required for graduation
Academic Journals: *Gonzaga Law Review, Across Borders International On-Line Journal*

STUDENT INFORMATION
Enrollment of Law School: 501
% Out of State: 47
% Male/Female: 53/47
% Full Time: 96
% Full Time That Are International: 1
% Minority: 16
Average Age of Entering Class: 27

RESEARCH FACILITIES
Research Resources Available: Foley Center Library

EXPENSES/FINANCIAL AID
Annual Tuition: $20,340
Room and Board (Off Campus): $7,375
Books and Supplies: $900
Financial Aid Application Deadline: 2/1
Average Grant: $6,000
Average Loan: $30,000
% of Aid That Is Merit-Based: 10
% Receiving Some Sort of Aid: 95
Average Total Aid Package: $35,215
Average Debt: $60,000
Tuition Per Credit: $678
Fees Per Credit: $50

ADMISSIONS INFORMATION
Application Fee: $40
Regular Application Deadline: 4/1
Regular Notification: Rolling
LSDAS Accepted? Yes
Average GPA: 3.1
Range of GPA: 2.9–3.5
Average LSAT: 152
Range of LSAT: 148–155
Transfer Students Accepted? Yes
Other Schools to Which Students Applied: California Western, Seattle University, Whittier College, Willamette University
Other Admissions Factors Considered: Personal statements, work experience, letters of recommendation, community service, life experiences
Number of Applications Received: 943
Number of Applicants Accepted: 568
Number of Applicants Enrolled: 205

EMPLOYMENT INFORMATION

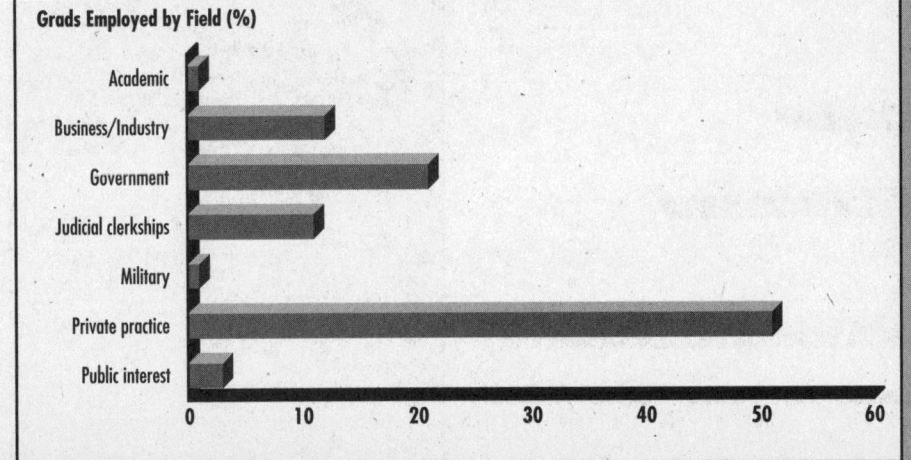

Grads Employed by Field (%)

Field	%
Academic	~1
Business/Industry	~12
Government	~21
Judicial clerkships	~12
Military	~0
Private practice	~51
Public interest	~2

Rate of Placement: 84%
Average Starting Salary: $43,333
Employers Who Frequently Hire Grads: Various law firms in Spokane and throughout Washington, various local and state government entities
State for Bar Exam: WA
Pass Rate for First-Time Bar: 67%

HAMLINE UNIVERSITY
School of Law

Admissions Contact: Director, Michael States
1536 Hewitt Avenue, St. Paul, MN 55104-1284
Admissions Phone: 651-523-2461 • Admissions Fax: 651-523-3064
Admissions E-mail: lawadm@gw.hamline.edu • Web Address: www.hamline.edu/law

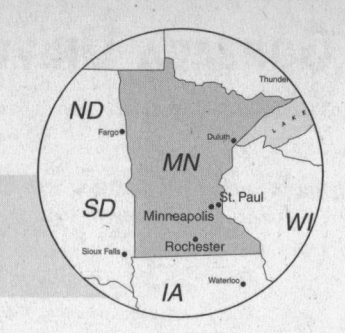

INSTITUTIONAL INFORMATION
Public/Private: Private
Affiliation: Methodist
Student/Faculty Ratio: 19:1
Total Faculty: 35
% Female: 40
% Minority: 8

PROGRAMS
Academic Specialties: Law, Religion, and Ethics; Commercial Law, Children and The Law; Corporate Law; Government and Regulatory Affairs; Labor and Employment Law; Criminal Law; Law and Slavery; Alternative Dispute Resolution; Corporation Securities Law; Government Services; Intellectual Property Law; International Law; Labor Law; Social Justice
Advanced Degrees Offered: JD (3 years), LLM for international lawyers (1 year)
Combined Degrees Offered: JD/MAPA (4 years), JD/AMBA (4 years), JD/MANM, JD/MAM, JD/MLIS (4 years), JD/MAOL (4 years)
Grading System: Letter grades on a 4.0 scale: A, A–, B+, B, B–, C+, C, C–, D+, D, D–, F; a few courses offered on Pass/No Pass basis
Clinical Program Required? No
Clinical Programs Description: General Practice Clinic, Mediation, Child Advocacy, Legal Assistance to Minnesota Prisoners (LAMP), Alternative Dispute Resolution Clinic, Education Law Clinic, Small Business/Nonprofit Clinic, Immigration Law
Legal Writing Course Requirements? Yes
Legal Writing Description: Legal Research and Writing is a full-year course required of all first-year law students. It is taught by full-time instructors in classes of approximately 20 students.
Legal Methods Course Requirements? No
Legal Research Course Requirements? Yes
Legal Research Description: See Legal Writing.
Moot Court Requirement? No
Public Interest Law Requirement? No
Academic Journals: Hamline Law Review, Hamline Journal of Public Law and Policy, Journal of Law and Religion

STUDENT INFORMATION
Enrollment of Law School: 548
% Out of State: 63
% Male/Female: 44/56
% Full Time: 85
% Full Time That Are International: 1
% Minority: 11
Average Age of Entering Class: 28

RESEARCH FACILITIES
Research Resources Available: Minnesota Innocence Project
School-Supported Research Centers: Dispute Resolution Institute, Dred and Harriet Scott Institute

EXPENSES/FINANCIAL AID
Annual Tuition: $19,090
Room and Board (On/Off Campus): $8,200/$11,200
Books and Supplies: $800
Average Grant: $6,631
Average Loan: $23,000
% of Aid That Is Merit-Based: 98
% Receiving Some Sort of Aid: 88
Average Debt: $67,000
Tuition Per Credit: $686
Fees Per Credit: $5

ADMISSIONS INFORMATION
Application Fee: $40
Regular Application Deadline: Rolling
Regular Notification: Rolling
LSDAS Accepted? Yes
Average GPA: 3.2
Range of GPA: 3.0–3.6
Average LSAT: 151
Range of LSAT: 148–154
Transfer Students Accepted? Yes
Other Schools to Which Students Applied: Drake University, Marquette University, University of Minnesota, University of Wisconsin—Madison, William Mitchell College of Law
Other Admissions Factors Considered: Motivation, personal experiences, employment history, graduate education, maturity, letters of recommendation, ability to articulate interest in and suitability for the study of law
Number of Applications Received: 990
Number of Applicants Accepted: 635
Number of Applicants Enrolled: 219

INTERNATIONAL STUDENTS
TOEFL Required of International Students? Yes
Minimum TOEFL: 250

EMPLOYMENT INFORMATION

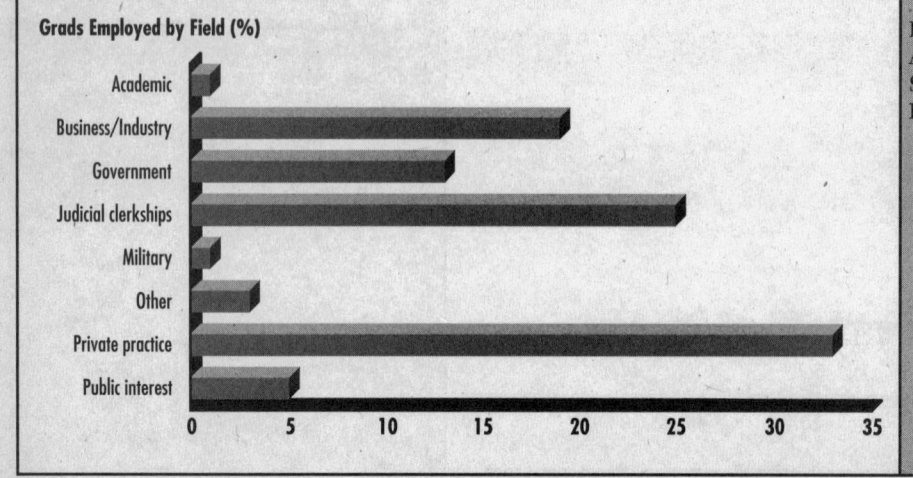

Grads Employed by Field (%)
- Academic
- Business/Industry
- Government
- Judicial clerkships
- Military
- Other
- Private practice
- Public interest

Rate of Placement: 89%
Average Starting Salary: $43,166
State for Bar Exam: MN
Pass Rate for First-Time Bar: 89%

HARVARD UNIVERSITY
Law School

Admissions Contact: Assistant Dean for Admissions and Financial Aid, Joyce Curll
1563 Massachusetts Avenue, Cambridge, MA 02138
Admissions Phone: 617-495-3109 • Admissions Fax: 617-496-7290
Admissions E-mail: jdadmiss@law.harvard.edu • Web Address: www.law.harvard.edu

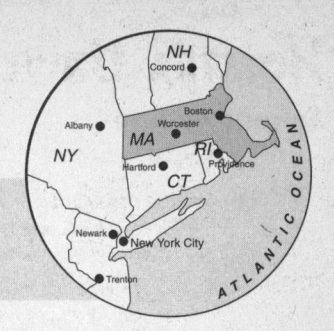

INSTITUTIONAL INFORMATION
Public/Private: Private
Environment: Urban
Academic Calendar: Semester
Schedule: Full time only
Student/Faculty Ratio: 19:1
Total Faculty: 142
% Part Time: 44
% Female: 20
% Minority: 11

PROGRAMS
Academic Specialties: 251 courses offered; International Law, Taxation, Human Rights, Constitutional Law, Negotiation/Alternative Dispute Resolution, Comparative Law, Family Law
Advanced Degrees Offered: LLM (18/20 credit hours with optional paper), SJD (8 hours of course work, exam, and dissertation)
Combined Degrees Offered: JD/MBA (4 years), JD/MPP-concurrent, JD/MALD-concurrent
Grading System: A+ to F
Clinical Program Required? No
Clinical Program Description: One of the largest clinical programs in U.S., 3 clinics, 5 student practice organizations
Legal Writing/Methods Course Requirements: Fall semester course

STUDENT INFORMATION
Enrollment of Law School: 1,658
% Male/Female: 57/43
% Full Time: 100
% Full Time That Are International: 3
% Minority: 27
Average Age of Entering Class: 24

RESEARCH FACILITIES
Computers/Workstations Available: 167

EXPENSES/FINANCIAL AID
Annual Tuition: $25,000
Room and Board: $12,618
Books and Supplies: $900
Average Grant: $12,000
Average Loan: $24,300
% of Aid That Is Merit-Based: 0
% Receiving Some Sort of Aid: 80
Average Total Aid Package: $28,000
Average Debt: $70,000

ADMISSIONS INFORMATION
Application Fee: $70
Regular Application Deadline: 2/1
Regular Notification: Rolling
LSDAS Accepted? Yes
Average GPA: 3.8
Range of GPA: 3.7–3.9
Average LSAT: 170
Range of LSAT: 167–173
Transfer Students Accepted? Yes
Other Schools to Which Students Applied: Yale University, Stanford University
Other Admissions Factors Considered: Letter of reccomendation, extracurricular activities, work experience, leadership, commitment to helping others, personal statement, ability to overcome obstacles. We try to evaluate each applicant in the context of their achievements
Number of Applications Received: 5,818
Number of Applicants Accepted: 845
Number of Applicants Enrolled: 556

EMPLOYMENT INFORMATION

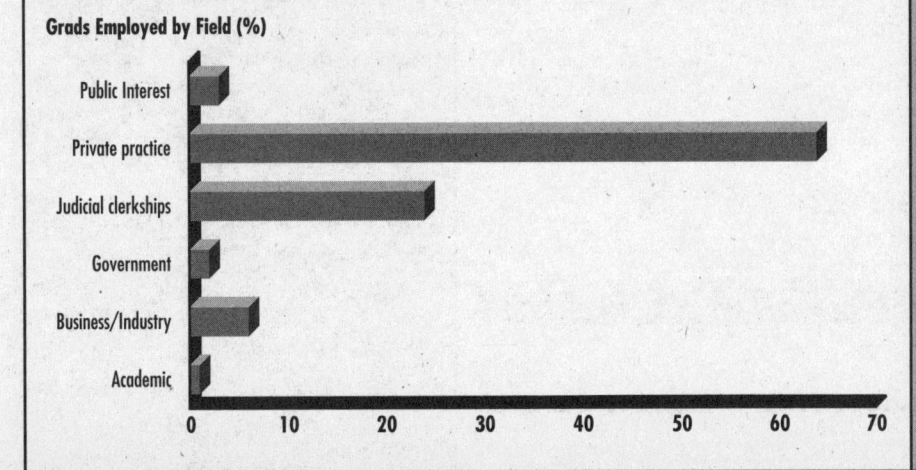

Grads Employed by Field (%)
- Public Interest
- Private practice
- Judicial clerkships
- Government
- Business/Industry
- Academic

Rate of Placement: 97%
Average Starting Salary: $81,000
Employers Who Frequently Hire Grads: Major national law firms, federal and state government, investment banks, consulting firms, law schools
Prominent Alumni: Supreme Court Justices Breyer, Ginsburg, Souter, Scalia, Kennedy; Attorney General Janet Reno; Mary Robinson, former president of The Republic of Ireland
State for Bar Exam: MA/NY
Number Taking Bar Exam: 68/199
Pass Rate for First-Time Bar: 100%/92%

HOFSTRA UNIVERSITY
School of Law

Admissions Contact: Assistant Dean for Enrollment Management, Tina Sneed
121 Hofstra University, Hempstead, NY 11549
Admissions Phone: 516-463-5916 • Admissions Fax: 516-463-6264
Admissions E-mail: lawadmissions@Hofstra.edu • Web Address: www.hofstra.edu/law

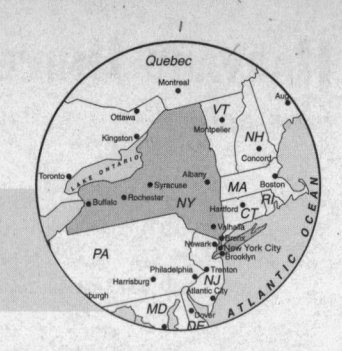

INSTITUTIONAL INFORMATION
Public/Private: Private
Student/Faculty Ratio: 17:1
Total Faculty: 86
% Part Time: 52
% Female: 22
% Minority: 5

PROGRAMS
Academic Specialties: Hofstra has a history of excellence in skills training and Trial Advocacy, including 3 clinical programs and an extensive array of simulation-based skills courses, both in traditional Litigation and Alternative Dispute Resolution. The Center for Children, Families, and the Law offers an innovative interdisciplinary curriculum in Child Advocacy and Family Law. Other specialties include Commercial Law, Corporate and Securities Law, Criminal Law, International Law, Civil Procedure, Constitutional Law, Environmental Law, Government Services, Intellectual Property Law, Labor Law, Property, Taxation, and Health Law.
Advanced Degrees Offered: JD (3 years full time, 4 years part time), LLM (1 year full time, 2 years part time)
Combined Degrees Offered: JD/MBA (4 years)
Grading System: A (4.0), A– (3.67), B+ (3.3) through D (1.00) and F (0.00)
Clinical Program Required? No
Clinical Programs Description: Child Advocacy Clinic, Criminal Justice Clinic, Housing Rights Clinic

Legal Writing Course Requirements? Yes
Legal Writing Description: Legal Writing (2 credits) taken in second semester of first year
Legal Methods Course Requirements? Yes
Legal Methods Description: A 2-week introduction prior to orientation, and a variety of sessions during the first semester of first year
Legal Research Course Requirements? Yes
Legal Research Description: Legal Research, while not a separate course, begins in the first semester of the first year and continues in the Legal Writing course.
Moot Court Requirement? Yes
Moot Court Description: Appellate Advocacy (2 credits) is a required course taken in the first semester; the second year includes a required appellate argument.
Public Interest Law Requirement? No
Academic Journals: *Law Review, Labor and Employment Law Journal, Family Courts Review*

STUDENT INFORMATION
Enrollment of Law School: 819
% Out of State: 22
% Male/Female: 53/47
% Full Time: 87
% Minority: 26
Average Age of Entering Class: 26

RESEARCH FACILITIES
Research Resources Available: Completely wireless Internet and network access both inside and outside of the building, access to discount Internet service through local providers

EXPENSES/FINANCIAL AID
Annual Tuition: $25,752
Room and Board (On/Off Campus): $8,350/$15,600
Books and Supplies: $900
Financial Aid Application Deadline: 6/1
Average Grant: $8,553
Average Loan: $3,161
% of Aid That Is Merit-Based: 66
% Receiving Some Sort of Aid: 96
Average Total Aid Package: $9,352

ADMISSIONS INFORMATION
Application Fee: $60
Regular Application Deadline: Rolling
Regular Notification: Rolling
LSDAS Accepted? Yes
Average GPA: 3.3
Range of GPA: 2.9–3.6
Average LSAT: 156
Range of LSAT: 152–158
Transfer Students Accepted? Yes
Other Schools to Which Students Applied: Brooklyn Law School, Fordham University, New York Law School, New York University, St. John's University, Touro College, Yeshiva University
Other Admissions Factors Considered: LSAT, GPA, undergraduate school curriculum, work experience, extracurricular activities, recommendations
Number of Applications Received: 2,678
Number of Applicants Accepted: 966
Number of Applicants Enrolled: 206

EMPLOYMENT INFORMATION

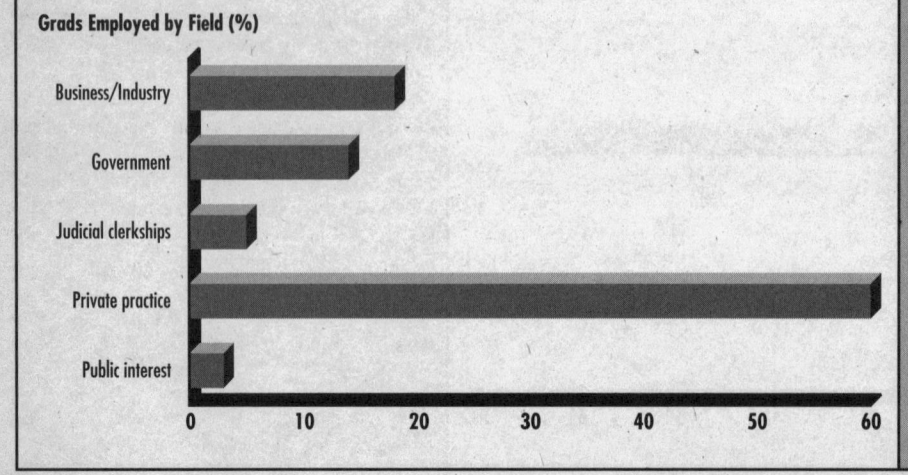

Grads Employed by Field (%)
- Business/Industry: ~18
- Government: ~14
- Judicial clerkships: ~5
- Private practice: ~60
- Public interest: ~3

Rate of Placement: 98%
Average Starting Salary: $68,799
Employers Who Frequently Hire Grads: The most prestigious law firms in New York City and Long Island regularly recruit at the law school. Government agencies and public interest organizations are well represented
State for Bar Exam: NY, NJ, CT, FL, CA
Pass Rate for First-Time Bar: 84%

HOWARD UNIVERSITY
School of Law

Admissions Contact: Assistant Dean, Ruby J. Sherrod
2900 Van Ness Street NW, Washington, DC 20008
Admissions Phone: 202-806-8008 • Admissions Fax: 202-806-8162
Admissions E-mail: admissions@law.howard.edu • Web Address: www.law.howard.edu

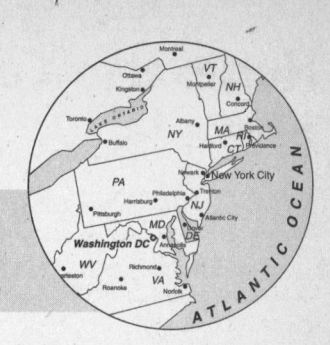

INSTITUTIONAL INFORMATION
Public/Private: Private
Environment: Urban
Academic Calendar: Semester
Schedule: Full time only
Student/Faculty Ratio: 16:1
Total Faculty: 56
% Part Time: 14
% Female: 35
% Minority: 60

PROGRAMS
Academic Specialties: Strong faculty with a wide range of interests including Antitrust Law and Religion, Evidence, Critical Race Scholarship, Feminist Scholarship
Advanced Degrees Offered: LLM (foreign lawyers only) (1–2 years)
Combined Degrees Offered: JD/MBA (4 years)
Grading System: Numerical system; grading is subject to a normalization system
Clinical Program Required? No
Clinical Program Description: Criminal Law, Elder Law, Civil Law, Immigration Law, Small Business Law
Legal Writing/Methods Course Requirements: Integrated program across 3 years

STUDENT INFORMATION
Enrollment of Law School: 415
% Male/Female: 40/60
% Full Time: 100
% Minority: 94
Average Age of Entering Class: 25

RESEARCH FACILITIES
Computers/Workstations Available: 100
School-Supported Research Centers: Law students have access to numerous research libraries in Washington, D.C., and the surrounding area, including the Library of Congress and numerous other public research centers.

EXPENSES/FINANCIAL AID
Annual Tuition: $12,650
Room and Board: $9,051
Books and Supplies: $1,050
Financial Aid Application Deadline: 2/1
Average Grant: $12,000
Average Loan: $15,000
% of Aid That Is Merit-Based: 28
% Receiving Some Sort of Aid: 95
Average Total Aid Package: $23,000
Average Debt: $55,500
Tuition Per Credit: $505
Fees Per Credit: $703

ADMISSIONS INFORMATION
Application Fee: $60
Regular Application Deadline: 3/31
Regular Notification: Rolling
Average GPA: 3.0
Range of GPA: 2.7–3.2
Average LSAT: 152
Range of LSAT: 148–154
Transfer Students Accepted? Yes
Other Schools to Which Students Applied: Georgetown University, University of Maryland, George Washington University, American University, New York University, Temple University, University of Baltimore, Harvard University
Number of Applications Received: 1,225
Number of Applicants Accepted: 372
Number of Applicants Enrolled: 140

INTERNATIONAL STUDENTS
TOEFL Required of International Students? Yes
Minimum TOEFL: 550

EMPLOYMENT INFORMATION

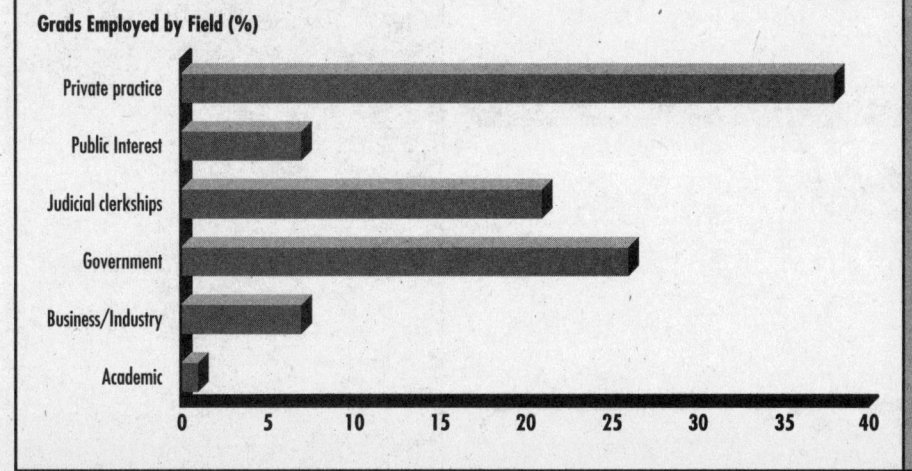

Grads Employed by Field (%)
- Private practice: ~39
- Public Interest: ~7
- Judicial clerkships: ~21
- Government: ~26
- Business/Industry: ~7
- Academic: ~1

Average Starting Salary: $85,200
State for Bar Exam: MD/NY
Number Taking Bar Exam: 41/17
Pass Rate for First-Time Bar: 29%/82%

HUMPHREYS COLLEGE
School of Law

Admissions Contact: Admission Officer, Santa Lopez
6650 Inglewood Avenue, Stockton, CA 95207
Admissions Phone: 209-478-0800 • Admissions Fax: 209-478-8721
Admissions E-mail: admissions@humphreys.edu • Web Address: www.humphreys.edu

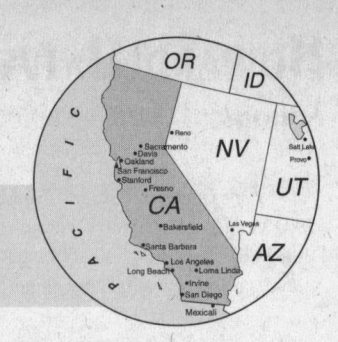

INSTITUTIONAL INFORMATION
Public/Private: Private
Academic Calendar: Quarter
Schedule: Part time only
Student/Faculty Ratio: 6:1
Total Faculty: 12
% Part Time: 83
% Female: 17
% Minority: 0

PROGRAMS
Academic Specialties: All faculty are practicing attorneys, including private practitioners and public defenders. Several judges are on the faculty.
Grading System: 100–90 Excellent, 89–80 Good, 79–70 Satisfactory, 69–55 Unsatisfactory, below 55 Failure
Clinical Program Required? No
Legal Writing/Methods Course Requirements: 1 quarter in first and fourth years each

STUDENT INFORMATION
Enrollment of Law School: 60
% Male/Female: 100/0
% Full Time: 0
% Full Time That Are International: 0
% Minority: 0
Average Age of Entering Class: 33

EXPENSES/FINANCIAL AID
Annual Tuition: $7,062
Books and Supplies: $650
Average Loan: $14,658
% Receiving Some Sort of Aid: 66
Average Total Aid Package: $14,658
Average Debt: $48,000
Fees Per Credit: $214

ADMISSIONS INFORMATION
Application Fee: $20
Regular Application Deadline: 6/1
Regular Notification: Rolling
LSDAS Accepted? No
Average GPA: 2.8
Average LSAT: 149
Transfer Students Accepted? Yes
Other Schools to Which Students Applied: California State University—Stanislaus, Delta College, California State University—Sacramento
Number of Applications Received: 52
Number of Applicants Accepted: 32
Number of Applicants Enrolled: 19

INTERNATIONAL STUDENTS
TOEFL Required of International Students? Yes
Minimum TOEFL: 450

EMPLOYMENT INFORMATION

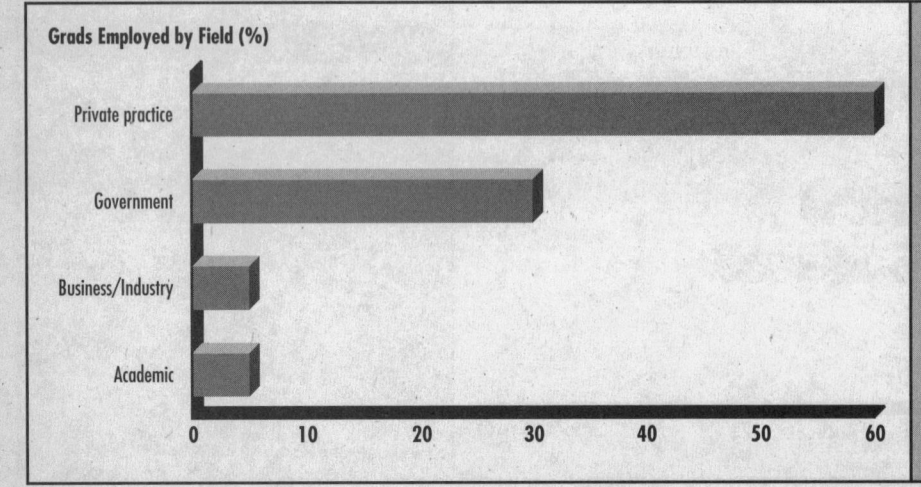

Grads Employed by Field (%)

Field	%
Private practice	60
Government	30
Business/Industry	5
Academic	5

Employers Who Frequently Hire Grads: District Attorney's Offices; police departments
Prominent Alumni: Patti Gharamendi

ILLINOIS INSTITUTE OF TECHNOLOGY
Chicago-Kent College of Law

Admissions Contact: Assistant Dean for Admissions, Michael S. Burns
565 West Adams Street, Chicago, IL 60661
Admissions Phone: 312-906-5020 • Admissions Fax: 312-906-5274
Admissions E-mail: admit@kentlaw.edu • Web Address: www.kentlaw.edu

INSTITUTIONAL INFORMATION
Public/Private: Private
Student/Faculty Ratio: 6:1
Total Faculty: 161
% Part Time: 62
% Female: 24
% Minority: 4

PROGRAMS
Academic Specialties: Biotechnology, Information Technology, Environmental Law and Protection, International Business Transactions, Corporation Securities Law, Human Rights Law, Intellectual Property Law, International Law, Labor Law, Technology, Financial Services, Litigation
Advanced Degrees Offered: JD (3 years full time, 4 years part time), LLM (2 to 8 semesters)
Combined Degrees Offered: JD/MBA (3.5 to 5 years); JD/LLM (4 to 5 years), JD/MS Financial Markets (4 to 5 years), JD/MPA (3.5 to 5 years), JD/MSEM (3.5 to 5 years), JD/MPH (3.5 years)
Grading System: A (4.0) to E (0.0); students must maintain a 2.3 to graduate
Clinical Program Required? No
Clinical Programs Description: Employment Discrimination/Civil Rights Litigation, Criminal Defense Litigation, Health Law Litigation, Alternative Dispute Resolution, Tax Litigation, Advice Desk, Mediation, Judicial Externship
Legal Writing Course Requirements? Yes
Legal Writing Description: 3-year, 5-course curriculum
Legal Methods Course Requirements? No
Legal Research Course Requirements? Yes
Legal Research Description: Basic legal research and writing courses during the first year, 2 additional courses during the second year
Moot Court Requirement? Yes
Moot Court Description: First-year Moot Court Competition. Outstanding students are invited to join the Moot Court Honor Society.
Public Interest Law Requirement? No
Public Interest Law Description: The Public Interest Resource Center acts as a link to nonprofit organizations and other public service projects.
Academic Journals: *Chicago-Kent Law Review, Employee Rights and Employment Policy Journal, Illinois Public Employee Relations Report,* and more

STUDENT INFORMATION
Enrollment of Law School: 967
% Out of State: 34
% Male/Female: 50/50
% Full Time: 73
% Full Time That Are International: 1
% Minority: 11
Average Age of Entering Class: 25

RESEARCH FACILITIES
Research Resources Available: U.S. District Cour, the U.S. Court of Appeals, numerous federal agencies
School-Supported Research Centers: Global Law and Policy Initiative; Institute for Law and the Humanities; Institute for Law and the Workplace; Institute for Science, Law, and Technology

EXPENSES/FINANCIAL AID
Annual Tuition: $24,220
Room and Board (On/Off Campus): $6,144/$13,860
Books and Supplies: $890
Financial Aid Application Deadline: 4/15
Average Grant: $8,797
Average Loan: $27,411
% of Aid That Is Merit-Based: 17
% Receiving Some Sort of Aid: 89
Average Total Aid Package: $29,376
Average Debt: $70,684
Tuition Per Credit: $855

ADMISSIONS INFORMATION
Application Fee: $45
Regular Application Deadline: 3/1
Regular Notification: Rolling
LSDAS Accepted? Yes
Average GPA: 3.3
Average LSAT: 156
Transfer Students Accepted? Yes
Other Schools to Which Students Applied: American University, DePaul, Loyola Chicago, Northwestern, John Marshall Law School, U. of Chicago, U of I at Urbana-Champaign
Other Admissions Factors Considered: Academic letters of recommendation, ability to write clearly and effectively, personal statement
Number of Applications Received: 2,054
Number of Applicants Accepted: 936
Number of Applicants Enrolled: 226

INTERNATIONAL STUDENTS
TOEFL Required of International Students? Yes
Minimum TOEFL: 250

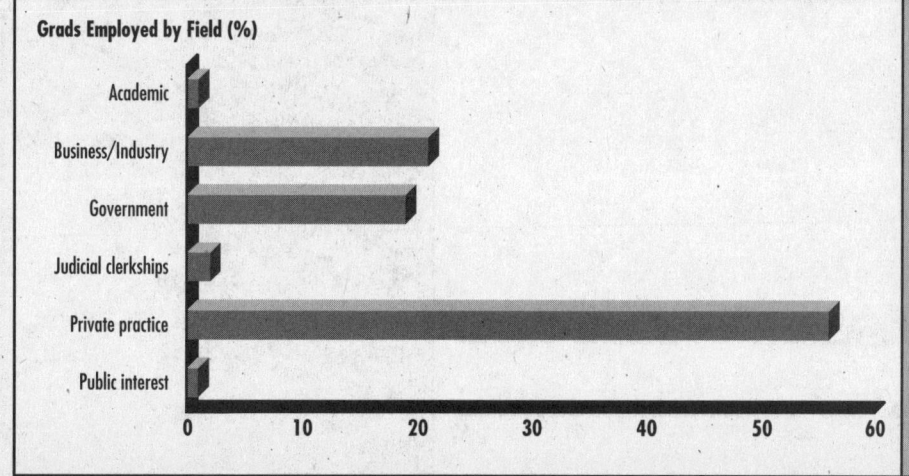

EMPLOYMENT INFORMATION

Grads Employed by Field (%)
- Academic
- Business/Industry
- Government
- Judicial clerkships
- Private practice
- Public interest

Rate of Placement: 95%
Average Starting Salary: $65,061
Employers Who Frequently Hire Grads: Approximately 75 employers conduct on-campus interviews. Hundreds of additional employers request resume collection or direct contact from students, hire students through consortium job fairs, and post open job listings with the Career Services Office. About 56% of the Class of 2000 graduates entered private practice. Of these graduates, 2% were self-employed, 51% went to small firms (2–25 attorneys); 21% to medium firms (26–100 attorneys), and 26% to firms of more than 100 attorneys.
State for Bar Exam: IL
Pass Rate for First-Time Bar: 80%

INDIANA UNIVERSITY — BLOOMINGTON
School of Law

Admissions Contact: Director of Admissions, Patricia S. Clark
211 South Indiana Avenue, Bloomington, IN 47405
Admissions Phone: 812-855-4765 • Admissions Fax: 812-855-0555
Admissions E-mail: lawadmis@indiana.edu • Web Address: www.law.indiana.edu

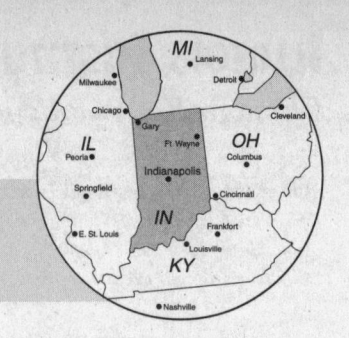

INSTITUTIONAL INFORMATION
Public/Private: Public
Student/Faculty Ratio: 14:1
Total Faculty: 48
% Part Time: 6
% Female: 29
% Minority: 6

PROGRAMS
Academic Specialties: International/Global Law, Communications Law, Environmental Law, Business/Corporations Law, Interdisciplinary Study of Law (Law and Economics, Law and Psychology, Law and Social Science, etc.), Intellectual Property and Biotechnology, Civil Procedure, Commercial Law, Constitutional Law, Corporation Securities Law, Criminal Law, Government Services, Human Rights Law, Labor Law, Legal History, Legal Philosophy, Property, Taxation
Advanced Degrees Offered: SJD (1 year in residence, completion of doctoral dissertation), LLM with thesis (completion of 20 credit hours of course work plus completion of thesis), LLM without thesis (completion of 24 credit hours plus a practicum) MCL (completion of 21 credit hours plus a practicum)
Combined Degrees Offered: JD/MBA (4 years), JD/MPA (4 years), JD/MSES (4 years), JD/MLIS (4 years), JD/MA or MS Telecommunications (4 years), PhD Law and Social Science (4 years), JD/MA Public Accountancy (4 years), JD/MA Journalism (4 years)
Grading System: 4.0 scale
Clinical Program Required? No

Clinical Programs Description: Community Clinic (students represent clients in family law cases), Child Advocacy, Protective Order Project (legal assistance to victims of domestic violence), Federal Courts Clinic
Legal Writing Course Requirements? Yes
Legal Writing Description: 3-year program
Legal Methods Course Requirements? No
Legal Research Course Requirements? Yes
Legal Research Description: See Legal Writing.
Moot Court Requirement? No
Moot Court Description: Sherman Minton Moot Court Competition for second-year students
Public Interest Law Requirement? No
Public Interest Law Description: In addition to IU clinics, students participate in the Environmental Law Research Group, the Inmate Legal Assistance Project, the Outreach for Legal Literacy, and the Public Interest Law Foundation.
Academic Journals: *Indiana Law Journal, Federal Communications Law Journal, Indiana Journal of Global Legal Studies*

STUDENT INFORMATION
Enrollment of Law School: 618
% Out of State: 46
% Male/Female: 58/42
% Full Time: 99
% Full Time That Are International: 1
% Minority: 16
Average Age of Entering Class: 24

EXPENSES/FINANCIAL AID
Annual Tuition (Residents/Nonresidents): $7,989/$20,491
Room and Board (On/Off Campus): $6,292/$6,480
Books and Supplies: $1,073
Financial Aid Application Deadline: 4/1
Average Grant: $5,223
Average Loan: $18,809
% of Aid That Is Merit-Based: 68
% Receiving Some Sort of Aid: 91
Average Total Aid Package: $20,502

ADMISSIONS INFORMATION
Application Fee: $35
Regular Application Deadline: Rolling
Regular Notification: Rolling
LSDAS Accepted? Yes
Average GPA: 3.4
Range of GPA: 2.9–3.7
Average LSAT: 161
Range of LSAT: 156–163
Transfer Students Accepted? Yes
Other Schools to Which Students Applied: George Washington U., Ohio State, U of I at Urbana-Champaign, U. of Michigan, U. of Notre Dame, U. of Wisconsin—Madison, Washington U.
Other Admissions Factors Considered: Faculty evaluations, strong writing and analytic skills
Number of Applications Received: 2,003
Number of Applicants Accepted: 773
Number of Applicants Enrolled: 214

INTERNATIONAL STUDENTS
TOEFL Required of International Students? Yes
Minimum TOEFL: 250

EMPLOYMENT INFORMATION

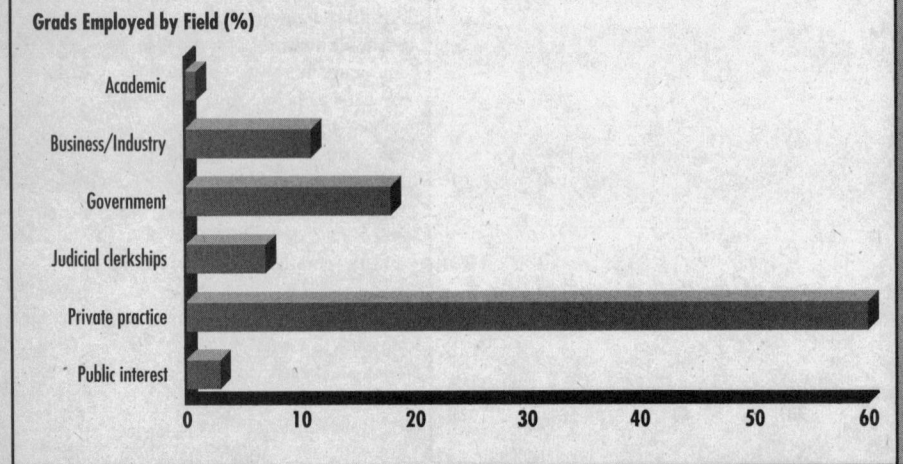

Grads Employed by Field (%)

Field	%
Academic	~1
Business/Industry	~11
Government	~18
Judicial clerkships	~5
Private practice	~60
Public interest	~2

Rate of Placement: 94%
Average Starting Salary: $65,000
Employers Who Frequently Hire Grads: Barnes & Thornburg; U.S. District Courts; Indiana Court of Appeals; Ice, Miller, Donadio & Ryan; Baker & Daniels; Warner, Norcross & Judd; Lord, Bissell & Brook; Katten, Muckin & Zavis; Kirkland & Ellis; Arnold & Porter
State for Bar Exam: IN
Pass Rate for First-Time Bar: 94%

INDIANA UNIVERSITY — INDIANAPOLIS
School of Law

Admissions Contact: Assistant Dean for Admissions, Angela Espada
530 West New York Street, Indianapolis, IN 46202-3225
Admissions Phone: 317-274-2459 • Admissions Fax: 317-278-4780
Admissions E-mail: khmiller@iupui.edu • Web Address: www.indylaw.indiana.edu

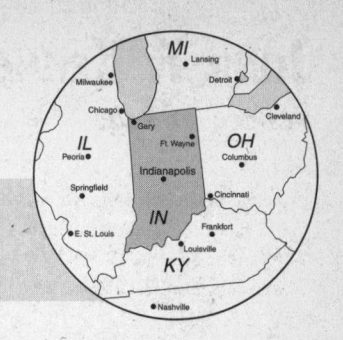

INSTITUTIONAL INFORMATION
Public/Private: Public
Student/Faculty Ratio: 18:1
Total Faculty: 64
% Part Time: 38
% Female: 27
% Minority: 1

PROGRAMS
Academic Specialties: Tax Law, Copyright Law, Human Rights Law, International Law, Health Law, Constitutional Law, Criminal Law, Government Services, Labor Law. The faculty includes practitioners as well as scholars, and the curriculum reflects the influence of both.
Combined Degrees Offered: JD/MPA (4 years), JD/MBA (4 years), JD/MHA (4 years), JD/MPH (4 years)
Grading System: 4.0 scale with a recommended curve
Clinical Program Required? No
Clinical Programs Description: Civil, Disability, and Criminal Law
Legal Writing Course Requirements? Yes
Legal Writing Description: 1 year
Legal Methods Course Requirements? Yes
Legal Research Course Requirements? Yes
Legal Research Description: 1 year
Moot Court Requirement? No
Public Interest Law Requirement? No
Academic Journals: *Indiana Law Review, Indiana International and Comparative Law Review*

STUDENT INFORMATION
Enrollment of Law School: 848
% Out of State: 10
% Male/Female: 69/31
% Full Time: 65
% Full Time That Are International: 2
% Minority: 17
Average Age of Entering Class: 27

RESEARCH FACILITIES
School-Supported Research Centers: Center for Law and Health, Center for State and Local Government

EXPENSES/FINANCIAL AID
Annual Tuition (Residents/Nonresidents): $8,569/$19,696
Room and Board: $13,902
Books and Supplies: $800
Average Grant: $5,300
Average Loan: $12,500
% of Aid That Is Merit-Based: 80
% Receiving Some Sort of Aid: 60
Average Total Aid Package: $4,500
Average Debt: $39,000
Tuition Per Credit (Residents/Nonresidents): $276/$635
Fees Per Credit: $83

ADMISSIONS INFORMATION
Application Fee: $35
Regular Application Deadline: 3/1
Regular Notification: Rolling
LSDAS Accepted? Yes
Average GPA: 3.3
Range of GPA: 3.0–3.5
Average LSAT: 154
Range of LSAT: 150–157
Transfer Students Accepted? Yes
Other Admissions Factors Considered: For international students: Test of Written English and a law degree from another institution in their home country
Number of Applications Received: 1,259
Number of Applicants Accepted: 553
Number of Applicants Enrolled: 262

INTERNATIONAL STUDENTS
TOEFL Required of International Students? Yes
Minimum TOEFL: 213

EMPLOYMENT INFORMATION

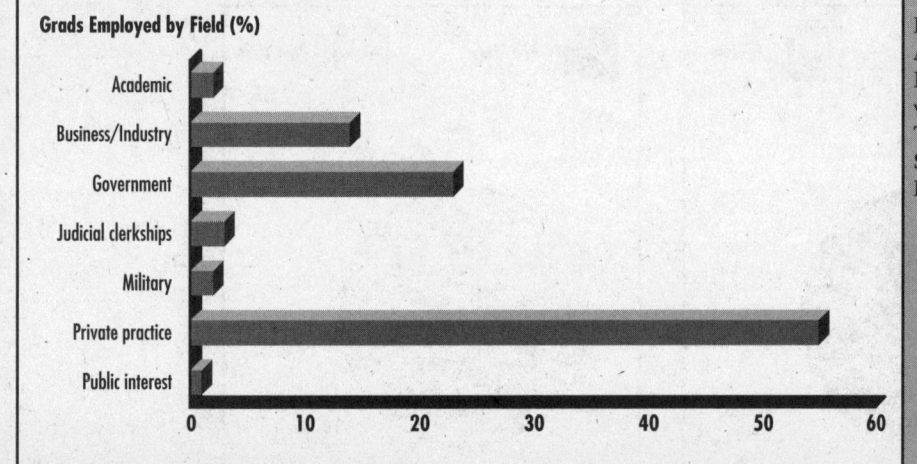

Grads Employed by Field (%)
- Academic: ~2
- Business/Industry: ~14
- Government: ~22
- Judicial clerkships: ~3
- Military: ~3
- Private practice: ~55
- Public interest: ~1

Rate of Placement: 97%
Average Starting Salary: $57,389
Employers Who Frequently Hire Grads: Private law firms; Baker & Daniels; Barnes & Thornburg; Ice Miller
State for Bar Exam: IN
Pass Rate for First-Time Bar: 85%

JOHN F. KENNEDY UNIVERSITY
School of Law

Admissions Contact: Admission Director, Ellena Bloedorn
547 Ygnacio Valley Road, Walnut Creek, CA 94596
Admissions Phone: 925-295-1800 • Admissions Fax: 925-933-0917
Admissions E-mail: law@jfku.edu • Web Address: www.jfku.edu/law

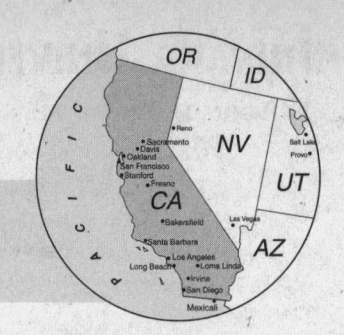

INSTITUTIONAL INFORMATION
Public/Private: Private
Student/Faculty Ratio: 30:1

PROGRAMS
Academic Specialties: Corporation Securities Law
Clinical Program Required? No
Legal Methods Course Requirements? No

STUDENT INFORMATION
Enrollment of Law School: 249
% Male/Female: 50/50
% Minority: 24
Average Age of Entering Class: 36

EXPENSES/FINANCIAL AID
Annual Tuition: $7,823

ADMISSIONS INFORMATION
Regular Application Deadline: 5/30
Regular Notification: Rolling
LSDAS Accepted? No
Transfer Students Accepted? No
Other Schools to Which Students Applied: University of California—Berkeley, Golden Gate University, Syracuse University, University of San Francisco, Stanford University

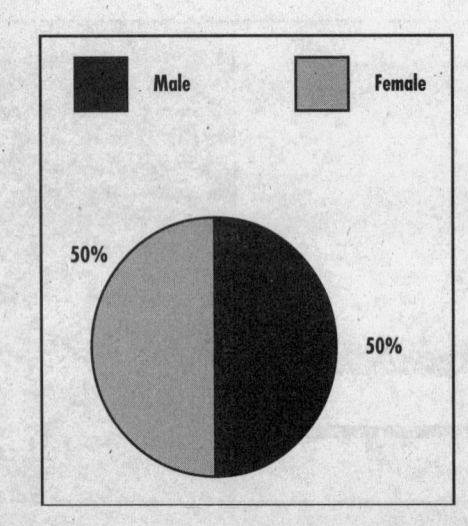

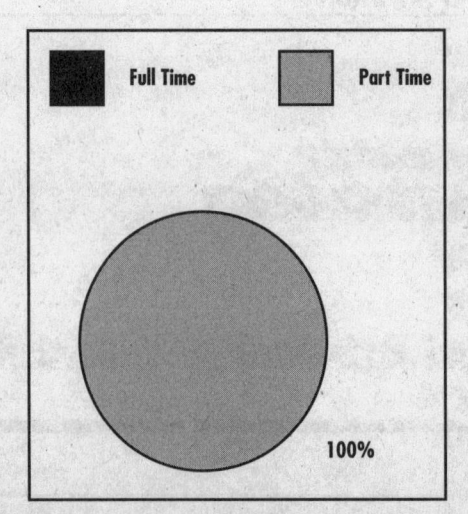

JOHN MARSHALL LAW SCHOOL

Admissions Contact: Associate Dean for Admission and Student Affairs, William B. Powers
315 South Plymouth Court, Chicago, IL 60604
Admissions Phone: 800-537-4280 • Admissions Fax: 312-427-5136
Admissions E-mail: admissions@jmls.edu • Web Address: www.jmls.edu

INSTITUTIONAL INFORMATION
Public/Private: Private
Student/Faculty Ratio: 15:1
Total Faculty: 290
% Part Time: 81
% Female: 17
% Minority: 4

PROGRAMS
Academic Specialties: Excellent programs in Lawyering Skills, Trial Advocacy and Moot Court; specialties include International Law, Property, and Taxation
Advanced Degrees Offered: LLM Taxation, Intellectual Property, Real Estate, Information Technology, Comparative Legal Studies, International Business and Trade Law, or Employee Benefits (1 year); MS Information Technology
Combined Degrees Offered: JD/MBA, JD/MPA, JD/MA, JD/LLM
Grading System: A+ (4.01), A (4.0), A– (3.5), B (3.0), B– (2.5), C (2.0), C– (1.5), D (1.0), F (0.0)
Clinical Program Required? Yes
Clinical Programs Description: Trial Advocacy, Fair Housing Clinic, extensive Legal Writing Program, numerous externships and simulation courses available
Legal Methods Course Requirements? Yes
Legal Methods Description: 4 semesters of legal writing are required for a total of 10 semester hours.

STUDENT INFORMATION
Enrollment of Law School: 1,152
% Out of State: 35
% Male/Female: 54/46
% Full Time: 62
% Full Time That Are International: 1
% Minority: 19
Average Age of Entering Class: 24

RESEARCH FACILITIES
School-Supported Research Centers: Center for Advocacy and Dispute Resolution, Center for Information and Privacy Law, Center for Intellectual Property Law, Center for International and Comparative Studies, Center for Real Estate Law, Center for Tax Law and Employee Benefits

EXPENSES/FINANCIAL AID
Annual Tuition: $21,000
Room and Board (Off Campus): $13,492
Books and Supplies: $700
Average Grant: $8,400
% of Aid That Is Merit-Based: 10
% Receiving Some Sort of Aid: 90
Average Total Aid Package: $18,500
Average Debt: $65,269
Tuition Per Credit: $700

ADMISSIONS INFORMATION
Application Fee: $50
Regular Application Deadline: 3/1
Regular Notification: Rolling
LSDAS Accepted? Yes
Average GPA: 3.0
Range of GPA: 2.7–3.2
Average LSAT: 150
Range of LSAT: 145–152
Transfer Students Accepted? Yes
Other Schools to Which Students Applied: University of Scranton, Illinois Institute of Technology, SUNY Stony Brook
Number of Applications Received: 1,543
Number of Applicants Accepted: 964
Number of Applicants Enrolled: 287

INTERNATIONAL STUDENTS
TOEFL Required of International Students? Yes

EMPLOYMENT INFORMATION

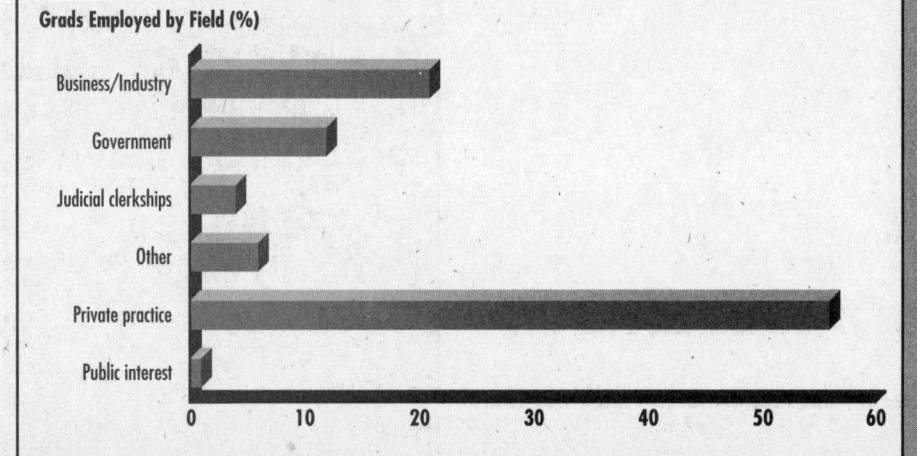

Grads Employed by Field (%)
- Business/Industry: ~21
- Government: ~12
- Judicial clerkships: ~3
- Other: ~3
- Private practice: ~57
- Public interest: ~1

Rate of Placement: 89%
Average Starting Salary: $45,076
Employers Who Frequently Hire Grads: Hinshaw & Culbertson, Cook County State's Attorney, Clausen Miller, City of Chicago Law Department
State for Bar Exam: IL
Pass Rate for First-Time Bar: 79%

LEWIS AND CLARK COLLEGE
Northwestern School of Law

Admissions Contact: Associate Dean, Martha Spence
10015 SW Terwilliger Boulevard, Portland, OR 97219
Admissions Phone: 503-768-6613 • Admissions Fax: 503-768-6850
Admissions E-mail: lawadmss@lclark.edu • Web Address: law.lclark.edu

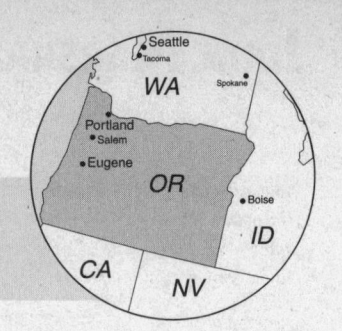

INSTITUTIONAL INFORMATION
Public/Private: Private
Student/Faculty Ratio: 15:1
Total Faculty: 71
% Part Time: 46
% Female: 39
% Minority: 6

PROGRAMS
Academic Specialties: The school has a top-ranked Environmental and Natural Resources Program; certificates in Business Law, Tax Law, Environmental Law, and Criminal Law; an emerging specialty in Intellectual Property; and a curriculum that supports specialization in several other subject areas including Tort Litigation, Public Interest Law, Family Law, Children's Rights, Real Estate Transactions, Employment Law, Commercial Law, Corporation Securities Law, Government Services, Labor Law, and Property.
Advanced Degrees Offered: LLM Environmental and Natural Resources (12 to 18 months)
Grading System: A+ to F (4.3 to 0.0)
Clinical Program Required? No
Clinical Programs Description: Live-client clinic in Law, Employment, Debtor-Creditor, Small Business, Tax, Landlord-Tenant, and Domestic Violence; clinical internship seminars in specific subject areas; summer and full-semester externships; environmental practicum
Legal Writing Course Requirements? Yes
Legal Writing Description: First-year students must take the year-long Legal Analysis and Writing course, which includes a number of research and drafting assignments including an appellate brief and a moot court argument.
Legal Methods Course Requirements? Yes
Legal Methods Description: See Legal Writing.
Legal Research Course Requirements? Yes
Legal Research Description: See Legal Writing.
Moot Court Requirement? No
Public Interest Law Requirement? No
Academic Journals: *Environmental Law Review, The Journal of Small and Emerging Business Law, Animal Law Journal, International Legal Perspectives*

STUDENT INFORMATION
Enrollment of Law School: 675
% Out of State: 67
% Male/Female: 51/49
% Full Time: 72
% Full Time That Are International: 2
% Minority: 14
Average Age of Entering Class: 28

RESEARCH FACILITIES
Research Resources Available: Boley Law Library, U.S. Patent Trademark Depository, The Pearl Environmental Law Library, The Johnson Public Land Law Collection

EXPENSES/FINANCIAL AID
Annual Tuition: $22,090
Room and Board (Off Campus): $7,425
Books and Supplies: $900
Financial Aid Application Deadline: 3/1
Average Grant: $7,595
Average Loan: $24,462
% of Aid That Is Merit-Based: 12
% Receiving Some Sort of Aid: 88
Average Total Aid Package: $26,349
Average Debt: $66,207

ADMISSIONS INFORMATION
Application Fee: $50
Regular Application Deadline: 3/15
Regular Notification: Rolling
LSDAS Accepted? Yes
Average GPA: 3.3
Range of GPA: 3.0–3.5
Average LSAT: 158
Range of LSAT: 154–162
Transfer Students Accepted? Yes
Other Schools to Which Students Applied: University of Oregon, University of Washington, Willamette University
Number of Applications Received: 1,758
Number of Applicants Accepted: 880
Number of Applicants Enrolled: 232

INTERNATIONAL STUDENTS
TOEFL Required of International Students? Yes
Minimum TOEFL: 250

EMPLOYMENT INFORMATION

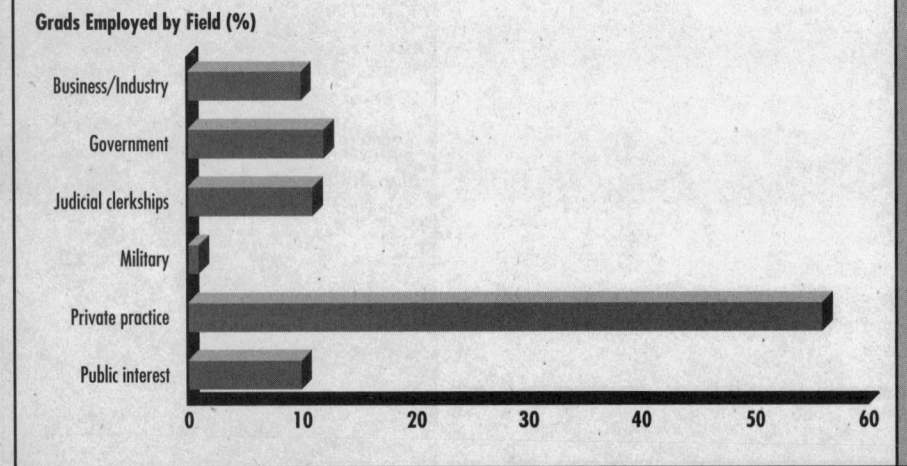

Grads Employed by Field (%)
- Business/Industry: ~10
- Government: ~12
- Judicial clerkships: ~12
- Military: ~0
- Private practice: ~57
- Public interest: ~10

Rate of Placement: 88%
Average Starting Salary: $50,643
Employers Who Frequently Hire Grads: Numerous small and medium-sized firms; state government (Oregon, Washington, Idaho); Multnomah County; U.S. government; state and federal judiciary; Stoel Rives LLP; Schwabe; Williamson; Bullivant Houser
State for Bar Exam: OR, CA, WA
Pass Rate for First-Time Bar: 76%

LINCOLN LAW SCHOOL OF SACRAMENTO

Admissions Contact: Registrar, Angelia Harlow
3140 J Street, Sacramento, CA 95816
Admissions Phone: 916-446-1275 • Admissions Fax: 916-446-5641
Admissions E-mail: lincolnlaw@lincolnlaw.edu • Web Address: www.lincolnlaw.edu

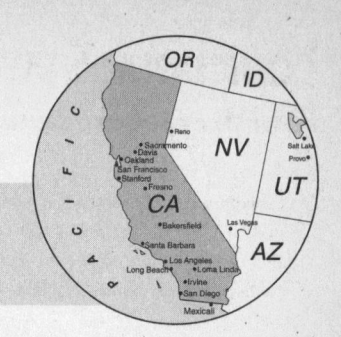

INSTITUTIONAL INFORMATION
Public/Private: Private
Student/Faculty Ratio: 50:1
Total Faculty: 25
% Part Time: 100
% Female: 20
% Minority: 10

PROGRAMS
Academic Specialties: Civil Procedure, Constitutional Law, Corporation Securities Law, Criminal Law, Environmental Law, Government Services, Intellectual Property Law, Labor Law, Legal History, Legal Philosophy, Property, Taxation; all faculty members teach in their field of expertise
Advanced Degrees Offered: JD (4 years)
Grading System: 4.0 scale
Clinical Program Required? No
Legal Writing Course Requirements? Yes
Legal Writing Description: 2 semesters of Legal Writing required for first-year students
Legal Methods Course Requirements? Yes
Legal Methods Description: Writing Law School exams (2 semesters)
Legal Research Course Requirements? Yes
Legal Research Description: 1 semester required for second-year students
Moot Court Requirement? Yes
Moot Court Description: Summer semester required for second-year students
Public Interest Law Requirement? No

STUDENT INFORMATION
Enrollment of Law School: 275
% Out of State: 0
% Male/Female: 100/0
% Full Time That Are International: 0
% Minority: 0
Average Age of Entering Class: 35

RESEARCH FACILITIES
Research Resources Available: Lexis/Nexis

EXPENSES/FINANCIAL AID
Annual Tuition: $6,000
Books and Supplies: $500
Financial Aid Application Deadline: 6/1
Average Grant: $500
Average Loan: $10,000
% of Aid That Is Merit-Based: 2
% Receiving Some Sort of Aid: 25
Average Total Aid Package: $5,000
Average Debt: $10,500
Fees Per Credit: $250

ADMISSIONS INFORMATION
Application Fee: $30
Regular Application Deadline: Rolling
Regular Notification: Rolling
LSDAS Accepted? Yes
Average GPA: 2.8
Range of GPA: 2.1–4.0
Average LSAT: 145
Transfer Students Accepted? Yes
Number of Applications Received: 150
Number of Applicants Accepted: 105
Number of Applicants Enrolled: 95

EMPLOYMENT INFORMATION

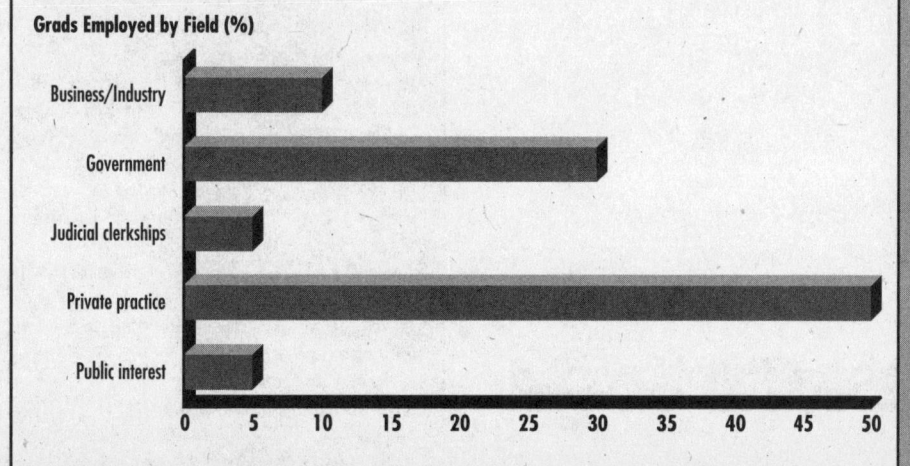

Grads Employed by Field (%)

Field	%
Business/Industry	~10
Government	~30
Judicial clerkships	~5
Private practice	~50
Public interest	~5

Rate of Placement: 80%
Average Starting Salary: $40,000
Employers Who Frequently Hire Grads: District Attorney's Office; Attorney General's Office; Public Defender's Office
State for Bar Exam: CA
Pass Rate for First-Time Bar: 60%

LOUISIANA STATE UNIVERSITY
Paul M. Hebert Law Center

Admissions Contact: Director of Admissions/Student Affairs, Michele Forbes
102 Law Center, Baton Rouge, LA 70803
Admissions Phone: 225-578-8646 • Admissions Fax: 225-578-8647
Admissions E-mail: admissions@law.lsu.edu • Web Address: www.law.lsu.edu

INSTITUTIONAL INFORMATION
Public/Private: Public
Student/Faculty Ratio: 20:1
Total Faculty: 60
% Part Time: 47
% Female: 10
% Minority: 5

PROGRAMS
Academic Specialties: The faculty and curriculum are particularly strong in the areas of Civil Law and International Law.
Advanced Degrees Offered: LLM (1 year), MCL (1 year)
Combined Degrees Offered: MPA/JD (3 years), JD/MBA (4 years)
Grading System: 4.0 scale: A (89–82), B (81–76), C (75–65), D (64–55), F (54–0)
Clinical Program Required? Yes
Clinical Programs Description: Trial Advocacy, Appellate Advocacy
Legal Writing Course Requirements? No
Legal Methods Course Requirements? Yes
Legal Methods Description: First year fall and spring, 1 hour/week
Legal Research Course Requirements? No
Moot Court Requirement? No
Public Interest Law Requirement? No

STUDENT INFORMATION
Enrollment of Law School: 637
% Out of State: 11
% Male/Female: 54/46
% Full Time: 100
% Full Time That Are International: 1
% Minority: 10

RESEARCH FACILITIES
School-Supported Research Centers: Center of Civil Law Studies

EXPENSES/FINANCIAL AID
Annual Tuition (Residents/Nonresidents): $6,711/$12,552
Room and Board (On/Off Campus): $10,550/$18,950
Books and Supplies: $1,500
Average Grant: $4,729
% of Aid That Is Merit-Based: 22
% Receiving Some Sort of Aid: 24

ADMISSIONS INFORMATION
Application Fee: $25

Regular Application Deadline: 2/2
Regular Notification: 1/2
LSDAS Accepted? Yes
Average GPA: 3.3
Range of GPA: 3.1–3.5
Average LSAT: 153
Range of LSAT: 149–156
Transfer Students Accepted? Yes
Number of Applications Received: 998
Number of Applicants Accepted: 553
Number of Applicants Enrolled: 261

INTERNATIONAL STUDENTS
TOEFL Required of International Students? Yes
Minimum TOEFL: 250

EMPLOYMENT INFORMATION

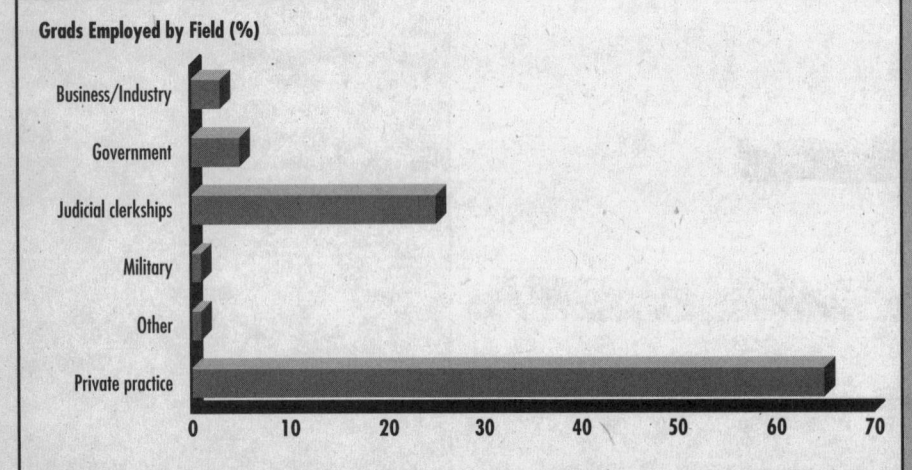

Grads Employed by Field (%):
- Business/Industry
- Government
- Judicial clerkships
- Military
- Other
- Private practice

Rate of Placement: 99%
Average Starting Salary: $49,195
Employers Who Frequently Hire Grads: Adams & Reese; Baker & Hostetler; Phelps Dunbar; McGinchey, Stafford, Lang; Stone Pigman; Vinson & Elkins; Cox & Smith; Crawford & Lewis; Fisher & Phillips; Jackson & Walker; Jones, Walker, Waechter, Poitevent, Carrerre; Kantrow, Spaht, Weaver & Blitzer; Laborde & Neuner; Lemle & Kelleher; Onebane, Bernard, Torian, Diaz, McNamara & Abell; Orleans Parish District Attorney's Office; Thompson & Knight; Voorhies & Labbe
State for Bar Exam: LA
Pass Rate for First-Time Bar: 89%

LOYOLA MARYMOUNT UNIVERSITY
Loyola Law School

Admissions Contact: Assistant Director of Admissions, Betty Vu
919 South Albany Street, Los Angeles, CA 90015
Admissions Phone: 213-736-1180 • Admissions Fax: 213-736-6523
Admissions E-mail: admissions@lls.edu • Web Address: www.lls.edu

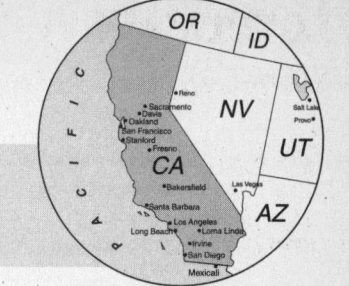

INSTITUTIONAL INFORMATION
Public/Private: Private
Student/Faculty Ratio: 19:1
Total Faculty: 136
% Part Time: 69
% Female: 45
% Minority: 21

PROGRAMS
Academic Specialties: International and Comparative Law, Law and Social Policy, Legal Skills and Litigation, Jurisprudence, Constitutional Law, Civil Procedure, Commercial Law, Corporation Securities Law, Criminal Law, Environmental Law, Government Services, Human Rights Law, Intellectual Property Law, Labor Law, Legal History, Property, Taxation, Entertainment Law, Mediation, Terrorism and the Law
Advanced Degrees Offered: LLM Taxation (1 year full time, 3 part time)
Combined Degrees Offered: JD/MBA (4 years)
Clinical Program Required? No
Clinical Programs Description: Business and Commercial, Civil Practice, Public Interest, Trial Advocacy, Judicial Administration, State and Local Government, Mediation, Entertainment Law
Legal Writing Course Requirements? No
Legal Methods Course Requirements? Yes
Legal Methods Description: The required Legal Research and Writing course covers ethical obligations to research, court structure, stare decisis, case reporting and precedent, digests, state and federal statutes and administrative law, periodicals, encyclopedias and treatises, citations form, research strategies, and computerized legal research. Students learn the fundamentals of drafting objective and persuasive legal documents. Students will prepare an office memorandum, a brief or memorandum of points and authorities, and other written work. Professors extensively critique student written work and meet individually with students to review their papers.
Legal Research Course Requirements? No
Moot Court Requirement? No
Public Interest Law Requirement? No

STUDENT INFORMATION
Enrollment of Law School: 1,353
% Male/Female: 48/52
% Full Time: 75
% Full Time That Are International: 1
% Minority: 37
Average Age of Entering Class: 24

RESEARCH FACILITIES
Research Resources Available: Loyola Marymount Westchester Campus facilities, online library catalogs from USC Law School, Columbia Law School, University of Texas Law School, University of California Libraries, Los Angeles Public Library

EXPENSES/FINANCIAL AID
Annual Tuition: $24,924
Room and Board (Off Campus): $9,405
Books and Supplies: $683
Financial Aid Application Deadline: 3/3
Average Grant: $15,469
Average Loan: $29,179
% of Aid That Is Merit-Based: 10
% Receiving Some Sort of Aid: 88
Average Total Aid Package: $31,701
Average Debt: $71,435

ADMISSIONS INFORMATION
Application Fee: $50
Regular Application Deadline: Rolling
Regular Notification: Rolling
LSDAS Accepted? Yes
Average GPA: 3.3
Range of GPA: 3.1–3.6
Average LSAT: 158
Range of LSAT: 155–160
Transfer Students Accepted? Yes
Other Admissions Factors Considered: Undergraduate record, LSAT score, personal statement, letters of recommendation, community/extracurricular involvement, work experience
Number of Applications Received: 2,921
Number of Applicants Accepted: 1,128
Number of Applicants Enrolled: 337

INTERNATIONAL STUDENTS
TOEFL Required of International Students? Yes
Minimum TOEFL: 250

EMPLOYMENT INFORMATION

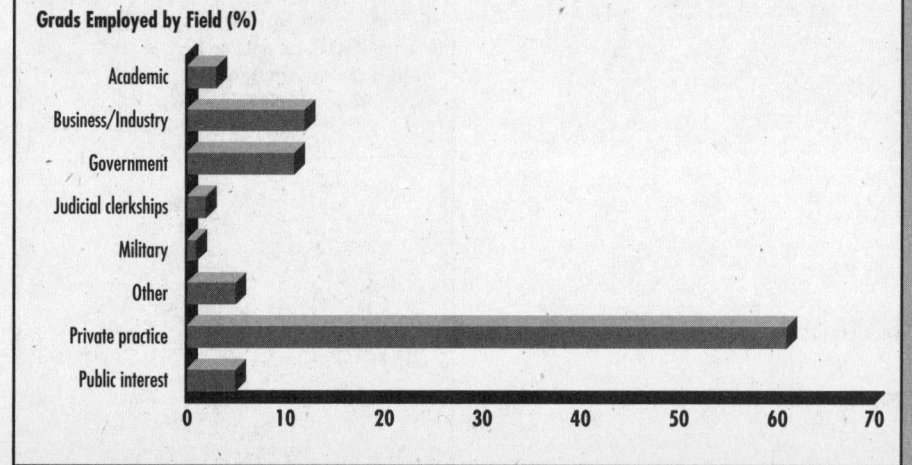

Grads Employed by Field (%)

Rate of Placement: 96%
Average Starting Salary: $81,401
Employers Who Frequently Hire Grads: O'Melveny & Myers; Manatt, Phelps & Phillips; California Attorney General; Los Angeles District Attorney; Dependency Court Legal Services; Skadden, Arps, Slate, Meagher & Flom; Legal Aid Foundation of Los Angeles; Paul, Hastings; Jones, Day, Reavis & Pogue; Brobeck, Phleger & Harrison; Shepherd, Mullin, Richter & Hampton; Gibson, Dunn & Crutcher
State for Bar Exam: CA
Pass Rate for First-Time Bar: 81%

LOYOLA UNIVERSITY CHICAGO
School of Law

Admissions Contact: Office of Admission and Financial Aid
1 East Pearson, 4th Floor, Chicago, IL 60611
Admissions Phone: 312-915-7170 • Admissions Fax: 312-915-7906
Admissions E-mail: law-admissions@luc.edu • Web Address: www.luc.edu/schools/law

INSTITUTIONAL INFORMATION
Public/Private: Private
Affiliation: Roman Catholic
Student/Faculty Ratio: 16:1
Total Faculty: 114
% Part Time: 71
% Female: 40
% Minority: 7

PROGRAMS
Academic Specialties: Health Law, Corporate Law, Child and Family Law, Litigation, Tax Law, Corporation Securities Law, Intellectual Property Law, International Law, Labor Law, Child and Family Law,
Advanced Degrees Offered: MJ Health Law (22 semester hours), MJ Child Law (22 semester hours), MJ Corporate Law (22 semester hours), LLM Health Law (24 semester hours), LLM Child Law (24 semester hours), LLM Corporate Law (24 semester hours), SJD Health Law, DLaw in Health Law (2 years full time)
Combined Degrees Offered: JD/MBA, JD/MSW, JD/HRIR, JD/MA Political Science, (each 4 years)
Grading System: Letter and numerical system on a 4.0 scale
Clinical Program Required? No
Clinical Programs Description: Community Law, Tax Law, Child Law, Family Law, Business Law
Legal Writing Course Requirements? Yes
Legal Writing Description: 3 semesters
Legal Methods Course Requirements? No
Legal Research Course Requirements? Yes
Legal Research Description: 1 semester
Moot Court Requirement? Yes
Moot Court Description: 1 semester course, which includes intraschool competition
Public Interest Law Requirement? No
Academic Journals: *Law Journal, Consumer Law Review, Annals of Health Law, Public Interest Law Reporter, Child Rights Journal, Forum on International Law*

STUDENT INFORMATION
Enrollment of Law School: 714
% Out of State: 39
% Male/Female: 48/52
% Full Time: 75
% Full Time That Are International: 1
% Minority: 19
Average Age of Entering Class: 26

RESEARCH FACILITIES
Research Resources Available: Numerous free computing resources that allow students to access computers, printers, the Internet, law journals, and various databases from the Law Library, classrooms, and home; free home Internet access provided through the University; Westlaw and Lexis available for home use for a small fee; Pro Bono Students America computerized job databases
School-Supported Research Centers: Childlaw Computer Resource Center, Community Law Computer Resource Center, Health Law Institute Computer Resources, Tax Clinic Computer Resource Center, National Institute of Trial Advocacy

EXPENSES/FINANCIAL AID
Annual Tuition: $24,380
Room and Board (Off Campus): $13,240
Books and Supplies: $900
Financial Aid Application Deadline: 3/1
Average Grant: $6,600
Average Loan: $18,500
% of Aid That Is Merit-Based: 41
% Receiving Some Sort of Aid: 90
Average Total Aid Package: $24,200
Average Debt: $64,000
Tuition Per Credit: $810

ADMISSIONS INFORMATION
Application Fee: $50
Regular Application Deadline: 4/1
Regular Notification: Rolling
LSDAS Accepted? Yes
Average GPA: 3.3
Range of GPA: 3.1–3.5
Average LSAT: 158
Range of LSAT: 156–160
Transfer Students Accepted? Yes
Other Admissions Factors Considered: Work experience, rigor of academic curriculum, applicant's ability to overcome hardships or disabilities
Number of Applications Received: 2,168
Number of Applicants Accepted: 769
Number of Applicants Enrolled: 164

INTERNATIONAL STUDENTS
TOEFL Required of International Students? Yes

EMPLOYMENT INFORMATION

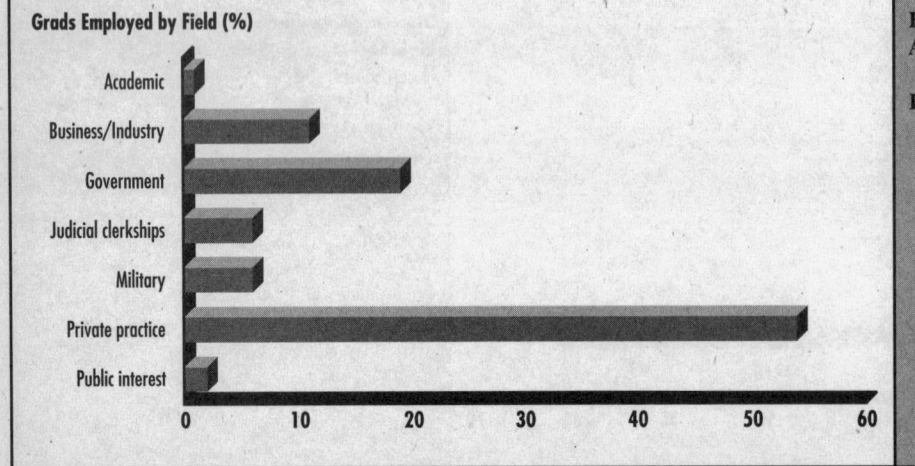

Grads Employed by Field (%)
- Academic: ~2
- Business/Industry: ~10
- Government: ~20
- Judicial clerkships: ~3
- Military: ~1
- Private practice: ~55
- Public interest: ~2

Rate of Placement: 94%
Average Starting Salary: $77,583
State for Bar Exam: IL
Pass Rate for First-Time Bar: 93%

LOYOLA UNIVERSITY NEW ORLEANS
School of Law

Admissions Contact: Dean of Admissions, K. Michele Allison-Davis
7214 Saint Charles Avenue, Box 904, New Orleans, LA 70118
Admissions Phone: 504-861-5575 • Admissions Fax: 504-861-5772
Admissions E-mail: ladmit@loyno.edu • Web Address: law.loyno.edu

INSTITUTIONAL INFORMATION
Public/Private: Private
Affiliation: Roman Catholic
Student/Faculty Ratio: 21:1
Total Faculty: 85
% Part Time: 69
% Female: 25
% Minority: 1

PROGRAMS
Academic Specialties: International Law, Pro Bono Program
Combined Degrees Offered: JD/MBA, JD/Masters of Religious Studies, JD/Masters of Communications, JD/MPA, JD/MURP (all combined degree programs add an additional year to the JD program)
Grading System: A, B+, B, C+, C, D+, D, F
Clinical Program Required? No
Clinical Programs Description: Criminal Prosecution and Defenses, Immigration, Civil, Juvenile, Domestic, Civil Rights
Legal Writing Course Requirements? Yes
Legal Writing Description: Legal Research and Writing (2 credit hours) required during the fall semester of the first year
Legal Methods Course Requirements? Yes
Legal Methods Description: See Legal Research and Writing.
Legal Research Course Requirements? Yes
Legal Research Description: See Legal Research and Writing.
Moot Court Requirement? Yes
Moot Court Description: 2 credit hours during the spring semester of the first year. Students submit appellate briefs and present oral arguments for grades.
Public Interest Law Requirement? Yes
Public Interest Law Description: Students must take the Law and Poverty course. They may substitute the Street Law class or participation in the Pro Bono Project, which requires 50 hours of legal representation to indigent clients in the community.
Academic Journals: Loyola Law Review, Journal of Public Interest Law, Maritime Law Journal, Loyola Intellectual Property and High Technology Journal

STUDENT INFORMATION
Enrollment of Law School: 766
% Out of State: 25
% Male/Female: 43/57
% Full Time: 73
% Full Time That Are International: 1
% Minority: 20
Average Age of Entering Class: 26

EXPENSES/FINANCIAL AID
Annual Tuition: $22,568
Room and Board (On/Off Campus): $5,000/$8,600
Books and Supplies: $1,000
Average Grant: $8,591
Average Loan: $21,099
% of Aid That Is Merit-Based: 41
Average Debt: $62,863
Tuition Per Credit: $728
Fees Per Credit: $642

ADMISSIONS INFORMATION
Application Fee: $40
Regular Application Deadline: Rolling
Regular Notification: Rolling
LSDAS Accepted? Yes
Average GPA: 3.0
Range of GPA: 2.8–3.3
Average LSAT: 151
Range of LSAT: 147–153
Transfer Students Accepted? Yes
Other Schools to Which Students Applied: Southern University, Louisiana State University, American University, University of Miami, Tulane University
Other Admissions Factors Considered: Graduate GPA, date of undergraduate degree, age, undergraduate major, undergraduate school, diversity, letters of recommendation, work experience
Number of Applications Received: 1,518
Number of Applicants Accepted: 839
Number of Applicants Enrolled: 313

INTERNATIONAL STUDENTS
TOEFL Required of International Students? Yes
Minimum TOEFL: 237

EMPLOYMENT INFORMATION

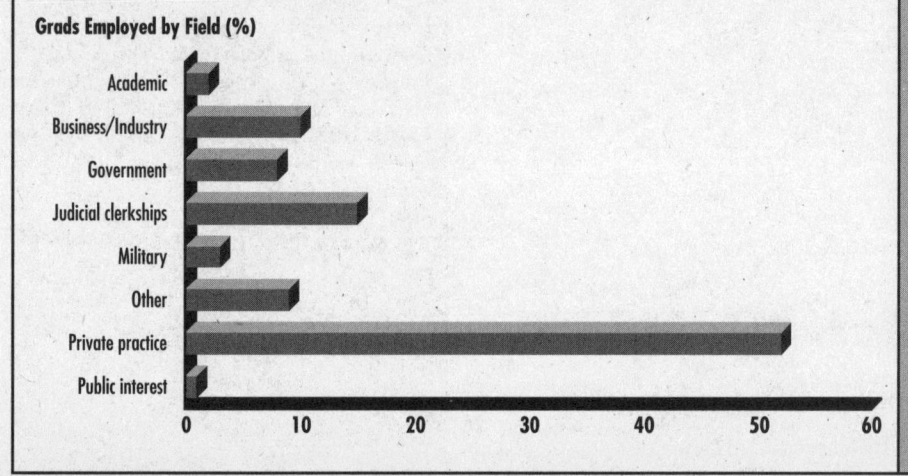

Grads Employed by Field (%)
- Academic
- Business/Industry
- Government
- Judicial clerkships
- Military
- Other
- Private practice
- Public interest

Rate of Placement: 100%
Employers Who Frequently Hire Grads: Private firms, the judiciary, and government agencies
State for Bar Exam: LA, FL, TX, CA, NY
Pass Rate for First-Time Bar: 65%

MARQUETTE UNIVERSITY
Law School

Admissions Contact: Assistant Dean for Admissions, Edward A. Kawczynski Jr.
1103 West Wisconsin Avenue, Milwaukee, WI 53201
Admissions Phone: 414-288-6767 • Admissions Fax: 414-288-0676
Admissions E-mail: law.admission@marquette.edu • Web Address: www.marquette.edu/law

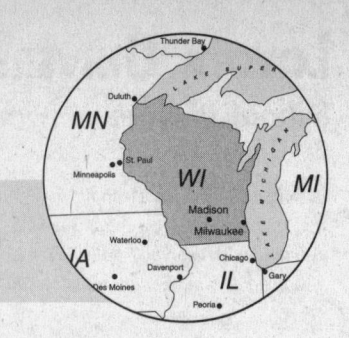

INSTITUTIONAL INFORMATION
Public/Private: Private
Affiliation: Roman Catholic
Student/Faculty Ratio: 15:1
Total Faculty: 35
% Female: 30
% Minority: 3

PROGRAMS
Academic Specialties: Intellectual Property Law, Sports Law, Criminal Law, Civil Litigation, Alternative Dispute Resolution, Civil Procedure, Commercial Law, Constitutional Law, Corporation Securities Law, Environmental Law, Government Services, International Law, Labor Law, Legal History, Property, Taxation
Combined Degrees Offered: JD/MBA, JD/MA Political Science, JD/MA International Relations, JD/MA Bioethics (all 4-year programs)
Grading System: A, B, C, D, F
Clinical Program Required? No
Legal Writing Course Requirements? Yes
Legal Writing Description: Communication skills are emphasized in all core classes. In addition, all students must take specific introductory courses in legal writing, research, and communication.
Legal Methods Course Requirements? Yes
Legal Methods Description: See Legal Writing; students must also take specially designated courses to meet advanced research and advanced oral communication requirements.

Legal Research Course Requirements? Yes
Legal Research Description: Advanced research required
Moot Court Requirement? No
Public Interest Law Requirement? No
Academic Journals: *Marquette Law Review, Intellectual Property Law Review, Sports Law Review, Elder's Advisor*

STUDENT INFORMATION
Enrollment of Law School: 587
% Out of State: 38
% Male/Female: 55/45
% Full Time: 81
% Full Time That Are International: 0
% Minority: 11
Average Age of Entering Class: 25

RESEARCH FACILITIES
Research Resources Available: Westlaw, Lexis/Nexis

EXPENSES/FINANCIAL AID
Annual Tuition: $21,550
Room and Board: $8,290
Books and Supplies: $1,065
Financial Aid Application Deadline: 3/1
Average Grant: $10,000
Average Loan: $30,000
% of Aid That Is Merit-Based: 25
% Receiving Some Sort of Aid: 90
Average Total Aid Package: $21,550
Average Debt: $62,000
Tuition Per Credit: $895

ADMISSIONS INFORMATION
Application Fee: $40
Regular Application Deadline: 4/1
Regular Notification: Rolling
LSDAS Accepted? Yes
Average GPA: 3.3
Range of GPA: 2.9–3.5
Average LSAT: 155
Range of LSAT: 152–157
Transfer Students Accepted? Yes
Other Schools to Which Students Applied: University of Wisconsin—Madison, Loyola University Chicago, DePaul University, Hamline University
Other Admissions Factors Considered: Cultural, educational, and experiential diversity
Number of Applications Received: 984
Number of Applicants Accepted: 490
Number of Applicants Enrolled: 151

INTERNATIONAL STUDENTS
TOEFL Required of International Students? Yes
Minimum TOEFL: 250

EMPLOYMENT INFORMATION

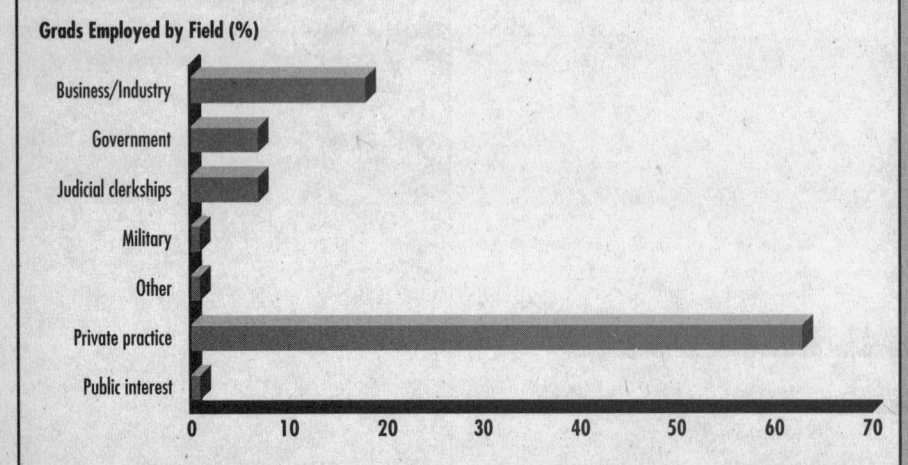

Grads Employed by Field (%)

Field	%
Business/Industry	~18
Government	~7
Judicial clerkships	~8
Military	~1
Other	~1
Private practice	~63
Public interest	~1

Rate of Placement: 95%
Average Starting Salary: $58,500
Employers Who Frequently Hire Grads: Michael, Best & Friedrich; Quarles & Brady; Godfrey & Kahn; Von Briesen, Purtell & Roport; Foley & Lardner; Davis & Kualthay, SC; Whyte, Hirschboeck, Dudek.
State for Bar Exam: WI
Pass Rate for First-Time Bar: 100%

MERCER UNIVERSITY
Walter F. George School of Law

Admissions Contact: Assistant Dean of Admissions and Financial Aid, Marilyn E. Sutton
1021 Georgia Avenue, Macon, GA 31207
Admissions Phone: 478-301-2605 • Admissions Fax: 478-301-2989
Admissions E-mail: martin_sv@mercer.edu • Web Address: www.law.mercer.edu

INSTITUTIONAL INFORMATION
Public/Private: Private
Affiliation: Baptist
Student/Faculty Ratio: 16:1
Total Faculty: 55
% Part Time: 46
% Female: 22
% Minority: 11

PROGRAMS
Academic Specialties: In 1996 Mercer received the Gambrell Professionalism Award from the ABA because of the depth and excellence of the curriculum and its commitment to professionalism. Specialties include: Civil Procedure, Commercial Law, Constitutional Law, Corporation Securities Law, Criminal Law, Environmental Law, Government Services, Intellectual Property Law, International Law, Labor Law, Legal History, Property, Taxation, and the Legal Writing Certificate Program.
Advanced Degrees Offered: JD (3 years)
Combined Degrees Offered: JD/MBA (4 years)
Grading System: A (99–90), B (89–82), C (81–76), D (75–70), F (69–65)
Clinical Program Required? No
Legal Writing Course Requirements? Yes
Legal Writing Description: A 3-year, 4-semester series of writing courses that progress in difficulty and rigor as the student moves toward excellence in writing for legal practice
Legal Methods Course Requirements? Yes
Legal Methods Description: The fall-semester, first-year Legal Analysis course covers formulating a rule of law from 1 or more legal authorities, placing the rule in a rule-structure, analyzing the application of that rule to a set of facts, and organizing a written legal discussion of that analysis.
Legal Research Course Requirements? Yes
Legal Research Description: Introduction to Legal Research is a 1-credit, first-year legal research course taught by the professional librarians and covering print and electronic formats used for researching a wide range of legal sources. Training in legal research continues throughout the Legal Writing Program.
Moot Court Requirement? Yes
Moot Court Description: During the fall semester of their second year, all students draft appellate briefs and present oral arguments as part of the Legal Writing program.
Public Interest Law Requirement? No
Academic Journals: Mercer Law Review, Journal of Southern Legal History

STUDENT INFORMATION
Enrollment of Law School: 436
% Out of State: 35
% Male/Female: 50/50
% Full Time: 99
% Full Time That Are International: 1
% Minority: 15
Average Age of Entering Class: 25

EXPENSES/FINANCIAL AID
Annual Tuition: $21,190
Room and Board (Off Campus): $11,900
Books and Supplies: $600
Financial Aid Application Deadline: 4/1
Average Grant: $14,243
Average Loan: $23,000
% of Aid That Is Merit-Based: 21
% Receiving Some Sort of Aid: 89
Average Total Aid Package: $29,000
Average Debt: $70,410
Tuition Per Credit: $882

ADMISSIONS INFORMATION
Application Fee: $45
Regular Application Deadline: 3/15
Regular Notification: Rolling
LSDAS Accepted? Yes
Average GPA: 3.3
Range of GPA: 2.9–3.5
Average LSAT: 153
Range of LSAT: 150–155
Transfer Students Accepted? Yes
Other Schools to Which Students Applied: Emory University, Florida State University, Georgia State University, Samford University, University of Georgia, University of South Carolina, Wake Forest University
Other Admissions Factors Considered: Letters of recommendation, personal statement, grade point trend, military experience, work experience, community service, evidence of obstacles overcome, writing proficiency
Number of Applications Received: 954
Number of Applicants Accepted: 366
Number of Applicants Enrolled: 136

EMPLOYMENT INFORMATION

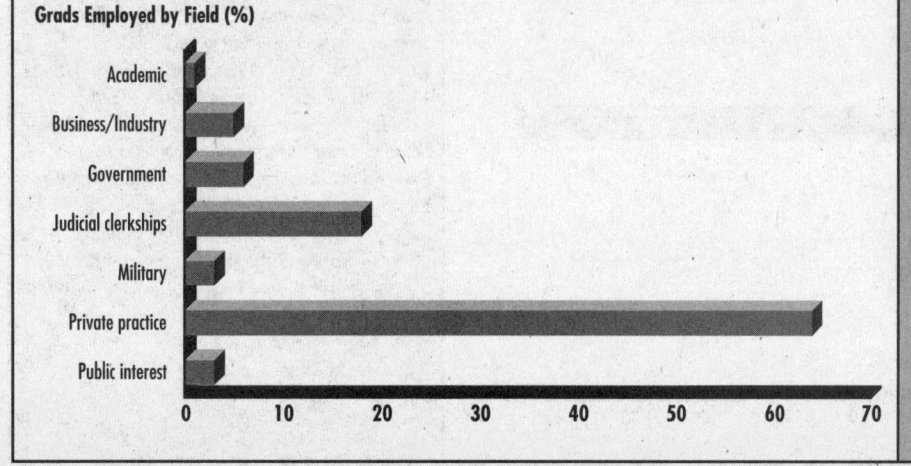

Grads Employed by Field (%)

Field	%
Academic	~1
Business/Industry	~5
Government	~6
Judicial clerkships	~18
Military	~1
Private practice	~65
Public interest	~2

Rate of Placement: 95%
Average Starting Salary: $51,255
Employers Who Frequently Hire Grads: King & Spalding (Atlanta); Long, Aldridge & Norman (Atlanta); Moore, Ingram, Johnson & Steele (Marietta, GA); Martin, Snow, Grant & Napier (Macon, GA); Alston & Bird (Atlanta, GA)
State for Bar Exam: GA
Pass Rate for First-Time Bar: 92%

Michigan State University
Detroit College of Law

Admissions Contact: Director of Admissions, Andrea Heatley
316 Law Building, East Lansing, MI 48824-1300
Admissions Phone: 517-432-0222 • Admissions Fax: 517-432-0098
Admissions E-mail: law@msu.edu • Web Address: www.dcl.edu

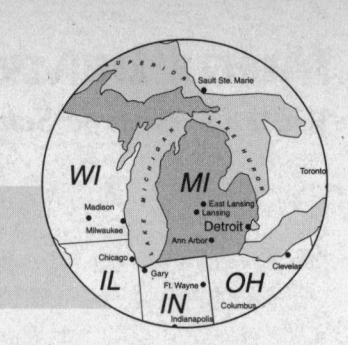

INSTITUTIONAL INFORMATION
Public/Private: Private
Environment: Urban
Schedule: Full time or part time
Student/Faculty Ratio: 23:1
Total Faculty: 30
% Part Time: 40
% Female: 30
% Minority: 2

PROGRAMS
Academic Specialties: 2 concentrations, International Law and Taxation; summer programs in Romania and Ottawa, Canada; joint JD/MBA program
Combined Degrees Offered: JD/MBA (4 years), JD/MPA (4 years), JD/MLIR (4 years), JD/MA (4 years)
Grading System: A (4.0) to F (0)
Clinical Program Required? No
Clinical Program Description: Externships with various courts and government agencies

STUDENT INFORMATION
Enrollment of Law School: 715
% Male/Female: 61/39
% Full Time: 78
% Full Time That Are International: 3
% Minority: 19
Average Age of Entering Class: 28

RESEARCH FACILITIES
Computers/Workstations Available: 70
School-Supported Research Centers: The Michigan State University Library System

EXPENSES/FINANCIAL AID
Annual Tuition: $15,584
Room and Board: $6,364
Books and Supplies: $872
Financial Aid Application Deadline: 6/30
Average Grant: $17,000
Average Loan: $16,925
% of Aid That Is Merit-Based: 7
% Receiving Some Sort of Aid: 80
Average Total Aid Package: $18,300
Average Debt: $59,381
Fees Per Credit: $535

ADMISSIONS INFORMATION
Application Fee: $50
Regular Application Deadline: Rolling
Regular Notification: Rolling
Average GPA: 3.2
Range of GPA: 2.9–3.4
Average LSAT: 152
Range of LSAT: 149–156
Transfer Students Accepted? Yes
Other Schools to Which Students Applied: Wayne State University
Number of Applications Received: 1,055
Number of Applicants Accepted: 701
Number of Applicants Enrolled: 210

INTERNATIONAL STUDENTS
TOEFL Required of International Students? Yes
Minimum TOEFL: 600

EMPLOYMENT INFORMATION

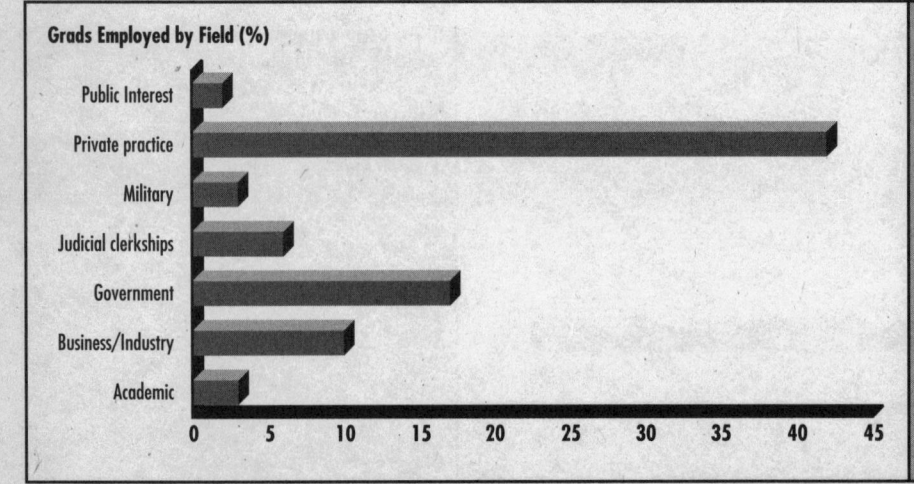

Grads Employed by Field (%)
- Public Interest
- Private practice
- Military
- Judicial clerkships
- Government
- Business/Industry
- Academic

Rate of Placement: 92%
Average Starting Salary: $43,285
Employers Who Frequently Hire Grads: Clark Hill, PLC; Dykema Gossett, PLLC; Kitch, Drutchas, Wagner and Kenney, PC; Secrest, Wardle, Lynch, Hampton; Truex and Morley
Prominent Alumni: Dennis Archer, mayor of Detroit and former Michigan Supreme Court judge, Hon. Richard Suhrheinrich, judge, U.S. Court of Appeals 6th District Circuit, Michael G. Morris, president and CEO of Consumers Power Company
State for Bar Exam: MI
Number Taking Bar Exam: 194
Pass Rate for First-Time Bar: 76%

MISSISSIPPI COLLEGE
School of Law

Admissions Contact: Director of Admissions, Patricia H. Evans
151 East Griffith Street, Jackson, MS 39201
Admissions Phone: 601-925-7150 • Admissions Fax: 601-925-7185
Admissions E-mail: hweaver@mc.edu • Web Address: www.law.mc.edu

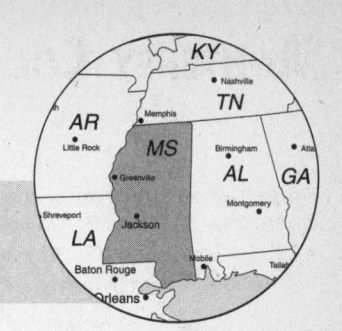

INSTITUTIONAL INFORMATION
Public/Private: Private
Affiliation: Southern Baptist
Student/Faculty Ratio: 18:1
Total Faculty: 36
% Part Time: 17
% Female: 50
% Minority: 7

PROGRAMS
Academic Specialties: Antitrust, Evidence, Bankruptcy Law
Advanced Degrees Offered: JD (3 years)
Combined Degrees Offered: JD/MBA (3 years JD, 1 year MBA)
Grading System: A to F
Clinical Program Required? No
Legal Writing Course Requirements? No
Legal Methods Course Requirements? Yes
Legal Methods Description: 2 semesters first year; upper-level writing requirement
Legal Research Course Requirements? No
Moot Court Requirement? No
Public Interest Law Requirement? No

STUDENT INFORMATION
Enrollment of Law School: 383
% Out of State: 48
% Male/Female: 56/44
% Full Time: 100
% Full Time That Are International: 0
% Minority: 9
Average Age of Entering Class: 26

EXPENSES/FINANCIAL AID
Annual Tuition: $15,600
Room and Board (On/Off Campus): $3,900/$7,400
Books and Supplies: $900
Financial Aid Application Deadline: 5/1
Average Grant: $9,000
Average Loan: $18,500
% of Aid That Is Merit-Based: 25
% Receiving Some Sort of Aid: 93
Average Total Aid Package: $24,000
Average Debt: $55,000
Tuition Per Credit: $499

ADMISSIONS INFORMATION
Application Fee: $40
Regular Application Deadline: Rolling
Regular Notification: Rolling
LSDAS Accepted? Yes
Average GPA: 3.1
Range of GPA: 2.8–3.4
Average LSAT: 149
Range of LSAT: 145–152
Transfer Students Accepted? Yes
Other Admissions Factors Considered: Extracurricular activities, work experience, letters of recommendation
Number of Applications Received: 574
Number of Applicants Accepted: 342
Number of Applicants Enrolled: 143

EMPLOYMENT INFORMATION

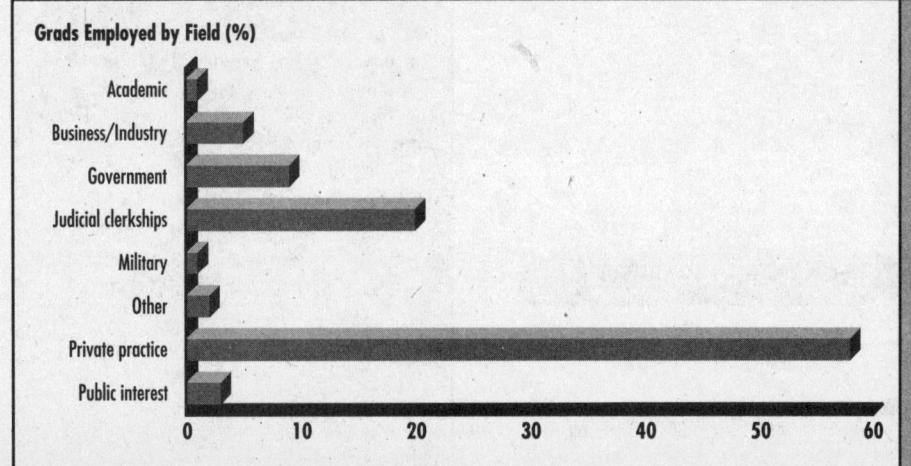

Grads Employed by Field (%)
- Academic
- Business/Industry
- Government
- Judicial clerkships
- Military
- Other
- Private practice
- Public interest

Rate of Placement: 92%
Average Starting Salary: $39,171
State for Bar Exam: MS, AL, TN, GA, FL
Pass Rate for First-Time Bar: 85%

MONTEREY COLLEGE OF LAW

Admissions Contact: Director of Admissions and Student Services
404 West Franklin Street, Monterey, CA 93940
Admissions Phone: 831-373-3301 • Admissions Fax: 831-373-0143
Admissions E-mail: wfl@montereylaw.edu • Web Address: www.montereylaw.edu

INSTITUTIONAL INFORMATION
Public/Private: Private
Student/Faculty Ratio: 25:1
Total Faculty: 44
% Part Time: 100
% Female: 23
% Minority: 2

PROGRAMS
Academic Specialties: Convenient evening classes taught by practicing attorneys and judges who bring real-world perspectives and experiences into the classroom
Advanced Degrees Offered: JD (4-year evening program)
Grading System: Numerical system (100 to 0)
Clinical Program Required? Yes
Clinical Programs Description: Under the supervision of a Clinical Studies professor, students give legal advice to clients in a pro bono legal clinic focusing on small claims issues.
Legal Writing Course Requirements? Yes
Legal Writing Description: 2-semester Legal Writing course during first year, 2-semester Advanced Legal Writing course during second year
Legal Methods Course Requirements? Yes
Legal Methods Description: Legal Writing classes are required in the first and second years. In the third and fourth years, they are integrated into the curriculum.

Legal Research Course Requirements? Yes
Legal Research Description: Legal Research is a required course for first-year students. Computer Assisted Legal Research is an elective course available after the second year of study.
Moot Court Requirement? Yes
Moot Court Description: The Heisler Moot Court gives students an opportunity to study and write about constitutional issues. Starting with drafting an appellate brief, the semester culminates in a series of hearings, where local judges hear the students' oral arguments on each side of a current civil liberties issue. The public is invited to witness the final round of arguments by 4 students in front of an appellate panel of judges.
Public Interest Law Requirement? No

STUDENT INFORMATION
Enrollment of Law School: 100
% Male/Female: 100/0
% Minority: 0
Average Age of Entering Class: 37

RESEARCH FACILITIES
Research Resources Available: Monterey Courthouse Law Library, Santa Cruz County Law Library, Salinas Law Library, Watsonville Law Library

EXPENSES/FINANCIAL AID
Average Grant: $750
Average Loan: $5,000
% of Aid That Is Merit-Based: 40
% Receiving Some Sort of Aid: 55
Tuition Per Credit: $380
Fees Per Credit: $70

ADMISSIONS INFORMATION
Application Fee: $75
Regular Application Deadline: 6/2
Regular Notification: 7/31
LSDAS Accepted? No
Average GPA: 3.0
Range of GPA: 2.3–4.0
Average LSAT: 150
Range of LSAT: 140–160
Transfer Students Accepted? Yes
Other Schools to Which Students Applied: Lincoln Law School of San Jose
Other Admissions Factors Considered: Selection of students for admissions to Monterey College of Law is based on a combination of factors and each application is considered on its own merit. The Admission Committee reviews each applicant's entire file prior to making a decision.
Number of Applications Received: 38
Number of Applicants Accepted: 28
Number of Applicants Enrolled: 27

EMPLOYMENT INFORMATION

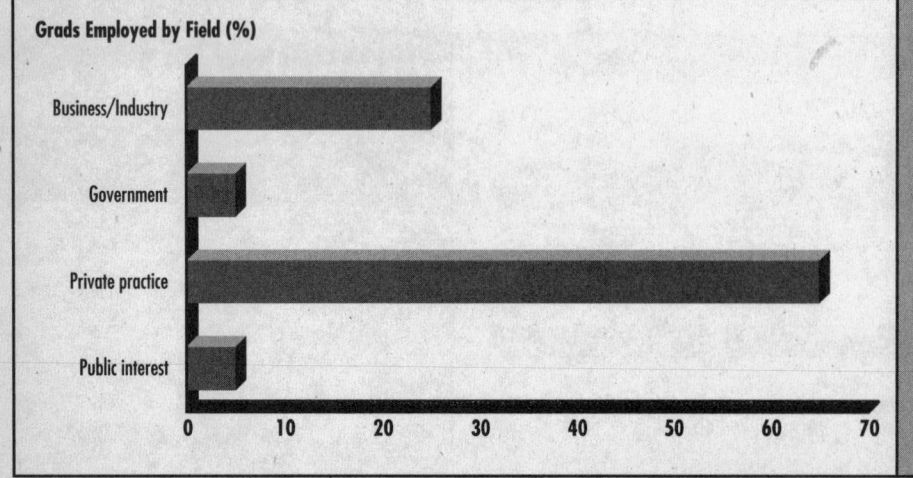

Grads Employed by Field (%)

Field	%
Business/Industry	~25
Government	~5
Private practice	~65
Public interest	~5

Rate of Placement: 85%
Employers Who Frequently Hire Grads: Governmental offices, public agencies, private law firms, Public Defender's Office, District Attorney's Office
State for Bar Exam: CA
Pass Rate for First-Time Bar: 54%

NEW COLLEGE OF CALIFORNIA
School of Law

Admissions Contact: Assistant Dean of Admissions, Sabrina Baptiste, JD
50 Fell Street, San Francisco, CA 94102
Admissions Phone: 415-241-1374 • Admissions Fax: 415-241-9525
Admissions E-mail: Brina72@aol.com • Web Address: www.newcollege.edu

INSTITUTIONAL INFORMATION
Public/Private: Private
Student/Faculty Ratio: 15:1

PROGRAMS
Academic Specialties: Constitutional Law, Environmental Law, Government Services, Human Rights Law, Labor Law, Property
Grading System: Letter grades based on a bar standard
Clinical Program Required? No
Legal Writing Course Requirements? Yes
Legal Writing Description: 1 year Legal Research and Writing
Legal Methods Course Requirements? Yes
Legal Methods Description: 1 semester
Legal Research Course Requirements? Yes
Legal Research Description: 1 year Legal Research and Writing
Moot Court Requirement? No
Public Interest Law Requirement? Yes
Public Interest Law Description: 600–800 hours of Public Interest Internship
Academic Journals: *Journal of Public Interest Law*

STUDENT INFORMATION
Enrollment of Law School: 160
% Male/Female: 45/55
% Full Time: 75
% Full Time That Are International: 4
% Minority: 43

EXPENSES/FINANCIAL AID
Annual Tuition: $10,540
Books and Supplies: $400
Average Loan: $18,500

ADMISSIONS INFORMATION
Application Fee: $45
Regular Application Deadline: 5/1
Regular Notification: Rolling
LSDAS Accepted? Yes
Average GPA: 3.0
Range of GPA: 2.0–4.0
Average LSAT: 145
Transfer Students Accepted? Yes
Number of Applications Received: 150
Number of Applicants Accepted: 78
Number of Applicants Enrolled: 58

EMPLOYMENT INFORMATION
State for Bar Exam: CA
Pass Rate for First-Time Bar: 38%

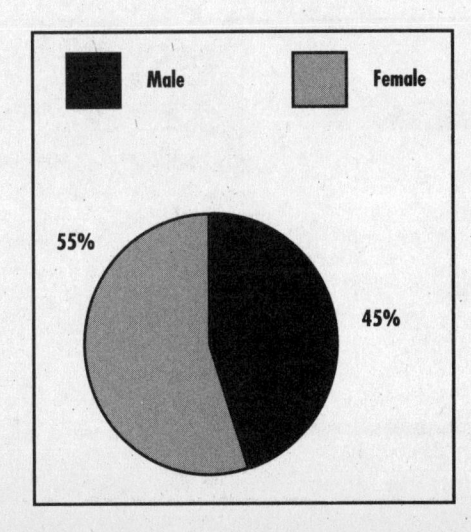

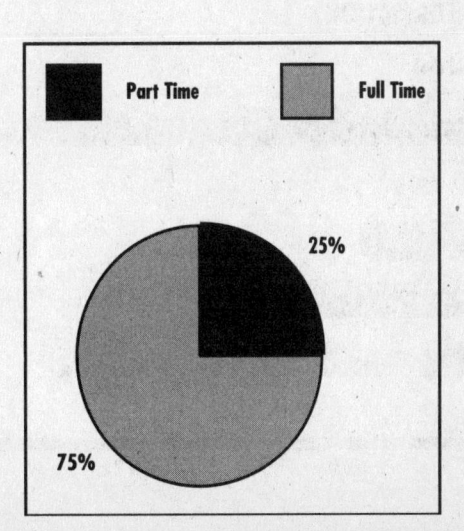

New England School of Law

Admissions Contact: Director of Admissions, Pamela Jorgensen
154 Stuart Street, Boston, MA 02116
Admissions Phone: 617-422-7210 • Admissions Fax: 617-422-7200
Admissions E-mail: admit@admin.nesl.edu • Web Address: www.nesl.edu

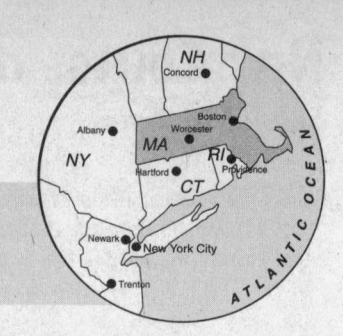

INSTITUTIONAL INFORMATION
Public/Private: Private
Environment: Urban
Academic Calendar: Semester
Schedule: Full time or part time
Student/Faculty Ratio: 20:1
Total Faculty: 93
% Part Time: 60
% Female: 27
% Minority: 8

PROGRAMS
Academic Specialties: International Law, Environmental Law, Business and Tax Law
Grading System: Letter and numerical system on a 4.0 scale
Clinical Program Required? No
Clinical Program Description: The Lawyering Process (Civil Litigation Clinic), The Lawyering Process (Summer Version), The Government Lawyer, Tax Clinic, Administrative Law Clinic, Criminal Procedure II Clinic, Environmental Law Clinic, Family Law Clinic, Health and Hospital Law Clinic
Legal Writing/Methods Course Requirements: There are five major objectives of the Legal Methods program: 1) learning to find and analyze the law and to place the law into a variety of legal formats; 2) learning the legal process from initial client interview through final disposition; 3) learning the relationship between courts and other branches of government; 4) learning how legal doctrines develop and change; and 5) learning to recognize and resolve ethical issues that arise in the practice of law.

STUDENT INFORMATION
Enrollment of Law School: 937
% Male/Female: 48/52
% Full Time: 61
% Full Time That Are International: 1
% Minority: 24
Average Age of Entering Class: 27

RESEARCH FACILITIES
Computers/Workstations Available: 79
School-Supported Research Centers: Memberships: New England Law Library Consortium (NELLCO) provides access to 19 major law libraries in the Northeast. Boston Regional Library System (BRLS) provides research and interlibrary loan service amongst its members—from the largest university library, to mid-size public libraries to small corporate libraries. Bilateral agreements exist between New England and Tufts Health Sciences Library and between New England and Wentworth Institute of Technology Library.

EXPENSES/FINANCIAL AID
Annual Tuition: $15,950
Room and Board (Off Campus): $12,600
Books and Supplies: $850
Financial Aid Application Deadline: 4/15
Average Grant: $5,340
Average Loan: $19,125
% of Aid That Is Merit-Based: 65
% Receiving Some Sort of Aid: 78
Average Total Aid Package: $20,950
Average Debt: $62,870
Tuition Per Credit: $610

ADMISSIONS INFORMATION
Application Fee: $50
Regular Application Deadline: 6/1
Regular Notification: Rolling
LSDAS Accepted? Yes
Range of GPA: 2.7–3.3
Average LSAT: 148
Range of LSAT: 143–153
Transfer Students Accepted? Yes
Other Schools to Which Students Applied: Suffolk University, Boston College, Northeastern University, Boston University, Western New England College, New York Law School, Syracuse University, Quinnipac University School of Law
Number of Applications Received: 2,224
Number of Applicants Accepted: 1,524
Number of Applicants Enrolled: 337

INTERNATIONAL STUDENTS
TOEFL Required of International Students? Yes

EMPLOYMENT INFORMATION

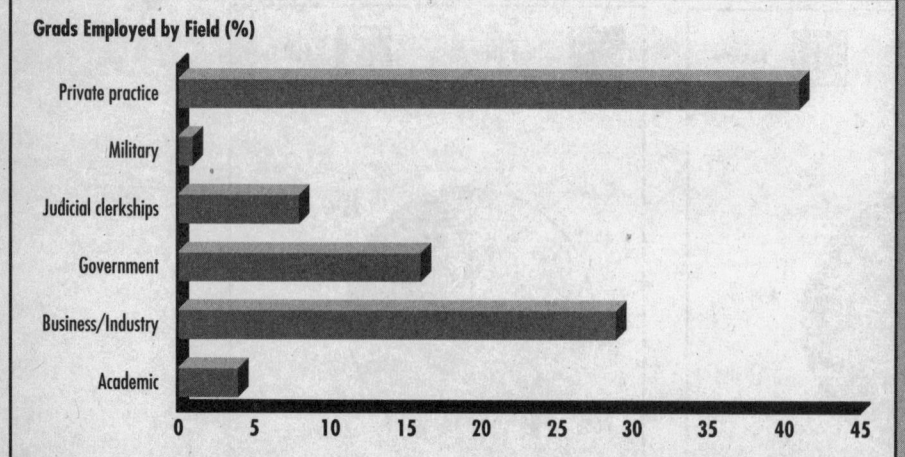

Grads Employed by Field (%)

Field	%
Private practice	~42
Military	~1
Judicial clerkships	~7
Government	~16
Business/Industry	~29
Academic	~3

Rate of Placement: 89%
Average Starting Salary: $46,287
Employers Who Frequently Hire Grads: A partial list of employers who have hired New England School of Law graduates can be found on our website www.nesl.edu/career/employ.htm
Prominent Alumni: Susan Crawford, judge, U.S. Court of Appeals for the Armed Forces; John Simpson, former director of the Secret Service; Gregory Phillips, presiding justice, Roxbury District Court; Joyce London Alexander, chief U.S. magistrate judge, U.S. District Court for District of Massachusetts; Judge Thomas A. Adams, New York Supreme Court; Joseph Mondello, Republican National Comitteeman for New York

NEW YORK LAW SCHOOL

Admissions Contact: Director of Admissions, Pamela McKenna
57 Worth Street, New York, NY 10013
Admissions Phone: 212-431-2888 • Admissions Fax: 212-966-1522
Admissions E-mail: admissions@nyls.edu • Web Address: www.nyls.edu

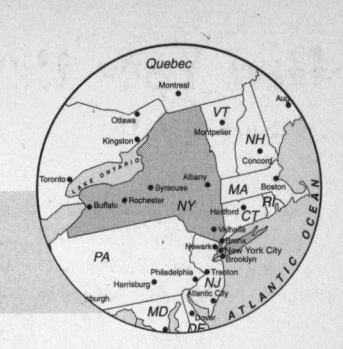

INSTITUTIONAL INFORMATION
Public/Private: Private
Environment: Urban
Academic Calendar: Semester
Schedule: Full time or part time
Student/Faculty Ratio: 21:1
Total Faculty: 124
% Part Time: 56
% Female: 32
% Minority: 8

PROGRAMS
Academic Specialties: Constitutional Law, Civil and Human Rights, Corporations and Business Transactions, Communications and Media Law, externships and judicial internships
Advanced Degrees Offered: JD (3 years full time, 4 years part time)
Combined Degrees Offered: JD/MBA with Baruch College (4 years of full-time course load)
Grading System: A to F, with some courses designated P/F
Clinical Program Required? No
Clinical Program Description: Civil and Human Rights Clinic focusing on housing discrimination and political asylum cases

STUDENT INFORMATION
Enrollment of Law School: 1,405
% Male/Female: 52/48
% Full Time: 66
% Full Time That Are International: 1
% Minority: 23
Average Age of Entering Class: 27

EXPENSES/FINANCIAL AID
Annual Tuition: $22,114
Room and Board (Off Campus): $9,945
Books and Supplies: $800
Average Grant: $7,150
Average Loan: $21,000
% Receiving Some Sort of Aid: 84
Average Total Aid Package: $29,000
Average Debt: $49,000

ADMISSIONS INFORMATION
Application Fee: $50
Regular Application Deadline: Rolling
Regular Notification: Rolling
LSDAS Accepted? Yes
Average GPA: 3.1
Range of GPA: 2.9–3.3
Average LSAT: 154
Range of LSAT: 151–156
Transfer Students Accepted? Yes
Other Schools to Which Students Applied: Brooklyn Law School, Fordham University, St. John's University, Hofstra University, Seton Hall University, New York University, American University, Pace University
Number of Applications Received: 4,240
Number of Applicants Accepted: 2,035
Number of Applicants Enrolled: 509

INTERNATIONAL STUDENTS
TOEFL Required of International Students? Yes
Minimum TOEFL: 600

EMPLOYMENT INFORMATION

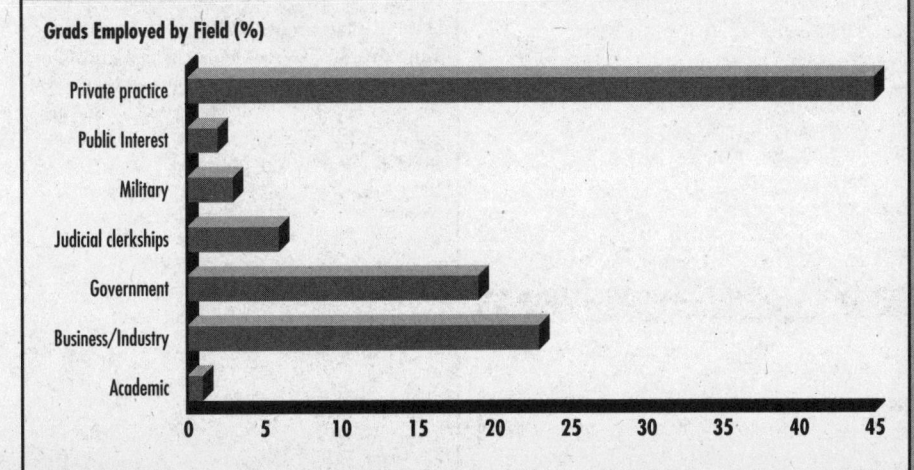

Grads Employed by Field (%):
- Private practice: ~45
- Public Interest: ~3
- Military: ~4
- Judicial clerkships: ~5
- Government: ~19
- Business/Industry: ~23
- Academic: ~1

Rate of Placement: 93%
Average Starting Salary: $60,000
Prominent Alumni: U.S. Supreme Court Justice John Marshall Harlan; Arnold Kopelson, Academy Award–winning producer (*Platoon*)

NEW YORK UNIVERSITY
School of Law

Admissions Contact: Assistant Dean of Admissions
110 West Third Street, New York, NY 10012
Admissions Phone: 212-998-6060 • Admissions Fax: 212-995-4527
Admissions E-mail: law.moreinfo@nyu.edu • Web Address: www.law.nyu.edu

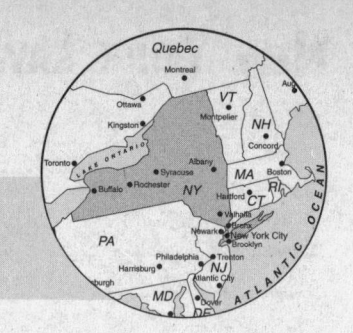

INSTITUTIONAL INFORMATION
Public/Private: Private
Student/Faculty Ratio: 13:1
Total Faculty: 197
% Part Time: 37
% Female: 33
% Minority: 8

PROGRAMS
Academic Specialties: NYU's curriculum is distinguished by its strength in traditional areas of legal study, interdisciplinary study, and clinical education, and has long been committed to educating lawyers who will use their degrees to serve the public. The Root-Tilden-Kern Program and the Public Interest Center sponsor speakers, offer academic and career counseling, and administer summer internship, volunteer, and mentoring programs. Specialties include Commercial Law, Constitutional Law, Corporation Securities Law, Criminal Law, Environmental Law, Human Rights Law, International Law, Labor Law, Legal History, Legal Philosophy, and Taxation.
Advanced Degrees Offered: LLM, JSD
Combined Degrees Offered: JD/LLM, JD/MBA, JD/MPA, JD/MUP, JD/MSW, JD/MA, JD/PhD
Clinical Program Required? No
Clinical Programs Description: 15 different clinics offered

Legal Writing Course Requirements? No
Legal Methods Course Requirements? No
Legal Research Course Requirements? No
Moot Court Requirement? No
Public Interest Law Requirement? No
Academic Journals: Student-edited publications are *New York University Law Review*, *Annual Survey of American Law*, *Clinical Law Review*, *Eastern European Constitutional Review*, *Environmental Law Review*, *Journal of International Law and Politics*, *Journal of Legislation and Public Policy*, *Review Law and Social Change*, and *Tax Law Review*. *The Commentator* is the law school newspaper.

STUDENT INFORMATION
Enrollment of Law School: 1,368
% Male/Female: 50/50
% Full Time: 100
% Full Time That Are International: 4
% Minority: 25

EXPENSES/FINANCIAL AID
Annual Tuition: $30,024
Room and Board: $19,025
Books and Supplies: $650
Financial Aid Application Deadline: 4/15
Average Grant: $15,000

ADMISSIONS INFORMATION
Application Fee: $65
Regular Application Deadline: 2/1
Regular Notification: 4/15
LSDAS Accepted? Yes
Average GPA: 3.7
Range of GPA: 3.6–3.8
Average LSAT: 169
Range of LSAT: 167–171
Transfer Students Accepted? Yes
Other Admissions Factors Considered: Evidence of significant nonacademic or professional achievement, rigor of thought, maturity, judgement, motivation, leadership, imagination, social commitment
Number of Applications Received: 6,954
Number of Applicants Accepted: 1,547
Number of Applicants Enrolled: 426

EMPLOYMENT INFORMATION

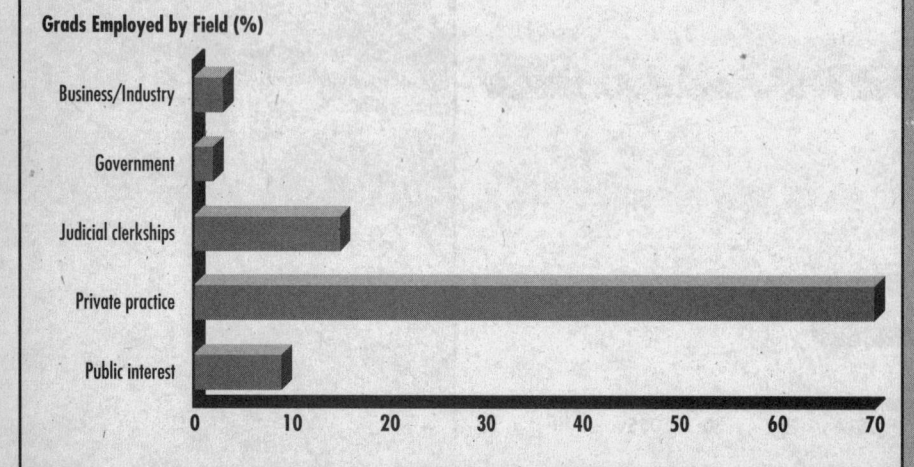

Grads Employed by Field (%)
- Business/Industry: ~2
- Government: ~3
- Judicial clerkships: ~15
- Private practice: ~70
- Public interest: ~8

Rate of Placement: 100%
Employers Who Frequently Hire Grads: Private law firms, public interest organizations, government agencies, corporations, public accounting firms
State for Bar Exam: NY
Pass Rate for First-Time Bar: 94%

NORTH CAROLINA CENTRAL UNIVERSITY
School of Law

Admissions Contact: Interim Director of Recruitment/Enrollment Manager, Karen Frasier Alston
1512 South Alston Avenue, Durham, NC 27707
Admissions Phone: 919-530-7173 • Admissions Fax: 919-560-6339
Admissions E-mail: recruiter@wpo.nccu.edu • Web Address: www.nccu.edu/law

INSTITUTIONAL INFORMATION
Public/Private: Public
Student/Faculty Ratio: 17:1

PROGRAMS
Advanced Degrees Offered: JD (3-year day program, 4-year evening program)
Combined Degrees Offered: JD/MBA (4 years), JD/MLS (4 years)
Grading System: A to F
Clinical Program Required? No
Clinical Programs Description: Third-year students in good standing are eligible to participate in the Clinical Program, in which students practice law under the supervision of a licensed attorney, after completing a required classroom component. The following clinical experiences are offered: Civil Litigation Clinic, Criminal Litigation Clinic, Family Law Clinic, Alternative Dispute Resolution Clinic, Pro Bono Legal Clinic, Small Business Clinic, and Juvenile Justice Clinic.
Legal Writing Course Requirements? Yes
Legal Writing Description: The School of Law emphasizes the development of effective writing and analytical skills. This commitment is reflected in an intensive writing program that begins in the first semester and continues through the student's tenure in law school. The required upper-level writing courses are Appellate Advocacy I, Legal Letters, Pleadings and Practice, and Senior Writing (evening program only).
Legal Methods Course Requirements? Yes

Legal Methods Description: First-year students must successfully complete Legal Reasoning and Analysis I and II. These courses cover the basics of legal reasoning, research, analysis, and writing, and citation form. Students practice the preparation of case briefs, issue identification, identification of key facts, analogy, distinction, case synthesis, and statutory construction.
Legal Research Course Requirements? Yes
Legal Research Description: Legal Bibliography is a required first-year, first-semester course that includes an overview of legal concepts, such as the structure of the court system and how law is made.
Moot Court Requirement? No
Moot Court Description: Student who have excelled in Appellate Advocacy I are chosen through in-house competitions to participate in various regional and national moot court competitions.
Public Interest Law Requirement? No
Academic Journals: *Law Journal*

STUDENT INFORMATION
Enrollment of Law School: 344
% Out of State: 0
% Male/Female: 39/61
% Full Time: 74
% Full Time That Are International: 0
% Minority: 63

RESEARCH FACILITIES
Research Resources Available: The Law School operates in an IBM PC-compatible environment running Windows 98 and 2000 and has 2 computer labs for word processing, legal research, Internet access, and e-mail in the Law Library.

EXPENSES/FINANCIAL AID
Annual Tuition (Residents/Nonresidents): $2,956/$12,060
Room and Board (On/Off Campus): $6,500/$10,205
Books and Supplies: $1,250
Financial Aid Application Deadline: 4/15
Average Grant: $2,200
Average Loan: $16,500
% of Aid That Is Merit-Based: 65
% Receiving Some Sort of Aid: 97

ADMISSIONS INFORMATION
Application Fee: $40
Regular Application Deadline: 4/15
Regular Notification: 5/31
LSDAS Accepted? Yes
Average GPA: 3.0
Average LSAT: 149
Transfer Students Accepted? Yes
Other Admissions Factors Considered: Selected applicants have excellent intellectual abilities, strong academic credentials, and diverse talents and personal experiences. Applicants who have overcome economic, social, or educational obstacles make a very important contribution to the diversity of the student body and serve as role models of achievement.
Number of Applications Received: 996
Number of Applicants Accepted: 256
Number of Applicants Enrolled: 132

INTERNATIONAL STUDENTS
TOEFL Required of International Students? Yes

EMPLOYMENT INFORMATION

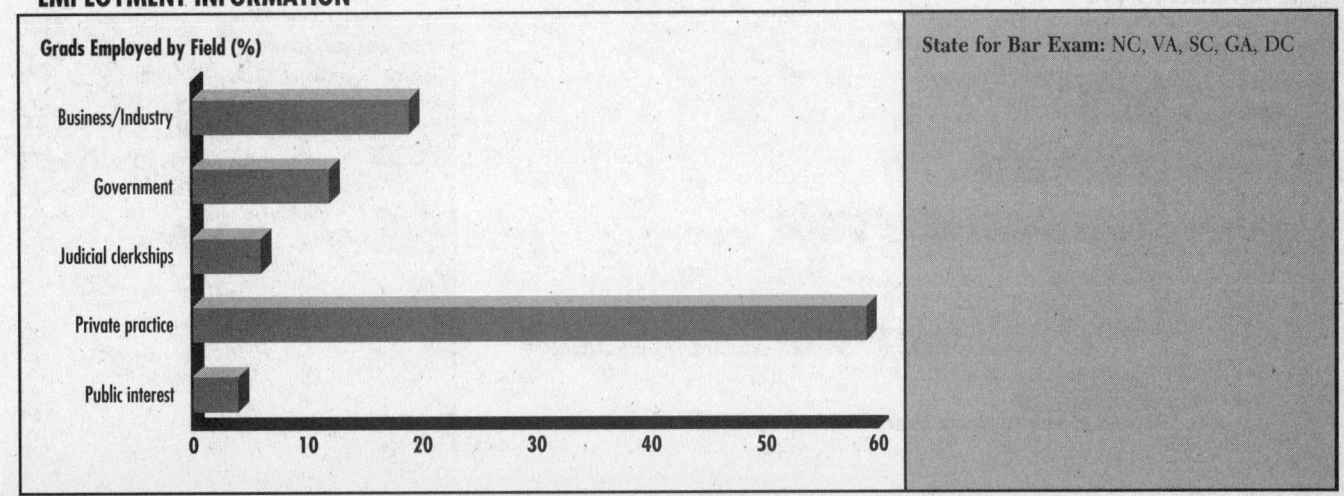

Grads Employed by Field (%)
- Business/Industry: ~20
- Government: ~12
- Judicial clerkships: ~5
- Private practice: ~60
- Public interest: ~3

State for Bar Exam: NC, VA, SC, GA, DC

NORTHEASTERN UNIVERSITY
School of Law

Admissions Contact: Assistant Dean and Director of Admissions, M.J. Knoll
400 Huntington Avenue, Boston, MA 02115
Admissions Phone: 617-373-2395 • Admissions Fax: 617-373-8865
Admissions E-mail: lawadmissions@neu.edu • Web Address: www.slaw.neu.edu

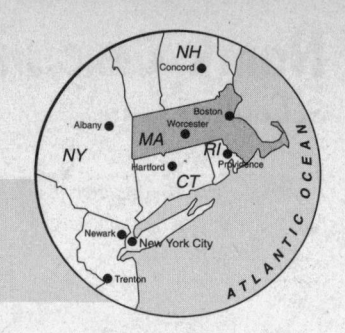

INSTITUTIONAL INFORMATION
Public/Private: Private
Student/Faculty Ratio: 20:1
Total Faculty: 81
% Part Time: 59
% Female: 25
% Minority: 10

PROGRAMS
Academic Specialties: Northeastern University School of Law offers the only Cooperative Legal Education Program in the country. Specializations include Environmental Law, Intellectual Property, Employment Law, Civil Procedure, Commercial Law, Constitutional Law, Corporation Securities Law, Criminal Law, Human Rights Law, International Law, Labor Law, Property, Taxation. The faculty combine energetic and innovative teaching, participation in scholarly debate on pressing contemporary issues of law and social policy, and active involvement in the local, national, and international communities.
Combined Degrees Offered: JD/MBA (45 months), JD/MBA/MS Accountancy (45 months), JD/MPH (42 months)
Grading System: In lieu of grades, students receive narrative evaluations in each academic course and co-op placement. All evaluations become part of the student's permanent transcript.
Clinical Program Required? No
Clinical Programs Description: The school offers 6 clinical programs for students interested in hands-on experience during their academic quarters. The clinics are: Ceriorari/Criminal Appeals, Criminal Advocacy, Domestic Violence, Poverty Law and Practice, Prisoners' Rights, and Tobacco Control.
Legal Writing Course Requirements? Yes
Legal Writing Description: Legal Practice is a 6-month (2-quarter) required first-year research and writing course.
Legal Methods Course Requirements? Yes
Legal Methods Description: See Legal Writing.
Legal Research Course Requirements? No
Moot Court Requirement? No
Public Interest Law Requirement? Yes
Public Interest Law Description: The requirement can be satisfied by successfully completing a public interest co-op, an approved clinical program, a 30-hour pro bono public interest project, or a special credit public interest independent study project.

STUDENT INFORMATION
Enrollment of Law School: 590
% Out of State: 66
% Male/Female: 40/60
% Full Time: 100
% Full Time That Are International: 3
% Minority: 27
Average Age of Entering Class: 25

RESEARCH FACILITIES
School-Supported Research Centers: Domestic Violence Institute, Tobacco Products Liability Project, Urban Law and Public Policy Institute, Disability Resource Center

EXPENSES/FINANCIAL AID
Annual Tuition: $26,820
Room and Board (On/Off Campus): $6,500/$12,150
Books and Supplies: $1,200
Financial Aid Application Deadline: 2/15
Average Grant: $8,000
% Receiving Some Sort of Aid: 83
Average Debt: $60,000

ADMISSIONS INFORMATION
Application Fee: $65
Regular Application Deadline: 3/1
Regular Notification: 4/15
LSDAS Accepted? Yes
Average GPA: 3.2
Range of GPA: 3.0–3.5
Average LSAT: 157
Range of LSAT: 152–160
Transfer Students Accepted? Yes
Other Schools to Which Students Applied: American University, Boston College, Boston University, Fordham University, George Washington University, New England School of Law, Suffolk University
Other Admissions Factors Considered: Significant work and/or community service experience, diversity of applicant's background
Number of Applications Received: 1,980
Number of Applicants Accepted: 793
Number of Applicants Enrolled: 206

INTERNATIONAL STUDENTS
TOEFL Required of International Students? Yes
Minimum TOEFL: 250

EMPLOYMENT INFORMATION

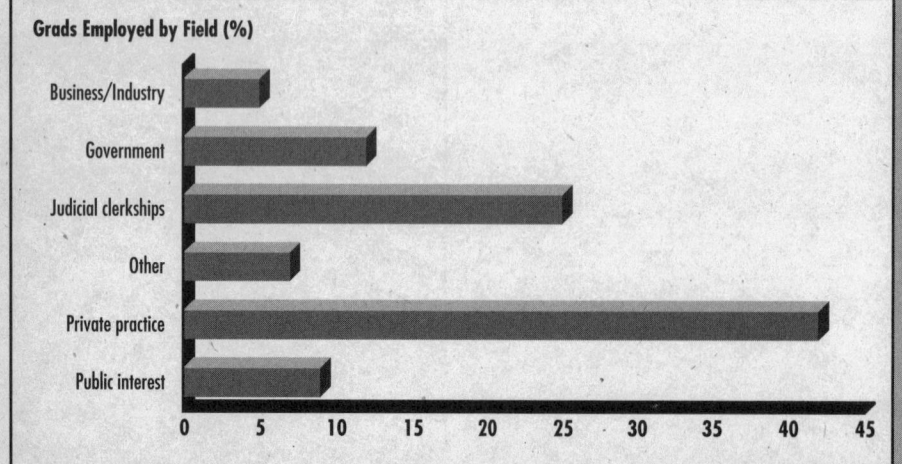

Grads Employed by Field (%)

Field	%
Business/Industry	~7
Government	~13
Judicial clerkships	~25
Other	~7
Private practice	~42
Public interest	~9

Rate of Placement: 91%
Average Starting Salary: $65,000
Employers Who Frequently Hire Grads: Mintz, Levin, Cohen, Ferris, Glovsky, & Popeo, PC; Testa, Hurwitz & Thibeault, PC; Hale & Dorr; Goodwin, Procter & Hoar; Massachusetts Superior Court; Suffolk County District Attorney's Office; Middlesex District Attorney's Office; Public Defender's Offices
State for Bar Exam: MA, NY, CA, FL
Pass Rate for First-Time Bar: 84%

NORTHERN ILLINOIS UNIVERSITY
College of Law

Admissions Contact: Director of Admission and Financial Aid, Judith L. Malen
Swen Parson Hall, College of Law, Room 276, De Kalb, IL 60115
Admissions Phone: 815-753-8559 • Admissions Fax: 815-753-4501
Admissions E-mail: lawadm@niu.edu • Web Address: www.niu.edu/col

INSTITUTIONAL INFORMATION
Public/Private: Public
Student/Faculty Ratio: 12:1
Total Faculty: 34
% Part Time: 35
% Female: 29
% Minority: 18

PROGRAMS
Academic Specialties: Public Interest, Mediation and Alternative Dispute Resolution, Corporate Law, Civil Procedure, Commercial Law, Constitutional Law, Corporation Securities Law, Criminal Law, Environmental Law, Government Services, Human Rights Law, International Law, Labor Law, Property, Taxation
Combined Degrees Offered: JD/MBA (4 years), other joint degrees can be arranged
Grading System: A to F on a 4.0 scale
Clinical Program Required? No
Clinical Programs Description: Students gain practical legal experience by representing clients in the Zeke Giorgi Legal Clinic. Though not required, students may also choose to directly experience the practice of law by enrolling in Criminal and Civil Externships, Judicial Externship, or the Appellate Defender Clinic.
Legal Writing Course Requirements? Yes
Legal Writing Description: Legal Writing and Advocacy (4 credit hours)
Legal Methods Course Requirements? Yes
Legal Methods Description: Legal Writing and Advocacy (4 credit hours) and Basic Legal Research (1 credit hour) are a 2-part course taken during the first year.

Legal Research Course Requirements? Yes
Legal Research Description: Basic Legal Research (2 credit hours)
Moot Court Requirement? No
Moot Court Description: Students have the opportunity to participate in the moot court experience during their second year. The Moot Court Society sends teams to participate in various national and regional competitions.
Public Interest Law Requirement? No
Academic Journals: *Northern Illinois University Law Review*

STUDENT INFORMATION
Enrollment of Law School: 287
% Out of State: 15
% Male/Female: 59/41
% Full Time: 90
% Full Time That Are International: 1
% Minority: 24
Average Age of Entering Class: 27

RESEARCH FACILITIES
Research Resources Available: Westlaw/Dow Jones, Lexis/Nexis, interlibrary loan access to library resources nationwide and abroad, Internet and e-mail access, help desk and technical support staff

EXPENSES/FINANCIAL AID
Annual Tuition (Residents/Nonresidents): $6,360/$13,883
Room and Board (On/Off Campus): $5,396/$6,296

Books and Supplies: $1,500
Financial Aid Application Deadline: 3/1
Average Grant: $4,045
Average Loan: $13,700
% Receiving Some Sort of Aid: 73
Average Total Aid Package: $17,830
Average Debt: $35,000

ADMISSIONS INFORMATION
Application Fee: $50
Regular Application Deadline: Rolling
Regular Notification: Rolling
LSDAS Accepted? Yes
Average GPA: 3.1
Range of GPA: 2.7–3.5
Average LSAT: 153
Range of LSAT: 150–156
Transfer Students Accepted? Yes
Other Admissions Factors Considered: Leadership qualities, good citizenship, integrity, initiative
Number of Applications Received: 897
Number of Applicants Accepted: 336
Number of Applicants Enrolled: 107

INTERNATIONAL STUDENTS
TOEFL Required of International Students? Yes
Minimum TOEFL: 250

EMPLOYMENT INFORMATION
Rate of Placement: 93%
Employers Who Frequently Hire Grads: State's attorneys, public defenders, Illinois Attorney General, private firms
State for Bar Exam: IL

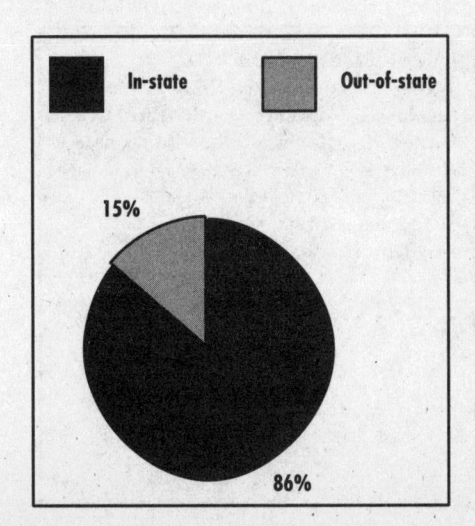

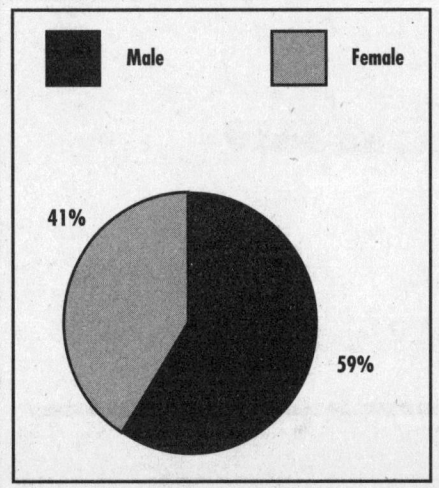

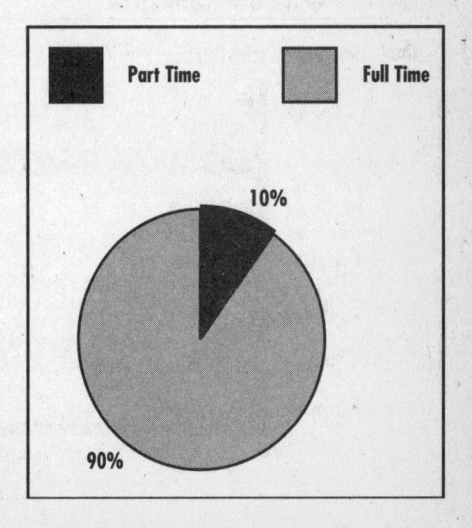

In-state / Out-of-state: 86% / 15%

Male / Female: 59% / 41%

Part Time / Full Time: 10% / 90%

NORTHERN KENTUCKY UNIVERSITY
Salmon P. Chase College of Law

Admissions Contact: Admissions Specialist, Gina Bray
Nunn Hall, Room 541, Highland Heights, KY 41099
Admissions Phone: 859-572-6476 • Admissions Fax: 859-572-6081
Admissions E-mail: brayg@nku.edu • Web Address: www.nku.edu

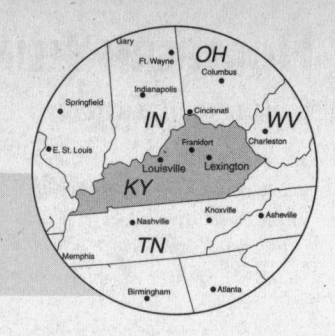

INSTITUTIONAL INFORMATION
Public/Private: Public
Student/Faculty Ratio: 13:1
Total Faculty: 65
% Part Time: 60
% Female: 34
% Minority: 12

PROGRAMS
Academic Specialties: Every first-year student is placed in a small section of one of his or her first-year classes. Each teacher in a small section uses varied teaching techniques and gives students individualized attention. We also offer the Academic Development Program to help students learn time management and study techniques. The Academic Learning Center offers a central clearinghouse for academic support and development programs.
Combined Degrees Offered: JD/MBA (3 years full time, 4 years part time)
Grading System: Letter system on a 4.3 scale, with designations for Incomplete, Satisfactory, Unsatisfactory, Pass, Credit, No Credit, Withdrew, and Audit
Clinical Program Required? No
Clinical Programs Description: The Clinical Extern Program includes placement with state and federal judges, prosecutors and public defenders, legal aid programs, and various governmental agencies.
Legal Writing Course Requirements? Yes
Legal Writing Description: Year-long course covering skills instruction and exercises in legal research and analysis of common and statutory law, legal writing and reasoning, written and oral advocacy
Legal Methods Course Requirements? No
Legal Research Course Requirements? Yes
Legal Research Description: See Legal Writing.
Moot Court Requirement? No
Moot Court Description: The Moot Court Program provides opportunities for students to develop various legal skills including research, brief writing, and presentation of oral arguments. The Moot Court Board conducts 2 intramural competitions annually and administers the National Environmental Law Moot Court Competition.
Public Interest Law Requirement? No
Academic Journals: Northern Kentucky Law Review

STUDENT INFORMATION
Enrollment of Law School: 376
% Out of State: 30
% Male/Female: 54/46
% Full Time: 55
% Full Time That Are International: 0
% Minority: 3
Average Age of Entering Class: 29

EXPENSES/FINANCIAL AID
Annual Tuition (Residents/Nonresidents): $6,396/$14,004
Room and Board: $13,526
Books and Supplies: $500
Financial Aid Application Deadline: 3/1
Average Grant: $7,352
Average Loan: $15,605
% of Aid That Is Merit-Based: 7
% Receiving Some Sort of Aid: 65
Average Total Aid Package: $12,047
Average Debt: $52,691
Tuition Per Credit (Residents/Nonresidents): $267/$584
Fees Per Credit: $33

ADMISSIONS INFORMATION
Application Fee: $30
Regular Application Deadline: 3/1
Regular Notification: Rolling
LSDAS Accepted? Yes
Average GPA: 3.3
Range of GPA: 3.0–3.5
Average LSAT: 152
Range of LSAT: 149–154
Transfer Students Accepted? Yes
Other Schools to Which Students Applied: University of Cincinnati, University of Dayton, University of Kentucky, University of Louisville
Other Admissions Factors Considered: Undergraduate institution, undergraduate major, work experience, writing ability
Number of Applications Received: 619
Number of Applicants Accepted: 307
Number of Applicants Enrolled: 127

EMPLOYMENT INFORMATION

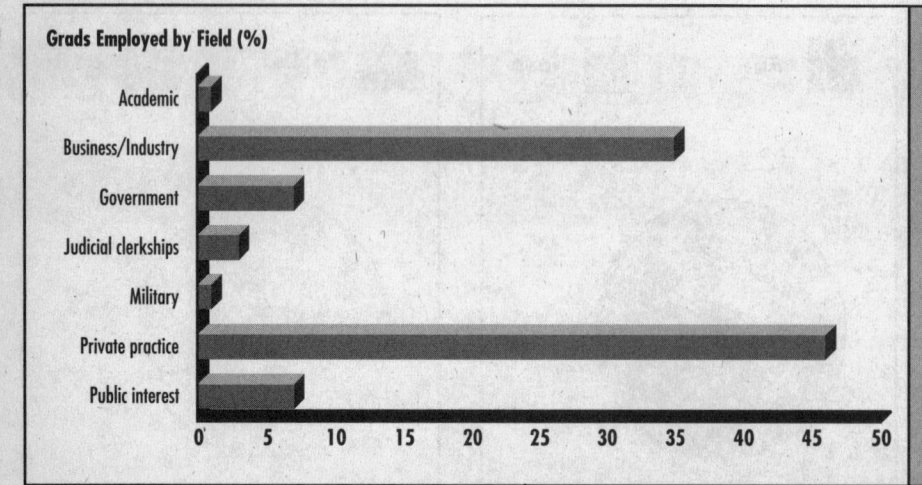

Grads Employed by Field (%)
- Academic: ~1
- Business/Industry: ~35
- Government: ~5
- Judicial clerkships: ~5
- Military: 0
- Private practice: ~47
- Public interest: ~7

Rate of Placement: 91%
Average Starting Salary: $52,630
Employers Who Frequently Hire Grads: Proctor & Gamble; Cincinnati Financial; Hamilton County Prosecutor; Dinsmore & Shoh; Taft, Stettinius & Hollister
State for Bar Exam: KY, OH, IN
Pass Rate for First-Time Bar: 88%

NORTHWESTERN UNIVERSITY
School of Law

Admissions Contact: Associate Dean of Enrollment, Don Rebstock
357 East Chicago Avenue, Chicago, IL 60611
Admissions Phone: 312-503-8465 • Admissions Fax: 312-503-0178
Admissions E-mail: nulawadm@law.northwestern.edu • Web Address: www.law.northwestern.edu

INSTITUTIONAL INFORMATION
Public/Private: Private
Student/Faculty Ratio: 12:1
Total Faculty: 210
% Part Time: 68
% Female: 25
% Minority: 5

PROGRAMS
Academic Specialties: Civil Rights, Constitutional Law, Contracts, Corporate Law, Criminal Law, Dispute Resolution, Employment/Labor Law, Environmental Law, Feminist Legal Theory, Health Law, International Private Law, International Human Rights, Intellectual Property, Jury Selection/Psychology, Law and Economics, Legal History, Public Interest, Torts, Trial Advocacy, Corporation Securities Law, International Law, Taxation, Law and Social Policy, Civil Litigation
Advanced Degrees Offered: JD (3 years), LLM (1 year), SJD (2 years), Tax LLM (1 year)
Combined Degrees Offered: JD/MBA (3 years), JD/PhD (6 years), JD/MA (4 years), LLM/Certificate in Management (1 year)
Grading System: A to F with plus and minus grades
Clinical Program Required? No
Clinical Programs Description: The Bluhm Legal Clinic offers the following programs: Children's and Family Justice Center, Center for International Human Rights, Trial Advocacy Program, Center on Wrongful Convictions, and Small Business Opportunity Center, as well as various civil clinical opportunities.

Legal Writing Course Requirements? Yes
Legal Writing Description: Communication and Legal Reasoning is a 1-year required course for first-year students.
Legal Methods Course Requirements? No
Legal Research Course Requirements? Yes
Legal Research Description: Incorporated into Communication and Legal Reasoning
Moot Court Requirement? Yes
Moot Court Description: Required participation during the first year as part of the Communication and Legal Reasoning Program
Public Interest Law Requirement? No
Academic Journals: *Northwestern University Law Review, Journal of Criminal Law and Criminology, Journal of International Law and Business*

STUDENT INFORMATION
Enrollment of Law School: 650
% Out of State: 80
% Male/Female: 50/50
% Full Time: 100
% Full Time That Are International: 2
% Minority: 30
Average Age of Entering Class: 25

EXPENSES/FINANCIAL AID
Annual Tuition: $30,226
Room and Board: $10,484
Books and Supplies: $7,868
Financial Aid Application Deadline: 3/1
Average Grant: $14,000
Average Loan: $24,000
% of Aid That Is Merit-Based: 30
% Receiving Some Sort of Aid: 80
Average Total Aid Package: $40,000
Average Debt: $80,000

ADMISSIONS INFORMATION
Application Fee: $80
Regular Application Deadline: 2/15
Regular Notification: Rolling
LSDAS Accepted? Yes
Average GPA: 3.6
Range of GPA: 3.3–3.7
Average LSAT: 167
Range of LSAT: 164–169
Transfer Students Accepted? Yes
Other Schools to Which Students Applied: Columbia University, Duke University, Georgetown University, New York University, University of Chicago, University of Michigan, University of Pennsylvania
Other Admissions Factors Considered: Applicants are strongly encouraged to conduct an admissions interview. We offer both on-campus interviews with a staff member or student and off-campus interviews with alumni.
Number of Applications Received: 4,083
Number of Applicants Accepted: 796
Number of Applicants Enrolled: 205

EMPLOYMENT INFORMATION

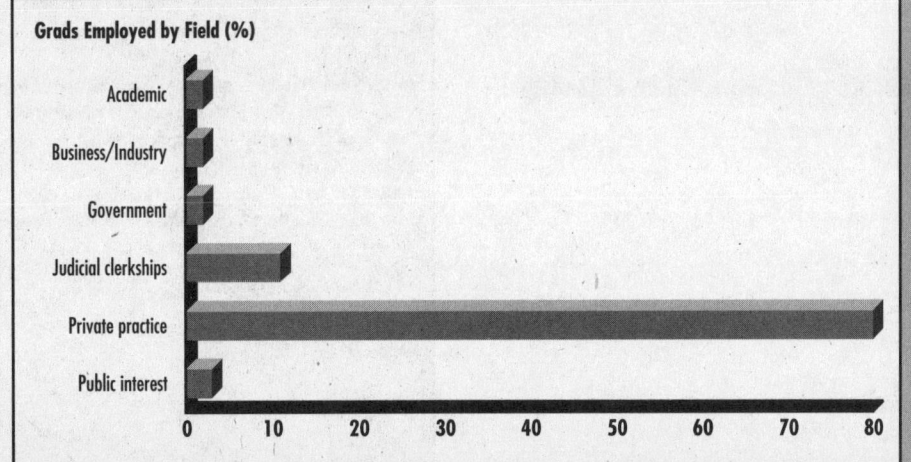

Grads Employed by Field (%)
- Academic
- Business/Industry
- Government
- Judicial clerkships
- Private practice
- Public interest

Rate of Placement: 100%
Average Starting Salary: $125,000
Employers Who Frequently Hire Grads: Sidley & Austin; Kirkland & Ellis; Latham & Watkins; Jones, Day, Reavis, & Pogue; Katten, Muchin & Zavis; Morrison & Foerster; Winston & Strawn; Baker & McKenzie; Mayer, Brown & Platt; Schiff, Hardin & Waite
State for Bar Exam: IL
Pass Rate for First-Time Bar: 93%

NOVA SOUTHEASTERN UNIVERSITY
Shepard Broad Law Center

Admissions Contact: Director of Admissions, Nancy Kelly Sanguigni
3305 College Avenue, Fort Lauderdale, FL 33314
Admissions Phone: 954-452-6115 • Admissions Fax: 954-452-6109
Admissions E-mail: admission@nsu.law.nova.edu • Web Address: www.nsulaw.nova.edu

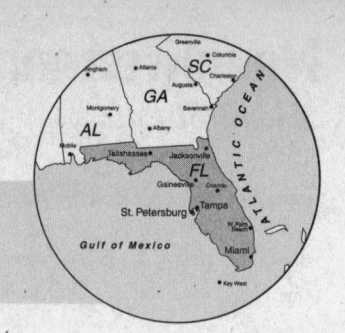

INSTITUTIONAL INFORMATION
Public/Private: Private
Environment: Urban
Academic Calendar: Semester
Schedule: Full time or part time
Student/Faculty Ratio: 16:1
Total Faculty: 93
% Part Time: 48
% Female: 32
% Minority: 13

PROGRAMS
Clinical Program Required? No

STUDENT INFORMATION
Enrollment of Law School: 953
% Male/Female: 54/46
% Full Time: 82
% Full Time That Are International: 3
% Minority: 28
Average Age of Entering Class: 27

RESEARCH FACILITIES
School-Supported Research Centers: Environmental and Land Use Law Center, Inter American Center for Human Rights

EXPENSES/FINANCIAL AID
Annual Tuition: $19,770
Room and Board (On/Off Campus): $12,668/$13,435
Books and Supplies: $1,200
Average Grant: $6,166
Average Loan: $20,882
% of Aid That Is Merit-Based: 6
% Receiving Some Sort of Aid: 90
Average Total Aid Package: $25,739
Average Debt: $78,889
Fees Per Credit: $820

ADMISSIONS INFORMATION
Regular Application Deadline: 2/15
Regular Notification: March–April
LSDAS Accepted? Yes
Average GPA: 2.9
Range of GPA: 2.5–3.1
Average LSAT: 147
Range of LSAT: 143–151
Transfer Students Accepted? Yes
Other Schools to Which Students Applied: University of Miami, St. Thomas University, Florida State University, University of Florida, Stetson University, Georgia State University, New York Law School, Emory University
Other Admissions Factors Considered: Age; trend of grades; hardships overcome; distinctive cultural point of view or life; socioeconomic, educational or personal experiences; other factors indicating motivation and discipline

EMPLOYMENT INFORMATION

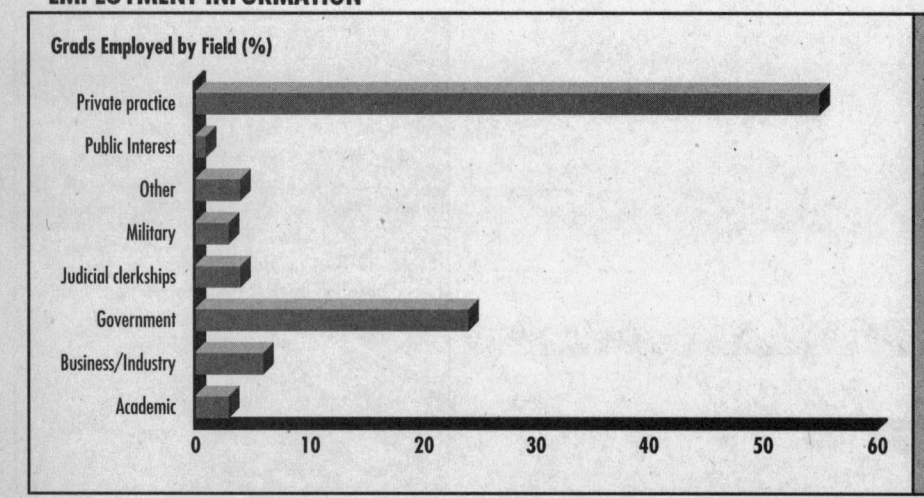

Grads Employed by Field (%)
- Private practice: ~55
- Public Interest: ~2
- Other: ~3
- Military: ~2
- Judicial clerkships: ~2
- Government: ~23
- Business/Industry: ~5
- Academic: ~1

Rate of Placement: 86%
Average Starting Salary: $39,354
Employers Who Frequently Hire Grads: Private law firms, local and state agencies, State Attorney's Office, Public Defender's Office
Prominent Alumni: Hon. Rex Ford, U.S. Immigration judge; Hon. John Rodstrom, chair, Broward County Commission; Hon. Ilene Lieberman, Broward County commissioner

OHIO NORTHERN UNIVERSITY
Claude W. Pettit College of Law

Admissions Contact: Assistant Dean and Director of Law Admissions, Linda K. English
Ohio Northern University, Pettit College, Ada, OH 45810-1599
Admissions Phone: 419-772-2211 • Admissions Fax: 419-772-1487
Admissions E-mail: l-english@onu.edu • Web Address: www.law.onu.edu

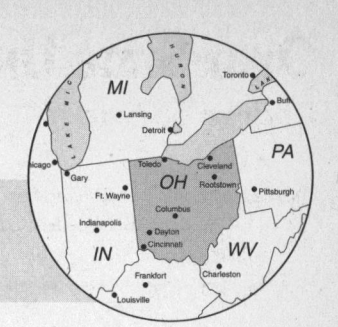

INSTITUTIONAL INFORMATION
Public/Private: Private
Affiliation: Methodist
Student/Faculty Ratio: 12:1
Total Faculty: 22
% Part Time: 30
% Female: 36
% Minority: 5

PROGRAMS
Academic Specialties: Criminal Law, Federal Income Taxation, International Law, Civil Procedure, Commercial Law, Constitutional Law, Corporation Securities Law, Environmental Law, Human Rights Law, Labor Law, Legal History, Legal Philosophy, Property, Capital Punishment
Grading System: 4.0 scale
Clinical Program Required? No
Clinical Programs Description: Criminal (Prosecution and Defense), Civil, Bankruptcy, Legal Aid, Environmental, Governmental, Legislative, Transactional, Guardian Ad Litem, Alternative Dispute Resolution, Education Seminar, several judicial externships
Legal Writing Course Requirements? Yes
Legal Writing Description: All first-year students are required to take a year-long course in Legal Research and Writing. Students complete a number of research and drafting assignments, including client memos, motions, discovery materials, an appellate brief, and an oral argument based on the appellate brief.
Legal Methods Course Requirements? Yes
Legal Methods Description: See Legal Writing.
Legal Research Course Requirements? Yes
Legal Research Description: See Legal Writing.
Moot Court Requirement? No
Moot Court Description: Ohio Northern's Moot Court program is administered by the Moot Court Executive Board, composed of second- and third-year law students. The Executive Board is assisted by the Moot Court Board of Advocates. All students are eligible to compete in both intra- and inter-scholastic competitions.
Public Interest Law Requirement? No
Academic Journals: *Ohio Northern University Law Review*

STUDENT INFORMATION
Enrollment of Law School: 266
% Out of State: 60
% Male/Female: 60/40
% Full Time: 100
% Full Time That Are International: 1
% Minority: 15
Average Age of Entering Class: 24

RESEARCH FACILITIES
Research Resources Available: Lexis/Nexis, Westlaw

EXPENSES/FINANCIAL AID
Annual Tuition: $19,740
Room and Board: $6,640
Books and Supplies: $900
Average Grant: $10,500
Average Loan: $23,270
% of Aid That Is Merit-Based: 30
% Receiving Some Sort of Aid: 95
Average Total Aid Package: $30,197
Average Debt: $65,000

ADMISSIONS INFORMATION
Application Fee: $40
Regular Application Deadline: Rolling
Regular Notification: Rolling
LSDAS Accepted? Yes
Average GPA: 3.0
Range of GPA: 2.6–3.4
Average LSAT: 147
Range of LSAT: 144–152
Transfer Students Accepted? Yes
Other Schools to Which Students Applied: Ohio State University, University of Cincinnati, University of Pittsburgh, Capital University, Case Western Reserve University, University of Toledo, University of Dayton
Other Admissions Factors Considered: Quality of undergraduate/graduate school(s), type of degree(s) earned, diversity of background and heritage, transcript, degree interpretation for international students
Number of Applications Received: 990
Number of Applicants Accepted: 650
Number of Applicants Enrolled: 111

EMPLOYMENT INFORMATION

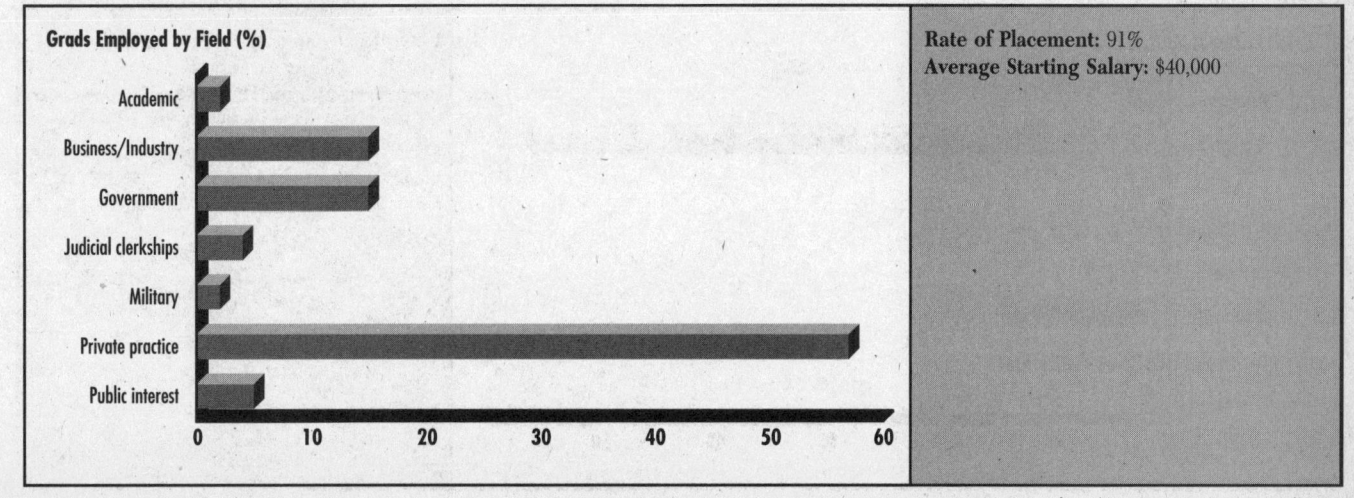

Grads Employed by Field (%)
- Academic
- Business/Industry: ~15
- Government: ~15
- Judicial clerkships: ~5
- Military: ~1
- Private practice: ~58
- Public interest: ~3

Rate of Placement: 91%
Average Starting Salary: $40,000

Ohio State University
College of Law

Admissions Contact: Assistant Dean, Kathy Northern
55 West 12th Avenue, Columbus, OH 43210
Admissions Phone: 614-292-8810 • Admissions Fax: 614-292-1492
Admissions E-mail: lawadmin@osu.edu • Web Address: www.osu.edu/units/law

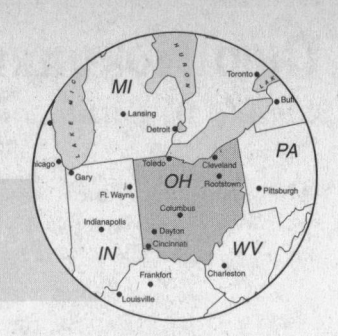

INSTITUTIONAL INFORMATION
Public/Private: Public
Environment: Urban
Academic Calendar: Semester
Schedule: Full time only
Student/Faculty Ratio: 14:1
Total Faculty: 41
% Female: 32
% Minority: 15

PROGRAMS
Clinical Program Required? No

STUDENT INFORMATION
Enrollment of Law School: 640
% Male/Female: 52/48
% Full Time: 99
% Minority: 18
Average Age of Entering Class: 24

RESEARCH FACILITIES
Computers/Workstations Available: 75

EXPENSES/FINANCIAL AID
Annual Tuition (Residents/Nonresidents): $8,424/$18,288
Room and Board: $8,184
Books and Supplies: $1,588
Financial Aid Application Deadline: 3/1
Average Grant: $2,135
% of Aid That Is Merit-Based: 2
% Receiving Some Sort of Aid: 70
Average Debt: $40,000

ADMISSIONS INFORMATION
Application Fee: $30
Regular Application Deadline: 3/15
Regular Notification: Rolling
LSDAS Accepted? Yes
Average GPA: 3.6
Range of GPA: 3.3–3.8
Average LSAT: 157
Range of LSAT: 153–160
Transfer Students Accepted? Yes
Other Schools to Which Students Applied: Case Western Reserve University, University of Cincinnati, University of Michigan, Georgetown University, George Washington University, University of Wisconsin, University of Dayton, Harvard University
Other Admissions Factors Considered: Resume, personal statement
Number of Applications Received: 1,482
Number of Applicants Accepted: 583
Number of Applicants Enrolled: 215

INTERNATIONAL STUDENTS
TOEFL Required of International Students? Yes
Minimum TOEFL: 600

EMPLOYMENT INFORMATION

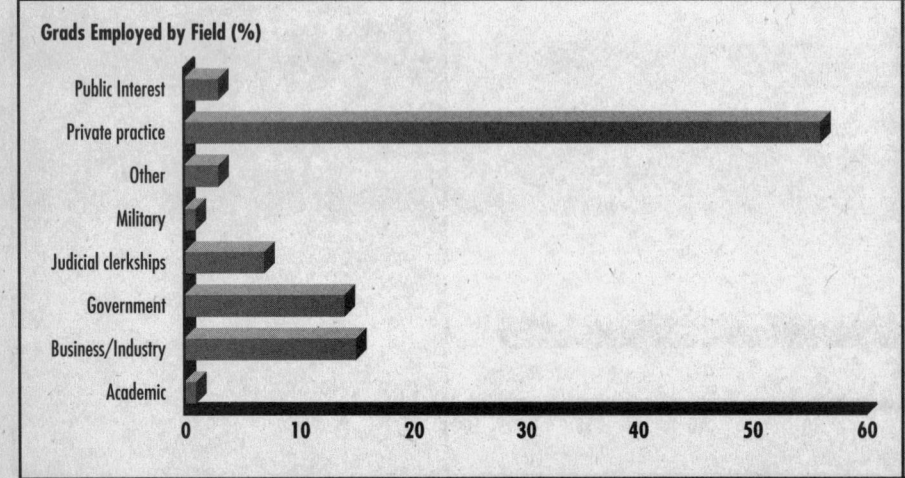

Grads Employed by Field (%)
- Public Interest
- Private practice
- Other
- Military
- Judicial clerkships
- Government
- Business/Industry
- Academic

Rate of Placement: 96%
Average Starting Salary: $50,419
Prominent Alumni: Howard Metzenbaum, U.S. senator; George Voinovich, U.S. senator; Thomas Moyer, chief justice, Ohio Supreme Court; Robert Duncan, former federal district court judge; Erin Moriarty, *CBS News* correspondent

OKLAHOMA CITY UNIVERSITY
School of Law

Admissions Contact: Director of Admission, Peter Storandt
PO Box 61310, Oklahoma City, OK 73146-1310
Admissions Phone: 405-521-5354 • Admissions Fax: 405-521-5814
Admissions E-mail: lawadmit@okcu.edu • Web Address: www.okcu.edu/law

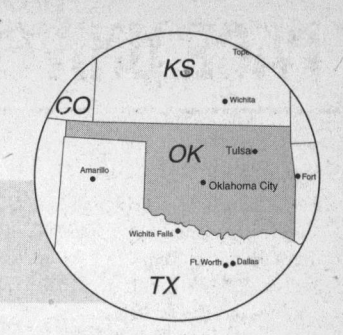

INSTITUTIONAL INFORMATION
Public/Private: Private
Affiliation: Methodist
Student/Faculty Ratio: 18:1
Total Faculty: 44
% Part Time: 30
% Female: 32
% Minority: 9

PROGRAMS
Combined Degrees Offered: JD/MBA (3 years)
Clinical Program Required? No
Legal Writing Course Requirements? Yes
Legal Writing Description: 2 semesters of Legal Writing and Research taught in small classes by full-time faculty
Legal Methods Course Requirements? No
Legal Research Course Requirements? Yes
Legal Research Description: See Legal Writing.
Moot Court Requirement? No
Public Interest Law Requirement? No
Academic Journals: *Law Review*

STUDENT INFORMATION
Enrollment of Law School: 537
% Out of State: 46
% Male/Female: 60/40
% Full Time: 74
% Full Time That Are International: 1
% Minority: 23
Average Age of Entering Class: 29

RESEARCH FACILITIES
Research Resources Available: State and county libraries, libraries at other universities in the area
School-Supported Research Centers: Center for the Study of State Constitutional Law and Government, Center on Alternative Dispute Resolution, Early Settlement Central Mediation Program, Native American Legal Resource Center

EXPENSES/FINANCIAL AID
Annual Tuition: $15,120
Room and Board (On/Off Campus): $6,509/$8,791
Books and Supplies: $750
Average Grant: $4,297
% of Aid That Is Merit-Based: 5
% Receiving Some Sort of Aid: 88
Average Debt: $42,042
Fees Per Credit: $504

ADMISSIONS INFORMATION
Application Fee: $35
Regular Application Deadline: Rolling
Regular Notification: Rolling
LSDAS Accepted? Yes
Average GPA: 2.9
Range of GPA: 2.5–4.0
Average LSAT: 149
Transfer Students Accepted? Yes
Other Admissions Factors Considered: The admissions committee tries to identify the level of motivation, tenacity, and integrity of each applicant through personal statements and letters of recommendation.
Number of Applications Received: 1,445
Number of Applicants Accepted: 796
Number of Applicants Enrolled: 220

INTERNATIONAL STUDENTS
TOEFL Required of International Students? Yes

EMPLOYMENT INFORMATION

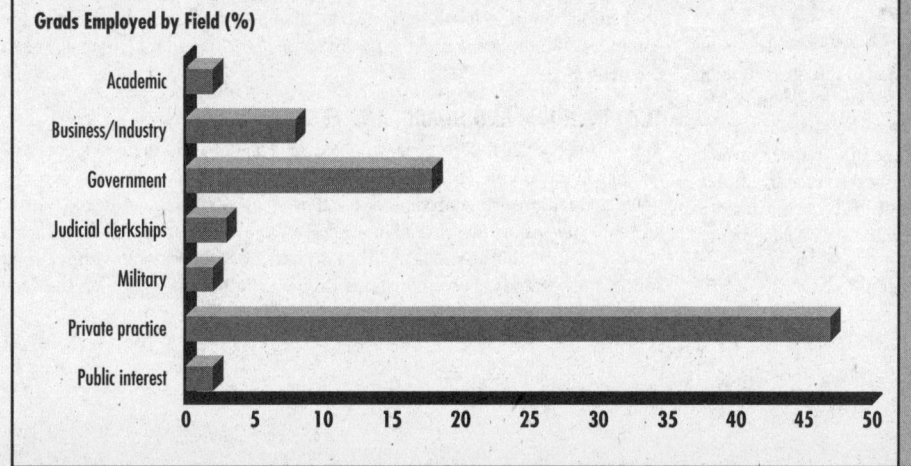

Grads Employed by Field (%)
- Academic: ~1
- Business/Industry: ~8
- Government: ~18
- Judicial clerkships: ~2
- Military: ~1
- Private practice: ~47
- Public interest: ~2

Average Starting Salary: $48,166
Employers Who Frequently Hire Grads: Small to medium-sized law firms, government agencies
State for Bar Exam: OK, TX, FL, KS, MO
Pass Rate for First-Time Bar: 76%

PACE UNIVERSITY

AT A GLANCE
Pace Law School, a division of Pace University, is fully accredited by the American Bar Association and is a member of the Association of American Law Schools. Known for an outstanding Environmental Program and excellent clinical opportunities, Pace also offers over 70 electives, more than those offered at most comparable law schools. The school offers an excellent student/faculty ratio (17:1) and over 60 percent of elective classes have less than 20 students enrolled.

CAMPUS AND LOCATION
Dedicated entirely to Pace's legal program, the White Plains campus houses the Law School's academic facilities, student activities center, and residence hall. The Law School has recently expanded and now includes a new, state-of-the-art classroom building on its sprawling, 12-acre campus. Students are attracted from all over the United States and from abroad. The school is known for its congenial atmosphere, diverse population, and for the closeness that exists between the student body, faculty, and alumni.

Located just 20 miles from New York City, the Law School provides convenient access to metropolitan New York, Connecticut, and New Jersey. White Plains is the headquarters of some of the nation's largest corporations and has a large legal community as well as county, state, and federal courts. This concentration of resources and the Law School's proximity to New York City have enabled Pace to attract highly qualified professors, speakers, and advisors, as well as offering excellent opportunities for internships and employment after graduation.

Pace Law School is soon to be the location for the Judicial Institute of the State of New York, an innovative center for judicial education that will be housed in a state-of-the-art facility on the campus. The $15 million project will be sponsored by the state, and students will participate in a curricular program that will provide opportunities for judicial fellowships. The Institute will be a 27,000-square-foot building with a great hall for public events, a 160-seat auditorium, and three 40-seat classrooms.

DEGREES OFFERED
Pace Law School offers the JD, JD/MBA, JD/MPA, a JD/MEM with Yale University, an LLM and SJD in Environmental Law, and an LLM in Comparative Legal Studies.

PROGRAMS AND CURRICULUM
The programs of the law school are national in perspective. They do not emphasize the law in any state, and are based on the concept that rigorous standards and high-quality teaching can coexist with an atmosphere congenial to learning and enjoyment. Students can obtain Certificates in Environmental Law, International Law, and Health Law by completing a sequence of courses with a specified GPA in the applicable area. Pace offers the opportunity to pursue joint degrees in the JD/MBA and JD/MPA programs. These programs can be completed in four years of full-time study. Part-time evening study is also possible.

The academic program prepares students to practice law competently in any jurisdiction in the United States. The curriculum is designed to give students practical knowledge of the law. The majority of classes have less than 25 students, which enables close faculty-student relationships. The range of scholarship reflects a faculty diverse in interests, and the curriculum offers courses in the traditional areas of legal study and specialized studies. Among the fundamental areas of law covered are Civil Litigation, Civil Procedure, Constitutional Law, Contracts, Corporate Law, Criminal Law and Criminal Practice, Evidence, Family Law, Property, and Torts.

SPECIAL PROGRAMS
The Women's Justice Center is a training, resource, and direct legal services center. Each year the center trains thousands of judges, attorneys, and others who work to eradicate injustice to women. Pace Law students participate in all aspects of the program, including direct representation of clients in family court. The Land Use Law Center teaches students to understand how best to develop and conserve the land. It brings students into the process in their first year of law school in such projects as research and publications, outreach and community service, and project management and technology. The Social Justice Center gives students exposure to public interest lawyering that addresses allegations of discrimination, police abuse of power, and governmental inaction at the community level. The Pace London Law program, in affiliation with University College Faculty of Laws, University of London, provides both an academic and an internship experience during the spring semester for 30 to 40 students from Pace and other law schools.

Direct representation clinics are designed and structured to enable students to take their extensive classroom training and make the transition to representing clients or prosecuting charges. They allow students to take full responsibility for their own caseload under the direct supervision of a full-time faculty member. Externship programs are also available and are clinical courses in which fieldwork is conducted under the supervision of practicing attorneys who are not full-time members of the faculty. Simulation courses give students the opportunity to learn specific components of lawyering work, including written and oral advocacy, interviewing and counseling clients, negotiation, analyzing a trial record, developing strategy, open and closing arguments, selecting a jury and drafting jury instructions, and witness preparation and examination.

LIBRARY AND PHYSICAL FACILITIES
Pace Law School's campus in White Plains features green space, student housing, recreational facilities and on-site parking. The centerpiece of the campus is a new $10 million classroom building, which joins four other buildings. The five classrooms in this three-story facility feature horseshoe-shaped seating with raised tiers designed to promote interaction between teachers and students. Each classroom is equipped for audio-visual and computer presentations and is capable of supporting computer-wired desks. Wide corridors on each of the three floors accommodate computer-wired work and lounge stations. Special moot courtrooms for the Trial Advocacy program and a fully connected distance-learning classroom are housed in adjoining Aloysia Hall.

The Pace Law Library is housed in an airy, modern facility, the Glass Law Center. The Law Library contains over 345,000 volumes of law and law-related publications, provides access to materials in other libraries in metropolitan New York and throughout the United States, and subscribes to national online research systems such as LEXIS/NEXIS, WESTLAW, and DIALOG. Pace Law students have free access to these databases from computer terminals distributed throughout the law library, in the student lounge and from their home computers. Study carrels and the student lounges are wired for laptop access to the network.

TUITION, ROOM AND BOARD, AND FEES
Tuition for the 2001–2002 year was $25,294. Dannat Hall, the residence center, has been completely renovated with rooms for 100 single, full-time students and features single rooms with Ethernet access, telephones, voice mail, and cable television. A variety of housing is available off campus in White Plains and the surrounding area. The Admissions Office assists students with securing suitable off-campus accommodations through the housing pages on the Law School's Web page.

Pace Law School

EXPENSES & FINANCIAL AID
A comprehensive aid program has been developed to include scholarships, need-based grants, employment, loans, and a loan forgiveness program for graduates who choose a public interest career. In 2001, the Law School established a number of new scholarships targeted toward first-year students interested in specific areas of the law such as Health, International, Environmental, Land Use, Social Justice, and Women's Justice. Funds are available based on a variety of criteria, including financial need, academic merit, education costs, or credit considerations.

FACULTY
The Law School includes 119 total faculty members, of whom 44 are full time and 75 are adjunct. Faculty scholarship covers fundamental areas of law such as Civil Litigation, Civil Procedure, Constitutional Law, Contracts, Evidence, Family Law, Federalism and Separation of Powers, Federal Jurisdiction, Federal Law and Procedure, Property, and Torts. Also covered are specialized areas of the law such as the Americans with Disabilities Act, Cable Franchising and Regulations, Children's Legal Representation, Environmental and Toxic Torts, Equal Pay, Hazardous Waste, Health Care Fraud, International Commercial Law, Land Use, Law of the Sea, Legal and Ethical Issues in Health Care, Non-profit Organizations, Prosecutorial and Judicial Ethics, Racially Motivated Violence, Securities Fraud, and White Collar Crime. Many of the faculty members are authors of widely circulated legal textbooks and books influential in the profession and are drafters of ground-breaking state laws.

STUDENTS
The entering class of 2000 was a diverse group, representing 23 states including Arizona, Puerto Rico, Michigan, Massachusetts, Rhode Island, California, Texas, Tennessee, Georgia, Florida, New York, New Jersey, and Connecticut as well as Canada and Japan. The average age for the full-time class was 23 and the part-time class was 31. There were over 130 undergraduate schools represented and a 18 percent minority population.

ADMISSIONS
At Pace, as at many law schools, the most important admissions criteria are the undergraduate grade point average (GPA) and the Law School Admissions Test. Reliance on these purely academic criteria is appropriate in making many decisions. Other factors, such as interpreting the GPA by carefully evaluating an applicant's transcript to determine the strength of the curriculum, or the quality of the institution at which undergraduate work was done, are also considered. Class rank and the progression of grades may be significant where there has been an interval of some years between college graduation and application to law school. Proven capacity for leadership; dedication to community service; excellence in a particular field; ethnic, socio-economic, and cultural background; motivation; graduate study in another discipline; work experience; and extracurricular activities all receive careful consideration in appropriate cases.

Approximately 130 students enter the three-year day program and 100 students enter the part-time day and evening programs. The average LSAT and GPA for students offered admissions is a 154 and 3.2.

STUDENT ACTIVITIES
Pace Law School publishes three law reviews, the *Pace Law Review*, the *Pace Environmental Law Review*, and the *Pace International Law Review*. Students compete in interscholastic moot court competitions and Pace hosts the largest environmental moot court competition in the country. The school offers more than 30 organizations in which students can participate. Available activities include professional organizations, minority student groups, issue-centered organizations, political groups, social action groups, religious groups, a student bar association, and a student newspaper. For a complete list of student organizations, please visit Pace's website at www.law.pace.edu.

CAREER SERVICES
Through a variety of outreach activities, the Office of Career Development actively solicits job listings for part-time, summer, and permanent positions after graduation as well as full-time jobs for evening students while they are in school. In addition to regularly contacting legal employers through mailings and surveys regarding immediate hiring needs, visits with law firms and other organizations are scheduled throughout the year to establish and maintain relationships that result in the receipt of additional job notices. Respondents to the 2000 graduating class survey reported 92 percent employment within the six months following graduation.

78 North Broadway, White Plains, NY 10603
Admissions Phone: 914-422-4210
Admissions E-mail: admissions@law.pace.edu
Web Address: www.law.pace.edu

PACE UNIVERSITY
School of Law

Admissions Contact: Director of Admissions, Cathy M. Alexander
78 North Broadway, White Plains, NY 10603
Admissions Phone: 914-422-4210 • Admissions Fax: 914-422-4010
Admissions E-mail: admissions@law.pace.edu • Web Address: www.law.pace.edu

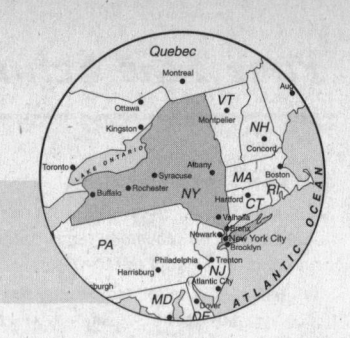

INSTITUTIONAL INFORMATION
Public/Private: Private
Student/Faculty Ratio: 16:1
Total Faculty: 75
% Part Time: 52
% Female: 37
% Minority: 5

PROGRAMS
Academic Specialties: Environmental Law, Health Law, International Law, Legal Analysis and Writing, clinical education
Advanced Degrees Offered: SJD Environmental Law (1 year), LLM Environmental Law (1 to 2 years), LLM Comparative Legal Studies (1 year)
Combined Degrees Offered: JD/MBA (4 to 6 years), JD/MPA (4 to 6 years), JD/MEM (4 to 6 years)
Grading System: A, A–, B+, B, B–, C+, C, C-, D, F; some courses graded P (pass) or F (fail).
Clinical Program Required? No
Clinical Programs Description: Appellate Litigation Clinic, Criminal Defense Clinic, Equal Justice American Disability Rights Clinic, Environmental Litigation Clinic, Prosecution of Domestic Violence Clinic, Securities Arbitration Clinic
Legal Writing Course Requirements? Yes
Legal Writing Description: Criminal Law Analysis and Writing I and II is an integrated 2-semester, 6-credit course that explores the substantive aspects of criminal law through legal analysis and writing. Students learn about the criminalization decision, goals of punishment, elements of criminal conduct, and defenses to criminal charges by reading statutes and using and distinguishing cases. Students also learn about legal research and the legislative process, and complete numerous writing exercises in the area of criminal law. This course finishes with students writing an appellate brief and arguing before a moot court.
Legal Methods Course Requirements? Yes
Legal Methods Description: See Legal Writing.
Legal Research Course Requirements? No
Moot Court Requirement? Yes
Moot Court Description: See Legal Writing.
Public Interest Law Requirement? No
Academic Journals: *Pace Law Review, Pace Environmental Law Review, Pace International Law Review*

STUDENT INFORMATION
Enrollment of Law School: 723
% Out of State: 60
% Male/Female: 40/60
% Full Time: 56
% Full Time That Are International: 1
% Minority: 18
Average Age of Entering Class: 27

RESEARCH FACILITIES
Research Resources Available: Westlaw, Lexis/Nexis, Dialog, e-mail, Virtual Law Library
School-Supported Research Centers: Pace Women's Justice Center, Pace Land Use Law Center, Pace Social Justice Center, Pace Energy Project, Pace Institute of International Commercial Law

EXPENSES/FINANCIAL AID
Annual Tuition: $25,294
Room and Board (On/Off Campus): $9,600/$10,200
Books and Supplies: $1,000
Financial Aid Application Deadline: 2/1
Average Grant: $10,800
Average Loan: $22,390
% of Aid That Is Merit-Based: 65
% Receiving Some Sort of Aid: 84
Average Total Aid Package: $24,220
Average Debt: $66,330

ADMISSIONS INFORMATION
Application Fee: $55
Regular Application Deadline: 2/15
Regular Notification: Rolling
LSDAS Accepted? Yes
Average GPA: 3.1
Average LSAT: 152
Transfer Students Accepted? Yes
Other Schools to Which Students Applied: Touro College, Hofstra University, St. John's University, New York Law School, Brooklyn Law School, Fordham University, Seton Hall University
Other Admissions Factors Considered: Undergraduate coursework, community service
Number of Applications Received: 1,794
Number of Applicants Accepted: 819
Number of Applicants Enrolled: 229

INTERNATIONAL STUDENTS
TOEFL Required of International Students? Yes
Minimum TOEFL: 250

EMPLOYMENT INFORMATION

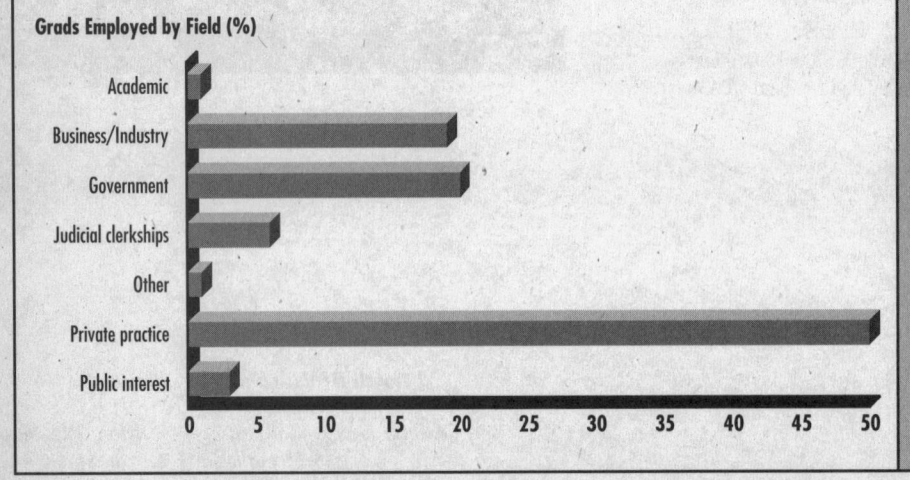

Grads Employed by Field (%)

Field	%
Academic	~1
Business/Industry	~20
Government	~20
Judicial clerkships	~5
Other	~2
Private practice	~50
Public interest	~3

Rate of Placement: 90%
Average Starting Salary: $60,552
Employers Who Frequently Hire Grads: Large law firms, large corporations, government and public interest offices
State for Bar Exam: NY, CT, NJ, PA, DC

PENNSYLVANIA STATE UNIVERSITY
The Dickinson School of Law

Admissions Contact: Director, Law Admissions, Barbara Guillaume
150 South College Street, Carlisle, PA 17013
Admissions Phone: 717-240-5207 • Admissions Fax: 717-241-3503
Admissions E-mail: dsladmit@psu.edu • Web Address: www.dsl.psu.edu

INSTITUTIONAL INFORMATION
Public/Private: Public
Student/Faculty Ratio: 19:1
Total Faculty: 88
% Part Time: 59
% Female: 23
% Minority: 2

PROGRAMS
Academic Specialties: Comparative and International Law, Advocacy, Corporate and Commercial Law, Clinical Education, Civil Procedure, Constitutional Law, Corporation Securities Law, Criminal Law, Environmental Law, Human Rights Law, Labor Law, Property, Taxation
Advanced Degrees Offered: JD (3 years), LLM Comparative Law (1 year)
Combined Degrees Offered: JD/MBA with Smeal College of Business Administration; JD/MBA, JD/MPA, JD and 3 Environmental Pollution Control degrees, all with Penn State Harrisburg; JD/MSIS with Penn State Harrisburg
Grading System: Distinguished (90 and above), Excellent (89–85), Good (84–80), Satisfactory (79–75), Passing (74–70), Conditional Failure (69–65), Failure (below 65)
Clinical Program Required? No
Clinical Program Description: Family Law; Disability Law; Art, Sports and Entertainment Law; externships in judges' chambers, district attorneys' and public defenders' offices, government agencies, legal services offices

Legal Writing Course Requirements? Yes
Legal Writing Description: Lawyering Skills (first-year, 2 semesters) involves teaching skills such as research, analysis of cases and statutes, writing of legal memoranda and briefs, and oral argument.
Legal Methods Course Requirements? Yes
Legal Methods Description: 2 semesters, involves small-group instruction
Legal Research Course Requirements? Yes
Legal Research Description: See Legal Writing above.
Moot Court Requirement? Yes
Moot Court Description: Fall semester, second year
Public Interest Law Requirement? No
Academic Journals: *Dickinson Law Review*, *Dickinson Journal of Environmental Law & Policy*, *Dickinson Journal of International Law*

STUDENT INFORMATION
Enrollment of Law School: 532
% Out of State: 26
% Male/Female: 57/43
% Full Time: 99
% Full Time That Are International: 1
% Minority: 8
Average Age of Entering Class: 25

RESEARCH FACILITIES
Research Resources Available: All Penn State libraries and libraries of Big Ten; Lexis, Westlaw, Loislaw, and member libraries of Association of College Libraries of Central Pennsylvania Consortium
% of JD Classrooms Wired: 75

EXPENSES/FINANCIAL AID
Annual Tuition: $17,160
Room and Board (On/Off Campus): $6,200/$7,700
Books and Supplies: $800
Financial Aid Application Deadline: 2/15
Average Grant: $5,779
Average Loan: $21,762
% of Aid That Is Merit-Based: 14
% Receiving Some Sort of Aid: 82
Average Total Aid Package: $24,489
Average Debt: $55,376

ADMISSIONS INFORMATION
Application Fee: $50
Regular Application Deadline: 3/1
Regular Notification: Rolling
LSDAS Accepted? Yes
Average GPA: 3.3
Range of GPA: 3.1–3.6
Average LSAT: 154
Range of LSAT: 151–157
Transfer Students Accepted? Yes
Other Schools to Which Students Applied: Temple University, University of Pittsburgh, Villanova University, Widener University
Other Admissions Factors Considered: Evidence of maturity, leadership, and initiative
Number of Applications Received: 1,803
Number of Applicants Accepted: 831
Number of Applicants Enrolled: 183

EMPLOYMENT INFORMATION

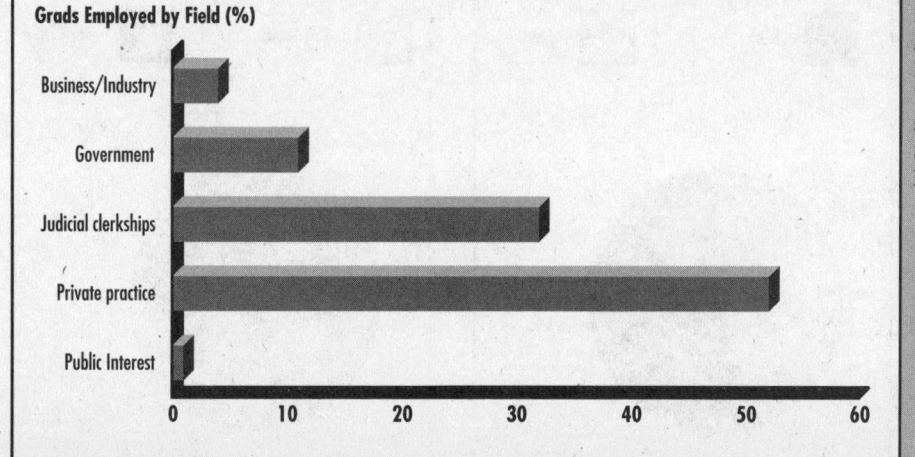

Grads Employed by Field (%)

Field	%
Business/Industry	~3
Government	~11
Judicial clerkships	~32
Private practice	~53
Public Interest	~1

Rate of Placement: 91%
Average Starting Salary: $49,529
Employers Who Frequently Hire Grads: Leading law firms, smaller firms, federal and state judges
State for Bar Exam: PA, NJ, NY, DE, VA
Pass Rate for First-Time Bar: 84%

PEPPERDINE UNIVERSITY
School of Law

Admissions Contact: Director of Admissions, Ms. Shannon Phillips
24255 Pacific Coast Highway, Malibu, CA 90263
Admissions Phone: 310-456-4631 • Admissions Fax: 310-317-1668
Admissions E-mail: soladmis@pepperdine.edu • Web Address: law.pepperdine.edu

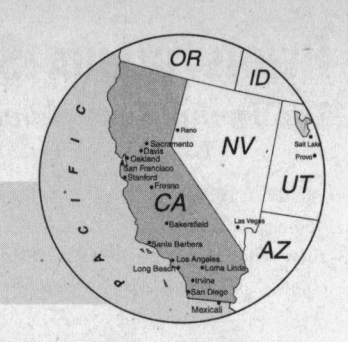

INSTITUTIONAL INFORMATION
Public/Private: Private
Affiliation: Church Of Christ
Environment: Urban
Academic Calendar: Semester
Schedule: Full time only
Student/Faculty Ratio: 20:1
Total Faculty: 77
% Female: 27
% Minority: 9

PROGRAMS
Grading System: Letter and numerical system on a 100 to 55 point scale; students must maintain a 72 average to remain in good standing
Clinical Program Required? No
Clinical Program Description: Public Interest Dispute Resolution, Commercial and International Dispute Resolution, Domestic Relations Dispute Resolution, Dispute Resolution in Education
Legal Writing/Methods Course Requirements: Identification, description, and use of source materials for the solution of legal problems; introduction to the law library and its use. Each student will be required to produce one or more papers dealing with approved legal subjects and to engage in oral argument thereon.

STUDENT INFORMATION
Enrollment of Law School: 652
% Male/Female: 55/45
% Full Time: 100
% Full Time That Are International: 1
% Minority: 16
Average Age of Entering Class: 23

EXPENSES/FINANCIAL AID
Annual Tuition: $23,810
Room and Board: $10,004
Books and Supplies: $700
Average Grant: $8,975
Average Loan: $24,560
% of Aid That Is Merit-Based: 60
% Receiving Some Sort of Aid: 84
Average Total Aid Package: $32,000
Average Debt: $74,515
Tuition Per Credit: $845
Fees Per Credit: $730

ADMISSIONS INFORMATION
Application Fee: $50
Regular Application Deadline: 3/1
Regular Notification: Rolling
LSDAS Accepted? Yes
Average GPA: 3.3
Range of GPA: 3.0–3.5
Average LSAT: 157
Range of LSAT: 154–160
Transfer Students Accepted? Yes
Other Schools to Which Students Applied: UCLA School of Law, Loyola Marymount University, University of Southern California, University of San Diego, Southwestern University, Santa Clara University, University of California—Hastings, Whittier College
Other Admissions Factors Considered: Community service, work experience
Number of Applications Received: 1,176

INTERNATIONAL STUDENTS
TOEFL Required of International Students? Yes

EMPLOYMENT INFORMATION
Rate of Placement: 92%
Average Starting Salary: $64,234
Employers Who Frequently Hire Grads: Gibson, Dunn & Crutcher; Latham & Watkins; Jones, Day, Reavis, & Pogue; McKenna & Cuneo; Los Angeles and Ventura County District Attorney's Offices and various other law firms and governmental agencies
Prominent Alumni: James K. Hahn, city attorney of Los Angeles; Terry Giles, trial lawyer, youngest person to be admitted to Horatio Alger Society; Mark Hiepler, trial lawyer, tried and received jury verdicts in significant cases against Health Maintenance Organizations

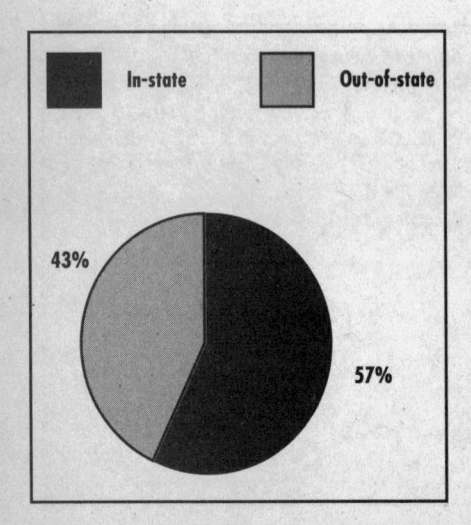

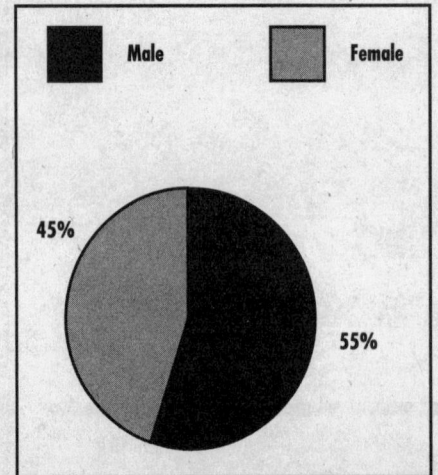

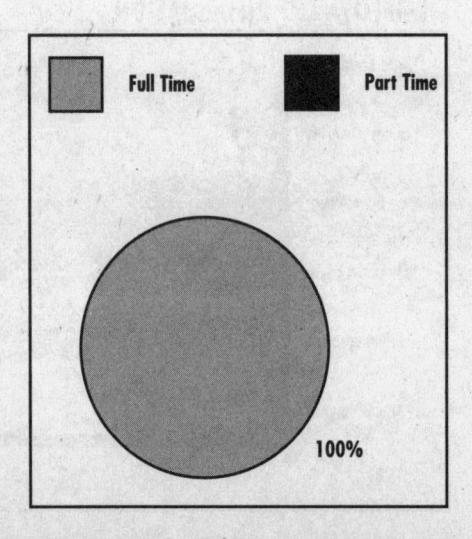

In-state 57% / Out-of-state 43%

Male 55% / Female 45%

Full Time 100%

QUEEN'S UNIVERSITY
Faculty of Law

Admissions Contact: Registrar of Law, Jane Emrich
Macdonald Hall, Union Street, Queen's University, Kingston, ON K7L 3N6 Canada
Admissions Phone: 613-533-2220 • Admissions Fax: 613-533-6611
Admissions E-mail: llb@qsilver.queensu.ca • Web Address: qsilver.queensu.ca/law/

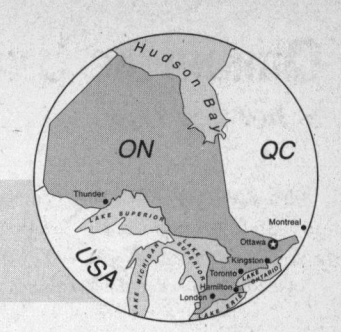

INSTITUTIONAL INFORMATION
Public/Private: Public
Student/Faculty Ratio: 7:1
Total Faculty: 70
% Part Time: 61
% Female: 34

PROGRAMS
Academic Specialties: Queen's has a leading reputation in Criminal Law, Labor Law, Family Law, Public Law, and Feminist Legal Studies with additional strong programs in Constitutional Law, Tax Law, Corporate Law, Health Law, International Law, Alternative Dispute Resolution, Civil Procedure, Commercial Law, Constitutional Law, Corporation Securities Law, Environmental Law, Government Services, Human Rights Law, Intellectual Property Law, International Law, Legal History, Legal Philosophy, and Property.
Advanced Degrees Offered: LLM (12 months)
Combined Degrees Offered: LLB/MIR (4 years), LLB/MPA (4 years)
Grading System: A (exceptional), A– (excellent), B+ (very good), B (good), B– (satisfactory), C+ (fair), C (adequate), D (marginal), F (failure), PA (pass), ED (exam deferred), IP (in progress)
Clinical Program Required? Yes
Clinical Programs Description: Clinical Correctional Law, Clinical Litigation, Clinical Family; practice skills degree requirement can be satisfied by completion of clinical programs and other related courses
Legal Writing Course Requirements? Yes
Legal Writing Description: First-Year Skills Introduction course introduces students to legal education and legal skills, with particular emphasis on legal research and writing; upper-level students must complete at least one substantial term paper
Legal Methods Course Requirements? Yes
Legal Methods Description: Students may fulfill this requirement either by taking a Practice Skills course, in which they undertake legal research and develop skills of drafting, client interaction, oral advocacy, negotiation, or mediation or by completing a clinical legal experience.
Legal Research Course Requirements? No
Moot Court Requirement? Yes
Moot Court Description: In order to satisfy the Moot Court Requirement, a student must successfully complete one of the following in his or her second year: a Faculty Moot, a Competitive Moot, or an upper-year course certified by the instructor as satisfying the Faculty's Moot Court Requirement.
Public Interest Law Requirement? Yes
Public Interest Law Description: In addition to Civil Procedure, each student must complete an upper-year course with a significant legal ethics element.
Academic Journals: *Queen's Law Journal*

STUDENT INFORMATION
Enrollment of Law School: 488
% Male/Female: 100/0
% Full Time: 100
% Minority: 0
Average Age of Entering Class: 25

RESEARCH FACILITIES
Research Resources Available: William R. Lederman Law Library, Electronic Law Library, numerous computer workstations and Internet connections, wide range of academic exchange programs with universities across Canada and abroad

EXPENSES/FINANCIAL AID
Annual Tuition: $3,657
Books and Supplies: $690

ADMISSIONS INFORMATION
Application Fee: $150
Regular Application Deadline: 11/1
Regular Notification: Rolling
LSDAS Accepted? No
Average LSAT: 159
Range of LSAT: 154–169
Transfer Students Accepted? Yes
Other Schools to Which Students Applied: University of Toronto, York University, University of Windsor, University of British Columbia, McGill University, University of Calgary, Dalhousie
Other Admissions Factors Considered: Interviews are not part of the admissions process, but admissions officers will meet with applicants upon request to answer questions about the programs.
Number of Applications Received: 1,893
Number of Applicants Accepted: 595
Number of Applicants Enrolled: 163

INTERNATIONAL STUDENTS
TOEFL Required of International Students? Yes

QUINNIPIAC UNIVERSITY
School of Law

Admissions Contact: Dean of Law School Admissions, John J. Noonan
275 Mount Carmel Avenue, Hamden, CT 06518-1950
Admissions Phone: 203-582-3400 • Admissions Fax: 203-582-3339
Admissions E-mail: ladm@quinnipiac.edu • Web Address: law.quinnipiac.edu

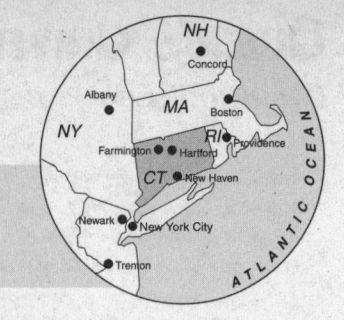

INSTITUTIONAL INFORMATION
Public/Private: Private
Student/Faculty Ratio: 16:1
Total Faculty: 90
% Part Time: 51
% Female: 32
% Minority: 5

PROGRAMS
Academic Specialties: Quinnipiac University School of Law offers a rich curriculum, with specialized practice courses, skills training, and hands-on experience. Specialties include Civil Procedure, Commercial Law, Corporation Securities Law, Criminal Law, International Law, and Taxation.
Advanced Degrees Offered: JD (3 years full time, 4 years part time)
Combined Degrees Offered: JD/MBA (4 years), JD/MHA (4 years)
Grading System: Letter grades with quality point equivalent based upon a 4.0 scale
Clinical Program Required? No
Clinical Programs Description: Civic Clinic, Appellate Clinic, Health Law Clinic, Tax Clinic
Legal Writing Course Requirements? Yes
Legal Writing Description: Year-long course trains students in the fundamentals of legal writing, analysis, and research
Legal Methods Course Requirements? No
Legal Research Course Requirements? No
Moot Court Requirement? No
Public Interest Law Requirement? No
Academic Journals: Quinnipiac Law Review, Health Law Journal, Probate Law Journal

STUDENT INFORMATION
Enrollment of Law School: 188
% Out of State: 48
% Male/Female: 53/47
% Full Time: 71
% Full Time That Are International: 1
% Minority: 11
Average Age of Entering Class: 26

RESEARCH FACILITIES
Research Resources Available: Lexis, Westlaw, CALI, digital video production and editing

EXPENSES/FINANCIAL AID
Annual Tuition: $26,550
Room and Board (Off Campus): $10,715
Books and Supplies: $1,000
Average Grant: $7,500
Average Loan: $19,265
% of Aid That Is Merit-Based: 40
% Receiving Some Sort of Aid: 87
Average Total Aid Package: $20,000
Average Debt: $65,100
Tuition Per Credit: $885

ADMISSIONS INFORMATION
Application Fee: $40
Regular Application Deadline: Rolling
Regular Notification: Rolling
LSDAS Accepted? Yes
Average GPA: 2.9
Range of GPA: 2.6–3.4
Average LSAT: 150
Range of LSAT: 147–153
Transfer Students Accepted? Yes
Other Admissions Factors Considered: Personal statement, recommendations, interview (optional)
Number of Applications Received: 2,017
Number of Applicants Accepted: 670
Number of Applicants Enrolled: 188

EMPLOYMENT INFORMATION

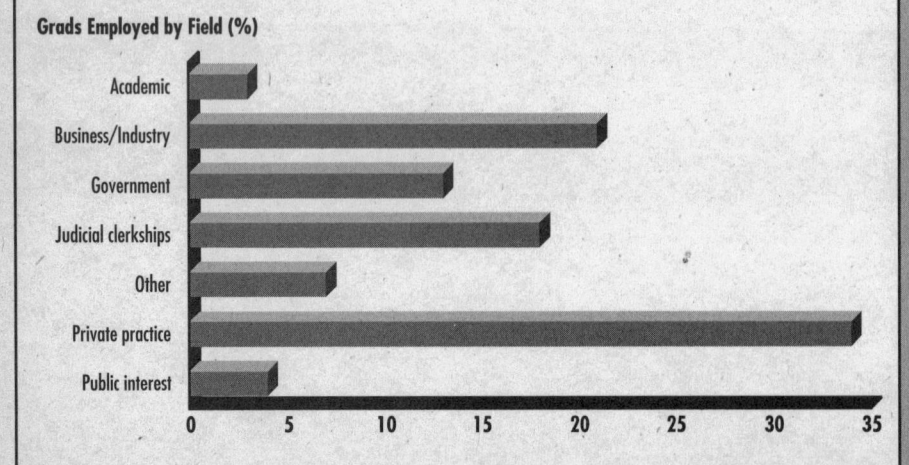

Grads Employed by Field (%)

Field	%
Academic	~2
Business/Industry	~21
Government	~13
Judicial clerkships	~18
Other	~7
Private practice	~35
Public interest	~4

Rate of Placement: 95%
Average Starting Salary: $50,655
Employers Who Frequently Hire Grads: Law firms, corporations, public defenders' offices, prosecutors' offices, various government and public interest organizations
State for Bar Exam: CT, NY, NJ, MA, RI
Pass Rate for First-Time Bar: 78%

REGENT UNIVERSITY
School of Law

Admissions Contact: Assistant to the Director of Admissions and Financial Aid, Marie Markham
1000 Regent University Drive, Virginia Beach, VA 23464
Admissions Phone: 757-226-4584 • Admissions Fax: 757-226-4139
Admissions E-mail: lawschool@regent.edu • Web Address: www.regent.edu/acad/schlaw/admit/home.html

INSTITUTIONAL INFORMATION
Public/Private: Private
Student/Faculty Ratio: 19:1
Total Faculty: 27
% Part Time: 0
% Female: 22
% Minority: 22

PROGRAMS
Academic Specialties: The opportunity to work alongside attorneys for the American Center for Law and Justice, one of the nation's foremost public interest law firms, in developing legal strategies to defend life, liberty and family; the opportunity for selected third-year students to meet regularly with federal and state judges, leading attorneys, and law faculty in the James Kent American Inn of Court to discuss ethical and practical concerns related to the practice of law.
Combined Degrees Offered: JD/MBA, JD/MPA (4 years), JD/MPP (4 years), JD/Masters of Political Management (4 years), JD/MAM (4 years), JD/MA in Counseling (4 years), JD/MA in Communication (4 years)
Grading System: A+ (4.00), A (4.00), A– (3.67), B+ (3.33), B (3.00), B– (2.67), C+ (2.33), C (2.00), C– (1.67), D+ (1.33), D (1.00), D– (0.67), F (0.00)
Clinical Program Required? No
Clinical Programs Description: Litigation Clinic, Family Mediation Clinic
Legal Writing Course Requirements? Yes
Legal Writing Description: The required Legal Research and Writing Program consists of 2 sequential, 3-hour courses in the first year that prepare students in the area of legal reasoning, research, and brief writing. All legal writing courses are taught by full-time instructors or by the director of the Legal Writing Program. An oral advocacy portion is taught in conjunction with the Moot Court Board.
Legal Methods Course Requirements? Yes
Legal Methods Description: See Legal Writing.
Legal Research Course Requirements? Yes
Legal Research Description: The Legal Research component of the Legal Research and Writing Program includes information on the state and federal court systems, reporters, finding tools, and basic jurisdictional issues. It also includes intensive lectures on 5 basic areas of legal research: secondary sources, finding common law, researching state statutes, researching federal statutes, and researching administrative law. During the second semester, students write a trial brief and an appellate brief.
Moot Court Requirement? Yes
Moot Court Description: The annual Moot Court Competition is an integral component of the first-year legal writing curriculum. Students argue 2 rounds of the competition and may proceed to later rounds if the quality of their argument warrants.
Public Interest Law Requirement? No
Academic Journals: *Regent Law Review, Journal of Maritime Law and International Trade, Regent Journal of International Law, Journal of Entertainment, Sports and Intellectual Property*

STUDENT INFORMATION
Enrollment of Law School: 475
% Male/Female: 52/48
% Full Time: 77
% Minority: 26
Average Age of Entering Class: 29

EXPENSES/FINANCIAL AID
Annual Tuition: $17,050
Room and Board (Off Campus): $6,111
Books and Supplies: $1,120
Financial Aid Application Deadline: 6/2
Average Grant: $5,372
Average Loan: $18,786
% of Aid That Is Merit-Based: 29
% Receiving Some Sort of Aid: 97
Average Total Aid Package: $29,949
Average Debt: $59,525
Tuition Per Credit: $550
Fees Per Credit: $64

ADMISSIONS INFORMATION
Application Fee: $40
Regular Application Deadline: 6/1
Regular Notification: Rolling
LSDAS Accepted? Yes
Average GPA: 3.0
Range of GPA: 2.7–3.4
Average LSAT: 149
Range of LSAT: 145–154
Transfer Students Accepted? Yes
Other Admissions Factors Considered: Compatibility with the mission of the law school
Number of Applications Received: 546
Number of Applicants Accepted: 317
Number of Applicants Enrolled: 170

INTERNATIONAL STUDENTS
TOEFL Required of International Students? Yes

EMPLOYMENT INFORMATION

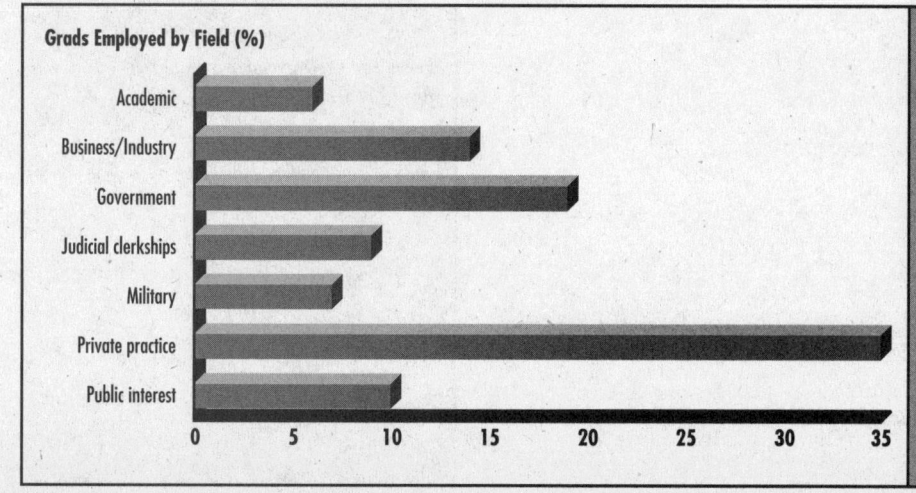

Grads Employed by Field (%)
- Academic: ~6
- Business/Industry: ~14
- Government: ~19
- Judicial clerkships: ~6
- Military: ~6
- Private practice: ~35
- Public interest: ~10

Rate of Placement: 87%
Average Starting Salary: $39,883
Employers Who Frequently Hire Grads: American Center for Law and Justice; Bopp, Coleson & Bostrom; U.S. Air Force JAG Corps; U.S. Army JAG Corps; Law Office of David McCormick; Portsmouth Commonwealth's Attorney; Virginia Beach Public Defender; Lexis/Nexis; Winters, King & Associates, Inc.; Smink, Thomas & Associates, P.C.
State for Bar Exam: VA, NC, TX, CA, FL

ROGER WILLIAMS UNIVERSITY
Ralph R. Papitto School of Law

Admissions Contact: Dean of Admissions, Christel Ertel
10 Metacom Avenue, Bristol, RI 02809
Admissions Phone: 401-254-4555 • Admissions Fax: 401-254-4516
Admissions E-mail: admissions@rwulaw.rwu.edu • Web Address: law.rwu.edu

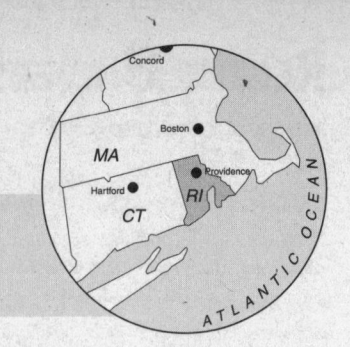

INSTITUTIONAL INFORMATION
Public/Private: Private
Student/Faculty Ratio: 15:1
Total Faculty: 39
% Part Time: 41
% Female: 38
% Minority: 7

PROGRAMS
Academic Specialties: Extensive Maritime Law Program, special emphasis on Intellectual Property Law and Labor Law; other specialties include Commercial Law, Constitutional Law, Corporation Securities Law, Criminal Law, Environmental Law, International Law, Legal History, and summer study abroad programs in London and Lisbon
Advanced Degrees Offered: JD (3 years full time, 4 years part time)
Combined Degrees Offered: JD/MCP (4 years), JD/MMA (3.5 years), JD/MS Labor Relations and Human Resources (4 years)
Grading System: A to F (4.0–0.0)
Clinical Program Required? No
Clinical Programs Description: Third-year students may participate in 2 clinics in Providence, a Family Law Clinic and a Criminal Defense Clinic. Under Rhode Island law, students are able to represent their clients in court.
Legal Writing Course Requirements? No
Legal Methods Course Requirements? Yes
Legal Methods Description: 4 separate courses over the first 2 years of law school: Analysis, Research, and Writing; Appellate Advocacy; Interviewing and Client Counseling; and Trial Advocacy
Legal Research Course Requirements? No
Moot Court Requirement? No
Public Interest Law Requirement? Yes
Public Interest Law Description: 20 hours of community service
Academic Journals: *Roger Williams University Law Review*

STUDENT INFORMATION
Enrollment of Law School: 365
% Out of State: 67
% Male/Female: 50/50
% Full Time: 64
% Full Time That Are International: 0
% Minority: 10
Average Age of Entering Class: 28

EXPENSES/FINANCIAL AID
Annual Tuition: $22,200
Room and Board: $12,900
Books and Supplies: $1,000
Financial Aid Application Deadline: 5/15
Average Grant: $5,605
Average Loan: $23,443
% of Aid That Is Merit-Based: 66
% Receiving Some Sort of Aid: 95
Average Total Aid Package: $25,619
Average Debt: $74,557
Tuition Per Credit: $740

ADMISSIONS INFORMATION
Application Fee: $60
Regular Application Deadline: Rolling
Regular Notification: Rolling
LSDAS Accepted? Yes
Average GPA: 3.0
Range of GPA: 2.7–3.3
Average LSAT: 148
Range of LSAT: 145–153
Transfer Students Accepted? Yes
Other Admissions Factors Considered: Graduate work
Number of Applications Received: 711
Number of Applicants Accepted: 384
Number of Applicants Enrolled: 134

INTERNATIONAL STUDENTS
TOEFL Required of International Students? Yes

EMPLOYMENT INFORMATION

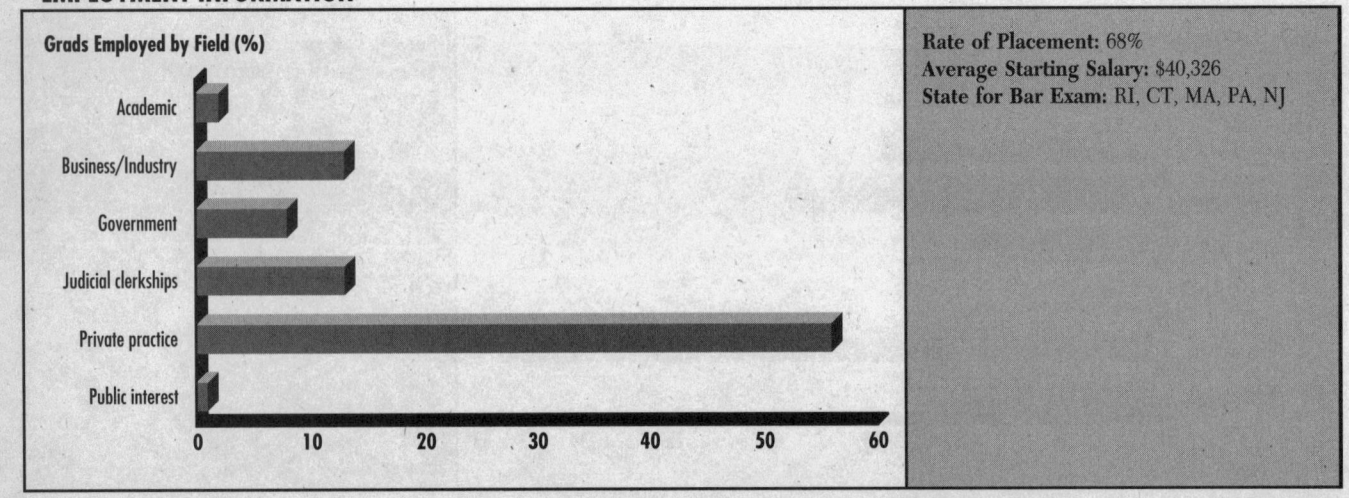

Grads Employed by Field (%):
- Academic
- Business/Industry
- Government
- Judicial clerkships
- Private practice
- Public interest

Rate of Placement: 68%
Average Starting Salary: $40,326
State for Bar Exam: RI, CT, MA, PA, NJ

RUTGERS UNIVERSITY — CAMDEN
Rutgers School of Law at Camden

Admissions Contact: Assistant Director of Admissions, Maureen O'Boyle
406 Penn Street, 3rd floor, Camden, NJ 08102
Admissions Phone: 800-466-7561 • Admissions Fax: 856-225-6537
Admissions E-mail: admissions@camlaw.rutgers.edu • Web Address: www-camden.rutgers.edu/

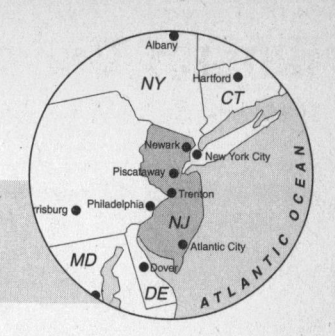

INSTITUTIONAL INFORMATION
Public/Private: Public
Student/Faculty Ratio: 6:1
Total Faculty: 121
% Part Time: 58
% Female: 31
% Minority: 9

PROGRAMS
Academic Specialties: International and Comparative Law, Commercial Law, Family Law and Domestic Violence, Health Law, Lawyering Skills, Advocacy, Constitutional Law, Corporation Securities Law, Criminal Law, Environmental Law, Labor Law, Taxation, and Litigation
Advanced Degrees Offered: JD (3 years full time, 4 years part time)
Combined Degrees Offered: JD/MBA (4 years), JD/MPA (4 years), JD/MSW (4 years), JD/MSPP (3.5 years), JD/MCRP (4 years), JD/MD and JD/DO with University of Medicine and Dentistry of New Jersey, JD/MPA Health Care Management and Policy (4 years)
Grading System: A+ to F with plus and minus
Clinical Program Required? No
Clinical Programs Description: Civil practice clinics, including a live-client clinic that represents elderly and disabled clients, as well as a clinic for children and their families who seek free education and related services. Students also participate in Domestic Violence, Mediation, Bankruptcy, Legal Education, and Income Tax assistance pro bono programs.
Legal Writing Course Requirements? Yes
Legal Writing Description: All students must complete legal writing credits in each year of study.
Legal Methods Course Requirements? Yes
Legal Methods Description: Required year-long, first-year course covering research, analysis, writing, and oral advocacy. The school also has a unique upper-level writing requirement, in which every student takes an average of 1 intensive writing course every semester.
Legal Research Course Requirements? No
Legal Research Description: First-year students are required to take Legal Research and Writing during their first semester.
Moot Court Requirement? Yes
Moot Court Description: Required Moot Court during spring semester of first year
Public Interest Law Requirement? No
Academic Journals: *Rutgers Law Journal, Rutgers Journal of Law and Religion*

STUDENT INFORMATION
Enrollment of Law School: 756
% Out of State: 40
% Male/Female: 51/49
% Full Time: 73
% Full Time That Are International: 1
% Minority: 20
Average Age of Entering Class: 26

EXPENSES/FINANCIAL AID
Annual Tuition (Residents/Nonresidents): $11,394/$16,600
Room and Board (On Campus): $4,796
Books and Supplies: $1,000
Financial Aid Application Deadline: 4/1
Average Grant: $5,000
Average Loan: $15,000
% of Aid That Is Merit-Based: 20
% Receiving Some Sort of Aid: 83
Average Total Aid Package: $18,000
Average Debt: $50,000
Tuition Per Credit (Residents/Nonresidents): $472/$691
Fees Per Credit: $28

ADMISSIONS INFORMATION
Application Fee: $50
Regular Application Deadline: 4/1
Regular Notification: Rolling
LSDAS Accepted? Yes
Average GPA: 3.2
Range of GPA: 2.9–3.5
Average LSAT: 159
Range of LSAT: 157–161
Transfer Students Accepted? Yes
Other Schools to Which Students Applied: Fordham, Rutgers Newark, UCLA, U. of Maryland, Penn, UT—Austin, Villanova
Other Admissions Factors Considered: Quality of undergraduate and graduate institutions, undergraduate major, graduate schools and GPA, life and work experiences, general background
Number of Applications Received: 1,929
Number of Applicants Accepted: 592
Number of Applicants Enrolled: 244

INTERNATIONAL STUDENTS
TOEFL Required of International Students? Yes
Minimum TOEFL: 250

EMPLOYMENT INFORMATION

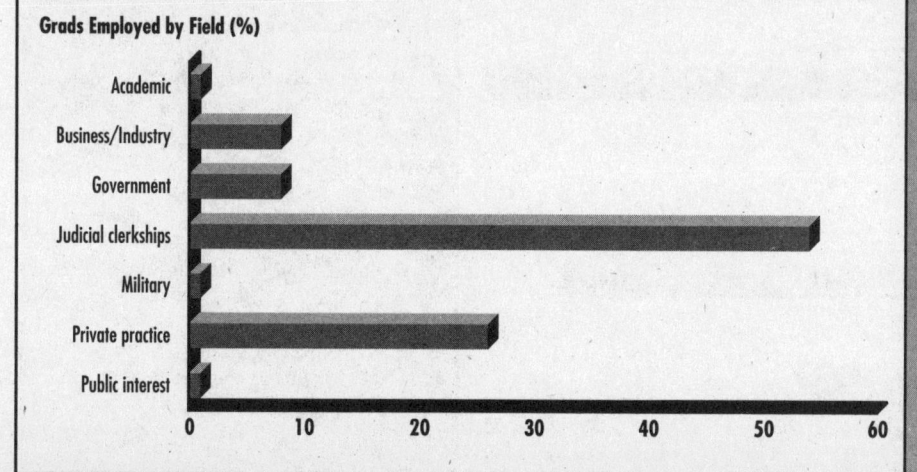

Grads Employed by Field (%)

Field	%
Academic	~1
Business/Industry	~8
Government	~8
Judicial clerkships	~55
Military	~1
Private practice	~27
Public interest	~2

Rate of Placement: 97%
Average Starting Salary: $76,000
Employers Who Frequently Hire Grads: All major Philadelphia, New Jersey, and Delaware law firms hire from Rutgers-Camden, as do numerous prestigious firms from New York City, Washington D.C., California, and other major metropolitan areas. Rutgers also ranks second in the country in placing its law graduates in highly desirable judicial clerkships.
State for Bar Exam: NJ, NY, PA, CA, TX
Pass Rate for First-Time Bar: 81%

RUTGERS UNIVERSITY — NEWARK
Rutgers School of Law at Newark

Admissions Contact: Director of Admissions, Anita Walton
123 Washington Street, Newark, NJ 07102
Admissions Phone: 973-353-5554 • Admissions Fax: 973-353-3459
Admissions E-mail: geddis@andromeda.rutgers.edu • Web Address: www.rutgers.edu

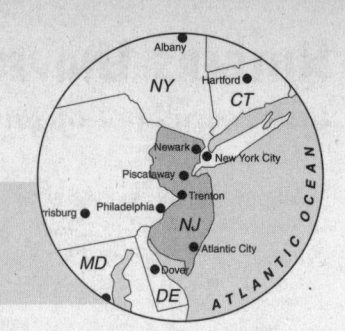

INSTITUTIONAL INFORMATION
Public/Private: Public
Environment: Urban
Academic Calendar: Semester
Schedule: Full time or part time
Student/Faculty Ratio: 16:1
Total Faculty: 68
% Part Time: 44
% Female: 34
% Minority: 19

PROGRAMS
Academic Specialties: Strengths include a diverse faculty with specialties over a broad range of topics. Public Interest Law is a point of intersection for many faculty members and is a driving commitment of the school.
Combined Degrees Offered: JD/MBA (4 years), JD/MBA (6 years), JD/PhD Jurisprudence (5 years), JD/MA Criminal Justice (4 years), JD/MCRP (4 years)
Grading System: Semester system; 4.0 cumulative system; mandatory curve in first year
Clinical Program Required? No
Clinical Program Description: Constitutional Litigation Clinic, Environmental Law Clinic, Federal Tax Clinic, Urban Legal Clinic, Women's Rights Clinic, Animal Rights Clinic, Women and AIDS, and Special Education Clinic
Legal Writing/Methods Course Requirements: 1 year, 3 credits, first year

STUDENT INFORMATION
Enrollment of Law School: 685
% Male/Female: 51/49
% Full Time: 74
% Full Time That Are International: 2
% Minority: 42
Average Age of Entering Class: 27

EXPENSES/FINANCIAL AID
Annual Tuition (Residents/Nonresidents): $10,106/$14,828
Room and Board (On/Off Campus): $7,000/$8,490
Books and Supplies: $3,618
Average Grant: $2,045
Average Loan: $17,992
% of Aid That Is Merit-Based: 39
% Receiving Some Sort of Aid: 80
Average Debt: $33,455

ADMISSIONS INFORMATION
Regular Application Deadline: 3/15
Regular Notification: Rolling
LSDAS Accepted? Yes
Average GPA: 3.2
Range of GPA: 2.9–3.4
Average LSAT: 157
Range of LSAT: 151–160
Transfer Students Accepted? Yes
Other Schools to Which Students Applied: Seton Hall University, New York University, Fordham University, George Washington University, Temple, Columbia University, Rutgers University—Camden, Boston College
Other Admissions Factors Considered: Graduate degree, work experience, socio-economic factors, community activities, personal essay, letters of recommendation
Number of Applications Received: 2,001
Number of Applicants Accepted: 910
Number of Applicants Enrolled: 289

INTERNATIONAL STUDENTS
Minimum TOEFL: 610

EMPLOYMENT INFORMATION

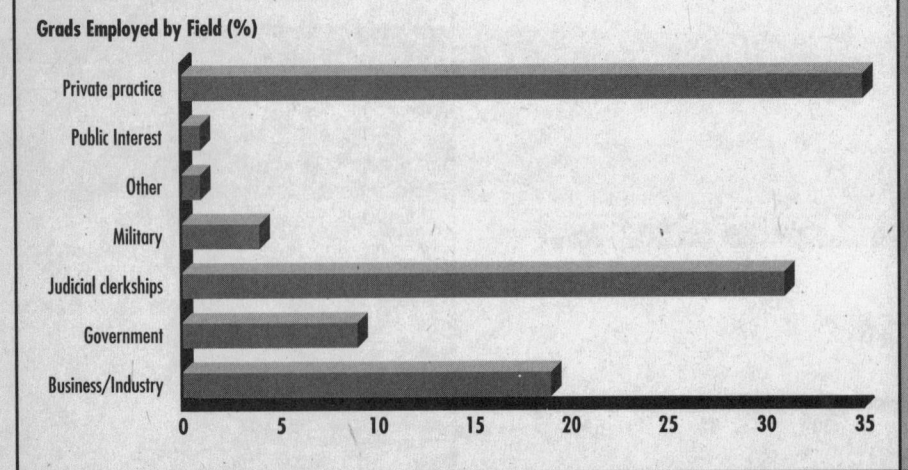

Grads Employed by Field (%)
- Private practice: ~35
- Public Interest: ~1
- Other: ~1
- Military: ~2
- Judicial clerkships: ~31
- Government: ~9
- Business/Industry: ~19

Rate of Placement: 98%
Average Starting Salary: $60,737
Employers Who Frequently Hire Grads: Federal judges, New Jersey State Court judges, large New Jersey and New York law firms, medium New Jersey firms, New York and New Jersey corporations, legal services
Prominent Alumni: Robert Torricelli, U.S. senator; Ida Castro, chair, Equal Employment Opportunity Commission; Louis Freeh, FBI director
State for Bar Exam: NJ
Number Taking Bar Exam: 175
Pass Rate for First-Time Bar: 80%

St. John's University
School of Law

Admissions Contact: Assistant Dean for Admissions, Robert M. Harrison
8000 Utopia Parkway, Jamaica, NY 11439
Admissions Phone: 718-990-6474 • Admissions Fax: 718-990-2526
Admissions E-mail: rsvp@stjohns.edu • Web Address: www.stjohns.edu/law

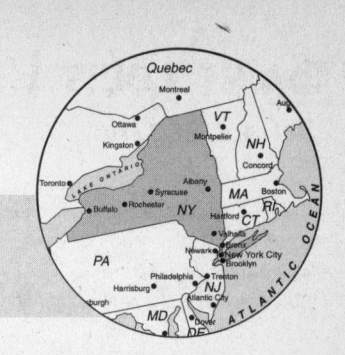

INSTITUTIONAL INFORMATION
Public/Private: Private
Student/Faculty Ratio: 19:1

PROGRAMS
Academic Specialties: Securities Law, Government Service, Labor Law, Real Estate, Bankruptcy, Criminal Law, Taxation, Environmental, Domestic and International Commercial, Legal Philosophy
Advanced Degrees Offered: JD (3 years day, 2.5 years day, 4 years evening), LLM Bankruptcy (1 year full time, 2 to 3 years part time)
Combined Degrees Offered: JD/MBA, JD/MA, JD/MS, BA/JD, BS/JD
Grading System: Letter system
Clinical Program Required? No
Clinical Program Description: Elder Law, Civil, Criminal, Judicial, and Domestic Violence Clinics
Legal Writing Course Requirements? Yes
Legal Writing Description: First-year required course
Legal Methods Course Requirements? Yes
Legal Methods Description: First-year required course
Legal Research Course Requirements? Yes
Legal Research Description: First-year required course
Moot Court Requirement? Yes
Moot Court Description: Part of the first-year research and writing program
Public Interest Law Requirement? No

Academic Journals: *Law Review, Journal of Legal Commentary, N.Y. International Law Review, N.Y. Real Property Law Journal, Bankruptcy Law Review, Catholic Lawyer*

STUDENT INFORMATION
Enrollment of Law School: 259
% Male/Female: 55/45
% Full Time: 80
% Minority: 18

EXPENSES/FINANCIAL AID
Annual Tuition: $22,000
Room and Board: $8,500
Average Grant: $6,904
Average Loan: $16,911
% of Aid That Is Merit-Based: 17
% Receiving Some Sort of Aid: 89
Average Total Aid Package: $18,496
Average Debt: $53,619
Tuition Per Credit: $800

ADMISSIONS INFORMATION
Application Fee: $60
Regular Application Deadline: Rolling
Regular Notification: Rolling
LSDAS Accepted? Yes
Average GPA: 3.2
Range of GPA: 2.9–3.5
Average LSAT: 156
Range of LSAT: 153–160
Transfer Students Accepted? Yes
Other Admissions Factors Considered: Undergraduate major, undergraduate educational institution, graduate work, work experience, extracurricular activities, community activities
Number of Applications Received: 2,617
Number of Applicants Accepted: 1,186
Number of Applicants Enrolled: 259

EMPLOYMENT INFORMATION

Grads Employed by Field (%)
- Academic
- Business/Industry
- Government
- Judicial clerkships
- Private practice

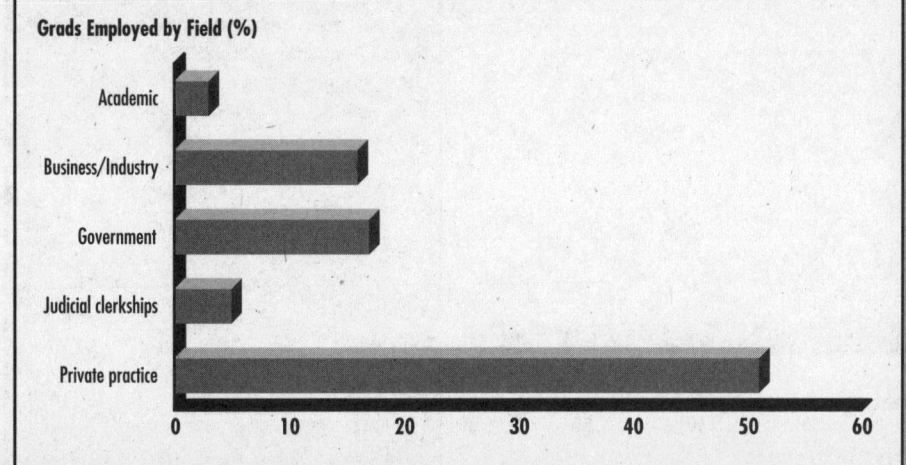

Rate of Placement: 98%
Average Starting Salary: $75,000
Employers Who Frequently Hire Grads: Private law firms, corporations, governmental agencies
State for Bar Exam: NY
Pass Rate for First-Time Bar: 78%

Saint Louis University
School of Law

Admissions Contact: Assistant Dean and Director of Admissions, Michael J. Kolnik
3700 Lindell Boulevard, St. Louis, MO 63108
Admissions Phone: 314-977-2800 • Admissions Fax: 314-977-1464
Admissions E-mail: admissions@law.slu.edu • Web Address: law.slu.edu

INSTITUTIONAL INFORMATION
Public/Private: Private
Affiliation: Roman Catholic
Student/Faculty Ratio: 18:1
Total Faculty: 65
% Part Time: 48
% Female: 23
% Minority: 7

PROGRAMS
Academic Specialties: Certificate programs in Employment Law, Health Law, and International and Comparative Law; clinic programs; other specialties include Civil Procedure, Commercial Law, Constitutional Law, Corporation Securities Law, Criminal Law, Environmental Law, Government Services, Human Rights Law, Intellectual Property Law, Labor Law, Legal History, Legal Philosophy, Property, and Taxation
Advanced Degrees Offered: LLM Health Law, (1 year full time, 2 years part time), LLM for foreign lawyers (1 year full time)
Combined Degrees Offered: JD/MBA (3.5 to 4 years), JD/MHA (4 years), JD/MAPA, JD/MAUA, (3.5 to 4 years), JD/MPH (4 years)
Grading System: Letter and numerical system on a 4.0 scale
Clinical Program Required? No
Clinical Programs Description: In-House Clinic, Externship Program, Judicial Process Clinic, Criminal Public Defender Clinic, Corporate Counsel Externship Clinic
Legal Writing Course Requirements? Yes
Legal Methods Course Requirements? No
Legal Methods Description: 1 year
Legal Research Course Requirements? Yes
Moot Court Requirement? No
Public Interest Law Requirement? No
Academic Journals: *Saint Louis University Law Journal, Public Law Review, The Journal of Health Law, The Saint Louis Warsaw Transatlantic Law Journal*

STUDENT INFORMATION
Enrollment of Law School: 749
% Out of State: 41
% Male/Female: 52/48
% Full Time: 74
% Full Time That Are International: 1
% Minority: 13
Average Age of Entering Class: 26

EXPENSES/FINANCIAL AID
Annual Tuition: $23,300
Room and Board (Off Campus): $11,192
Books and Supplies: $1,000
Financial Aid Application Deadline: 6/2
Average Grant: $8,968
Average Loan: $21,582
% of Aid That Is Merit-Based: 19
% Receiving Some Sort of Aid: 92
Average Total Aid Package: $24,799

Average Debt: $54,981
Tuition Per Credit: $17,000
Fees Per Credit: $55

ADMISSIONS INFORMATION
Application Fee: $55
Regular Application Deadline: 3/2
Regular Notification: Rolling
LSDAS Accepted? Yes
Average GPA: 3.3
Range of GPA: 3.0–3.6
Average LSAT: 154
Range of LSAT: 151–158
Transfer Students Accepted? Yes
Other Admissions Factors Considered: Graduate degrees earned, undergraduate institution, major, leadership positions, motivation, work experience, service
Number of Applications Received: 1,351
Number of Applicants Accepted: 729
Number of Applicants Enrolled: 263

INTERNATIONAL STUDENTS
TOEFL Required of International Students? Yes
Minimum TOEFL: 232

EMPLOYMENT INFORMATION

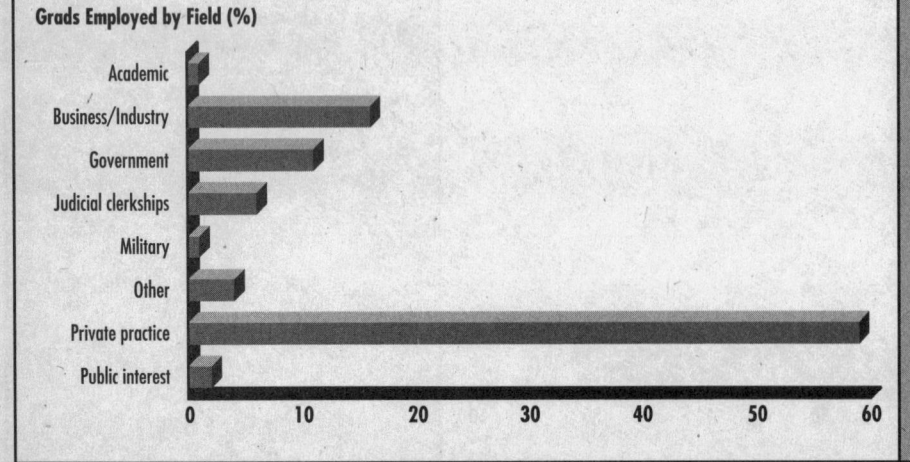

Grads Employed by Field (%)
- Academic
- Business/Industry
- Government
- Judicial clerkships
- Military
- Other
- Private practice
- Public interest

Rate of Placement: 94%
Average Starting Salary: $58,605
State for Bar Exam: MO
Pass Rate for First-Time Bar: 83%

ST. MARY'S UNIVERSITY
School of Law

Admissions Contact: Assistant Dean and Director of Admissions
One Camino Santa Maria, San Antonio, TX 78228-8601
Admissions Phone: 866-639-5831 • Admissions Fax: 210-431-4202
Admissions E-mail: admissions@law.stmarytx.edu • Web Address: www.stmarylaw.stmarytx.edu

INSTITUTIONAL INFORMATION
Public/Private: Private
Affiliation: Roman Catholic
Student/Faculty Ratio: 18:1
Total Faculty: 95
% Part Time: 53
% Female: 35
% Minority: 22

PROGRAMS
Academic Specialties: International Law, Criminal Law, clinical offerings
Advanced Degrees Offered: LLM International and Comparative Law for U.S.-educated students, LLM American Legal Studies for foreign-educated students
Combined Degrees Offered: JD/MBA Accounting, JD/MA Economics, JD/MA International Relations with concentration in Justice Administration, JD/MA Public Administration, JD/MA English Communications-Arts, JD/MA Theology, JD/MS Computer Science, JD/MS Engineering, JD/MBA (all 3.5 to 4 years)
Grading System: Letter system on a 4.0 scale with 10 tiers
Clinical Program Required? No
Clinical Programs Description: Civil Justice Clinic, Community Development Clinic, Criminal Justice Clinic, Immigration Clinic, Human Rights Clinic
Legal Writing Course Requirements? Yes
Legal Writing Description: Part of first-year, 2-semester course
Legal Methods Course Requirements? Yes
Legal Methods Description: Part of first-year, 2-semester course
Legal Research Course Requirements? Yes
Legal Research Description: Part of first-year, 2-semester course
Moot Court Requirement? No
Moot Court Description: First-year moot court is basically a requirement.
Public Interest Law Requirement? No
Academic Journals: *St. Mary's Law Journal, St. Mary's Law Review on Minority Issues*

STUDENT INFORMATION
Enrollment of Law School: 705
% Out of State: 10
% Male/Female: 52/48
% Full Time: 100
% Full Time That Are International: 2
% Minority: 46
Average Age of Entering Class: 28

EXPENSES/FINANCIAL AID
Annual Tuition: $17,970
Room and Board (On/Off Campus): $5,535/$7,055
Books and Supplies: $1,100
Financial Aid Application Deadline: 4/1
Average Grant: $2,861
Average Loan: $26,984
% of Aid That Is Merit-Based: 4
% Receiving Some Sort of Aid: 90
Average Total Aid Package: $27,673
Average Debt: $78,936
Tuition Per Credit: $599

ADMISSIONS INFORMATION
Application Fee: $45
Regular Application Deadline: 3/1
Regular Notification: 5/1
LSDAS Accepted? Yes
Average GPA: 3.0
Range of GPA: 2.7–3.2
Average LSAT: 149
Range of LSAT: 146–152
Transfer Students Accepted? Yes
Other Schools to Which Students Applied: Baylor University, Oklahoma City University, Southern Methodist University, Texas A&M University, Texas Southern University, Texas Tech University, Texas Wesleyan University
Other Admissions Factors Considered: Evidence of having overcome hardships or obstacles in attaining education
Number of Applications Received: 1,066
Number of Applicants Accepted: 692
Number of Applicants Enrolled: 240

INTERNATIONAL STUDENTS
TOEFL Required of International Students? Yes

EMPLOYMENT INFORMATION

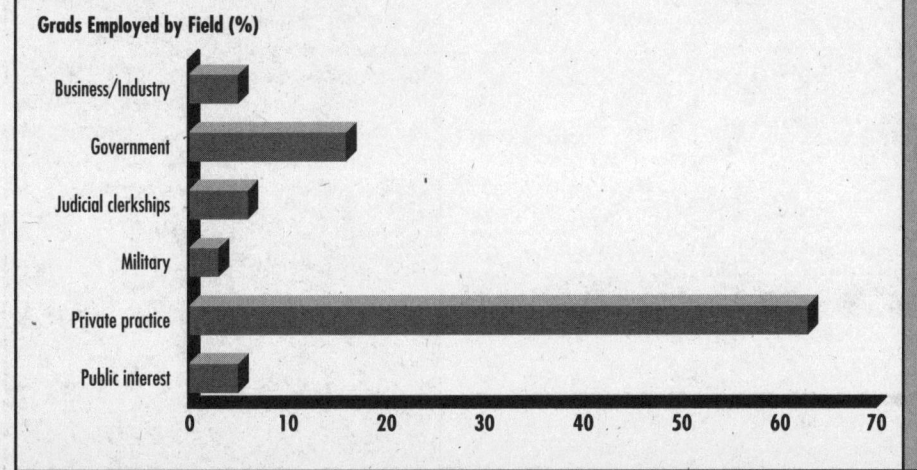

Grads Employed by Field (%)
- Business/Industry
- Government
- Judicial clerkships
- Military
- Private practice
- Public interest

Rate of Placement: 74%
Average Starting Salary: $55,000
Employers Who Frequently Hire Grads: Small and medium-sized firms, government agencies, business (banking/financial)
State for Bar Exam: TX, FL, MO, OK, NM
Pass Rate for First-Time Bar: 59%

ST. THOMAS UNIVERSITY
School of Law

Admissions Contact: Assistant Dean for Enrollment Services
16400 Northwest 32nd Avenue, Miami, FL 33054
Admissions Phone: 305-623-2310 • Admissions Fax: 305-623-2357
Admissions E-mail: admitme@stu.edu • Web Address: www.stu.edu

INSTITUTIONAL INFORMATION
Public/Private: Private
Affiliation: Roman Catholic
Student/Faculty Ratio: 19:1
Total Faculty: 24
% Part Time: 39
% Female: 41
% Minority: 25

PROGRAMS
Academic Specialties: Human Rights Law, International Law, Taxation
Advanced Degrees Offered: LLM International Tax (2 years online), LLM Intercultural Human Rights (1 year)
Combined Degrees Offered: JD/MS Marriage and Family Counseling, JD/MS Sports Administration, JD/MBA Accounting, JD/MBA International Business, JD/BA 3+3 Program
Grading System: A, B+, B, C+, C, C–, D, F, P/NP
Clinical Program Required? No
Clinical Programs Description: Immigration Clinic; Family Court Clinic; Tax Clinic; Bankruptcy Clinic; Public Defender, State's Attorney, and Legal Services externships
Legal Writing Course Requirements? Yes
Legal Writing Description: Legal Analysis, Writing, and Research (3 credits) required first semester; Advanced Legal Research (2 credits) required fourth semester; senior writing requirement
Legal Methods Course Requirements? Yes
Legal Methods Description: See Legal Writing.
Legal Research Course Requirements? Yes
Legal Research Description: See Legal Writing.
Moot Court Requirement? Yes
Moot Court Description: Students write briefs and present oral arguments in the Appellate Advocacy course taken in the spring of the first year.
Public Interest Law Requirement? Yes
Public Interest Law Description: 20 hours per year of pro bono work in second and third year of school
Academic Journals: *St. Thomas Law Review*

STUDENT INFORMATION
Enrollment of Law School: 475
% Out of State: 35
% Male/Female: 51/49
% Full Time: 100
% Full Time That Are International: 1
% Minority: 46
Average Age of Entering Class: 27

RESEARCH FACILITIES
Research Resources Available: Off-campus housing with wireless Internet access
School-Supported Research Centers: St. Thomas University Human Rights Institute

EXPENSES/FINANCIAL AID
Annual Tuition: $22,400
Room and Board (On/Off Campus): $7,900/$9,000
Books and Supplies: $1,000
Financial Aid Application Deadline: 5/1
Average Grant: $12,500
Average Loan: $26,089
% of Aid That Is Merit-Based: 28
% Receiving Some Sort of Aid: 90
Average Total Aid Package: $25,570
Average Debt: $84,000

ADMISSIONS INFORMATION
Application Fee: $40
Regular Application Deadline: Rolling
Regular Notification: Rolling
LSDAS Accepted? Yes
Average GPA: 2.8
Range of GPA: 2.4–3.1
Average LSAT: 148
Range of LSAT: 145–151
Transfer Students Accepted? Yes
Other Schools to Which Students Applied: Nova Southeastern University, University of Miami
Number of Applications Received: 1,466
Number of Applicants Accepted: 853
Number of Applicants Enrolled: 186

EMPLOYMENT INFORMATION

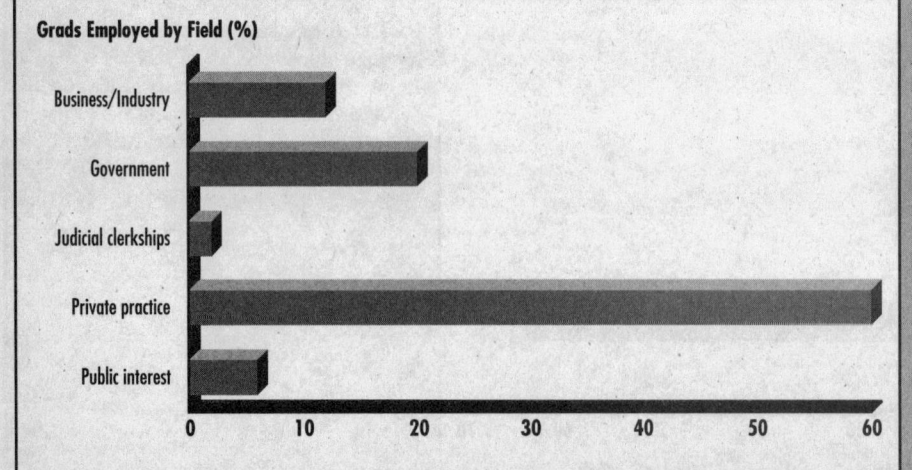

Grads Employed by Field (%)
- Business/Industry: ~12
- Government: ~20
- Judicial clerkships: ~3
- Private practice: ~60
- Public interest: ~6

Rate of Placement: 94%
Average Starting Salary: $36,610
Employers Who Frequently Hire Grads: Private law firms of all sizes; government agencies, including the U.S. Department of Justice, the Florida State Attorney's Office, Prosecutors' and Public Defenders' Offices; public interest organizations, and corporations
State for Bar Exam: FL, NY, GA
Pass Rate for First-Time Bar: 78%

Samford University
Cumberland School of Law

Admissions Contact: Director of Admissions, M. Giselle Gauthier
800 Lakeshore Drive, Birmingham, AL 35229
Admissions Phone: 205-726-2702 • Admissions Fax: 205-726-2057
Admissions E-mail: law.admissions@samford.edu • Web Address: cumberland.samford.edu

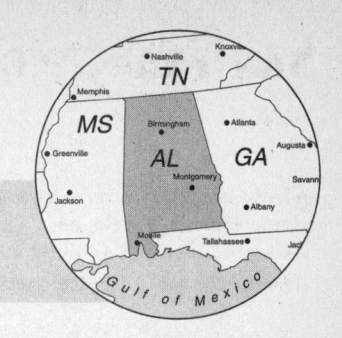

INSTITUTIONAL INFORMATION
Public/Private: Private
Affiliation: Southern Baptist
Student/Faculty Ratio: 20:1
Total Faculty: 46
% Part Time: 41
% Female: 21
% Minority: 13

PROGRAMS
Academic Specialties: 6-credit Lawyering and Legal Reasoning courses
Advanced Degrees Offered: MCL; LLM/SJD in Law, Religion, and Culture
Combined Degrees Offered: JD/MAcc (3.5 to 4 years), JD/MBA (3.5 to 4 years), JD/MDiv (5 years), JD/MPA (3.5 to 4 years), JD/MPH (3.5 to 4 years), JD/MS in Environmental Management (3.5 to 4 years)
Grading System: Letter grades with quality points assigned
Clinical Program Required? No
Clinical Programs Description: State court judges, federal court judges, corporate, U.S. Attorney's Office, IRS legal internship, District Attorney's Office (Adult Prosecution, Juvenile Prosecution), Public Defender's Office, Legal Services, Legal Aid Society (Criminal Defense, Juvenile Defense), Family Court
Legal Writing Course Requirements? Yes
Legal Methods Course Requirements? Yes
Legal Methods Description: 1 full year; all first-year law students receive intensive instructions in prelitigation skills, such as client interviewing, counseling, memorandum preparation, and negotiation; pretrial litigation skills, including summary judgement motions and making compelling oral arguments; and appellate litigation skills.
Legal Research Course Requirements? Yes
Moot Court Requirement? No
Public Interest Law Requirement? No
Academic Journals: Cumberland Law Review, The American Journal of Trial Advocacy

STUDENT INFORMATION
Enrollment of Law School: 511
% Out of State: 45
% Male/Female: 58/42
% Full Time: 100
% Full Time That Are International: 0
% Minority: 6
Average Age of Entering Class: 23

EXPENSES/FINANCIAL AID
Annual Tuition: $20,528
Room and Board (Off Campus): $9,900
Books and Supplies: $1,200
Financial Aid Application Deadline: 3/1
Average Grant: $2,822
Average Loan: $27,254
% of Aid That Is Merit-Based: 4
% Receiving Some Sort of Aid: 85
Average Total Aid Package: $28,661
Average Debt: $68,445
Tuition Per Credit: $693
Fees Per Credit: $20

ADMISSIONS INFORMATION
Application Fee: $40
Regular Application Deadline: Rolling
Regular Notification: Rolling
LSDAS Accepted? Yes
Average GPA: 3.1
Range of GPA: 2.7–3.4
Average LSAT: 152
Range of LSAT: 150–153
Transfer Students Accepted? Yes
Other Admissions Factors Considered: Undergraduate major, grade trend, graduate studies, cultural or ethnic diversity, clarity and content of personal statement
Number of Applications Received: 886
Number of Applicants Accepted: 461

INTERNATIONAL STUDENTS
TOEFL Required of International Students? Yes
Minimum TOEFL: 213

EMPLOYMENT INFORMATION

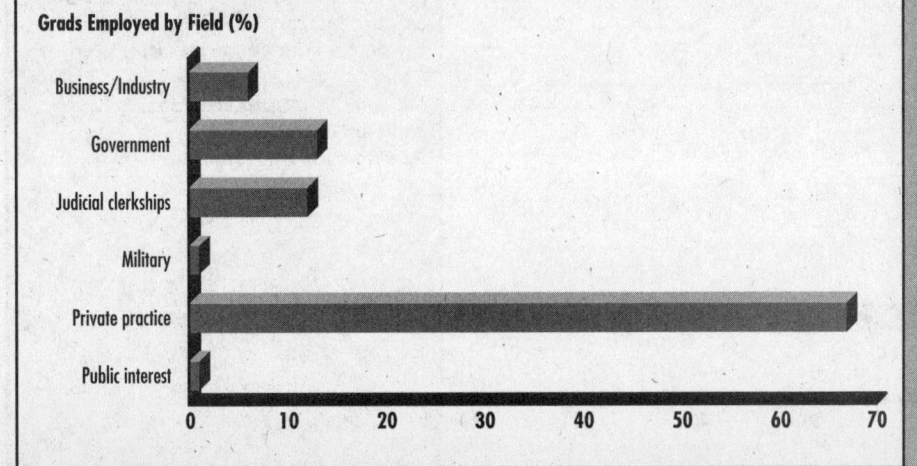

Grads Employed by Field (%)

Field	%
Business/Industry	~5
Government	~12
Judicial clerkships	~12
Military	0
Private practice	~68
Public interest	~1

Rate of Placement: 86%
Average Starting Salary: $50,000
Employers Who Frequently Hire Grads: Bradley, Arant, Rose & White; Burr & Forman; Balch & Bingham; Lange, Simpson, Robinson & Somerville; Carbaniss, Johnston, Gardner, Dumas & O'Neal; Sirote & Permutt (Birmingham); Attorney General's Office (Montgomery); Hand & Arendall, Lyons, Pipes, & Cook (Mobile); Leitner, Williams, Dooley & Neopolitan (Chattanooga, TN); Watkins & Ludlam, Winter and Stennis (Jackson, MS)
State for Bar Exam: AL, FL, TN, GA, VA
Pass Rate for First-Time Bar: 85%

SAN FRANCISCO LAW SCHOOL

Admissions Contact: Director of Admissions
20 Haight Street, San Francisco, CA 94102
Admissions Phone: 415-626-5550 • Admissions Fax: 415-626-5584
Admissions E-mail: admin@sfls.edu • Web Address: www.sfls.edu

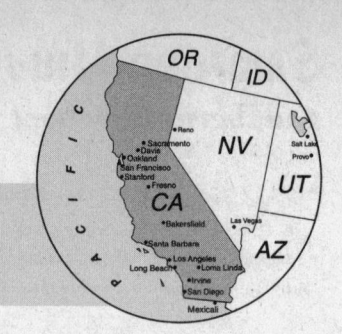

INSTITUTIONAL INFORMATION
Public/Private: Private
Student/Faculty Ratio: 5:1
Total Faculty: 32
% Part Time: 100
% Female: 31
% Minority: 6

PROGRAMS
Academic Specialties: All faculty are adjunct and are practicing judges and attorneys who teach in their field.
Grading System: Numerical system up to 100
Clinical Program Required? No
Clinical Programs Description: Private practice/judges
Legal Writing Course Requirements? Yes
Legal Methods Course Requirements? Yes
Legal Methods Description: 1 semester
Legal Research Course Requirements? Yes
Legal Research Description: 2 semesters
Moot Court Requirement? Yes
Moot Court Description: 1 semester
Public Interest Law Requirement? No
Academic Journals: San Francisco Law Review

STUDENT INFORMATION
Enrollment of Law School: 150
% Male/Female: 100/0
Average Age of Entering Class: 34

EXPENSES/FINANCIAL AID
Annual Tuition $6,489
Books and Supplies: $250
% of Aid That Is Merit-Based: 40
Tuition Per Credit: $309

ADMISSIONS INFORMATION
Application Fee: $50
Regular Application Deadline: 6/15
Regular Notification: Rolling
LSDAS Accepted? No
Average GPA: 2.8
Range of GPA: 2.0–3.8
Transfer Students Accepted? Yes
Number of Applications Received: 51
Number of Applicants Enrolled: 31

EMPLOYMENT INFORMATION

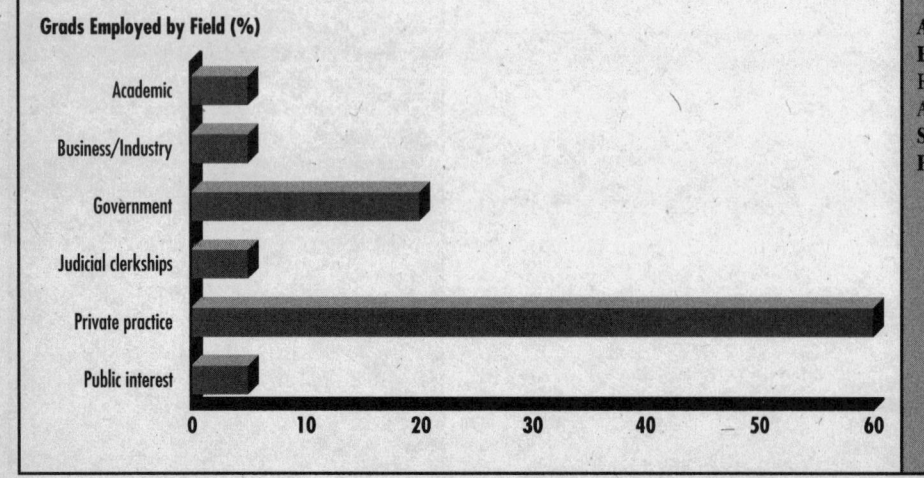

Grads Employed by Field (%)

Field	%
Academic	~3
Business/Industry	~3
Government	~20
Judicial clerkships	~3
Private practice	~60
Public interest	~3

Average Starting Salary: $40,000
Employers Who Frequently Hire Grads: San Francisco Public Defender's and District Attorney's Offices, private sector
State for Bar Exam: CA
Pass Rate for First-Time Bar: 50%

SAN JOAQUIN COLLEGE OF LAW

Admissions Contact: Admissions Officer
901 Fifth Street, Clovis, CA 93612-1312
Admissions Phone: 559-323-2100 • Admissions Fax: 559-323-5566
Admissions E-mail: jcanalin@sjcl.org • Web Address: www.sjcl.org

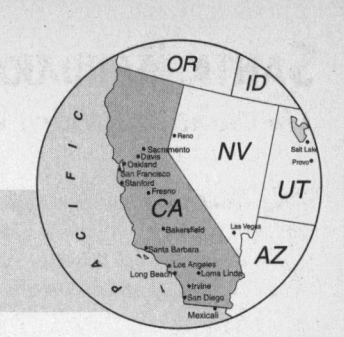

INSTITUTIONAL INFORMATION
Public/Private: Private
Student/Faculty Ratio: 16:1
Total Faculty: 36
% Part Time: 83
% Female: 45
% Minority: 14

PROGRAMS
Academic Specialties: Practice-orientated curriculum with many skills classes; law review devoted to issues surrounding agriculture; specialties include Commercial Law, Corporation Securities Law, Criminal Law, Environmental Law, International Law, Labor Law, and Taxation
Advanced Degrees Offered: JD (3 to 5 years), MS Taxation (2 years)
Grading System: A (100–85), B (84–75), C (74–65), D (64–55), F (54–0)
Clinical Program Required? Yes
Clinical Programs Description: Alternative Dispute Resolution, Small Claims
Legal Methods Course Requirements? Yes
Legal Methods Description: Legal analysis/research writing

STUDENT INFORMATION
Enrollment of Law School: 185
% Male/Female: 54/46
% Full Time: 13
% Minority: 26
Average Age of Entering Class: 33

EXPENSES/FINANCIAL AID
Annual Tuition: $10,212
Books and Supplies: $550
Average Grant: $1,600
Average Loan: $14,500
% of Aid That Is Merit-Based: 12
% Receiving Some Sort of Aid: 75
Average Total Aid Package: $18,500
Average Debt: $62,500
Fees Per Credit: $475

ADMISSIONS INFORMATION
Application Fee: $40
Regular Application Deadline: 6/30
Regular Notificatión: Rolling
LSDAS Accepted? No
Average GPA: 2.9
Range of GPA: 1.8–3.9
Average LSAT: 148
Range of LSAT: 139–174
Transfer Students Accepted? Yes
Number of Applications Received: 135
Number of Applicants Accepted: 108
Number of Applicants Enrolled: 91

EMPLOYMENT INFORMATION

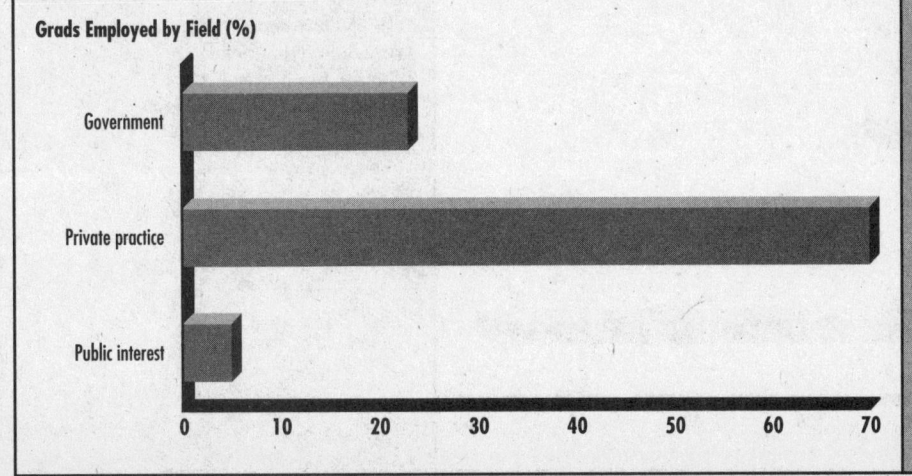

Grads Employed by Field (%)
- Government: ~22
- Private practice: ~70
- Public interest: ~5

Rate of Placement: 70%
Employers Who Frequently Hire Grads: Local District Attorney and District Defender's Offices and various small firms
State for Bar Exam: CA
Pass Rate for First-Time Bar: 56%

SANTA BARBARA COLLEGE OF LAW
The Santa Barbara and Ventura Colleges of Law

Admissions Contact: Assistant Dean, Mary Osborne
20 East Victoria Street, Santa Barbara, CA 93101
Admissions Phone: 805-966-0010 • Admissions Fax: 805-966-7181
Admissions E-mail: sbcl@santabarbaralaw.edu • Web Address: www.santabarbaralaw.edu

INSTITUTIONAL INFORMATION
Public/Private: Private
Student/Faculty Ratio: 11:1
Total Faculty: 19
% Part Time: 100
% Female: 26
% Minority: 5

PROGRAMS
Academic Specialties: All faculty are practicing attorneys or judges.
Grading System: A to F
Clinical Program Required? Yes
Clinical Programs Description: Off-site government or private pro bono
Legal Writing Course Requirements? Yes
Legal Writing Description: Basic Legal Writing (30 hours), Advanced Legal Writing (30 hours)
Legal Methods Course Requirements? No
Legal Research Course Requirements? Yes
Legal Research Description: 30 hours of instruction
Moot Court Requirement? No
Public Interest Law Requirement? No

STUDENT INFORMATION
Enrollment of Law School: 917
% Male/Female: 51/49
% Full Time: 100

EXPENSES/FINANCIAL AID
Annual Tuition: $22,000
Room and Board: $9,787
Books and Supplies: $903
Average Grant: $8,071
% of Aid That Is Merit-Based: 7
% Receiving Some Sort of Aid: 85
Average Debt: $60,379

ADMISSIONS INFORMATION
Application Fee: $40
Regular Application Deadline: Rolling
Regular Notification: Rolling
LSDAS Accepted? No
Average GPA: 3.2
Range of GPA: 3.0–3.5
Average LSAT: 156
Range of LSAT: 153–158
Transfer Students Accepted? No
Other Schools to Which Students Applied: University of California—Berkeley, University of California—Davis, University of California—Hastings, Syracuse University, University of San Francisco
Number of Applications Received: 2,528
Number of Applicants Accepted: 1,265
Number of Applicants Enrolled: 291

EMPLOYMENT INFORMATION

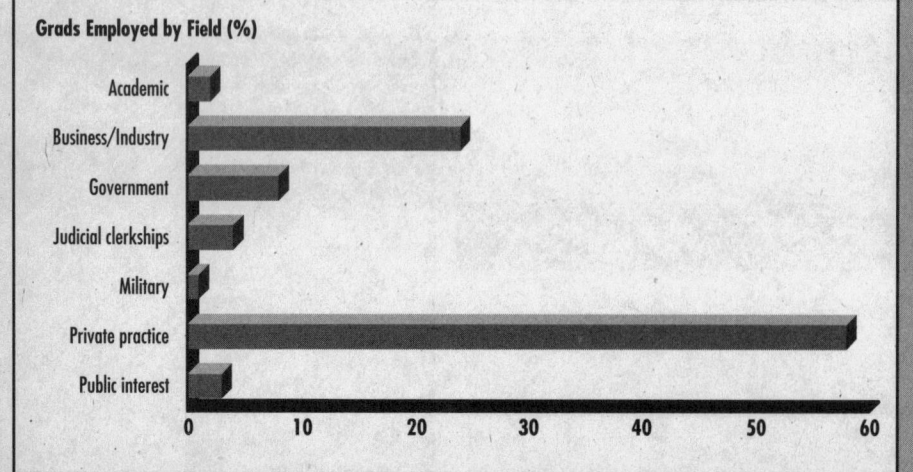

Grads Employed by Field (%)

Rate of Placement: 96%
Average Starting Salary: $58,000
State for Bar Exam: CA
Pass Rate for First-Time Bar: 71%

SANTA CLARA UNIVERSITY
School of Law

Admissions Contact: Director of Admissions and Diversity Services, Jeanette J. Leach
500 El Camino Real, Santa Clara, CA 95053
Admissions Phone: 408-554-4800 • Admissions Fax: 408-554-7897
Admissions E-mail: lawadmissions@scu.edu • Web Address: www.scu.edu/law

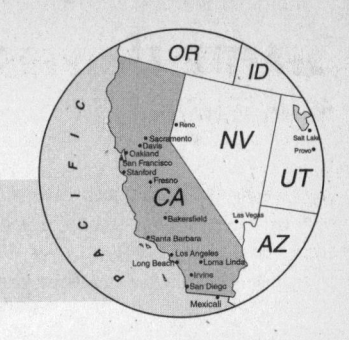

INSTITUTIONAL INFORMATION
Public/Private: Private
Student/Faculty Ratio: 19:1
Total Faculty: 112
% Part Time: 43
% Female: 41
% Minority: 12

PROGRAMS
Academic Specialties: Certificates in Intellectual Property and High Technology, International and Comparative Law, and Public Interest Law; summer programs in 13 countries
Advanced Degrees Offered: LLM for foreign lawyers, LLM International and Comparative Law, LLM Intellectual Property Law
Combined Degrees Offered: JD/MBA (3.5 to 4 years)
Grading System: A to F: A (4.33), B (3.33), C (2.33), etc.; student must maintain 2.33 GPA to graduate
Clinical Program Required? No
Clinical Programs Description: Criminal Defense Law Clinic (Northern California Innocence Project), East San Jose Community Law Center
Legal Writing Course Requirements? Yes
Legal Writing Description: 3-unit, 2-semester Legal Analysis, Research, and Writing course required for first-year students
Legal Methods Course Requirements? No
Legal Research Course Requirements? Yes
Legal Research Description: See Legal Writing.

Moot Court Requirement? Yes
Moot Court Description: First-year students are required to write a brief and present oral argument as part of the required Legal Research, Analysis, and Writing course.
Public Interest Law Requirement? No
Academic Journals: Santa Clara Law Review, Computer and High Technology Law Journal

STUDENT INFORMATION
Enrollment of Law School: 891
% Male/Female: 46/54
% Full Time: 75
% Minority: 37
Average Age of Entering Class: 26

RESEARCH FACILITIES
Research Resources Available: A good portion of the carrels in the Law Library are wired for full access to the University's network. The Law Library contains three computer labs, and the University has 2 large labs that the law students may access. The University also has a large multi-media department.

EXPENSES/FINANCIAL AID
Annual Tuition: $25,560
Room and Board: $11,822
Books and Supplies: $1,304
Financial Aid Application Deadline: 3/1
Average Grant: $8,071
Average Loan: $21,877
% of Aid That Is Merit-Based: 7
% Receiving Some Sort of Aid: 85

Average Total Aid Package: $24,089
Average Debt: $60,379
Tuition Per Credit: $852
Fees Per Credit: $852

ADMISSIONS INFORMATION
Application Fee: $60
Regular Application Deadline: 3/1
Regular Notification: Rolling
LSDAS Accepted? Yes
Average GPA: 3.2
Range of GPA: 3.0–3.5
Average LSAT: 156
Range of LSAT: 153–159
Transfer Students Accepted? Yes
Other Schools to Which Students Applied: Pepperdine, University of California Hastings, University of San Diego, University of San Francisco
Other Admissions Factors Considered: Academic record including course of study and quality of institution, graduate work, employment history, maturity, community activities, extracurricular achievements, honors and awards, personal statement
Number of Applications Received: 2,371
Number of Applicants Accepted: 1,173
Number of Applicants Enrolled: 233

EMPLOYMENT INFORMATION

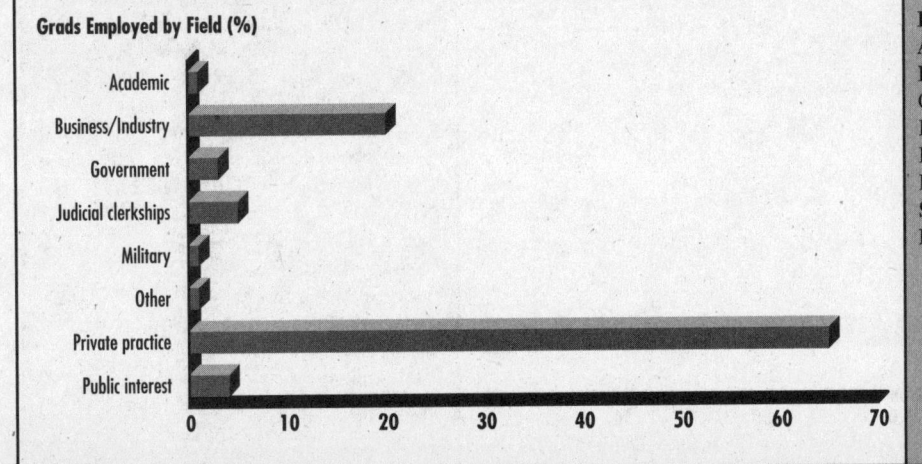

Grads Employed by Field (%)
- Academic
- Business/Industry: ~20
- Government
- Judicial clerkships
- Military
- Other
- Private practice: ~65
- Public interest

Rate of Placement: 96%
Average Starting Salary: $96,086
Employers Who Frequently Hire Grads: Cooley, Godward; McCutchen Doyle; Crosby Heafey; Morrison & Foerster; Skjerven Morrill; Brobeck, Phleger & Harrison; Ropers Majeski; Fenwick & West; Wilson Sonsini
State for Bar Exam: CA
Pass Rate for First-Time Bar: 69%

SEATTLE UNIVERSITY
School of Law

Admissions Contact: Director of Admission, Carol Cochran
900 Broadway, Seattle, WA 98122-4340
Admissions Phone: 206-398-4200 • Admissions Fax: 206-398-4058
Admissions E-mail: lawadmis@seattleu.edu • Web Address: www.law.seattleu.edu

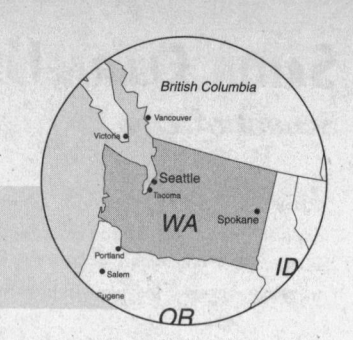

INSTITUTIONAL INFORMATION
Public/Private: Private
Affiliation: Roman Catholic
Student/Faculty Ratio: 21:1
Total Faculty: 88
% Part Time: 45
% Female: 48
% Minority: 9

PROGRAMS
Academic Specialties: Business, Tax, Civil Advocacy, Commercial Law, Criminal Practice, Environmental Law, Estate Planning, Intellectual Property, Labor and Employment Law, Poverty Law, Real Estate, Civil Procedure, Constitutional Law, Corporation Securities Law, Human Rights Law, International Law, Property
Advanced Degrees Offered: JD (3 years)
Combined Degrees Offered: JD/MBA, JD/MIB, JD/MS Finance (all 4 years)
Grading System: A to F: A+ (4.33), A (4.00), A– (3.67), etc.; Pass/Fail grades awarded for limited number of classes
Clinical Program Required? Yes
Clinical Programs Description: Law Practice Clinic, Bankruptcy Clinic, Immigration, Health, Law and Psychology, Housing Law, Ethics, Environmental Law, Intellectual Property, Administrative Law, Trust and Estates
Legal Writing Course Requirements? Yes
Legal Writing Description: 3 semesters of Legal Writing I and II with legal research element included

Legal Methods Course Requirements? No
Legal Research Course Requirements? Yes
Legal Research Description: See Legal Writing.
Moot Court Requirement? No
Public Interest Law Requirement? No
Academic Journals: Seattle University Law Review, Seattle Journal of Social Justice

STUDENT INFORMATION
Enrollment of Law School: 955
% Out of State: 21
% Male/Female: 43/57
% Full Time: 76
% Full Time That Are International: 1
% Minority: 23
Average Age of Entering Class: 28

EXPENSES/FINANCIAL AID
Annual Tuition: $21,210
Room and Board (Off Campus): $9,036
Books and Supplies: $903
Financial Aid Application Deadline: 3/1
Average Grant: $5,813
Average Loan: $23,855
% Receiving Some Sort of Aid: 97
Average Total Aid Package: $27,117
Average Debt: $68,600
Tuition Per Credit: $707

ADMISSIONS INFORMATION
Application Fee: $50
Regular Application Deadline: 4/1
Regular Notification: Rolling
LSDAS Accepted? Yes
Average GPA: 3.2
Range of GPA: 2.9–3.5
Average LSAT: 155
Range of LSAT: 151–157
Transfer Students Accepted? Yes
Other Schools to Which Students Applied: Gonzaga University, Lewis and Clark College, Santa Clara University, University of California—Hastings, University of Oregon, University of Washington, Willamette University
Other Admissions Factors Considered: Personal accomplishments including (but not limited to) exceptional professional achievement or community service, outstanding performance in a rigorous program of study, or unique talent
Number of Applications Received: 1,379
Number of Applicants Accepted: 846
Number of Applicants Enrolled: 345

INTERNATIONAL STUDENTS
TOEFL Required of International Students? Yes
Minimum TOEFL: 250

EMPLOYMENT INFORMATION

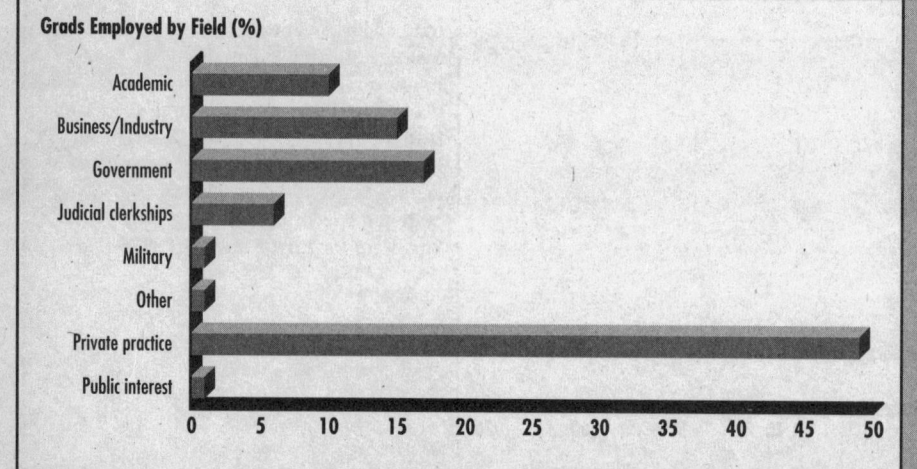

Grads Employed by Field (%)

Field	%
Academic	~1
Business/Industry	~10
Government	~17
Judicial clerkships	~6
Military	~1
Other	~2
Private practice	~50
Public interest	~1

Rate of Placement: 84%
Average Starting Salary: $45,914
Employers Who Frequently Hire Grads: Perkins Coie; Lane, Powell, Spears, Lubersky; King County Prosecutors; Washington State Attorney General; Williams, Kastner & Gibbs; Cozen & O'Connor; Ridell Williams; Foster, Pepper, Shefelman; Preston, Gates & Ellis; Reed McClure; Lee, Smart, Cook; Deloitte & Touche; Bullivant, Houser & Bailey; Stokes Lawrence; Schwabe, Williamson & Wyatt; Davis, Wright, Tremaine; Dorsey & Whitney; Seattle City Attorney; Stoel Rives
State for Bar Exam: WA, CA, AZ, CO, WV
Pass Rate for First-Time Bar: 78%

SETON HALL UNIVERSITY
School of Law

Admissions Contact: Dean of Admissions/Financial Resource Management, Mr. William Perez
One Newark Center, Newark, NJ 07102
Admissions Phone: 973-642-8747 • Admissions Fax: 973-642-8876
Admissions E-mail: admitme@shu.edu • Web Address: www.shu.edu/law

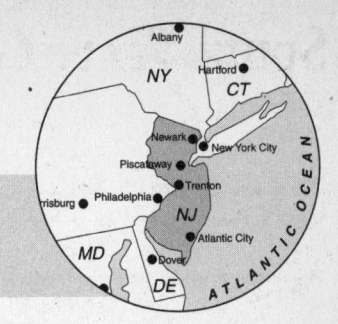

INSTUTIONAL INFORMATION

Public/Private: Private
Affiliation: Roman Catholic
Student/Faculty Ratio: 20:1
Total Faculty: 58
% Faculty Female: 39
% Faculty Minority: 22

PROGRAMS

Academic Specialties: Criminal Law, Environmental Law, International Law, Labor Law, Intellectual Property, Health Law, Commercial Law, Corporation Securities Law, Government Services, Human Rights Law, Legal History, Legal Philosophy Property, Taxation
Advanced Degrees Offered: JD (3 years full time, 4 years part time), LLM (2 years part time), MSJ (1 year full time, 2 years part time)
Combined Degreees Offered: JD/MBA (4 years full-time), JD/MA International Relations (4 years and 1 summer full time), JD/MD (6 years), MSJ (1 to 2 years)
Grading System: Letter and numerical grading system ranging from A+ (4.5) to F (0.0)
Clinical Program Required? No
Clinical Programs Description: Housing Law Clinic, Immigration Law/Human Rights Clinic, Juvenile Justice Clinic, Civil Litigation Clinic, Family Law Clinic, Appellate Litigation Clinic, Pro Bono Service Program
Legal Writing Course Requirements? Yes
Legal Writing Description: Full-year, 3-credit course
Legal Methods Course Requirements? No
Legal Research Course Requirements? Yes
Legal Research Description: Required as part of the Legal Research & Writing full-year, 3-credit course
Moot Court Requirement? No
Public Interest Law Requirement? No
Academic Journals: Seton Hall Law Journal, Seton Hall Constitutional Law Journal, Seton Hall Legislative Bureau

STUDENT INFORMATION

Enrollment of Law School: 1,109
% Out of State: 25
% Male/Female: 52/48
% Full-Time: 70
% Minority: 22
Average Age of Entering Class: 26

RESEARCH FACILITIES

Research Resources Available: Lexis, Westlaw, Findlaw, Lawcrawler, Loislaw
School-Supported Research Centers: Institute of Law, Science, and Technology; Center for Social Justice; Health Law & Policy Program; Institute for Law & Mental Health

EXPENSES/FINANCIAL AID

Annual Tuition: $22,680
Room and Board: $10,800
Books and Supplies: $850
Financial Aid Application Deadline: 4/18
Average Grant: $8,000
Average Loan: $18,000
% of Aid That Is Merit-Based: 17
% Receiving Some Sort of Aid: 85
Average Total Aid Package: $21,000
Average Debt: $68,279
Tuition Per Credit: $810
Fees Per Credit: $90

ADMISSIONS INFORMATION

Application Fee: $50
Regular Application Deadline: 4/1
Regular Notification: 1/1
LSDAS Accepted? Yes
Average GPA: 3.4
Range of GPA: 2.9–3.5
Average LSAT: 155
Range of LSAT: 153–158
Transfer Students Accepted? Yes
Other Admissions Factors Considered: Life experiences
Number of Applications Received: 2,384
Number of Applicants Accepted: 1,035
Number of Applicants Enrolled: 356

EMPLOYMENT INFORMATION

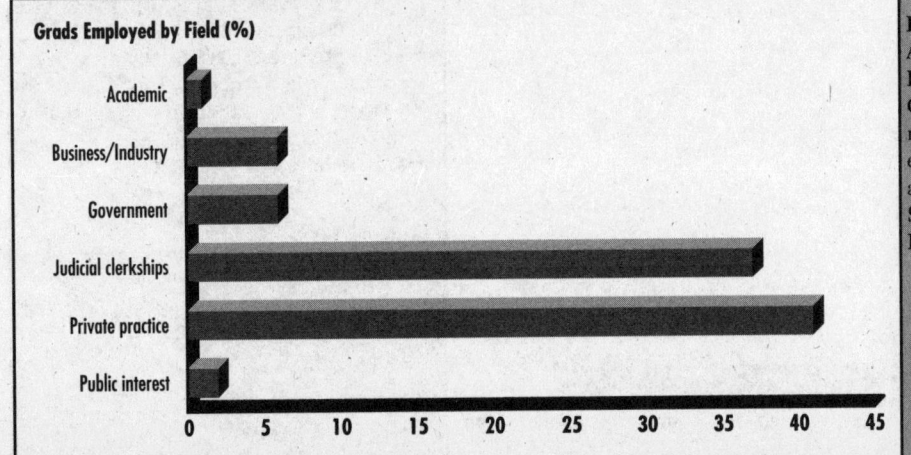

Grads Employed by Field (%)

Field	%
Academic	~1
Business/Industry	~5
Government	~6
Judicial clerkships	~37
Private practice	~41
Public interest	~2

Rate of Placement: 96%
Average Starting Salary: $61,000
Employers Who Frequently Hire Grads: Graduates are frequently hired by the nation's most prestigious firms, all national and state government agencies, public interest organizations, and state federal judges nationwide.
State for Bar Exam: NJ, NY
Pass Rate for First Time Bar: 83%

SOUTH TEXAS COLLEGE OF LAW

Admissions Contact: Assistant Dean of Admissions, Alicia K. Cramer
1303 San Jacinto Street, Houston, TX 77002-7000
Admissions Phone: 713-646-1810 • Admissions Fax: 713-646-2906
Admissions E-mail: admissions@stcl.edu • Web Address: www.stcl.edu

INSTITUTIONAL INFORMATION
Public/Private: Private
Student/Faculty Ratio: 19:1
Total Faculty: 95
% Part Time: 41
% Female: 27

PROGRAMS
Academic Specialties: Emerging programs in International Law, Environmental Law, and Dispute Resolution; nationally-recognized program in Advocacy. The college is a recognized leader for its Legal Research and Writing program. Hands-on live client clinics and extensive externship opportunities provide both a community service and valuable practical experience to students.
Grading System: Letter system with select courses graded Honors Pass, Pass, or Fail
Clinical Program Required? No
Clinical Programs Description: General Civil Clinic, Criminal Process Clinic, Judicial Process Clinic, Public and Governmental Interest Clinic, Meditation Clinic
Legal Writing Course Requirements? Yes
Legal Writing Description: Students are required to take a semester each of Legal Research and Writing I and II (for a total of 4 semester hours of credit). These courses cover the fundamentals of research and writing techniques and advance to the research and writing of an appellate brief. Students are also required to present an oral argument based on their brief.
Legal Methods Course Requirements? Yes
Legal Methods Description: Incorporated into the college's Legal Research and Writing courses
Legal Research Course Requirements? No
Moot Court Requirement? No
Public Interest Law Requirement? No
Academic Journals: *Corporate Counsel Review, CURRENTS: International Trade Law Journal, South Texas Law Review*

STUDENT INFORMATION
Enrollment of Law School: 1,250
% Out of State: 7
% Male/Female: 52/48
% Full Time: 66
% Minority: 24
Average Age of Entering Class: 28

RESEARCH FACILITIES
School-Supported Research Centers: Law Institute for Medical Studies, Center for Legal Responsibility

EXPENSES/FINANCIAL AID
Annual Tuition: $17,100
Room and Board (Off Campus): $7,418
Books and Supplies: $912
Financial Aid Application Deadline: 5/1
Average Grant: $2,473
Average Loan: $23,666
% of Aid That Is Merit-Based: 2
% Receiving Some Sort of Aid: 85
Average Total Aid Package: $23,315
Average Debt: $66,222
Tuition Per Credit: $11,400
Fees Per Credit: $600

ADMISSIONS INFORMATION
Application Fee: $50
Regular Application Deadline: 2/25
Regular Notification: 5/25
LSDAS Accepted? Yes
Average GPA: 3.0
Range of GPA: 2.7–3.3
Average LSAT: 149
Range of LSAT: 146–152
Transfer Students Accepted? Yes
Other Schools to Which Students Applied: Southern Methodist University, St. Mary's University, Texas Tech University, University of Texas at Austin, University of Houston
Other Admissions Factors Considered: Information provided in the essay regarding personal background, accomplishments and/or achievements; letters of recommendation speaking strongly on the applicant's behalf; competitive LSAT score; upward grade trend over a significant number of hours
Number of Applications Received: 1,394
Number of Applicants Accepted: 934
Number of Applicants Enrolled: 368

EMPLOYMENT INFORMATION

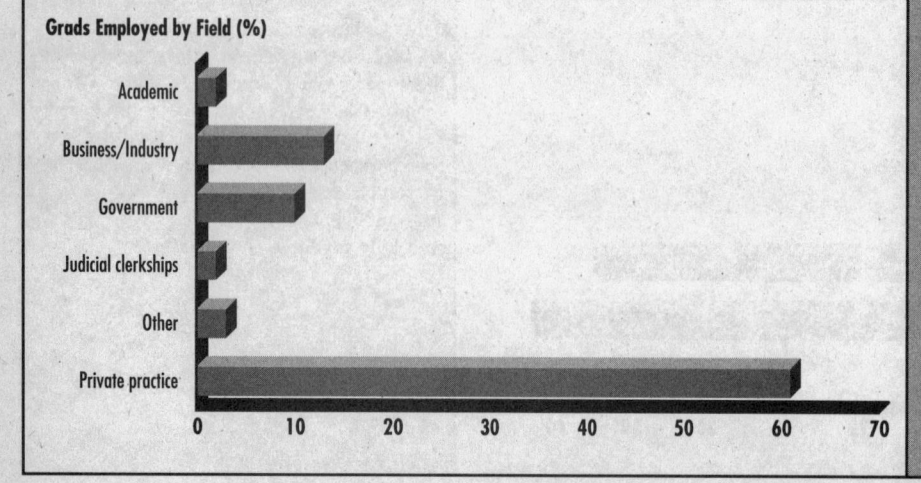

Grads Employed by Field (%)
- Academic: ~1
- Business/Industry: ~13
- Government: ~10
- Judicial clerkships: ~3
- Other: ~3
- Private practice: ~62

Rate of Placement: 79%
Average Starting Salary: $70,606
Employers Who Frequently Hire Grads: Private law firms, corporations, government entities
State for Bar Exam: TX
Pass Rate for First-Time Bar: 78%

SOUTHERN CALIFORNIA INSTITUTE OF LAW
College of Law

Admissions Contact: Dean, Dr. Stanislaus Pulle
877 S. Victoria, Ventura, CA 93003
Admissions Phone: 805-644-2327 • Admissions Fax: 805-644-2367
Web Address: www.lawdegree.com

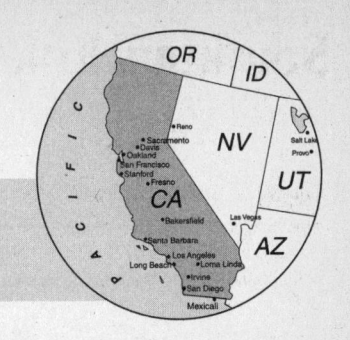

INSTITUTIONAL INFORMATION
Public/Private: Private
Affiliation: Conservative
Academic Calendar: Semester
Student/Faculty Ratio: 5:1
% Part Time: 75
% Female: 50
% Minority: 10

PROGRAMS
Academic Specialties: Strong emphasis on legal writing. Professors teach in subjects in which they have a specialized practice.

STUDENT INFORMATION
Enrollment of Law School: 50
% Male/Female: 60/40
% Full Time: 0
% Minority: 15
Average Age of Entering Class: 32

RESEARCH FACILITIES
School-Supported Research Centers: Local courthouse library

EXPENSES/FINANCIAL AID
Annual Tuition: $6,480
Books and Supplies: $500
% of Aid That Is Merit-Based: 100
Tuition Per Credit: $200
Fees Per Credit: $200

ADMISSIONS INFORMATION
LSDAS Accepted? No
Transfer Students Accepted? No
Other Schools to Which Students Applied: Ventura College of Law, San Francisco Law School, Santa Barbara College of Law, Western State University
Other Admissions Factors Considered: Working professionals

INTERNATIONAL STUDENTS
TOEFL Required of International Students? Yes

EMPLOYMENT INFORMATION
Average Starting Salary: $30,000
Employers Who Frequently Hire Grads: Local law firms, government and state agencies
Prominent Alumni: Dr. Michael Clare, vice president, HCIA; Sally La Macchia, associate general counsel, National Association of Government Employees; Dr. Jim Forrest, senior scientist, P.E. Muger Base

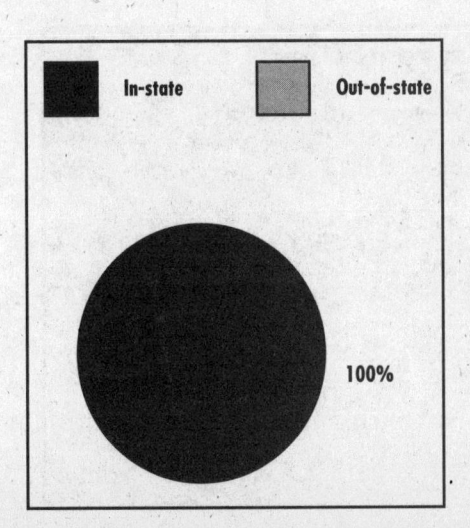

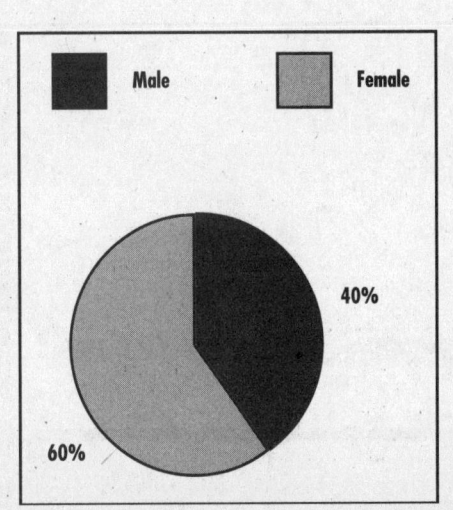

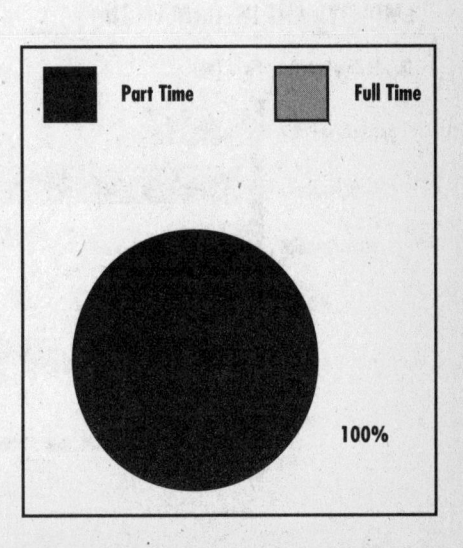

SOUTHERN ILLINOIS UNIVERSITY
School of Law

Admissions Contact: Assistant Dean, Michael Ruiz
SIU School of Law, Carbondale, IL 62901-6804
Admissions Phone: 618-453-8858 • Admissions Fax: 618-453-8769
Admissions E-mail: lawadmit@siu.edu • Web Address: www.law.siu.edu

INSTITUTIONAL INFORMATION
Public/Private: Public
Student/Faculty Ratio: 13:1
Total Faculty: 46
% Part Time: 22
% Female: 41
% Minority: 1

PROGRAMS
Academic Specialties: Health Law, Alternative Dispute Resolution, Clinical Programs
Advanced Degrees Offered: JD (3 years)
Combined Degrees Offered: JD/MD (6 years), JD/MBA (4 years), JD/MPA (4 years), JD/MAcc (4 years), JD/MSW, JD/PhD
Grading System: 4.0 scale with a fixed median
Clinical Program Required? No
Clinical Programs Description: Elderly Law, Domestic Violence, Alternative Dispute Resolution, Self-Help Legal Center, Agricultural Mediation
Legal Writing Course Requirements? No
Legal Methods Course Requirements? Yes
Legal Methods Description: Required Lawyering Skills Program includes legal research, writing, argumentation, negotiation
Legal Research Course Requirements? No
Moot Court Requirement? No
Public Interest Law Requirement? No
Academic Journals: *Southern Illinois University Law Journal, Journal of Legal Medicine*

STUDENT INFORMATION
Enrollment of Law School: 369
% Male/Female: 60/40
% Full Time: 100
% Full Time That Are International: 1
% Minority: 9
Average Age of Entering Class: 26

RESEARCH FACILITIES
Research Resources Available: Lexis, Westlaw, 4 on-campus computer labs

EXPENSES/FINANCIAL AID
Annual Tuition (Residents/Nonresidents): $5,178/$15,534
Room and Board: $9,086
Books and Supplies: $810
Financial Aid Application Deadline: 4/1
Average Grant: $1,500
Average Loan: $13,380
% of Aid That Is Merit-Based: 99
% Receiving Some Sort of Aid: 95
Average Total Aid Package: $15,380
Average Debt: $27,370

ADMISSIONS INFORMATION
Application Fee: $40
Regular Application Deadline: Rolling
Regular Notification: Rolling
LSDAS Accepted? Yes
Average GPA: 3.1
Range of GPA: 2.8–3.5
Average LSAT: 152
Range of LSAT: 149–154
Transfer Students Accepted? Yes
Other Schools to Which Students Applied: Northern Illinois University
Other Admissions Factors Considered: Leadership ability, character, maturity, motivation, ability to contribute to diversity, overcoming of obstacles
Number of Applications Received: 592
Number of Applicants Accepted: 381
Number of Applicants Enrolled: 128

INTERNATIONAL STUDENTS
TOEFL Required of International Students? Yes

EMPLOYMENT INFORMATION

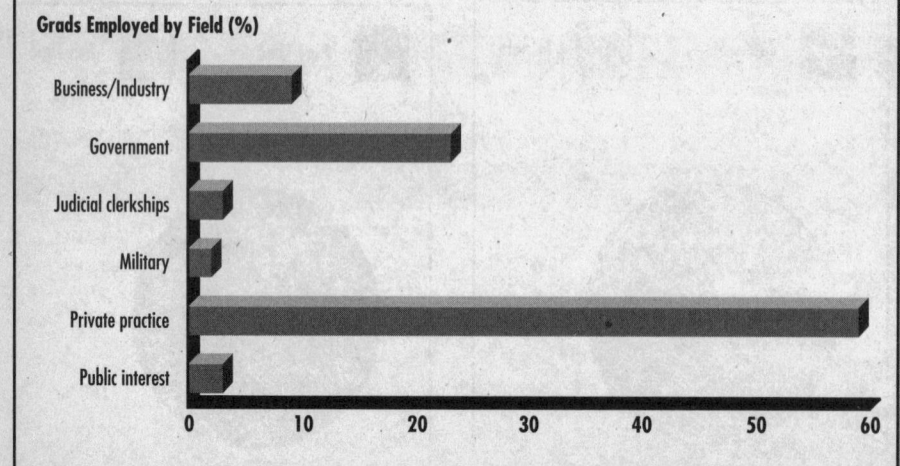

Grads Employed by Field (%):
- Business/Industry: ~8
- Government: ~23
- Judicial clerkships: ~3
- Military: ~2
- Private practice: ~60
- Public interest: ~2

Rate of Placement: 97%
Average Starting Salary: $38,500
Employers Who Frequently Hire Grads: Various Illinois State's Attorney's Offices; various large and small law firms, public interest organizations
State for Bar Exam: IL, MO, KY, TN, IN
Pass Rate for First-Time Bar: 83%

SOUTHERN METHODIST UNIVERSITY
Dedman School of Law

Admissions Contact: Assistant Dean and Director of Admissions, Lynn Bozalis
PO Box 750110, Dallas, TX 75275
Admissions Phone: 214-768-2550 • Admissions Fax: 214-768-2549
Admissions E-mail: lawadmit@mail.smu.edu • Web Address: www.law.smu.edu/

INSTITUTIONAL INFORMATION
Public/Private: Private
Affiliation: Methodist
Student/Faculty Ratio: 18:1
Total Faculty: 36
% Part Time: 0
% Female: 30
% Minority: 14

PROGRAMS
Academic Specialties: Business, Tax, Securities, International Law, Litigation, Environmental, Health Care, Internet, Dispute Resolution
Advanced Degrees Offered: LLM Taxation (1 year), LLM (1 year)
Combined Degrees Offered: JD/MBA (4.5 years), JD/MA (4 years)
Grading System: Letter and numerical system on a 4.0 scale with no C–, D+, or D–
Clinical Program Required? Yes
Clinical Programs Description: Civil, Criminal Defense, Tax, Domestic Violence, Criminal Prosecution, Poverty Law
Legal Writing Course Requirements? No
Legal Methods Course Requirements? Yes
Legal Methods Description: 1 year (2 hours in fall, 4 hours in spring)
Legal Research Course Requirements? No
Moot Court Requirement? No
Public Interest Law Requirement? No

STUDENT INFORMATION
Enrollment of Law School: 741
% Out of State: 35
% Male/Female: 56/44
% Full Time: 98
% Full Time That Are International: 1
% Minority: 11
Average Age of Entering Class: 25

EXPENSES/FINANCIAL AID
Annual Tuition: $22,550
Room and Board: $8,400
Books and Supplies: $1,300
Financial Aid Application Deadline: 6/1
Average Grant: $8,000
Average Loan: $22,500
% of Aid That Is Merit-Based: 100
% Receiving Some Sort of Aid: 80
Average Total Aid Package: $35,000
Average Debt: $70,000
Tuition Per Credit: $770
Fees Per Credit: $99

ADMISSIONS INFORMATION
Application Fee: $50
Regular Application Deadline: 2/15
Regular Notification: 4/30
LSDAS Accepted? Yes
Average GPA: 3.5
Range of GPA: 3.1–3.7
Average LSAT: 159
Range of LSAT: 156–161
Transfer Students Accepted? Yes
Other Schools to Which Students Applied: University of Texas at Austin, Tulane University, University of Houston, Baylor University
Number of Applications Received: 1,582
Number of Applicants Accepted: 595
Number of Applicants Enrolled: 262

EMPLOYMENT INFORMATION

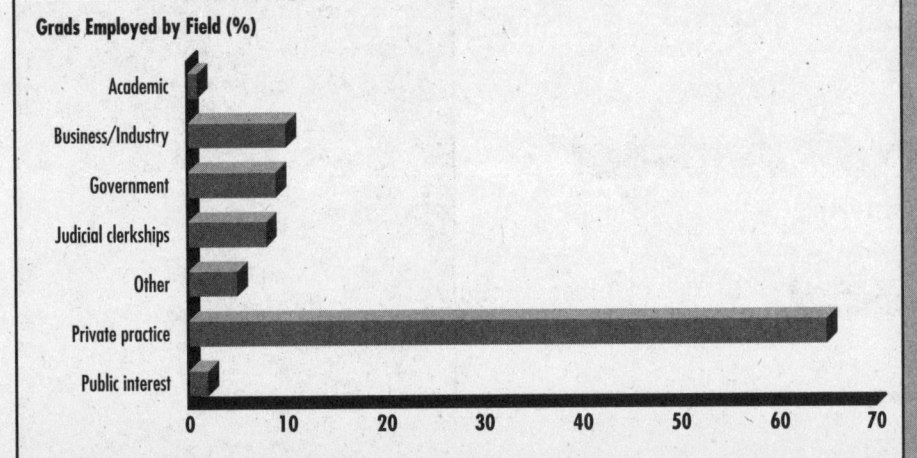

Grads Employed by Field (%)
- Academic
- Business/Industry
- Government
- Judicial clerkships
- Other
- Private practice
- Public interest

Rate of Placement: 98%
Average Starting Salary: $74,000
Employers Who Frequently Hire Grads: Akin, Gump, Strauss, Hauer & Feld; Baker Botts; Haynes and Boone; Jones, Day, Reavis & Pogue; Vinson & Elkins; Dallas County District Attorney's Office; Texas Supreme Court
State for Bar Exam: TX
Pass Rate for First-Time Bar: 84%

SOUTHERN UNIVERSITY
Law Center

Admissions Contact: Gloria Simon
PO Box 9294, Baton Rouge, LA 70813
Admissions Phone: 225-771-5340 • Admissions Fax: 225-771-7424
Web Address: www.sus.edu

INSTITUTIONAL INFORMATION
Public/Private: Public
Environment: Urban
Academic Calendar: Semester
Schedule: Full time only
Student/Faculty Ratio: 12:1
Total Faculty: 44
% Female: 30
% Minority: 64

PROGRAMS
Academic Specialties: Law and Technology (Artificial Intelligence)
Grading System: 4.0 grade point scale; A (90–100), B+ (85–89), B (84–80), C+ (79–75), C (74–70), D+ (69–65), D (64–60), F (59–0)
Clinical Program Required? No
Clinical Program Description: 4 Clinics: Criminal, Juvenile, Elder Law, Administrative/Civil. Clinical Education Program is restricted to third-year law students in good standing.
Legal Writing/Methods Course Requirements: First year: Legal Writing, 2 hours/semester; second year: Advanced Legal Writing 1 hour/semester

STUDENT INFORMATION
Enrollment of Law School: 311
% Male/Female: 50/50
% Full Time: 100
% Minority: 66
Average Age of Entering Class: 27

RESEARCH FACILITIES
School-Supported Research Centers: Through a cooperative aggreement with Paul M. Herbert Law Center at Louisiana State University, students at both institutions have unlimited and free access to each institution's facilities and materials.

EXPENSES/FINANCIAL AID
Annual Tuition (Residents/Nonresidents): $3,128/$7,728

ADMISSIONS INFORMATION
Regular Application Deadline: 3/1
Regular Notification: January–May
Average GPA: 3.6
Average LSAT: 145
Other Schools to Which Students Applied: Loyola University Chicago, Howard University, Tulane University, Texas Southern University, Georgia State University, Florida State University, George Mason University, Georgetown University

EMPLOYMENT INFORMATION

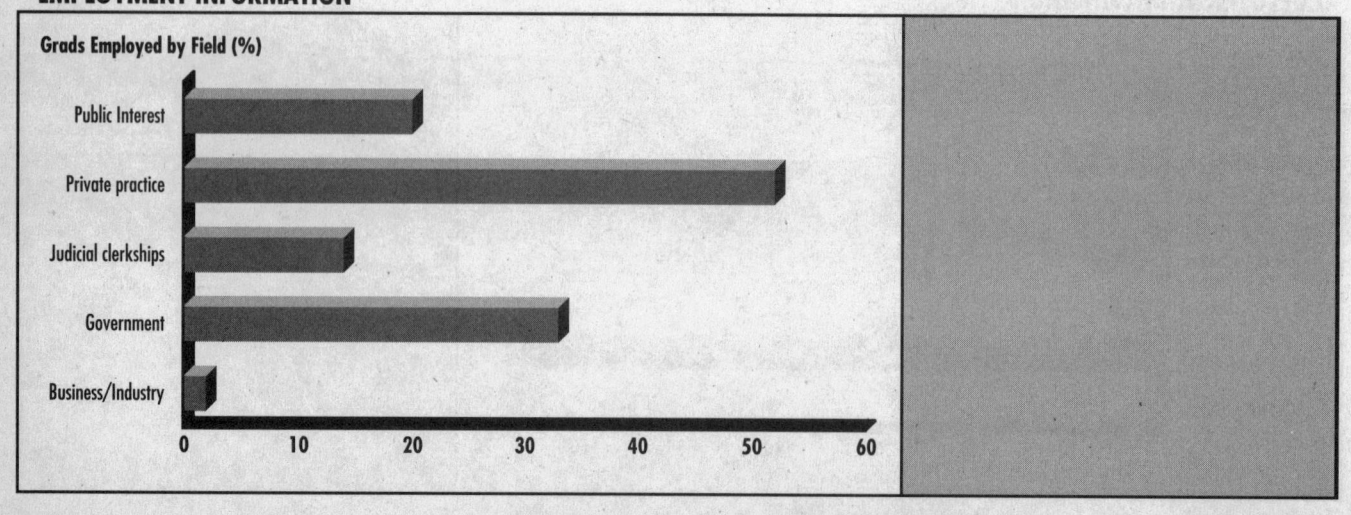

Grads Employed by Field (%)

Field	%
Public Interest	~20
Private practice	~52
Judicial clerkships	~15
Government	~33
Business/Industry	~2

SOUTHWESTERN UNIVERSITY SCHOOL OF LAW

Admissions Contact: Director of Admissions
675 South Westmoreland Avenue, Los Angeles, CA 90005
Admissions Phone: 213-738-6717 • Admissions Fax: 213-383-1688
Admissions E-mail: admissions@swlaw.edu • Web Address: www.swlaw.edu

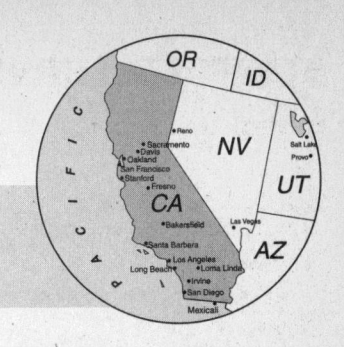

INSTITUTIONAL INFORMATION
Public/Private: Private
Student/Faculty Ratio: 16:1
Total Faculty: 90
% Part Time: 44
% Female: 36
% Minority: 20

PROGRAMS
Academic Specialties: Nationally recognized experts in Antitrust Law, Criminal Law, Environmental Law, Family Law, Housing and Urban Development, Intellectual Property Law, Entertainment and Media Law, International Law, and Taxation. Other specialties include Civil Procedure, Commercial Law, Constitutional Law, Corporation Securities Law, Government Services, Human Rights Law, Labor Law, Legal History, Legal Philosophy, and Property.
Grading System: A+/A (4.0) to F (0); some courses are Pass/Fail
Clinical Program Required? No
Clinical Programs Description: Externships in over 100 legal settings in judicial, public interest, federal/state/local government, or entertainment entities; clinical/simulation courses on a variety of topics from Alternative Dispute Resolution to White-Collar Crime
Legal Writing Course Requirements? No
Legal Methods Course Requirements? Yes
Legal Methods Description: Legal Research and Writing in the first year, culminating in Moot Court Intramural Competition

Legal Research Course Requirements? No
Moot Court Requirement? Yes
Moot Court Description: Each first-year student prepares a written appellate brief in the Legal Research and Writing course and participates in 2 mandatory rounds of oral argument. Following the third optional round, 16 students are selected to compete in 4 final rounds judged by distinguished members of the bench and bar.
Public Interest Law Requirement? No
Academic Journals: *Southwestern University Law Review*, *Southwestern Journal of Law and Trade in the Americas*

STUDENT INFORMATION
Enrollment of Law School: 826
% Out of State: 20
% Male/Female: 46/54
% Full Time: 70
% Full Time That Are International: 1
% Minority: 34
Average Age of Entering Class: 27

EXPENSES/FINANCIAL AID
Annual Tuition: $23,310
Room and Board (Off Campus): $11,000
Books and Supplies: $620
Financial Aid Application Deadline: 6/1
Average Grant: $7,051
Average Loan: $22,853
% of Aid That Is Merit-Based: 30
% Receiving Some Sort of Aid: 93
Average Total Aid Package: $24,975
Average Debt: $82,449
Tuition Per Credit: $777

ADMISSIONS INFORMATION
Application Fee: $50
Regular Application Deadline: 6/30
Regular Notification: Rolling
LSDAS Accepted? Yes
Range of GPA: 2.8–3.3
Range of LSAT: 148–153
Transfer Students Accepted? Yes
Number of Applications Received: 1,968
Number of Applicants Accepted: 1,078
Number of Applicants Enrolled: 342

EMPLOYMENT INFORMATION

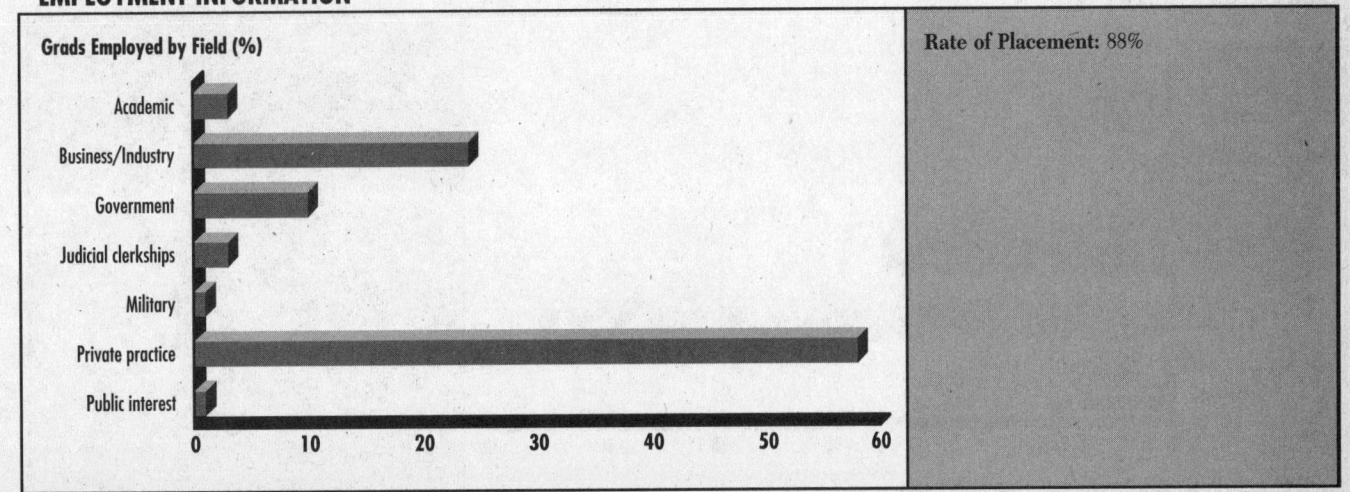

Grads Employed by Field (%)

Field	%
Academic	~2
Business/Industry	~23
Government	~10
Judicial clerkships	~3
Military	~1
Private practice	~58
Public interest	~1

Rate of Placement: 88%

STANFORD UNIVERSITY
School of Law

Admissions Contact: Associate Dean for Admissions and Financial Aid, Faye K. Deal
559 Nathan Abbott Way, Stanford, CA 94305-8610
Admissions Phone: 650-723-4985 • Admissions Fax: 650-723-0838
Admissions E-mail: law.admissions@forsythe.stanford.edu • Web Address: www.law.stanford.edu

INSTITUTIONAL INFORMATION
Public/Private: Private
Student/Faculty Ratio: 13:1
Total Faculty: 38
% Female: 24
% Minority: 15

PROGRAMS
Academic Specialties: Civil Procedure, Commercial Law, Constitutional Law, Corporation Securities Law, Criminal Law, Environmental Law, Government Services, Human Rights Law, Intellectual Property Law, International Law, Labor Law, Legal History, Legal Philosophy, Property, Taxation
Advanced Degrees Offered: MLS (1 year), JSM (1 year), LLM (1 year), JSD (2 years)
Combined Degrees Offered: JD/MBA (4 years), JD/MA (4 years)
Grading System: Letter system
Clinical Program Required? No
Legal Writing Course Requirements? Yes
Legal Writing Description: 1 year
Legal Methods Course Requirements? No
Legal Research Course Requirements? Yes
Legal Research Description: 1 year
Moot Court Requirement? No
Public Interest Law Requirement? No

Academic Journals: *Stanford Agora: An Online Journal of Legal Perspectives; Stanford Environmental Law Journal; Stanford Law Review; Stanford Journal of International Law; Stanford Journal of Law, Business, and Finance; Stanford Law and Public Policy Review; Stanford Technology and Law Review*

STUDENT INFORMATION
Enrollment of Law School: 559
% Male/Female: 52/48
% Full Time: 100
% Full Time That Are International: 2
% Minority: 32
Average Age of Entering Class: 25

EXPENSES/FINANCIAL AID
Annual Tuition: $29,398
Room and Board (On/Off Campus): $12,040/$18,535
Books and Supplies: $1,360

Financial Aid Application Deadline: 3/15
Average Grant: $11,147
Average Loan: $34,727
% of Aid That Is Merit-Based: 0
% Receiving Some Sort of Aid: 84
Average Total Aid Package: $39,550
Average Debt: $74,000

ADMISSIONS INFORMATION
Application Fee: $65
Regular Application Deadline: Rolling
Regular Notification: 4/30
LSDAS Accepted? Yes
Average GPA: 3.7
Range of GPA: 3.7–3.9
Average LSAT: 168
Range of LSAT: 165–170
Transfer Students Accepted? Yes
Number of Applications Received: 4,273
Number of Applicants Accepted: 478
Number of Applicants Enrolled: 178

EMPLOYMENT INFORMATION

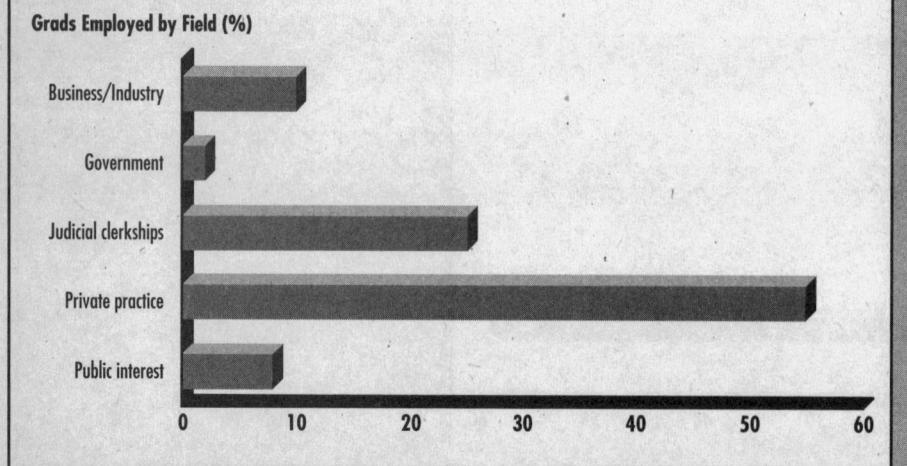

Grads Employed by Field (%)

Field	%
Business/Industry	10
Government	2
Judicial clerkships	25
Private practice	55
Public interest	8

Rate of Placement: 100%
Average Starting Salary: $89,876
State for Bar Exam: CA
Pass Rate for First-Time Bar: 85%

STETSON UNIVERSITY
College of Law

Admissions Contact: Assistant Dean of Admissions, Pamela B. Coleman
1401 61st Street South, St. Petersburg, FL 33707
Admissions Phone: 727-562-7802 • Admissions Fax: 727-343-0136
Admissions E-mail: lawadmit@law.stetson.edu • Web Address: www.law.stetson.edu

INSTITUTIONAL INFORMATION
Public/Private: Private
Student/Faculty Ratio: 18:1
Total Faculty: 76
% Part Time: 48
% Female: 38
% Minority: 14

PROGRAMS
Academic Specialties: Nationally ranked Stetson Advocacy Program; award-winning Moot Court Program; "Centers for Excellence" in Advocacy, Health Law, Elder Law, and Alternative Dispute Resolution; Honors program for students who earn a 3.5 GPA after the first or second full academic semester; comprehensive academic success program; other specialties include International Law, Advocacy, Health Law, and Elder Law
Advanced Degrees Offered: JD (3 years full time, 4 years part time), LLM (1 year), JD/MBA (3 years)
Combined Degrees Offered: JD/MBA (3 years)
Grading System: 4.0 scale
Clinical Program Required? No
Clinical Programs Description: Criminal Defense, Criminal Prosecution, Civil Poverty, Elder Law, Employment Discrimination, Local Government, Alternative Dispute Resolution, Labor Law
Legal Writing Course Requirements? Yes
Legal Writing Description: 2-semester course that focuses on legal research, objective and persuasive writing, and oral advocacy.
Legal Methods Course Requirements? No
Legal Research Course Requirements? Yes
Legal Research Description: Legal research is taught as part of the Research and Writing course, with a focus on print and computer-assisted research. Students have the opportunity to participate in small-group lab sessions.
Moot Court Requirement? Yes
Moot Court Description: First-year students are taught oral advocacy in the second semester and give 4 oral presentations. Top oralists compete in a first-year appellate advocacy competition for cash prizes and positions on the Moot Court Board.
Public Interest Law Requirement? Yes
Public Interest Law Description: Students must complete 20 hours of pro bono work before graduation.
Academic Journals: *Stetson Law Review*, *Stetson Law Forum* (online publication)

STUDENT INFORMATION
Enrollment of Law School: 650
% Out of State: 27
% Male/Female: 45/55
% Full Time: 100
% Full Time That Are International: 1
% Minority: 18
Average Age of Entering Class: 26

EXPENSES/FINANCIAL AID
Annual Tuition: $21,905
Room and Board (On/Off Campus): $7,500/$10,000
Books and Supplies: $1,200
Average Grant: $12,724
Average Loan: $30,000
% of Aid That Is Merit-Based: 63
% Receiving Some Sort of Aid: 90
Average Total Aid Package: $36,000
Average Debt: $94,306

ADMISSIONS INFORMATION
Application Fee: $50
Regular Application Deadline: Rolling
Regular Notification: Rolling
LSDAS Accepted? Yes
Average GPA: 3.2
Range of GPA: 2.9–3.5
Average LSAT: 151
Range of LSAT: 148–155
Transfer Students Accepted? Yes
Other Schools to Which Students Applied: Florida State University, Mercer University, University of Florida, University of Miami
Other Admissions Factors Considered: Personal statements, grade trends, letters of recommendation, campus activities/work experience, diversity factors
Number of Applications Received: 1,215
Number of Applicants Accepted: 621
Number of Applicants Enrolled: 181

INTERNATIONAL STUDENTS
TOEFL Required of International Students? Yes
Minimum TOEFL: 250

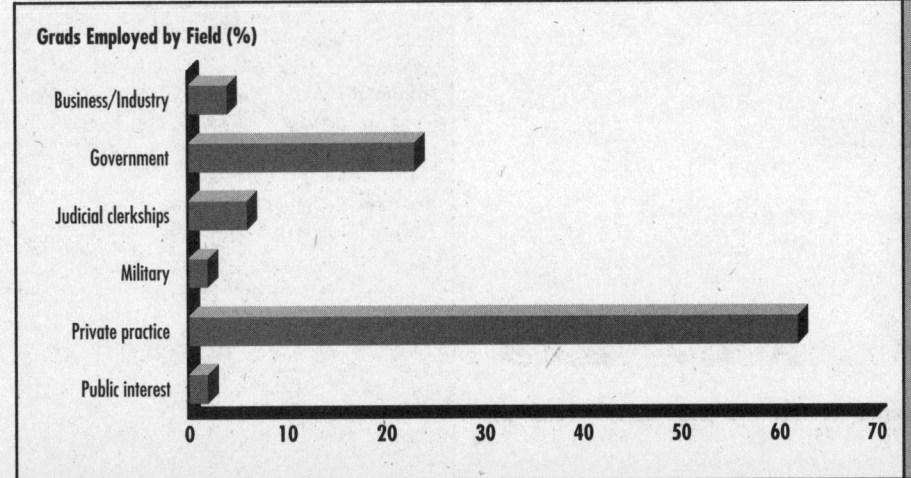

EMPLOYMENT INFORMATION

Grads Employed by Field (%)

Field	%
Business/Industry	~3
Government	~22
Judicial clerkships	~7
Military	~2
Private practice	~62
Public interest	~3

Rate of Placement: 97%
Average Starting Salary: $45,554
Employers Who Frequently Hire Grads: Small, medium, and large firms in the Greater Tampa Bay area; State Attorney's Offices; Public Defender's Office
State for Bar Exam: FL
Pass Rate for First-Time Bar: 85%

Suffolk University
Law School

Admissions Contact: Dean of Admissions, Gail Ellis
120 Tremont Street, Boston, MA 02114
Admissions Phone: 617-573-8144 • Admissions Fax: 617-523-1367
Admissions E-mail: lawadm@admin.suffolk.edu • Web Address: www.law.suffolk.edu

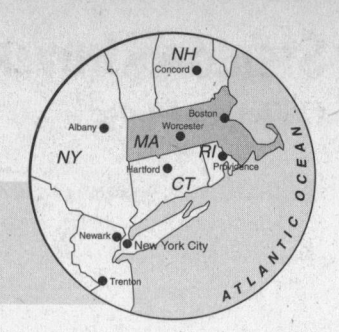

INSTITUTIONAL INFORMATION
Public/Private: Private
Student/Faculty Ratio: 20:1
Total Faculty: 160
% Part Time: 60
% Female: 17
% Minority: 5

PROGRAMS
Academic Specialties: High Technology/Intellectual Property, Health Care/Biomedical Law, Financial Services, Civil Litigation, International Law, Human Rights/Civil Rights, Labor and Employment Law, Juvenile Law, Civil Procedure, Commercial Law, Constitutional Law, Corporation Securities Law, Criminal Law, Environmental Law, Government Services, Legal History, Legal Philosophy, Property, Taxation; study abroad program at University of Lund, Sweden
Advanced Degrees Offered: JD (3 years full time, 4 years part time)
Combined Degrees Offered: JD/MBA, JD/MPA, JD/MSIE, JD/MSF, JD/MSCJ (all 3 years full time, 5 years part time)
Grading System: Letter and numerical system ranging from A+ = 4.3 to F = 0
Clinical Program Required? Yes
Clinical Programs Description: Voluntary Defenders/Prosecutors Program, Battered Women's Advocacy Program, Center for Juvenile Justice, SU Clinica (works with Hispanic community), Suffolk University Legal Assistance Bureau, Macaronis Institute for Trial and Appellate Advocacy

Legal Writing Course Requirements? No
Legal Methods Course Requirements? Yes
Legal Methods Description: 2 semesters
Legal Research Course Requirements? No
Moot Court Requirement? No
Public Interest Law Requirement? No
Academic Journals: Suffolk University Law Review, Transnational Law Review, Suffolk Journal of Trial and Appellate Advocacy, Journal of High Technology Law

STUDENT INFORMATION
Enrollment of Law School: 1,690
% Out of State: 46
% Male/Female: 46/54
% Full Time: 67
% Full Time That Are International: 5
% Minority: 12
Average Age of Entering Class: 25

RESEARCH FACILITIES
Research Resources Available: 2,700 data ports in the new Law School facility; laptop computer accessibility at all classroom desktops, library study carrels, and table spaces; extensive laptop hookups in all student lounges and cafeteria

EXPENSES/FINANCIAL AID
Annual Tuition: $24,870
Room and Board (Off Campus): $14,370
Books and Supplies: $900
Financial Aid Application Deadline: 3/2
Average Grant: $4,000
Average Loan: $26,035
% of Aid That Is Merit-Based: 39
% Receiving Some Sort of Aid: 82
Average Total Aid Package: $24,500
Average Debt: $65,785
Tuition Per Credit: $850

ADMISSIONS INFORMATION
Application Fee: $50
Regular Application Deadline: 3/1
Regular Notification: Rolling
LSDAS Accepted? Yes
Average GPA: 3.2
Range of GPA: 2.9–3.4
Average LSAT: 153
Range of LSAT: 150–155
Transfer Students Accepted? Yes
Other Admissions Factors Considered: Community service
Number of Applications Received: 2,200
Number of Applicants Enrolled: 547

INTERNATIONAL STUDENTS
TOEFL Required of International Students? Yes

EMPLOYMENT INFORMATION

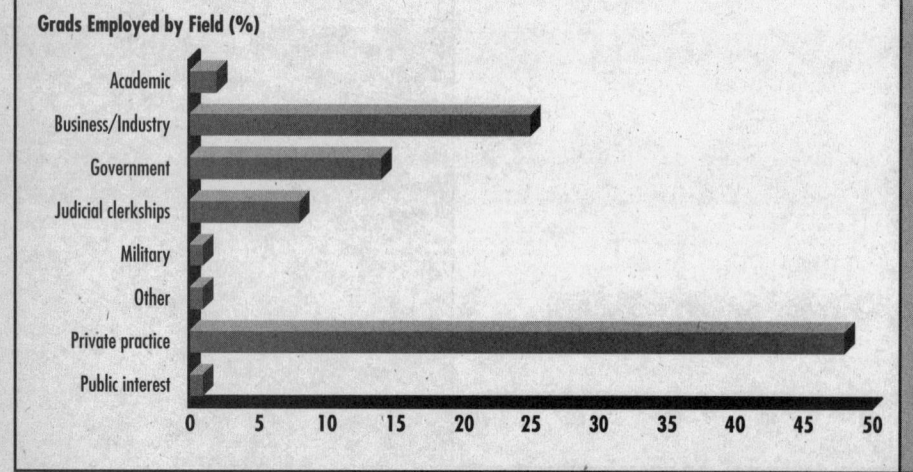

Grads Employed by Field (%)
- Academic
- Business/Industry: ~25
- Government: ~15
- Judicial clerkships: ~8
- Military
- Other
- Private practice: ~48
- Public interest

Rate of Placement: 94%
Average Starting Salary: $54,850
Employers Who Frequently Hire Grads: Testa, Hurwitz & Thibeault, LLP; Navy JAG; Massachusetts Superior Court; Suffolk County District Attorney's Office
State for Bar Exam: MA
Pass Rate for First-Time Bar: 84%

SYRACUSE UNIVERSITY
College of Law

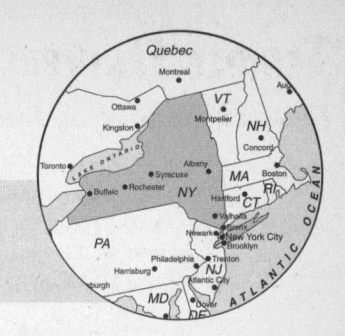

Admissions Contact: Director of Admissions, Nikki S. Laubenstein
Office of Admissions and Financial Aid, Suite 340, Syracuse, NY 13244
Admissions Phone: 315-443-1962 • Admissions Fax: 315-443-9568
Admissions E-mail: admissions@law.syr.edu • Web Address: www.law.syr.edu

INSTITUTIONAL INFORMATION
Public/Private: Private
Student/Faculty Ratio: 17:1
Total Faculty: 39
% Female: 33
% Minority: 15

PROGRAMS
Academic Specialties: Syracuse programs are designed to integrate theory and practical training by providing hands-on experience in a variety of fields. Specialties include Trial Practice; Law, Technology, and Management; Law and Economics; Clinical Training; Commercial Law; Constitutional Law; Corporation Securities Law; Criminal Law; Environmental Law; Government Services; Human Rights Law; International Law; Labor Law; Taxation; Technology Law; and Family Law.
Combined Degrees Offered: JD/MS Accounting, Library Science, Environmental Science, Communications, Speech Communications, News/Magazine, Media, Language Arts, or Nutrition; JD/MBA; JD/MA Economics, History, International Relations, Engineering, or Geography; JD/PhD Political Science; JD/MSW; JD/MPA
Grading System: A, A–, B+, B, B–, C+, C, C–, D, and F or Pass/Fail.
Clinical Program Required? No
Clinical Programs Description: Community Development, Criminal Law, Public Interest Law, Children's Rights, and Family Law; externships in Judicial, Advocacy, Public Interest, and Washington, D.C.

Legal Writing Course Requirements? Yes
Legal Writing Description: First-year course "Law Firm" (2 semesters)
Legal Methods Course Requirements? Yes
Legal Methods Description: First-year course "Law Firm" (2 semesters)
Legal Research Course Requirements? Yes
Legal Research Description: First-year course "Law Firm" (2 semesters)
Moot Court Requirement? No
Public Interest Law Requirement? No
Academic Journals: *Law Review, Syracuse Journal of International Law and Commerce, The Digest, The Labor Lawyer, The Journal of Law and Technology*

STUDENT INFORMATION
Enrollment of Law School: 763
% Male/Female: 53/47
% Full Time: 99
% Full Time That Are International: 4
% Minority: 18
Average Age of Entering Class: 25

RESEARCH FACILITIES
Research Resources Available: 84 PCs available in the College of Law

EXPENSES/FINANCIAL AID
Annual Tuition: $25,940
Room and Board: $9,620
Books and Supplies: $1,100
Financial Aid Application Deadline: 2/1

Average Grant: $8,673
Average Loan: $24,900
Average Debt: $65,000
Tuition Per Credit: $1,135
Fees Per Credit: $189

ADMISSIONS INFORMATION
Application Fee: $50
Regular Application Deadline: Rolling
Regular Notification: Rolling
LSDAS Accepted? Yes
Average GPA: 3.2
Range of GPA: 3.0–3.5
Average LSAT: 151
Range of LSAT: 147–154
Transfer Students Accepted? Yes
Other Admissions Factors Considered: Trend of undergraduate performance and course selection, graduate coursework and degree, writing ability, overcoming personal hardship such as poverty or disability, age, race/ethnicity, gender, and, community activities
Number of Applications Received: 1,901
Number of Applicants Accepted: 1,095
Number of Applicants Enrolled: 280

INTERNATIONAL STUDENTS
TOEFL Required of International Students? Yes

EMPLOYMENT INFORMATION

Grads Employed by Field (%)
- Academic
- Business/Industry
- Government
- Judicial clerkships
- Other
- Private practice
- Public interest

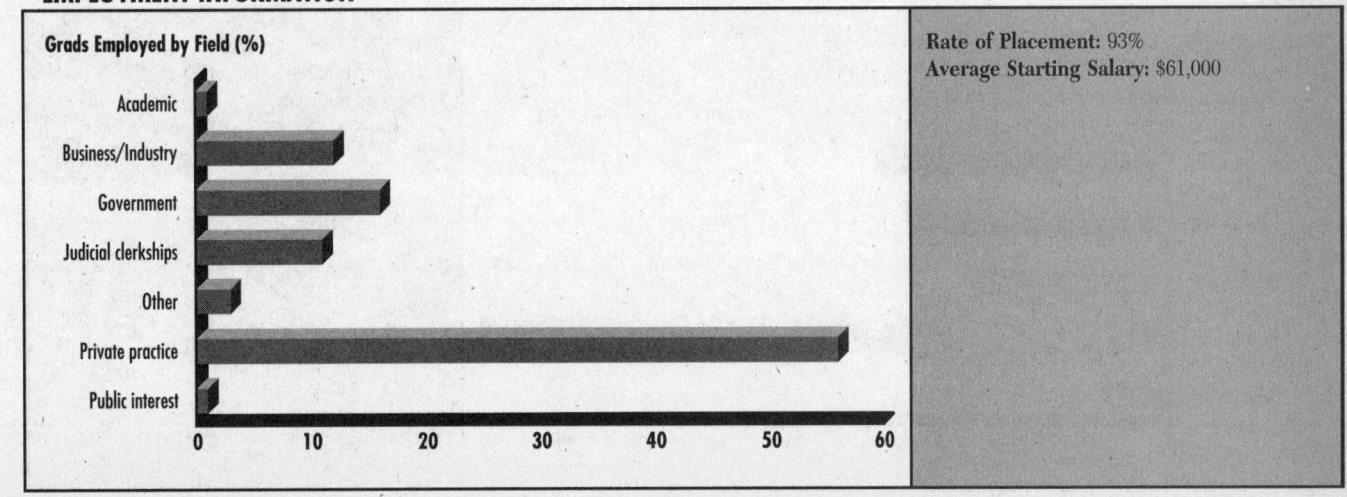

Rate of Placement: 93%
Average Starting Salary: $61,000

TEMPLE UNIVERSITY
Beasley School of Law

Admissions Contact: Director of Admissions and Financial Aid, Johanne L. Johnston
1719 North Broad Street, Philadelphia, PA 19122
Admissions Phone: 800-560-1428 • Admissions Fax: 215-204-9319
Admissions E-mail: lawadmis@blue.temple.edu • Web Address: www.temple.edu/lawschool

INSTITUTIONAL INFORMATION
Public/Private: Public
Student/Faculty Ratio: 16:1
Total Faculty: 61
% Female: 33
% Minority: 25

PROGRAMS
Academic Specialties: Trial Advocacy, Business and Tax Law, International Law, Public Interest Law, Criminal Law, Transactional Law, Technology Law/ Intellectual Property, Civil Procedure, Commercial Law, Constitutional Law, Corporation Securities Law, Property
Advanced Degrees Offered: JD (3 years full time, 4 years part time), LLM Trial Advocacy (1 year), LLM Taxation (1 year), LLM Transnational Law (1 year), Graduate Teaching Fellowships (1 year), LLM for graduates of foreign law schools (1 year)
Combined Degrees Offered: JD/MBA (approximately 4 years), JD/LLM degree programs in Taxation and Transnational Law (3.5 years), JD with individually-designed joint degrees
Grading System: 4.0 scale
Clinical Program Required? No
Clinical Programs Description: Temple has extensive clinical offerings in 25 areas ranging from Civil Litigation to Business and Criminal Law. All students are guaranteed at least 1 clinical offering.
Legal Writing Course Requirements? Yes
Legal Writing Description: 1-year intensive program that includes drafting briefs, memos, and conducting an oral argument
Legal Methods Course Requirements? Yes
Legal Methods Description: Semester-long course that includes an introduction to legal methods and legal reasoning and analysis
Legal Research Course Requirements? Yes
Legal Research Description: 1-year intensive program that includes drafting briefs, memos, and conducting an oral argument
Moot Court Requirement? No
Public Interest Law Requirement? No
Academic Journals: *Temple Law Review, Temple International and Comparative Law Review, Temple Political and Civil Rights Law Review, Temple Environmental Law and Technology Journal*

STUDENT INFORMATION
Enrollment of Law School: 1,074
% Male/Female: 51/49
% Full Time: 73
% Full Time That Are International: 1
% Minority: 19
Average Age of Entering Class: 26

RESEARCH FACILITIES
School-Supported Research Centers: Brand new state-of-the-art conference center, Shusterman Hall, devoted entirely to Law School activities

EXPENSES/FINANCIAL AID
Annual Tuition (Residents/Nonresidents): $10,308/$17,864
Room and Board: $6,720
Books and Supplies: $1,500
Financial Aid Application Deadline: 3/1
Average Grant: $2,749
Average Loan: $19,238
% of Aid That Is Merit-Based: 83
% Receiving Some Sort of Aid: 80
Average Total Aid Package: $20,606
Average Debt: $53,524
Tuition Per Credit (Residents/Nonresidents): $398/$729

ADMISSIONS INFORMATION
Application Fee: $50
Regular Application Deadline: 3/1
Regular Notification: Rolling
LSDAS Accepted? Yes
Average GPA: 3.3
Range of GPA: 3.0–3.6
Average LSAT: 157
Range of LSAT: 154–160
Transfer Students Accepted? Yes
Other Schools to Which Students Applied: American University, George Washington University, Rutgers University, Villanova University, Widener University
Other Admissions Factors Considered: Graduate coursework; demonstrated leadership ability in college, community, or career activities; economic disadvantage; academic honors; commitment to service (Peace Corps, VISTA, military); serious disabilities
Number of Applications Received: 3,226
Number of Applicants Accepted: 1,276
Number of Applicants Enrolled: 345

INTERNATIONAL STUDENTS
TOEFL Required of International Students? Yes

EMPLOYMENT INFORMATION

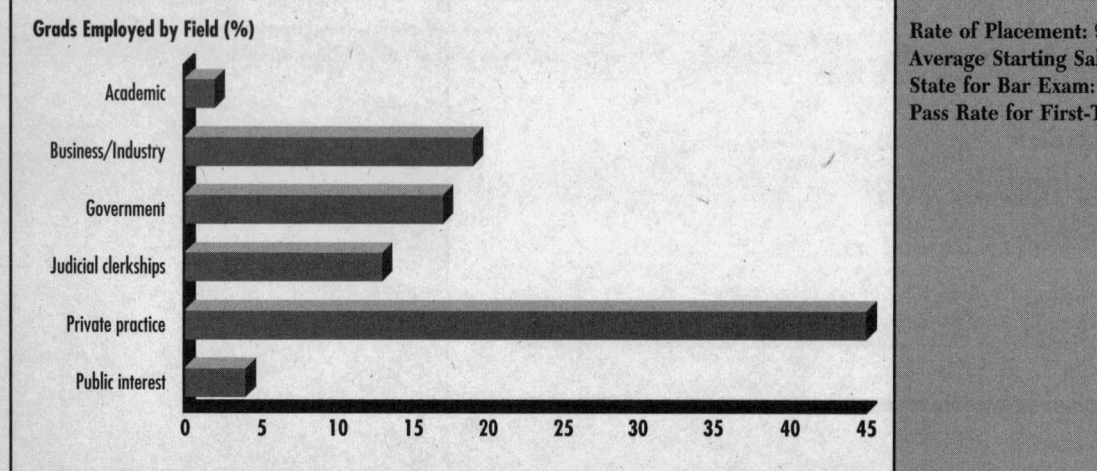

Grads Employed by Field (%)
- Academic: ~2
- Business/Industry: ~19
- Government: ~17
- Judicial clerkships: ~14
- Private practice: ~45
- Public interest: ~3

Rate of Placement: 93%
Average Starting Salary: $65,450
State for Bar Exam: PA
Pass Rate for First-Time Bar: 75%

TEXAS SOUTHERN UNIVERSITY
Thurgood Marshall School of Law

Admissions Contact: Dean of Admissions
3100 Cleburne Avenue, Houston, TX 77004
Admissions Phone: 713-313-7114 • Web Address: www.tsulaw.edu

INSTITUTIONAL INFORMATION
Public/Private: Public
Student/Faculty Ratio: 17:1
Total Faculty: 35
% Female: 20
% Minority: 83

PROGRAMS
Academic Specialties: Commercial Law, Corporation Securities Law
Clinical Program Required? No
Legal Methods Course Requirements? No

STUDENT INFORMATION
Enrollment of Law School: 541
% Male/Female: 57/43
% Full Time: 100
% Minority: 77

EXPENSES/FINANCIAL AID
Annual Tuition (Residents/Nonresidents): $4,466/$7,562
Room and Board (Off Campus): $6,000
Books and Supplies: $700

ADMISSIONS INFORMATION
Application Fee: $40
Regular Application Deadline: 4/1
Regular Notification: Rolling
LSDAS Accepted? No
Average GPA: 3.0
Transfer Students Accepted? Yes
Number of Applications Received: 1,460
Number of Applicants Accepted: 540
Number of Applicants Enrolled: 265

EMPLOYMENT INFORMATION

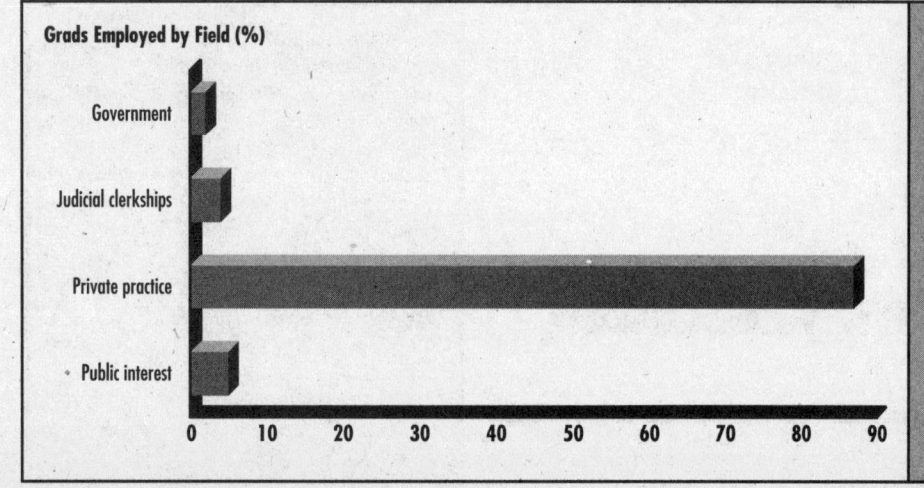

Grads Employed by Field (%)
- Government
- Judicial clerkships
- Private practice
- Public interest

State for Bar Exam: TX
Pass Rate for First-Time Bar: 68%

TEXAS TECH UNIVERSITY
School of Law

Admissions Contact: Admissions Counselor, Donna Williams
Texas Tech University School of Law, 1802 Hartford Avenue, Lubbock, TX 79409
Admissions Phone: 806-742-3990 • Admissions Fax: 806-742-1629
Admissions E-mail: donna.williams@ttu.edu • Web Address: www.law.ttu.edu

INSTITUTIONAL INFORMATION
Public/Private: Public
Student/Faculty Ratio: 20:1
Total Faculty: 47
% Part Time: 43
% Female: 28
% Minority: 28

PROGRAMS
Academic Specialties: Litigation Skills, Civil Procedure, Commercial Law, Constitutional Law, Corporation Securities Law, Criminal Law, Environmental Law, Government Services, Human Rights Law, International Law, Labor Law, Legal History, Legal Philosophy, Property, Taxation
Combined Degrees Offered: JD/MBA (3 years), JD/MPA (3.5 years), JD/MS Agriculture and Applied Science (3 to 3.5 years), JD/MS Accounting/Taxation (3 to 3.5 years), JD/MS Environmental Toxicology (3 to 3.5 years), JD/FFP Family Financial Planning (3 to 3.5 years)
Grading System: A– (4.0), B+ (3.5), B– (3.0), C+ (2.5), C– (2.0), D+ (1.5), D– (1.0), F (0.0)
Clinical Program Required? No
Clinical Programs Description: Tax Clinic, Civil Litigation Clinic, Criminal Prosecution Clinic
Legal Writing Course Requirements? No
Legal Methods Course Requirements? Yes
Legal Methods Description: 2-semester course, 6 total credits, meets in classes of approximately 22 students
Legal Research Course Requirements? No
Moot Court Requirement? No

Public Interest Law Requirement? No
Academic Journals: Texas Tech Law Review, Administrative Law Journal, The Texas Bank Lawyer, Texas Judges Bench Book

STUDENT INFORMATION
Enrollment of Law School: 663
% Out of State: 9
% Male/Female: 54/46
% Full Time: 100
% Full Time That Are International: 1
% Minority: 13
Average Age of Entering Class: 25

EXPENSES/FINANCIAL AID
Annual Tuition (Residents/Nonresidents): $4,800/$9,870
Room and Board: $6,198
Books and Supplies: $866
Average Grant: $1,750
Average Loan: $13,428
% of Aid That Is Merit-Based: 68
% Receiving Some Sort of Aid: 79
Average Total Aid Package: $19,934
Average Debt: $44,685

ADMISSIONS INFORMATION
Application Fee: $50
Regular Application Deadline: 2/1
Regular Notification: Rolling
LSDAS Accepted? Yes
Average GPA: 3.4
Range of GPA: 3.1–3.6
Average LSAT: 153
Range of LSAT: 150–157
Transfer Students Accepted? Yes
Other Schools to Which Students Applied: Baylor University, Southern Methodist University, University of Texas at Austin, University of Houston
Other Admissions Factors Considered: Socioeconomic background, including the percentage by which the applicant's family is above or below any recognized measure of poverty; household income; parents' level of education
Number of Applications Received: 1,123
Number of Applicants Accepted: 548
Number of Applicants Enrolled: 234

INTERNATIONAL STUDENTS
TOEFL Required of International Students? Yes
Minimum TOEFL: 213

EMPLOYMENT INFORMATION

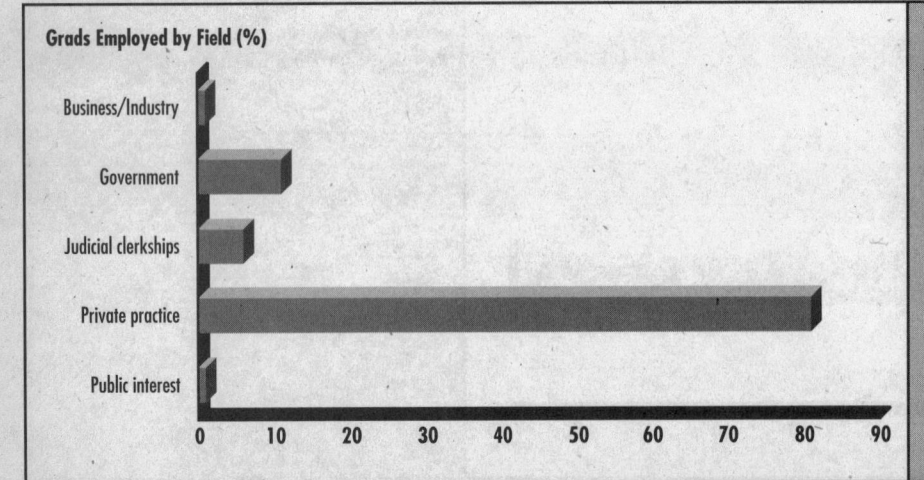

Grads Employed by Field (%)
- Business/Industry: ~2
- Government: ~10
- Judicial clerkships: ~5
- Private practice: ~82
- Public interest: ~1

Rate of Placement: 92%
Average Starting Salary: $51,500
Employers Who Frequently Hire Grads: Jones, Day, Reavis & Pogue; Thompson & Knight; Haynes & Boone; Thompson & Coe; Cousins & Irons; Strasburger & Price; Cooper & Aldous; Kemp, Smith, Duncan & Hammond; Mehaffy & Weber; Orgain, Bell & Tucker; state and federal judiciary
State for Bar Exam: TX, NM
Pass Rate for First-Time Bar: 89%

TEXAS WESLEYAN UNIVERSITY
School of Law

Admissions Contact: Assistant Dean and Director of Admissions, Sonel Y. Shropshire
1515 Commerce Street, Fort Worth, TX 76102
Admissions Phone: 800-733-9529 • Admissions Fax: 817-212-4002
Admissions E-mail: law_admissions@law.txwes.edu • Web Address: www.txwesleyan.edu/law

INSTITUTIONAL INFORMATION
Public/Private: Private
Affiliation: Methodist
Student/Faculty Ratio: 16:1
Total Faculty: 29
% Part Time: 20
% Female: 30
% Minority: 10

PROGRAMS
Academic Specialties: Innovative program of skills courses called Practicum Courses—a course of study designed especially for the preparation of practitioners that involves the supervised practical application of previously studied theory. Other specialties include Corporation Securities Law, Environmental Law, and International Law.
Advanced Degrees Offered: JD (3 years full time, 4 years part time)
Grading System: Numerical system
Clinical Program Required? No
Legal Writing Course Requirements? No
Legal Methods Course Requirements? No
Legal Methods Description: 2-semester course that includes briefing and meets court component
Legal Research Course Requirements? No
Moot Court Requirement? No
Public Interest Law Requirement? Yes
Public Interest Law Description: Pro bono requirement

STUDENT INFORMATION
% Out of State: 0
% Male/Female: 100/0
% Full Time: 100
% Full Time That Are International: 0
% Minority: 0
Average Age of Entering Class: 34

RESEARCH FACILITIES
Research Resources Available: Various city and state bar associations, legal and judicial internship program

EXPENSES/FINANCIAL AID
Annual Tuition: $17,100
Books and Supplies: $1,500
Financial Aid Application Deadline: 4/15
Average Grant: $2,500
Average Loan: $17,681
% of Aid That Is Merit-Based: 20
% Receiving Some Sort of Aid: 82
Average Total Aid Package: $20,000
Average Debt: $56,500
Tuition Per Credit: $570
Fees Per Credit: $570

ADMISSIONS INFORMATION
Application Fee: $50
Regular Application Deadline: 3/31
Regular Notification: Rolling
LSDAS Accepted? Yes
Average GPA: 3.0
Range of GPA: 2.7–3.4
Average LSAT: 150
Range of LSAT: 146–154
Transfer Students Accepted? Yes
Other Schools to Which Students Applied: Baylor University, Southern Methodist University, Texas Tech University
Number of Applications Received: 1,177
Number of Applicants Accepted: 486

EMPLOYMENT INFORMATION

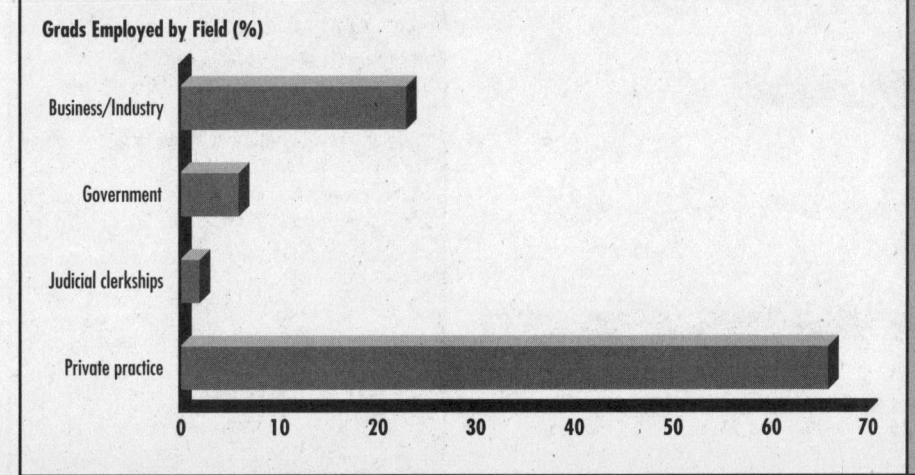

Grads Employed by Field (%)
- Business/Industry: ~23
- Government: ~5
- Judicial clerkships: ~2
- Private practice: ~67

Rate of Placement: 85%
Average Starting Salary: $42,000
Employers Who Frequently Hire Grads: Small to medium-size private firms, district attorney's offices, government agencies, various corporations and businesses
State for Bar Exam: TX
Pass Rate for First-Time Bar: 71%

Thomas Jefferson School of Law

Admissions Contact: Assistant Dean, Jennifer Keller
2121 San Diego Avenue, San Diego, CA 92110
Admissions Phone: 619-297-9700 • Admissions Fax: 619-294-4713
Admissions E-mail: adm@tjsl.edu • Web Address: www.tjsl.edu

INSTITUTIONAL INFORMATION
Public/Private: Private
Student/Faculty Ratio: 19:1
Total Faculty: 56
% Part Time: 54
% Female: 39
% Minority: 5

PROGRAMS
Academic Specialties: Curriculum emphasizes professional skills. Specialties include International Law, Constitutional Law, Criminal Law, Environmental Law, Government Services, and Taxation.
Advanced Degrees Offered: JD (3 years full time, 4 years part time)
Grading System: 4.0 system
Clinical Program Required? No
Legal Writing Course Requirements? Yes
Legal Writing Description: 2 semesters
Legal Methods Course Requirements? No
Legal Research Course Requirements? No
Moot Court Requirement? No
Public Interest Law Requirement? No
Academic Journals: *Thomas Jefferson Law Review*

STUDENT INFORMATION
Enrollment of Law School: 611
% Out of State: 68
% Male/Female: 58/42
% Full Time: 68
% Full Time That Are International: 16
% Minority: 24
Average Age of Entering Class: 28

EXPENSES/FINANCIAL AID
Annual Tuition: $22,180
Room and Board (Off Campus): $8,181
Books and Supplies: $1,074
Financial Aid Application Deadline: 4/30
Average Grant: $9,144
Average Loan: $22,772
% Receiving Some Sort of Aid: 93
Average Total Aid Package: $20,703
Average Debt: $87,000
Tuition Per Credit: $745
Fees Per Credit: $150

ADMISSIONS INFORMATION
Application Fee: $35
Regular Application Deadline: Rolling
Regular Notification: Rolling
LSDAS Accepted? Yes
Average GPA: 2.9
Range of GPA: 2.6–3.2
Average LSAT: 148
Range of LSAT: 145–153
Transfer Students Accepted? Yes
Other Schools to Which Students Applied: California Western, University of San Diego, Southwestern University School of Law, University of the Pacific, Whittier College
Number of Applications Received: 1,522
Number of Applicants Accepted: 1,048
Number of Applicants Enrolled: 226

EMPLOYMENT INFORMATION

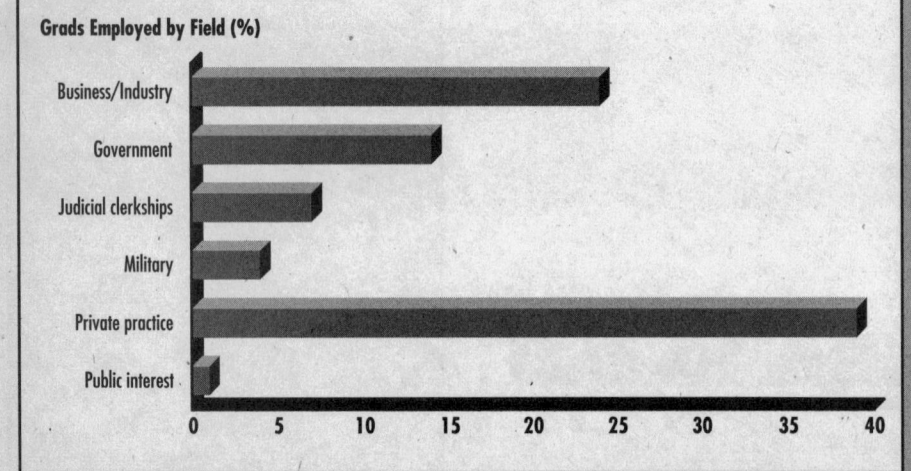

Grads Employed by Field (%)
- Business/Industry: ~24
- Government: ~14
- Judicial clerkships: ~7
- Military: ~2
- Private practice: ~39
- Public interest: ~1

Rate of Placement: 87%
Average Starting Salary: $50,315
Employers Who Frequently Hire Grads: District attorneys, attorney generals, public defenders, various alumni small firms, other medium-sized local firms in San Diego and Orange County
State for Bar Exam: CA
Pass Rate for First-Time Bar: 59%

Thomas M. Cooley Law School

Admissions Contact: Assistant Dean of Admissions, Stephanie Gregg
PO Box 13038, Lansing, MI 48901
Admissions Phone: 517-371-5140 • Admissions Fax: 517-334-5718
Admissions E-mail: admissions@cooley.edu • Web Address: www.cooley.edu

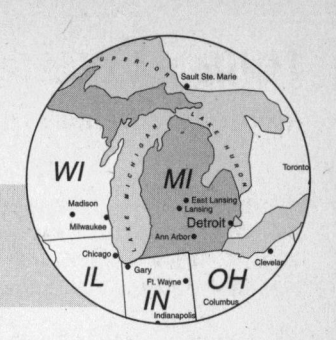

INSTITUTIONAL INFORMATION
Public/Private: Private
Student/Faculty Ratio: 24:1
Total Faculty: 144
% Part Time: 67
% Female: 37
% Minority: 8

PROGRAMS
Academic Specialties: Constitutional Law, Environmental Law, Government Services, International Law, Business Transactions, General Practice, Litigation, Administrative Law
Advanced Degrees Offered: JD (2 to 4 years)
Combined Degrees Offered: JD/MPA with Western Michigan University (3 to 6 years)
Grading System: In most courses, grades are based on written final exams. Professors adhere to established grade definitions.
Clinical Program Required? Yes
Clinical Programs Description: 4 clinical options: 1) an extensive third-year externship program which places senior students in real work situations throughout the U.S. 2) Sixty Plus, an award-winning in-house clinical program, providing representation to senior citizens in mid-Michigan; 3) Estate Planning Clinic, an evening or weekend clinic with students providing estate planning services to seniors; and 4) Innocence Project, where students use forensic science to aid innocent persons wrongfully convicted of crimes.
Legal Writing Course Requirements? Yes
Legal Writing Description: Research and Writing (first year) and Advanced Research and Writing (third year) are required of all students.
Legal Methods Course Requirements? Yes
Legal Methods Description: Introduction to Law I is required of all students, exposing them to law school briefing, examinations, and jurisprudence.
Legal Research Course Requirements? Yes
Legal Research Description: In 2 sequenced courses, students learn both traditional book research and efficient and effective computer research. Additional instruction is available in Advanced Computer Research elective.
Moot Court Requirement? No
Moot Court Description: We offer a first-year moot court competition to all interested students, a second-year class, and several invitation-only teams that compete in national programs.
Public Interest Law Requirement? No
Academic Journals: *The Thomas M. Cooley Law Review, The Thomas M. Cooley Journal of Practical and Clinical Law*

STUDENT INFORMATION
Enrollment of Law School: 1,819
% Out of State: 75
% Male/Female: 51/49
% Full Time: 21
% Full Time That Are International: 1
% Minority: 27
Average Age of Entering Class: 30

RESEARCH FACILITIES
Research Resources Available: 2 computer labs; Academic Resource Center provides access to a variety of CALI instruction materials; clinical programs are networked to assist interns and their clients

EXPENSES/FINANCIAL AID
Annual Tuition: $20,460
Room and Board (Off Campus): $6,860
Books and Supplies: $800
Financial Aid Application Deadline: 9/1
Average Grant: $3,251
Average Loan: $18,500
% of Aid That Is Merit-Based: 5
% Receiving Some Sort of Aid: 97
Average Total Aid Package: $18,500
Average Debt: $82,330
Tuition Per Credit: $682

ADMISSIONS INFORMATION
Regular Application Deadline: Rolling
Regular Notification: Rolling
LSDAS Accepted? Yes
Average GPA: 2.9
Range of GPA: 2.4–3.2
Average LSAT: 142
Range of LSAT: 138–146
Transfer Students Accepted? Yes
Other Schools to Which Students Applied: Michigan State, New England School of Law, Ohio Northern, Florida Coastal, Thomas Jefferson School of Law, Widener, The John Marshall Law School
Other Admissions Factors Considered: None other than character and fitness
Number of Applications Received: 2,061
Number of Applicants Accepted: 1,513
Number of Applicants Enrolled: 273

EMPLOYMENT INFORMATION

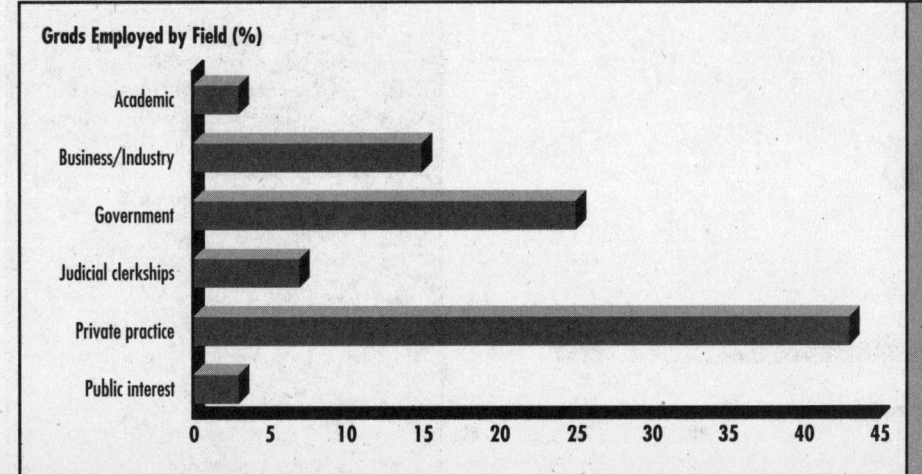

Grads Employed by Field (%):
- Academic: ~3
- Business/Industry: ~15
- Government: ~25
- Judicial clerkships: ~7
- Private practice: ~43
- Public interest: ~3

Rate of Placement: 96%
Average Starting Salary: $41,895
Employers Who Frequently Hire Grads: Michigan Court of Appeals, prosecutors, Legal Services programs, Michigan law firms
State for Bar Exam: MI, NY, NJ, FL, IN
Pass Rate for First-Time Bar: 63%

TOURO COLLEGE
Jacob D. Fuchsberg Law Center

Admissions Contact: Director of Admissions, Grant Keener
300 Nassau Road, Huntington, NY 11743
Admissions Phone: 631-421-2244 • Admissions Fax: 631-421-9708
Admissions E-mail: admissions@tourolaw.edu • Web Address: www.tourolaw.edu

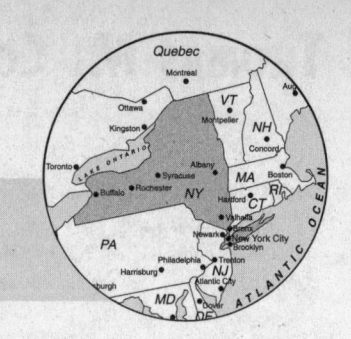

INSTITUTIONAL INFORMATION
Public/Private: Private
Student/Faculty Ratio: 16:1
Total Faculty: 50
% Part Time: 28
% Female: 35
% Minority: 7

PROGRAMS
Academic Specialties: Business Law, Criminal Law, Family Law, Health Law, Intellectual Property Law, International Law, Public Interest Law, Commercial Law, Human Rights Law
Advanced Degrees Offered: JD (3 years full time, 4 years part time), LLM for foreign-trained attorneys (1 year full time, 3 semesters part time), LLM General Studies (1 year full time, 3 semesters part time)
Combined Degrees Offered: JD/MBA, JD/MPA, JD/MSW (add one year of study for joint degree programs)
Grading System: Clinics and courses are graded, pro bono work is Pass/Fail
Clinical Program Required? No
Clinical Programs Description: Civil Rights Litigation Clinic, Elder Law Clinic, International Human Rights Litigation Clinic, Family Law Clinic, Judicial Clerkship Clinic, Not-for-Profit Corporation Law, Civil Practice Clinic, Criminal Law Clinic
Legal Writing Course Requirements? No
Legal Methods Course Requirements? Yes
Legal Methods Description: 2 semesters, 2 credits each semester
Legal Research Course Requirements? Yes
Legal Research Description: Part of Legal Methods
Moot Court Requirement? No
Moot Court Description: Membership is by grade-on and by competition (combination of brief and oral argument). Members must serve for 4 consecutive semesters.
Public Interest Law Requirement? Yes
Public Interest Law Description: Successful completion of 1 of the following: a clinic, a course plus 20 hours pro bono work, or 40 hours of pro bono work.
Academic Journals: *Touro Law Review, Journal of the Suffolk Academy of Law*

STUDENT INFORMATION
Enrollment of Law School: 558
% Male/Female: 49/51
% Full Time: 55
% Minority: 26
Average Age of Entering Class: 29

EXPENSES/FINANCIAL AID
Annual Tuition: $22,410
Room and Board: $10,000
Books and Supplies: $750
Average Grant: $4,500
Average Loan: $38,500
% of Aid That Is Merit-Based: 53
% Receiving Some Sort of Aid: 90
Average Total Aid Package: $30,000
Average Debt: $65,000
Tuition Per Credit: $825

ADMISSIONS INFORMATION
Application Fee: $50
Regular Application Deadline: Rolling
Regular Notification: Rolling
LSDAS Accepted? Yes
Range of GPA: 2.6–3.3
Range of LSAT: 144–150
Transfer Students Accepted? Yes
Other Admissions Factors Considered: Personal statement, work experience, graduate degree
Number of Applications Received: 1,547
Number of Applicants Accepted: 733
Number of Applicants Enrolled: 224

INTERNATIONAL STUDENTS
TOEFL Required of International Students? Yes
Minimum TOEFL: 250

EMPLOYMENT INFORMATION

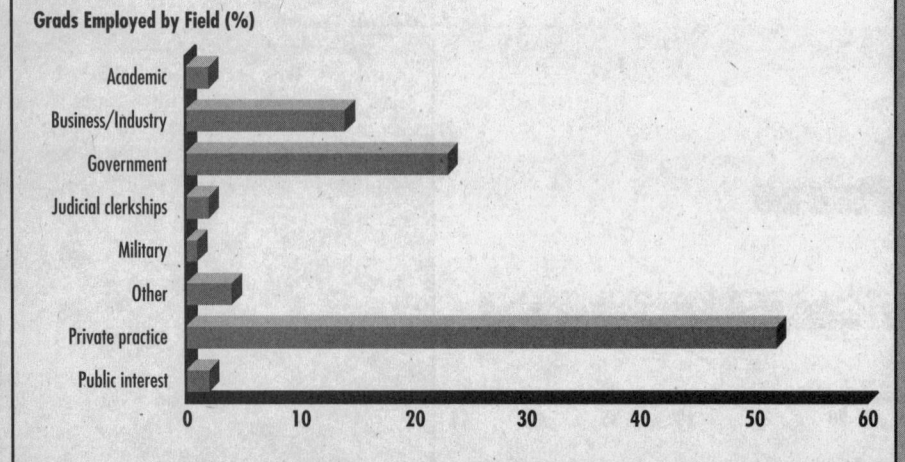

Grads Employed by Field (%)

Field	%
Academic	0
Business/Industry	~14
Government	~23
Judicial clerkships	~3
Military	~1
Other	~3
Private practice	~52
Public interest	~3

Rate of Placement: 89%
Average Starting Salary: $45,000
Employers Who Frequently Hire Grads: District Attorney's Offices, public interest employers, small and medium law firms
State for Bar Exam: NY
Pass Rate for First-Time Bar: 63%

TULANE UNIVERSITY
School of Law

Admissions Contact: Admission Coordinator, Carl Hudson
Weinmann Hall, 6329 Freret Street, New Orleans, LA 70118-6231
Admissions Phone: 504-865-5930 • Admissions Fax: 504-865-6710
Admissions E-mail: admissions@law.tulane.edu • Web Address: www.law.tulane.edu

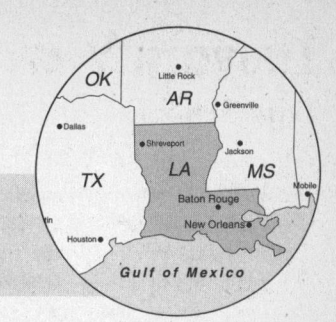

INSTITUTIONAL INFORMATION
Public/Private: Private
Environment: Urban
Academic Calendar: Semester
Schedule: Full time only
Student/Faculty Ratio: 20:1
Total Faculty: 50
% Female: 24
% Minority: 12

PROGRAMS
Academic Specialties: International and Comparative Law, Maritime Law, Environmental Law, Intellectual Property
Advanced Degrees Offered: JD (1 to 3 years), LLM (1 year full time), LLM Admiralty (1 year full time, 2 years part time), LLM Energy and Environment (1 year full time, 2 years part time), LLM International and Comparative Law (1 year full time)
Combined Degrees Offered: JD/BA or JD/BS (6 years), JD/MBA (4–4.5 years), JD/MHA (4–4.5 years), JD/MPH (4–4.5 years), LLM/MPH (2 years), JD/MSW (4–4.5 years), JD/MA International Affairs, Latin American Studies (3–3.5 years)
Grading System: Letter and numerical system on a 4.0 scale
Clinical Program Required? No
Legal Writing/Methods Course Requirements: 1 year, taught in 8 sections

STUDENT INFORMATION
Enrollment of Law School: 952
% Male/Female: 50/50
% Full Time: 100
% Full Time That Are International: 1
% Minority: 23
Average Age of Entering Class: 24

RESEARCH FACILITIES
Computers/Workstations Available: 150
Computer Labs: 3
Campuswide Network? Yes

EXPENSES/FINANCIAL AID
Annual Tuition: $23,500
Room and Board (Off Campus): $7,250
Books and Supplies: $1,270
Average Grant: $9,788
Average Loan: $26,837
% Receiving Some Sort of Aid: 86
Average Total Aid Package: $35,128
Average Debt: $65,220

ADMISSIONS INFORMATION
Application Fee: $50
Regular Application Deadline: 8/10
Regular Notification: Rolling
LSDAS Accepted? Yes
Average GPA: 3.3
Range of GPA: 3.0–3.5
Average LSAT: 159
Range of LSAT: 155–161
Transfer Students Accepted? Yes
Other Schools to Which Students Applied: Emory University, American University, Boston University, Vanderbilt University, George Washington University, Georgetown University, Boston College, Loyola University New Orleans
Other Admissions Factors Considered: Membership in a minority group or other group in which the institution is interested, life experience, qualities or characteristics that may be underrepresented and/or that indicate special motivation, leadership skills, industriousness, seriousness of purpose
Number of Applications Received: 2,993
Number of Applicants Accepted: 1,204

EMPLOYMENT INFORMATION

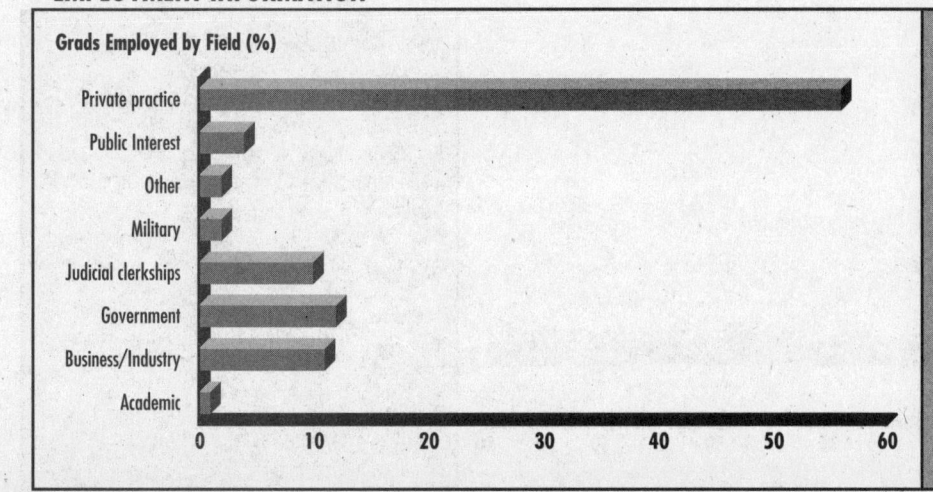

Grads Employed by Field (%)
- Private practice
- Public Interest
- Other
- Military
- Judicial clerkships
- Government
- Business/Industry
- Academic

Average Starting Salary: $56,588
Employers Who Frequently Hire Grads: Fulbright and Jaworski; Skadden Arps; Arnold and Porter; White and Case; Mayer, Brown and Platt; Cleary Gottlieb; Winthrop Stimson; McGlinchey; Adams and Reese; Exxon Co.; U.S. Army; U.S. Department of Justice
Prominent Alumni: Judge J. Wisdom, U.S. 5th Circuit Court of Appeals; Joseph Parkinson, founder, Micron Corp.; Hon. William Suter, clerk of the U.S. Supreme Court
State for Bar Exam: NY
Number Taking Bar Exam: 57
Pass Rate for First-Time Bar: 85%

UNIVERSITY AT BUFFALO, STATE UNIVERSITY OF NY
Law School

Admissions Contact: Associate Dean for Admissions and Financial Aid, Jack D. Cox, Jr.
309 O'Brian Hall, Buffalo, NY 14260
Admissions Phone: 716-645-2907 • Admissions Fax: 716-645-6676
Admissions E-mail: law-admissions@buffalo.edu • Web Address: www.law.buffalo.edu

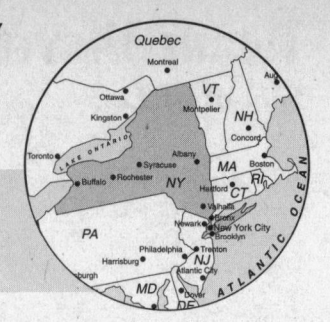

INSTITUTIONAL INFORMATION
Public/Private: Public
Student/Faculty Ratio: 17:1
Total Faculty: 115
% Part Time: 63
% Female: 28
% Minority: 8

PROGRAMS
Academic Specialties: Law and Society, Corporate Finances, International Human Rights, Affordable Housing, Labor and Employment Law, Health Law and Management, Community Economic Development, Environmental Law, Government Services, Intellectual Property Law, International Law, Property, Civil Litigation
Advanced Degrees Offered: LLM Criminal Law (1 year)
Combined Degrees Offered: JD/MSW (4 years), JD/MBA (4 years), JD/MPH (4 years), JD/PhD (5 to 6 years)
Grading System: A, B+, B, C, D, F
Clinical Program Required? No
Clinical Programs Description: Affordable Housing Clinic, Community Economic Development Clinic, Family Violence Clinic, Education Law Clinic, Health-Related Legal Concerns of the Elderly Clinic, Criminal Law Clinic, Securities Law, Environment and Development Clinic, judicial and legislative externships
Legal Writing Course Requirements? Yes
Legal Writing Description: 7-credit, 2-semester course during first year
Legal Methods Course Requirements? No
Legal Research Course Requirements? Yes
Legal Research Description: See Legal Writing.
Moot Court Requirement? No
Moot Court Description: 2 separate moot court boards, regional and international competitions.
Public Interest Law Requirement? No
Academic Journals: *Buffalo Law Review, Buffalo Criminal Law Review, Buffalo Environmental Law Review*, and more

STUDENT INFORMATION
Enrollment of Law School: 717
% Out of State: 6
% Male/Female: 51/49
% Full Time: 98
% Full Time That Are International: 4
% Minority: 16
Average Age of Entering Class: 25

RESEARCH FACILITIES
Research Resources Available: Charles B. Sears Law Library, Lexis/Nexis; city, state, and federal courthouses with legal libraries
School-Supported Research Centers: Baldy Center for Law and Social Policy, Criminal Law Center, Human Rights Center, Ewin F. Jaeckle Center for State and Local Government, Center for the Study of Business Transactions, Environment and Society Institute, Institute for Research and Education on Women and Gender

EXPENSES/FINANCIAL AID
Annual Tuition (Residents/Nonresidents): $9,900/$15,450
Room and Board (On/Off Campus): $7,159/$7,433
Books and Supplies: $1,323
Financial Aid Application Deadline: 3/1
Average Grant: $4,550
Average Loan: $14,500
% of Aid That Is Merit-Based: 45
% Receiving Some Sort of Aid: 57
Average Total Aid Package: $18,500
Average Debt: $34,973
Tuition Per Credit (Residents/Nonresidents): $353/$584
Fees Per Credit: $39

ADMISSIONS INFORMATION
Application Fee: $50
Regular Application Deadline: 3/15
Regular Notification: Rolling
LSDAS Accepted? Yes
Average GPA: 3.3
Average LSAT: 154
Transfer Students Accepted? Yes
Other Schools to Which Students Applied: American University, Brooklyn Law School, Case Western Reserve, Hofstra, Syracuse, U. at Albany, U. of Pittsburgh
Other Admissions Factors Considered: Achievements or activities that suggest a high probability of scholastic excellence or distinctive intellectual contribution while in law school
Number of Applications Received: 1,225
Number of Applicants Accepted: 489
Number of Applicants Enrolled: 235

INTERNATIONAL STUDENTS
TOEFL Required of International Students? Yes
Minimum TOEFL: 280

EMPLOYMENT INFORMATION

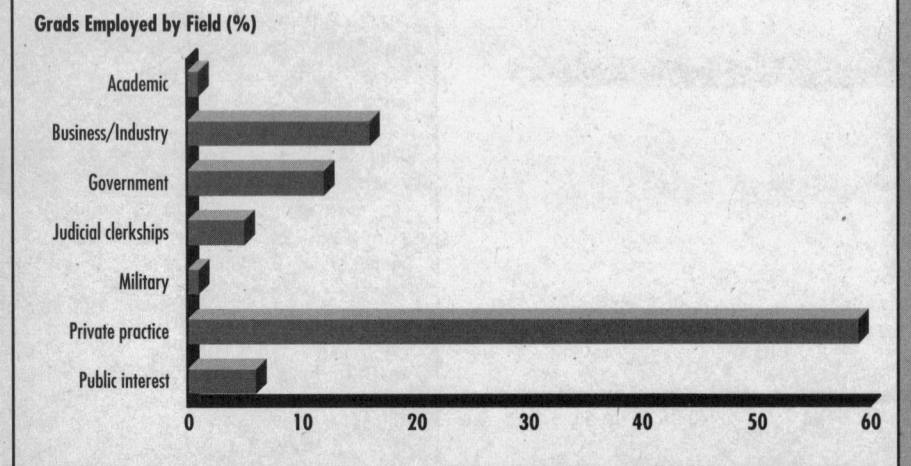

Grads Employed by Field (%):
- Academic
- Business/Industry
- Government
- Judicial clerkships
- Military
- Private practice
- Public interest

Rate of Placement: 95%
Average Starting Salary: $52,848
Employers Who Frequently Hire Grads: LeBoeuf Lamb; Hodgson Russ; New York State Appellate Division 4th Department; Dewey Ballantine; Nixon Peabody; Phillips Lytle; Harris, Beach & Wilcox; New York County District Attorney's Office; National Labor Relations Board; White & Case; Bond, Schoeneck, Schulte, Roth & Zabel
State for Bar Exam: NY
Pass Rate for First-Time Bar: 74%

UNIVERSITY OF AKRON
School of Law

Admissions Contact: Director of Admissions and Financial Assistance, Lauri S. File
The University of Akron School of Law, Akron, OH 44325-2901
Admissions Phone: 800-425-7668 • Admissions Fax: 330-258-2343
Admissions E-mail: lawadmissions@uakron.edu • Web Address: www.uakron.edu/law

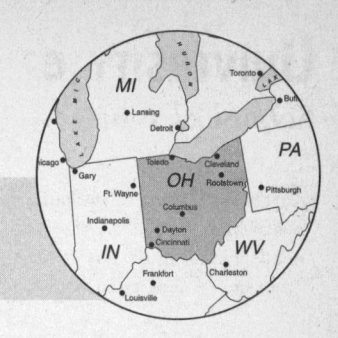

INSTITUTIONAL INFORMATION
Public/Private: Public
Student/Faculty Ratio: 17:1
Total Faculty: 74
% Part Time: 57
% Female: 41
% Minority: 8

PROGRAMS
Academic Specialties: Strengths include small class sizes and nationally recognized Intellectual Property and Trial Advocacy Programs; other specialties include Corporate Law, Criminal Law, International Law, Litigation, Labor/Employment Law, Public Interest Law, Taxation, and Corporation Securities Law
Combined Degrees Offered: JD/MBA, JD/Master of Science and Management in Human Resources, JD/MT, JD/MPA (each usually takes 1 additional semester to finish)
Grading System: 4.0 scale; students must maintain at least a 2.0 accumulative GPA (C average) in order to continue law studies
Clinical Program Required? No
Clinical Programs Description: Legal Clinic, Appellate Review, Trial Litigation Clinic, Clinical Seminar, Inmate Assistance Program
Legal Writing Course Requirements? Yes
Legal Writing Description: Legal Analysis Research and Writing I (3 credits), Legal Analysis Research and Writing II (2 credits), Legal Drafting (1 credit), all 1-semester courses
Legal Methods Course Requirements? Yes
Legal Methods Description: Introduction to Law and Legal Systems is a week-long intensive course held before the first semester of law school.
Legal Research Course Requirements? Yes
Legal Research Description: 1 credit hour, Westlaw and Lexis instruction, manual research skills training
Moot Court Requirement? No
Public Interest Law Requirement? No
Academic Journals: Akron Law Review, Akron Tax Journal

STUDENT INFORMATION
Enrollment of Law School: 590
% Male/Female: 54/46
% Full Time: 62
% Full Time That Are International: 0
% Minority: 13
Average Age of Entering Class: 28

RESEARCH FACILITIES
Research Resources Available: Wireless laptop program, licensing agreement with Microsoft to offer products at substantially reduced rate, low-cost high-speed Internet access offered

EXPENSES/FINANCIAL AID
Annual Tuition (Residents/Nonresidents): $8,067/$13,482
Room and Board: $11,664
Books and Supplies: $860
Financial Aid Application Deadline: 5/1
Average Grant: $7,601
Average Loan: $12,250
% of Aid That Is Merit-Based: 99
% Receiving Some Sort of Aid: 91
Average Total Aid Package: $13,325
Average Debt: $32,510
Tuition Per Credit (Residents/Nonresidents): $269/$449
Fees Per Credit: $9

ADMISSIONS INFORMATION
Application Fee: $0
Regular Application Deadline: Rolling
Regular Notification: Rolling
LSDAS Accepted? Yes
Average GPA: 3.1
Range of GPA: 2.9–3.4
Average LSAT: 152
Range of LSAT: 149–155
Transfer Students Accepted? Yes
Other Schools to Which Students Applied: Cleveland State University, Case Western Reserve University, Ohio State University, University of Toledo, University of Cincinnati, University of Dayton, Capital University
Other Admissions Factors Considered: Whether or not the applicant had to overcome special challenges such as economic hardship, educational deprivation, physical disability, discrimination, assimilation to a different culture/society
Number of Applications Received: 1,419
Number of Applicants Accepted: 595
Number of Applicants Enrolled: 228

INTERNATIONAL STUDENTS
TOEFL Required of International Students? Yes

EMPLOYMENT INFORMATION

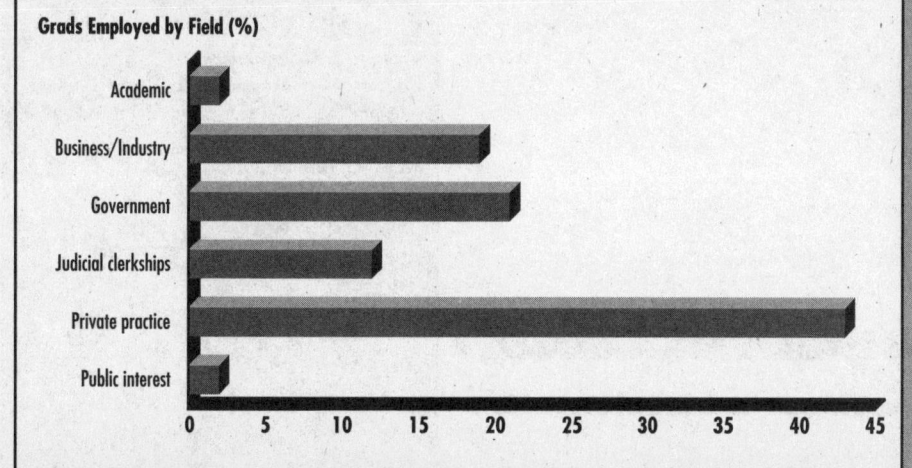

Grads Employed by Field (%)

Field	%
Academic	~1
Business/Industry	~20
Government	~21
Judicial clerkships	~12
Private practice	~44
Public interest	~2

Rate of Placement: 88%
Average Starting Salary: $47,679
Employers Who Frequently Hire Grads: Buckingham, Doolittle, & Burroughs; Brouse & McDowell; Roetzel & Andress; County Prosecutor Offices; Stark & Summit; County Courts of Common Pleas; 9th District Court of Appeals; Ernst & Young; Arthur Andersen; U.S. Army JAG Corps; CSFA; City of Akron Law Department; Jones, Day, Reavis & Pogue
State for Bar Exam: OH
Pass Rate for First-Time Bar: 85%

UNIVERSITY OF ALABAMA
School of Law

Admissions Contact: Coordinator of Recruitment and Scholarships, Ms. Claude Beers
Box 870382, Tuscaloosa, AL 35487
Admissions Phone: 205-348-5440 • Admissions Fax: 205-348-3917
Admissions E-mail: admissions@law.ua.edu • Web Address: www.law.ua.edu

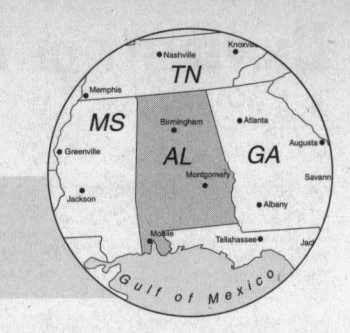

INSTITUTIONAL INFORMATION
Public/Private: Public
Student/Faculty Ratio: 16:1
Total Faculty: 81
% Part Time: 51
% Female: 14
% Minority: 7

PROGRAMS
Academic Specialties: Business and Tax Law, Criminal Law, Commercial Law, Bankruptcy Law, Intellectual Property, Environmental Law, Trial Advocacy, International Law
Advanced Degrees Offered: LLM Taxation (2 years part time), LLM International Graduate Program LLM (1 year)
Combined Degrees Offered: JD/MBA (4 years)
Grading System: Letter and numerical system on a 4.0 scale
Clinical Program Required? No
Clinical Programs Description: Summer and academic year externship programs; 6 in-house clinics offered for 3 credit hours each
Legal Writing Course Requirements? Yes
Legal Writing Description: First year (both semesters)
Legal Methods Course Requirements? No
Legal Methods Description: 2 semesters
Legal Research Course Requirements? Yes
Legal Research Description: First year (both semesters)
Moot Court Requirement? Yes
Moot Court Description: Legal Writing/Research II in second semester of first year
Public Interest Law Requirement? No
Academic Journals: *Alabama Law Review, The Journal of the Legal Profession, Law and Psychology Review*

STUDENT INFORMATION
Enrollment of Law School: 523
% Out of State: 0
% Male/Female: 61/39
% Full Time: 100
% Full Time That Are International: 0
% Minority: 11
Average Age of Entering Class: 25

RESEARCH FACILITIES
School Supported Research Centers: John Payne Special Collections Room, which houses Alabama historical legal materials; Howell Hefflin Papers; Hugo Black Special Collection

EXPENSES/FINANCIAL AID
Annual Tuition (Residents/Nonresidents): $5,764/$11,972
Room and Board (On Campus): $5,776
Books and Supplies: $1,068
Average Grant: $5,764

ADMISSIONS INFORMATION
Application Fee: $25
Regular Application Deadline: 3/2
Regular Notification: Rolling
LSDAS Accepted? Yes
Average GPA: 3.3
Range of GPA: 3.1–3.6
Average LSAT: 159
Range of LSAT: 157–161
Transfer Students Accepted? Yes
Other Admissions Factors Considered: Difficulty of undergraduate coursework, graduate study, writing ability, trends in academic performance, leadership qualities, unique work or service experience, career achievement, history of overcoming adversity
Number of Applications Received: 991
Number of Applicants Accepted: 366
Number of Applicants Enrolled: 186

INTERNATIONAL STUDENTS
TOEFL Required of International Students? Yes

EMPLOYMENT INFORMATION

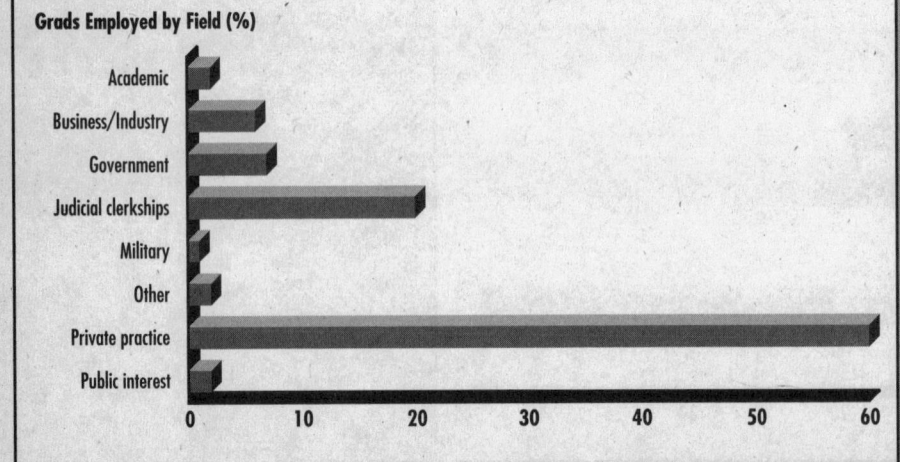

Grads Employed by Field (%)
- Academic: ~1
- Business/Industry: ~5
- Government: ~5
- Judicial clerkships: ~20
- Military: ~1
- Other: ~2
- Private practice: ~60
- Public interest: ~2

Rate of Placement: 99%
Average Starting Salary: $55,875
Employers Who Frequently Hire Grads: Private practices, government agencies, public interest agencies
State for Bar Exam: AL
Pass Rate for First-Time Bar: 91%

UNIVERSITY OF ARIZONA
James E. Rogers College of Law

Admissions Contact: Assistant Dean for Admissions, Terry Sue Holpert
College of Law, Room 114, PO Box 210176, Tucson, AZ 85721-0176
Admissions Phone: 520-621-3477 • Admissions Fax: 520-621-9140
Admissions E-mail: admissions@nt.law.arizona.edu • Web Address: www.law.arizona.edu

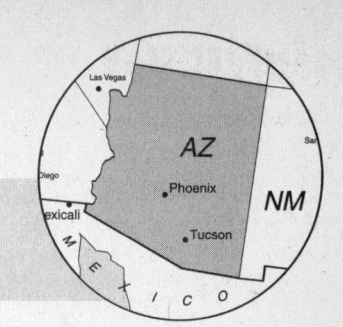

INSTITUTIONAL INFORMATION
Public/Private: Public
Affiliation: Not Applicable
Environment: Urban
Academic Calendar: Semester
Schedule: Full time only
Student/Faculty Ratio: 15:1
Total Faculty: 80
% Part Time: 50
% Female: 33
% Minority: 20

PROGRAMS
Academic Specialties: Outstanding teaching faculty with extraordinary strength in all first-year classes. In addition, there is particular strength in Tax, Estates, and Trust; Corporate and Securities; Indian Law; Water Law; Constitutional Law; Employment Law; Remedies and Trial Advocacy; Family Law; International Trade; International Trade Rights; and Environmental Law.
Advanced Degrees Offered: LLM International Trade Law (24 units, 1 year), JD (85 units, 3 years)
Combined Degrees Offered: JD/PhD in Philosophy, Psychology, or Economics (6 years.), JD/MBA (4 years), JD/MPA (4 years), JD/MA American Indian Studies (4 years), JD/MA Economics (4 years), JD/MA Women's Studies (4 years)
Grading System: There is a curve for all courses of 21 or more students: 25% A, 55% B, 20% C, D, and E. For classes of 20 or less, the mean GPA for courses shall not exceed 3.5.

Clinical Program Required? No
Clinical Program Description: Criminal Prosecution and Defense, Immigration Law, Domestic Violence, Child Advocacy, Indian/Tribal Law Clinics
Legal Writing/Methods Course Requirements: 1-semester Legal Research and Writing class required in the first semester of first year and Research and Writing seminar in second or third year.

STUDENT INFORMATION
Enrollment of Law School: 460
% Male/Female: 50/50
% Full Time: 100
% Full Time That Are International: 1
% Minority: 25
Average Age of Entering Class: 26

RESEARCH FACILITIES
Computers/Workstations Available: 50
School-Supported Research Centers: The University of Arizona is a top-ranked research university with a plethora of library and cultural opportunities and venues for interdisiplinary study and extracurricular involvement.

EXPENSES/FINANCIAL AID
Annual Tuition (Residents/Nonresidents): $5,125/$12,500
Room and Board (On/Off Campus): $6,000/$7,500
Books and Supplies: $750
Financial Aid Application Deadline: 3/1
Average Grant: $4,000
Average Loan: $13,500

% of Aid That Is Merit-Based: 35
% Receiving Some Sort of Aid: 81
Average Total Aid Package: $15,000
Average Debt: $42,000

ADMISSIONS INFORMATION
Application Fee: $45
Regular Application Deadline: 2/15
Regular Notification: Rolling
LSDAS Accepted? Yes
Average GPA: 3.5
Range of GPA: 2.6–4.0
Average LSAT: 161
Range of LSAT: 145–173
Transfer Students Accepted? Yes
Other Schools to Which Students Applied: Arizona State University, UCLA School of Law, University of San Diego, University of Texas, University of Colorado, University of California—Berkeley, University of California—Davis, University of California—Hastings
Other Admissions Factors Considered: The College seeks to enroll a class that is intellectually dynamic and culturally diverse. Each file is therefore reviewed with care and in the context of the student's strengths, background, academic experience, test scores, work experience, community and public service.
Number of Applications Received: 1,667
Number of Applicants Accepted: 420
Number of Applicants Enrolled: 150

INTERNATIONAL STUDENTS
TOEFL Required of International Students? Yes

EMPLOYMENT INFORMATION

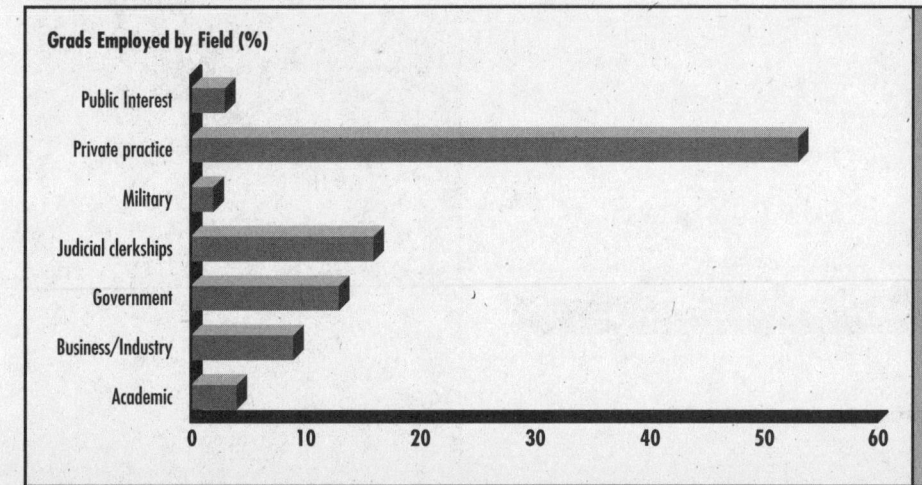

Grads Employed by Field (%)
- Public Interest
- Private practice
- Military
- Judicial clerkships
- Government
- Business/Industry
- Academic

Rate of Placement: 94%
Average Starting Salary: $49,031
Employers Who Frequently Hire Grads: Snell and Wilmer; Quarles and Brady; Bryan Cave; Gibson, Dunn and Crutcher; O'Conner Cavanagh; Streich Lang; Squire Sanders; Arizona Supreme Court and court of Appeals; U.S. District and Circuit Courts; Department of Justice; District Attorney's, Public Defender's, City Attorney's Offices
Prominent Alumni: Morris K. Udall, former congressman; Stewart Udall, former congressman and secretary of interior; former Senator Dennis Deconcini
State for Bar Exam: CA/FL/NV/NY/AK/AZ
Number Taking Bar Exam: 137
Pass Rate for First-Time Bar: 93

UNIVERSITY OF ARKANSAS — FAYETTEVILLE
School of Law

Admissions Contact: Associate Dean for Students, James K. Miller
Leflar Law Center, Fayetteville, AR 72701
Admissions Phone: 479-575-3102 • Admissions Fax: 479-575-3320
Admissions E-mail: jkmiller@uark.edu • Web Address: law.uark.edu/

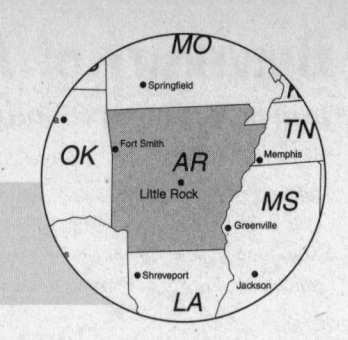

INSTITUTIONAL INFORMATION
Public/Private: Public
Student/Faculty Ratio: 14:1
Total Faculty: 49
% Part Time: 31
% Female: 31
% Minority: 16

PROGRAMS
Academic Specialties: The graduate law program is the only program in the U.S. offering the LLM in Agricultural Law. These specialized agricultural law courses are generally open to JD students. The comprehensive Legal Research and Writing Program is staffed by 5 full-time faculty members whose primary or exclusive focus is on the legal research and writing courses that are required of all students. All students are required to complete 1 skills course before graduation and are provided a number of specially designed skills courses that can satisfy this requirement. The skills requirement also fosters widespread student interest in various skills competitions.
Advanced Degrees Offered: LLM Agricultural Law (1 academic year)
Combined Degrees Offered: JD/MBA (3.5 years), JD/MPA (3.5 years), LLM/MS (1.5 years)
Grading System: A (4.0), A– (3.67), B+ (3.33), B (3.0), B– (2.67), C+ (2.33), C (2.0), C– (1.67), D+ (1.33), D (1.0), D– (0.67), F (0.0)
Clinical Program Required? No
Clinical Programs Description: Students may take 3-hour credit clinic courses in Civil Litigation, Criminal Prosecution, Criminal Defense, and Federal Practice.
Legal Writing Course Requirements? Yes
Legal Writing Description: Legal Research and Writing I (3 credits) is required the first semester; Legal Research and Writing II (2 credits) is required the second semester; Legal Research and Writing III (2 credits) must be taken by the end of the second year.
Legal Methods Course Requirements? No
Legal Research Course Requirements? No
Legal Research Description: See Legal Writing.
Moot Court Requirement? No
Moot Court Description: Second-year students are invited to participate in an intraschool competition. This is a feeder program for our interschool competition squad, which competes in multiple moot court competitions each year.
Public Interest Law Requirement? No
Academic Journals: *Arkansas Law Review*

STUDENT INFORMATION
Enrollment of Law School: 373
% Male/Female: 56/44
% Full Time: 100
% Full Time That Are International: 1
% Minority: 17
Average Age of Entering Class: 26

EXPENSES/FINANCIAL AID
Annual Tuition (Residents/Nonresidents): $5,707/$12,285
Room and Board: $5,312
Books and Supplies: $6,188
Financial Aid Application Deadline: 7/1
Average Grant: $4,680
Average Loan: $13,840
% of Aid That Is Merit-Based: 48
Average Debt: $42,458

ADMISSIONS INFORMATION
Regular Application Deadline: Rolling
Regular Notification: Rolling
LSDAS Accepted? Yes
Average GPA: 3.3
Range of GPA: 3.0–3.6
Average LSAT: 152
Range of LSAT: 148–156
Transfer Students Accepted? Yes
Other Schools to Which Students Applied: University of Arkansas at Little Rock
Other Admissions Factors Considered: In order to ensure a diverse student body, the Admissions Committee is given the authority to admit a limited number of students on a discretionary basis, considering such factors as age, gender, cultural, ethnic and racial background; and geographic origin.
Number of Applications Received: 591
Number of Applicants Accepted: 320
Number of Applicants Enrolled: 141

INTERNATIONAL STUDENTS
TOEFL Required of International Students? Yes

EMPLOYMENT INFORMATION

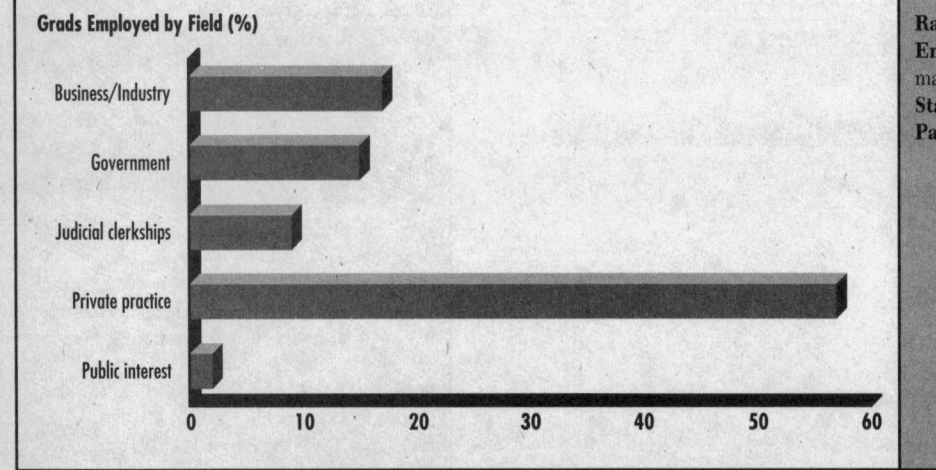

Grads Employed by Field (%)
- Business/Industry: ~17
- Government: ~15
- Judicial clerkships: ~13
- Private practice: ~57
- Public interest: ~2

Rate of Placement: 96%
Employers Who Frequently Hire Grads: The majority of graduates go into small firms.
State for Bar Exam: AR
Pass Rate for First-Time Bar: 85%

UNIVERSITY OF ARKANSAS — LITTLE ROCK
William H. Bowen School of Law

Admissions Contact: Director of Admissions, Jean Probasco
1201 McAlmont, Little Rock, AR 72202-5142
Admissions Phone: 501-324-9903 • Admissions Fax: 501-324-9433
Admissions E-mail: lawadm@ualr.edu • Web Address: www.ualr.edu/~lawschool

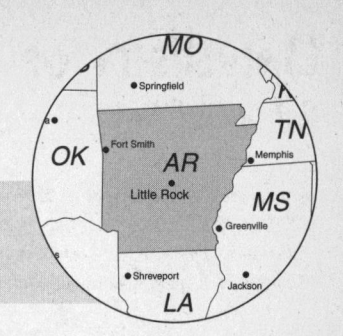

INSTITUTIONAL INFORMATION
Public/Private: Public
Student/Faculty Ratio: 17:1
Total Faculty: 48
% Part Time: 38
% Female: 38
% Minority: 8

PROGRAMS
Academic Specialties: Our curriculum offers a strong foundation in traditional areas as well as requiring all students to take Trial Advocacy. Other specialties include Civil Procedure, Commercial Law, Constitutional Law, Corporation Securities Law, Criminal Law, Environmental Law, International Law, Labor Law, Legal History, Property, and Taxation.
Combined Degrees Offered: JD/MBA, JD/MPA (both approximately 3.5 years)
Grading System: Letter grades converted to a 4.0 scale
Clinical Program Required? No
Clinical Programs Description: 2 clinics, Litigation and Mediation. Areas of practice include Family Law, Administrative Law, Mental Health Law, and Child Dependency and Neglect.
Legal Writing Course Requirements? Yes
Legal Methods Course Requirements? Yes
Legal Methods Description: First-year and upper level requirement
Legal Research Course Requirements? Yes
Moot Court Requirement? No
Public Interest Law Requirement? No

STUDENT INFORMATION
Enrollment of Law School: 385
% Out of State: 13
% Male/Female: 52/48
% Full Time: 65
% Minority: 11
Average Age of Entering Class: 27

EXPENSES/FINANCIAL AID
Annual Tuition (Residents/Nonresidents): $5,100/$11,460
Room and Board (Off Campus): $9,000
Books and Supplies: $800
Average Grant: $4,784
Average Loan: $12,004
% of Aid That Is Merit-Based: 14
% Receiving Some Sort of Aid: 64
Average Total Aid Package: $14,300
Average Debt: $26,000
Tuition Per Credit (Residents/Nonresidents): $170/$383
Fees Per Credit: $12

ADMISSIONS INFORMATION
Application Fee: $40
Regular Application Deadline: 5/1
Regular Notification: Rolling
LSDAS Accepted? Yes
Average GPA: 3.3
Range of GPA: 3.0–3.7
Average LSAT: 153
Range of LSAT: 150–157
Transfer Students Accepted? Yes

Other Schools to Which Students Applied: The University of Tulsa, University of Arkansas at Fayetteville, Mercer University
Other Admissions Factors Considered: Background and experience relevant to success in law school and to diversity of the student body and the profession
Number of Applications Received: 430
Number of Applicants Accepted: 253
Number of Applicants Enrolled: 135

EMPLOYMENT INFORMATION

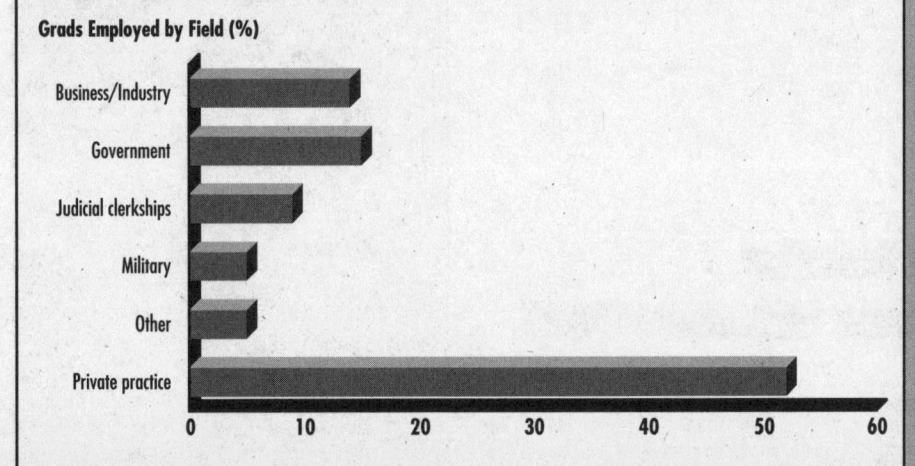

Grads Employed by Field (%)
- Business/Industry: ~15
- Government: ~15
- Judicial clerkships: ~10
- Military: ~3
- Other: ~3
- Private practice: ~53

Rate of Placement: 91%
Average Starting Salary: $40,493
Employers Who Frequently Hire Grads: Wright, Lindsey & Jennings; Friday, Eldredge & Clark; Prosecuting Attorney; Mitchell, Williams, Selig, Gates & Woodyard; State Supreme Court; State Court of Appeals
State for Bar Exam: AR, TN, TX, GA, FL
Pass Rate for First-Time Bar: 73%

UNIVERSITY OF BALTIMORE
School of Law

Admissions Contact: Assistant Director of Admissions, Lisa Lawler
1420 North Charles Street, Baltimore, MD 21201
Admissions Phone: 410-837-4459 • Admissions Fax: 410-837-4450
Admissions E-mail: lwadmiss@ubmail.ubalt.edu • Web Address: www.law.ubalt.edu

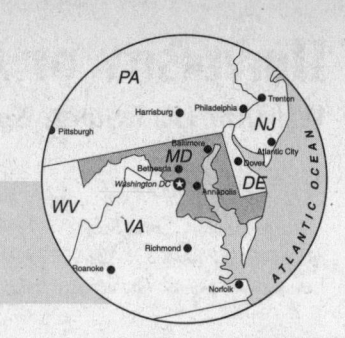

INSTITUTIONAL INFORMATION
Public/Private: Public
Student/Faculty Ratio: 18:1
Total Faculty: 104
% Part Time: 58
% Female: 32
% Minority: 11

PROGRAMS
Academic Specialties: 12 concentrations as well as an LLM in Taxation. Specialities include Family Law, Intellectual Property, Evidence, Antitrust, Environmental, Commercial Law, Corporation Securities Law, Criminal Law, Government Services, International Law, Labor Law, Legal History, Legal Philosophy, Property, and Taxation.
Advanced Degrees Offered: LLM Taxation
Combined Degrees Offered: JD/MBA, JD/MS Criminal Justice, JD/MPA, JD/PhD Policy Science in conjunction with University of Maryland at Baltimore, JD/LLM Taxation, JD/MS Negotiation and Conflict Management. Most combined degrees add 1 year of study.
Grading System: 4.0 quality scale from A to F
Clinical Program Required? No
Clinical Program Description: Family Law Clinic, Criminal Practice Clinic, Community Development Clinic, Appellate Advocacy Clinic, Civil Clinic, Disability Law Clinic
Legal Writing Course Requirements? Yes
Legal Writing Description: 3 semesters of legal writing and an upper-level writing requirement
Legal Methods Course Requirements? Yes
Legal Methods Description: Part of 3-semester program encompassing legal writing and research
Legal Research Course Requirements? Yes
Legal Research Description: Part of 3-semester writing program
Moot Court Requirement? No
Public Interest Law Requirement? No
Academic Journals: *Law Review, Law Forum, Environmental Law Journal, Intellectual Property Law Journal*

STUDENT INFORMATION
Enrollment of Law School: 889
% Out of State: 15
% Male/Female: 51/49
% Full Time: 66
% Full Time That Are International: 1
% Minority: 21
Average Age of Entering Class: 27

EXPENSES/FINANCIAL AID
Annual Tuition (Residents/Nonresidents): $10,116/$17,552
Room and Board (Off Campus): $10,000
Books and Supplies: $850
Financial Aid Application Deadline: 4/1
Average Grant: $4,000
Average Loan: $12,500
% Receiving Some Sort of Aid: 68
Average Debt: $38,300
Tuition Per Credit (Residents/Nonresidents): $392/$662
Fees Per Credit: $22

ADMISSIONS INFORMATION
Application Fee: $35
Regular Application Deadline: Rolling
Regular Notification: Rolling
LSDAS Accepted? Yes
Average GPA: 2.9
Range of GPA: 2.7–3.3
Average LSAT: 149
Range of LSAT: 147–152
Transfer Students Accepted? Yes
Other Schools to Which Students Applied: Widener University, Catholic University of America, American University, University of Maryland, College Park
Other Admissions Factors Considered: Difficulty of the undergraduate major, graduate degrees, work experience, ability to overcome adversity, individual achievement, motivation, character
Number of Applications Received: 1,463
Number of Applicants Accepted: 684
Number of Applicants Enrolled: 269

EMPLOYMENT INFORMATION

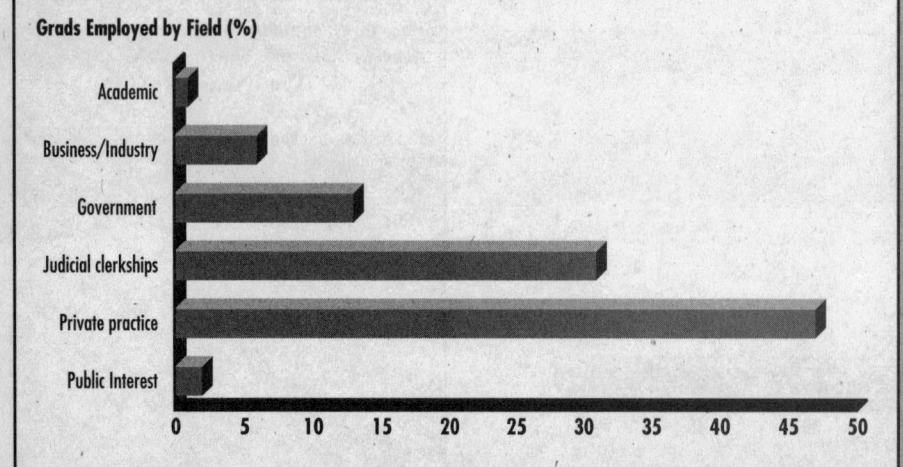

Grads Employed by Field (%)

Field	%
Academic	~1
Business/Industry	~6
Government	~13
Judicial clerkships	~31
Private practice	~47
Public Interest	~2

Rate of Placement: 92%
Average Starting Salary: $39,391
Employers Who Frequently Hire Grads: Law firms, judges, government agencies, corporations
State for Bar Exam: MD
Pass Rate for First-Time Bar: 72%

UNIVERSITY OF BRITISH COLUMBIA
Faculty of Law

Admissions Contact: Admissions Officer, Elaine L. Borthwick
1822 East Mall, Vancouver, BC V6T 1Z1 Canada
Admissions Phone: 604-822-6303 • Admissions Fax: 604-822-8108
Admissions E-mail: borthwick@law.ubc.ca • Web Address: www.law.ubc.ca

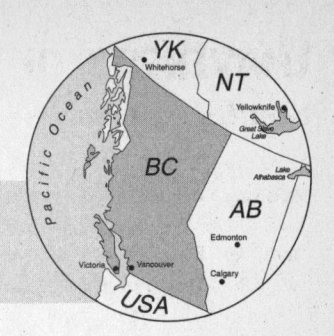

INSTITUTIONAL INFORMATION
Public/Private: Public
Student/Faculty Ratio: 5:1
Total Faculty: 118
% Part Time: 67
% Female: 45

PROGRAMS
Academic Specialties: UBC Faculty of Law does not have specialization programs that are reflected on the graduate's degree; however it is possible for students to concentrate their electives in certain areas of study. UBC Law School does offer formal programs: the Centre for Asian Legal Studies; the Centre for Feminist Legal Studies; the First Nations Legal Studies Program; the Environment, Sustainable Development, and the Law; the International Centre for Criminal Law Reform and Criminal Justice Policy; Legal History; Law and Computers; and the new Alternate Dispute Resolution Program. Other specialties include Civil Procedure, Commercial Law, Constitutional Law, Corporation Securities Law, Criminal Law, Government Services, Human Rights Law, Intellectual Property Law, International Law, Labor Law, Legal Philosophy, Property, and Taxation.
Advanced Degrees Offered: LLB (3 years), LLM (12 months), PhD (1 to 2 years)
Combined Degrees Offered: LLB/MBA (4 years; 86 credits in law and 45 credits in the MBA program)
Grading System: Percentages
Clinical Program Required? No

Clinical Programs Description: The Law Students Legal Advice Program is a student-run organization that provides legal advice to those who would otherwise not be able to afford such assistance. LSLAP also operates specialized legal clinics: the Women's Clinic, the Persons with AIDS Clinic, the Street Youth Clinic, the Chinese Clinic, and the First Nations Clinic.
Legal Writing Course Requirements? Yes
Legal Writing Description: The Legal Research and Writing Program is 1 full year during the first year of study.
Legal Methods Course Requirements? No
Legal Research Course Requirements? Yes
Legal Research Description: See Legal Writing.
Moot Court Requirement? No
Moot Court Description: All first-year students are required to participate in a moot court program, in which they write an appeal factum and participate as an advocate in the mock appeal in front of a bench of legal practitioners acting as judges.
Public Interest Law Requirement? No

STUDENT INFORMATION
Enrollment of Law School: 693
% Out of State: 26
% Male/Female: 46/54
% Full Time: 90
% Full Time That Are International: 1
% Minority: 10
Average Age of Entering Class: 26

RESEARCH FACILITIES
Research Resources Available: Quicklaw, Westlaw, Lexis/Nexis, Canadian Bar Association

School-Supported Research Centers: Centre for Asian Legal Studies, Chinese Legal Studies, Southeast Asian Legal Studies; Centre for Feminist Legal Studies; First Nations Legal Studies Program; Environment, Sustainable Development, and Law; International Centre for Criminal Law Reform and Criminal Justice Policy; Alternate Dispute Resolution Program; Legal History; Law and Computers

EXPENSES/FINANCIAL AID
Annual Tuition (Residents/Nonresidents): $3,199/$15,000
Room and Board (On/Off Campus): $27,018/$15,000
Books and Supplies: $1,300
Financial Aid Application Deadline: 5/15
Average Loan: $5,350
% Receiving Some Sort of Aid: 70
Average Total Aid Package: $5,500
Average Debt: $25,000

ADMISSIONS INFORMATION
Application Fee: $45
Regular Application Deadline: 2/1
Regular Notification: Rolling
LSDAS Accepted? No
Average GPA: 3.6
Range of GPA: 3.2–4.0
Average LSAT: 163
Range of LSAT: 152–173
Transfer Students Accepted? Yes
Other Schools to Which Students Applied: U. of Calgary, U. of Toronto, U. of Victoria, York
Number of Applications Received: 1,385
Number of Applicants Accepted: 445
Number of Applicants Enrolled: 207

EMPLOYMENT INFORMATION

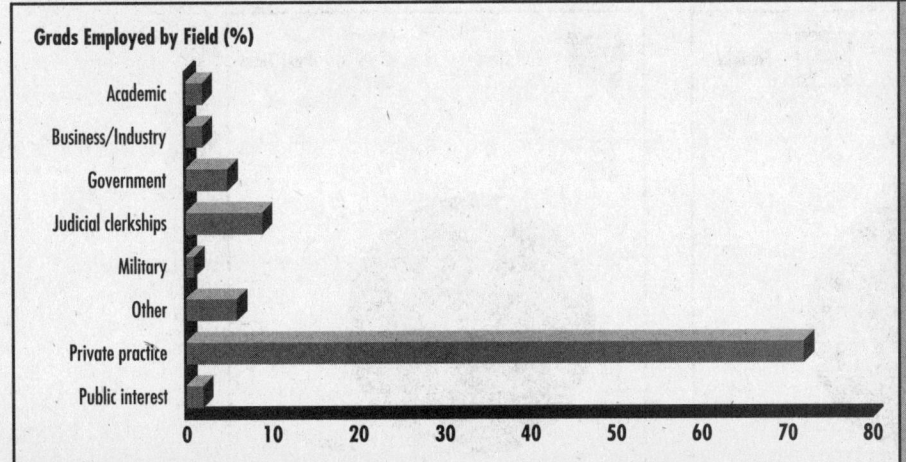

Grads Employed by Field (%)

Field	%
Academic	~2
Business/Industry	~3
Government	~5
Judicial clerkships	~8
Military	0
Other	~2
Private practice	~73
Public interest	~1

Rate of Placement: 97%
Average Starting Salary: $49,000
Employers Who Frequently Hire Grads: Law firms and government agencies in British Columbia, Ontario, and Alberta; law firms in Nova Scotia, New York, Boston, and California; Canadian public interest groups; Canadian courts both federal and provincial; corporate legal departments; Canadian Crown Corporations
State for Bar Exam: BC, AB, NY, MA, ON
Pass Rate for First-Time Bar: 99%

UNIVERSITY OF CALGARY
Faculty of Law

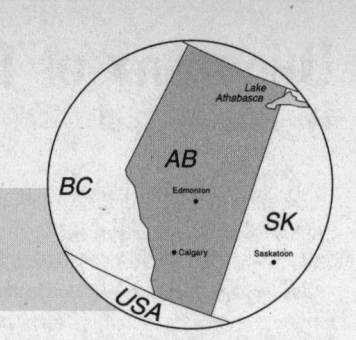

Admissions Contact: Admissions/Student Services Officer, Karen Argento
2500 University Drive NW, Calgary, AB T2N 1NY Canada
Admissions Phone: 403-220-8154 • Admissions Fax: 403-282-8325
Admissions E-mail: law@ucalgary.ca • Web Address: www.ucalgary.ca/faculties/law/

INSTITUTIONAL INFORMATION
Public/Private: Public
Student/Faculty Ratio: 15:1
Total Faculty: 17
% Female: 47

PROGRAMS
Advanced Degrees Offered: LLB (3 years)
Advanced Degrees Offered: LLB (3 years), LLM (15–18 months)
Combined Degrees Offered: LLB/MBA (4 years), LLB/MED
Grading System: 11-band grading system, 4-point scale
Clinical Program Required? No
Clinical Program Description: Criminal Seminar, Family Seminar, Natural Resources Seminar, Business Seminar

STUDENT INFORMATION
Enrollment of Law School: 216
% Male/Female: 46/54
% Full Time: 94
Average Age of Entering Class: 28

EXPENSES/FINANCIAL AID
Annual Tuition: $4,488
Room and Board (On/Off Campus): $4,400/ $7,000
Books and Supplies: $1,450

ADMISSIONS INFORMATION
Regular Application Deadline: 2/1
Regular Notification: Rolling
Average GPA: 3.4
Range of GPA: 2.2–3.9
Transfer Students Accepted? No
Other Schools to Which Students Applied: University of Alberta

EMPLOYMENT INFORMATION
Rate of Placement: 90%

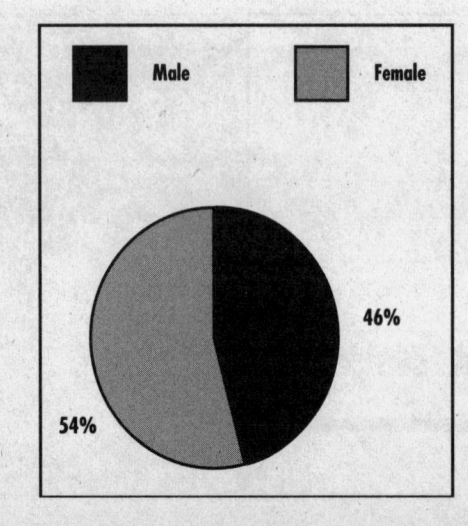

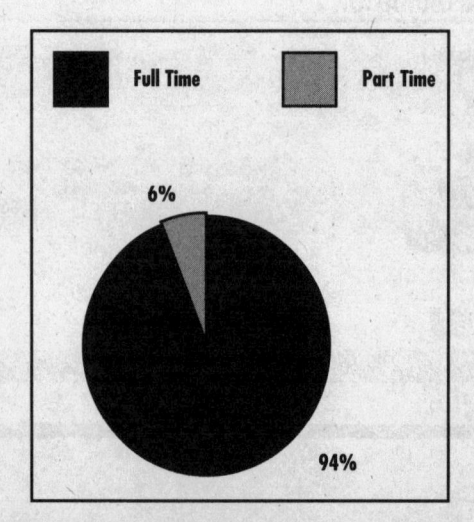

UNIVERSITY OF CALIFORNIA, BERKELEY
School of Law (Boalt Hall)

Admissions Contact: Director of Admissions, Edward Tom
5 Boalt Hall, Berkeley, CA 94720-7200
Admissions Phone: 510-642-2274 • Admissions Fax: 510-643-6222
Admissions E-mail: admissions@law.berkeley.edu • Web Address: www.law.berkeley.edu

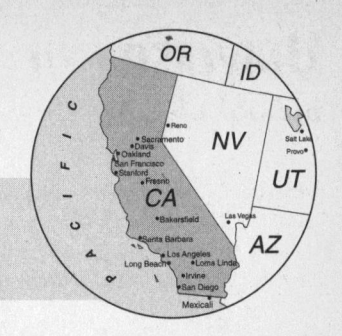

INSTITUTIONAL INFORMATION
Public/Private: Public
Student/Faculty Ratio: 16:1
Total Faculty: 164
% Part Time: 58
% Female: 56
% Minority: 9

PROGRAMS
Academic Specialties: Corporation Securities Law, Environmental Law, International Law, Intellectual Property Law, Law & Technology, Comparative Legal Studies, Law & Economics, Social Justice/Public Interest.
Advanced Degrees Offered: LLM (1 year), JSD, PhD in Jurisprudence and Social Policy (approximately 6 years)
Combined Degrees Offered: JD/MA and JD/PhD Economics, JD/MA Asian Studies, JD/MA International Area Studies, JD/MBA, JD/MCP Department of City and Regional Planning, JD/MJ Graduate School of Journalism, JD/MPP, JD/MSW, JD/MA and JD/PhD Information Management Systems, JD/PhD History (Legal History), JD/MS Energy and Resources Group, plus other combined degree programs on an individual basis. JD/Masters degrees average four years to completion. JD/PhD degrees vary in years to completion.
Grading System: High Honors, assigned to the top 10% of the first-year class (10% to 15% of the second- and third-year classes); Honors, to the next 30% of the first-year class (30% to 35% of the second- and third-year classes); and Pass to the remainder. Substandard Pass or No Credit is used when work is unsatisfactory; these grades are not governed by a curve.
Clinical Program Required? No.
Clinical Programs Description: Death Penalty; International Human Rights Law; Law, Technology, and Public Policy; East Bay Community Law Center; faculty-supervised clinics; a field placement program; professional lawyering skills courses; student-initiated projects; Disability Rights; Street Law Clinic
Legal Writing Course Requirements? Yes
Legal Writing Description: Required first-year course.
Legal Methods Course Requirements? Yes
Legal Methods Description: Required first-year course.
Legal Research Course Requirements? Yes
Legal Research Description: Required first-year course.
Moot Court Requirement? Yes.
Moot Court Description: Required first-year course during Spring semester.
Public Interest Law Requirement? No.
Academic Journals: *African-American Law and Policy Report, Asian Law Journal, Berkeley Journal of Employment and Labor Law, Berkeley Journal of International Law, Berkeley Technology Law Journal, Berkeley Women's Law Journal, California Criminal Law Review, California Law Review, Ecology Law Quarterly, La Raza Law Journal*

STUDENT INFORMATION
Enrollment of Law School: 893
% Out of State: 13
% Male/Female: 40/60
% Full Time: 100
% Full Time That Are International: 3
% Minority: 26
Average Age of Entering Class: 24

RESEARCH FACILITIES
School-Supported Research Centers: Student computing labs, network access from library reading rooms, Disabled Students Program on the Berkeley campus

EXPENSES/FINANCIAL AID
Annual Tuition (Residents/Nonresidents): $0/$10,704
Room and Board: $11,258
Books and Supplies: $1,170
Financial Aid Application Deadline: 3/2
Average Grant: $5,915
Average Loan: $18,380
% Receiving Some Sort of Aid: 84
Average Total Aid Package: $21,872
Average Debt: $46,553
Full-Time Annual Fees: $10,945

ADMISSIONS INFORMATION
Application Fee: $65
Regular Application Deadline: 2/1
Regular Notification: Rolling
LSDAS Accepted? Yes
Average GPA: 3.7
Average LSAT: 165
Transfer Students Accepted? Yes
Other Schools to Which Students Applied: Harvard, NYU, Stanford, UCLA
Number of Applications Received: 5,632
Number of Applicants Accepted: 873
Number of Applicants Enrolled: 299

EMPLOYMENT INFORMATION

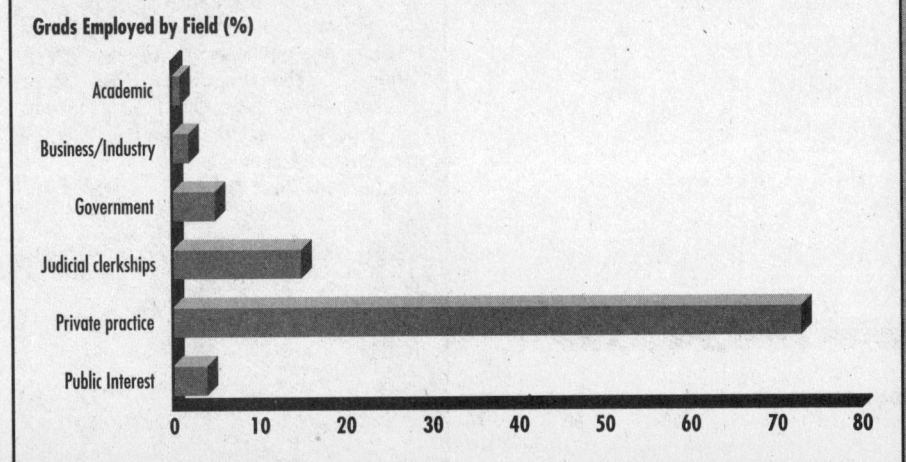

Grads Employed by Field (%)

Field	%
Academic	~2
Business/Industry	~3
Government	~5
Judicial clerkships	~15
Private practice	~73
Public Interest	~3

Rate of Placement: 100%
Average Starting Salary: $103,335
Employers Who Frequently Hire Grads: Over 400 employers recruit at Boalt Hall each fall including national firms, multinational corporations, public interest groups, and governmental agencies.
State for Bar Exam: CA
Pass Rate for First-Time Bar: 94%

UNIVERSITY OF CALIFORNIA, DAVIS
School of Law

Admissions Contact: Director of Admission, Sharon L. Pinkney
School of Law-King Hall, Davis, CA 95616-5201
Admissions Phone: 530-752-6477 • Admissions Fax:
Admissions E-mail: lawadmissions@ucdavis.edu • Web Address: www.kinghall.ucdavis.edu

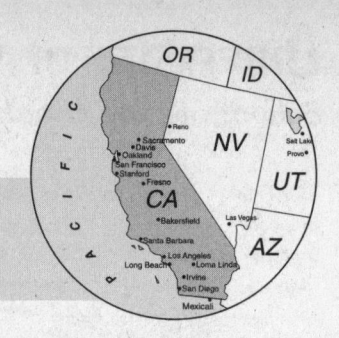

INSTITUTIONAL INFORMATION
Public/Private: Public
Student/Faculty Ratio: 15:1
Total Faculty: 61
% Part Time: 41
% Female: 36
% Minority: 19

PROGRAMS
Academic Specialties: International Law, Immigration Law, Public Interest Law, Skills Training, Environmental Law, Civil Rights Law, Human Rights Law, Clinical Programs, Criminal Law, Intellectual Property Law, Taxation
Advanced Degrees Offered: LLM (1 year)
Combined Degrees Offered: JD/MBA (4 years), JD/MA, JD/MS (4 years)
Grading System: A to F, with some courses graded S/U (satisfactory/unsatisfactory); some skills courses and all clinicals graded Pass/Fail
Clinical Program Required? No
Clinical Programs Description: In-house clinics in Prison Law, Civil Rights, Immigration and Family Protection; externships in Tax, Labor, Criminal, Public Interest, Judicial, and Environmental
Legal Writing Course Requirements? Yes
Legal Writing Description: 1 semester of Legal Writing, instruction in the form and substance of writing. A variety of law-related documents are discussed and drafted. An experience in oral advocacy is included.
Legal Methods Course Requirements? Yes
Legal Methods Description: See Legal Writing.

Legal Research Course Requirements? Yes
Legal Research Description: Legal Research, a description of the evolution and use of sources of law and secondary authority.
Moot Court Requirement? No
Moot Court Description: The Appellate Advocacy (Moot Court) course teaches basic appellate practice and procedure. The course also provides beginning instruction in oral advocacy skills and an opportunity to practice these skills in front of a moot court.
Public Interest Law Requirement? No
Academic Journals: *Environs* (environmental law and policy journal), *UC Davis Journal of International Law & Policy*, *UC Davis Law Review*, *UC Davis Journal of Juvenile Law & Policy*

STUDENT INFORMATION
Enrollment of Law School: 540
% Out of State: 14
% Male/Female: 43/57
% Full Time: 100
% Full Time That Are International: 1
% Minority: 32
Average Age of Entering Class: 25

RESEARCH FACILITIES
Research Resources Available: Additional computer labs located on the campus outside the law school
School-Supported Research Centers: Civil Rights Clinic, Immigration Clinic, Family Protection and Legal Assistance Clinic

EXPENSES/FINANCIAL AID
Annual Tuition (Residents/Nonresidents): $0/$10,704
Room and Board (On/Off Campus): $9,438/$9,479
Books and Supplies: $973
Financial Aid Application Deadline: 3/2
Average Grant: $4,952
Average Loan: $15,903
% of Aid That Is Merit-Based: 1
% Receiving Some Sort of Aid: 91
Average Total Aid Package: $18,596
Average Debt: $45,650

ADMISSIONS INFORMATION
Application Fee: $70
Regular Application Deadline: 2/1
Regular Notification: Rolling
LSDAS Accepted? Yes
Average GPA: 3.5
Range of GPA: 3.3–3.7
Average LSAT: 159
Range of LSAT: 157–162
Transfer Students Accepted? Yes
Other Admissions Factors Considered: Rigor of undergraduate course of study, undergraduate school attended, advanced degrees or coursework, diversity of background and experiences, significant work experience
Number of Applications Received: 2,779
Number of Applicants Accepted: 863
Number of Applicants Enrolled: 214

INTERNATIONAL STUDENTS
TOEFL Required of International Students? Yes

EMPLOYMENT INFORMATION

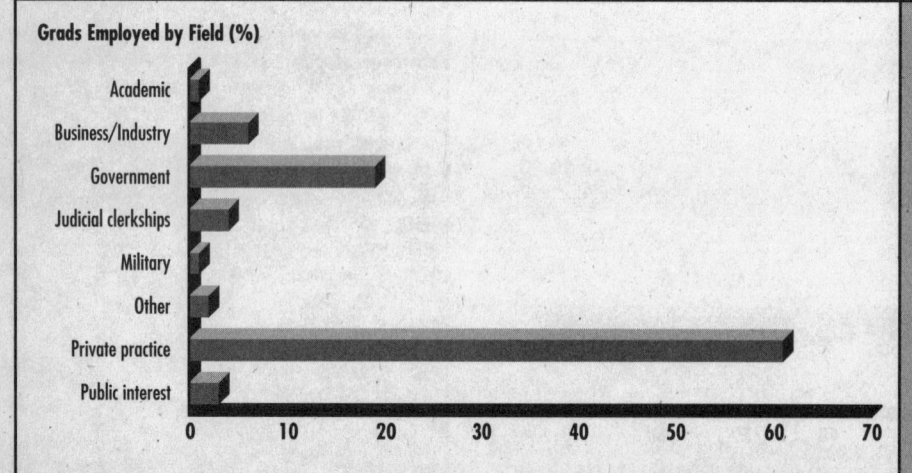

Grads Employed by Field (%)

Field	%
Academic	~1
Business/Industry	~2
Government	~19
Judicial clerkships	~3
Military	0
Other	~1
Private practice	~62
Public interest	~3

Rate of Placement: 94%
Average Starting Salary: $83,079
Employers Who Frequently Hire Grads: State of California, private law firms, district attorneys, public defenders, public interest entities
State for Bar Exam: CA
Pass Rate for First-Time Bar: 91%

UNIVERSITY OF CALIFORNIA, HASTINGS
College of Law

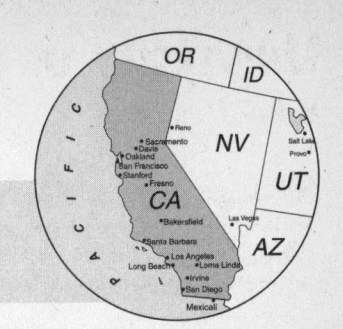

Admissions Contact: Director of Admissions, Akira Shiroma
200 McAllister Street #214, San Francisco, CA 94102
Admissions Phone: 415-565-4623 • Admissions Fax: 415-565-4863
Admissions E-mail: admiss@uchastings.edu • Web Address: www.uchastings.edu

INSTITUTIONAL INFORMATION
Public/Private: Public
Student/Faculty Ratio: 21:1
Total Faculty: 137
% Part Time: 60
% Female: 11
% Minority: 10

PROGRAMS
Academic Specialties: Civil Litigation, International Law, Public Interest Law, Taxation, Civil Procedure, International
Advanced Degrees Offered: JD (3 years)
Combined Degrees Offered: JD/MBA; other master's degrees (4 to 5 years)
Grading System: Traditional 4.0 scale, except C– is 1.5 and there are no D+ or D– grades
Clinical Program Required? No
Clinical Programs Description: As early as the fourth semester, enrollment is permitted in 1 of the clinics, which contain a class component and placement in a designated Bay Area law office. Current clinics are Civil Justice Clinic, Criminal Practice Clinic, Environmental Law, Immigrants' Rights, Local Government, and Workers' Rights.
Legal Writing Course Requirements? Yes
Legal Writing Description: No
Legal Methods Course Requirements? No
Legal Research Course Requirements? Yes
Legal Research Description: Comprehensive Legal Writing and Research
Moot Court Requirement? Yes
Moot Court Description: 1 semester, introduces students to oral and written appellate advocacy
Public Interest Law Requirement? No
Academic Journals: Hastings Communications and Entertainment Law Journal, Hastings Constitutional Law Quarterly, Hastings International and Comparative Law Review, Hastings Law Journal, Hastings West-Northwest Journal of Environmental Law and Policy, Hastings Women's Law Journal

STUDENT INFORMATION
Enrollment of Law School: 1,252
% Out of State: 12
% Male/Female: 47/53
% Full Time: 100
% Full Time That Are International: 1
% Minority: 33
Average Age of Entering Class: 24

RESEARCH FACILITIES
Research Resources Available: The Land Conservation Institute
School-Supported Research Centers: Public Law Research Institute, Civil Justice Clinic

EXPENSES/FINANCIAL AID
Annual Tuition (Residents/Nonresidents): $10,175/$19,661
Room and Board (Off Campus): $18,825
Books and Supplies: $863
Financial Aid Application Deadline: 3/1
Average Grant: $4,648
Average Loan: $20,106
% of Aid That Is Merit-Based: 1
% Receiving Some Sort of Aid: 95
Average Total Aid Package: $24,207
Average Debt: $50,372

ADMISSIONS INFORMATION
Application Fee: $60
Regular Application Deadline: 3/1
Regular Notification: 5/1
LSDAS Accepted? Yes
Average GPA: 3.5
Range of GPA: 3.3–3.7
Average LSAT: 161
Range of LSAT: 159–164
Transfer Students Accepted? Yes
Other Admissions Factors Considered: Writing ability and obstacles overcome
Number of Applications Received: 4,800
Number of Applicants Accepted: 1,496
Number of Applicants Enrolled: 420

EMPLOYMENT INFORMATION

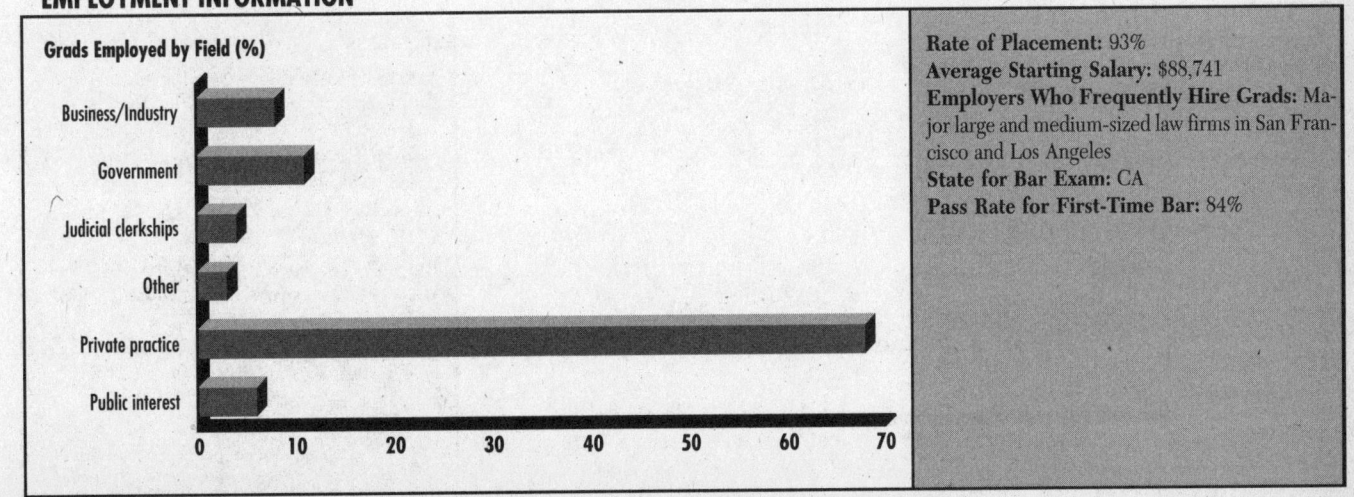

Grads Employed by Field (%)
- Business/Industry
- Government
- Judicial clerkships
- Other
- Private practice
- Public interest

Rate of Placement: 93%
Average Starting Salary: $88,741
Employers Who Frequently Hire Grads: Major large and medium-sized law firms in San Francisco and Los Angeles
State for Bar Exam: CA
Pass Rate for First-Time Bar: 84%

UNIVERSITY OF CALIFORNIA, LOS ANGELES
School of Law

Admissions Contact: Assistant Dean and Director of Admissions, Andrea Sossin-Bergman
Box 951445, Los Angeles, CA 90095-1445
Admissions Phone: 310-825-4041 • Admissions Fax: 310-825-9450
Admissions E-mail: admissions@law.ucla.edu • Web Address: www.law.ucla.edu

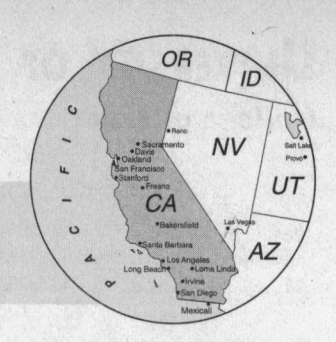

INSTITUTIONAL INFORMATION
Public/Private: Public
Student/Faculty Ratio: 15:1
Total Faculty: 110
% Part Time: 25
% Female: 30
% Minority: 7

PROGRAMS
Academic Specialties: Public Law (Constitutional and Criminal Law), Intellectual Property, Legal and Moral Philosophy, Communications and Cyberlaw, Public Interest Law and Policy, International Law, Environmental Law, Civil Procedure, Commercial Law, Constitutional Law, Corporation Securities Law, Government Services, Human Rights Law, International Law, Labor Law, Legal History, and Taxation
Advanced Degrees Offered: JD, LLM for advanced foreign scholars (1 year)
Combined Degrees Offered: JD/MA African American Studies, JD/MA American Indian Studies, JD/MBA, JD/MA Public Policy, JD/MSW, JD/MA Urban Planning (all 4 years).
Grading System: A+ (4.3) to F (0.0), mandatory curve in all first-year classes and advanced courses with 40 or more students
Clinical Program Required? Yes
Clinical Programs Description: Required first-year Lawyering Skills course has a clinical component; additional clinical programs include a working mediation clinic.
Legal Writing Course Requirements? No
Legal Methods Course Requirements? Yes
Legal Methods Description: Students are introduced to the fundamentals of legal research, reasoning, client counseling, and fact investigation using clinical methods.
Legal Research Course Requirements? No
Moot Court Requirement? No
Public Interest Law Requirement? No
Public Interest Law Description: Partnership with Public Counsel, the pro bono arm of the Los Angeles County and Beverly Hills bar associations; Environmental Law Clinic; access to a wide variety of volunteer opportunities.
Academic Journals: *Asian Pacific American Law Journal, Journal of Law and Technology, Chicano/Latino Law Review, Entertainment Law Review, Journal of Environmental Law and Policy, Journal of International Law & Foreign Policy, Pacific Basin Law Journal, UCLA Law Review, Women's Law Journal*

STUDENT INFORMATION
Enrollment of Law School: 951
% Out of State: 26
% Male/Female: 48/52
% Full Time: 100
% Full Time That Are International: 0
% Minority: 28
Average Age of Entering Class: 25

RESEARCH FACILITIES
Research Resources Available: One of the top university research libraries in the nation

EXPENSES/FINANCIAL AID
Room and Board (Off Campus): $13,575
Books and Supplies: $1,425
Financial Aid Application Deadline: 3/2
Average Grant: $6,250
Average Loan: $17,626
% of Aid That Is Merit-Based: 5
% Receiving Some Sort of Aid: 87
Average Total Aid Package: $26,156
Average Debt: $52,701

ADMISSIONS INFORMATION
Application Fee: $70
Regular Application Deadline: 2/1
Regular Notification: 5/1
LSDAS Accepted? Yes
Average GPA: 3.6
Average LSAT: 164
Transfer Students Accepted? Yes
Other Schools to Which Students Applied: U. of Southern California, UC—Berkeley, UC—Hastings, Georgetown, NYU
Other Admissions Factors Considered: Undergraduate program, graduate study, awards or publications, unusual or exceptional career or personal achievements, diversity characteristics, challenges overcome, other significant experience
Number of Applications Received: 5,091
Number of Applicants Accepted: 967
Number of Applicants Enrolled: 304

EMPLOYMENT INFORMATION

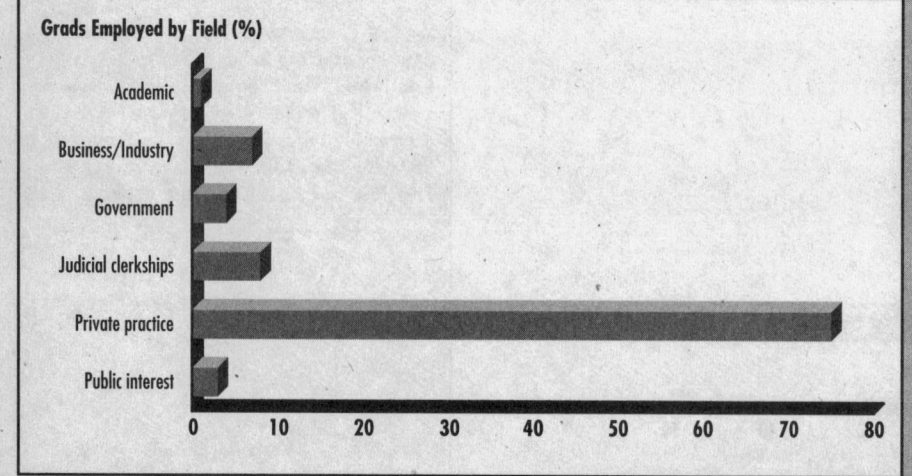

Grads Employed by Field (%):
- Academic: ~1
- Business/Industry: ~4
- Government: ~5
- Judicial clerkships: ~8
- Private practice: ~76
- Public interest: ~3

Rate of Placement: 98%
Average Starting Salary: $96,000
Employers Who Frequently Hire Grads: Latham & Watkins; O'Melveny & Myers; Irell & Manella; Gibson, Dunn & Crutcher; Morrison & Foerster; Skadden, Arps, et al.; Brobeck, Phleger & Harrison; Foley & Lardner; Gray, Cary, Ware & Freidenrich; Kirkland & Ellis; Orrick, Herrington & Sutcliffe; Riordan & McKinzie; Wilson, Sonsini, Goodrich & Rosati; U.S. Securities and Exchange Commission
State for Bar Exam: CA
Pass Rate for First-Time Bar: 90%

UNIVERSITY OF CHICAGO
Law School

Admissions Contact: Dean of the JD and Graduate Programs, Anna Praschma and Genita Robinson
1111 East 60th Street, Chicago, IL 60637
Admissions Phone: 773-702-9484 • Admissions Fax: 773-834-0942
Admissions E-mail: admissions@law.uchicago.edu • Web Address: www.law.uchicago.edu

INSTITUTIONAL INFORMATION
Public/Private: Private
Environment: Urban
Academic Calendar: Quarter
Schedule: Full time only
Student/Faculty Ratio: 19:1
Total Faculty: 30
% Female: 17
% Minority: 13

PROGRAMS
Academic Specialties: Interdisciplinary Studies
Advanced Degrees Offered: LLM (1 year), JSD (length depends on dissertation)
Combined Degrees Offered: JD/MBA (4 years), JD/PhD (length depends on dissertation)
Grading System: A (80 and above), B (79–74), C (73–68), D (67–60), F (59–55)
Clinical Program Required? No
Clinical Program Description: Anti-Poverty, Employment Discrimination, Criminal Justice, Child Support, Mental Health, Homelessness Assistance, Entrepreneurship
Legal Writing/Methods Course Requirements: Year-long program during first year—students are divided into 6 sections of 30 and taught by full-time fellows.

STUDENT INFORMATION
Enrollment of Law School: 565
% Male/Female: 58/42
% Full Time: 100
% Full Time That Are International: 1
% Minority: 20
Average Age of Entering Class: 24

EXPENSES/FINANCIAL AID
Annual Tuition: $27,276
Room and Board: $10,100
Books and Supplies: $1,300
Average Grant: $8,000
% Receiving Some Sort of Aid: 82

ADMISSIONS INFORMATION
Application Fee: $60
Regular Application Deadline: 2/1
Regular Notification: 3/30
LSDAS Accepted? Yes
Average GPA: 3.7
Range of GPA: 3.5–3.8
Average LSAT: 170
Range of LSAT: 165–172
Transfer Students Accepted? Yes
Other Schools to Which Students Applied: Harvard University, Yale University, University of Michigan, Stanford University, Columbia University, New York University, Duke University, Georgetown University
Other Admissions Factors Considered: Quality of undergraduate school, quality of academic record, interview

INTERNATIONAL STUDENTS
TOEFL Required of International Students? Yes
Minimum TOEFL: 600

EMPLOYMENT INFORMATION

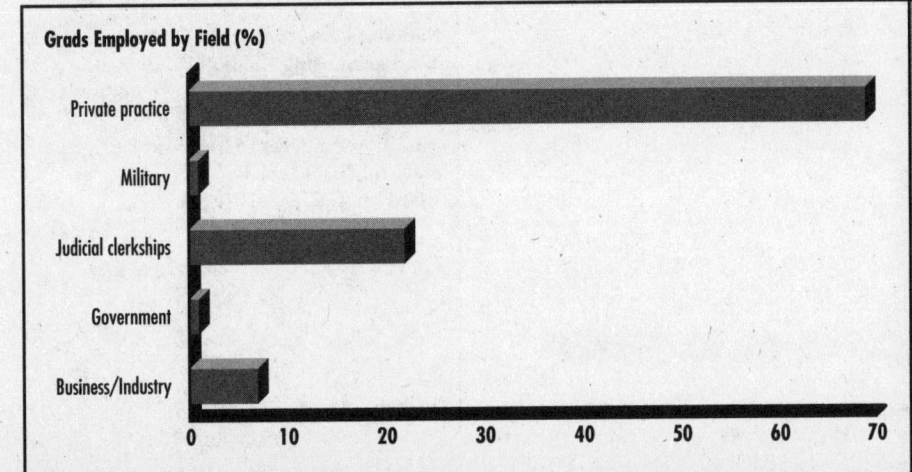

Grads Employed by Field (%)
- Private practice: ~68
- Military: ~1
- Judicial clerkships: ~22
- Government: ~2
- Business/Industry: ~7

Rate of Placement: 99%
Average Starting Salary: $125,000
Employers Who Frequently Hire Grads: Cravath, Swain and Moore; Mayer, Brown and Platt; Gibson, Dunn and Crutcher; Sidley and Austin; Kirkland and Ellis; Skadden, Arps, Slate, Meagher and Flom
State for Bar Exam: IL
Number Taking Bar Exam: 77
Pass Rate for First-Time Bar: 97%

UNIVERSITY OF CINCINNATI
College of Law

Admissions Contact: Assistant Dean and Director of Admission and Financial Aid
PO Box 210040, Cincinnati, OH 45221
Admissions Phone: 513-556-6805 • Admissions Fax: 513-556-2391
Admissions E-mail: admissions@law.uc.edu • Web Address: www.law.uc.edu

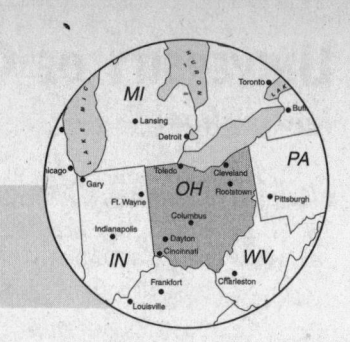

INSTITUTIONAL INFORMATION
Public/Private: Public
Student/Faculty Ratio: 14:1
Total Faculty: 24
% Female: 36
% Minority: 17

PROGRAMS
Academic Specialties: National program with experienced and dedicated faculty to help advocate a selective and diverse student body of 385 students; specialties include Human Rights Law.
Advanced Degrees Offered: JD (3 years), JD/MBA, JD/MA Women's Studies, JD/MCP
Combined Degrees Offered: JD/MBA (4 years), JD/MCP (4.5 years), JD/MA Women's Studies (4 years)
Grading System: Numerical system on a 4.0 scale. First-year courses are graded on a B curve; after the first year there is no mandatory curve.
Clinical Program Required? No
Clinical Program Description: We offer a very wide range of internships and externships, including judicial.
Legal Writing Course Requirements? Yes
Legal Writing Description: Full-time instructors teach small sections of legal research and writing.
Legal Methods Course Requirements? Yes
Legal Research Course Requirements? Yes
Moot Court Requirement? No
Moot Court Description: Moot court teams participate in all national competitions and host the annual Product Liability Competition.

Public Interest Law Requirement? No
Public Interest Law Description: A full-time director supervises externship programs and public interest externships and programs.
Academic Journals: *Law Review, Immigration and Nationality, Law Journal*

STUDENT INFORMATION
Enrollment of Law School: 392
% Out of State: 35
% Male/Female: 46/54
% Full Time: 100
% Full Time That Are International: 1
% Minority: 20
Average Age of Entering Class: 25

RESEARCH FACILITIES
% of JD Classrooms Wired: 95

EXPENSES/FINANCIAL AID
Annual Tuition (Residents/Nonresidents): $9,164/$17,466
Room and Board: $6,429
Books and Supplies: $4,478
Financial Aid Application Deadline: 4/1
Average Grant: $5,159
% Receiving Some Sort of Aid: 75
Average Debt: $43,000

ADMISSIONS INFORMATION
Application Fee: $35
Regular Application Deadline: 4/1
Regular Notification: Rolling
LSDAS Accepted? Yes
Average GPA: 3.5
Range of GPA: 3.2–3.7
Average LSAT: 158
Range of LSAT: 154–161
Transfer Students Accepted? Yes
Other Schools to Which Students Applied: Indiana University, Ohio State University, University of Dayton, University of Pittsburgh
Other Admissions Factors Considered: Quality of applicant's previous education, trend of academic performance, community service, graduate work
Number of Applications Received: 1,066
Number of Applicants Accepted: 475
Number of Applicants Enrolled: 140

EMPLOYMENT INFORMATION

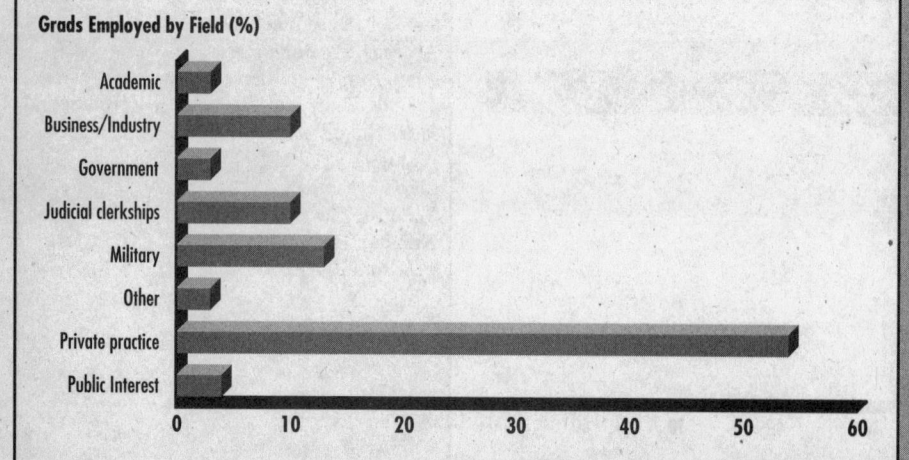

Grads Employed by Field (%)

Field	%
Academic	~2
Business/Industry	~10
Government	~8
Judicial clerkships	~13
Military	~1
Other	~2
Private practice	~55
Public Interest	~2

Rate of Placement: 94%
Average Starting Salary: $56,777
Employers Who Frequently Hire Grads: All major law firms in Cincinnati and other Ohio cities as well as other midwestern cities
State for Bar Exam: OH
Pass Rate for First-Time Bar: 93%

UNIVERSITY OF COLORADO
School of Law

Admissions Contact: Assistant Dean for Admissions and Financial Aid, Carol Nelson-Douglas
403 UCB, Boulder, CO 80309-0403
Admissions Phone: 303-492-7203 • Admissions Fax: 303-492-2542
Admissions E-mail: lawadmin@colorado.edu • Web Address: www.colorado.edu/law

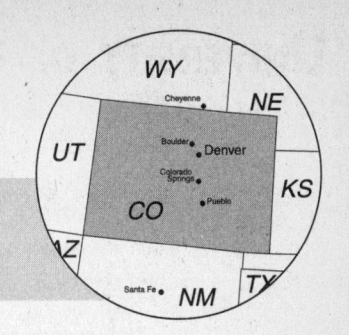

INSTITUTIONAL INFORMATION
Public/Private: Public
Student/Faculty Ratio: 14:1
Total Faculty: 76
% Part Time: 28
% Female: 23
% Minority: 15

PROGRAMS
Academic Specialties: Natural Resources and Environmental Law, Constitutional Law, Legal Theory, Corporate Law, International Law, Alternative Dispute Resolution, Tax Law, American Indian Law, Telecommunications Law
Advanced Degrees Offered: JD (3 years)
Combined Degrees Offered: JD/MBA (4 years), JD/MPA (4 years), Tax Certificate (3 years), Environmental Policy Certificate (3 years)
Grading System: Letter and numerical system on a 4.0 and 99–50 point scale; designations offered for Incomplete, No Credit-Audit Pass, Transfer Credit, and Withdrew
Clinical Program Required? No
Clinical Programs Description: Entrepreneurial Law Clinic, Indian Law Clinic, Legal Aid and Defender Program, Natural Resources Litigation Clinic
Legal Writing Course Requirements? Yes
Legal Writing Description: First-year Legal Writing and Appellate Court Advocacy courses and a seminar with a major research paper.
Legal Methods Course Requirements? Yes
Legal Methods Description: See Legal Writing.
Legal Research Course Requirements? Yes
Legal Research Description: See Legal Writing.
Moot Court Requirement? No
Moot Court Description: Moot court competitions.
Public Interest Law Requirement? No
Academic Journals: *University of Colorado Law Review, Colorado Journal of International Environmental Law and Policy, Journal on Telecommunications and High Technology Law*

STUDENT INFORMATION
Enrollment of Law School: 485
% Out of State: 13
% Male/Female: 46/54
% Full Time: 100
% Full Time That Are International: 0
% Minority: 19
Average Age of Entering Class: 26

RESEARCH FACILITIES
Research Resources Available: Native American Rights Fund, Law and Water Fund
School-Supported Research Centers: Natural Resources Law Center, Byron R. White Center for the Study of American Constitutional Law, Center for the Study of Race and Ethnicity, Center of the American West, Environmental Center, Center for Entrepreneurial Law, Silicon Flatirons Telecommunications Program

EXPENSES/FINANCIAL AID
Annual Tuition (Residents/Nonresidents): $6,069/$18,549
Room and Board (On/Off Campus): $5,495/$8,325
Books and Supplies: $720
Average Grant: $2,855
Average Loan: $16,855
% of Aid That Is Merit-Based: 5
% Receiving Some Sort of Aid: 83
Average Total Aid Package: $18,959
Average Debt: $46,912

ADMISSIONS INFORMATION
Application Fee: $55
Regular Application Deadline: 2/15
Regular Notification: Rolling
LSDAS Accepted? Yes
Average GPA: 3.5
Average LSAT: 161
Transfer Students Accepted? Yes
Other Schools to Which Students Applied: University of Denver, George Washington University, University of Texas at Austin, University of California—Hastings, Georgetown University, Boston College, University of Arizona
Other Admissions Factors Considered: Diversity of backgrounds, experiences, and viewpoints; variation in geographic, economic, social or cultural background; variation in undergraduate or graduate program or institution; unusual employment or other experience
Number of Applications Received: 2,239
Number of Applicants Accepted: 601
Number of Applicants Enrolled: 165

EMPLOYMENT INFORMATION

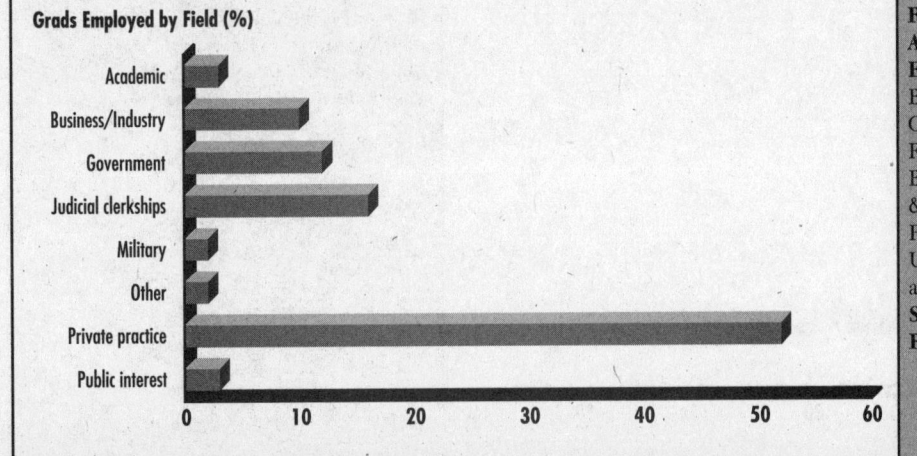

Grads Employed by Field (%)

Field	%
Academic	~1
Business/Industry	~11
Government	~12
Judicial clerkships	~17
Military	~1
Other	~2
Private practice	~52
Public interest	~3

Rate of Placement: 91%
Average Starting Salary: $61,357
Employers Who Frequently Hire Grads: Brownstein, Hyatt; Bullivant, Houser; Campbell, Carr; Faegre & Benson; Featherstone & Shea; Fenwick, West; Freeborn & Peters; Hutchinson, Black & Cook; Icenogle, Norton Seter; McKenna & Cuneo; Merchant & Gould; Modrall Law Firm; Ruegsegger, Thomas; Security Life of Denver; U.S. Marine Corps; U.S. Navy; U.S. Securities and Exchange Commission
State for Bar Exam: CO
Pass Rate for First-Time Bar: 91%

UNIVERSITY OF CONNECTICUT
School of Law

Admissions Contact: Associate Dean
45 Elizabeth Street, Hartford, CT 06105
Admissions Phone: 860-570-5159 • Admissions Fax: 860-570-5153
Admissions E-mail: admit@law.uconn.edu • Web Address: www.law.uconn.edu

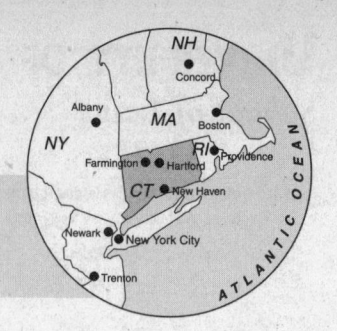

INSTITUTIONAL INFORMATION
Public/Private: Public
Student/Faculty Ratio: 11:1
Total Faculty: 126
% Part Time: 59
% Female: 29
% Minority: 11

PROGRAMS
Academic Specialties: Commercial Law, Constitutional Law, Corporation Securities Law, Criminal Law, Environmental Law, Government Services, Human Rights Law, Intellectual Property Law, International Law, Labor Law, Legal History, Legal Philosophy, Property, Taxation
Advanced Degrees Offered: LLM, (1 year), JD (3 to 4 years), LLM Insurance (1year)
Combined Degrees Offered: JD/MA Public Policy Studies, JD/MBA, JD/MLS, JD/MPA, JD/MSW, JD/MPH, JD/LLM Insurance Law
Grading System: Letter system; Pass/Fail designation available
Clinical Program Required? No
Clinical Programs Description: Clinic and externship programs in Administrative Law, Civil Rights, Disability Law, Criminal Law, Tax Law, Street Law, Judicial Clerkship, Women's Rights, Children's Rights, Labor Relations, Mediation, Poverty Law, Health Law, and Legislative Process
Legal Writing Course Requirements? No
Legal Methods Course Requirements? Yes
Legal Methods Description: Year-long Lawyering Process course covers writing and lawyering skills

Legal Research Course Requirements? Yes
Legal Research Description: Year-long Lawyering Process course also focuses on legal research
Moot Court Requirement? Yes
Moot Court Description: Required first-year Moot Court course, 6 weeks of intensive brief writing and appellate arguments.
Public Interest Law Requirement? No
Academic Journals: *Connecticut Law Review, Connecticut Journal of International Law, Connecticut Insurance Law Journal, Connecticut Public Interest Law Journal*

STUDENT INFORMATION
Enrollment of Law School: 571
% Out of State: 33
% Male/Female: 50/50
% Full Time: 67
% Full Time That Are International: 1
% Minority: 18
Average Age of Entering Class: 25

RESEARCH FACILITIES
Research Resources Available: Center for Children's Advocacy, Connecticut Urban Legal Initiative

EXPENSES/FINANCIAL AID
Annual Tuition (Residents/Nonresidents): $11,374/$23,992
Room and Board (Off Campus): $8,152
Books and Supplies: $964
Financial Aid Application Deadline: 3/15
Average Grant: $7,172
Average Loan: $15,555
% of Aid That Is Merit-Based: 19
% Receiving Some Sort of Aid: 76
Average Total Aid Package: $19,075
Average Debt: $43,439
Tuition Per Credit (Residents/Nonresidents): $397/$837
Fees Per Credit: $527

ADMISSIONS INFORMATION
Application Fee: $30
Regular Application Deadline: 3/15
Regular Notification: Rolling
LSDAS Accepted? Yes
Average GPA: 3.3
Range of GPA: 3.1–3.5
Average LSAT: 160
Range of LSAT: 158–161
Transfer Students Accepted? Yes
Other Admissions Factors Considered: Quality and maturity of written essays, strength of undergraduate/graduate curriculum, achievement of academic awards and honors
Number of Applications Received: 1,465
Number of Applicants Accepted: 505
Number of Applicants Enrolled: 118

INTERNATIONAL STUDENTS
TOEFL Required of International Students? Yes

EMPLOYMENT INFORMATION

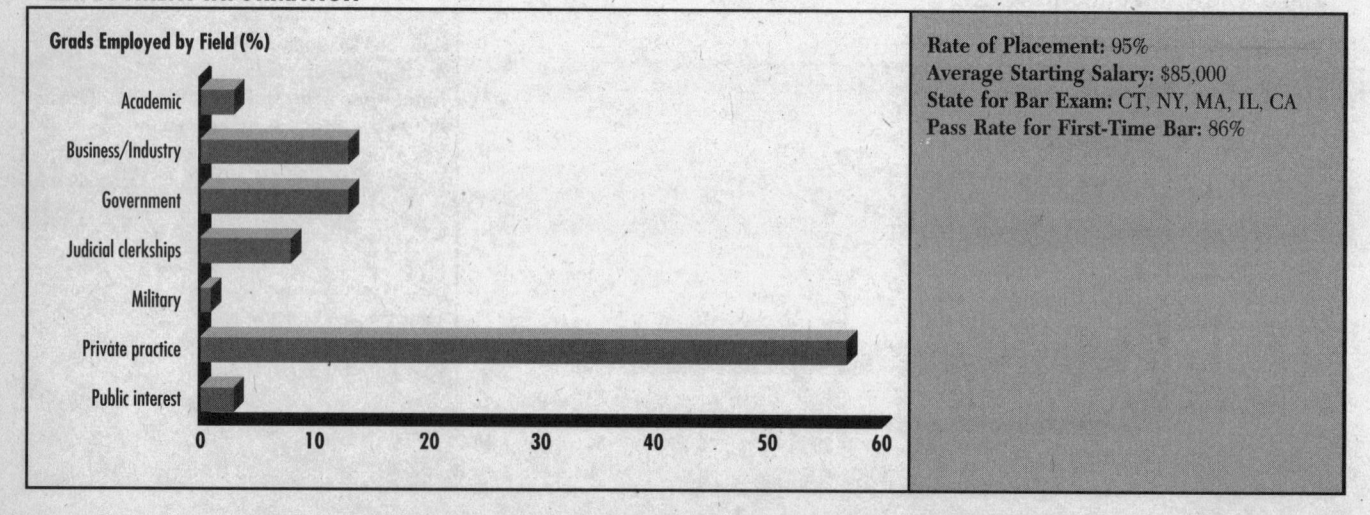

Grads Employed by Field (%)
- Academic
- Business/Industry
- Government
- Judicial clerkships
- Military
- Private practice
- Public interest

Rate of Placement: 95%
Average Starting Salary: $85,000
State for Bar Exam: CT, NY, MA, IL, CA
Pass Rate for First-Time Bar: 86%

UNIVERSITY OF DAYTON
School of Law

Admissions Contact: Assistant Dean, Director of Admissions and Financial Aid, Janet L. Hein
300 College Park, Dayton, OH 45469-2760
Admissions Phone: 937-229-3555 • Admissions Fax: 937-229-4194
Admissions E-mail: lawinfo@notes.udayton.edu • Web Address: www.law.udayton.edu

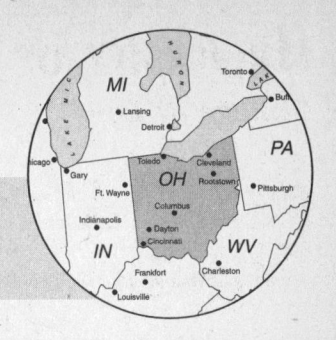

INSTITUTIONAL INFORMATION
Public/Private: Private
Affiliation: Roman Catholic
Student/Faculty Ratio: 15:1
Total Faculty: 28
% Part Time: 0
% Female: 36
% Minority: 11

PROGRAMS
Academic Specialties: UDSL has 1 of the top Law and Technology programs in the country, with 15 courses offered in Intellectual Property, Copyright and Trademark, Computer-Related Law, Cyberspace Law and Electronic Commerce, and Entertainment Law. The Legal Profession Program is a unique 3-semester, 8-credit-hour series of required legal writing, analysis, and research training. Other specialties include Civil Procedure, Commercial Law, Constitutional Law, Corporation Securities Law, Criminal Law, and Taxation.
Advanced Degrees Offered: JD (3 years)
Combined Degrees Offered: JD/MBA (4 years)
Grading System: 4.0 scale
Clinical Program Required? No
Clinical Programs Description: Students are responsible for assisting low-income clients in real legal disputes. The combination of fieldwork and class sessions helps the students assume the role of lawyer and analyze decisions made in that role.
Legal Writing Course Requirements? Yes
Legal Writing Description: There are 3 required semesters of legal research, writing and analysis under the title Legal Profession I, II, and III. The courses are client-simulation driven and introduce students to research in several media, objective writing, and persuasive writing and oral argument at the trial and appellate level.
Legal Methods Course Requirements? Yes
Legal Methods Description: See Legal Writing.
Legal Research Course Requirements? Yes
Legal Research Description: See Legal Writing.
Moot Court Requirement? No
Moot Court Description: Second- and third-year students represent the School of Law in interschool and national competitions.
Public Interest Law Requirement? No
Academic Journals: *University of Dayton Law Review*

STUDENT INFORMATION
Enrollment of Law School: 424
% Out of State: 48
% Male/Female: 59/41
% Full Time: 100
% Full Time That Are International: 0
% Minority: 16
Average Age of Entering Class: 25

RESEARCH FACILITIES
Research Resources Available: Lexis/Nexis, Westlaw, Index Master, TA Campus, separate Law School server

EXPENSES/FINANCIAL AID
Annual Tuition: $21,766
Room and Board: $7,900
Books and Supplies: $900
Financial Aid Application Deadline: 3/1
Average Grant: $9,800
Average Loan: $22,000
% Receiving Some Sort of Aid: 90
Average Total Aid Package: $32,116
Average Debt: $60,000
Tuition Per Credit: $870

ADMISSIONS INFORMATION
Application Fee: $50
Regular Application Deadline: 5/1
Regular Notification: Rolling
LSDAS Accepted? Yes
Average GPA: 3.0
Range of GPA: 2.7–3.4
Average LSAT: 151
Range of LSAT: 147–154
Transfer Students Accepted? Yes
Other Schools to Which Students Applied: Capital University, Cleveland State University, Ohio Northern University, Ohio State University, The University of Akron, University of Cincinnati, University of Toledo
Other Admissions Factors Considered: Diversity of experiences, leadership, motivation, the ability to overcome hardships, breadth and depth of skills and interests
Number of Applications Received: 1,340
Number of Applicants Accepted: 857
Number of Applicants Enrolled: 172

INTERNATIONAL STUDENTS
TOEFL Required of International Students? Yes
Minimum TOEFL: 250

EMPLOYMENT INFORMATION

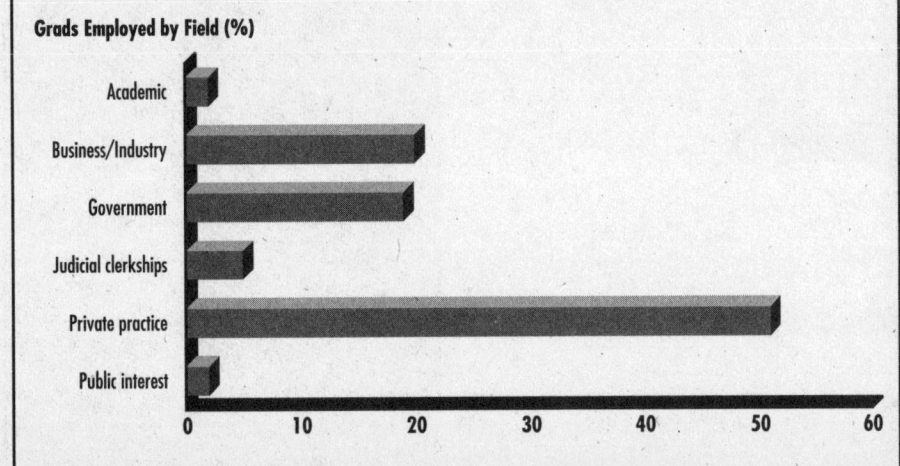

Grads Employed by Field (%)
- Academic: ~1
- Business/Industry: ~20
- Government: ~18
- Judicial clerkships: ~5
- Private practice: ~52
- Public interest: ~2

Rate of Placement: 91%
Average Starting Salary: $50,286
Employers Who Frequently Hire Grads: Procter and Gamble; Porter, Wright, Morris, and Arthur; Thompson, Hine, and Flory; Dinsmore and Shohl; Chernesky, Heyman & Kress; Faruki, Gilliam & Ireland; Sebaly, Shillito and Dyer
State for Bar Exam: OH, PA, MI, KY, IN
Pass Rate for First-Time Bar: 79%

UNIVERSITY OF DENVER
College of Law

Admissions Contact: Assistant Director of Admissions
7039 East 18th Avenue, Denver, CO 80220
Admissions Phone: 303-871-6135 • Admissions Fax: 303-871-6100
Admissions E-mail: admissions@adm.law.du.edu • Web Address: www.law.du.edu

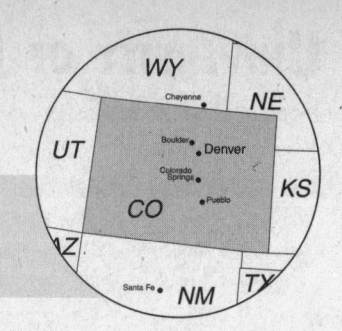

INSTITUTIONAL INFORMATION
Public/Private: Private
Student/Faculty Ratio: 17:1
Total Faculty: 61
% Female: 30
% Minority: 16

PROGRAMS
Academic Specialties: Civil Procedure, Corporation Securities Law, Environmental Law, Human Rights Law, International Law, Taxation
Combined Degrees Offered: Business, Geography, History, International Management, International Studies, Legal Administration, Mass Communications, Professional Psychology, Psychology, Social Work, Sociology
Clinical Program Required? No
Clinical Programs Description: Natural Resources and Environmental Law Program, Public Interest, Transportation, Litigation, Child Advocacy, Metro Volunteer Lawyers, Low-Income Taxpayer Representation Clinic, Domestic Violence Clinic, Civil Justice Project, EarthJustice, MACLAW, MSLA, Spanish for Lawyers
Legal Writing Course Requirements? Yes
Legal Methods Course Requirements? Yes
Legal Methods Description: 2 semesters
Legal Research Course Requirements? No
Moot Court Requirement? No
Public Interest Law Requirement? No
Academic Journals: *Law Journal, Trans Law Journal, Water Law*

STUDENT INFORMATION
Enrollment of Law School: 1,182
% Out of State: 48
% Male/Female: 48/52
% Full Time: 72
% Full Time That Are International: 2
% Minority: 13
Average Age of Entering Class: 25

EXPENSES/FINANCIAL AID
Annual Tuition: $21,960
Room and Board (On Campus): $7,984
Books and Supplies: $900
Financial Aid Application Deadline: 3/30
Average Grant: $10,000
Average Loan: $18,500
% of Aid That Is Merit-Based: 33
% Receiving Some Sort of Aid: 80
Average Total Aid Package: $36,000
Average Debt: $60,000
Tuition Per Credit: $732

ADMISSIONS INFORMATION
Application Fee: $45
Regular Application Deadline: 5/30
Regular Notification: Rolling
LSDAS Accepted? Yes
Average GPA: 3.1
Range of GPA: 2.8–3.4
Average LSAT: 155
Range of LSAT: 150–157
Transfer Students Accepted? Yes
Other Admissions Factors Considered: Resume is required
Number of Applications Received: 2,054
Number of Applicants Accepted: 1,041
Number of Applicants Enrolled: 375

INTERNATIONAL STUDENTS
TOEFL Required of International Students? Yes

EMPLOYMENT INFORMATION

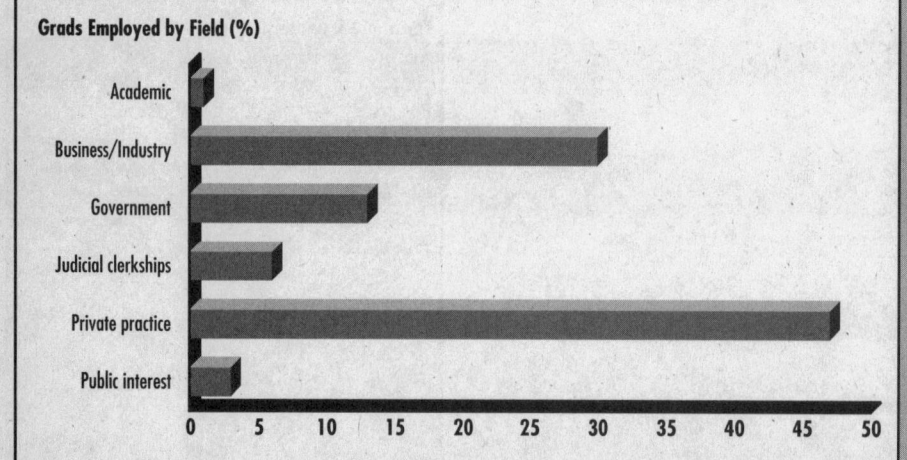

Grads Employed by Field (%)
- Academic: ~1
- Business/Industry: ~30
- Government: ~8
- Judicial clerkships: ~5
- Private practice: ~47
- Public interest: ~3

Rate of Placement: 94%
Average Starting Salary: $50,000
Employers Who Frequently Hire Grads: Small, medium, and large law firms; government agencies such as District Attorney's and Attorney General's Offices; corporations.
State for Bar Exam: CO
Pass Rate for First-Time Bar: 81%

230 • COMPLETE BOOK OF LAW SCHOOLS

UNIVERSITY OF DETROIT MERCY
School of Law

Admissions Contact: Admissions Counselor, Bernard Dobranski
651 East Jefferson Avenue, Detroit, MI 48226
Admissions Phone: 313-596-9848 • Admissions Fax: 313-596-0280
Admissions E-mail: udmlawao@udmercy.edu • Web Address: www.law.udmercy.edu

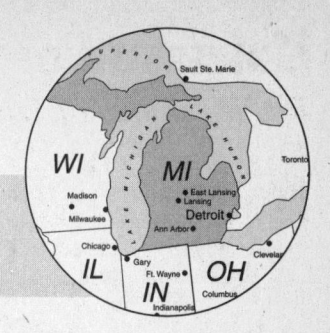

INSTITUTIONAL INFORMATION
Public/Private: Private
Affiliation: Society of Jesus
Schedule: Full time or part time
Total Faculty: 24
% Part Time: 50
% Female: 20
% Minority: 9

PROGRAMS
Academic Specialties: London Law Program available fall and winter semesters
Advanced Degrees Offered: JD (3 years full time), JD/MBA (4 years)
Combined Degrees Offered: JD/MBA (3.5–4 years full time), JD/LLB (2 years), JD for Canadian lawyers (1 year full time)
Grading System: 4.5 system
Clinical Program Required? No
Clinical Program Description: 4-credit in-house Urban Law Clinic, numerous externships
Legal Writing/Methods Course Requirements: Full year, 5 credits, integrated with contracts course

STUDENT INFORMATION
Enrollment of Law School: 429
% Male/Female: 50/50
% Full Time: 57
% Full Time That Are International: 1
% Minority: 11
Average Age of Entering Class: 29

EXPENSES/FINANCIAL AID
Annual Tuition : $18,000
Books and Supplies: $900
Average Grant: $8,000
% of Aid That Is Merit-Based: 5
Average Debt: $55,541
Fees Per Credit: $600

ADMISSIONS INFORMATION
Regular Application Deadline: 4/15
Regular Notification: Rolling
Average GPA: 3.2
Average LSAT: 150
Transfer Students Accepted? Yes
Other Schools to Which Students Applied: Wayne State University, University of Michigan, Detroit College of Law at Michigan State University, Thomas M. Cooley Law School, University of Notre Dame, Loyola University Chicago, DePaul University, University of Toledo
Other Admissions Factors Considered: Strong writing skills, undergraduate course work

EMPLOYMENT INFORMATION

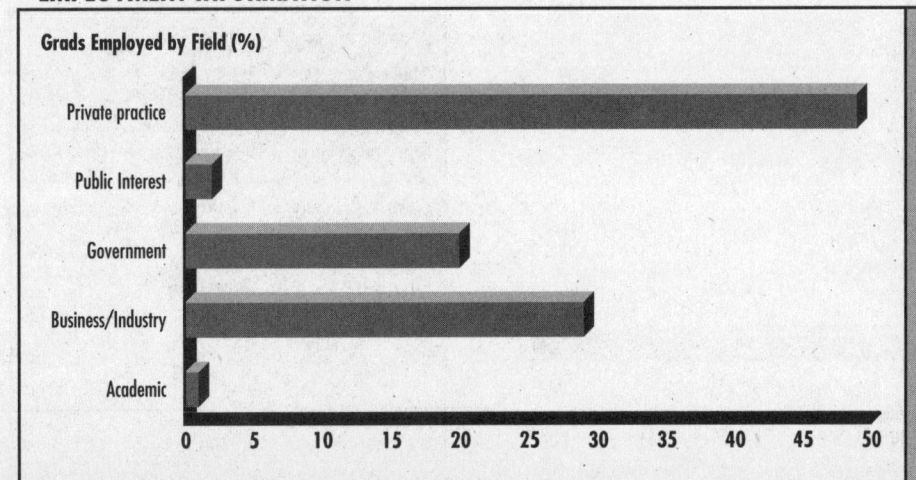

Grads Employed by Field (%)

- Private practice: ~49
- Public Interest: ~1
- Government: ~20
- Business/Industry: ~29
- Academic: ~1

Rate of Placement: 86%
Average Starting Salary: $439,000
Employers Who Frequently Hire Grads: County prosecutors; Dickinson Wright, PLLC; Dykema Gossett, PLLC; Michigan Court of Appeals; Butzel Long; Bodman Longley; Howard and Howard; Michigan Supreme Court
Prominent Alumni: Hon. Michael F. Cacanagh, Michigan Supreme Court; Hon. James H. Brickley, Michigan Supreme Court; Hon. Maura D. Corrigan, Michigan Supreme Court
State for Bar Exam: MI
Number Taking Bar Exam: 142
Pass Rate for First-Time Bar: 57%

UNIVERSITY OF FLORIDA
Levin College of Law

Admissions Contact: Assistant Dean for Admissions, J. Michael Patrick
Box 117622, Gainesville, FL 32611
Admissions Phone: 352-392-2087 • Admissions Fax: 352-392-4087
Admissions E-mail: patrick@law.ufl.edu • Web Address: www.law.ufl.edu

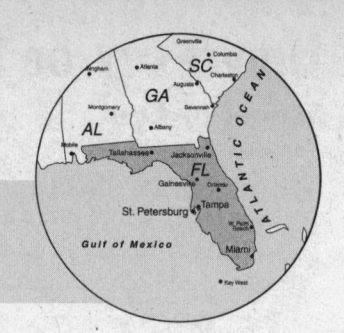

INSTITUTIONAL INFORMATION
Public/Private: Public
Student/Faculty Ratio: 15:1
Total Faculty: 74
% Female: 35
% Minority: 9

PROGRAMS
Academic Specialties: Centers or degree programs in Taxation, International and Comparative Law, Environmental and Land Use Law, Intellectual Property, Dispute Resolution, and Race and Race Relations. Other specialties include Civil Procedure, Commercial Law, Constitutional Law, Corporation Securities Law, Criminal Law, Government Services, Human Rights Law, Labor Law, Legal History, Legal Philosophy, and Property
Advanced Degrees Offered: LLM Taxation, (1 year), LLM Comparative Law (1 year), SJD Taxation
Combined Degrees Offered: JD/MA Urban and Regional Planning, JD/MBA, JD/MA Political Science—Public Administration, JD/MA Sociology, JD/PhD History, JD/MA Accounting, JD/MA Mass Communication, JD/PhD Psychology, JD/PhD Mass Communication, JD/MA Forest Conservation, JD/PhD Education Leadership, JD/MA Sports Management, JD/MD, JD/MA Biotechnology, JD/MA Environmental Engineering. JD/MA Latin American Studies
Grading System: Letter and numerical system on a 4.0 scale. Minimum 2.0 GPA required for good academic standing and graduation.

Clinical Program Required? Yes
Clinical Programs Description: Civil, Criminal and Mediation Clinics; Juvenile Clinic; Pro Se Clinic; Conservation Clinic
Legal Methods Course Requirements? Yes
Legal Methods Description: First semester, Legal Research and Writing; second semester, Appellate Advocacy; second year, Legal Drafting

STUDENT INFORMATION
Enrollment of Law School: 1,186
% Out of State: 10
% Male/Female: 52/48
% Full Time: 100
% Full Time That Are International: 2
% Minority: 28
Average Age of Entering Class: 25

RESEARCH FACILITIES
School-Supported Research Centers: Center for Governmental Responsibility, Public Policy and Law Research Center, Legal Technology Institute

EXPENSES/FINANCIAL AID
Room and Board (On/Off Campus): $6,130/$6,540
Books and Supplies: $3,690
Financial Aid Application Deadline: 3/15
Average Grant: $8,300
Average Loan: $10,500
% of Aid That Is Merit-Based: 14
% Receiving Some Sort of Aid: 83
Average Total Aid Package: $13,000
Average Debt: $49,000

ADMISSIONS INFORMATION
Application Fee: $20
Regular Application Deadline: 2/1
Regular Notification: 4/1
LSDAS Accepted? Yes
Average GPA: 3.5
Range of GPA: 3.3–3.8
Average LSAT: 156
Range of LSAT: 152–161
Transfer Students Accepted? Yes
Other Admissions Factors Considered: Undergraduate or other academic performance, undergraduate institution, post-bachelor's degree coursework, leadership or other relevant activities, maturing experiences, economic background
Number of Applications Received: 1,798
Number of Applicants Accepted: 486
Number of Applicants Enrolled: 209

INTERNATIONAL STUDENTS
TOEFL Required of International Students? Yes
Minimum TOEFL: 213

EMPLOYMENT INFORMATION

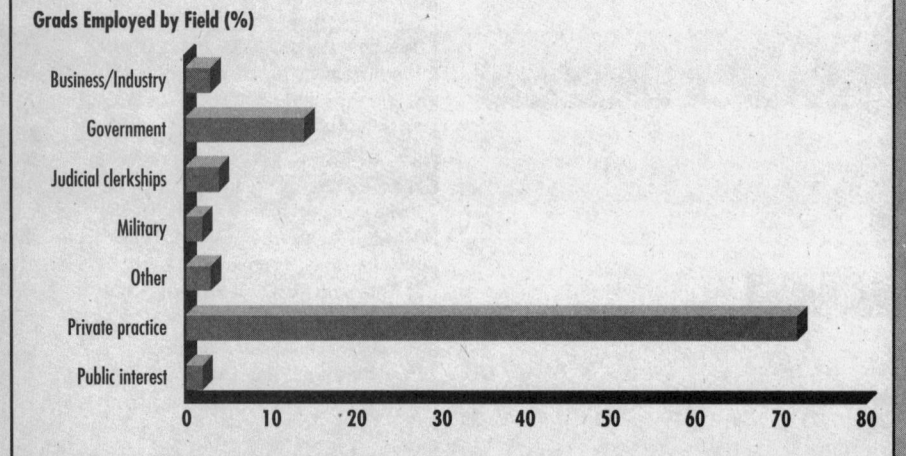

Grads Employed by Field (%)
- Business/Industry
- Government
- Judicial clerkships
- Military
- Other
- Private practice
- Public interest

Rate of Placement: 84%
Average Starting Salary: $48,628
Employers Who Frequently Hire Grads: Foley & Lardner; King & Spalding; Holland & Knight; Troutman Sanders; Steel, Hector & Davis; Gunster Yoakley; Powell Goldstein; Lowndes Drosdick; Kilpatrick Stockton; federal and state judges; State Attorneys' Offices
State for Bar Exam: FL
Pass Rate for First-Time Bar: 91%

UNIVERSITY OF GEORGIA
School of Law

Admissions Contact: Director of Law Admissions, Giles Kennedy
University of Georgia School of Law, Athens, GA 30602-6012
Admissions Phone: 706-542-7060 • Admissions Fax: 706-542-5556
Admissions E-mail: ugajd@arches.uga.edu • Web Address: www.lawsch.uga.edu

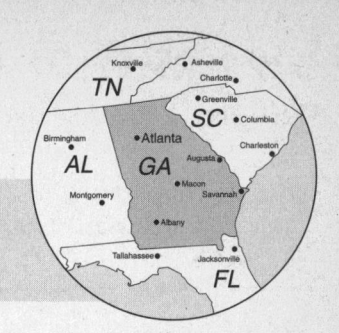

INSTITUTIONAL INFORMATION
Public/Private: Public
Environment: Urban
Academic Calendar: Quarter
Schedule: Full time only
Student/Faculty Ratio: 17:1
Total Faculty: 84
% Part Time: 43
% Female: 17
% Minority: 2

PROGRAMS
Advanced Degrees Offered: LLM (1 year)
Combined Degrees Offered: JD/MBA (4 years), JD/Master of Historic Preservation (4 years)
Clinical Program Required? No
Clinical Program Description: Legal Aid Clinic, Prosecutorial Clinic, Civil Clinic, Public Interest Practicum, civil externships, Family Violence Clinic
Legal Writing/Methods Course Requirements: 2 semesters, 2 hours per semester

STUDENT INFORMATION
Enrollment of Law School: 640
% Male/Female: 53/47
% Full Time: 100
% Full Time That Are International: 1
% Minority: 12
Average Age of Entering Class: 25

RESEARCH FACILITIES
Computers/Workstations Available: 50

EXPENSES/FINANCIAL AID
Annual Tuition (Residents/Nonresidents): $4,736/$17,084
Room and Board (On/Off Campus): $6,726/$8,714
Books and Supplies: $1,000
Financial Aid Application Deadline: 3/1

ADMISSIONS INFORMATION
Application Fee: $30
Regular Application Deadline: 3/1
Regular Notification: Rolling
Average GPA: 3.6
Range of GPA: 3.3–3.8
Average LSAT: 161
Range of LSAT: 157–164
Transfer Students Accepted? Yes
Number of Applications Received: 1,680

EMPLOYMENT INFORMATION

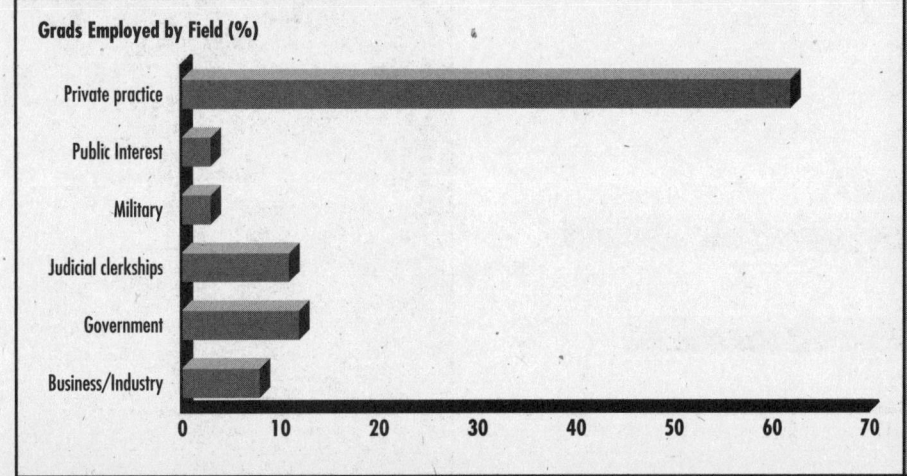

Grads Employed by Field (%)
- Private practice: ~63
- Public Interest: ~3
- Military: ~3
- Judicial clerkships: ~12
- Government: ~13
- Business/Industry: ~8

Rate of Placement: 98%
Average Starting Salary: $47,957
State for Bar Exam: GA
Number Taking Bar Exam: 190
Pass Rate for First-Time Bar: 93%

UNIVERSITY OF HAWAII—MANOA
William S. Richardson School of Law

Admissions Contact: Assistant Dean, Laurie Tochiki
2515 Dole Street, Honolulu, HI 96822
Admissions Phone: 808-956-3000 • Admissions Fax: 808-956-3813
Admissions E-mail: lawadm@hawaii.edu • Web Address: www.hawaii.edu/law

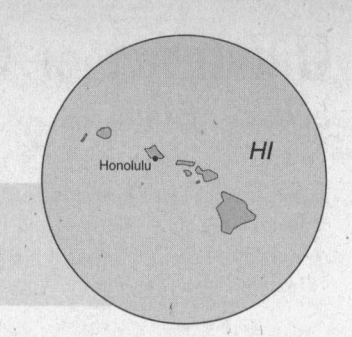

INSTITUTIONAL INFORMATION
Public/Private: Public
Student/Faculty Ratio: 13:1
Total Faculty: 18
% Female: 50
% Minority: 22

PROGRAMS
Academic Specialties: Pacific Asian Legal Studies with emphasis on China, Japan, and Pacific Rim; Environmental Law Studies with emphasis on ocean and water resources; International Law
Advanced Degrees Offered: JD (3 years)
Combined Degrees Offered: JD Environmental Law (3 years), JD Pacific-Asian Legal Studies (3 years), JD/Grad. Ocean Policy (varies), JD/MA (varies), JD/MBA (varies), JD/MS (varies), JD/MSW (varies), JD/PhD (varies)
Grading System: Grades are on a C+/B– curve, and this standard is in effect for all classes except writing classes. Median GPA is 2.60. Grading allowances within curve are: A (0–15 percent), B (25–45 percent), C (40–65 percent), D (0–20 percent), and F (0–10 percent).
Clinical Program Required? Yes
Clinical Program Description: Elder Law, Family, Prosecution, Mediation, Native Hawaiian Rights, Estate Planning, Defense, Trial Practice
Legal Writing Course Requirements? Yes
Legal Writing Description: Appellate Advocacy, first year, second semester (2 credits); Second Year Seminar (4 credits)
Legal Methods Course Requirements? Yes
Legal Methods Description: First semester, 3 credits
Legal Research Course Requirements? Yes
Legal Research Description: 1 credit
Moot Court Requirement? No
Public Interest Law Requirement? Yes
Public Interest Law Description: 60 hours of pro bono work
Academic Journals: Law Review, Asian-Pacific Law and Policy Journal

STUDENT INFORMATION
Enrollment of Law School: 241
% Out of State: 22
% Male/Female: 46/54
% Full Time: 100
% Full Time That Are International: 2
% Minority: 68
Average Age of Entering Class: 27

RESEARCH FACILITIES
% of JD Classrooms Wired: 100

EXPENSES/FINANCIAL AID
Annual Tuition (Residents/Nonresidents): $9,624/$16,344
Room and Board (On/Off Campus): $7,550/$8,900
Books and Supplies: $2,800
Financial Aid Application Deadline: 3/1
Average Grant: $3,951
Average Loan: $13,332
% of Aid That Is Merit-Based: 31
% Receiving Some Sort of Aid: 65
Average Total Aid Package: $16,642
Average Debt: $41,265

ADMISSIONS INFORMATION
Application Fee: $45
Regular Application Deadline: 3/1
Regular Notification: 4/15
LSDAS Accepted? Yes
Average GPA: 3.3
Range of GPA: 3.1–3.6
Average LSAT: 157
Range of LSAT: 153–160
Transfer Students Accepted? Yes
Other Schools to Which Students Applied: Santa Clara University, University of California—Los Angeles, University of California—Berkeley, University of California Hastings, University of San Diego
Other Admissions Factors Considered: Personal factors such as writing ability, work experience, volunteer or community involvement, letters of recommendation, honors, and awards as well as a history of overcoming adversity
Number of Applications Received: 594
Number of Applicants Accepted: 189
Number of Applicants Enrolled: 74

EMPLOYMENT INFORMATION

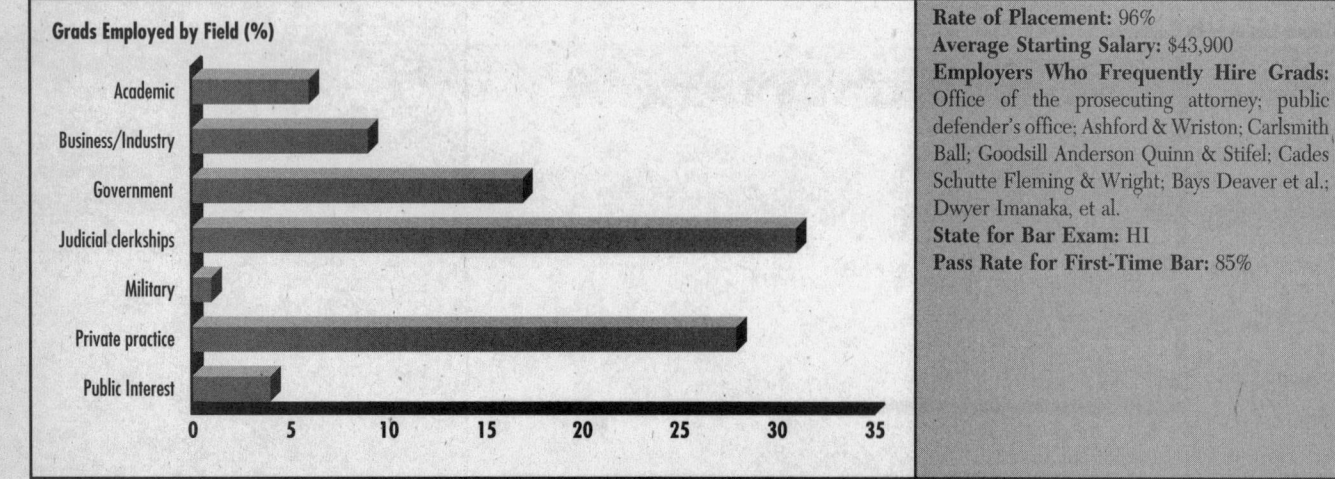

Grads Employed by Field (%)
Field	%
Academic	~5
Business/Industry	~9
Government	~17
Judicial clerkships	~31
Military	~1
Private practice	~28
Public Interest	~4

Rate of Placement: 96%
Average Starting Salary: $43,900
Employers Who Frequently Hire Grads: Office of the prosecuting attorney; public defender's office; Ashford & Wriston; Carlsmith Ball; Goodsill Anderson Quinn & Stifel; Cades Schutte Fleming & Wright; Bays Deaver et al.; Dwyer Imanaka, et al.
State for Bar Exam: HI
Pass Rate for First-Time Bar: 85%

UNIVERSITY OF HOUSTON
Law Center

Admissions Contact: Assistant Dean for Admissions, Sondra R. Tennessee
100 Law Center, Houston, TX 77204-6060
Admissions Phone: 713-743-2280 • Admissions Fax: 713-743-2194
Admissions E-mail: admissions@www.law.uh.edu • Web Address: www.law.uh.edu

INSTITUTIONAL INFORMATION
Public/Private: Public
Student/Faculty Ratio: 15:1
Total Faculty: 103
% Part Time: 54
% Female: 24
% Minority: 9

PROGRAMS
Academic Specialties: Health Law, Intellectual Property Law, International Law, Corporate Law, Taxation, Corporation Securities Law, Environmental Law, Legal History
Advanced Degrees Offered: LLM Health, Intellectual Property, Tax, Energy and Natural Resources, International Law (24 credit hours); LLM for foreign students
Combined Degrees Offered: JD/MBA (4 years), JD/MPH (3.5 years), JD/MA History (4 years), JD/PhD (5 years), JD/MSW (4 years)
Grading System: A (4.00), A– (3.67), B+ (3.33), B (3.00), B– (2.67), C+ (2.33), C (2.00), C– (1.67), D+ (1.33), D (1.00), D– (0.67), F (0.00)
Clinical Program Required? No
Clinical Programs Description: Family and Poverty Law Clinic, Criminal Defense, Criminal Prosecution, Health, Judicial, Environmental, Mediations, Immigration Clinic
Legal Writing Course Requirements? Yes
Legal Writing Description: Year-long first-year legal research and writing includes small-group instruction
Legal Methods Course Requirements? Yes
Legal Methods Description: See Legal Writing.
Legal Research Course Requirements? Yes
Legal Research Description: See Legal Writing.
Moot Court Requirement? Yes
Moot Court Description: First-year students have a moot court competition.
Public Interest Law Requirement? No
Academic Journals: *Houston Law Review, Houston Business and Tax Law Journal, Houston Journal of Health Law and Policy, Houston Journal of International Law, Consumer Law Journal*

STUDENT INFORMATION
Enrollment of Law School: 931
% Out of State: 17
% Male/Female: 50/50
% Full Time: 80
% Full Time That Are International: 1
% Minority: 19
Average Age of Entering Class: 25

EXPENSES/FINANCIAL AID
Annual Tuition (Residents/Nonresidents): $5,600/$9,520
Room and Board (On/Off Campus): $5,150/$6,344
Books and Supplies: $864
Financial Aid Application Deadline: 4/1
Average Grant: $2,695
Average Loan: $14,934
% of Aid That Is Merit-Based: 27
% Receiving Some Sort of Aid: 79
Average Total Aid Package: $14,857
Average Debt: $44,762
Tuition Per Credit (Residents/Nonresidents): $240/$340
Fees Per Credit: $534

ADMISSIONS INFORMATION
Application Fee: $50
Regular Application Deadline: 2/15
Regular Notification: 5/15
LSDAS Accepted? Yes
Average GPA: 3.4
Range of GPA: 3.2–3.6
Average LSAT: 157
Range of LSAT: 155–161
Transfer Students Accepted? Yes
Other Schools to Which Students Applied: Baylor University, Texas A&M University, Southern Methodist University, Texas Tech University, University of Texas at Austin
Number of Applications Received: 2,385
Number of Applicants Accepted: 836
Number of Applicants Enrolled: 306

INTERNATIONAL STUDENTS
TOEFL Required of International Students? Yes
Minimum TOEFL: 250

EMPLOYMENT INFORMATION

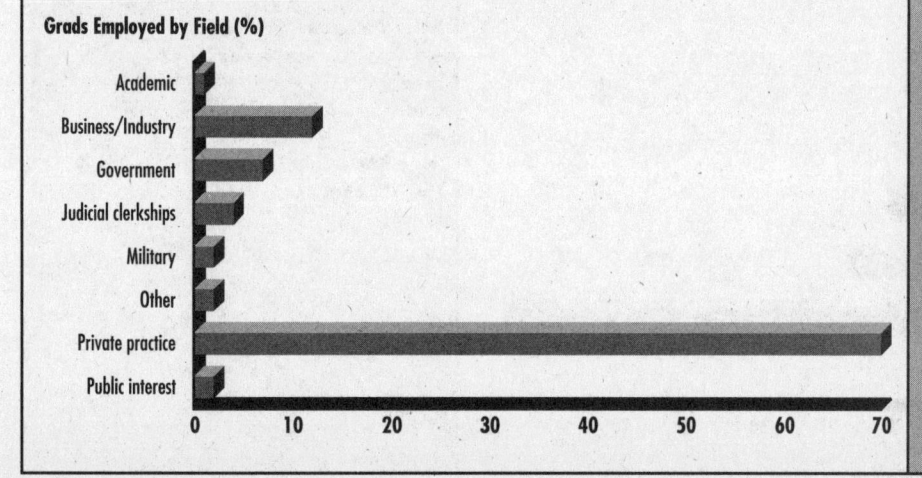

Grads Employed by Field (%)
- Academic
- Business/Industry
- Government
- Judicial clerkships
- Military
- Other
- Private practice
- Public interest

Rate of Placement: 90%
Average Starting Salary: $79,202
Employers Who Frequently Hire Grads: Baker & Botts; Locke Liddel & Sapp; Fulbright & Jaworski; Arthur Andersen; Jenkins, Gilcrest; Bracewell & Patterson; Harris County District Attorney; Weil, Gotshal & Manges
State for Bar Exam: TX
Pass Rate for First-Time Bar: 90%

UNIVERSITY OF IDAHO
College of Law

Admissions Contact: Admissions Coordinator, Erick J. Larson
Sixth and Rayburn, Moscow, ID 83844-2321
Admissions Phone: 208-885-2300 • Admissions Fax: 208-885-5709
Admissions E-mail: lawadmit@uidaho.edu • Web Address: www.uidaho.edu/law

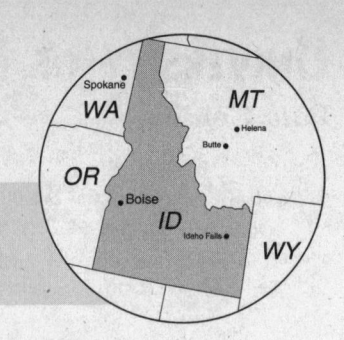

INSTITUTIONAL INFORMATION
Public/Private: Public
Student/Faculty Ratio: 18:1
Total Faculty: 28
% Part Time: 1

PROGRAMS
Academic Specialties: Business Law, Environmental and Natural Resource Law, Professional and Litigation Skills
Combined Degrees Offered: JD/MS Environmental Science (4 years), JD/MBA with Washington State University (4 years), JD/MA Business and Economics (4 years)
Grading System: A (4.00), A– (3.67), B+ (3.33), B (3.00), B– (2.67), etc.
Clinical Program Required? No
Clinical Programs Description: Tax Clinic, Tribal Clinic, Appellate Clinic, General Clinic. Students will get the opportunity to interview, represent, and research actual cases.
Legal Writing Course Requirements? Yes
Legal Methods Course Requirements? Yes
Legal Methods Description: 1 year for all first-year students
Legal Research Course Requirements? No
Moot Court Requirement? No
Public Interest Law Requirement? No
Academic Journals: Law Review. After completing the first year of law school, students in the top 10 percent are invited into Law Review. If students are not in the top 10 percent, they may enter a writing competition to enter (up to 15 slots). Law Review will fulfill all upper-division writing requirements. Law Review will publish two reviews a year.

STUDENT INFORMATION
Enrollment of Law School: 304
% Out of State: 20
% Male/Female: 62/38
% Full Time: 100
% Minority: 7
Average Age of Entering Class: 27

RESEARCH FACILITIES
Research Resources Available: Students may enroll in graduate-level courses at Washington State University; up to 6 graduate-level credits may be accepted towards the JD.
School-Supported Research Centers: Legal Aid Clinic In-House, External Program Office (Boise, ID)

EXPENSES/FINANCIAL AID
Annual Tuition (Residents/Nonresidents): $0/$6,000
Fee (Full-Time) per Academic Year (Residential/Nonresidents): $5,160/$11,160
Room and Board (On/Off Campus): $4,740/$5,400
Books and Supplies: $700
Financial Aid Application Deadline: 2/15
Average Grant: $2,075
Average Loan: $9,000
% of Aid That Is Merit-Based: 20
Average Total Aid Package: $18,500
Average Debt: $40,000

ADMISSIONS INFORMATION
Application Fee: $40
Regular Application Deadline: 2/1
Regular Notification: 4/1
LSDAS Accepted? Yes
Average GPA: 3.3
Range of GPA: 3.1–3.6
Average LSAT: 152
Range of LSAT: 148–155
Transfer Students Accepted? Yes
Other Admissions Factors Considered: Personal statement, resume, letters of recommendation, work experience
Number of Applications Received: 460
Number of Applicants Accepted: 284
Number of Applicants Enrolled: 124

INTERNATIONAL STUDENTS
TOEFL Required of International Students? Yes
Minimum TOEFL: 280

EMPLOYMENT INFORMATION

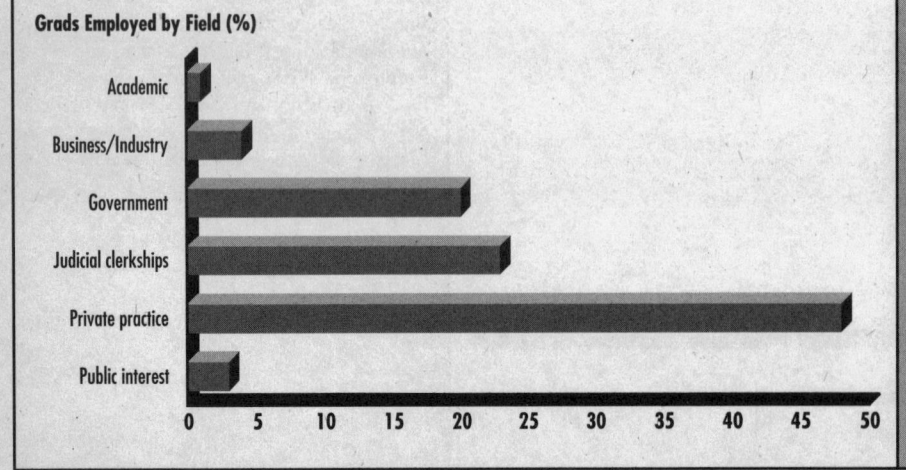

Grads Employed by Field (%)
- Academic
- Business/Industry
- Government
- Judicial clerkships
- Private practice
- Public interest

Rate of Placement: 98%
Average Starting Salary: $41,385
Employers Who Frequently Hire Grads: Employers with offices in Idaho, Washington, Oregon, Utah
State Bar Exam: ID, WA, UT, OR, NV
Pass Rate for First-Time Bar: 77%

UNIVERSITY OF ILLINOIS
College of Law

Admissions Contact: Director of Admissions, Maggie D. Austin
504 East Pennsylvania Avenue, Champaign, IL 61820
Admissions Phone: 217-244-6415 • Admissions Fax: 217-244-1478
Admissions E-mail: admissions@law.uiuc.edu • Web Address: www.law.uiuc.edu

INSTITUTIONAL INFORMATION
Public/Private: Public
Student/Faculty Ratio: 12:1
Total Faculty: 86
% Part Time: 39
% Female: 34
% Minority: 15

PROGRAMS
Academic Specialties: Constitutional Law, Criminal Law, Intellectual Property Law, Professional Responsibility, International Law, Environmental Law, Property Law, Family Law, Civil Procedure, Commercial Law, Corporation Securities Law, Government Services, Human Rights Law, Labor Law, Legal History, Legal Philosophy, Taxation
Advanced Degrees Offered: JD (3 years), LLM (1 year)
Combined Degrees Offered: JD/MBA (4 years), JD/MA (4 years), JD/PhD (varies), JD/DVM (6 years), JD/MD (6 years), JD/MUP (4 years), JD/MHRIR (4 years)
Grading System: Letter and numerical system on a 4.0 scale
Clinical Program Required? No
Clinical Programs Description: Civil Clinic, International Human Rights Clinic, Appellate Defender Clinic
Legal Writing Course Requirements? Yes
Legal Writing Description: First-year students learn objective writing first term and writing as an advocate second term.
Legal Methods Course Requirements? No
Legal Research Course Requirements? Yes

Legal Research Description: Students learn research skills throughout their first year through hands-on training offered by full-time faculty and librarians in of the best law libraries in the country. This is taught as a part of both the Legal Research and Writing and Introduction to Advocacy courses.
Moot Court Requirement? No
Moot Court Description: Second-year students can participate in and receive credit for many different internal moot court competitions, ranging in subject matter from constitutional law to intellectual property. Those who advance internally participate in regional and national competitions.
Public Interest Law Requirement? No
Academic Journals: *University of Illinois Law Review; The Elder Law Journal; Journal of Law, Technology, and Policy; Comparative Labor Law and Policy Journal; Illinois Law Update*

STUDENT INFORMATION
Enrollment of Law School: 660
% Out of State: 24
% Male/Female: 60/40
% Full Time: 100
% Full Time That Are International: 0
% Minority: 27
Average Age of Entering Class: 24

RESEARCH FACILITIES
Research Resources Available: Wireless access available beginning fall 2002

EXPENSES/FINANCIAL AID
Annual Tuition (Residents/Nonresidents): $9,872/$21,770
Room and Board: $7,848
Books and Supplies: $960
Average Grant: $4,300
Average Loan: $18,500
% of Aid That Is Merit-Based: 31
% Receiving Some Sort of Aid: 95
Average Total Aid Package: $22,000
Average Debt: $51,000

ADMISSIONS INFORMATION
Application Fee: $50
Regular Application Deadline: 3/15
Regular Notification: 1/1
LSDAS Accepted? Yes
Average GPA: 3.5
Average LSAT: 160
Transfer Students Accepted? Yes
Other Schools to Which Students Applied: Northwestern, U. of Chicago, U. of Iowa, U. of Michigan, U. of Wisconsin—Madison, Washington U.
Other Admissions Factors Considered: Graduate work in other fields, demonstrated leadership
Number of Applications Received: 1,843
Number of Applicants Accepted: 608
Number of Applicants Enrolled: 224

INTERNATIONAL STUDENTS
TOEFL Required of International Students? Yes
Minimum TOEFL: 250

EMPLOYMENT INFORMATION

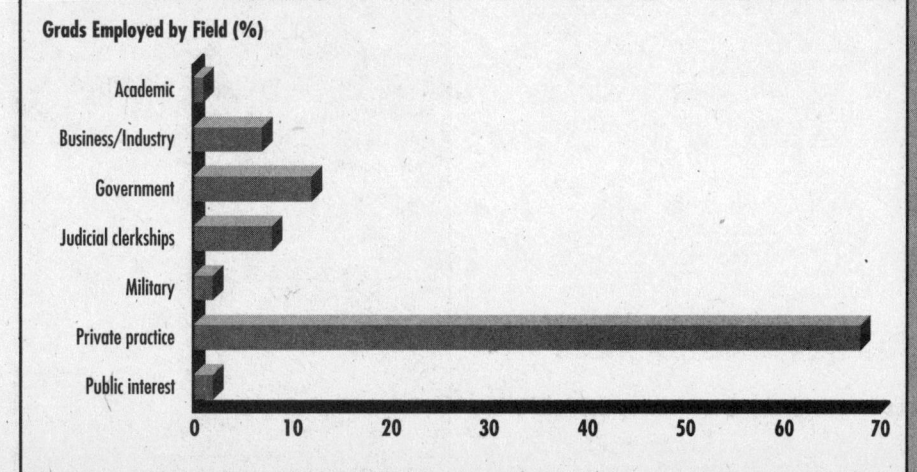

Grads Employed by Field (%)
- Academic: ~2
- Business/Industry: ~7
- Government: ~12
- Judicial clerkships: ~10
- Military: ~1
- Private practice: ~68
- Public interest: ~2

Rate of Placement: 99%
Average Starting Salary: $80,265
Employers Who Frequently Hire Grads: Baker & McKenzie; Bell, Boyd & Lloyd; Foley & Lardner; Gardner, Carton & Douglas; Jenner & Block; Jones, Day, Reavis & Pogue; Lord, Bissell & Brook; Mayer, Brown & Platt; Piper, Marbury, Rudnick & Wolfe; Sidley, Austin, Brown & Wood; Skadden, Arps, Slate, Meagher & Flom; Sonnenschein, Nath & Rosenthal; Winston & Strawn
State for Bar Exam: IL, CA, DC, NY, TX
Pass Rate for First-Time Bar: 96%

UNIVERSITY OF IOWA
College of Law

Admissions Contact: Admissions Coordinator, Jan Barnes
Melrose at Byington Streets, Iowa City, IA 52242
Admissions Phone: 319-335-9095 • Admissions Fax: 319-335-9019
Admissions E-mail: law-admissions@uiowa.edu • Web Address: www.law.uiowa.edu

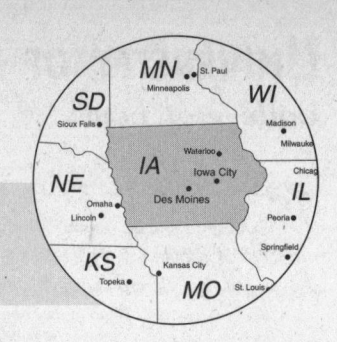

INSTITUTIONAL INFORMATION
Public/Private: Public
Student/Faculty Ratio: 12:1
Total Faculty: 50
% Part Time: 2
% Female: 26
% Minority: 15

PROGRAMS
Academic Specialties: The University of Iowa College of Law is renowned for its writing program as well as other strengths. Specialties include International Law; other specialties and a complete curriculum description can be found at www.law.uiowa.edu.
Advanced Degrees Offered: LLM International and Comparative Law (24 hours of academic credit and a thesis)
Combined Degrees Offered: JD/MBA (4 years), JD/MA (4 years), JD/MHA (4 years), JD/MSW (4 years)
Grading System: Letter and numerical system, 90–55 range
Clinical Program Required? No
Legal Writing Course Requirements? Yes
Legal Writing Description: Students must complete 2 first-year small-section classes (for a total of 3 credits) in research and writing under the direct supervision of a faculty member. All students must also complete 5 upper-class writing credits, 2 of which must be faculty-supervised.
Legal Methods Course Requirements? Yes
Legal Research Course Requirements? Yes

Legal Research Description: At the beginning of the first year, students attend 4 one-hour sessions in Legal Research training, evenly divided between lecture and library exercises. During the course of the first semester, each student completes a series of research and writing assignments under the direction of professor. In the second semester, students are trained in Westlaw and Lexis. Early in the second year, students attend 3 further lectures on advanced legal research topics. An advanced legal research class for credit is also offered.
Moot Court Requirement? Yes
Moot Court Description: All students participate in a for-credit Appellate Advocacy course in which they write a brief and present an oral argument.
Public Interest Law Requirement? No
Academic Journals: *Journal of Gender, Race, and Justice; Journal of Corporation Law; Law Review; Transnational Law and Contemporary Problems Journal*

STUDENT INFORMATION
Enrollment of Law School: 707
% Out of State: 37
% Male/Female: 53/47
% Full Time: 100
% Full Time That Are International: 2
% Minority: 15
Average Age of Entering Class: 25

EXPENSES/FINANCIAL AID
Annual Tuition (Residents/Nonresidents): $8,152/$20,274
Room and Board (Off Campus): $5,220
Books and Supplies: $1,350
Average Grant: $7,416
Average Loan: $15,590
% of Aid That Is Merit-Based: 6
% Receiving Some Sort of Aid: 97
Average Total Aid Package: $18,090
Average Debt: $43,010

ADMISSIONS INFORMATION
Application Fee: $30
Regular Application Deadline: 3/2
Regular Notification: Rolling
LSDAS Accepted? Yes
Average GPA: 3.5
Range of GPA: 3.2–3.8
Average LSAT: 158
Range of LSAT: 156–163
Transfer Students Accepted? Yes
Other Schools to Which Students Applied: George Washington University, Indiana University, University of Texas at Austin, University of Illinois at Urbana-Champaign, University of Minnesota, University of Wisconsin—Madison, Washington University
Other Admissions Factors Considered: Letters of recommendation reflecting academic or professional ability, extracurricular activities, any other information that addresses the applicant's potential for law study
Number of Applications Received: 1,273
Number of Applicants Accepted: 523
Number of Applicants Enrolled: 245

INTERNATIONAL STUDENTS
TOEFL Required of International Students? Yes

EMPLOYMENT INFORMATION

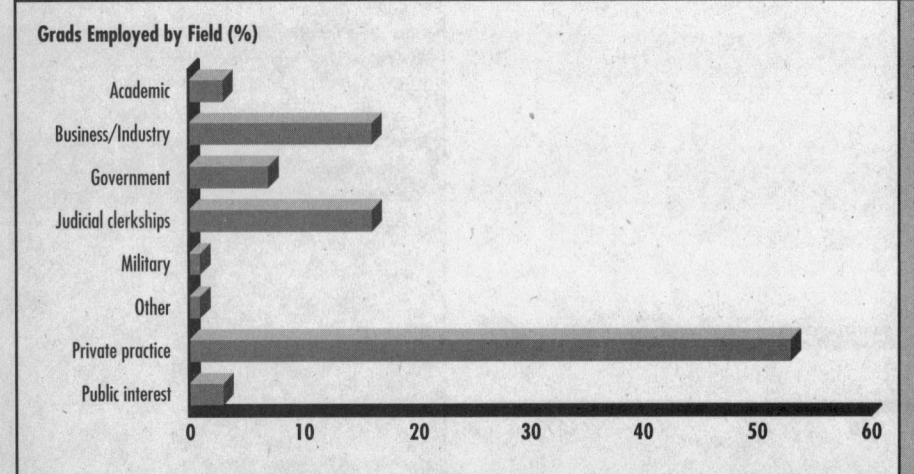

Grads Employed by Field (%)

Field	%
Academic	~2
Business/Industry	~17
Government	~10
Judicial clerkships	~17
Military	~0
Other	~1
Private practice	~53
Public interest	~2

Rate of Placement: 99%
Average Starting Salary: $53,208
Employers Who Frequently Hire Grads: National law firms, government agencies, state and federal judges
State for Bar Exam: IA
Pass Rate for First-Time Bar: 87%

UNIVERSITY OF KANSAS
School of Law

Admissions Contact: Assistant Dean of Admissions, Rachel Smith
1535 W. 15th Street, Lawrence, KS 66045-7577
Admissions Phone: 785-864-4378 • Admissions Fax: 785-864-5054
Admissions E-mail: admissions@ku.edu • Web Address: www.law.ku.edu

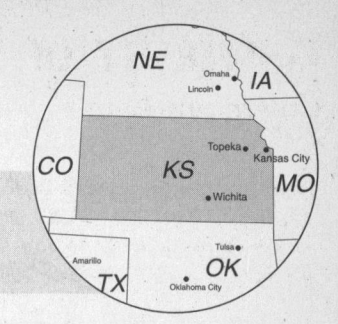

INSTITUTIONAL INFORMATION
Public/Private: Public
Student/Faculty Ratio: 20:1
Total Faculty: 55
% Part Time: 35
% Female: 33
% Minority: 5

PROGRAMS
Academic Specialties: Tax and Business Law, Criminal Law, Family Law, Environmental/Natural Resource Law, International Law, Agriculture Law, Media Law and Policy, Public Law, Litigation, Constitutional Law, Commercial Law, Elder Law Certificate, Native American Law Certificate
Advanced Degrees Offered: JD (3 years; accelerated 26-month option also available)
Combined Degrees Offered: JD/MBA, JD/MA Economics, JD/MPA, JD/MA Philosophy, JD/MSW, JD/MUP, JD/MHSA (all 4 years)
Grading System: A to F, using the PLUS system; some courses graded on a Credit/No Credit, A/Credit/No credit or A/Credit/F basis
Clinical Program Required? No
Clinical Programs Description: Legal Aid Clinic, Judicial Clerkship Clinic, Criminal Justice Clinic, Defender Project, Elder Law Clinic, Public Policy Clinic, Legislative Clinic, Media Law Clinic
Legal Writing Course Requirements? Yes
Legal Writing Description: Required 2-semester Lawyering course for first-year students teaches legal writing, motions drafting, and other practical skills; there is also an upper-level writing requirement.
Legal Methods Course Requirements? Yes
Legal Methods Description: 2 semesters, legal writing exercises implemented
Legal Research Course Requirements? Yes
Legal Research Description: Taught during the Lawyering class
Moot Court Requirement? No
Public Interest Law Requirement? No
Academic Journals: *Kansas Law Review, Kansas Journal of Law and Public Policy*

STUDENT INFORMATION
Enrollment of Law School: 497
% Out of State: 22
% Male/Female: 56/44
% Full Time: 100
% Minority: 9
Average Age of Entering Class: 24

RESEARCH FACILITIES
Research Resources Available: Law School has a wireless network

EXPENSES/FINANCIAL AID
Annual Tuition (Residents/Nonresidents): $6,829/$14,648
Room and Board: $6,546
Books and Supplies: $650
Financial Aid Application Deadline: 3/15
Average Grant: $8,500
Average Loan: $8,500
% of Aid That Is Merit-Based: 85
% Receiving Some Sort of Aid: 80
Average Total Aid Package: $18,500
Average Debt: $40,000

ADMISSIONS INFORMATION
Application Fee: $50
Regular Application Deadline: 3/15
Regular Notification: Rolling
LSDAS Accepted? Yes
Average GPA: 3.4
Range of GPA: 2.0–4.0
Average LSAT: 155
Range of LSAT: 135–175
Transfer Students Accepted? Yes
Other Schools to Which Students Applied: University of Texas at Austin, Tulane University, University of Denver, University of Missouri—Columbia, University of Missouri—Kansas City, University of Nebraska—Lincoln, Washburn University
Other Admissions Factors Considered: Demonstrated ability to overcome cultural, financial, or other disadvantages; Kansas residents receive preference
Number of Applications Received: 861
Number of Applicants Accepted: 428
Number of Applicants Enrolled: 192

INTERNATIONAL STUDENTS
TOEFL Required of International Students? Yes

EMPLOYMENT INFORMATION

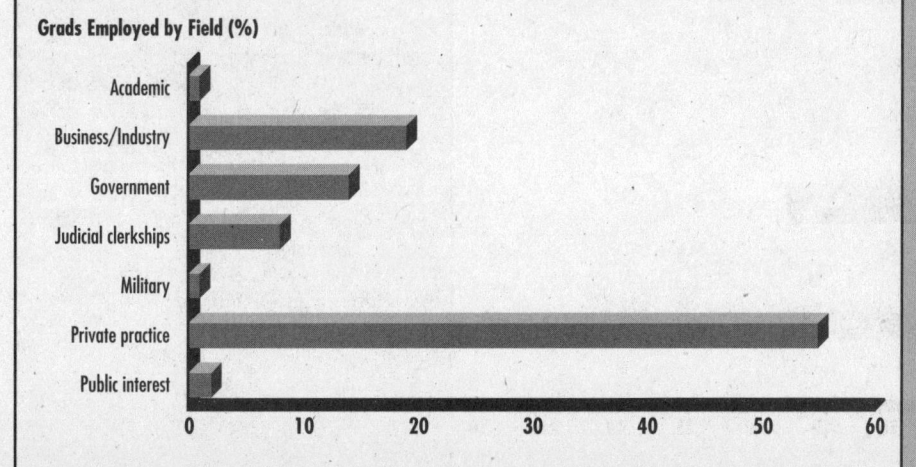

Grads Employed by Field (%)
- Academic: ~1
- Business/Industry: ~20
- Government: ~15
- Judicial clerkships: ~8
- Military: ~1
- Private practice: ~55
- Public interest: ~2

Rate of Placement: 96%
Average Starting Salary: $55,140
State for Bar Exam: KS, MO, TX
Pass Rate for First-Time Bar: 89%

UNIVERSITY OF KENTUCKY
College of Law

Admissions Contact: Associate Dean, Drusilla V. Bakert
209 Law Building, Lexington, KY 40506-0048
Admissions Phone: 859-257-6770 • Admissions Fax: 859-323-1061
Admissions E-mail: dbakert@uky.edu • Web Address: www.uky.edu/law

INSTITUTIONAL INFORMATION
Public/Private: Public
Student/Faculty Ratio: 14:1
Total Faculty: 29
% Part Time: 0
% Female: 30
% Minority: 10

PROGRAMS
Academic Specialties: Family Law, Fair Housing Law, Bankruptcy Law, White Collar Crime, Professional Responsibility, Civil Procedure, Commercial Law, Constitutional Law, Corporation Securities Law, Criminal Law, Environmental Law, Human Rights Law, Intellectual Property Law, International Law, Labor Law, Property, Taxation, Health Law, Advocacy
Combined Degrees Offered: JD/MPA (4 years), JD/MBA (4 years)
Grading System: A+(4.3) to E (0.0); typical curve is 2.7 median grade for first-years, 2.8 median grade for second- and third-years
Clinical Program Required? No
Clinical Programs Description: UK Law Legal Clinic (students represent elderly and low-income clients), Judicial Clerkship externship, Kentucky Innocence Project externship, prosecutorial externship, prison externship
Legal Writing Course Requirements? Yes
Legal Writing Description: Year-long course for first-year students in legal research and writing taught in small groups of 10–12 students
Legal Methods Course Requirements? No
Legal Research Course Requirements? Yes
Legal Research Description: See Legal Writing.
Moot Court Requirement? Yes
Moot Court Description: All first-year students write and argue a brief before an appellate panel. Second- and third-year programs in moot court and trial advocacy are optional.
Public Interest Law Requirement? No
Academic Journals: Kentucky Law Journal, Journal of Natural Resources and Environmental Law

STUDENT INFORMATION
Enrollment of Law School: 379
% Out of State: 14
% Male/Female: 56/44
% Full Time: 100
% Full Time That Are International: 1
% Minority: 6
Average Age of Entering Class: 23

RESEARCH FACILITIES
Research Resources Available: New M. I. King Library has state-of-the-art resources; Law Library has computer lab and laptops that students may checkout for use in the library; Law Library is a member of the National Law Library Consortium; students also have access to the State Loan Library and the State Library System; Law School is in the process of renovating a majority of classrooms for Internet access and laptop use

EXPENSES/FINANCIAL AID
Annual Tuition (Residents/Nonresidents): $6,250/$16,064
Room and Board: $7,400
Books and Supplies: $650
Financial Aid Application Deadline: 4/1
Average Grant: $2,500
Average Loan: $17,000
% of Aid That Is Merit-Based: 0
% Receiving Some Sort of Aid: 75
Average Total Aid Package: $20,000
Average Debt: $42,000

ADMISSIONS INFORMATION
Application Fee: $35
Regular Application Deadline: 3/1
Regular Notification: Rolling
LSDAS Accepted? Yes
Average GPA: 3.5
Range of GPA: 3.2–3.7
Average LSAT: 158
Range of LSAT: 154–160
Transfer Students Accepted? Yes
Other Schools to Which Students Applied: Indiana University, Northern Kentucky University, University of Cincinnati, University of Georgia, University of Louisville, University of Tennessee, Vanderbilt University
Other Admissions Factors Considered: Geographic, racial, ethnic diversity; diversity of experience; success in career prior to law school
Number of Applications Received: 925
Number of Applicants Accepted: 395
Number of Applicants Enrolled: 131

INTERNATIONAL STUDENTS
TOEFL Required of International Students? Yes
Minimum TOEFL: 280

EMPLOYMENT INFORMATION

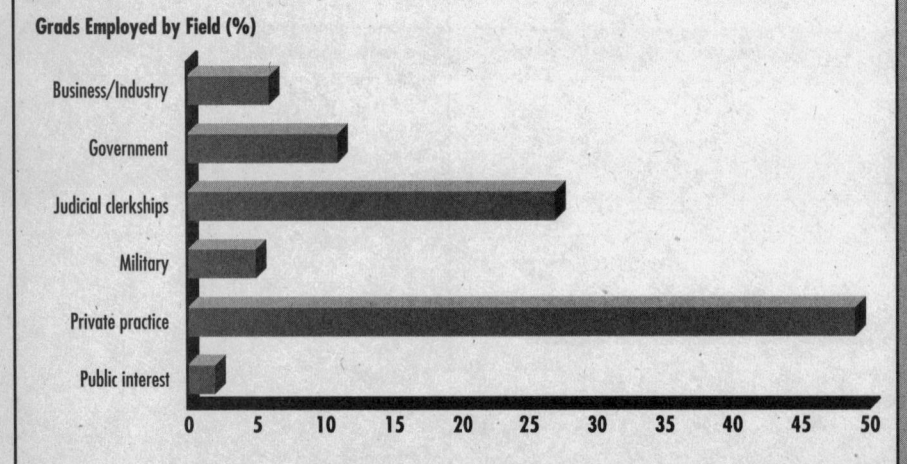

Grads Employed by Field (%)
- Business/Industry: ~5
- Government: ~11
- Judicial clerkships: ~27
- Military: ~3
- Private practice: ~50
- Public interest: ~2

Rate of Placement: 99%
Average Starting Salary: $50,500
Employers Who Frequently Hire Grads: All Kentucky legal employers; major firms in Cincinnati, Nashville, West Virginia, D.C., and Atlanta. Through job fairs students also have access to employers nationwide, with most popular locations being New York City, Chicago, California, Florida, Texas, and Arizona.
State for Bar Exam: KY
Pass Rate for First-Time Bar: 92%

UNIVERSITY OF LA VERNE
College of Law

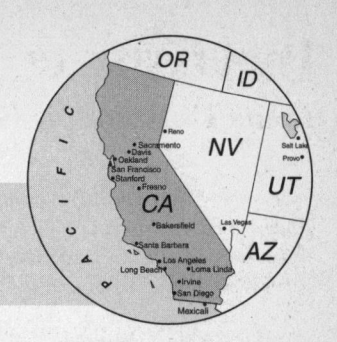

Admissions Contact: Director of Admissions, John Osborne
1950 3rd Street, La Verne, CA 91715
Admissions Phone: 909-596-1848 • Admissions Fax: 909-392-2707
Admissions E-mail: osborne@ulv.edu • Web Address: www.ulv.edu

INSTITUTIONAL INFORMATION
Public/Private: Private
Academic Calendar: Semester
Schedule: Full time or part time
Student/Faculty Ratio: 25:1

PROGRAMS
Advanced Degrees Offered: JD (3 years full time, 4 years part time)
Grading System: A to F
Clinical Program Required? No
Legal Writing/Methods Course Requirements: Legal Analysis, 2-unit class

STUDENT INFORMATION
Enrollment of Law School: 160
% Male/Female: 50/50
% Full Time: 50

EXPENSES/FINANCIAL AID
Books and Supplies: $1,500
Tuition Per Credit: $575

ADMISSIONS INFORMATION
Regular Application Deadline: 8/1
Transfer Students Accepted? Yes

EMPLOYMENT INFORMATION
Employers Who Frequently Hire Grads: County government and law firms

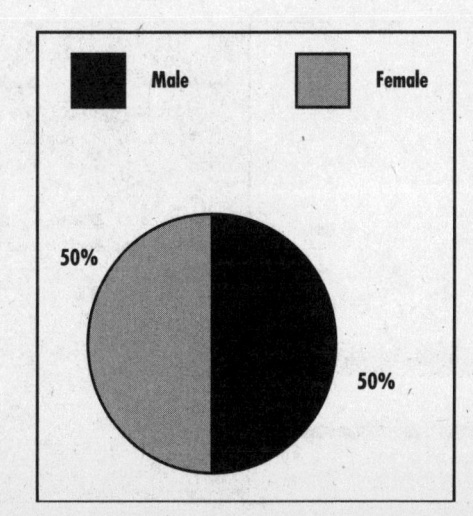

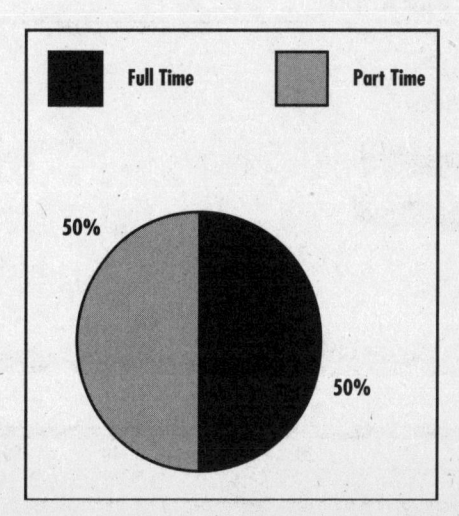

University of Louisville
Louis D. Brandeis School of Law

Admissions Contact: Assistant Dean for Admissions, Connie Shumake
University of Louisville, Louisville, KY 40292
Admissions Phone: 502-852-6364 • Admissions Fax: 502-852-0862
Admissions E-mail: lawadmissions@louisville.edu • Web Address: www.louisville.edu/brandeislaw

INSTITUTIONAL INFORMATION
Public/Private: Public
Student/Faculty Ratio: 12:1
Total Faculty: 32
% Part Time: 18
% Female: 36
% Minority: 15

PROGRAMS
Academic Specialties: Commercial Law, Corporation Securities Law, Criminal Law, Environmental Law, Government Services, International Law, Labor Law, Taxation
Advanced Degrees Offered: JD (3 years full time, 4 years part time)
Combined Degrees Offered: JD/MBA, JD/MSW, JD/MDiv, JD/MA Humanities (4 to 5 years)
Grading System: Numerical system on a 4.0 scale
Clinical Program Required? Yes
Clinical Program Description: Public service program, 6 externship programs
Legal Writing Course Requirements? Yes
Legal Writing Description: 3 credits—Basic Legal Skill Writing (first year)
Legal Methods Course Requirements? Yes
Legal Methods Description: 3 credits—Basic Legal Skill Writing (first year)
Legal Research Course Requirements? Yes
Legal Research Description: 1 credit—Research and Writing (first semester)
Moot Court Requirement? Yes
Moot Court Description: Basic Legal Skills—course requirement, second semester oral arguments
Public Interest Law Requirement? Yes
Public Interest Law Description: 30 work hours of public service
Academic Journals: Brandeis Law Journal, Journal of Law and Education

STUDENT INFORMATION
Enrollment of Law School: 368
% Out of State: 21
% Male/Female: 51/49
% Full Time: 71
% Full Time That Are International: 1
% Minority: 13
Average Age of Entering Class: 25

RESEARCH FACILITIES
Research Resources Available: Westlaw, Lexis-Nexis, CALI, Kentucky Commonwealth Virtual University
% of JD Classrooms Wired: 95

EXPENSES/FINANCIAL AID
Annual Tuition (Residents/Nonresidents): $6,425/$17,253
Room and Board: $10,030
Books and Supplies: $854
Financial Aid Application Deadline: 6/1
Average Grant: $3,000
Average Loan: $14,650
% of Aid That Is Merit-Based: 20
% Receiving Some Sort of Aid: 79
Average Total Aid Package: $17,000
Average Debt: $23,000
Tuition Per Credit (Residents/Nonresidents): $293/$745
Fees Per Credit: $15

ADMISSIONS INFORMATION
Application Fee: $40
Regular Application Deadline: 5/15
Regular Notification: Rolling
LSDAS Accepted? Yes
Average GPA: 3.3
Range of GPA: 2.8–3.7
Average LSAT: 157
Range of LSAT: 154–159
Transfer Students Accepted? Yes
Other Schools to Which Students Applied: Indiana University, Northern Kentucky University, University of Memphis, University of Dayton, University of Kentucky, University of Tennessee, Vanderbilt University
Other Admissions Factors Considered: Academic improvement, overcoming adversity, diversity factors, community service
Number of Applications Received: 850
Number of Applicants Accepted: 310
Number of Applicants Enrolled: 120

EMPLOYMENT INFORMATION

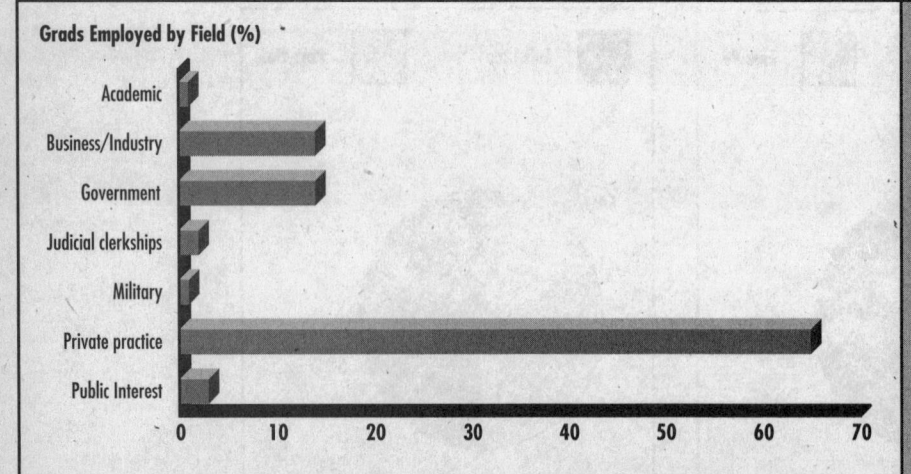

Grads Employed by Field (%)
- Academic: ~1
- Business/Industry: ~13
- Government: ~14
- Judicial clerkships: ~3
- Military: ~1
- Private practice: ~65
- Public Interest: ~3

Rate of Placement: 99%
Average Starting Salary: $42,000
Employers Who Frequently Hire Grads: Frost, Brown & Todd; Dinsmore & Shohl; Greenebaum, Doll & McDonald; Wyatt, Tarrant & Combs
State for Bar Exam: KY, IN, FL, TN, DC
Pass Rate for First-Time Bar: 83%

UNIVERSITY OF MARYLAND
School of Law

Admissions Contact: Director of Admission, Patricia Scott
500 West Baltimore Street, Baltimore, MD 21201
Admissions Phone: 410-706-3492 • Admissions Fax: 410-706-4045
Admissions E-mail: admissions@law.umaryland.edu • Web Address: www.law.umaryland.edu

INSTITUTIONAL INFORMATION
Public/Private: Public
Student/Faculty Ratio: 14:1
Total Faculty: 156
% Part Time: 63
% Female: 37
% Minority: 14

PROGRAMS
Academic Specialties: The school's location in the Baltimore/D.C./Annapolis triad provides students with access to local, regional, and national issues. The elective curriculum is especially rich in International and Comparative Law, Business and Intellectual Property Law, Trial and Appellate Advocacy, and Alternative Dispute Resolution. Other specialties include Environmental Law and Law and Health Care.
Advanced Degrees Offered: JD (3 years full time day; 4 years evening)
Combined Degrees Offered: JD/PhD Policy Sciences (7 years), JD/MBA (4 years), JD/MA Public Management (4 years), JD/MA Criminal Justice (3.5 to 4 years), JD/MSW (3.5 to 4 years), JD/MA Liberal Education (4 years), JD/MA Applied and Professional Ethics (4 years), JD/MACP (4 years), JD/PharmD (7 years), JD/MA Policy Sciences (4 years).
Grading System: Letter and numerical system on a 4.3 scale.
Clinical Program Required? Yes
Clinical Programs Description: Offerings vary from semester to semester, including AIDS Litigation and Counseling, Appellate Advocacy, Civil Rights of Persons with Disabilities, Community Legal Assistance, Employment Rights Clinical Workshop, Environmental Law, Family Investment Program Legal Clinic, Federal and State Criminal Defense Litigation, Housing and Community Development, Elder Law, Health Law, Low Income Tax Payer, Immigration Law, Juvenile Law, Children's Issues, Legislation Advocacy, and Advanced Criminal Procedure.
Legal Writing Course Requirements? Yes
Legal Writing Description: 3-semester Legal Analysis, Research, and Writing Program and an Advanced Legal Research course.
Legal Methods Course Requirements? Yes
Legal Methods Description: Covered in the first semester of the Legal Analysis, Research, and Writing series.
Legal Research Course Requirements? Yes
Legal Research Description: See Legal Writing.
Moot Court Requirement? Yes
Moot Court Description: The Moot Court requirement is met in LAWR III, a course required for all students in their third semester.
Public Interest Law Requirement? No
Academic Journals: *The Business Lawyer, The Maryland Law Review, The Journal of Health Care Law and Policy, MARGINS*

STUDENT INFORMATION
Enrollment of Law School: 958
% Out of State: 29
% Male/Female: 41/59
% Full Time: 75
% Full Time That Are International: 1
% Minority: 22
Average Age of Entering Class: 26

EXPENSES/FINANCIAL AID
Annual Tuition (Residents/Nonresidents): $10,692/$19,639
Room and Board (On/Off Campus): $11,291/$16,025
Books and Supplies: $1,500
Financial Aid Application Deadline: 3/1
Average Grant: $3,830
Average Loan: $19,098
% of Aid That Is Merit-Based: 1
% Receiving Some Sort of Aid: 72
Average Total Aid Package: $21,042
Average Debt: $52,238

ADMISSIONS INFORMATION
Application Fee: $60
Regular Application Deadline: Rolling
Regular Notification: Rolling
LSDAS Accepted? Yes
Average GPA: 3.4
Range of GPA: 3.1–3.7
Average LSAT: 156
Range of LSAT: 149–159
Transfer Students Accepted? Yes
Other Admissions Factors Considered: Geographic origin; language, cultural, social, disability, and economic barriers overcome; interpersonal skills; extracurricular activities; work or service experience; leadership record; potential for service to the institution
Number of Applications Received: 2,275
Number of Applicants Accepted: 910
Number of Applicants Enrolled: 302

EMPLOYMENT INFORMATION

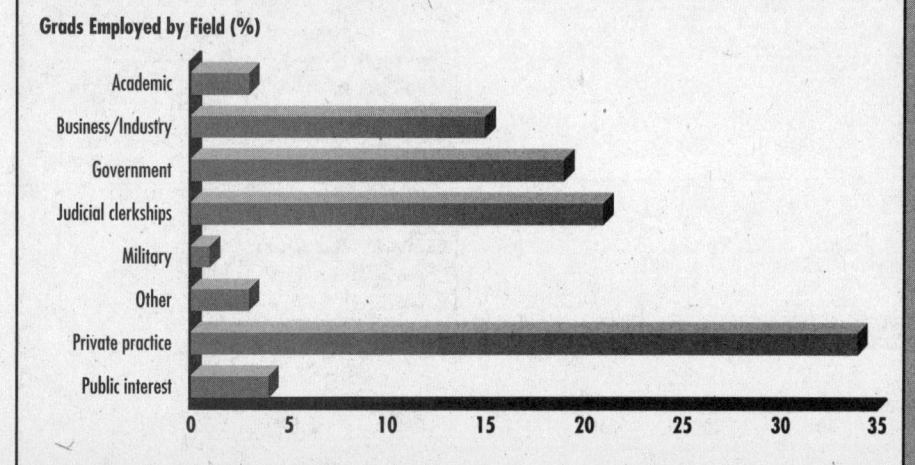

Grads Employed by Field (%)

Field	%
Academic	~1
Business/Industry	~15
Government	~19
Judicial clerkships	~20
Military	~1
Other	~3
Private practice	~34
Public interest	~4

Rate of Placement: 97%
Average Starting Salary: $47,717
Employers Who Frequently Hire Grads: Department of Justice; Dickstein, Shapiro & Morin, LLP; Environmental Protection Agency; Miles & Stockbridge; Ober, Kaler, Grimes & Shriver; Piper, Marbury, Rudnick & Wolfe, LLP; Public Defender's Office; Maryland Attorney General's Office; Venable, Baetjer, and Howard, LLP; Whiteford, Taylor & Preston, LLP
State for Bar Exam: MD
Pass Rate for First-Time Bar: 78%

UNIVERSITY OF MEMPHIS
Cecil C. Humphreys School of Law

Admissions Contact: Assistant Dean for Admissions, Dr. Sue Ann McClellan
207 Humphreys Law School, Memphis, TN 38152-3140
Admissions Phone: 901-678-5403 • Admissions Fax: 901-678-5210
Admissions E-mail: lawadmissions@spc75.law.memphis.edu • Web Address: www.law.memphis.edu

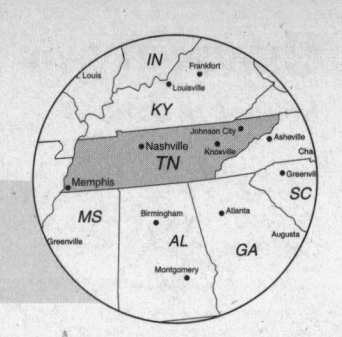

INSTITUTIONAL INFORMATION
Public/Private: Public
Student/Faculty Ratio: 18:1
Total Faculty: 63
% Part Time: 71
% Female: 29
% Minority: 5

PROGRAMS
Academic Specialties: Curriculum is designed to prepare students for general practice in civil and criminal matters through numerous required courses that expose students to all major facets of the practice of law. Specialties include Civil Procedure, Commercial Law, Constitutional Law, Corporation Securities Law, Criminal Law, Environmental Law, Human Rights Law, International Law, Labor Law, Property, and Taxation.
Advanced Degrees Offered: JD (6 semesters)
Combined Degrees Offered: JD/MBA (4 years/8 semesters)
Grading System: A+ to F; in some courses E (excellent), S (satisfactory), and U (unsatisfactory). A grade of D or better is passing, less than D is failing, and below C is unsatisfactory.
Clinical Program Required? No
Clinical Programs Description: Civil Litigation, Child Advocacy, Elder Law, Domestic Violence, General Sessions
Legal Writing Course Requirements? No
Legal Methods Course Requirements? Yes
Legal Methods Description: 3 credit hours in first year
Legal Research Course Requirements? Yes
Legal Research Description: Upper-class research requirement
Moot Court Requirement? No
Public Interest Law Requirement? No
Academic Journals: The University of Memphis Law Review, The Tennessee Journal of Practice and Procedure

STUDENT INFORMATION
Enrollment of Law School: 431
% Out of State: 12
% Male/Female: 59/41
% Full Time: 92
% Full Time That Are International: 0
% Minority: 10
Average Age of Entering Class: 26

RESEARCH FACILITIES
Research Resources Available: Law Library, Interlibrary loan programs with other law schools, Tiger Lan Labs

EXPENSES/FINANCIAL AID
Annual Tuition (Residents/Nonresidents): $6,290/$17,546
Room and Board: $6,570
Books and Supplies: $1,300
Financial Aid Application Deadline: 4/1
Average Grant: $5,500
Average Loan: $8,450
% of Aid That Is Merit-Based: 58
% Receiving Some Sort of Aid: 85
Average Total Aid Package: $8,701
Average Debt: $42,364
Tuition Per Credit (Residents/Nonresidents): $309/$821
Fees Per Credit: $6

ADMISSIONS INFORMATION
Application Fee: $25
Regular Application Deadline: 2/15
Regular Notification: 4/15
LSDAS Accepted? Yes
Average GPA: 3.2
Range of GPA: 3.0–3.6
Average LSAT: 153
Range of LSAT: 149–156
Transfer Students Accepted? Yes
Other Schools to Which Students Applied: Georgia State University, Mercer University, Mississippi College, Samford University, The University of Mississippi, University of Tennessee, Vanderbilt University
Number of Applications Received: 771
Number of Applicants Accepted: 320
Number of Applicants Enrolled: 146

INTERNATIONAL STUDENTS
TOEFL Required of International Students? Yes

EMPLOYMENT INFORMATION

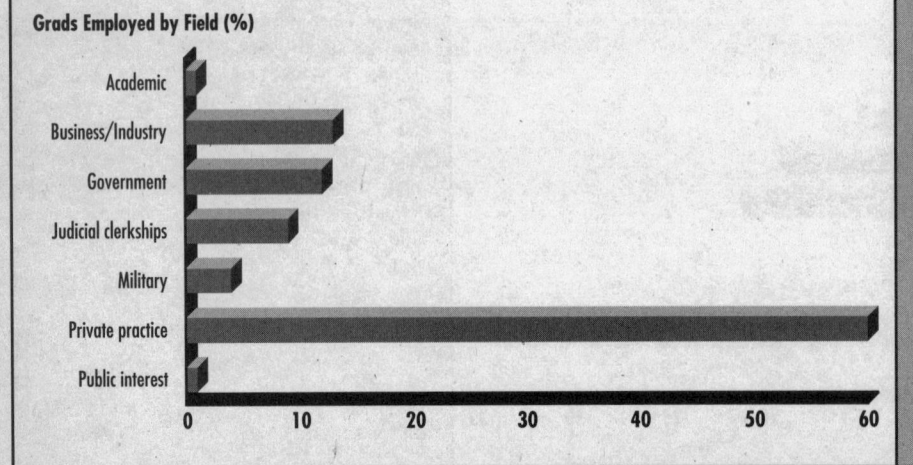

Grads Employed by Field (%)
- Academic
- Business/Industry
- Government
- Judicial clerkships
- Military
- Private practice
- Public interest

Rate of Placement: 98%
Average Starting Salary: $42,500
Employers Who Frequently Hire Grads: Major area and regional law firms, Tennessee Attorney General, Public Defender's Office, Tennessee Supreme Court and Court of Appeals, major area corporate legal departments, city and county government
State for Bar Exam: TN
Pass Rate for First-Time Bar: 92%

UNIVERSITY OF MIAMI
School of Law

Admissions Contact: Director of Student Recruiting, Therese Lambert
PO Box 248087, Coral Gables, FL 33124-8087
Admissions Phone: 305-284-6746 • Admissions Fax: 305-284-3084
Admissions E-mail: admissions@law.miami.edu • Web Address: www.law.miami.edu

INSTITUTIONAL INFORMATION
Public/Private: Private
Student/Faculty Ratio: 16:1
Total Faculty: 153
% Female: 25
% Minority: 10

PROGRAMS
Academic Specialties: International Law (3 courses are offered in Spanish); Taxation and Litigation Skills; Labor Law, Entertainment and Sports Law, Computer Law, Estate Panning, Human Rights Law, Public Interest Law, Civil Procedure, Commercial Law, Constitutional Law, Corporation Securities Law, Criminal Law, Environmental Law, Legal History, Legal Philosophy, Property
Advanced Degrees Offered: LLM Comparative Law (for graduates of foreign law schools), LLM Estate Planning, LLM Inter-American Law, LLM International Law, LLM Ocean and Coastal Law, LLM Real Property Development, LLM Taxation (all 1 year full time)
Combined Degrees Offered: JD/MBA, JD/MPH, JD/MSMA (all approximately 3.5 years)
Grading System: Letter system; some Pass/Fail
Clinical Program Required? No
Clinical Programs Description: Students enrolled in the Clinical Placement Program may represent indigent clients in both civil and criminal matters and may represent state and local agencies. Students may also enroll and work at a federal placement. Clinical students must also take Clinical Theory during the semester.
Legal Writing Course Requirements? Yes
Legal Writing Description: Legal Research and Writing is a required, 2-semester, first-year course that provides students with a strong grounding in legal writing, analysis, research, and oral advocacy. Students are assigned to writing instructors who work with students in small groups (approximately 20 students per group).
Legal Methods Course Requirements? Yes
Legal Methods Description: Required first-year course (see Legal Writing); advanced legal writing and research courses also available
Legal Research Course Requirements? Yes
Legal Research Description: See Legal Writing.
Moot Court Requirement? Yes
Moot Court Description: In the second semester of the Legal Research and Writing Program, students concentrate on brief writing and preparing for a moot court argument. Optional moot court competitions are sponsored by the Moot Court Board.
Public Interest Law Requirement? No
Academic Journals: *University of Miami Law Review, University of Miami Inter-American Law Review, Business Law Journal, International and Comparative Law Review, Tax Law Chronicle, Amicus Curiae, The Hearsay*

STUDENT INFORMATION
Enrollment of Law School: 1,079
% Out of State: 54
% Male/Female: 54/46
% Full Time: 88
% Full Time That Are International: 6
% Minority: 30
Average Age of Entering Class: 24

EXPENSES/FINANCIAL AID
Annual Tuition: $24,876
Room and Board: $9,360
Books and Supplies: $1,000
Financial Aid Application Deadline: 3/1
Average Grant: $15,755
Average Loan: $28,325
% of Aid That Is Merit-Based: 19
% Receiving Some Sort of Aid: 83
Average Total Aid Package: $31,700
Average Debt: $79,409
Tuition Per Credit: $848

ADMISSIONS INFORMATION
Application Fee: $50
Regular Application Deadline: 7/31
Regular Notification: Rolling
LSDAS Accepted? Yes
Average GPA: 3.3
Average LSAT: 153
Transfer Students Accepted? Yes
Other Schools to Which Students Applied: American University, Emory, Florida State, George Washington U., Nova Southeastern, Tulane, U. of Florida
Other Admissions Factors Considered: Undergraduate institution and major, LSAT writing sample, pattern and trend of grades, work and internship experience, graduate work, diversity
Number of Applications Received: 3,286
Number of Applicants Accepted: 1,569
Number of Applicants Enrolled: 418

INTERNATIONAL STUDENTS
TOEFL Required of International Students? Yes
Minimum TOEFL: 250

EMPLOYMENT INFORMATION

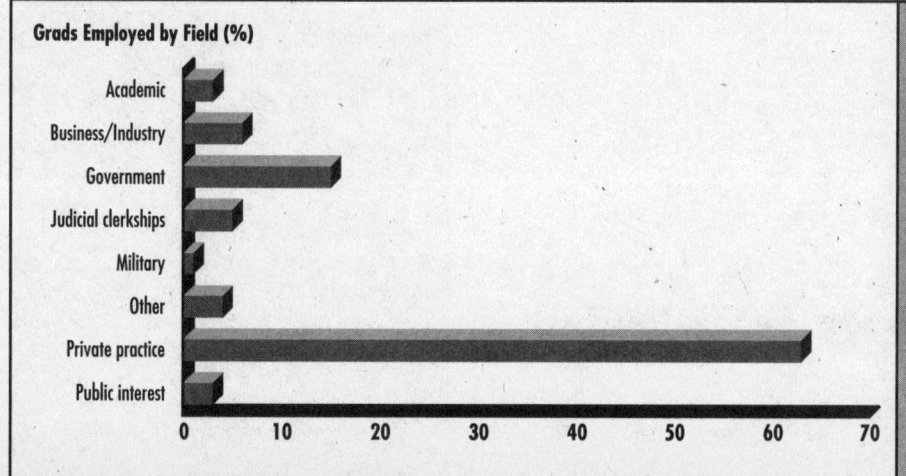

Grads Employed by Field (%)
- Academic
- Business/Industry
- Government
- Judicial clerkships
- Military
- Other
- Private practice
- Public interest

Rate of Placement: 90%
Average Starting Salary: $64,528
Employers Who Frequently Hire Grads: Steel, Hector & Davis; Greenberg, Traurig; Holland & Knight; White & Case; Weil, Gotshal & Manges; Morgan, Lewis & Bockius; Carlton Fields; Shutts & Bowen; Ruden, McClosky; Gunster, Yoakley; McDermott, Will & Emery; Dade County State Attorney; Dade County Public Defender; Broward County State Attorney; Broward County Public Defender; Legal Aid; Legal Services
State for Bar Exam: FL
Pass Rate for First-Time Bar: 86%

UNIVERSITY OF MICHIGAN
Law School

Admissions Contact: Assistant Dean and Director of Admissions, Sarah C. Zearfoss
726 Oakland Avenue, Ann Arbor, MI 48104-3031
Admissions Phone: 734-764-0537 • Admissions Fax: 734-647-3218
Admissions E-mail: law.jd.admissions@umich.edu • Web Address: www.law.umich.edu

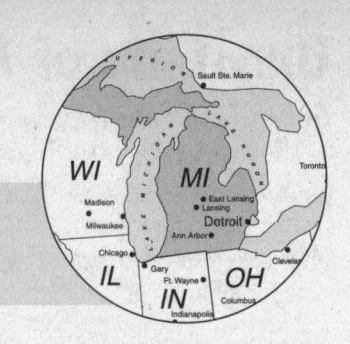

INSTITUTIONAL INFORMATION
Public/Private: Public
Student/Faculty Ratio: 14:1
Total Faculty: 122
% Part Time: 24
% Female: 27
% Minority: 6

PROGRAMS
Academic Specialties: Strong interdisciplinary legal scholarship and teaching; diverse clinical offerings. Specialties include Civil Procedure, Commercial Law, Constitutional Law, Corporation Securities Law, Criminal Law, Environmental Law, Government Services, Human Rights Law, Intellectual Property Law, International Law, Labor Law, Legal History, Legal Philosophy, Property, and Taxation.
Advanced Degrees Offered: LLM, MCL, SJD
Combined Degrees Offered: JD/MBA (4 years), JD/PhD Economics (5 years), JD/MA Modern Middle Eastern and North African Studies (3.5 to 4 years), JD/MPP (4 years), JD/MS Natural Resources (4 years), JD/MHSA (9 terms), JD/MA Russian and East European Studies (3.5 years), JD/MA World Politics (3.5 years), JD/MSW (8 terms), JD/MSI (8 terms), JD/MPH (8 terms), JD/MA Japanese Studies (3.5 years), JD/MUP (8 terms)
Clinical Program Required? No
Clinical Programs Description: General Clinic (civil or criminal concentration), Child Advocacy Law Clinic, Legal Assistance for Urban Communities Program, Environmental Law Clinic, Criminal Appellate Practice Clinic. In addition, there are student-run advocacy programs in which students volunteer to represent clients.
Legal Writing Course Requirements? Yes
Legal Writing Description: Michigan's unique Legal Practice Program provides first-year students with individual instruction in legal research and analysis, persuasive legal writing, and oral advocacy. Students are assigned to 1 of 9 full-time Legal Practice professors.
Legal Methods Course Requirements? Yes
Legal Methods Description: See Legal Writing.
Legal Research Course Requirements? Yes
Legal Research Description: See Legal Writing.
Moot Court Requirement? No
Public Interest Law Requirement? No
Academic Journals: *Michigan Law Review, Michigan Journal of Law Reform, Michigan Journal of International Law, Michigan Journal of Gender and Law, Michigan Journal of Race and Law, Michigan Telecommunications and Technology Law Review*

STUDENT INFORMATION
Enrollment of Law School: 1,098
% Male/Female: 57/43
% Full Time: 100
% Full Time That Are International: 0
% Minority: 23
Average Age of Entering Class: 24

RESEARCH FACILITIES
Research Resources Available: The Law School has one of the largest wireless Ethernet networks on campus, supporting law school students, faculty, and staff network access through multiple stationary access points located throughout the law school.

EXPENSES/FINANCIAL AID
Annual Tuition (Residents/Nonresidents): $23,164/$29,164
Room and Board: $8,150
Books and Supplies: $830
Average Grant: $10,737
Average Loan: $22,400
% of Aid That Is Merit-Based: 29
% Receiving Some Sort of Aid: 87
Average Total Aid Package: $31,718
Average Debt: $67,500

ADMISSIONS INFORMATION
Application Fee: $60
Regular Application Deadline: 2/15
Regular Notification: Rolling
LSDAS Accepted? Yes
Average GPA: 3.5
Range of GPA: 3.4–3.7
Average LSAT: 166
Range of LSAT: 164–168
Transfer Students Accepted? Yes
Other Schools to Which Students Applied: Columbia University, Georgetown University, Harvard University, New York University, University of California—Berkeley, University of Chicago, Yale University
Number of Applications Received: 4,022
Number of Applicants Accepted: 1,169
Number of Applicants Enrolled: 362

EMPLOYMENT INFORMATION

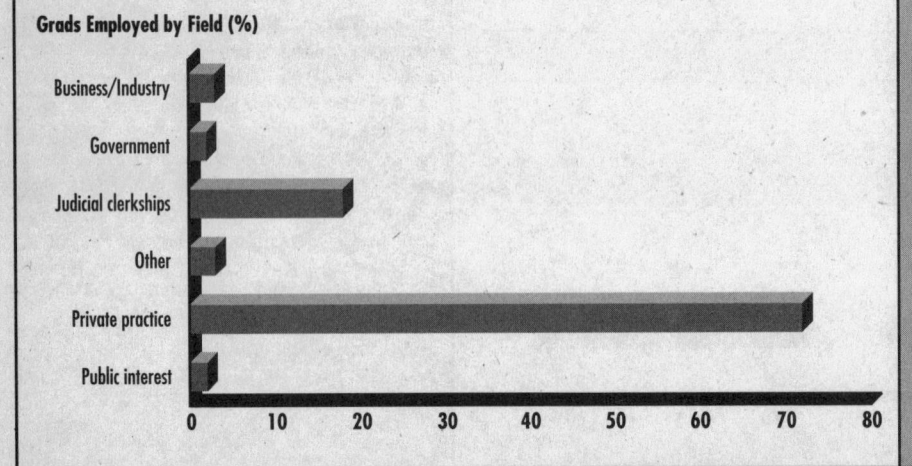

Grads Employed by Field (%):
- Business/Industry
- Government
- Judicial clerkships
- Other
- Private practice
- Public interest

Rate of Placement: 99%
Average Starting Salary: $102,615
State for Bar Exam: NY, IL, CA, MI, MA

UNIVERSITY OF MINNESOTA
Law School

Admissions Contact: Director of Admissions, Collins B. Byrd, Jr.
229 19th Avenue South, Minneapolis, MN 55455
Admissions Phone: 612-625-5005 • Admissions Fax: 612-625-2011
Admissions E-mail: umnlsadm@tc.umn.edu • Web Address: www.law.umn.edu

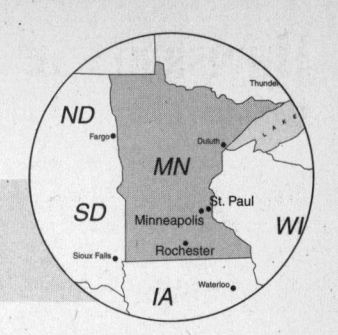

INSTITUTIONAL INFORMATION
Public/Private: Public
Environment: Urban
Academic Calendar: Semester
Schedule: Full time only
Student/Faculty Ratio: 16:1
Total Faculty: 44
% Part Time: 100
% Female: 30
% Minority: 11

PROGRAMS
Academic Specialties: Public Law, Public and Private International Law, Constitutional Law, Criminal Law, Corporate and Business Law, Regulatory Law, Legislation, Human Rights Law, Legal Philosophy, Law Clinic
Advanced Degrees Offered: LLM for foreign lawyers (1 year)
Combined Degrees Offered: JD/MBA, JD/MPA, joint degrees available with most graduate programs (all are 4 years)
Grading System: Numerical system on a 4 to 16 scale
Clinical Program Required? No
Clinical Program Description: 16 separate clinics, including Bankruptcy, Child Advocacy, Civil Litigation, Criminal Appeals, Disability, Domestic Abuse, Federal Prosecution, Federal Taxation, Housing, Immigration, Indian Child Welfare, Law and Violence Against Women, Legal Assistance
Legal Writing/Methods Course Requirements: 3 years of writing requirements

STUDENT INFORMATION
Enrollment of Law School: 744
% Male/Female: 53/47
% Full Time: 100
% Full Time That Are International: 2
% Minority: 17
Average Age of Entering Class: 24

RESEARCH FACILITIES
School-Supported Research Centers: 6 international exchanges programs in France, Germany, Ireland, the Netherlands, Spain, and Sweden

EXPENSES/FINANCIAL AID
Annual Tuition (Residents/Nonresidents): $9,000/$15,300
Average Grant: $6,300
Average Loan: $17,500
% Receiving Some Sort of Aid: 91
Average Debt: $38,000

ADMISSIONS INFORMATION
Application Fee: $40
Regular Application Deadline: 3/1
Regular Notification: Rolling
LSDAS Accepted? Yes
Average GPA: 3.6
Range of GPA: 3.3–3.8
Average LSAT: 162
Range of LSAT: 158–164
Transfer Students Accepted? Yes
Other Schools to Which Students Applied: University of Wisconsin, University of Michigan, William Mitchell College of Law, Hamline University, Yale University, Harvard University, Georgetown University, University of Iowa
Number of Applications Received: 1,467

INTERNATIONAL STUDENTS
TOEFL Required of International Students? Yes

EMPLOYMENT INFORMATION

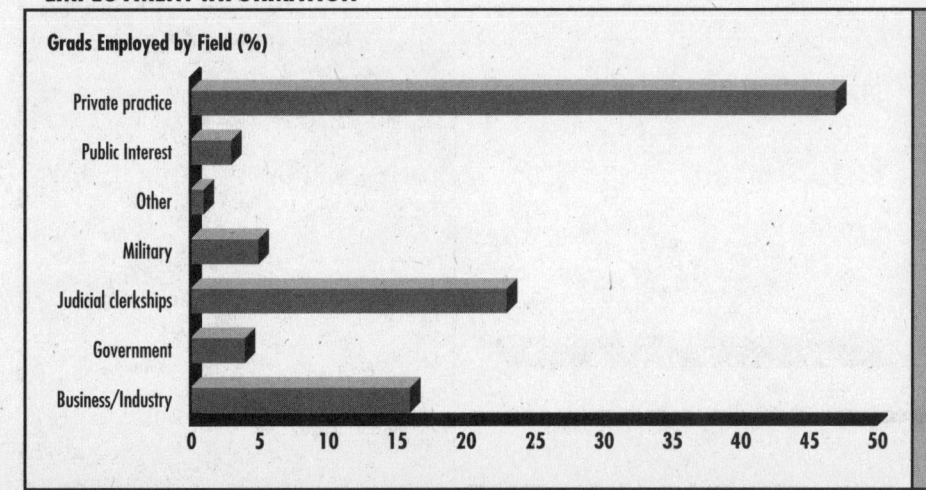

Grads Employed by Field (%)
- Private practice: ~48
- Public Interest: ~3
- Other: ~2
- Military: ~4
- Judicial clerkships: ~23
- Government: ~3
- Business/Industry: ~16

Rate of Placement: 99%
Average Starting Salary: $60,000
Prominent Alumni: Walter Mondale, former vice president and ambassador to Japan; James Blanchard, former governor of Michigan and ambassador to Canada; Constance Barry Newman, director of the U.S. Office of Personnel Management; Robert Stein, executive director of the American Bar Association; A. W. Clausen, former president of the World Bank, and CEO of Bank America; Michael Sullivan, president of International Dairy Queen; Michael Wright, President of SUPERVALU Inc.; over 250 federal and state court judges nationwide

UNIVERSITY OF MISSISSIPPI
Lamar Hall

Admissions Contact: Director of Admissions, Barbara Vinson
School of Law, Room 310, University, MS 38677
Admissions Phone: 662-915-6910 • Admissions Fax: 662-915-1289
Admissions E-mail: lawmiss@olemiss.edu • Web Address: www.olemiss.edu/depts/law_school/law-hom.html

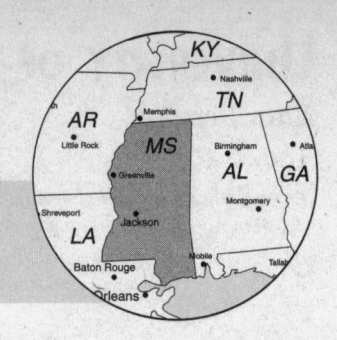

INSTITUTIONAL INFORMATION
Public/Private: Public
Student/Faculty Ratio: 22:1
Total Faculty: 36
% Part Time: 22
% Female: 19
% Minority: 8

PROGRAMS
Academic Specialties: Solid legal education in all areas with particular strength in Tax and Business, International, and Environmental Law
Combined Degrees Offered: JD/MBA (5 years)
Grading System: A (4.0), B+ (3.5), B (3.0), C+ (2.5), C (2.0), D+ (1.5), D (1.0), F (0.0), Z (pass), X (audit), W (withdraw), I (incomplete)
Clinical Program Required? No
Clinical Programs Description: Prosecutorial Externship, Criminal Appeals Clinic, Public Service Internships (3 to 6 hours)
Legal Writing Course Requirements? Yes
Legal Writing Description: A 6-credit hour course is required in the first year. The first semester (3 hours) covers the study and practice of basic legal research and legal writing skills, primarily using state materials and focusing on objective legal writing. The second semester (3 hours) continues with more complex legal problems, primarily federal materials, and a focus on persuasive legal writing.
Legal Methods Course Requirements? Yes
Legal Methods Description: 1-year Legal Research and Writing, advanced skills writing requirement

Legal Research Course Requirements? Yes
Legal Research Description: See Legal Writing.
Moot Court Requirement? Yes
Moot Court Description: First year, oral arguments; second/third year, appellate and trial requirement
Public Interest Law Requirement? No
Academic Journals: *Mississippi Law Journal, The Journal of National Security Law*

STUDENT INFORMATION
Enrollment of Law School: 480
% Out of State: 16
% Male/Female: 59/41
% Full Time: 100
% Full Time That Are International: 0
% Minority: 12
Average Age of Entering Class: 23

RESEARCH FACILITIES
School-Supported Research Centers: Sea Grant Legal Program, Mississippi Law Research Institute, National Center for Justice and the Rule of Law, National Center for Remote Sensing and Space Law

EXPENSES/FINANCIAL AID
Annual Tuition (Residents/Nonresidents): $5,654/$11,142
Room and Board: $9,828
Books and Supplies: $1,200
Average Grant: $3,393
Average Loan: $15,334
% of Aid That Is Merit-Based: 90

Average Total Aid Package: $15,417
Average Debt: $38,134

ADMISSIONS INFORMATION
Application Fee: $25
Regular Application Deadline: 3/1
Regular Notification: 4/15
LSDAS Accepted? Yes
Average GPA: 3.5
Range of GPA: 3.1–3.7
Average LSAT: 153
Range of LSAT: 150–157
Transfer Students Accepted? Yes
Other Schools to Which Students Applied: Mississippi College, University of Alabama, University of Tennessee
Other Admissions Factors Considered: Grade patterns and progression, difficulty of major field of study, job experience, social or economic circumstances, nonacademic achievements, letters of recommendation, residency
Number of Applications Received: 1,165
Number of Applicants Accepted: 411
Number of Applicants Enrolled: 163

INTERNATIONAL STUDENTS
TOEFL Required of International Students? Yes
Minimum TOEFL: 263

EMPLOYMENT INFORMATION

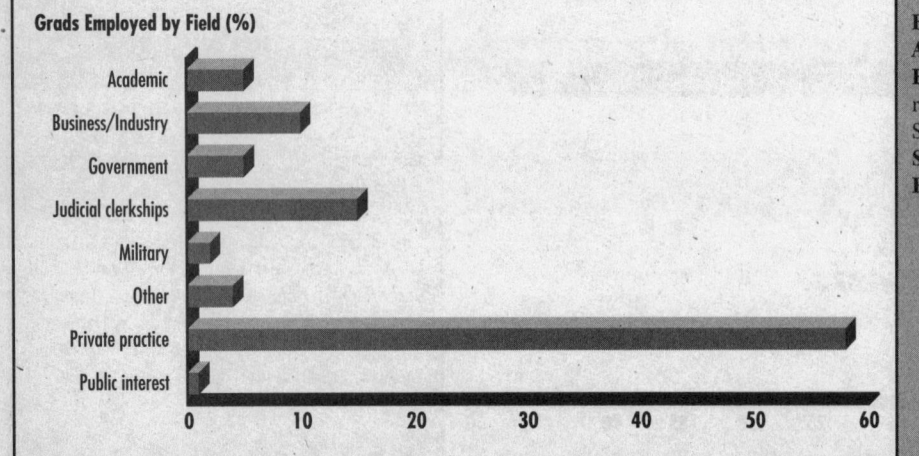

Grads Employed by Field (%)
- Academic
- Business/Industry
- Government
- Judicial clerkships
- Military
- Other
- Private practice
- Public interest

Rate of Placement: 98%
Average Starting Salary: $54,000
Employers Who Frequently Hire Grads: Top regional employers from across the South and Southeast
State for Bar Exam: MS, TN, GA, FL, TX
Pass Rate for First-Time Bar: 95%

UNIVERSITY OF MISSOURI—COLUMBIA
School of Law

Admissions Contact: Assistant Dean, Donna Pavlick
103 Hulston Hall, Columbia, MO 65211
Admissions Phone: 573-882-6042 • Admissions Fax: 573-882-9625
Admissions E-mail: umclawadmissions@missouri.edu • Web Address: www.law.missouri.edu

INSTITUTIONAL INFORMATION
Public/Private: Public
Student/Faculty Ratio: 16:1
Total Faculty: 36
% Part Time: 25
% Female: 27
% Minority: 1

PROGRAMS
Academic Specialties: Dispute Resolution, Criminal Law, Environmental Law, International Law, Labor Law, Property, Taxation
Advanced Degrees Offered: LLM Dispute Resolution (1 year)
Combined Degrees Offered: JD/MBA (4 years), JD/MPA (4 years), JD/MA Economics (4 years), JD/MA Human Development and Family Studies (4 years), JD/MA Educational Leadership and Policy Analysis (4 years), JD/MA Journalism (4 years), JD/PhD Journalism (5 years), JD/MALIS (4 years)
Grading System: Numerical system, ranging 100 to 55. Minimum 70 GPA required for graduation.
Clinical Program Required? No
Clinical Programs Description: Family Violence Clinic, Criminal Clinic, Mediation Clinic
Legal Writing Course Requirements? No
Legal Methods Course Requirements? Yes
Legal Methods Description: 2 hours fall and winter of first year; includes research, writing, and oral advocacy
Legal Research Course Requirements? No

Moot Court Requirement? Yes
Moot Court Description: Second- and third-year students selected based on competitions and GPA. Students are awarded credit for each competition. 1 full year of law school.
Public Interest Law Requirement? No
Academic Journals: *Missouri Law Review, Journal of Dispute Resolution, Missouri Environmental Law and Policy Review*

STUDENT INFORMATION
Enrollment of Law School: 543
% Out of State: 14
% Male/Female: 61/39
% Full Time: 99
% Full Time That Are International: 1
% Minority: 11
Average Age of Entering Class: 24

RESEARCH FACILITIES
School-Supported Research Centers: Center for the Study of Dispute Resolution

EXPENSES/FINANCIAL AID
Annual Tuition (Residents/Nonresidents): $10,462/$20,221
Room and Board (On/Off Campus): $6,912
Books and Supplies: $1,200
Financial Aid Application Deadline: 3/1

Average Grant: $4,000
Average Loan: $16,500
% Receiving Some Sort of Aid: 90
Average Debt: $48,442

ADMISSIONS INFORMATION
Application Fee: $40
Regular Application Deadline: Rolling
Regular Notification: Rolling
LSDAS Accepted? Yes
Average GPA: 3.3
Range of GPA: 3.0–3.7
Average LSAT: 155
Range of LSAT: 153–158
Transfer Students Accepted? Yes
Other Schools to Which Students Applied: Saint Louis University, University of Missouri—Kansas City, Washington University
Other Admissions Factors Considered: Applicant's suitability for career
Number of Applications Received: 733
Number of Applicants Accepted: 446
Number of Applicants Enrolled: 185

INTERNATIONAL STUDENTS
TOEFL Required of International Students? Yes
Minimum TOEFL: 250

EMPLOYMENT INFORMATION

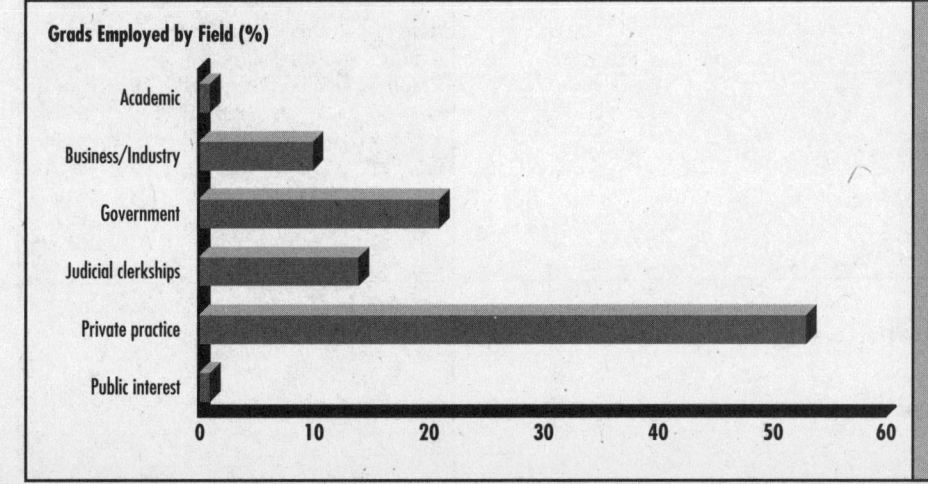

Grads Employed by Field (%)
- Academic: ~1
- Business/Industry: ~10
- Government: ~22
- Judicial clerkships: ~14
- Private practice: ~53
- Public interest: ~1

Rate of Placement: 92%
Average Starting Salary: $46,506
Employers Who Frequently Hire Grads: Shook, Hardy & Bacon (Kansas City); Missouri Attorney General's Office; Missouri Court of Appeals; Thompson Coburn (St. Louis); Missouri Supreme Court; Arthur Andersen; Blackwell, Sanders, Peper, Martin (Kansas City and St. Louis)
State for Bar Exam: MO, IL, TX, KS, CA
Pass Rate for First-Time Bar: 90%

UNIVERSITY OF MISSOURI—KANSAS CITY
School of Law

Admissions Contact: Director of Admissions, Jean Klosterman
5100 Rockhill Road, Kansas City, MO 64110
Admissions Phone: 816-235-1644 • Admissions Fax: 816-235-5276
Admissions E-mail: klostermanm@umkc.edu • Web Address: www.law.umkc.edu

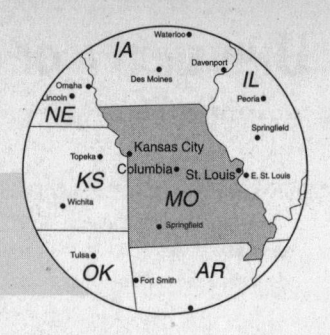

INSTITUTIONAL INFORMATION
Public/Private: Public
Student/Faculty Ratio: 18:1
Total Faculty: 34
% Part Time: 6
% Female: 30
% Minority: 6

PROGRAMS
Academic Specialties: Law students do not have a formal major, but many students desire to take a concentration of courses in one of the many practice areas, including Advocacy and Litigation, Business and Tax Law, Commercial Law, Estate Planning and Administration, Criminal Law and Procedure, Domestic Relations, Labor and Employment, International Law, Property and Real Estate, Civil Liberties and Civil Rights, and Environmental Law. In addition, through participation in the mentor program, externships, competitions, journals, and student organizations, students are able to develop skills and contacts in specialized areas of the law. Other specialties include Taxation.
Advanced Degrees Offered: LLM (1 to 3 years)
Combined Degrees Offered: JD/MBA (3 to 4 years), JD/LLM (3.5 to 4 years)
Grading System: A, B, C, D, F (with plus and minus)
Clinical Program Required? No
Clinical Programs: Students counsel clients in federal, state, and local tax controversy matters in the Kansas City Tax Clinic under the supervision and direction of tax faculty, clinic director, and volunteer attorneys.

Legal Writing Course Requirements? No
Legal Methods Course Requirements? Yes
Legal Methods Description: 5-hour course split between a student's first 2 semesters. First semester consists of an introduction to legal reasoning; case analysis and synthesis; case research; and structure and style in legal writing with emphasis on expository writing, including office memoranda. Second semester includes introduction to advocacy; introduction to interviewing, counseling, and negotiation; statutory and computerized research; writing to and on behalf of a client, including a trial or appellate brief; and oral advocacy.
Legal Research Course Requirements? No
Moot Court Requirement? Yes
Moot Court Description: Students write and argue an appellate brief in their Introduction to Law and Lawyering Processes class.
Public Interest Law Requirement? No
Academic Journals: *Law Review, Urban Lawyer, Journal of the American Academy of Matrimonial Lawyers*

STUDENT INFORMATION
Enrollment of Law School: 485
% Male/Female: 51/49
% Full Time: 94
% Full Time That Are International: 1
% Minority: 16
Average Age of Entering Class: 27

EXPENSES/FINANCIAL AID
Annual Tuition (Residents/Nonresidents): $8,814/$17,624
Room and Board (On/Off Campus): $9,740/$11,690
Books and Supplies: $1,520
Financial Aid Application Deadline: 3/1
Average Grant: $4,500
Average Loan: $18,512
% Receiving Some Sort of Aid: 33
Tuition Per Credit (Residents/Nonresidents): $315/$630
Fees Per Credit: $26

ADMISSIONS INFORMATION
Application Fee: $25
Regular Application Deadline: Rolling
Regular Notification: Rolling
LSDAS Accepted? Yes
Average GPA: 3.2
Range of GPA: 2.1–4.0
Average LSAT: 154
Range of LSAT: 150–156
Transfer Students Accepted? Yes
Other Admissions Factors Considered: Extracurricular activities, work experience, advanced degrees, efforts to overcome societally imposed disadvantages
Number of Applications Received: 646
Number of Applicants Accepted: 401
Number of Applicants Enrolled: 165

EMPLOYMENT INFORMATION

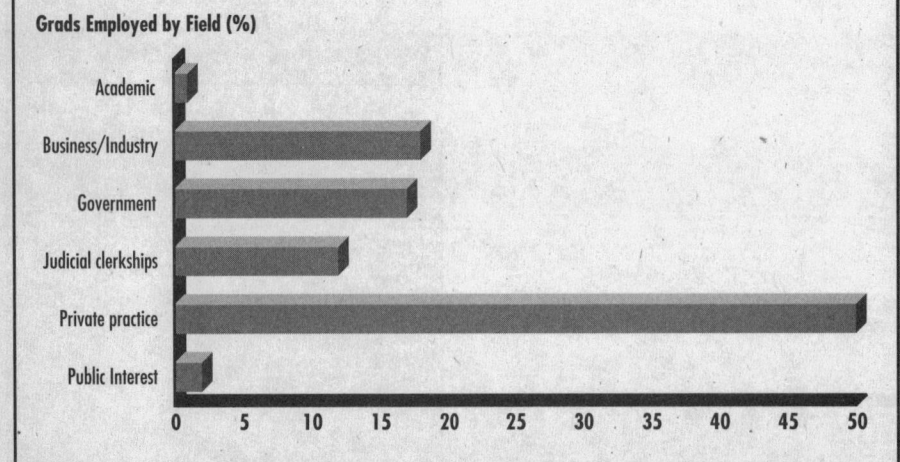

Grads Employed by Field (%)
- Academic: ~1
- Business/Industry: ~17
- Government: ~15
- Judicial clerkships: ~12
- Private practice: ~50
- Public Interest: ~2

Rate of Placement: 92%
Average Starting Salary: $46,088
Employers Who Frequently Hire Grads: Jackson County, Missouri, Prosecutor; Shook, Hardy & Bacon; Blackwell, Sanders, Peper, Martin, LLP; Bryan Cave, LLP; United Missouri Bank; Shughart, Thomson & Kilroy, PC; Lathrop & Gage, LC; Stinson, Mag & Fizzell, PC; Morrison & Hecker, LLP; Husch & Eppenberger, LLC
State for Bar Exam: MO
Pass Rate for First-Time Bar: 76%

UNIVERSITY OF MONTANA
School of Law

Admissions Contact: Director of Admissions, Heidi Fanslow
University of Montana School of Law, Missoula, MT 59812
Admissions Phone: 406-243-2698 • Admissions Fax: 406-243-2576
Admissions E-mail: lawadmis@selway.umt.edu • Web Address: www.umt.edu/law/

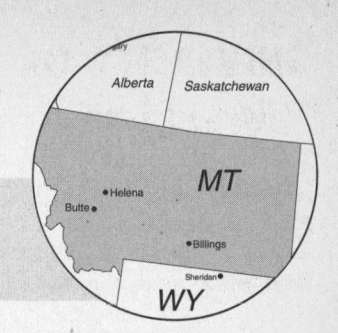

INSTITUTIONAL INFORMATION
Public/Private: Public
Environment: Urban
Academic Calendar: Semester
Schedule: Full time only
Student/Faculty Ratio: 15:1
Total Faculty: 22
% Part Time: 18
% Female: 32
% Minority: 5

PROGRAMS
Academic Specialties: Competency-based curriculum, Environmental and Indian Law
Advanced Degrees Offered: JD (3 years)
Combined Degrees Offered: JD/MPA (4 years), JD/MS Environmental Studies (4 years)
Grading System: Students are not graded on mandatory curve.
Clinical Program Required? Yes
Clinical Program Description: Criminal Defense, Indian Law, Prosecution, Legal Aid, Disability, Judicial

STUDENT INFORMATION
Enrollment of Law School: 235
% Male/Female: 58/42
% Full Time: 100
% Minority: 7
Average Age of Entering Class: 28

RESEARCH FACILITIES
Computers/Workstations Available: 45

EXPENSES/FINANCIAL AID
Annual Tuition (Residents/Nonresidents): $6,882/$12,484
Room and Board: $7,510
Books and Supplies: $910
Average Grant: $1,457
Average Loan: $14,349
% of Aid That Is Merit-Based: 3
% Receiving Some Sort of Aid: 87
Average Total Aid Package: $14,619
Average Debt: $35,507

ADMISSIONS INFORMATION
Application Fee: $60
Regular Application Deadline: 3/1
Regular Notification: Rolling
LSDAS Accepted? Yes
Average GPA: 3.2
Range of GPA: 3.0–3.4
Average LSAT: 153
Range of LSAT: 149–157
Transfer Students Accepted? Yes
Other Schools to Which Students Applied: Lewis and Clark College, University of Oregon, Gonzaga University, University of Idaho, Willamette University, University of Colorado, University of Wyoming, University of Denver
Other Admissions Factors Considered: Ability to overcome economic or other disadvantage
Number of Applications Received: 362
Number of Applicants Accepted: 225
Number of Applicants Enrolled: 73

INTERNATIONAL STUDENTS
TOEFL Required of International Students? Yes
Minimum TOEFL: 600

EMPLOYMENT INFORMATION

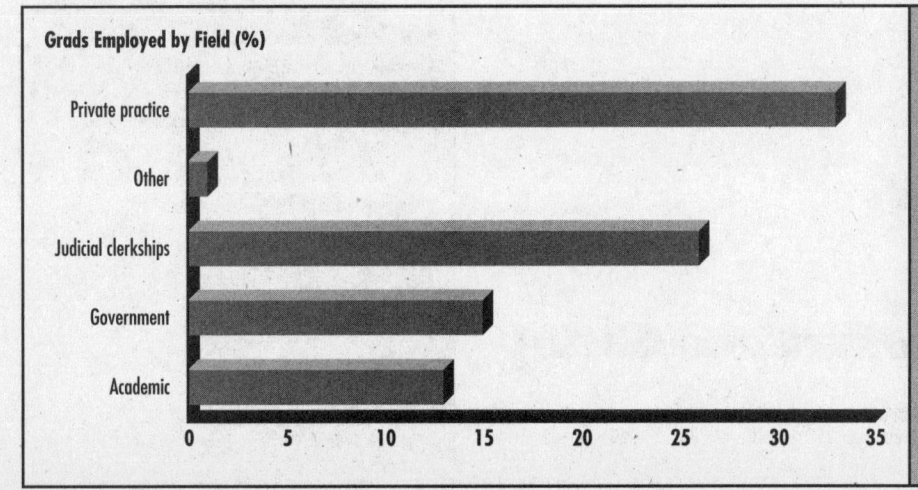

Grads Employed by Field (%)
- Private practice: ~33
- Other: ~1
- Judicial clerkships: ~26
- Government: ~15
- Academic: ~13

Rate of Placement: 93%
Average Starting Salary: $34,149
Employers Who Frequently Hire Grads: Church, Harris, Johnson and Williams; Moulton, Bellingham, Longo & Mather; Crowley, Haughy, Hanson, Toole & Dietrich
Prominent Alumni: Governor Marc Racicot; Hon. James R. Browning, 9th Circuit Court of Appeals; Hon. William J. Jameson (deceased) former American Bar Association president, former president of American Judicature Society, recipent of the American Bar Association Medal

UNIVERSITY OF NEBRASKA — LINCOLN
College of Law

Admissions Contact: Associate Dean, Glenda J. Pierce
PO Box 830902, Lincoln, NE 68583-0902
Admissions Phone: 402-472-2161 • Admissions Fax: 402-472-5185
Admissions E-mail: lawadm@unl.edu • Web Address: www.unl.edu/lawcoll

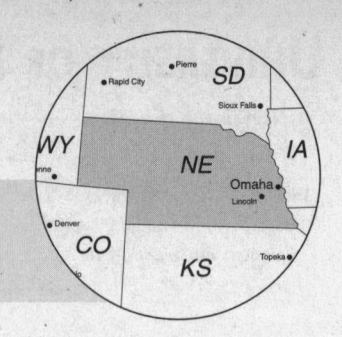

INSTITUTIONAL INFORMATION
Public/Private: Public
Student/Faculty Ratio: 14:1
Total Faculty: 56
% Part Time: 50
% Female: 28
% Minority: 4

PROGRAMS
Academic Specialties: Faculty with national/international reputations in Tort Law, Intellectual Property Law, and Labor and Employment Law. Eight College of Law faculty have published casebooks used as teaching materials in law schools throughout the country. Other specialties include Commercial Law, Corporation Securities Law, Environmental Law, International Law, Labor Law Taxation, and Litigation.
Advanced Degrees Offered: JD (3 years), MLS (1 year)
Combined Degrees Offered: JD/PhD Psychology (6 years), JD/MA Economics (4 years), JD/MBA (4 years), JD/MPA (4 years), JD/MA Political Science (4 years), JD/MCRP (4 years), JD/PhD Education Administration (5 years), JD/MAIA (4 years)
Grading System: A+ (9), A (8), B+ (7), B (6), C+ (5), C (4), D+ (3), D (2), F (0)
Clinical Program Required? No
Clinical Programs Description: Criminal Prosecution Clinic, Civil Clinic
Legal Writing Course Requirements? Yes
Legal Writing Description: Legal Research and Writing (6 credit hours, 2 semesters during the first year)
Legal Methods Course Requirements? No
Legal Research Course Requirements? Yes
Legal Research Description: See Legal Writing.
Moot Court Requirement? No
Moot Court Description: The Nebraska Moot Court Board is composed of students selected on the basis of either their class rank or their performance in an annual writing competition.
Public Interest Law Requirement? No
Academic Journals: *The Nebraska Law Journal*

STUDENT INFORMATION
Enrollment of Law School: 396
% Out of State: 29
% Male/Female: 54/46
% Full Time: 100
% Full Time That Are International: 1
% Minority: 8
Average Age of Entering Class: 24

RESEARCH FACILITIES
Research Resources Available: Thanks to the school's location in the state capital, students have access to government offices, the state legislature, and the courts.
School-Supported Research Centers: Center for Children, Families, and the Law; Center for the Teaching and Study of Applied Ethics

EXPENSES/FINANCIAL AID
Annual Tuition (Residents/Nonresidents): $4,743/$12,717
Room and Board (On/Off Campus): $7,926/$8,892
Books and Supplies: $1,040
Financial Aid Application Deadline: 3/1
Average Grant: $4,742
Average Loan: $13,394
% of Aid That Is Merit-Based: 50
% Receiving Some Sort of Aid: 85
Average Total Aid Package: $15,000
Average Debt: $39,300

ADMISSIONS INFORMATION
Application Fee: $25
Regular Application Deadline: 3/1
Regular Notification: Rolling
LSDAS Accepted? Yes
Average GPA: 3.6
Range of GPA: 3.3–3.8
Average LSAT: 153
Range of LSAT: 150–156
Transfer Students Accepted? Yes
Other Schools to Which Students Applied: Creighton University, Drake University, University of Iowa, University of Kansas, University of Minnesota, Washburn University
Other Admissions Factors Considered: Major, courses taken and their level of difficulty, upward or downward trend in undergraduate GPA, graduate study, work experience, extracurricular activities
Number of Applications Received: 551
Number of Applicants Accepted: 334
Number of Applicants Enrolled: 152

INTERNATIONAL STUDENTS
TOEFL Required of International Students? Yes
Minimum TOEFL: 250

EMPLOYMENT INFORMATION

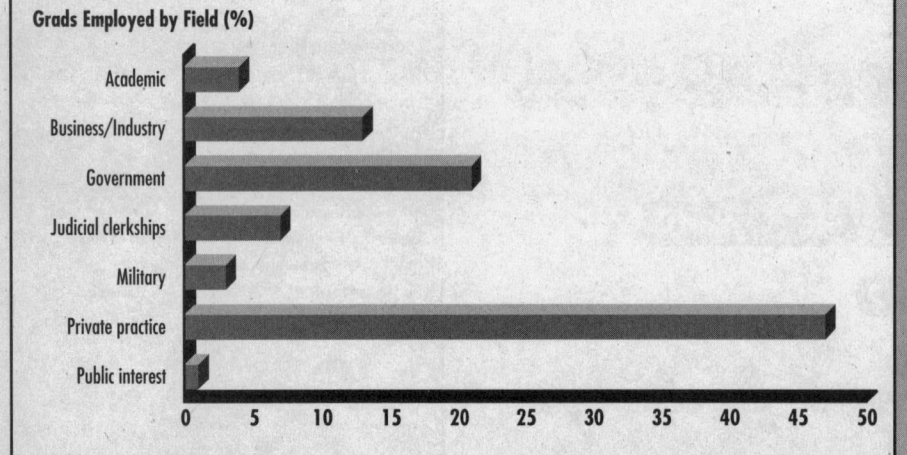

Grads Employed by Field (%)

Field	%
Academic	~2
Business/Industry	~8
Government	~21
Judicial clerkships	~7
Military	~3
Private practice	~47
Public interest	~1

Rate of Placement: 96%
Average Starting Salary: $43,500
Employers Who Frequently Hire Grads: Very small law firms (2–10 attorneys), small law firms (11–25 attorneys), state government
State for Bar Exam: NE, AZ, CA, IL, MO
Pass Rate for First-Time Bar: 90%

UNIVERSITY OF NEW MEXICO
School of Law

Admissions Contact: Director of Admissions, Susan Mitchell
1117 Stanford, NE, Albuquerque, NM 87131
Admissions Phone: 505-277-0158 • Admissions Fax: 505-277-9958
Admissions E-mail: mitchell@law.unm.edu • Web Address: lawschool.unm.edu

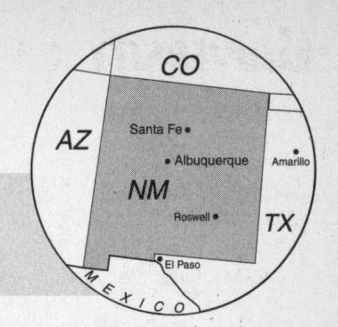

INSTITUTIONAL INFORMATION
Public/Private: Public
Student/Faculty Ratio: 12:1
Total Faculty: 34
% Female: 44
% Minority: 27

PROGRAMS
Advanced Degrees Offered: JD (3 years)
Combined Degrees Offered: JD/MA, JD/MS, JD/PhD, JD/MAPA, JD/MA Latin American Studies (4 years)
Grading System: 4.0 scale; students must maintain a GPA of at least 2.0
Clinical Program Required? Yes
Clinical Programs Description: Southwest Indian Law Clinic, District Attorney Clinic, Law Practice Clinic, Community Lawyering Clinic
Legal Writing Course Requirements? Yes
Legal Writing Description: Legal Research/Writing course required during first year
Legal Methods Course Requirements? No
Legal Research Course Requirements? Yes
Legal Research Description: Legal Research/Writing course required during first year
Moot Court Requirement? No
Public Interest Law Requirement? No
Academic Journals: *Natural Resources Journal, New Mexico Law Review, Tribal Law Journal* (online), *US-Mexico Law Journal*

STUDENT INFORMATION
Enrollment of Law School: 345
% Male/Female: 41/59
% Full Time: 100
% Minority: 36
Average Age of Entering Class: 30

EXPENSES/FINANCIAL AID
Annual Tuition (Residents/Nonresidents): $5,040/$16,872
Books and Supplies: $850
Financial Aid Application Deadline: 3/1
Average Grant: $4,600
Average Loan: $13,900

ADMISSIONS INFORMATION
Application Fee: $40
Regular Application Deadline: 2/15
Regular Notification: Rolling
LSDAS Accepted? Yes
Average GPA: 3.2
Range of GPA: 2.8–3.4
Average LSAT: 154
Range of LSAT: 150–158
Transfer Students Accepted? Yes
Other Admissions Factors Considered: Preference given to New Mexico residents
Number of Applications Received: 673
Number of Applicants Accepted: 251
Number of Applicants Enrolled: 104

INTERNATIONAL STUDENTS
TOEFL Required of International Students? Yes

EMPLOYMENT INFORMATION

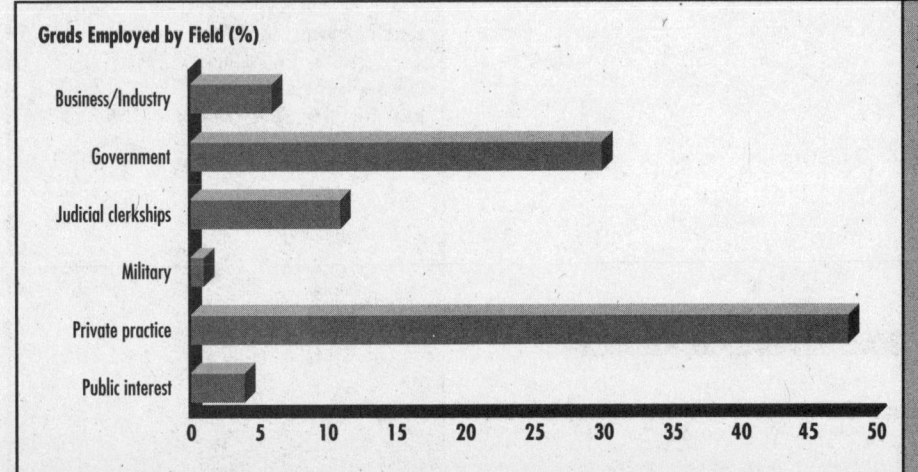

Grads Employed by Field (%)
- Business/Industry: ~5
- Government: ~30
- Judicial clerkships: ~10
- Military: ~1
- Private practice: ~48
- Public interest: ~5

Rate of Placement: 87%
Average Starting Salary: $41,000
State for Bar Exam: NM
Pass Rate for First-Time Bar: 95%

UNIVERSITY OF NORTH CAROLINA — CHAPEL HILL
School of Law

Admissions Contact: Assistant Dean for Admissions, Victoria Taylor Carter
Campus Box 3380, Chapel Hill, NC 27599
Admissions Phone: 919-962-5109 • Admissions Fax: 919-843-7939
Admissions E-mail: law_admission@unc.edu • Web Address: www.law.unc.edu

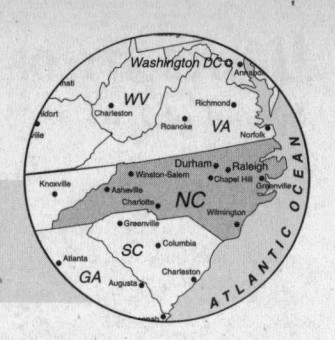

INSTITUTIONAL INFORMATION
Public/Private: Public
Student/Faculty Ratio: 15:1
Total Faculty: 84
% Part Time: 47
% Female: 32
% Minority: 6

PROGRAMS
Academic Specialties: Civil Procedure, Commercial Law, Constitutional Law, Corporation Securities Law, Criminal Law, Environmental Law, Government Services, Human Rights Law, International Law, Labor Law, Legal History, Legal Philosophy, Property, Taxation
Combined Degrees Offered: JD/MBA (4 years), JD/MPA (4 years), JD/MPPS (4 years), JD/MPH (4 years), JD/MRP (4 years), JD/MSW (4 years)
Grading System: Numerical system ranging from 4.3 to 0.0
Clinical Program Required? No
Clinical Program Description: Live Client Clinics in criminal and civil law, simulation programs in trial advocacy, dispute resolution
Legal Writing Course Requirements? Yes

Legal Writing Description: Research, Reasoning, Writing and Advocacy (RRWA) is a required first-year course that provides intensive instruction in the basics of legal reasoning and in communicating accurate legal analysis clearly, both orally and in writing.
Legal Methods Course Requirements? No
Legal Research Course Requirements? Yes
Legal Research Description: See Legal Writing.
Moot Court Requirement? No
Public Interest Law Requirement? No
Academic Journals: *North Carolina Banking Institute Journal, North Carolina Law Review, North Carolina Journal of International Law and Commercial Regulation, North Carolina Journal of Law and Technology*

STUDENT INFORMATION
Enrollment of Law School: 780
% Out of State: 25
% Male/Female: 48/52
% Full Time: 100
% Full Time That Are International: 1
% Minority: 14

EXPENSES/FINANCIAL AID
Annual Tuition (Residents/Nonresidents): $5,031/$17,131
Room and Board (On Campus): $7,695
Books and Supplies: $800
Average Grant: $2,800
Average Debt: $33,982

ADMISSIONS INFORMATION
Application Fee: $60
Regular Application Deadline: Rolling
Regular Notification: Rolling
LSDAS Accepted? Yes
Average GPA: 3.6
Range of GPA: 3.4–3.8
Average LSAT: 159
Range of LSAT: 156–164
Transfer Students Accepted? Yes
Other Schools to Which Students Applied: Villanova University
Number of Applications Received: 2,649
Number of Applicants Accepted: 718
Number of Applicants Enrolled: 325

EMPLOYMENT INFORMATION

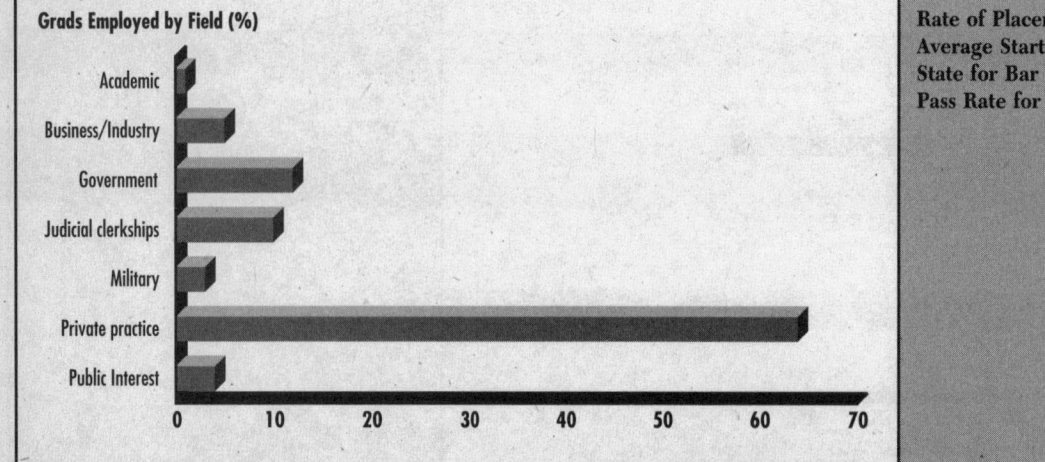

Grads Employed by Field (%)
- Academic: ~2
- Business/Industry: ~4
- Government: ~12
- Judicial clerkships: ~12
- Military: ~1
- Private practice: ~65
- Public Interest: ~3

Rate of Placement: 99%
Average Starting Salary: $53,781
State for Bar Exam: NC
Pass Rate for First-Time Bar: 81%

254 • COMPLETE BOOK OF LAW SCHOOLS

UNIVERSITY OF NORTH DAKOTA
School of Law

Admissions Contact: Admissions and Records Associate, Linda D. Kohoutek
Centennial Drive PO Box 9003, Grand Forks, ND 58202
Admissions Phone: 701-777-2260 • Admissions Fax: 701-777-2217
Admissions E-mail: mark.brickson@thor.law.und.nodak.edu • Web Address: www.law.und.nodak.edu

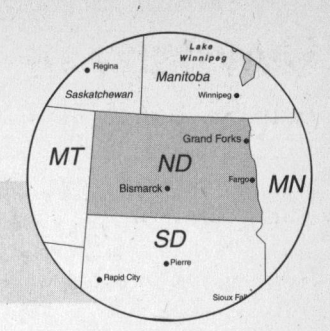

INSTITUTIONAL INFORMATION
Public/Private: Public
Student/Faculty Ratio: 11:1
Total Faculty: 18
% Part Time: 5
% Female: 39
% Minority: 1

PROGRAMS
Advanced Degrees Offered: JD (3 years)
Combined Degrees Offered: JD/MPA (4 years)
Grading System: A to F
Clinical Program Required? No
Legal Writing Course Requirements? Yes
Legal Writing Description: Fall and spring of first year
Legal Methods Course Requirements? Yes
Legal Methods Description: Fall and spring of first year
Legal Research Course Requirements? Yes
Legal Research Description: Fall and spring of first year
Moot Court Requirement? No
Public Interest Law Requirement? No
Academic Journals: *North Dakota Law Review*

STUDENT INFORMATION
Enrollment of Law School: 200
% Male/Female: 54/46
% Full Time: 100
% Full Time That Are International: 6
% Minority: 8

EXPENSES/FINANCIAL AID
Annual Tuition (Residents/Nonresidents): $3,174/$8,476
Room and Board: $7,200
Books and Supplies: $800
Financial Aid Application Deadline: 4/15
Average Grant: $500
Average Loan: $15,800
% of Aid That Is Merit-Based: 1
% Receiving Some Sort of Aid: 86
Average Total Aid Package: $16,200
Average Debt: $45,400
Tuition Per Credit (Residents/Nonresidents): $132/$353
Fees Per Credit: $47

ADMISSIONS INFORMATION
Application Fee: $35
Regular Application Deadline: 4/1
Regular Notification: Rolling
LSDAS Accepted? Yes
Average GPA: 3.3
Range of GPA: 3.0–3.5
Average LSAT: 150
Range of LSAT: 146–153
Transfer Students Accepted? Yes
Number of Applications Received: 201
Number of Applicants Accepted: 133
Number of Applicants Enrolled: 72

EMPLOYMENT INFORMATION

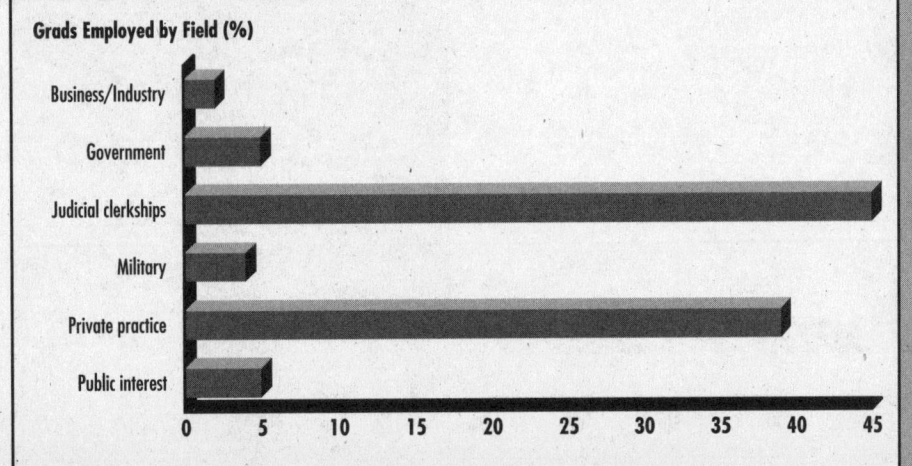

Grads Employed by Field (%)

Field	%
Business/Industry	~2
Government	~3
Judicial clerkships	~45
Military	~3
Private practice	~40
Public interest	~5

Rate of Placement: 93%
Average Starting Salary: $40,900
Employers Who Frequently Hire Grads: Judicial systems and private firms in North Dakota and Minnesota
State for Bar Exam: ND, MN, AZ, MT, IL
Pass Rate for First-Time Bar: 88%

UNIVERSITY OF NOTRE DAME
Law School

Admissions Contact: Director of Admissions, Charles W. Roboski
Notre Dame Law School PO Box 959, Notre Dame, IN 46556-0959
Admissions Phone: 219-631-6626 • Admissions Fax: 219-631-3980
Admissions E-mail: lawadmit@nd.edu • Web Address: www.law.nd.edu

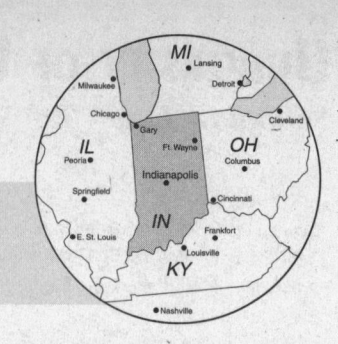

INSTITUTIONAL INFORMATION
Public/Private: Private
Affiliation: Roman Catholic
Student/Faculty Ratio: 17:1
Total Faculty: 60
% Part Time: 45
% Female: 22
% Minority: 4

PROGRAMS
Academic Specialties: Trial Advocacy, International Human Rights Law, Comparative Law, Law and Religion, Professionalism and Ethics, International Law
Advanced Degrees Offered: LLM International Human Rights (1 year), JSD International Human Rights (3 to 5 years, including 1 year of residency); LLM International Comparative Law (1 academic year, London campus only)
Combined Degrees Offered: JD/MBA (4 years), JD/ME (4 years), JD/MA English (3 to 4 years), JD/MA Peace Studies (3 to 4 years)
Grading System: A (4.000), A– (3.667), B+ (3.333), B (3.000), B– (2.667), C+ (2.333), C (2.000), C– (1.667), D (1.000), F (0.000). No mandated grading curve; students are not ranked. Faculty regard C as indicating satisfactory work, and therefore, a C is a respectable grade. The median grade point average for each class year is as follows: first year 3.000, second year 3.100, third year 3.300.
Clinical Program Required? No
Clinical Programs Description: Immigration Law, General Civil Practice
Legal Writing Course Requirements? Yes
Legal Writing Description: First-year year-long course
Legal Methods Course Requirements? Yes
Legal Methods Description: 2-credit legal writing course in the first semester, followed by a 2-credit Legal Research and Writing program (Moot Court) in the second semester
Legal Research Course Requirements? Yes
Legal Research Description: Fall semester of first year
Moot Court Requirement? Yes
Moot Court Description: Second semester of first year
Public Interest Law Requirement? No
Academic Journals: Notre Dame Law Review, Journal of College and University Law, Journal of Law, Ethics, and Public Policy, Journal of Legislation

STUDENT INFORMATION
Enrollment of Law School: 528
% Male/Female: 58/42
% Full Time: 100
% Minority: 19
Average Age of Entering Class: 24

RESEARCH FACILITIES
School-Supported Research Centers: Center for Civil and Human Rights, London Law Centre

EXPENSES/FINANCIAL AID
Annual Tuition: $24,920
Room and Board: $10,530
Books and Supplies: $1,200
Financial Aid Application Deadline: 3/1
Average Grant: $10,000
Average Loan: $23,900
% of Aid That Is Merit-Based: 100
Average Debt: $64,875

ADMISSIONS INFORMATION
Application Fee: $55
Regular Application Deadline: 3/1
Regular Notification: Rolling
LSDAS Accepted? Yes
Average GPA: 3.5
Range of GPA: 3.3–3.7
Average LSAT: 162
Range of LSAT: 159–164
Transfer Students Accepted? Yes
Other Schools to Which Students Applied: Boston College, Georgetown University, George Washington University, Northwestern University, Duke University
Other Admissions Factors Considered: Strong weight to an applicant's demonstrated leadership, record of participation in extracurricular activities and/or work experience, commitment to community service, strength of the personal statement, numerical data
Number of Applications Received: 1,904
Number of Applicants Accepted: 605
Number of Applicants Enrolled: 173

INTERNATIONAL STUDENTS
TOEFL Required of International Students? Yes

EMPLOYMENT INFORMATION

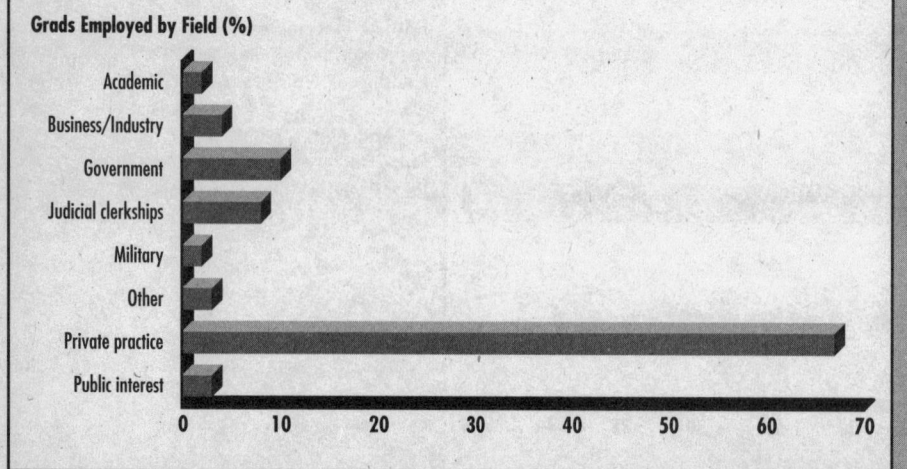

Grads Employed by Field (%)

- Academic
- Business/Industry
- Government
- Judicial clerkships
- Military
- Other
- Private practice
- Public interest

Rate of Placement: 98%
Average Starting Salary: $88,007
Employers Who Frequently Hire Grads: Major law firms in locations throughout the country and abroad, judges at all levels, government agencies, corporations, public interest organizations.
State for Bar Exam: IL
Pass Rate for First-Time Bar: 87%

UNIVERSITY OF OKLAHOMA
College of Law

Admissions Contact: Admissions Coordinator, Kathie G. Madden
300 Timberdell Road, Norman, OK 73019
Admissions Phone: 405-325-4726 • Admissions Fax: 405-325-0502
Admissions E-mail: kmadden@ou.edu • Web Address: www.law.ou.edu

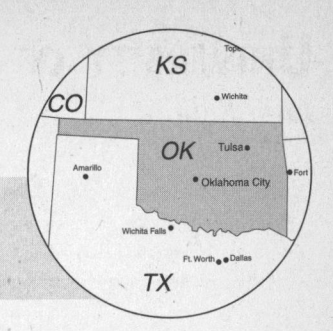

INSTITUTIONAL INFORMATION
Public/Private: Public
Student/Faculty Ratio: 15:1
Total Faculty: 67
% Part Time: 33
% Female: 18
% Minority: 6

PROGRAMS
Academic Specialties: Oil and Gas, Criminal Law, International Law, Taxation, Indian Law, Products Liability, Constitutional Law, Professional Responsibility, Environmental Law, Family Law, Commercial Law, Labor Law, Corporation Securities Law, Intellectual Property Law
Combined Degrees Offered: JD/MBA (4 years), JD/MPH (4 years), JD/generic dual degree (4 years)
Grading System: 12 point scale: A+ (12), A (11), A− (10), B+ (9), B (8), B− (7), C+ (6), C (5), C− (4), D+ (3), D (2), D− (1), F (0)
Clinical Program Required? No
Clinical Programs Description: Judicial Clinic, Civil Clinic, Criminal Defense Clinic
Legal Writing Course Requirements? Yes
Legal Writing Description: Required first-year course, both semesters
Legal Methods Course Requirements? No
Legal Research Course Requirements? Yes
Legal Research Description: Required first-year course, both semesters
Moot Court Requirement? No
Public Interest Law Requirement? No
Academic Journals: Oklahoma Law Review, American Indian Law Review

STUDENT INFORMATION
Enrollment of Law School: 505
% Out of State: 9
% Male/Female: 55/45
% Full Time: 100
% Full Time That Are International: 0
% Minority: 12
Average Age of Entering Class: 24

RESEARCH FACILITIES
Research Resources Available: Westlaw, Lexis/Nexis, Wilsonweb, CCH, LegalTrac

EXPENSES/FINANCIAL AID
Annual Tuition (Residents/Nonresidents): $5,259/$14,285
Room and Board (On/Off Campus): $6,600/$7,930
Books and Supplies: $913
Financial Aid Application Deadline: 3/1
Average Grant: $1,000
Average Loan: $17,900
% of Aid That Is Merit-Based: 22
% Receiving Some Sort of Aid: 81
Average Total Aid Package: $17,900
Average Debt: $54,373
Tuition Per Credit (Residents/Nonresidents): $175/$476

ADMISSIONS INFORMATION
Application Fee: $50
Regular Application Deadline: 3/15
Regular Notification: Rolling
LSDAS Accepted? Yes
Average GPA: 3.4
Range of GPA: 3.1–3.6
Average LSAT: 154
Range of LSAT: 151–158
Transfer Students Accepted? Yes
Other Admissions Factors Considered: Factors such as cultural, economic, and educational background; grade trends; extracurricular activities; work experience; military achievements; graduate studies; and adjustments to personal difficulties
Number of Applications Received: 746
Number of Applicants Accepted: 295
Number of Applicants Enrolled: 180

EMPLOYMENT INFORMATION

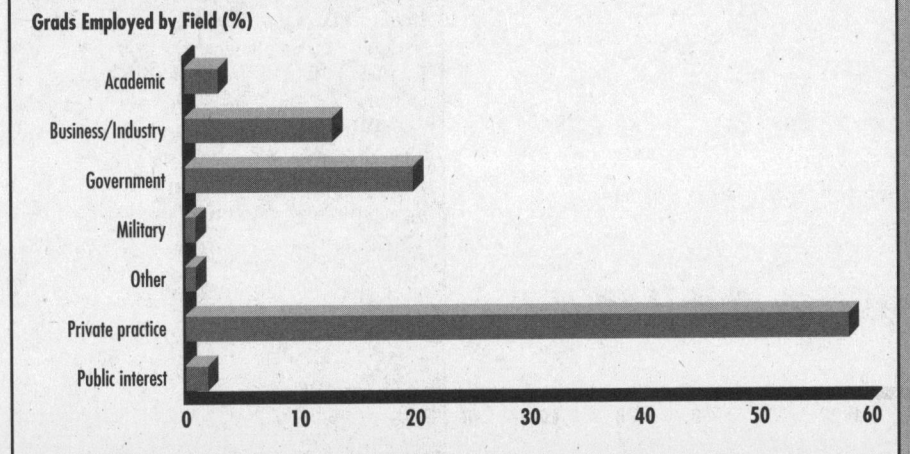

Grads Employed by Field (%)
- Academic: ~2
- Business/Industry: ~13
- Government: ~20
- Military: ~0
- Other: ~1
- Private practice: ~60
- Public interest: ~2

Rate of Placement: 93%
Average Starting Salary: $52,176
Employers Who Frequently Hire Grads: McAfee & Taft; Crowe & Dunlevy; McKinney & Stringer; Conner & Winters; Gable & Gotwals; Hall, Estill, Hardwick, Gable & Nelson; Phillips, McFall, McCaffrey, McVay & Murray; U.S. government; state of Oklahoma
State for Bar Exam: OK, TX, CO, NM, VA
Pass Rate for First-Time Bar: 88%

UNIVERSITY OF PENNSYLVANIA
Law School

Admissions Contact: Assistant Dean for Admissions, Janice Austin
3400 Chestnut Street, Philadelphia, PA 19104-6204
Admissions Phone: 215-898-7400 • Admissions Fax: 215-573-2025
Admissions E-mail: admissions@law.upenn.edu • Web Address: www.law.upenn.edu

INSTITUTIONAL INFORMATION
Public/Private: Private
Student/Faculty Ratio: 14:1
Total Faculty: 115
% Part Time: 47
% Female: 30

PROGRAMS
Academic Specialties: Administrative Law, Commercial Law, Constitutional Law, Criminal Law, Jurisprudence, Law and Economics, Civil Procedure, Corporation Securities Law, Environmental Law, Government Services, Human Rights Law, Intellectual Property Law, International Law, Labor Law, Legal History, Legal Philosophy, Property, Taxation
Advanced Degrees Offered: JD (3 years), LLM (1 year), SJD (at least 1 year), LLCM (1 year)
Combined Degrees Offered: JD/MBA (4 years), JD/MA or PhD Economics (4+ years), JD/MA or PhD Public Policy and Management (4+ years), JD/MA or PhD Philosophy (6 years), JD/MA Islamic Studies (3+ years), JD/MCP (4 years), JD/MSW (4 years), JD/MD, others as approved
Grading System: A+, A, B+, B, C, F; mandatory distribution in first-year courses
Clinical Program Required? No
Clinical Programs Description: Civil Practice Clinic, Advanced Civil Practice Clinic, Small Business Clinic, Mediation Clinic, Criminal Defense Clinic, Legislative Clinic
Legal Writing Course Requirements? Yes
Legal Writing Description: See Legal Methods.
Legal Methods Course Requirements? Yes
Legal Methods Description: A year-long course taught in small groups by third-year students under the supervision of the Legal Writing Instructor. The course covers legal research, basic legal analysis, objective and persuasive writing, and oral advocacy.
Legal Research Course Requirements? Yes
Legal Research Description: See Legal Methods.
Moot Court Requirement? No
Public Interest Law Requirement? Yes
Public Interest Law Description: 70 hours of public service
Academic Journals: Law Review, Journal of Constitutional Law, Journal of Labor and Employment Law, Journal of International Economic Law

STUDENT INFORMATION
Enrollment of Law School: 751
% Out of State: 83
% Male/Female: 50/50
% Full Time: 100
% Full Time That Are International: 4
% Minority: 31
Average Age of Entering Class: 24

EXPENSES/FINANCIAL AID
Annual Tuition: $27,960
Room and Board: $9,345
Books and Supplies: $850
Average Grant: $10,600
Average Loan: $29,940
% of Aid That Is Merit-Based: 5
% Receiving Some Sort of Aid: 73
Average Total Aid Package: $40,540
Average Debt: $81,518

ADMISSIONS INFORMATION
Application Fee: $70
Regular Application Deadline: 3/1
Regular Notification: Rolling
LSDAS Accepted? Yes
Average GPA: 3.6
Range of GPA: 3.4–3.7
Average LSAT: 166
Range of LSAT: 164–168
Transfer Students Accepted? Yes
Other Schools to Which Students Applied: Columbia University, Cornell University, Georgetown University, New York University
Other Admissions Factors Considered: Other life (professional and personal) accomplishments, interest in interdisciplinary academic curriculums or joint degrees
Number of Applications Received: 3,657
Number of Applicants Accepted: 897
Number of Applicants Enrolled: 261

EMPLOYMENT INFORMATION

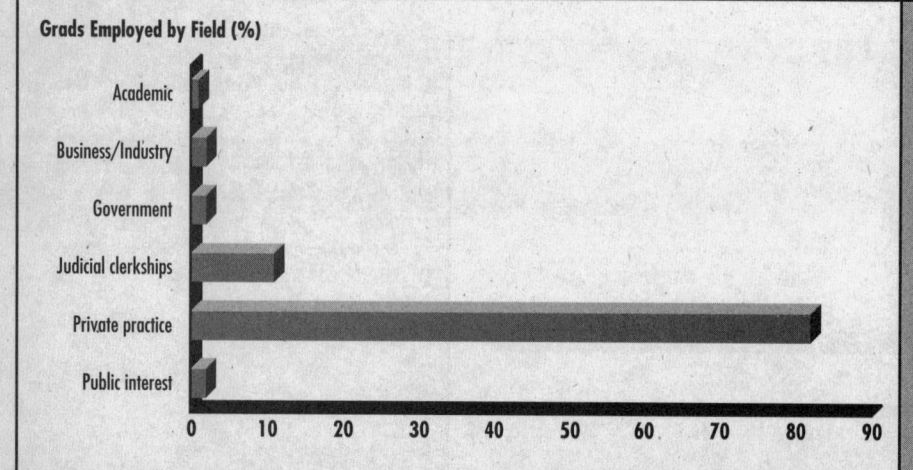

Grads Employed by Field (%)
- Academic: ~2
- Business/Industry: ~3
- Government: ~3
- Judicial clerkships: ~12
- Private practice: ~82
- Public interest: ~2

Rate of Placement: 99%
Average Starting Salary: $106,530
Employers Who Frequently Hire Grads: Major corporate law firms nationwide, prestigious national fellowship organizations and public interest organizations, federal and state judges
State for Bar Exam: NY
Pass Rate for First-Time Bar: 94%

258 • COMPLETE BOOK OF LAW SCHOOLS

UNIVERSITY OF PITTSBURGH
School of Law

Admissions Contact: Assistant Dean for Admissions and Financial Aid, Fredi G. Miller
3900 Forbes Avenue, Pittsburgh, PA 15260
Admissions Phone: 412-648-1413 • Admissions Fax: 412-648-2647
Admissions E-mail: admissions@law.pitt.edu • Web Address: www.law.pitt.edu

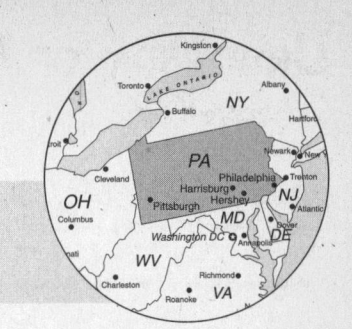

INSTITUTIONAL INFORMATION
Public/Private: Public
Student/Faculty Ratio: 15:1
Total Faculty: 73
% Part Time: 44
% Female: 26
% Minority: 0

PROGRAMS
Academic Specialties: New Certificate programs offered in Health Law, Environmental Law, International and Comparative Law, and Civil Litigation. Other specialties include Civil Procedure, Corporation Securities Law, and Taxation.
Advanced Degrees Offered: LLM for foreign-trained attorneys (2 semesters)
Combined Degrees Offered: JD/MPA (4 years), JD/MPIA (4 years), JD/MBA (3.5 years), JD/MPH (3.5 years), JD/MA Medical Ethics (3.5 years), JD/MSIA (4 years), JD/MS Public Management (4 years), JD/MAM (4 years)
Grading System: A to F; some seminars and clinics graded Honors/Pass/Fail
Clinical Program Required? No
Clinical Programs Description: Civil Practice Clinic (Health Law, Elder Law, Disability Law, Discrimination Law), Tax Clinic, Environmental Law Clinic
Legal Writing Course Requirements? Yes
Legal Writing Description: First-year Legal Writing class divided into 3 small sections; there is also an upper-level writing requirement for graduation
Legal Methods Course Requirements? No
Legal Research Course Requirements? Yes
Legal Research Description: 2-semester course combined with Legal Writing
Moot Court Requirement? No
Public Interest Law Requirement? No
Academic Journals: *University of Pittsburgh Law Review, University of Pittsburgh Journal of Law and Commerce, The Pittsburgh Journal of Technology Law & Policy*

STUDENT INFORMATION
Enrollment of Law School: 738
% Out of State: 30
% Male/Female: 53/47
% Full Time: 100
% Full Time That Are International: 1
% Minority: 10
Average Age of Entering Class: 24

EXPENSES/FINANCIAL AID
Annual Tuition (Residents/Nonresidents): $13,980/$21,854
Room and Board: $10,980
Books and Supplies: $1,150
Financial Aid Application Deadline: 3/1
Average Grant: $6,213
Average Loan: $18,500
% of Aid That Is Merit-Based: 57
% Receiving Some Sort of Aid: 87
Average Debt: $65,000

ADMISSIONS INFORMATION
Application Fee: $50
Regular Application Deadline: 3/1
Regular Notification: Rolling
LSDAS Accepted? Yes
Average GPA: 3.3
Range of GPA: 2.9–3.6
Average LSAT: 156
Range of LSAT: 153–159
Transfer Students Accepted? Yes
Other Schools to Which Students Applied: American University, Boston University, Case Western Reserve University, George Washington University, Temple University, The Pennsylvania State University, Villanova University
Other Admissions Factors Considered: Strength of the undergraduate institution, curriculum and campus activities
Number of Applications Received: 1,429
Number of Applicants Accepted: 732
Number of Applicants Enrolled: 272

INTERNATIONAL STUDENTS
TOEFL Required of International Students? Yes

EMPLOYMENT INFORMATION

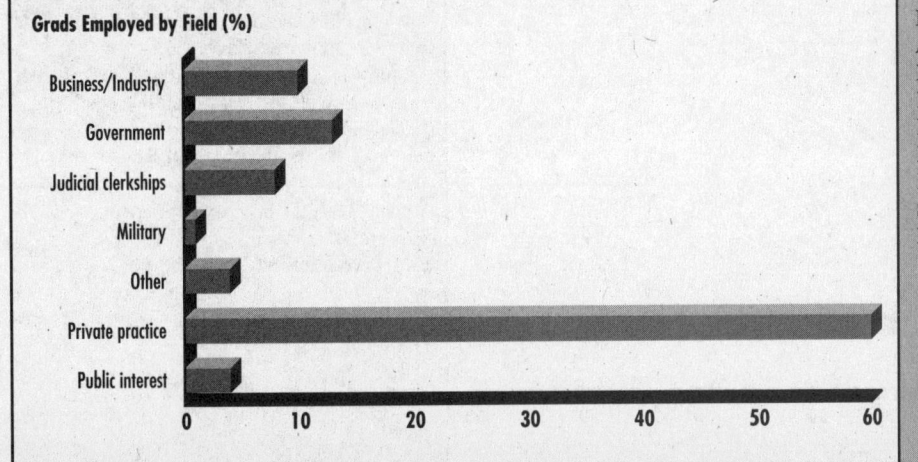

Grads Employed by Field (%)

Field	%
Business/Industry	~5
Government	~13
Judicial clerkships	~10
Military	~1
Other	~5
Private practice	~60
Public interest	~3

Rate of Placement: 99%
Average Starting Salary: $62,552
Employers Who Frequently Hire Grads: Buchanan, Ingersoll; Kirkpatrick & Lockhart; Reed, Smith, Shaw & McClay; Morgan, Lewis & Bockius; Jones, Day, Reavis & Pogue; Pepper, Hamilton; Milbank, Tweed
State for Bar Exam: PA, VA, MD, NY, CA
Pass Rate for First-Time Bar: 84%

UNIVERSITY OF RICHMOND
School of Law

Admissions Contact: Director of Admissions, Michelle Rahman
Law School Admissions Office, University of Richmond, VA 23173
Admissions Phone: 804-289-8189 • Admissions Fax: 804-287-6516
Admissions E-mail: admissions@uofrlaw.richmond.edu • Web Address: law.richmond.edu

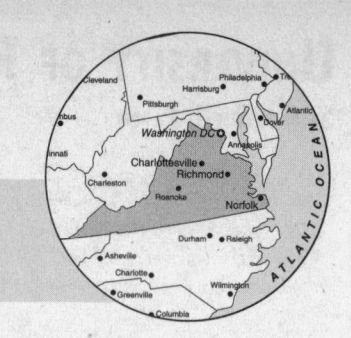

INSTITUTIONAL INFORMATION
Public/Private: Private
Student/Faculty Ratio: 16:1
Total Faculty: 101
% Part Time: 63
% Female: 33
% Minority: 12

PROGRAMS
Academic Specialties: First law school in country to require all students to have a laptop computer; numerous International and Comparative Law courses; several courses focus on lawyering skills (advanced trial practice, interviewing, counseling, negotiations, business transactions); other specialties include Civil Procedure, Commercial Law, Constitutional Law, Corporation Securities Law, Criminal Law, Environmental Law, International Law, Labor Law, Legal History, Property, and Taxation.
Advanced Degrees Offered: JD (3 years)
Combined Degrees Offered: JD/MBA, JD/MURP, JD/MHA, JD/MSW, JD/MPA (all 4 years)
Grading System: 4.0 scale
Clinical Program Required? No
Legal Writing Course Requirements? Yes
Legal Methods Course Requirements? Yes
Legal Methods Description: 4 semesters of Lawyering Skills
Legal Research Course Requirements? Yes
Legal Research Description: 4 semesters of Lawyering Skills
Moot Court Requirement? No

Public Interest Law Requirement? No
Academic Journals: Law and Public Policy, Journal of Law and Technology, Journal of Law and Public Interest, Journal of Global Law and Business

STUDENT INFORMATION
Enrollment of Law School: 472
% Out of State: 47
% Male/Female: 52/48
% Full Time: 100
% Full Time That Are International: 3
% Minority: 9
Average Age of Entering Class: 25

EXPENSES/FINANCIAL AID
Annual Tuition: $21,770
Room and Board (On/Off Campus): $4,924/$7,335
Books and Supplies: $900
Financial Aid Application Deadline: 2/25
Average Grant: $5,560
Average Loan: $22,515
% of Aid That Is Merit-Based: 31
% Receiving Some Sort of Aid: 96
Average Total Aid Package: $25,135
Average Debt: $62,200
Tuition Per Credit: $1,090

ADMISSIONS INFORMATION
Application Fee: $35
Regular Application Deadline: 1/15
Regular Notification: 4/15
LSDAS Accepted? Yes
Average GPA: 3.2
Range of GPA: 2.9–3.5
Average LSAT: 158
Range of LSAT: 156–160
Transfer Students Accepted? Yes
Other Schools to Which Students Applied: American University, College of William and Mary, George Washington University, University of Virginia, Wake Forest University, Washington and Lee University
Other Admissions Factors Considered: Community service, letters of recommendation, extracurricular activities
Number of Applications Received: 1,545
Number of Applicants Accepted: 575
Number of Applicants Enrolled: 171

EMPLOYMENT INFORMATION

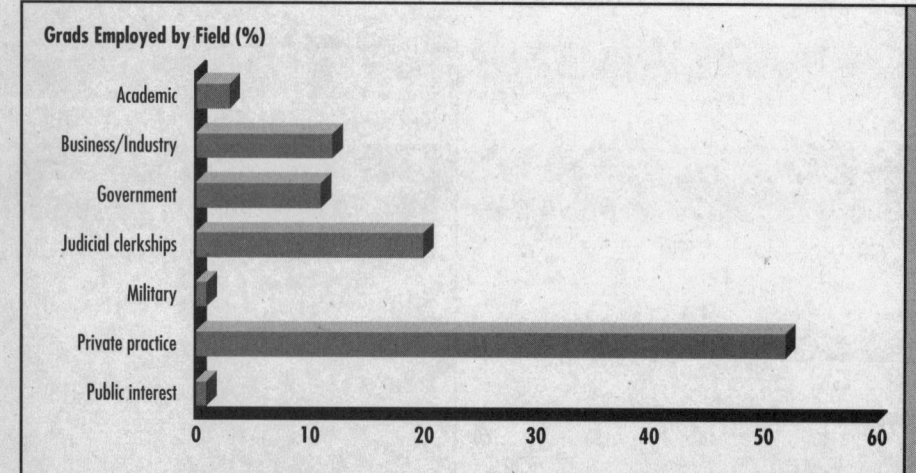

Grads Employed by Field (%):
- Academic: ~2
- Business/Industry: ~12
- Government: ~10
- Judicial clerkships: ~20
- Military: ~1
- Private practice: ~53
- Public interest: ~2

Rate of Placement: 100%
Average Starting Salary: $56,142
Employers Who Frequently Hire Grads: Hunton & Williams; Williams, Mullen, Christian & Dobbins; McGuire, Woods, Battle, & Booth; Kaufman & Canoles; Troutman, Sanders & Sanders; Woods, Rogers & Hazlegrove; Holland & Knight; Reed, Smith, Hazel & Thomas
State for Bar Exam: NC, NY, FL, VA, DC
Pass Rate for First-Time Bar: 90%

UNIVERSITY OF SAN DIEGO
School of Law

Admissions Contact: Director of Admissions and Financial Aid, Carl Eging
5998 Alcala Park, San Diego, CA 92110
Admissions Phone: 619-260-4528 • Admissions Fax: 619-260-2218
Admissions E-mail: jdinfo@SanDiego.edu • Web Address: www.sandiego.edu/usdlaw

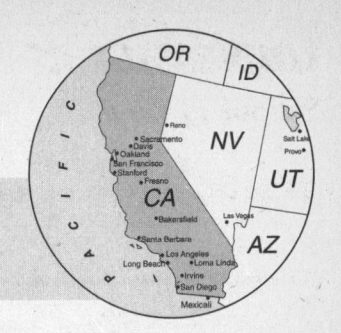

INSTITUTIONAL INFORMATION
Public/Private: Private
Affiliation: Roman Catholic
Student/Faculty Ratio: 18:1
Total Faculty: 173
% Part Time: 35
% Female: 28
% Minority: 14

PROGRAMS
Academic Specialties: USD's large faculty contains experts in virtually every field of law and includes authors of leading case books, treatises, and scholarly monographs. Specialties include Civil Procedure, Commercial Law, Constitutional Law, Criminal Law, Environmental Law, Human Rights Law, International Law, Labor Law, and Taxation.
Advanced Degrees Offered: JD (3 years day, 4 years evening), LLM General, LLM Taxation, LLM Business, LLM Corporate, LLM International, LLM Comparative Law for foreign lawyers (approximately 1 year)
Combined Degrees Offered: JD/MBA, JD/MA International Relations (4 to 4.5 years), JD/IMBA
Grading System: Letter and numerical system on 93–65 point scale; some courses may be graded Pass/Fail or Honors, Pass, Low Pass, Fail
Clinical Program Required? No
Clinical Programs Description: Children's Advocacy, Civil, Criminal, Environmental, Immigration, Mental Health, Public Interest, Judicial Internship, Land Development, Tax, Small Claims Clinic
Legal Writing Course Requirements? Yes

Legal Writing Description: Semester-long Lawyering Skills course taught in small sections with a low student-faculty ratio
Legal Methods Course Requirements? No
Legal Research Course Requirements? No
Moot Court Requirement? No
Moot Court Description: Students simulate the appellate advocacy process by researching and writing an appellate brief, then arguing the case before a distinguished panel of judges.
Public Interest Law Requirement? No
Academic Journals: San Diego Law Review, Journal of Contemporary Legal Issues, San Diego International Law Journal, California Regulatory Law Reporter, Children's Regulatory Law Reporter, California Children's Budget, Legal Theory, Motions

STUDENT INFORMATION
Enrollment of Law School: 991
% Out of State: 33
% Male/Female: 52/48
% Full Time: 72
% Full Time That Are International: 1
% Minority: 24
Average Age of Entering Class: 24

RESEARCH FACILITIES
School-Supported Research Centers: Academic support program, legal research and writing programs, alumni advisor program, clinical and internship opportunities, Children's Advocacy Institute, Center for Public Interest Law

EXPENSES/FINANCIAL AID
Annual Tuition: $24,880
Room and Board: $13,562
Books and Supplies: $750
Financial Aid Application Deadline: 3/1
Average Grant: $14,378
Average Loan: $22,744
% Receiving Some Sort of Aid: 76
Average Total Aid Package: $38,492
Average Debt: $65,000
Tuition Per Credit: $865

ADMISSIONS INFORMATION
Application Fee: $50
Regular Application Deadline: Rolling
Regular Notification: Rolling
LSDAS Accepted? Yes
Average GPA: 3.3
Range of GPA: 3.0–3.5
Average LSAT: 161
Range of LSAT: 157–161
Transfer Students Accepted? Yes
Other Admissions Factors Considered: Full application file is reviewed by Admissions Committee.
Number of Applications Received: 2,946

INTERNATIONAL STUDENTS
TOEFL Required of International Students? Yes
Minimum TOEFL: 250

EMPLOYMENT INFORMATION

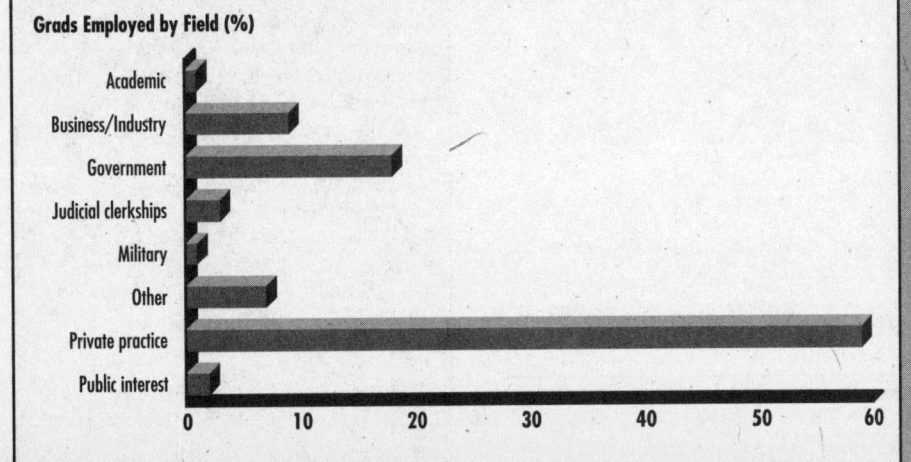

Grads Employed by Field (%)

Field	%
Academic	~1
Business/Industry	~7
Government	~18
Judicial clerkships	~5
Military	~1
Other	~5
Private practice	~60
Public interest	~2

Rate of Placement: 92%
Employers Who Frequently Hire Grads: Gibson, Dunn & Crutcher; Brobeck, Phleger, and Harrison; Cooley and Godward; Fulbright & Jaworski; Gray, Cary; Littler, Mendelson, Fastiff, Tichy & Mathiason; Pillsbury, Winthrop; Department of Justice; Luce, Forward, Hamilton & Scripps; Heller, Ehrman, White and Mcauliffe; Deloitte and Touche
State for Bar Exam: CA
Pass Rate for First-Time Bar: 73%

UNIVERSITY OF SAN FRANCISCO
School of Law

Admissions Contact: Director of Admissions, Alan Guerrero
2130 Fulton Street, San Francisco, CA 94117
Admissions Phone: 415-422-6586 • Admissions Fax: 415-422-6433
Admissions E-mail: lawadmissions@usfca.edu • Web Address: www.usfca.edu

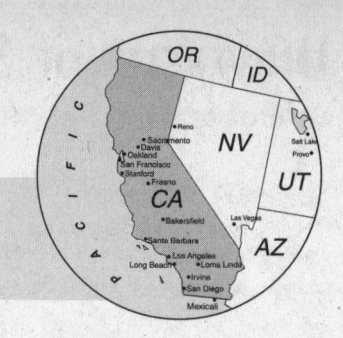

INSTITUTIONAL INFORMATION
Public/Private: Private
Affiliation: Roman Catholic
Student/Faculty Ratio: 20:1
Total Faculty: 39
% Part Time: 38
% Female: 30
% Minority: 20

PROGRAMS
Academic Specialties: The law school's program is especially strong in Trial Advocacy and Dispute Resolution, with courses taught by faculty nationally recognized as experts in these fields. Similarly, the school has a significant concentration of courses in Intellectual Property area taught by leading attorneys from firms and corporations in Silicon Valley, as well as by full-time faculty, one of whom is recognized as a preeminent international authority in these subjects. There is also a large number of offerings in International Law, again taught by full-time faculty experts in the field as well as by practitioners and scholars from the Bay Area and abroad. In addition, the school offers many courses in Maritime Law and publishes 1 of only 2 journals devoted to the subject. Other specialties include Civil Procedure, Commercial Law, Constitutional Law, Corporation Securities Law, Criminal Law, Environmental Law, Government Services, Human Rights Law, Labor Law, Legal History, Legal Philosophy, Property, and Taxation.
Advanced Degrees Offered: LLM International Transactions and Comparative Law (1 year)
Combined Degrees Offered: JD/MBA (4 years)
Grading System: Letter and numerical system on a 4.0 scale; Credit/No Credit available for some courses
Clinical Program Required? Yes
Clinical Programs Description: Criminal Law Clinic, Civil Law Clinic, Investigation Law Clinic, judicial externships.
Legal Writing Course Requirements? No
Legal Methods Course Requirements? Yes
Legal Methods Description: 2 semesters during the first year
Legal Research Course Requirements? No
Moot Court Requirement? No
Public Interest Law Requirement? No

STUDENT INFORMATION
Enrollment of Law School: 637
% Male/Female: 42/58
% Full Time: 80
% Full Time That Are International: 0
% Minority: 32
Average Age of Entering Class: 25

RESEARCH FACILITIES
Research Resources Available: USF Law Library, Gleeson Library/Ceschke Center, Other ABA law schools in the San Francisco Bay area, USF Law and Global Justice website, USF Intellectual Property website

EXPENSES/FINANCIAL AID
Annual Tuition: $22,938
Room and Board (On/Off Campus): $7,838/$9,900
Books and Supplies: $750
Average Grant: $9,721
Average Loan: $22,000
% of Aid That Is Merit-Based: 80
% Receiving Some Sort of Aid: 90
Average Total Aid Package: $22,500
Average Debt: $63,131
Tuition Per Credit: $792
Fees Per Credit: $125

ADMISSIONS INFORMATION
Application Fee: $50
Regular Application Deadline: 4/1
Regular Notification: Rolling
LSDAS Accepted? Yes
Average GPA: 3.2
Range of GPA: 2.9–3.4
Average LSAT: 155
Range of LSAT: 153–158
Transfer Students Accepted? Yes
Other Schools to Which Students Applied: Golden Gate University, Loyola Marymount University, Santa Clara University, University of California—Davis, University of California—Hastings, University of California—Berkeley, University of San Diego
Number of Applications Received: 2,002
Number of Applicants Accepted: 928
Number of Applicants Enrolled: 242

INTERNATIONAL STUDENTS
TOEFL Required of International Students? Yes

EMPLOYMENT INFORMATION

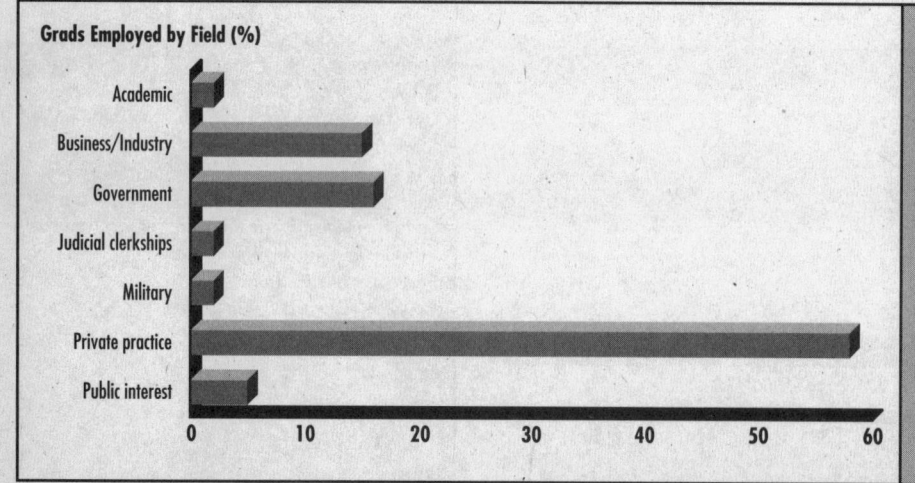

Grads Employed by Field (%)

Field	%
Academic	~1
Business/Industry	~15
Government	~17
Judicial clerkships	~3
Military	~1
Private practice	~58
Public interest	~3

Rate of Placement: 77%
Average Starting Salary: $62,863
Employers Who Frequently Hire Grads: Brobeck, Phleger & Harrison; Sedgewick, Detert, Moran & Arnold; Landels, Ripley & Diamond; Keesel, Young & Logan; Hanson, Bridgett, Marcus, Vlahos & Rudy; McCutchen, Doyle, Brown & Enersen; Miller, Starr & Regalia; Orrick, Herrington & Sutcliffe; Shook, Hardy & Bacon
State for Bar Exam: CA
Pass Rate for First-Time Bar: 71%

UNIVERSITY OF SOUTH CAROLINA
School of Law

Admissions Contact: Assistant Dean for Admissions
Main and Greene Streets, Columbia, SC 29208
Admissions Phone: 803-777-6605 • Admissions Fax: 803-777-7751
Admissions E-mail: usclaw@law.law.sc.edu • Web Address: www.law.sc.edu

INSTITUTIONAL INFORMATION
Public/Private: Public
Student/Faculty Ratio: 21:1
Total Faculty: 43
% Female: 4
% Minority: 2

PROGRAMS
Academic Specialties: Corporation Securities Law, Environmental Law, International Law, Property, Taxation, Criminal Law, Constitutional Law, Clinical Legal Education. Clinical Legal Education programs afford students the opportunity to gain practical experience while enrolled in the School of Law.
Advanced Degrees Offered: JD (3 years)
Combined Degrees Offered: JD/MIB (4 years), JD/MBA (4 years), JD/MPA (4 years), JD/Masters in Criminal Justice (4 years), JD/Masters in Economics (4 years), JD/Masters in Accounting (4 years), JD/Masters in Social Work (4 years), JD/Masters in Environmental Sciences (4 years), JD/Masters in Earth and Environmental Resource Management
Grading System: A to F (4.0 scale)

Clinical Program Required? No
Legal Writing Course Requirements? Yes
Legal Writing Description: 1 year
Legal Methods Course Requirements? Yes
Legal Methods Description: First year, 2 semesters
Legal Research Course Requirements? No
Moot Court Requirement? No
Public Interest Law Requirement? No
Public Interest Law Description: Outstanding pro bono program
Academic Journals: S.C. Law Review, ABA Real Property Trust and Probate

STUDENT INFORMATION
Enrollment of Law School: 669
% Out of State: 15
% Male/Female: 55/45
% Full Time: 100
% Full Time That Are International: 0
% Minority: 11
Average Age of Entering Class: 24

RESEARCH FACILITIES
% of JD Classrooms Wired: 40

EXPENSES/FINANCIAL AID
Annual Tuition (Residents/Nonresidents): $7,990/$16,530
Room and Board: $10,000
Books and Supplies: $500
Financial Aid Application Deadline: 4/15
Average Grant: $1,200
Average Loan: $18,000
% of Aid That Is Merit-Based: 15
% Receiving Some Sort of Aid: 69
Average Total Aid Package: $19,226
Average Debt: $42,000

ADMISSIONS INFORMATION
Application Fee: $40
Regular Application Deadline: 2/15
Regular Notification: Rolling
LSDAS Accepted? Yes
Average GPA: 3.2
Average LSAT: 156
Range of LSAT: 152–159
Transfer Students Accepted? Yes
Other Admissions Factors Considered: Undergraduate institution, undergraduate major, graduate work, diversity, joint degree candidacy, maturity
Number of Applications Received: 1,179
Number of Applicants Enrolled: 223

EMPLOYMENT INFORMATION

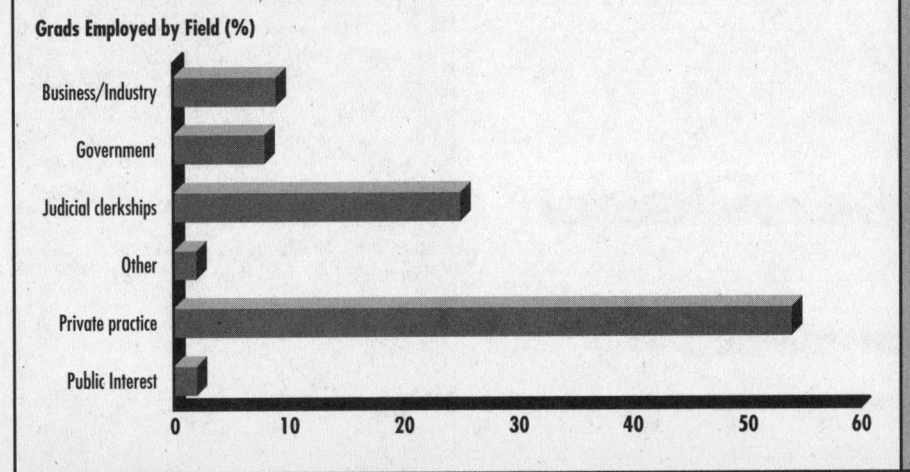

Grads Employed by Field (%)
- Business/Industry: ~8
- Government: ~8
- Judicial clerkships: ~25
- Other: ~3
- Private practice: ~54
- Public Interest: ~2

Rate of Placement: 90%
Average Starting Salary: $46,956
Employers Who Frequently Hire Grads: Nelson Mullins Riley & Scarborough; Kennedy, Covington, Labdell, & Hickman; Alston and Bird
State for Bar Exam: SC, NC, GA, TX, PA
Pass Rate for First-Time Bar: 82%

UNIVERSITY OF SOUTH DAKOTA
School of Law

Admissions Contact: Admission Officer/Registrar, Jean Henriques
414 East Clark Street, Vermillion, SD 57069-2390
Admissions Phone: 605-677-5443 • Admissions Fax: 605-677-5417
Admissions E-mail: lawreq@usd.edu • Web Address: www.usd.edu/law

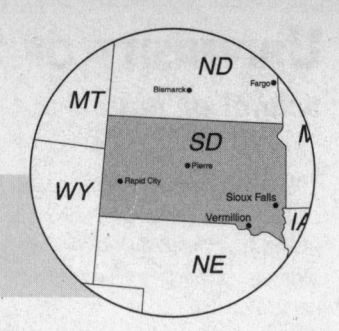

INSTITUTIONAL INFORMATION
Public/Private: Public
Student/Faculty Ratio: 13:1
Total Faculty: 17
% Part Time: 1
% Female: 17
% Minority: 5

PROGRAMS
Academic Specialties: Indian Law, Environmental Law, Business; opportunity to write for *Great Plains Natural Resources Journal*
Combined Degrees Offered: JD/MBA, JD/MPA, JD/Masters in Education Administration, English, History, Political Science, Psychology, Administrative Studies, or Professional Accountancy
Grading System: A (99–90), B (89–80), C (79–70), D (69–60), F (59–50)
Clinical Program Required? No
Legal Writing Course Requirements? Yes
Legal Writing Description: First-year course, fall semester
Legal Methods Course Requirements? Yes
Legal Methods Description: First-year course: Legal Research and Writing (first semester), Appellate Advocacy (second semester)
Legal Research Course Requirements? Yes
Legal Research Description: First-year course, fall semester
Moot Court Requirement? No
Public Interest Law Requirement? No
Academic Journals: *Law Review, Great Plains Natural Resources Journal*

STUDENT INFORMATION
Enrollment of Law School: 183
% Out of State: 25
% Male/Female: 49/51
% Full Time: 98
% Full Time That Are International: 1
% Minority: 9
Average Age of Entering Class: 27

EXPENSES/FINANCIAL AID
Annual Tuition (Residents/Nonresidents): $3,432/$9,948
Room and Board (On/Off Campus): $3,100/$5,500
Books and Supplies: $800
Average Grant: $1,645
Average Loan: $15,000
% of Aid That Is Merit-Based: 90
% Receiving Some Sort of Aid: 93
Average Total Aid Package: $17,300
Average Debt: $50,000
Tuition Per Credit (Residents/Nonresidents): $114/$332
Fees Per Credit: $93

ADMISSIONS INFORMATION
Application Fee: $35
Regular Application Deadline: Rolling
Regular Notification: Rolling
LSDAS Accepted? Yes

Average GPA: 3.2
Range of GPA: 3.0–3.5
Average LSAT: 150
Range of LSAT: 145–154
Transfer Students Accepted? Yes
Other Schools to Which Students Applied: Hamline University, University of Minnesota, University of Nebraska—Lincoln, University of Wyoming, University of North Dakota, William Mitchell College of Law
Number of Applications Received: 279
Number of Applicants Accepted: 180
Number of Applicants Enrolled: 79

INTERNATIONAL STUDENTS
TOEFL Required of International Students? Yes
Minimum TOEFL: 250

EMPLOYMENT INFORMATION

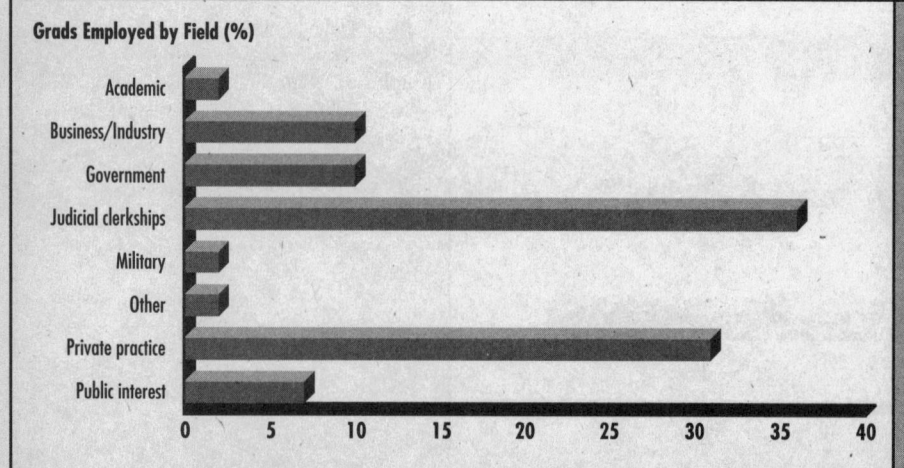

Grads Employed by Field (%)
- Academic: ~2
- Business/Industry: ~3
- Government: ~10
- Judicial clerkships: ~37
- Military: ~1
- Other: ~2
- Private practice: ~32
- Public interest: ~7

Rate of Placement: 90%
Average Starting Salary: $40,266
Employers Who Frequently Hire Grads: U.S. Eighth Circuit Court of Appeals, U.S. District Court, South Dakota Supreme Court, South Dakota Circuit Court, Minnehaha Public Defender's Office, firms, Minnesota State District Courts
State for Bar Exam: SD, MN, IA, NE, CO
Pass Rate for First-Time Bar: 98%

UNIVERSITY OF SOUTHERN CALIFORNIA
The Law School

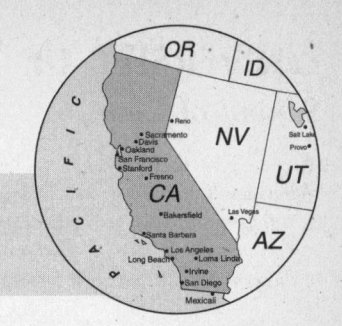

Admissions Contact: Associate Dean, William Hoye
USC Law School, Los Angeles, CA 90089-0074
Admissions Phone: 213-740-2523 • Admissions Fax: 213-740-4570
Admissions E-mail: admissions@law.usc.edu • Web Address: www.law.usc.edu

INSTITUTIONAL INFORMATION
Public/Private: Private
Student/Faculty Ratio: 13:1
Total Faculty: 110
% Part Time: 40
% Female: 21
% Minority: 14

PROGRAMS
Academic Specialties: Corporations and Business Government Relationships, Bioethics, International Law, Civil Rights and Liberties, Taxation, Civil Procedure, Commercial Law, Constitutional Law, Corporation Securities Law, Criminal Law, Environmental Law, Government Services, Human Rights Law, Intellectual Property Law, International Law, Labor Law, Legal History, Legal Philosophy, and Property.
Advanced Degrees Offered: JD (3 years)
Combined Degrees Offered: JD/MBA (3.5 to 4 years), JD/MPA (3 years), JD/MA Economics (3 years), JD/MA International Relations (3 years), JD/MA Communications Management (3 years), JD/MA Philosophy (3 years), JD/MA Religion (3 years), JD/MSW (4 years), JD/Master of Real Estate Development (3.5 years), JD/Master of Business Taxation (3.5 to 4 years), JD/MS Gerontology (4 years), JD/MPP (3 years), JD/PhD (5 years)
Grading System: 4.4 to 1.9, with explicit letter-grade equivalents ranging from A+ to F.
Clinical Program Required? No
Clinical Programs Description: Post Conviction Justice Project, Children's Legal Issues, Externship/Internship Program, Trial Advocacy, Pretrial Advocacy, Negotiations, Employment Law Advice Clinic, Family Violence Clinic, Immigration Clinic

Legal Writing Course Requirements? Yes
Legal Writing Description: 2-semester Introduction to Lawyering Skills.
Legal Methods Course Requirements? Yes
Legal Methods Description: See Legal Writing.
Legal Research Course Requirements? Yes
Legal Research Description: Legal Research examines the basic sources of law.
Moot Court Requirement? Yes
Moot Court Description: Part of first-year Lawyering Skills course.
Public Interest Law Requirement? No
Academic Journals: *Southern California Law Review, Southern California Interdisciplinary Law Journal, Southern California Review of Law and Women's Studies*

STUDENT INFORMATION
Enrollment of Law School: 628
% Out of State: 50
% Male/Female: 48/52
% Full Time: 100
% Full Time That Are International: 2
% Minority: 40
Average Age of Entering Class: 25

RESEARCH FACILITIES
Research Resources Available: CalTech, extensive alumni network, One Institute
School-Supported Research Centers: Pacific Center (Studies Law and Medicine Issues); Public Interest Law Foundation; Center for the Study of Law and Politics; Center for Law, Economics, and Organization; Center for Communication Law and Policy; Center for Feminist Research; Center for Law, History, and Culture

EXPENSES/FINANCIAL AID
Annual Tuition: $29,454
Room and Board: $12,412
Books and Supplies: $1,026
Financial Aid Application Deadline: 2/15
Average Grant: $9,677
Average Loan: $29,130
% Receiving Some Sort of Aid: 87
Average Total Aid Package: $42,906
Average Debt: $65,723

ADMISSIONS INFORMATION
Application Fee: $60
Regular Application Deadline: 2/1
Regular Notification: Rolling
LSDAS Accepted? Yes
Average GPA: 3.5
Average LSAT: 164
Transfer Students Accepted? Yes
Other Schools to Which Students Applied: Georgetown, NYU, Stanford, UC Berkeley, UCLA
Other Admissions Factors Considered: Outstanding academic and professional promise, background and experience that will enhance the diversity of the student body or the profession
Number of Applications Received: 4,669
Number of Applicants Accepted: 1,140
Number of Applicants Enrolled: 210

EMPLOYMENT INFORMATION
Employers Who Frequently Hire Grads: Private firms, corporations, federal judges, government, public interest nonprofits
State for Bar Exam: CA, NY, AZ, WA
Pass Rate for First-Time Bar: 89%

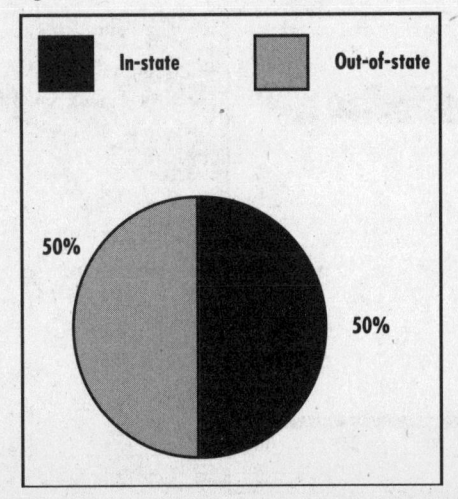

In-state / Out-of-state: 50% / 50%

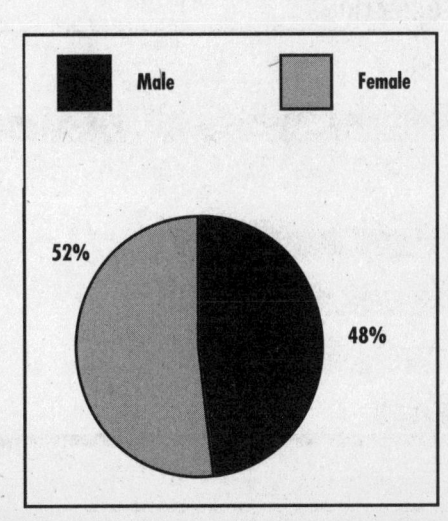

Male / Female: 48% / 52%

UNIVERSITY OF SOUTHERN MAINE
School of Law

Admissions Contact: Assistant Dean, Barbara Gauditz
246 Deering Avenue, Portland, ME 04102
Admissions Phone: 207-780-4341 • Admissions Fax: 207-780-4239
Admissions E-mail: law@usm.maine.edu • Web Address: www.law.usm.maine.edu

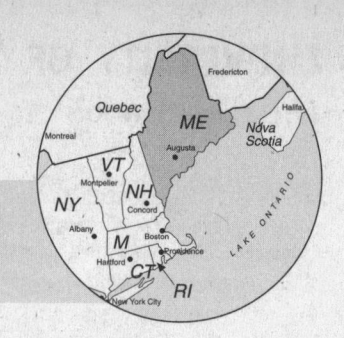

INSTITUTIONAL INFORMATION
Public/Private: Public
Environment: Urban
Schedule: Full time only
Student/Faculty Ratio: 17:1
Total Faculty: 17
% Female: 35

PROGRAMS
Advanced Degrees Offered: JD
Combined Degrees Offered: JD/MA
Grading System: Letter system
Clinical Program Required? No
Clinical Program Description: General Practice Clinic, Criminal Law Practicum, Family Law Clinic
Legal Writing/Methods Course Requirements: 3 credits first semester, 2 credits second semester

STUDENT INFORMATION
Enrollment of Law School: 262
% Male/Female: 57/43
% Full Time: 97
% Full Time That Are International: 2
% Minority: 5
Average Age of Entering Class: 30

RESEARCH FACILITIES
School-Supported Research Centers: CalTech; International Gay/Lesbian Archives

EXPENSES/FINANCIAL AID
Annual Tuition (Residents/Nonresidents): $9,900/$17,790
Room and Board: $7,496
Books and Supplies: $1,050
Average Grant: $2,961
Average Loan: $16,442
% of Aid That Is Merit-Based: 20
% Receiving Some Sort of Aid: 80
Average Debt: $38,000
Tuition Per Credit (Residents/Nonresidents): $276/$548
Fees Per Credit: $952

ADMISSIONS INFORMATION
Application Fee: $25
Regular Application Deadline: 2/15
Regular Notification: Rolling
LSDAS Accepted? Yes
Average GPA: 3.1
Range of GPA: 2.8–3.4
Average LSAT: 155
Range of LSAT: 149–157
Transfer Students Accepted? Yes
Other Schools to Which Students Applied: Vermont Law School, Suffolk University, Boston College, Northeastern University, Franklin Pierce Law Center, Boston University, Western New England College, American University
Other Admissions Factors Considered: Overall academic record, difficulty of courses taken, undergraduate institution, professional background
Number of Applicants Enrolled: 77

INTERNATIONAL STUDENTS
TOEFL Required of International Students? Yes

EMPLOYMENT INFORMATION

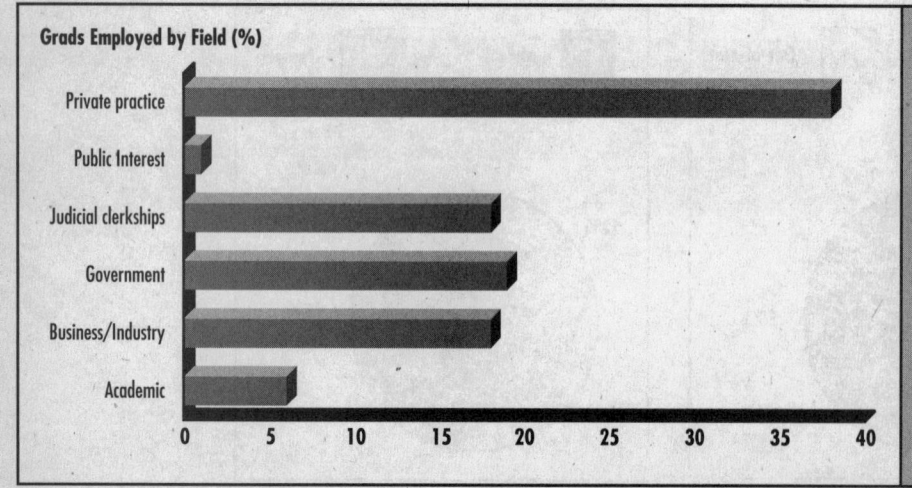

Grads Employed by Field (%)
- Private practice: ~38
- Public Interest: ~1
- Judicial clerkships: ~18
- Government: ~18
- Business/Industry: ~18
- Academic: ~5

Rate of Placement: 77%
State for Bar Exam: ME
Number Taking Bar Exam: 52
Pass Rate for First-Time Bar: 71%

UNIVERSITY OF TENNESSEE
College of Law

Admissions Contact: Director of Admissions and Career Services, Karen R. Britton
1505 West Cumberland Avenue, Knoxville, TN 37996
Admissions Phone: 865-974-4131 • Admissions Fax: 865-974-1572
Admissions E-mail: lawadmit@libra.law.utk.edu • Web Address: www.law.utk.edu

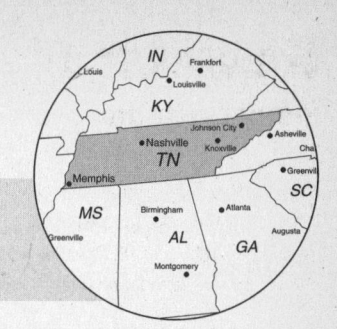

INSTITUTIONAL INFORMATION
Public/Private: Public
Student/Faculty Ratio: 13:1
Total Faculty: 57
% Part Time: 49
% Female: 37
% Minority: 5

PROGRAMS
Academic Specialties: Commercial Law; concentrations in Business Transactions and Advocacy and Dispute Resolution
Advanced Degrees Offered: JD (3 years/6 semesters)
Combined Degrees Offered: JD/MBA (4 years)
Grading System: Letter system; Pass/Fail available for some courses
Clinical Program Required? No
Legal Writing Course Requirements? No
Legal Methods Course Requirements? Yes
Legal Methods Description: Legal Process I and II are required in the first year of law school as an introduction to formal legal writing, appellate procedure, and oral advocacy.
Legal Research Course Requirements? No
Moot Court Requirement? No
Public Interest Law Requirement? No
Academic Journals: *Tennessee Law Review*

STUDENT INFORMATION
Enrollment of Law School: 467
% Out of State: 20
% Male/Female: 52/48
% Full Time: 100
% Full Time That Are International: 0
% Minority: 15
Average Age of Entering Class: 25

EXPENSES/FINANCIAL AID
Annual Tuition (Residents/Nonresidents): $6,118/$17,580
Room and Board: $6,216
Books and Supplies: $1,244
Financial Aid Application Deadline: 3/1
Average Grant: $6,200
Average Loan: $16,460
% of Aid That Is Merit-Based: 52
% Receiving Some Sort of Aid: 81
Average Total Aid Package: $16,874
Average Debt: $39,728
Tuition Per Credit (Residents/Nonresidents): $340/$977
Fees Per Credit (Residents/Nonresidents): $25/$42

ADMISSIONS INFORMATION
Application Fee: $15
Regular Application Deadline: 2/15
Regular Notification: 3/15
LSDAS Accepted? Yes
Average GPA: 3.5
Range of GPA: 3.2–3.7
Average LSAT: 156
Range of LSAT: 154–159
Transfer Students Accepted? Yes
Other Schools to Which Students Applied: The University of Memphis, Vanderbilt University, Mercer University, University of Kentucky, Samford University, University of Georgia, University of North Carolina at Chapel Hill
Other Admissions Factors Considered: Academic factors; employment; activities and service; economic, social or cultural background; evidence of maturity, responsibility, and motivation; circumstances that may have affected the applicant's GPA or LSAT
Number of Applications Received: 1,069
Number of Applicants Accepted: 386
Number of Applicants Enrolled: 156

INTERNATIONAL STUDENTS
TOEFL Required of International Students? Yes

EMPLOYMENT INFORMATION

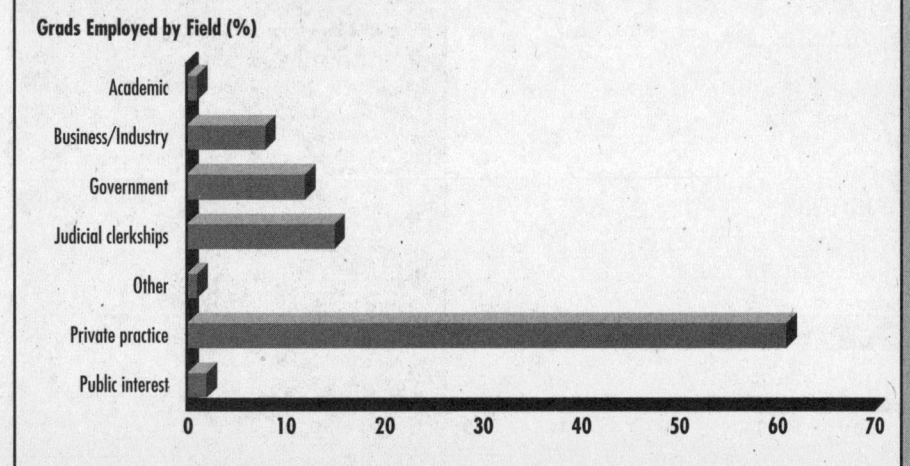

Grads Employed by Field (%)
- Academic: ~1
- Business/Industry: ~8
- Government: ~10
- Judicial clerkships: ~15
- Other: ~1
- Private practice: ~62
- Public interest: ~2

Rate of Placement: 99%
Average Starting Salary: $59,133
Employers Who Frequently Hire Grads: Law firms and judges across the Southeast and the United States
State for Bar Exam: TN
Pass Rate for First-Time Bar: 88%

UNIVERSITY OF TEXAS—AUSTIN
School of Law

Admissions Contact: Assistant Dean for Admissions
727 East Dean Keeton Street, Austin, TX 78705-3299
Admissions Phone: 512-232-1200 • Admissions Fax: 512-471-6988
Admissions E-mail: admissions@mail.law.utexas.edu • Web Address: www.utexas.edu/law

INSTITUTIONAL INFORMATION
Public/Private: Public
Student/Faculty Ratio: 18:1
Total Faculty: 176
% Part Time: 59
% Female: 26
% Minority: 9

PROGRAMS
Academic Specialties: Very broad and diverse curriculum. Specialties include Commercial Law, Constitutional Law, Criminal Law, Environmental Law, International Law, Labor Law, Property.
Advanced Degrees Offered: LLM (1 year)
Combined Degrees Offered: JD/MBA; JD/MPA; JD/MA Latin American Studies; JD/MSCRP; JD/MA in Russian, East European, and European Studies; JD/MA in Middle Eastern Studies; informal combined programs leading to the JD/PhD in Government, History, or Philosophy
Grading System: A+ (4.3), A (4.0), A– (3.7), B+ (3.3), B (3.0), B– (2.7), C+ (2.3), C (2.0), D (1.7), F (1.3)
Clinical Program Required? No
Clinical Programs Description: Mediation Clinic, Housing Law Clinic, Domestic Violence Clinic, Capital Punishment Clinic, Children's Rights Clinic, Criminal Defense Clinic, Juvenile Justice Clinic, Mental Health Clinic, Immigration Law Clinic
Legal Writing Course Requirements? Yes
Legal Writing Description: 1 semester, first year
Legal Methods Course Requirements? No

Legal Research Course Requirements? Yes
Legal Research Description: 1 semester, first year, combined with Legal Writing
Moot Court Requirement? Yes
Moot Court Description: Part of required first-year Legal Writing course
Public Interest Law Requirement? No
Academic Journals: *American Journal of Criminal Law, Texas Environmental Law Journal, Texas Forum on Civil Liberties and Civil Rights, Texas Hispanic Journal of Law and Policy, Texas Intellectual Property Law Journal, Texas International Law Journal, Texas Journal of Business Law, Texas Journal of Women and the Law, Texas Law Review, Texas Review of Entertainment and Sports Law, Texas Review of Law and Politics, The Review of Litigation*

STUDENT INFORMATION
Enrollment of Law School: 1,453
% Out of State: 20
% Male/Female: 51/49
% Full Time: 100
% Full Time That Are International: 1
% Minority: 22
Average Age of Entering Class: 26

EXPENSES/FINANCIAL AID
Annual Tuition (Residents/Nonresidents): $6,060/$15,060
Room and Board: $7,332
Books and Supplies: $898
Average Grant: $2,200
Average Loan: $18,130

% of Aid That Is Merit-Based: 25
% Receiving Some Sort of Aid: 93
Average Total Aid Package: $26,530
Average Debt: $48,000
Tuition Per Credit (Residents/Nonresidents): $202/$502

ADMISSIONS INFORMATION
Application Fee: $65
Regular Application Deadline: 2/1
Regular Notification: 4/30
LSDAS Accepted? Yes
Average GPA: 3.6
Range of GPA: 3.5–3.8
Average LSAT: 161
Range of LSAT: 158–165
Transfer Students Accepted? Yes
Other Schools to Which Students Applied: Duke University, Georgetown University, University of Houston, University of Michigan, University of Virginia
Other Admissions Factors Considered: The admissions committee attempts to identify those students with the greatest probability of success in law school by considering both proven predictors (LSAT, GPA, undergraduate school, and major) and all other factors in the applicant's file.
Number of Applications Received: 4,451
Number of Applicants Accepted: 1,050
Number of Applicants Enrolled: 484

INTERNATIONAL STUDENTS
TOEFL Required of International Students? Yes
Minimum TOEFL: 213

EMPLOYMENT INFORMATION

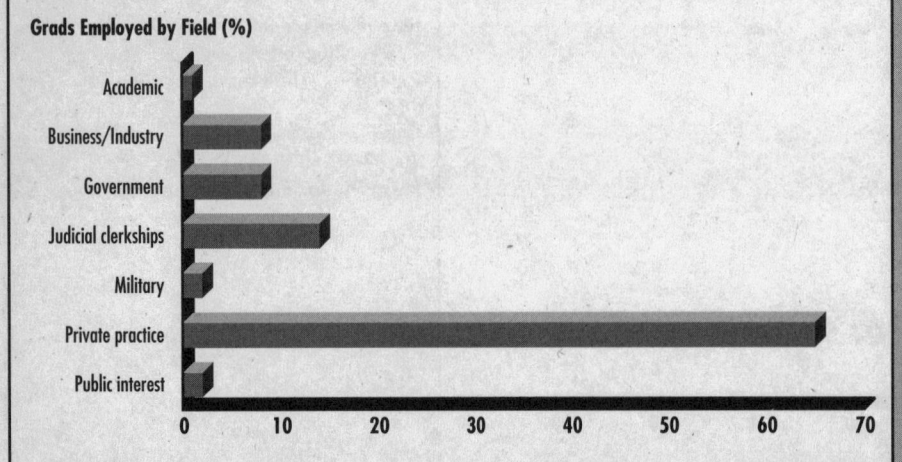

Grads Employed by Field (%):
- Academic
- Business/Industry
- Government
- Judicial clerkships
- Military
- Private practice
- Public interest

Rate of Placement: 99%
Average Starting Salary: $88,266
Employers Who Frequently Hire Grads: Baker Botts, LLP; Cravath, Swaine, and Moore; Ernst & Young, LLP; Fulbright & Jaworski, LLP; Skadden, Arps, Slate, Meagher & Flom, LLP; Supreme Court of Texas; U.S. Department of Justice; Vinson & Elkins, LLP; Winstead, Sechrest & Minick, PC
State for Bar Exam: TX
Pass Rate for First-Time Bar: 93%

UNIVERSITY OF THE DISTRICT OF COLUMBIA
David A. Clarke School of Law

Admissions Contact: Director of Admissions, Vivian Canty
4200 Connecticut Avenue, NW, Washington, DC 20008
Admissions Phone: 202-274-7336 • Admissions Fax: 202-274-5583
Admissions E-mail: vcanty@law.udc.edu • Web Address: www.law.udc.edu

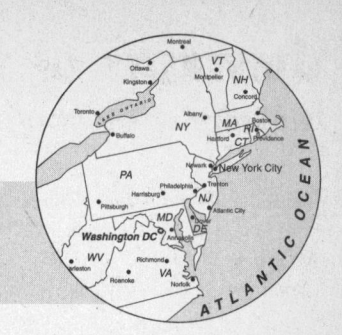

INSTITUTIONAL INFORMATION
Public/Private: Public
Student/Faculty Ratio: 9:1
Total Faculty: 23
% Female: 43
% Minority: 39

PROGRAMS
Academic Specialties: Public Interest and Civil Rights Law emphasis; 14 required credits in clinics serving indigent D.C. residents
Advanced Degrees Offered: JD (3 years)
Grading System: 4.0 scale: A (4.0), B (3.0), C (2.0), D (1.0)
Clinical Program Required? Yes
Clinical Programs Description: Legislation, Juvenile/Special Education, HIV/AIDS, Housing and Consumer, Community Development, Small Business
Legal Writing Course Requirements? Yes
Legal Writing Description: Lawyering Process I and II are required first-year courses and carry 5 credits. They are taught in small sections of approximately 12 students.
Legal Methods Course Requirements? No
Legal Research Course Requirements? No
Moot Court Requirement? Yes
Moot Court Description: Moot court is a required 2-credit course and is part of the Legal Writing curriculum.

Public Interest Law Requirement? Yes
Public Interest Law Description: Law and Justice is a required course offered in the first year. One component of the course is 40 hours of law-related community service which must be completed by the end of the first year.
Academic Journals: *University of the District of Columbia Law Review*

STUDENT INFORMATION
Enrollment of Law School: 126
% Out of State: 55
% Male/Female: 36/64
% Full Time: 100
% Minority: 74
Average Age of Entering Class: 30

RESEARCH FACILITIES
Research Resources Available: Library of Congress, 5 area law schools

EXPENSES/FINANCIAL AID
Annual Tuition (Residents/Nonresidents): $7,000/$14,000
Room and Board (Off Campus): $19,900
Books and Supplies: $2,000
Financial Aid Application Deadline: 5/1
Average Grant: $5,033
Average Loan: $21,000
% of Aid That Is Merit-Based: 12
% Receiving Some Sort of Aid: 96
Average Total Aid Package: $34,000

Average Debt: $63,000
Fees Per Credit (Residents/Nonresidents): $250/$500

ADMISSIONS INFORMATION
Application Fee: $35
Regular Application Deadline: 4/1
Regular Notification: Rolling
LSDAS Accepted? Yes
Average GPA: 2.7
Range of GPA: 2.3–3.0
Average LSAT: 148
Range of LSAT: 145–150
Transfer Students Accepted? Yes
Other Schools to Which Students Applied: American University, City University of New York, George Mason University, Howard University, The Catholic University of America, University of Baltimore, University of Maryland—College Park
Other Admissions Factors Considered: Goals, family background, community involvement, graduate work (if applicable), college attended, college major
Number of Applications Received: 427
Number of Applicants Accepted: 94
Number of Applicants Enrolled: 40

INTERNATIONAL STUDENTS
TOEFL Required of International Students? Yes

EMPLOYMENT INFORMATION

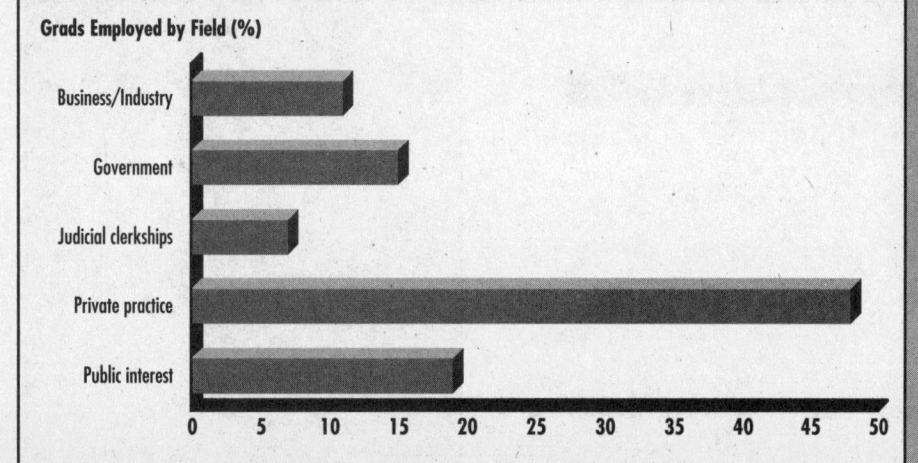

Grads Employed by Field (%)
- Business/Industry: ~11
- Government: ~15
- Judicial clerkships: ~7
- Private practice: ~48
- Public interest: ~19

Rate of Placement: 87%
Average Starting Salary: $55,200
Employers Who Frequently Hire Grads: District of Columbia Council, various U.S. agencies, legal services providers, smaller litigation-oriented law firms
State for Bar Exam: MD
Pass Rate for First-Time Bar: 55%

UNIVERSITY OF THE PACIFIC
McGeorge School of Law

Admissions Contact: Dean of Students, Admissions Office
3200 Fifth Avenue, Sacramento, CA 95817
Admissions Phone: 916-739-7105 • Admissions Fax: 916-739-7134
Admissions E-mail: admissionsmcgeorge@uop.edu • Web Address: www.mcgeorge.edu

INSTITUTIONAL INFORMATION
Public/Private: Private
Environment: Urban
Academic Calendar: Semester
Schedule: Full time or part time
Student/Faculty Ratio: 22:1
Total Faculty: 103
% Part Time: 57
% Female: 14
% Minority: 5

PROGRAMS
Academic Specialties: Governmental Affairs program offers certificate concurrently with JD degree; particular faculty strengths in areas of Criminal Law, Trial and Appellate Advocacy, Environmental Law, Taxation, Child and Elder Law, International Business Law, Government Affairs
Advanced Degrees Offered: JD (3-4 years), LLM Transnational Business Practice (1 year)
Combined Degrees Offered: JD/MBA, JD/MPPA, JD/MA or MS upon approval
Grading System: Letter and numerical system, A+ to F; A+ (4.33)
Clinical Program Required? No
Clinical Program Description: 5 on-campus live-client clinics and over 50 internships with local, state, and federal offices and courts.
Legal Writing/Methods Course Requirements: First-year, year-long program offered in small sections

STUDENT INFORMATION
Enrollment of Law School: 1,050
% Male/Female: 51/49
% Full Time: 66
% Full Time That Are International: 0
% Minority: 25
Average Age of Entering Class: 25

RESEARCH FACILITIES
Computers/Workstations Available: 70
School-Supported Research Centers: California State University—Sacramento and the Eberhardt School of Business of the University of the Pacific for joint degree programs.

EXPENSES/FINANCIAL AID
Annual Tuition: $22,956
Room and Board: $8,883
Books and Supplies: $610
Average Grant: $4,969
Average Loan: $18,500
% Receiving Some Sort of Aid: 92
Average Total Aid Package: $28,813
Average Debt: $64,409
Fees Per Credit: $739

ADMISSIONS INFORMATION
Application Fee: $40
Regular Application Deadline: 5/15
Regular Notification: Rolling
LSDAS Accepted? Yes
Average GPA: 3.0
Range of GPA: 2.7–3.3
Average LSAT: 151
Range of LSAT: 148–154
Transfer Students Accepted? Yes
Other Schools to Which Students Applied: University of California—Davis, Santa Clara University, University of San Diego, University of San Francisco, University of California—Hastings, Loyola Marymount University, Golden Gate University, Southwestern University
Other Admissions Factors Considered: Career experiences, graduate study, extracurricular leadership activities, recommendation letters, factors that contribute to student body diversity
Number of Applications Received: 1,680
Number of Applicants Accepted: 1,174
Number of Applicants Enrolled: 364

INTERNATIONAL STUDENTS
TOEFL Required of International Students? Yes
Minimum TOEFL: 600

EMPLOYMENT INFORMATION

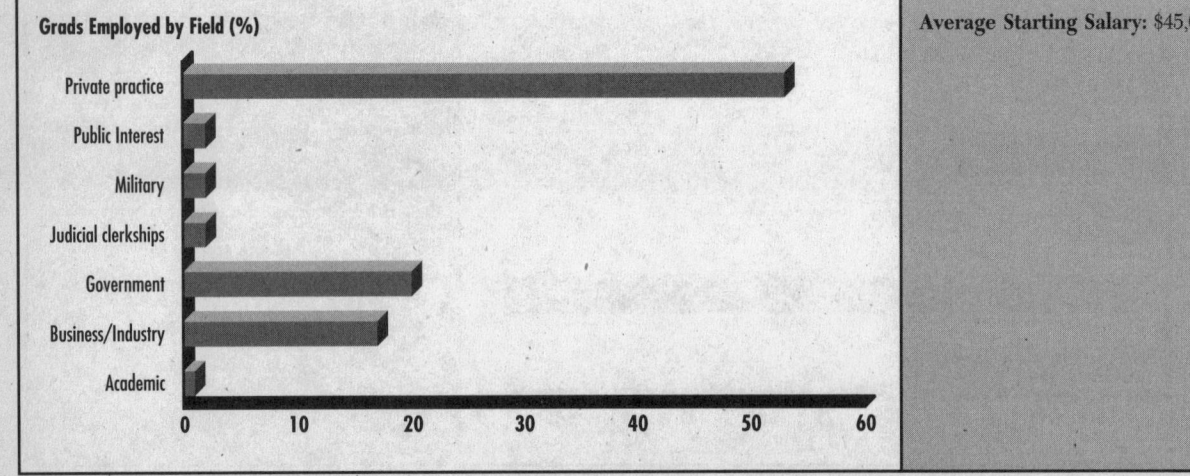

Grads Employed by Field (%)
- Private practice: ~53
- Public Interest: ~2
- Military: ~1
- Judicial clerkships: ~2
- Government: ~20
- Business/Industry: ~18
- Academic: ~1

Average Starting Salary: $45,000

UNIVERSITY OF TOLEDO
College of Law

Admissions Contact: Assistant Dean for Admissions
2801 West Bancroft, Toledo, OH 43606
Admissions Phone: 419-530-4131 • Admissions Fax: 419-530-4345
Admissions E-mail: law.admissions@utoledo.edu • Web Address: www.utlaw.edu

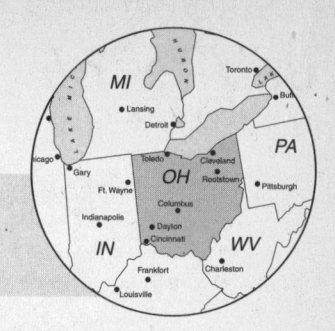

INSTITUTIONAL INFORMATION
Public/Private: Public
Student/Faculty Ratio: 14:1
Total Faculty: 51
% Part Time: 35
% Female: 31
% Minority: 4

PROGRAMS
Academic Specialties: Environmental Law, International Law, Intellectual Property Law, Civil Procedure, Commercial Law, Constitutional Law, Corporation Securities Law, Criminal Law, Government Services, Human Rights Law, Intellectual Property Law, International Law, Labor Law, Legal History, Legal Philosophy, Property, Taxation
Advanced Degrees Offered: JD (3 to 4 years)
Combined Degrees Offered: JD/MBA (3 to 3.5 years), JD/MSE, JD/MS, JD/PhD Engineering (3.5 to 4 years)
Grading System: A (4.0) to F (0.0), DR (0.0), W (0.0)
Clinical Program Required? No
Clinical Programs Description: The Criminal Law Practice Program (Prosecutor Intern Program) places legal interns in prosecutors' offices in Toledo and its environs. The Dispute Resolution Clinic trains law students in mediation skills and provides mediation services through the county juvenile court to families in conflict. Students are offered the opportunity for basic and advanced mediation training. The Domestic Violence Project provides students with an opportunity to engage in collaborative work with the local prosecutor's office, city and county law enforcement agencies, and area victim advocate groups. The Human Rights Project works to protect the rights of area gay, lesbian, bisexual, and transgendered persons through traditional legislation, educational outreach, legislative action, and community activism.
Legal Writing Course Requirements? No
Legal Methods Course Requirements? Yes
Legal Methods Description: 2 semesters of intensive study of research tools and techniques and their utilization in the preparation of memoranda of law.
Legal Research Course Requirements? Yes
Moot Court Requirement? No
Public Interest Law Requirement? No
Academic Journals: *Law Review*

STUDENT INFORMATION
Enrollment of Law School: 450
% Out of State: 28
% Male/Female: 52/48
% Full Time: 72
% Full Time That Are International: 0
% Minority: 6
Average Age of Entering Class: 27

RESEARCH FACILITIES
Research Resources Available: Toledo Lucas County Public Library, Medical College of Ohio, Toledo Museum of Art
School-Supported Research Centers: The Legal Institute of the Great Lakes (LIGL)

EXPENSES/FINANCIAL AID
Annual Tuition (Residents/Nonresidents): $7,860/$16,330
Room and Board (Off Campus): $6,355
Books and Supplies: $1,056
Financial Aid Application Deadline: 8/1
Average Grant: $7,726
Average Loan: $15,274
% of Aid That Is Merit-Based: 27
% Receiving Some Sort of Aid: 97
Average Total Aid Package: $17,499
Average Debt: $44,648
Tuition Per Credit: $327
Fees Per Credit: $50

ADMISSIONS INFORMATION
Application Fee: $30
Regular Application Deadline: Rolling
Regular Notification: Rolling
LSDAS Accepted? Yes
Average GPA: 3.2
Average LSAT: 154
Transfer Students Accepted? Yes
Number of Applications Received: 808
Number of Applicants Accepted: 429
Number of Applicants Enrolled: 123

EMPLOYMENT INFORMATION

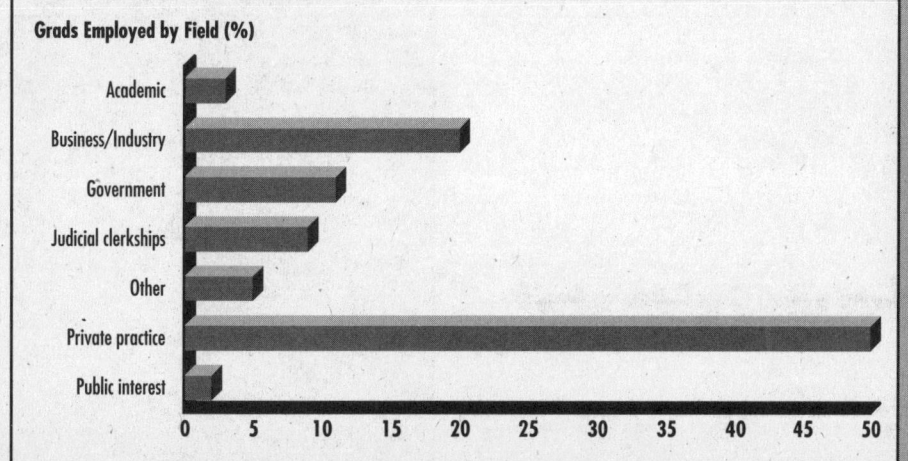

Grads Employed by Field (%)

Field	%
Academic	~2
Business/Industry	~20
Government	~11
Judicial clerkships	~6
Other	~5
Private practice	~50
Public interest	~2

Rate of Placement: 94%
Average Starting Salary: $53,491
Employers Who Frequently Hire Grads: Spengler, Nathanson; Shumaker, Loop & Kendrik; Eastman & Smith; DeNune & Killam; Gallon & Takacs; Wagoner & Steinberg; Kalniz, Iorio & Feldstein; Connelly, Soutar & Jackson; Marshall & Melhorn; Cooper, Walinski & Cramer; Fuller & Henry; Robison, Curphey & O'Connell; Newcomer, Shaffer & Spangler; Watkins, Bates & Carey; Williams, Jilek, Lafferty & Gallagher; Brown, Schlageter, Craig & Shindler
State for Bar Exam: OH, MI, FL, IN, IL
Pass Rate for First-Time Bar: 80%

UNIVERSITY OF TORONTO
Faculty of Law

Admissions Contact: Admissions Officer, Judy Finlay
84 Queens Park, Toronto, ON M5S 2C5 Canada
Admissions Phone: 416-978-3716 • Admissions Fax: 416-978-7899
Admissions E-mail: law.admissions@utoronto.ca • Web Address: www.law.utoronto.ca

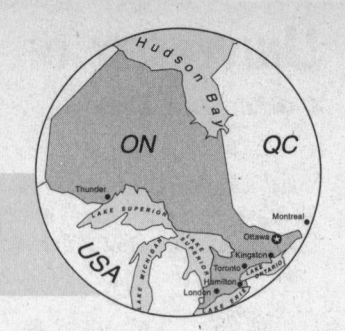

INSTITUTIONAL INFORMATION
Public/Private: Public
Student/Faculty Ratio: 9:1
Total Faculty: 54
% Female: 30

PROGRAMS
Academic Specialties: Administrative Law and Regulation Business Law, including Corporations, Commercial Law, and Taxation; Constitutional Law; Crime and Criminology; Family Law; Intellectual Property and Technology Law; International and Comparative Law; Labor Law and Social Justice Law; Law and Economics; Legal Research and Writing; Legal Theory; Litigation and Dispute Settlement; Women's Studies
Advanced Degrees Offered: LLM (1 year), SJD (1 year plus thesis), MSL (1 year)
Combined Degrees Offered: JD/MBA (4 years), JD/MSW (4 years), JD/MA Criminology (3 years), JD/MA Economics (3 years), JD/MA Political Science, Collaborative Program in International Relations (3 years), JD/MA Russian and East European Studies (4 years), Collaborative Program in Environmental Studies (3 years), JD/PhD Economics (4 years plus dissertation), JD/PhD Philosophy (4 years plus dissertation)
Grading System: Letter grades and overall standing for the year of A, B, or C
Clinical Program Required? Yes
Clinical Programs Description: Centre for Spanish Speaking People, Advocates for Injured Workers, Downtown Legal Services, Enterprise Legal Services; a majority of students take part in at least one clinic program
Legal Writing Course Requirements? Yes
Legal Writing Description: See Legal Methods.
Legal Methods Course Requirements? Yes
Legal Methods Description: The cornerstone of the first-year curriculum is the "small group," which permits students to study one of the first-year subjects with a member of the faculty and 15 classmates and introduces students to the techniques of legal research and writing in a personal and direct setting.
Legal Research Course Requirements? Yes
Legal Research Description: See Legal Methods.
Moot Court Requirement? Yes
Moot Court Description: Students complete a compulsory moot in the first term of their second year and can participate for credit in competitive moots in the second term of their second year. First-year students can compete in voluntary moots.
Public Interest Law Requirement? No
Public Interest Law Description: Many students participate in the Pro Bono Students Canada program, which offers students volunteer placements and summer internships doing pro bono work abroad or domestically.
Academic Journals: *University of Toronto Faculty of Law Review*

STUDENT INFORMATION
Enrollment of Law School: 523
% Male/Female: 50/50
% Full Time: 98
% Minority: 24
Average Age of Entering Class: 25

EXPENSES/FINANCIAL AID
Annual Tuition (Residents/Nonresidents): $12,000/$19,000
Room and Board (On Campus): $8,500
Books and Supplies: $1,000
Financial Aid Application Deadline: 9/30
Average Grant: $3,500
Average Loan: $7,700
% of Aid That Is Merit-Based: 2
Average Total Aid Package: $4,350

ADMISSIONS INFORMATION
Application Fee: $50
Regular Application Deadline: 11/1
Regular Notification: 1/4
LSDAS Accepted? No
Average GPA: 3.8
Range of GPA: 3.6–3.9
Average LSAT: 166
Range of LSAT: 163–169
Transfer Students Accepted? Yes
Other Admissions Factors Considered: Response to disadvantage due to adverse personal or socio-economic circumstances, barriers faced by cultural or linguistic minorities, motivation and involvement in academic and nonacademic activities, impact of temporary or permanent physical disability
Number of Applications Received: 1,640
Number of Applicants Accepted: 278
Number of Applicants Enrolled: 173

EMPLOYMENT INFORMATION

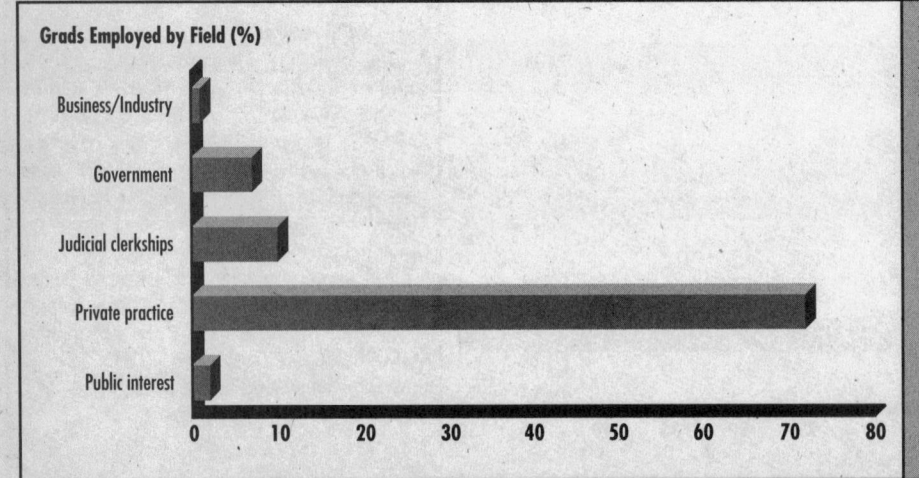

Grads Employed by Field (%)

Field	%
Business/Industry	~3
Government	~7
Judicial clerkships	~10
Private practice	~72
Public interest	~2

Rate of Placement: 95%
Average Starting Salary: $50,000
Employers Who Frequently Hire Grads: All major Toronto law firms; all provincial and federal government departments; many large New York and Boston law firms; large and midsized Vancouver, Halifax, and Calgary law firms
State for Bar Exam: NY, MA, CA

UNIVERSITY OF TULSA
College of Law

Admissions Contact: Assistant Dean of Admissions and Financial Aid
3120 East Fourth Place, Tulsa, OK 74104-3189
Admissions Phone: 918-631-2709 • Web Address: www.utulsa.edu/law

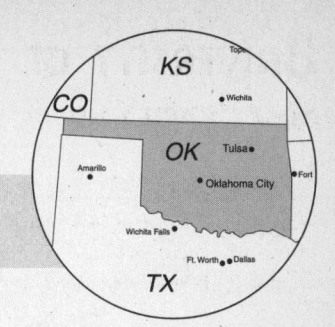

INSTITUTIONAL INFORMATION
Public/Private: Private
Student/Faculty Ratio: 14:1
Total Faculty: 68
% Part Time: 41
% Female: 36
% Minority: 12

PROGRAMS
Academic Specialties: Certificate programs in Alternative Methods of Dispute Resolution; Comparative and International Law; Health Law; Native American Public Policy and Regulation; Resources, Energy, and Environmental Law; and Practical Skills. Other specialties include Government Services.
Advanced Degrees Offered: LLM American Indian and Indigenous Law (1 to 2 years, both academic track and research track available)
Combined Degrees Offered: History, Industrial/Organizational Psychology, Geosciences, Biological Sciences, Anthropology, Accounting, Taxation, Business Administration, Clinical Psychology, English (each joint degree program takes approximately 4 years to complete)
Grading System: A (4.0), B+ (3.5), B (3.0), C+ (2.5), C (2.0), D+ (1.5), D (1.0), F (0.0)
Clinical Program Required? No
Clinical Programs Description: Older Americans Law Project, Health Law Project, Judicial and Legal internship programs

Legal Writing Course Requirements? Yes
Legal Methods Course Requirements? Yes
Legal Methods Description: 1-year, 6-credit-hour course teaches students to research and analyze the law and to communicate that analysis effectively in writing.
Legal Research Course Requirements? Yes
Moot Court Requirement? No
Moot Court Description: Although moot court is not required, we do participate on regional, national and international levels.
Public Interest Law Requirement? No
Academic Journals: *Law Review, International Law Journal, Energy Law Journal*

STUDENT INFORMATION
Enrollment of Law School: 577
% Out of State: 50
% Male/Female: 70/30
% Full Time: 81
% Full Time That Are International: 1
% Minority: 18
Average Age of Entering Class: 25

EXPENSES/FINANCIAL AID
Annual Tuition: $19,425
Room and Board (On/Off Campus): $6,000/$7,210
Books and Supplies: $1,500
Financial Aid Application Deadline: 4/1
Average Grant: $6,300
Average Loan: $24,468
% of Aid That Is Merit-Based: 25
% Receiving Some Sort of Aid: 89
Average Total Aid Package: $22,538
Average Debt: $69,021
Tuition Per Credit: $725

ADMISSIONS INFORMATION
Application Fee: $30
Regular Application Deadline: Rolling
Regular Notification: Rolling
LSDAS Accepted? Yes
Average GPA: 3.1
Range of GPA: 2.1–4.0
Average LSAT: 148
Range of LSAT: 134–167
Transfer Students Accepted? Yes
Number of Applications Received: 876
Number of Applicants Accepted: 543
Number of Applicants Enrolled: 223

INTERNATIONAL STUDENTS
TOEFL Required of International Students? Yes

EMPLOYMENT INFORMATION

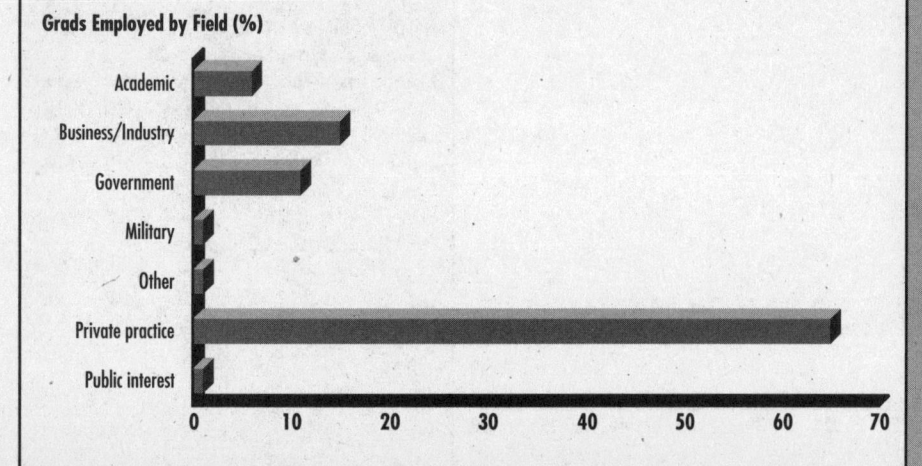

Grads Employed by Field (%)
- Academic: ~5
- Business/Industry: ~15
- Government: ~10
- Military: ~1
- Other: ~1
- Private practice: ~65
- Public interest: ~1

Rate of Placement: 83%
Average Starting Salary: $57,211
Employers Who Frequently Hire Grads: Shook, Hardy & Bacon (Kansas City, MO); Williams; Tulsa law firms
State for Bar Exam: OK, TX, MO, FL, GA
Pass Rate for First-Time Bar: 80%

UNIVERSITY OF UTAH
SJ Quinney College of Law

Admissions Contact: Coordinator for Admissions, Gwen Spotted Elk
Admissions, 332 South 1400 East, Room 101, Salt Lake City, UT 84112
Admissions Phone: 801-581-7479 • Admissions Fax: 801-581-6897
Admissions E-mail: admission@law.utah.edu • Web Address: www.law.utah.edu

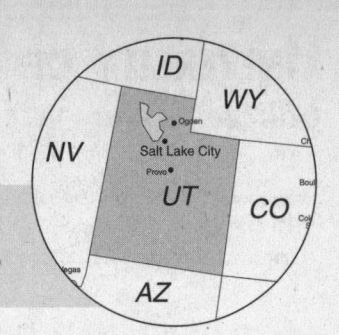

INSTITUTIONAL INFORMATION
Public/Private: Public
Student/Faculty Ratio: 13:1
Total Faculty: 65
% Part Time: 51
% Female: 30
% Minority: 13

PROGRAMS
Academic Specialties: Environmental, Resource, and Energy Law; Constitutional Law; Business and Commercial Law; Constitutional Law; Criminal Law; International Law
Advanced Degrees Offered: LLM Environmental Law (1 year)
Combined Degrees Offered: JD/MPA (4 years), JD/MBA (4 years), others by petition
Grading System: 4.0
Clinical Program Required? No
Clinical Programs Description: Mediation Clinic, Health Law Clinic, Legislative Clinic, Criminal Law Clinic, Civil Clinic (5 placement areas)
Legal Writing Course Requirements? Yes
Legal Writing Description: Full-year Legal Methods course covering legal writing and research
Legal Methods Course Requirements? Yes
Legal Methods Description: 2 semesters, 4 credits; see Legal Writing.
Legal Research Course Requirements? Yes
Legal Research Description: See Legal Writing.

Moot Court Requirement? No
Moot Court Description: 1-year intramural moot court competition program; finalists are invited to serve on the National Moot Court Competition team
Public Interest Law Requirement? No
Public Interest Law Description: Pro Bono Project facilitates volunteerism and public service
Academic Journals: *Utah Law Review, Journal of Land, Resources & Environmental Law, Journal of Law and Family Studies*

STUDENT INFORMATION
Enrollment of Law School: 388
% Out of State: 20
% Male/Female: 59/41
% Full Time: 100
% Full Time That Are International: 1
% Minority: 14
Average Age of Entering Class: 28

EXPENSES/FINANCIAL AID
Annual Tuition (Residents/Nonresidents): $6,213/$13,952
Room and Board: $6,264
Books and Supplies: $1,156
Financial Aid Application Deadline: 3/15
Average Grant: $4,340
Average Loan: $14,000
% of Aid That Is Merit-Based: 15

% Receiving Some Sort of Aid: 81
Average Total Aid Package: $16,400
Average Debt: $39,000

ADMISSIONS INFORMATION
Application Fee: $50
Regular Application Deadline: 2/1
Regular Notification: Rolling
LSDAS Accepted? Yes
Average GPA: 3.5
Range of GPA: 3.3–3.7
Average LSAT: 158
Range of LSAT: 154–162
Transfer Students Accepted? Yes
Other Schools to Which Students Applied: Arizona State University, Brigham Young University, George Washington University, University of Arizona, University of Colorado, University of Oregon, University of San Diego
Other Admissions Factors Considered: Personal statement; letter of recommendation; resume; leadership; diverse educational, cultural, economic, and/or ethnic background
Number of Applications Received: 908
Number of Applicants Accepted: 344
Number of Applicants Enrolled: 138

INTERNATIONAL STUDENTS
TOEFL Required of International Students? Yes
Minimum TOEFL: 250

EMPLOYMENT INFORMATION

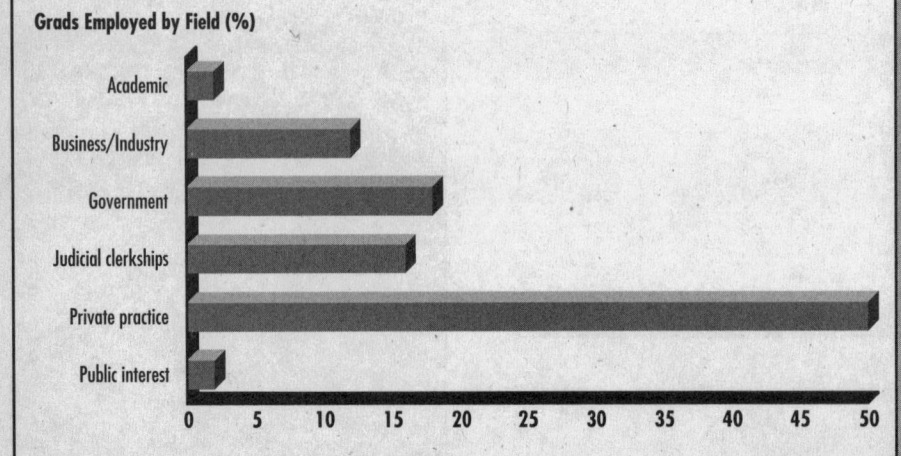

Grads Employed by Field (%):
- Academic
- Business/Industry
- Government
- Judicial clerkships
- Private practice
- Public interest

Rate of Placement: 96%
Average Starting Salary: $55,377
Employers Who Frequently Hire Grads: Utah Attorney General's Office; Van Cott, Bagley, Cornwall & McCarthy (Salt Lake City); Ray, Quinney & Nebeker (Salt Lake City); Jones, Waldo, Holbrook, & Mconough
State for Bar Exam: UT, CA, NV, AZ, ID
Pass Rate for First-Time Bar: 90%

UNIVERSITY OF VICTORIA
Faculty of Law

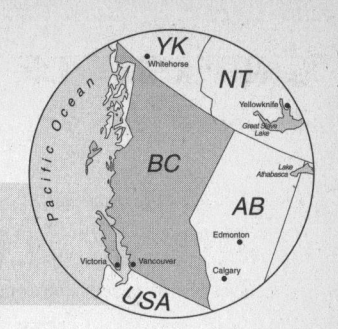

Admissions Contact: Admissions Assistant, Neela Paige
PO Box 2400, Victoria, BC V8W 3H7 Canada
Admissions Phone: 250-721-8151 • Admissions Fax: 250-721-6390
Admissions E-mail: lawadmss@uvic.ca • Web Address: www.law.uvic.ca

INSTITUTIONAL INFORMATION
Public/Private: Public
Student/Faculty Ratio: 7:1
Total Faculty: 57
% Part Time: 54
% Female: 20
% Minority: 5

PROGRAMS
Academic Specialties: Environmental Law, Intellectual Property Law, Aboriginal Law, Asia-Pacific Law, Dispute Resolution, International Law, Legal History, Property
Combined Degrees Offered: LLB/MPA (4 years), LLB/MBA (4 years), LLB/MIA (3.5 years), LLB/BCL (4.5 years), LLB/MA in Indigenous Government (4 years)
Grading System: 9 point system: A+ (9), A (8), A– (7), B+ (6), B (5), B– (4), C+ (3), C (2), D (1), F (0)
Clinical Program Required? No
Clinical Programs Description: Law 349-Business Law Clinic: Students apply knowledge gained in earlier courses to assist small business owners in assessing their legal requirements. Law 350-Clinical Law Term: Provides students with the opportunity to integrate legal theory, legal skills, and public service in a community law office. Law 353-Environmental Law Centre Clinic: Students study theory, conduct research projects, and engage in public interest environmental lawyering.
Legal Writing Course Requirements? Yes
Legal Writing Description: Law 110-Legal Research and Writing (8 months) acquaints first year students with the variety of materials in the Law Library and provides a knowledge of basic legal research techniques. Through a variety of written assignments, students become familiar with accepted principles pertaining to proper citation in legal writing and develop a degree of proficiency in legal writing and research.
Legal Methods Course Requirements? Yes
Legal Methods Description: Law 104-The Law, Legislation, and Policy (8 months during the first year) considers the development and interpretation of legislation.
Legal Research Course Requirements? Yes
Legal Research Description: Part of the Law 110 as listed under Legal Writing
Moot Court Requirement? Yes
Moot Court Description: All students must complete a moot court exercise in their first year as part of the Legal Research and Writing Course. In upper years, there are optional competitive mooting programs, in which students can take part for credit.
Public Interest Law Requirement? No
Academic Journals: *APPEAL: Review of Current Law and Law Reform*

STUDENT INFORMATION
Enrollment of Law School: 357
% Out of State: 50
% Male/Female: 42/58
% Full Time: 96
% Minority: 20
Average Age of Entering Class: 27

EXPENSES/FINANCIAL AID
Annual Tuition (Residents/Nonresidents): $2,896/$8,688
Room and Board (On/Off Campus): $7,000/$10,000
Books and Supplies: $1,000
Average Grant: $2,500
Average Loan: $10,000
% of Aid That Is Merit-Based: 60
% Receiving Some Sort of Aid: 54
Average Total Aid Package: $1,500
Average Debt: $30,000
Tuition Per Credit (Residents/Nonresidents): $191/$573

ADMISSIONS INFORMATION
Application Fee: $50
Regular Application Deadline: 2/1
Regular Notification: 5/31
LSDAS Accepted? No
Average GPA: 3.8
Average LSAT: 162
Transfer Students Accepted? Yes
Other Schools to Which Students Applied: University of British Columbia, University of Toronto
Other Admissions Factors Considered: Academically related extracurricular activities, community involvement, work experience, personal characteristics
Number of Applications Received: 963
Number of Applicants Accepted: 228
Number of Applicants Enrolled: 107

INTERNATIONAL STUDENTS
TOEFL Required of International Students? Yes
Minimum TOEFL: 250

EMPLOYMENT INFORMATION
Rate of Placement: 93%

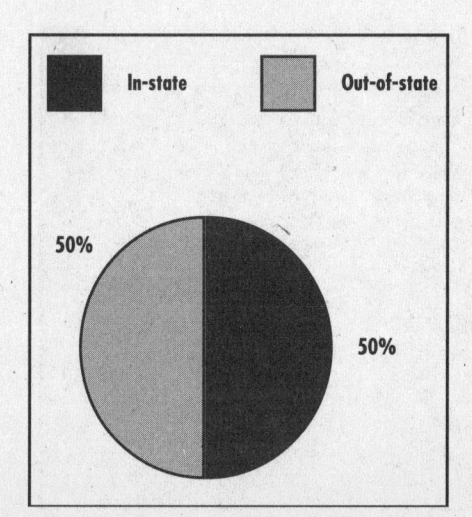

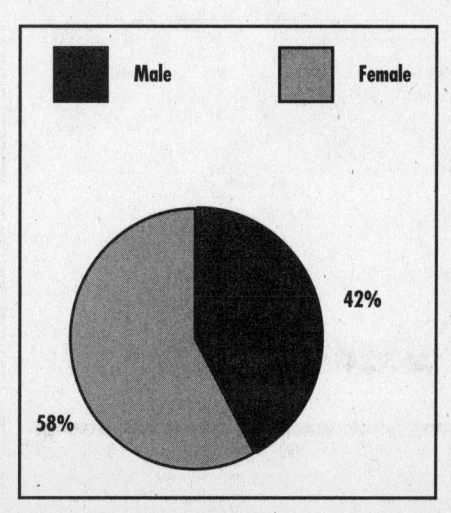

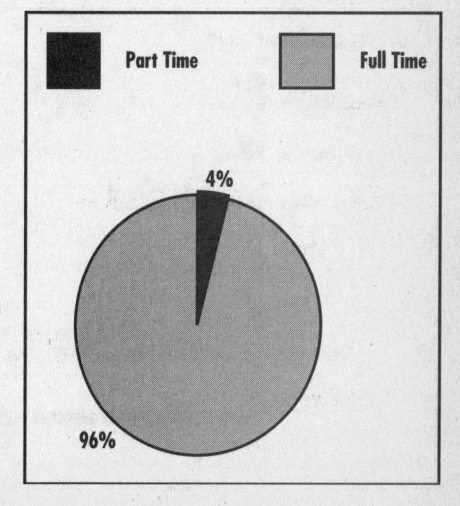

UNIVERSITY OF VIRGINIA
School of Law

Admissions Contact: Associate Dean for Admissions and Career Services, Albert R. Turnbull
580 Massie Road, Charlottesville, VA 22903-1789
Admissions Phone: 434-924-7351 • Admissions Fax: 434-982-2128
Admissions E-mail: lawadmit@virginia.edu • Web Address: www.law.virginia.edu

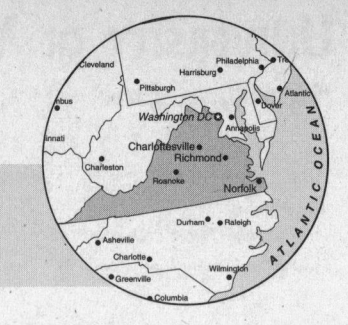

INSTITUTIONAL INFORMATION
Public/Private: Public
Student/Faculty Ratio: 14:1
Total Faculty: 129
% Part Time: 46
% Female: 17
% Minority: 7

PROGRAMS
Academic Specialties: Commercial Law, Constitutional Law, Corporation Securities Law, Criminal Law, Environmental Law, Government Services, Human Rights Law, International Law, Labor Law, Legal History, Taxation
Advanced Degrees Offered: SJD, LLM (1 year full time), JD (3 years full time)
Combined Degrees Offered: JD/PhD Government; JD/MA History, Government, Economics, English, Philosophy, Sociology, Marine Affairs; JD/MBA (4 years full time); JD/MPP; JD/MAcc
Grading System: Letter and numerical system; faculty policy requires adherence to a mean grade of B+ in most classes
Clinical Program Required? No
Clinical Programs Description: Appellate Litigation, Child Advocacy, Criminal Defense, Criminal Prosecution, Employment Discrimination, Environmental Practice, First Amendment, Human Rights, Public Practice, Psychiatry and Civil Practice, Housing Law, Patents and Licensing
Legal Writing Course Requirements? No
Legal Methods Course Requirements? Yes
Legal Methods Description: 2 semesters; small sections; research, writing, and oral argument
Legal Research Course Requirements? No
Moot Court Requirement? No
Moot Court Description: More than 200 second-year students, competing in 2-person teams, hone their oral argument skills in the annual William Minor Lile Moot Court Competition. Distinguished federal and state judges preside in the semifinal and final rounds. Winners receive a cash prize and their names are inscribed on a plaque located outside the 3 moot courtrooms. Teams of students chosen from among those entered in the competition may represent the Law School in the national Moot Court Competition and other extramural competitions.
Public Interest Law Requirement? No
Academic Journals: *Journal of Law and Politics, Virginia Environmental Law Journal, Virginia Journal of International Law, Virginia Journal of Law and Technology, Virginia Journal of Social Policy and the Law, Virginia Journal of Sports and the Law, Virginia Law Review, Virginia Tax Review*

STUDENT INFORMATION
Enrollment of Law School: 1,068
% Out of State: 54
% Male/Female: 55/45
% Full Time: 100
% Minority: 15
Average Age of Entering Class: 24

EXPENSES/FINANCIAL AID
Annual Tuition (Residents/Nonresidents): $16,866/$24,092
Room and Board: $11,280
Books and Supplies: $800
Financial Aid Application Deadline: 2/15
Average Grant: $9,000
Average Loan: $22,300
% of Aid That Is Merit-Based: 26
% Receiving Some Sort of Aid: 79
Average Total Aid Package: $25,143
Average Debt: $57,853

ADMISSIONS INFORMATION
Application Fee: $65
Regular Application Deadline: 1/15
Regular Notification: 4/15
LSDAS Accepted? Yes
Average GPA: 3.6
Range of GPA: 3.5–3.8
Average LSAT: 166
Range of LSAT: 163–169
Transfer Students Accepted? Yes
Other Schools to Which Students Applied: Columbia University, Duke University, Georgetown University, Harvard University, New York University, Stanford University, George Washington University
Other Admissions Factors Considered: Maturing effect of some years away from formal education, rising trend in academic performance, financial pressure requiring employment as undergraduate, significant personal achievement
Number of Applications Received: 3,562
Number of Applicants Accepted: 977
Number of Applicants Enrolled: 350

INTERNATIONAL STUDENTS
TOEFL Required of International Students? Yes

EMPLOYMENT INFORMATION

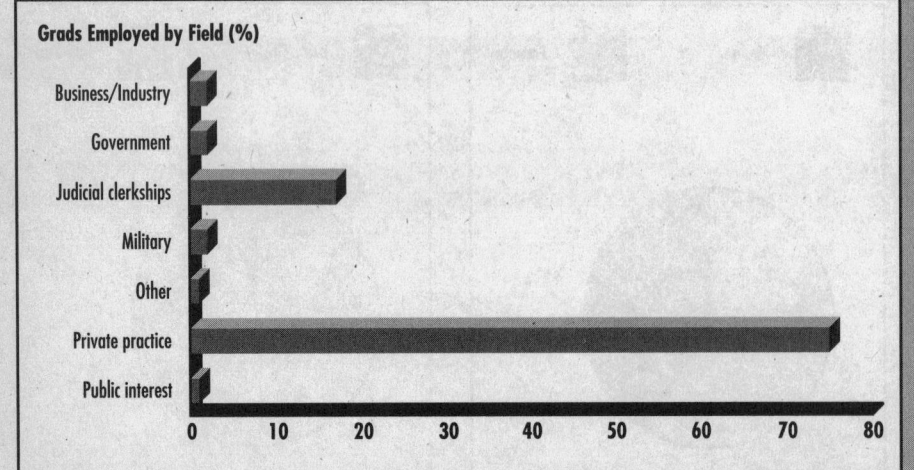

Grads Employed by Field (%)
- Business/Industry
- Government
- Judicial clerkships
- Military
- Other
- Private practice
- Public interest

Rate of Placement: 100%
Average Starting Salary: $100,000
Employers Who Frequently Hire Grads: Graduates are in all top 100 firms in the country.
State for Bar Exam: NY, VA
Pass Rate for First-Time Bar: 96%

UNIVERSITY OF WASHINGTON
School of Law

Admissions Contact: Admissions Supervisor, Kathy Swinehart
1100 NE Campus Parkway, Seattle, WA 98105-6617
Admissions Phone: 206-543-4078 • Admissions Fax: 206-543-5671
Admissions E-mail: admissions@law.washington.edu • Web Address: www.law.washington.edu

INSTITUTIONAL INFORMATION
Public/Private: Public
Student/Faculty Ratio: 13:1
Total Faculty: 47
% Female: 31
% Minority: 8

PROGRAMS
Academic Specialties: Civil Procedure, Commercial Law, Constitutional Law, Corporation Securities Law, Criminal Law, Environmental Law, Government Services, Human Rights Law, Intellectual Property Law, International Law, Labor Law, Legal History, Legal Philosophy, Property, Taxation, Dispute Resolution, Asian Law, International and Comparative Law, Health Law
Advanced Degrees Offered: LLM Asian Law, Law of Sustainable International Development, Taxation
Combined Degrees Offered: Can be arranged with 90 graduate programs at UW
Grading System: A to F
Clinical Program Required? No
Clinical Programs Description: 9 different programs offered
Legal Writing Course Requirements? Yes
Legal Writing Description: Analytic Writing required (full first year)
Legal Methods Course Requirements? Yes
Legal Methods Description: 1 year
Legal Research Course Requirements? No
Moot Court Requirement? No

Public Interest Law Requirement? Yes
Public Interest Law Description: 60 clock hours (2 credits)
Academic Journals: *Washington Law Review, Pacific Rim Law and Policy Journal*

STUDENT INFORMATION
Enrollment of Law School: 485
% Out of State: 20
% Male/Female: 49/51
% Full Time: 100
% Full Time That Are International: 1
% Minority: 6
Average Age of Entering Class: 25

EXPENSES/FINANCIAL AID
Annual Tuition (Residents/Nonresidents): $6,521/$16,724
Room and Board: $8,640
Books and Supplies: $1,000
Financial Aid Application Deadline: 2/28
Average Grant: $5,200
Average Loan: $12,881

% of Aid That Is Merit-Based: 4
% Receiving Some Sort of Aid: 70
Average Debt: $42,260

ADMISSIONS INFORMATION
Application Fee: $50
Regular Application Deadline: 1/15
Regular Notification: 4/1
LSDAS Accepted? Yes
Average GPA: 3.6
Range of GPA: 3.4–3.8
Average LSAT: 162
Range of LSAT: 159–165
Transfer Students Accepted? Yes
Other Schools to Which Students Applied: University of California—Berkeley, University of California—Hastings, Georgetown University, University of California—Los Angeles, George Washington University, Seattle University, University of Southern California
Number of Applications Received: 1,954
Number of Applicants Accepted: 468
Number of Applicants Enrolled: 177

EMPLOYMENT INFORMATION

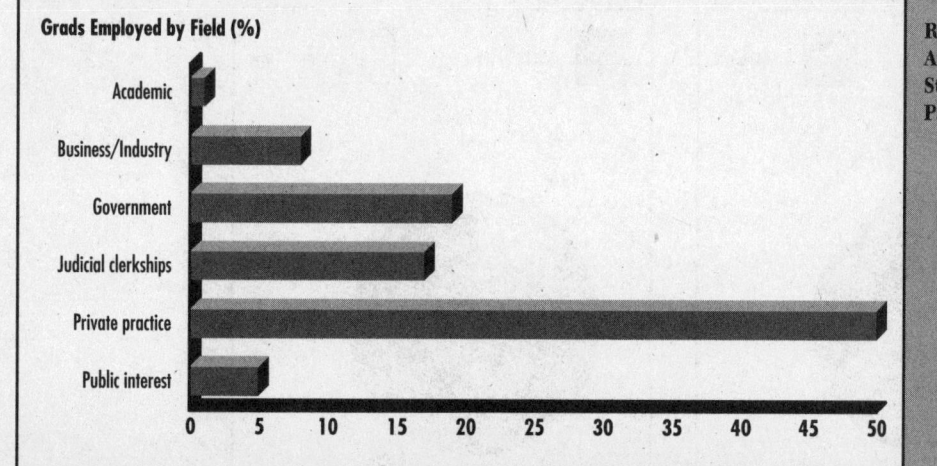

Grads Employed by Field (%)
- Academic
- Business/Industry
- Government
- Judicial clerkships
- Private practice
- Public interest

Rate of Placement: 98%
Average Starting Salary: $65,000
State for Bar Exam: WA
Pass Rate for First-Time Bar: 90%

UNIVERSITY OF WEST LOS ANGELES
School of Law

Admissions Contact: Director of Admissions, Lynda Freeman
1155 West Arbor Vitae Street, Inglewood, CA 90301-2902
Admissions Phone: 310-342-5254 • Admissions Fax: 310-342-5295
Admissions E-mail: lfreeman@uwla.edu • Web Address: www.uwla.edu

INSTITUTIONAL INFORMATION
Public/Private: Private
Student/Faculty Ratio: 40:1
Total Faculty: 36
% Part Time: 81
% Female: 19
% Minority: 17

PROGRAMS
Advanced Degrees Offered: JD (3 years full time, 4 years part time)
Grading System: Letter grade on a 4.0 scale
Clinical Program Required? No
Clinical Programs Description: Judicial externships and lawyer-supervised internships
Legal Writing Course Requirements? Yes
Legal Writing Description: 2 courses are required, a basic research and writing course in the first year and an advanced writing class in the second year
Legal Methods Course Requirements? Yes
Legal Methods Description: First-semester required course for all students.
Legal Research Course Requirements? Yes
Legal Research Description: Basic course required after completion of the first year; Students learn how to use print and on-line research tools
Moot Court Requirement? No
Public Interest Law Requirement? No
Academic Journals: *UWLA Law Review*

STUDENT INFORMATION
Enrollment of Law School: 158
% Male/Female: 50/50
% Full Time: 14
% Minority: 32
Average Age of Entering Class: 35

EXPENSES/FINANCIAL AID
Annual Tuition: $13,365
Books and Supplies: $1,000
Financial Aid Application Deadline: 3/1
Average Loan: $18,500
% Receiving Some Sort of Aid: 90
Average Total Aid Package: $18,500
Average Debt: $70,000
Tuition Per Credit: $495

ADMISSIONS INFORMATION
Application Fee: $55
Regular Application Deadline: Rolling
Regular Notification: Rolling
LSDAS Accepted? No
Range of GPA: 2.0–3.9
Transfer Students Accepted? Yes
Other Admissions Factors Considered: If an applicant has completed less than 60 academic semester units, 3 General CLEP exams are required.
Number of Applications Received: 22
Number of Applicants Accepted: 11
Number of Applicants Enrolled: 7

INTERNATIONAL STUDENTS
TOEFL Required of International Students? Yes
Minimum TOEFL: 213

EMPLOYMENT INFORMATION
State for Bar Exam: CA
Pass Rate for First-Time Bar: 30%

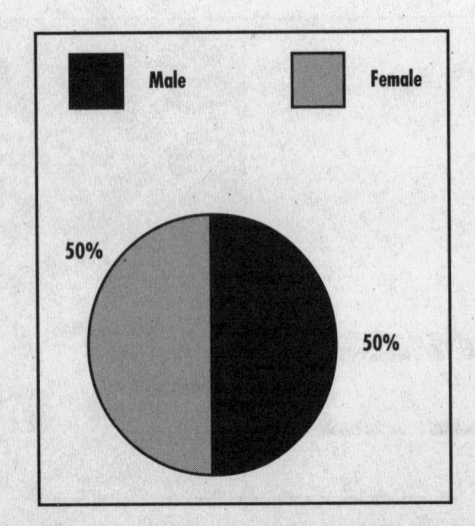

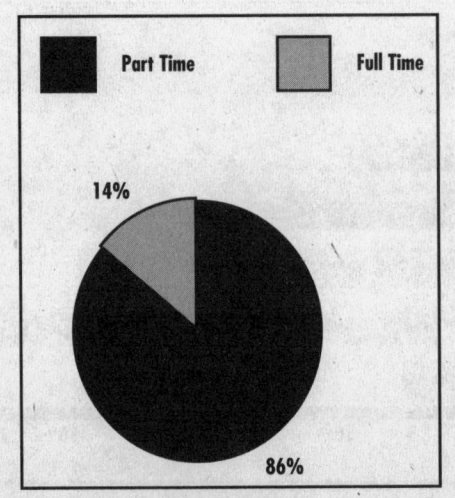

UNIVERSITY OF WINDSOR
Faculty of Law

Admissions Contact: Assistant to the Dean/Director of Admissions, Michelle Pilutti
Faculty of Law, 401 Sunset, Windsor, ON N9B 3P4 Canada
Admissions Phone: 519-253-3000 • Admissions Fax: 519-973-7064
Admissions E-mail: lawadmit@uwindsor.ca • Web Address: www.uwindsor.ca/law

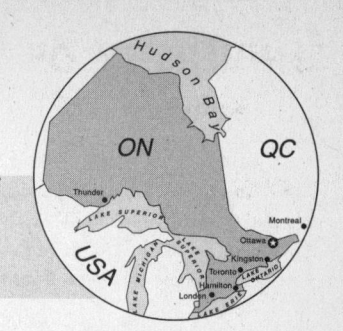

INSTITUTIONAL INFORMATION
Public/Private: Public
Student/Faculty Ratio: 20:1
Total Faculty: 23
% Part Time: 24
% Female: 30
% Minority: 10

PROGRAMS
Academic Specialties: Canada-U.S. Relations, Environmental Law, Intellectual Property, Access to Justice, Civil Procedure, Commercial Law, Constitutional Law, Corporation Securities Law, Criminal Law, Human Rights Law, International Law, Labor Law, Legal Philosophy, Property, Taxation
Combined Degrees Offered: MBA/LLB (3 to 4 years), JD/LLB (3 years)
Grading System: 13-point scale
Clinical Program Required? Yes
Clinical Programs Description: Legal Assistance of Windsor, Community Legal Aid, University of Windsor Mediation Service
Legal Writing Course Requirements? Yes
Legal Writing Description: 1 academic year culminating in the Moot Court
Legal Methods Course Requirements? Yes
Legal Methods Description: Part of the Legal Research and Writing course; see Legal Writing.
Legal Research Course Requirements? Yes
Legal Research Description: Part of the Legal Research and Writing course; see Legal Writing.
Moot Court Requirement? Yes
Moot Court Description: Required component of the first-year Legal Research and Writing Course
Public Interest Law Requirement? No
Academic Journals: *Windsor Review of Legal and Social Issues*

STUDENT INFORMATION
Enrollment of Law School: 454
% Out of State: 0
% Male/Female: 43/57
% Full Time: 98
% Full Time That Are International: 0
% Minority: 0
Average Age of Entering Class: 26

RESEARCH FACILITIES
School-Supported Research Centers: Canadian-American Research Centre for Law and Policy (CARC), Intellectual Property Law Institute (IPLI)

EXPENSES/FINANCIAL AID
Annual Tuition (Residents/Nonresidents): $6,300/$10,545
Room and Board (On Campus): $5,287
Books and Supplies: $1,000
Average Grant: $750
Average Loan: $8,626
% of Aid That Is Merit-Based: 60

ADMISSIONS INFORMATION
Application Fee: $50
Regular Application Deadline: 1/11
Regular Notification: Rolling
LSDAS Accepted? No
Transfer Students Accepted? Yes
Other Admissions Factors Considered: Community involvement, career objectives
Number of Applications Received: 1,462
Number of Applicants Accepted: 381
Number of Applicants Enrolled: 155

EMPLOYMENT INFORMATION

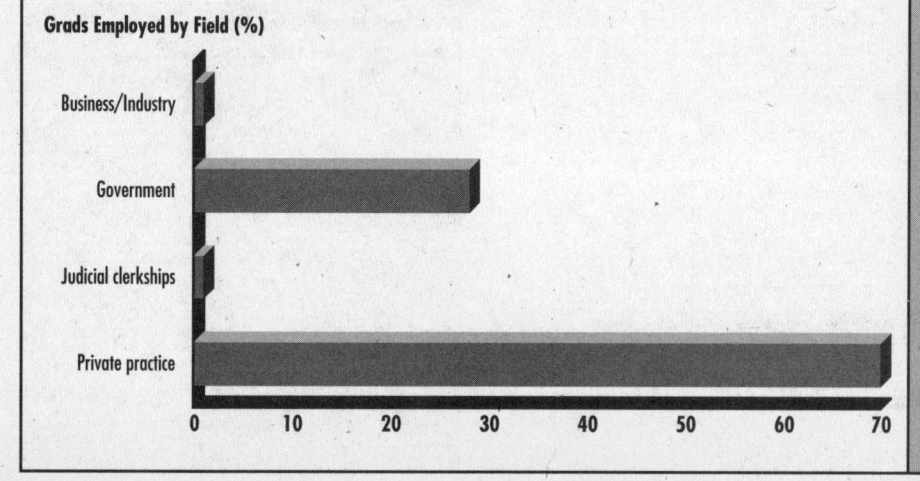

Grads Employed by Field (%)
- Business/Industry: ~1
- Government: ~28
- Judicial clerkships: ~1
- Private practice: ~70

Rate of Placement: 98%
Employers Who Frequently Hire Grads: Law firms
State for Bar Exam: ON, AB, BC, NS, NF
Pass Rate for First-Time Bar: 99%

UNIVERSITY OF WISCONSIN
Law School

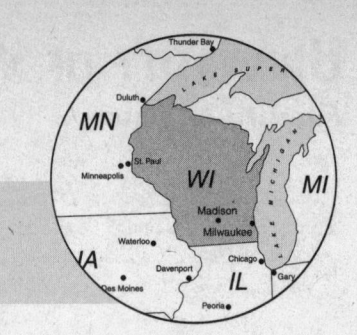

Admissions Contact: Dean of Admissions and Financial Aid, M. Elizabeth Kransberger
975 Bascom Mall, Madison, WI 53706
Admissions Phone: 608-262-5914 • Admissions Fax: 608-263-3190
Admissions E-mail: admissions@law.wisc.edu • Web Address: www.law.wisc.edu

INSTITUTIONAL INFORMATION
Public/Private: Public
Student/Faculty Ratio: 20:1
Total Faculty: 49
% Female: 20
% Minority: 15

PROGRAMS
Advanced Degrees Offered: JD, LLM, SJD
Combined Degrees Offered: Law and Environmental Studies; JD/MBA, Law and Industrial Relations; Law and Ibero-American Studies; Law and Sociology
Grading System: Letter and numerical system, ranging 95–65
Clinical Program Required? No
Legal Writing Course Requirements? No
Legal Methods Course Requirements? No
Legal Research Course Requirements? No
Moot Court Requirement? No
Public Interest Law Requirement? No

STUDENT INFORMATION
Enrollment of Law School: 796
% Out of State: 41
% Male/Female: 54/46
% Full Time: 100
% Minority: 26
Average Age of Entering Class: 26

EXPENSES/FINANCIAL AID
Annual Tuition (Residents/Nonresidents): $8,176/$22,480
Room and Board (On/Off Campus): $6,290
Books and Supplies: $1,820
Average Grant: $1,000
Average Loan: $12,797
% of Aid That Is Merit-Based: 10

ADMISSIONS INFORMATION
Application Fee: $45
Regular Application Deadline: 2/1
Regular Notification: Rolling
LSDAS Accepted? Yes
Average GPA: 3.3
Range of GPA: 3.1–3.6
Average LSAT: 160
Transfer Students Accepted? Yes
Other Admissions Factors Considered: Residency, trend of college grades, graduate study, time interval between college graduation and application to law school, undergraduate institution, college grading and course selection patterns, employment while in college
Number of Applications Received: 1,981
Number of Applicants Accepted: 695
Number of Applicants Enrolled: 236

EMPLOYMENT INFORMATION

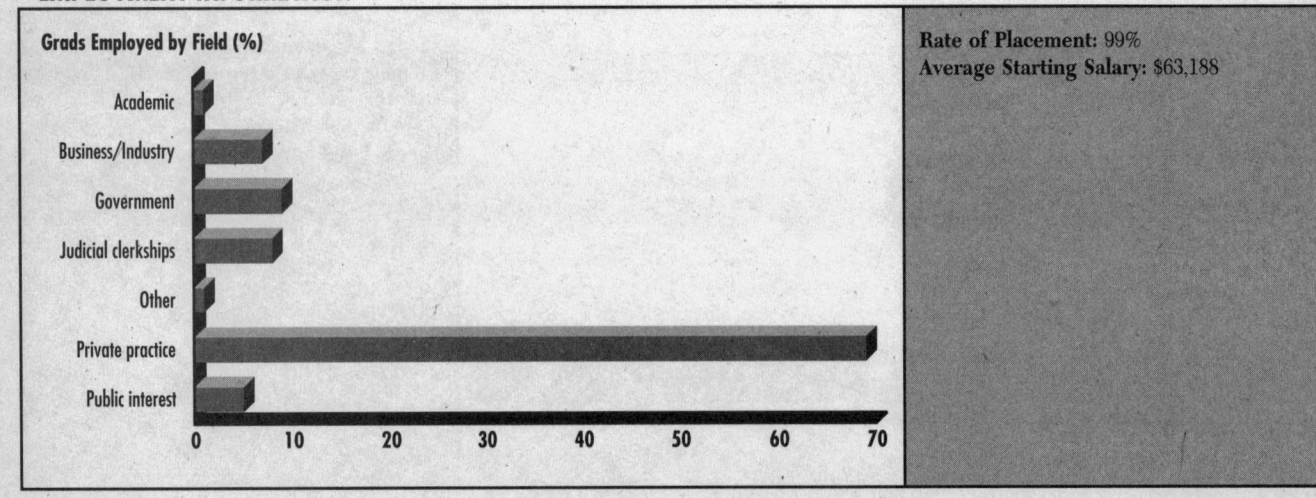

Grads Employed by Field (%)
- Academic
- Business/Industry
- Government
- Judicial clerkships
- Other
- Private practice
- Public interest

Rate of Placement: 99%
Average Starting Salary: $63,188

UNIVERSITY OF WYOMING
College of Law

Admissions Contact: Coordinator of Admissions, Robyn Kniffen
PO Box 3035, Laramie, WY 82071
Admissions Phone: 307-766-6416 • Admissions Fax: 307-766-6417
Admissions E-mail: lawadmis@uwyo.edu • Web Address: www.uwyo.edu/law

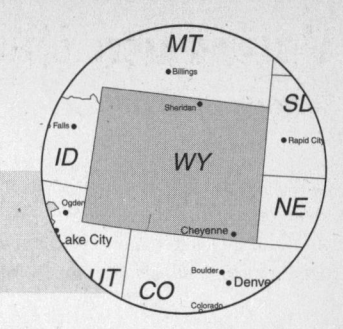

INSTITUTIONAL INFORMATION
Public/Private: Public
Student/Faculty Ratio: 15:1
Total Faculty: 25
% Part Time: 48
% Female: 45
% Minority: 0

PROGRAMS
Academic Specialties: The College offers a general curriculum designed to equip students for the general practice of law, with sufficient course work to develop some specializations (e.g. Environmental Law, Natural Resources Law). The College also offers 3 clinical programs, which give third-year students the opportunity to make court appearances, write appellate briefs, and appear before the Wyoming Supreme Court.
Advanced Degrees Offered: JD (3 years)
Combined Degrees Offered: JD/MPA (3.5 years), JD/MBA (3.5 to 4 years)
Grading System: A to F, with plus/minus designations; grades of Incomplete (X) and Withdrawn (W) are disregarded; Satisfactory (S) or Unsatisfactory (U) may be granted if the student so requests at the time of registration; courses taken for S/U credit do not count toward hours required for graduation unless the course is offered for the S/U grade only.
Clinical Program Required? No
Clinical Programs Description: Defender Aid, Legal Services, Prosecution Assistance
Legal Writing Course Requirements? Yes
Legal Writing Description: 2-credit course in the first semester
Legal Methods Course Requirements? No
Legal Research Course Requirements? Yes
Legal Research Description: 1 credit course in the first semester
Moot Court Requirement? No
Public Interest Law Requirement? No
Academic Journals: *Wyoming Law Review*

STUDENT INFORMATION
Enrollment of Law School: 233
% Out of State: 52
% Male/Female: 55/45
% Full Time: 100
% Full Time That Are International: 0
% Minority: 7
Average Age of Entering Class: 27

RESEARCH FACILITIES
Research Resources Available: Wireless Internet access throughout the Law Library

EXPENSES/FINANCIAL AID
Annual Tuition (Residents/Nonresidents): $4,359/$9,831
Room and Board: $4,744
Books and Supplies: $800
Financial Aid Application Deadline: 3/1
Average Grant: $1,870
Average Loan: $11,160
% of Aid That Is Merit-Based: 52
% Receiving Some Sort of Aid: 82
Average Total Aid Package: $13,030
Average Debt: $37,905

ADMISSIONS INFORMATION
Application Fee: $35
Regular Application Deadline: 3/15
Regular Notification: 4/15
LSDAS Accepted? Yes
Average GPA: 3.3
Range of GPA: 3.0–3.6
Average LSAT: 151
Range of LSAT: 149–154
Transfer Students Accepted? Yes
Other Schools to Which Students Applied: Gonzaga University, University of Colorado, University of Denver, University of Idaho, University of Montana, University of Oregon, University of Utah
Other Admissions Factors Considered: Grade progression
Number of Applications Received: 435
Number of Applicants Accepted: 249
Number of Applicants Enrolled: 90

INTERNATIONAL STUDENTS
TOEFL Required of International Students? Yes
Minimum TOEFL: 195

EMPLOYMENT INFORMATION

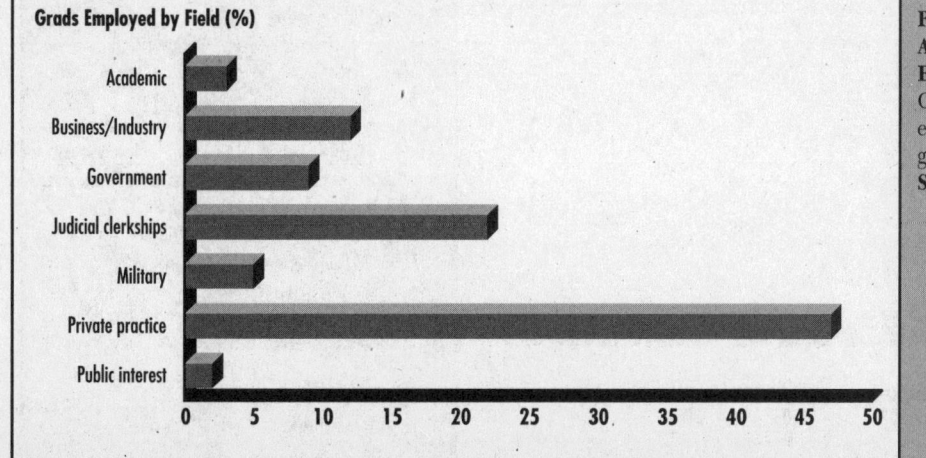

Grads Employed by Field (%)
- Academic: ~2
- Business/Industry: ~12
- Government: ~10
- Judicial clerkships: ~22
- Military: ~5
- Private practice: ~47
- Public interest: ~2

Rate of Placement: 97%
Average Starting Salary: $39,050
Employers Who Frequently Hire Grads: Government (attorney general, district and federal courts, public defender, county attorney); general practice firms
State for Bar Exam: WY, CO

VALPARAISO UNIVERSITY
School of Law

Admissions Contact: Assistant Dean of Admissions and Student Services, Marilyn Olson
Wesemann Hall, Valparaiso, IN 46383
Admissions Phone: 888-825-7652 • Admissions Fax: 219-465-7808
Admissions E-mail: valpolaw@valpo.edu • Web Address: www.valpo.edu/law

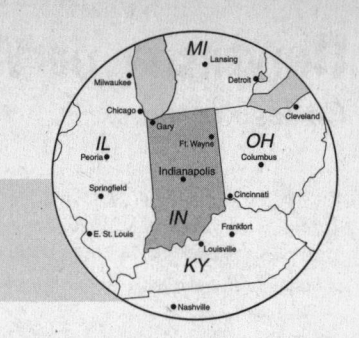

INSTITUTIONAL INFORMATION
Public/Private: Private
Affiliation: Lutheran
Student/Faculty Ratio: 17:1
Total Faculty: 72
% Part Time: 51
% Female: 38
% Minority: 4

PROGRAMS
Academic Specialties: Opportunity to select a minor or concentration area; each includes course work, practical experience, and a scholarly paper. Specialties include Civil Procedure, Criminal Law, Environmental Law, International Law, and Labor Law.
Advanced Degrees Offered: JD (3 years full time, 5 years part time), LLM (1 year full time, 2 years part time)
Combined Degrees Offered: JD/MA Psychology (4 years), JD/MBA (4 years)
Grading System: Numerical and letter system, A (4.0) to F (0.0)
Clinical Program Required? No
Clinical Program Description: 6 clinical options: Civil, Criminal, Domestic Violence, Tax, Mediation, and Juvenile.
Legal Writing Course Requirements? Yes
Legal Writing Description: Legal writing required each of the 3 years

Legal Methods Course Requirements? Yes
Legal Research Course Requirements? Yes
Legal Research Description: Legal research is a first-year course taught by the law librarians.
Moot Court Requirement? No
Public Interest Law Requirement? No

STUDENT INFORMATION
Enrollment of Law School: 420
% Out of State: 41
% Male/Female: 54/46
% Full Time: 87
% Full Time That Are International: 1
% Minority: 13
Average Age of Entering Class: 26

RESEARCH FACILITIES
% of JD Classrooms Wired: 90

EXPENSES/FINANCIAL AID
Annual Tuition: $19,950
Room and Board: $6,600
Books and Supplies: $750
Average Grant: $11,502
Average Loan: $20,200
% Receiving Some Sort of Aid: 90
Average Total Aid Package: $23,210
Average Debt: $56,916
Tuition Per Credit: $740
Fees Per Credit: $18

ADMISSIONS INFORMATION
Application Fee: $30
Regular Application Deadline: 4/15
Regular Notification: Rolling
LSDAS Accepted? Yes
Average GPA: 3.2
Range of GPA: 2.9–3.6
Average LSAT: 152
Range of LSAT: 148–157
Transfer Students Accepted? Yes
Other Admissions Factors Considered: Undergraduate institution, undergraduate major, graduate work, life/work experience
Number of Applications Received: 692
Number of Applicants Accepted: 491
Number of Applicants Enrolled: 167

EMPLOYMENT INFORMATION

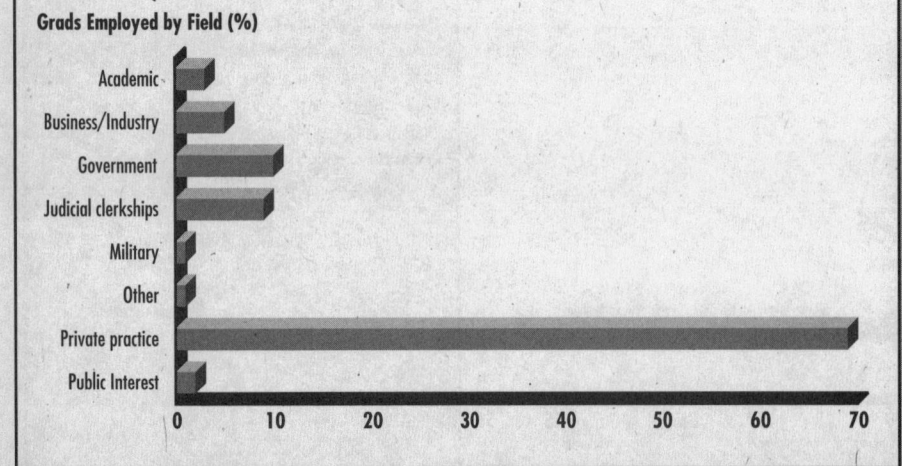

Grads Employed by Field (%)

Field	%
Academic	~1
Business/Industry	~5
Government	~10
Judicial clerkships	~8
Military	~0
Other	~1
Private practice	~70
Public Interest	~2

Rate of Placement: 96%
Average Starting Salary: $50,000
Employers Who Frequently Hire Grads: Jenner & Block; Sidley & Austin; Foley & Lardner; Hinshaw & Culbertson; Querrey & Harrow; Ungaaretti & Harris; Thacher, Proffitt & Wood; Beckman Lawson; Bose, McKinney & Evans; Barnes & Thornburg; Baker & Daniels; Ice, Miller, Donadio & Ryan; Locke Reynolds; May, Oberfell & Lorber; Hoeppner, Wagner & Evans; Ruman, Clements, Tobin & Holub; Kightlinger & Gray; Lucas, Holcomb, & Medrea; Warner, Norcross & Judd; Briggs and Morgan
State for Bar Exam: IN
Pass Rate for First-Time Bar: 88%

VANDERBILT UNIVERSITY
Law School

Admissions Contact: Assistant Dean, Sonya G. Smith
131 21st Avenue South, Nashville, TN 37203
Admissions Phone: 615-322-6452 • Admissions Fax: 615-322-1531
Admissions E-mail: admissions@law.vanderbilt.edu • Web Address: www.vanderbilt.edu/Law/

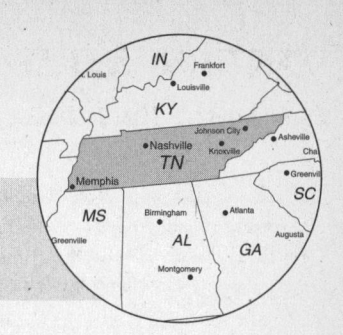

INSTITUTIONAL INFORMATION
Public/Private: Private
Student/Faculty Ratio: 13:1
Total Faculty: 69
% Part Time: 52
% Female: 30
% Minority: 10

PROGRAMS
Academic Specialties: Public and Constitutional Law, Corporate Law, Intellectual Property Law, Entertainment Law and Practice, Cyberspace & Technology Law, Civil Procedure, Commercial Law, Criminal Law, Environmental Law, Government Services, Human Rights Law, International Law, Labor Law, Legal History, Legal Philosophy, Property, Taxation
Advanced Degrees Offered: LLM (1 year)
Combined Degrees Offered: JD/MBA (4 years), JD/MA (5 years), JD/PhD (7 years), JD/MDiv (5 years), JD/MTS (4 years), JD/MD (6 years)
Grading System: A+ to F
Clinical Program Required? No
Clinical Programs Description: Civil Practice Clinic, Criminal Practice Clinic, Juvenile Practice Clinic, Child and Family Practice Clinic
Legal Writing Course Requirements? Yes
Legal Writing Description: Required first year
Legal Methods Course Requirements? Yes
Legal Methods Description: 2 semesters first year

Legal Research Course Requirements? No
Moot Court Requirement? No
Public Interest Law Requirement? No
Academic Journals: The Vanderbilt Law Review, Journal of Transnational Law, Journal of Sports and Entertainment Law

STUDENT INFORMATION
Enrollment of Law School: 564
% Out of State: 84
% Male/Female: 52/48
% Full Time: 100
% Full Time That Are International: 5
% Minority: 24
Average Age of Entering Class: 24

EXPENSES/FINANCIAL AID
Annual Tuition: $26,960
Room and Board (On/Off Campus): $14,225/ $15,585
Books and Supplies: $1,255
Financial Aid Application Deadline: 2/15
Average Grant: $9,000
Average Loan: $28,500
% Receiving Some Sort of Aid: 80
Average Total Aid Package: $42,588
Average Debt: $70,000

ADMISSIONS INFORMATION
Application Fee: $50
Regular Application Deadline: 3/15
Regular Notification: 4/15
LSDAS Accepted? Yes
Average GPA: 3.6
Range of GPA: 3.4–3.8
Average LSAT: 162
Range of LSAT: 160–164
Transfer Students Accepted? Yes
Other Schools to Which Students Applied: Duke University, Emory University, Georgetown University, Harvard University, Stanford University, The University of Texas at Austin, University of Virginia
Other Admissions Factors Considered: Letters of recommendation, personal statements, rigor of academic courses, extracurricular activities, work experience, diverse background
Number of Applications Received: 2,341
Number of Applicants Accepted: 757
Number of Applicants Enrolled: 198

INTERNATIONAL STUDENTS
TOEFL Required of International Students? Yes

EMPLOYMENT INFORMATION

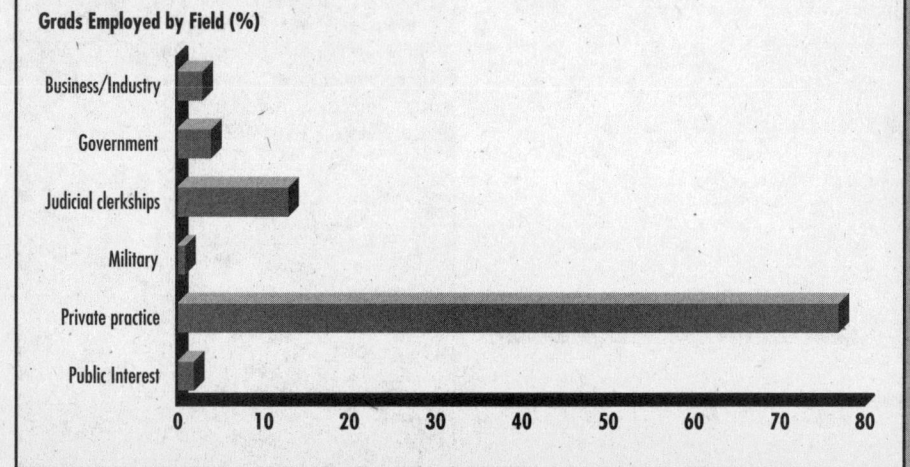

Grads Employed by Field (%)
- Business/Industry
- Government
- Judicial clerkships
- Military
- Private practice
- Public Interest

Rate of Placement: 99%
Average Starting Salary: $107,000
State for Bar Exam: TN
Pass Rate for First-Time Bar: 93%

VENTURA COLLEGE OF LAW
The Santa Barbara and Ventura Colleges of Law

Admissions Contact: Assistant Dean, Barbara Doyle
4475 Market Street, Ventura, CA 93003
Admissions Phone: 805-658-0511 • Admissions Fax: 805-658-0529
Admissions E-mail: vcl@venturalaw.edu • Web Address: www.venturalaw.edu

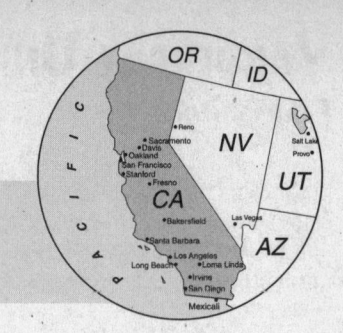

INSTITUTIONAL INFORMATION
Public/Private: Private
Student/Faculty Ratio: 6:1
Total Faculty: 16
% Part Time: 100
% Female: 13
% Minority: 19

PROGRAMS
Academic Specialties: All faculty are practicing attorneys or judges.
Advanced Degrees Offered: JD (4-year part-time evening program)
Grading System: A to F on a 4.0 scale
Clinical Program Required? Yes
Clinical Programs Description: Off-campus internships
Legal Writing Course Requirements? Yes
Legal Writing Description: 2 separate 2-unit courses
Legal Methods Course Requirements? No
Legal Research Course Requirements? Yes
Legal Research Description: One 2-unit course is required
Moot Court Requirement? No
Public Interest Law Requirement? Yes
Public Interest Law Description: 65-hour internship (1 unit)

STUDENT INFORMATION
Enrollment of Law School: 89
% Out of State: 0
% Male/Female: 100/0
% Full Time That Are International: 0
% Minority: 0
Average Age of Entering Class: 36

EXPENSES/FINANCIAL AID
Annual Tuition: $5,355
Books and Supplies: $400
Average Grant: $1,000
Average Loan: $10,000
Tuition Per Credit: $255

ADMISSIONS INFORMATION
Application Fee: $45
Regular Application Deadline: 8/1
Regular Notification: Rolling
LSDAS Accepted? No
Average GPA: 3.2
Average LSAT: 150
Transfer Students Accepted? Yes

EMPLOYMENT INFORMATION

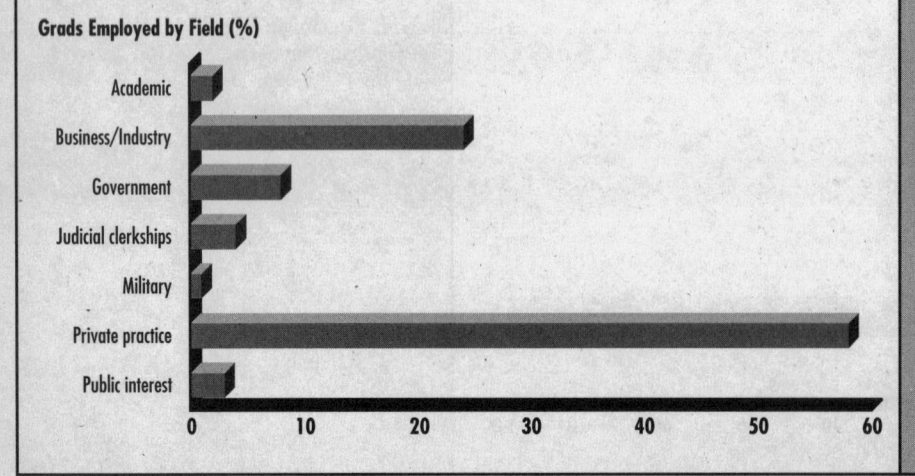

Grads Employed by Field (%):
- Academic: ~1
- Business/Industry: ~25
- Government: ~8
- Judicial clerkships: ~4
- Military: ~0
- Private practice: ~58
- Public interest: ~2

Employers Who Frequently Hire Grads: County of Ventura District Attorneys' and Public Defenders' Offices
State for Bar Exam: CA
Pass Rate for First-Time Bar: 35%

VERMONT LAW SCHOOL

Admissions Contact: Assistant Dean for Admissions and Financial Aid, Kathy Hartman
Chelsea Street, South Royalton, VT 05068-0096
Admissions Phone: 888-277-5985 • Admissions Fax: 802-763-7071
Admissions E-mail: admiss@vermontlaw.edu • Web Address: www.vermontlaw.edu

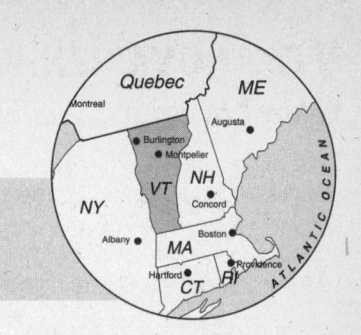

INSTITUTIONAL INFORMATION
Public/Private: Private
Student/Faculty Ratio: 18:1
Total Faculty: 36
% Part Time: 0
% Female: 38
% Minority: 1

PROGRAMS
Academic Specialties: Clinical/experiential programs, Environmental Law, Public Interest Law, General Practice Program Certificate, Canadian Studies Program, First Nations Environmental Law Program, Civil Procedure, Commercial Law, Constitutional Law, Corporation Securities Law, Criminal Law, Government Services, Human Rights Law, International Law, Labor Law, Legal History, Legal Philosophy, Property, Taxation
Advanced Degrees Offered: JD (3 years), Master of Studies Environmental Law (MSEL) (1 year), LLM Environmental Law (1 year)
Combined Degrees Offered: JD/MSEL (3 years total; 6 regular semesters and 2 summer semesters)
Grading System: A to F
Clinical Program Required? No
Clinical Programs Description: South Royalton Legal Clinic, Semester in Practice, Environmental Semester in Washington, Legislation Clinic, Environmental Law Clinic, etc.
Legal Writing Course Requirements? Yes
Legal Writing Description: 2 courses over 3 years
Legal Methods Course Requirements? Yes
Legal Methods Description: 4 courses over 3 years
Legal Research Course Requirements? Yes
Legal Research Description: 2 courses over 1 year
Moot Court Requirement? Yes
Moot Court Description: 1 semester course
Public Interest Law Requirement? No
Academic Journals: *Vermont Law Review, Res Communes*

STUDENT INFORMATION
Enrollment of Law School: 510
% Out of State: 90
% Male/Female: 54/46
% Full Time: 100
% Full Time That Are International: 2
% Minority: 12
Average Age of Entering Class: 26

EXPENSES/FINANCIAL AID
Annual Tuition: $22,164
Room and Board (Off Campus): $8,636
Books and Supplies: $900
Financial Aid Application Deadline: 3/1
Average Grant: $7,000
Average Loan: $18,500
% of Aid That Is Merit-Based: 0
% Receiving Some Sort of Aid: 90
Average Total Aid Package: $27,500
Average Debt: $72,000

ADMISSIONS INFORMATION
Application Fee: $50
Regular Application Deadline: 3/15
Regular Notification: 4/1
LSDAS Accepted? Yes
Average GPA: 3.1
Range of GPA: 2.8–3.3
Average LSAT: 151
Range of LSAT: 148–154
Transfer Students Accepted? Yes
Other Schools to Which Students Applied: Franklin Pierce Law Center, Lewis and Clark College, Pace University, Suffolk University, University at Albany, University of Colorado, University of Denver
Number of Applications Received: 781
Number of Applicants Accepted: 515
Number of Applicants Enrolled: 185

INTERNATIONAL STUDENTS
TOEFL Required of International Students? Yes

EMPLOYMENT INFORMATION

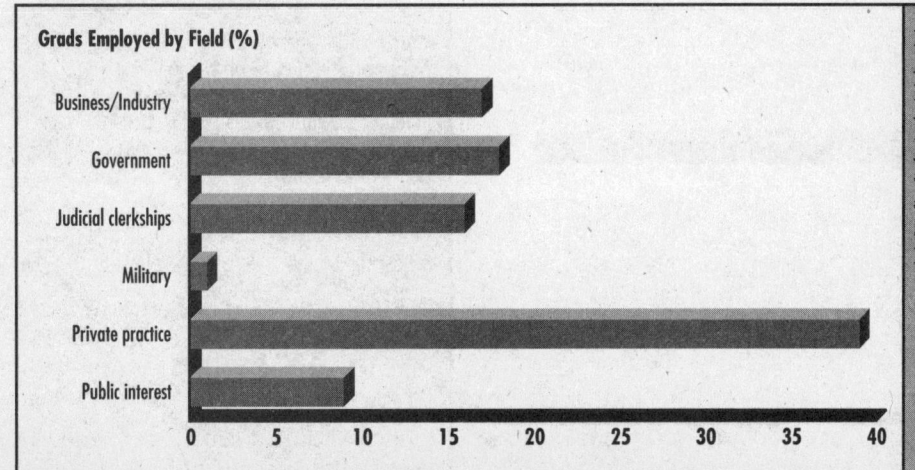

Grads Employed by Field (%):
- Business/Industry: ~17
- Government: ~17
- Judicial clerkships: ~16
- Military: ~1
- Private practice: ~40
- Public interest: ~9

Rate of Placement: 85%
Average Starting Salary: $46,001
Employers Who Frequently Hire Grads: Environmental Protection Agency, Department of Justice, various nonprofit legal aid organizations and advocacy groups, various state and federal appellate and trial court systems
State for Bar Exam: VT, MA, NY
Pass Rate for First-Time Bar: 65%

VILLANOVA UNIVERSITY
School of Law

Admissions Contact: Director of Admissions, David Pallozzi
299 North Spring Mill Road, Villanova, PA 19085
Admissions Phone: 610-519-7010 • Admissions Fax: 610-519-6291
Admissions E-mail: shaiko@law.vill.edu • Web Address: vls.law.vill.edu

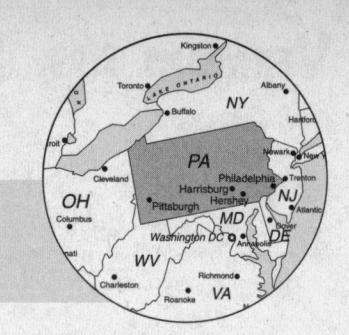

INSTITUTIONAL INFORMATION
Public/Private: Private
Affiliation: Roman Catholic
Environment: Suburban
Academic Calendar: Semester
Schedule: Full time only
Student/Faculty Ratio: 16:1
Total Faculty: 84
% Part Time: 46
% Female: 32
% Minority: 8

PROGRAMS
Advanced Degrees Offered: JD (3 years), LLM Tax (24 credits)
Combined Degrees Offered: JD/MBA (3–4.5 years), JD/PhD Psychology (7–8 years)
Grading System: 4.00 scale
Clinical Program Required? No
Clinical Program Description: Tax Clinic, Informational Law Clinic, Juvenile Justice Clinic, Villanova Community Legal Services, externships, Law and Entrepreneurship, Immigration Law Clinic

STUDENT INFORMATION
Enrollment of Law School: 710
% Male/Female: 53/47
% Full Time: 100
% Full Time That Are International: 2
% Minority: 15
Average Age of Entering Class: 24

EXPENSES/FINANCIAL AID
Annual Tuition: $20,000
Room and Board (Off Campus): $10,990
Books and Supplies: $1,000
Average Grant: $6,414
Average Loan: $26,003
% Receiving Some Sort of Aid: 74
Average Total Aid Package: $26,893
Average Debt: $73,076

ADMISSIONS INFORMATION
Application Fee: $75
Regular Application Deadline: 3/1
Regular Notification: Rolling
Average GPA: 3.3
Range of GPA: 3.0–3.5
Average LSAT: 157
Range of LSAT: 153–158
Transfer Students Accepted? Yes
Other Schools to Which Students Applied: Temple University, George Washington University, University of Pennsylvania, Boston University, Boston College

EMPLOYMENT INFORMATION

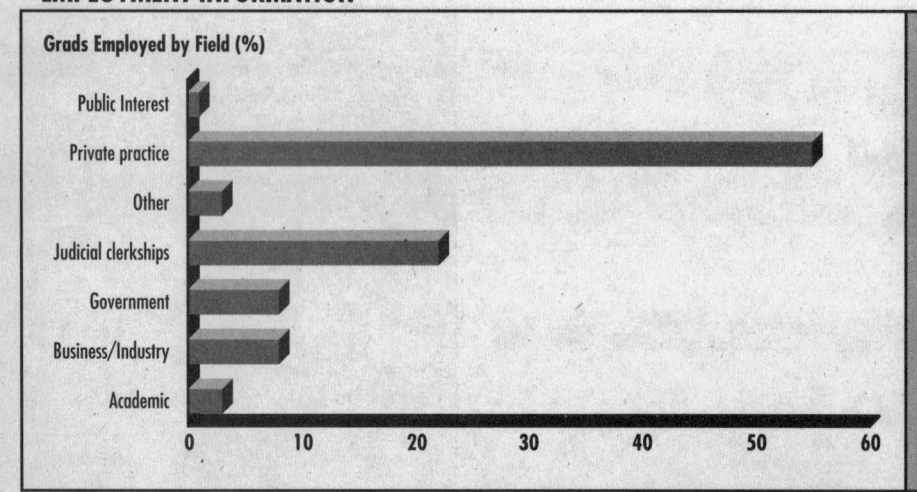

Grads Employed by Field (%)
- Public Interest
- Private practice: ~57
- Other
- Judicial clerkships: ~22
- Government
- Business/Industry
- Academic

Rate of Placement: 86%
Average Starting Salary: $55,000
Employers Who Frequently Hire Grads: State judges and government law firms in Philadelphia, New York, New Jersey, Washington, D.C., and Delaware
Prominent Alumni: Ed Rendell, Mayor of Philadelphia; Mattew McHugh, former U.S. congressman, now general counsel to the World Bank; Sandra Schultz Newman, first elected woman to Supreme Court of Pennsylvania; Mattew Ryan, Speaker of the Pennsylvania House of Representatives; John J. LaFalce, U.S. congressman; William Green, Former U.S. congressman and former mayor of Philadelphia

WAKE FOREST UNIVERSITY
School of Law

Admissions Contact: Director of Admissions and Financial Aid, Melanie E. Nutt
PO Box 7206, Winston-Salem, NC 27109
Admissions Phone: 336-758-5437 • Admissions Fax: 336-758-4632
Admissions E-mail: admissions@law.wfu.edu • Web Address: www.law.wfu.edu

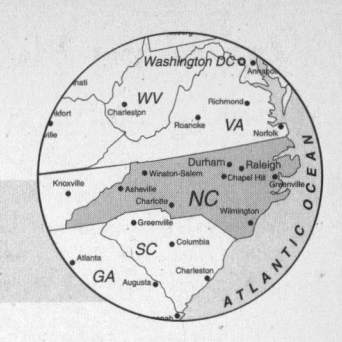

INSTITUTIONAL INFORMATION
Public/Private: Private
Student/Faculty Ratio: 13:1
Total Faculty: 28
% Part Time: 18
% Female: 32
% Minority: 4

PROGRAMS
Academic Specialties: Commercial Law, Constitutional Law, Corporation Securities Law, Criminal Law, International Law, Taxation
Advanced Degrees Offered: LLM American Law (for foreign lawyers only)
Combined Degrees Offered: JD/MBA
Grading System: A (100–91), B (90–81), C (80–71), D (70–66), and F (65–59)
Clinical Program Required? No
Clinical Programs Description: Over half of students participate in either Traditional Clinic or Elder Care Clinic; approximately 80 students participate in a Domestic Advocacy project
Legal Writing Course Requirements? Yes
Legal Writing Description: 3 semesters required; complete course description available at www.law.wfu.edu
Legal Methods Course Requirements? Yes
Legal Methods Description: 3 semesters; begins with instruction in legal methods and ethics
Legal Research Course Requirements? Yes
Legal Research Description: See Legal Writing.
Moot Court Requirement? No
Public Interest Law Requirement? Yes

Public Interest Law Description: Each entering student is assigned a pro bono project the first week of school to encourage them to become involved throughout their career.
Academic Journals: *Wake Forest Law Review, Virtual Intellectual Property Journal* (online)

STUDENT INFORMATION
Enrollment of Law School: 464
% Out of State: 60
% Male/Female: 55/45
% Full Time: 100
% Full Time That Are International: 1
% Minority: 10
Average Age of Entering Class: 25

RESEARCH FACILITIES
Research Resources Available: Lexis, Westlaw, library resources available electronically and via CD, 53 computers available in student computer lab at law school, another 28 PCs available in library, all library carrels wired for laptop access to network and Internet

EXPENSES/FINANCIAL AID
Annual Tuition: $22,950
Room and Board (Off Campus): $11,000
Books and Supplies: $700
Financial Aid Application Deadline: 4/1
Average Grant: $14,700
Average Loan: $18,500
% of Aid That Is Merit-Based: 40
% Receiving Some Sort of Aid: 80
Average Total Aid Package: $33,940
Average Debt: $66,600

ADMISSIONS INFORMATION
Application Fee: $60
Regular Application Deadline: 3/15
Regular Notification: Rolling
LSDAS Accepted? Yes
Average GPA: 3.4
Range of GPA: 2.5–4.0
Average LSAT: 159
Range of LSAT: 156–161
Transfer Students Accepted? Yes
Other Schools to Which Students Applied: University of North Carolina at Chapel Hill, George Washington University, College of William and Mary, Emory University, American University, Tulane University, University of Georgia
Other Admissions Factors Considered: Undergraduate institution; undergraduate coursework; maturity; trend in academic performance; employment during undergraduate years; military service; experience acquired in business, industry, or the community
Number of Applications Received: 1,724
Number of Applicants Accepted: 630
Number of Applicants Enrolled: 160

INTERNATIONAL STUDENTS
TOEFL Required of International Students? Yes

EMPLOYMENT INFORMATION

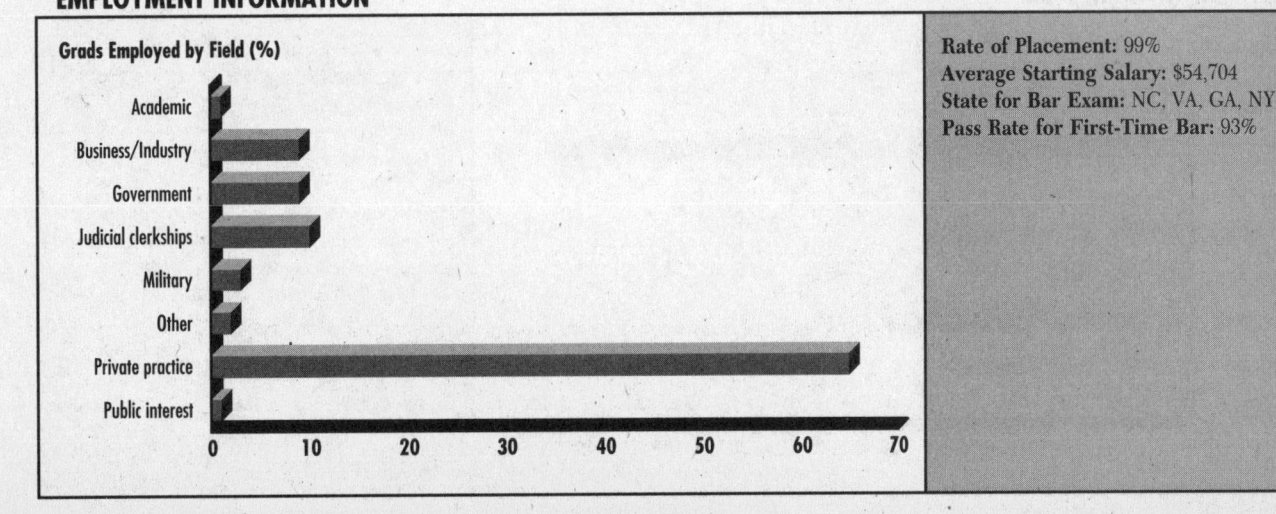

Grads Employed by Field (%)

Rate of Placement: 99%
Average Starting Salary: $54,704
State for Bar Exam: NC, VA, GA, NY
Pass Rate for First-Time Bar: 93%

WASHBURN UNIVERSITY
School of Law

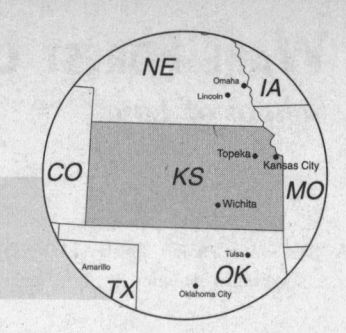

Admissions Contact: Director of Admissions, Janet K. Kerr
1700 College, Topeka, KS 66621
Admissions Phone: 785-231-1185 • Admissions Fax: 785-232-8087
Admissions E-mail: admissions@washburnlaw.edu • Web Address: washburnlaw.edu

INSTITUTIONAL INFORMATION
Public/Private: Public
Environment: Urban
Academic Calendar: Semester
Schedule: Full time only
Student/Faculty Ratio: 14:1
Total Faculty: 29
% Female: 31
% Minority: 21

PROGRAMS
Advanced Degrees Offered: JD (90 credit hours, 3 years)
Combined Degrees Offered: MBA may be completed in conjunction with the JD; 9 hours of the 30 hours required for the MBA are met by completing the JD, leaving only 21 hours of MBA course work to complete. This may be completed within the 3-year JD program or can extend an additional semester or two. MCJ may be completed with JD. Up to 18 hours of 36 hours required for the MCJ may be met by JD courses, leaving only 12 hours of course work and 6 hours of thesis or practicum to complete.
Grading System: A (4.0), B+ (3.5), C+ (2.5), C (2.0), D+ (1.5), D (1.0), F (0.0). Must have 2.0 GPA or above to graduate. Some courses may be designated as Outstanding, Credit, or No Credit rather than graded.
Clinical Program Required? No

Clinical Program Description: Washburn has one of the oldest clinical programs in the country, offering a General Practice Clinic that also includes a strong mediation program. It is staffed by 5 full-time faculty and is housed in a model law office building adjacent to the law school.

STUDENT INFORMATION
Enrollment of Law School: 411
% Male/Female: 58/42
% Full Time: 100
% Full Time That Are International: 2
% Minority: 15
Average Age of Entering Class: 27

RESEARCH FACILITIES
Computers/Workstations Available: 110

EXPENSES/FINANCIAL AID
Annual Tuition (Residents/Nonresidents): $8,220/$12,750
Room and Board (On/Off Campus): $3,500/$7,000
Books and Supplies: $800
Financial Aid Application Deadline: 4/1
Average Grant: $3,454
Average Loan: $17,500
% of Aid That Is Merit-Based: 95
% Receiving Some Sort of Aid: 90
Average Total Aid Package: $17,950
Average Debt: $37,000
Fees Per Credit (Residents/Nonresidents): $251/$378

ADMISSIONS INFORMATION
Application Fee: $30
Regular Application Deadline: 3/15
Regular Notification: 6/1
Average GPA: 3.1
Range of GPA: 2.8–3.5
Average LSAT: 151
Range of LSAT: 146–154
Transfer Students Accepted? Yes
Other Schools to Which Students Applied: University of Kansas, University of Missouri—Kansas City, Creighton University, University of Tulsa, Oklahoma State University, Drake University, University of Nebraska, University of Missouri—Columbia
Number of Applications Received: 543
Number of Applicants Accepted: 353
Number of Applicants Enrolled: 141

EMPLOYMENT INFORMATION

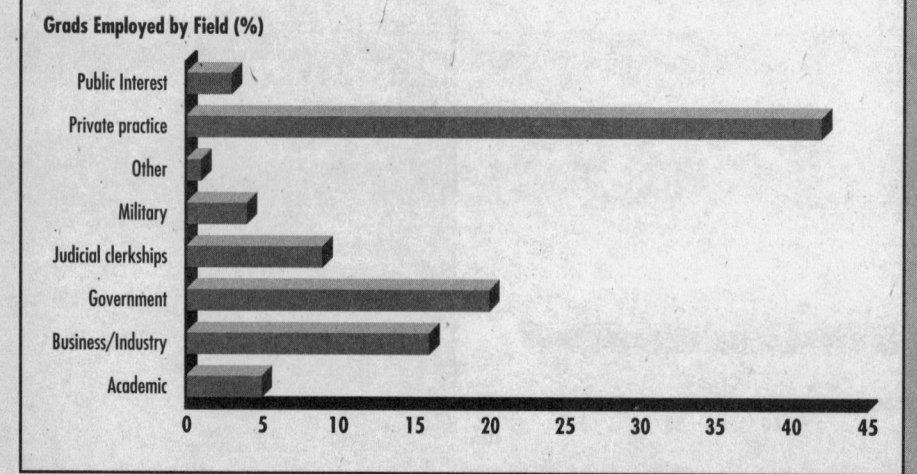

Grads Employed by Field (%)

Field	%
Public Interest	~2
Private practice	~43
Other	~2
Military	~3
Judicial clerkships	~8
Government	~20
Business/Industry	~17
Academic	~4

Rate of Placement: 91%
Average Starting Salary: $36,440
Employers Who Frequently Hire Grads: Koch Industries, many large law firms in the Kansas City and Wichita areas, various state and federal courts
Prominent Alumni: Bob Dole, former majority leader of the U.S. Senate, 1996 Republican presidential nominee; Delano Lewis, former CEO and president of the National Public Radio and current nominee for U.S. ambassador to South Africa; Ronald K. Richey, CEO and president of Torchmark Corporation; Bill Kurtis, broadcast journalist

WASHINGTON AND LEE UNIVERSITY
School of Law

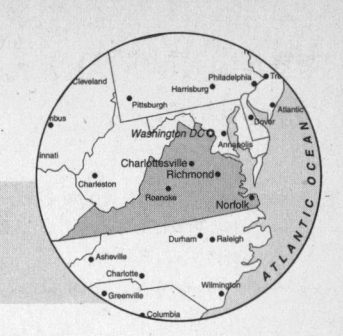

Admissions Contact: Director of Admissions, Sidney Evans
Sydney Lewis Hall, Lexington, VA 24450
Admissions Phone: 540-463-8504 • Admissions Fax: 540-463-8586
Admissions E-mail: lawadm@wlu.edu • Web Address: www.law.wlu.edu

INSTITUTIONAL INFORMATION
Public/Private: Private
Student/Faculty Ratio: 11:1
Total Faculty: 52
% Part Time: 36
% Female: 23
% Minority: 7

PROGRAMS
Grading System: system: A, A–, B, B–, C+, C, C–, D+, D, D–, F, I (incomplete)
Clinical Program Required? Yes
Clinical Programs Description: Prison Practicum (a legal services clinic at a federal women's prison; the Black Lung Administrative/Labor Law Clinic; the Virginia Capital Case Clearinghouse (a death penalty clinic); Public Defender Service; U.S. Attorney's Prosecutorial Clinic; Legal Aid Society; judicial clerkships in a trial, juvenile, and domestic relations, or federal bankruptcy court.
Legal Writing Course Requirements? No
Legal Methods Course Requirements? Yes
Legal Methods Description: Each semester of the first year 1 substantive course is taught by full-time tenure-track faculty in small sections of no more than 20 students; legal research, writing, and advocacy exercises are incorporated into classroom teaching and course assignments.
Legal Research Course Requirements? No
Moot Court Requirement? No
Public Interest Law Requirement? No

Academic Journals: *Washington and Lee Law Review, Capital Defense Journal, Washington and Lee Race and Ethnic Ancestry Law Journal, Environmental Law News*

STUDENT INFORMATION
Enrollment of Law School: 363
% Out of State: 78
% Male/Female: 57/43
% Full Time: 100
% Full Time That Are International: 1
% Minority: 15
Average Age of Entering Class: 24

RESEARCH FACILITIES
School-Supported Research Centers: The Frances Lewis Law Center supports research in the area of legal reform and brings visiting scholars, lawyers, and judges to the School of Law to research, write, and teach.

EXPENSES/FINANCIAL AID
Annual Tuition: $21,320
Room and Board (Off Campus): $10,519
Books and Supplies: $1,100
Financial Aid Application Deadline: 2/15
Average Grant: $9,311
Average Loan: $19,524
% of Aid That Is Merit-Based: 100
% Receiving Some Sort of Aid: 95
Average Total Aid Package: $28,735
Average Debt: $54,350

ADMISSIONS INFORMATION
Application Fee: $50
Regular Application Deadline: 2/1
Regular Notification: 4/1
LSDAS Accepted? Yes
Average GPA: 3.4
Range of GPA: 3.1–3.6
Average LSAT: 165
Range of LSAT: 161–167
Transfer Students Accepted? Yes
Other Schools to Which Students Applied: College of William and Mary, University of Virginia, Vanderbilt University
Other Admissions Factors Considered: Trends in grades, rigor of undergraduate curriculum, length of time out of school, history of standardized test performance and how accurately tests have predicted classroom performance, obstacles overcome, alumni connection, special talents, interests
Number of Applications Received: 1,637
Number of Applicants Accepted: 506
Number of Applicants Enrolled: 122

EMPLOYMENT INFORMATION

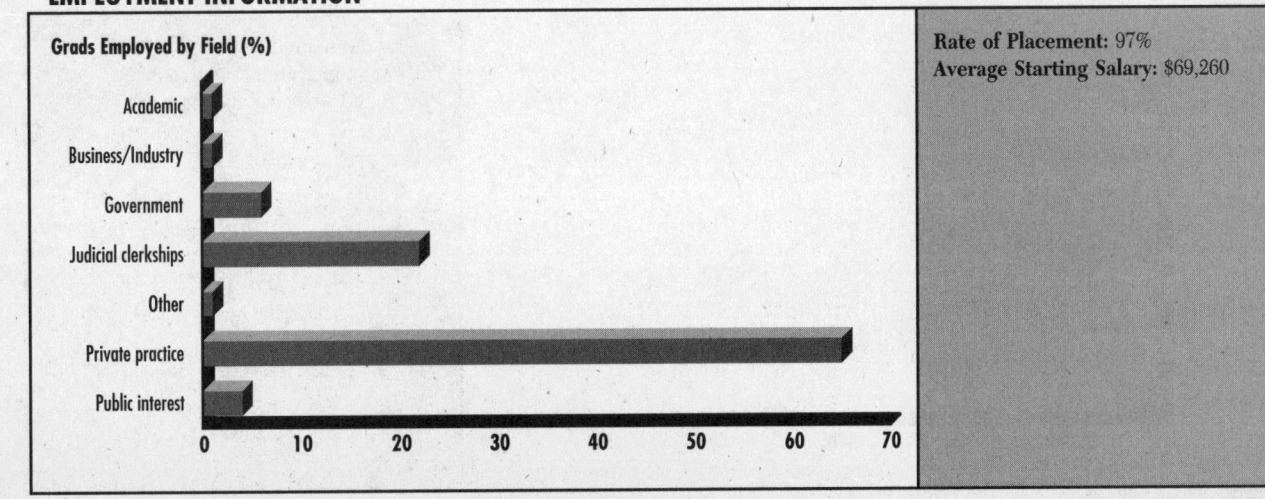

Grads Employed by Field (%)
- Academic: ~1
- Business/Industry: ~2
- Government: ~5
- Judicial clerkships: ~22
- Other: ~1
- Private practice: ~65
- Public interest: ~3

Rate of Placement: 97%
Average Starting Salary: $69,260

WASHINGTON UNIVERSITY
School of Law

Admissions Contact: Assistant Dean of Admissions and Financial Aid, Janet Bolin
1 Brookings Drive, Campus Box 1120, St. Louis, MO 63130
Admissions Phone: 314-935-4525 • Admissions Fax: 314-935-8778
Admissions E-mail: admiss@wulaw.wustl.edu • Web Address: ls.wustl.edu

INSTITUTIONAL INFORMATION
Public/Private: Private
Student/Faculty Ratio: 15:1
Total Faculty: 77
% Part Time: 41
% Female: 46
% Minority: 2

PROGRAMS
Academic Specialties: International Law, Corporate Law, Environmental Law, Intellectual Property Law, Trial Advocacy and Transactional Skills Training, Civil Procedure, Commercial Law, Constitutional Law, Corporation Securities Law, Criminal Law, Government Services, Human Rights Law, Labor Law, Legal History, Legal Philosophy, Property, Taxation, clinical programs, interdisciplinary offerings
Advanced Degrees Offered: JD (3 years), JSD, LLM, MJS
Combined Degrees Offered: JD/MA East Asian Studies, Political Science, European Studies, Islamic Studies; JD/PhD; JD/MBA; JD/MHA; JD/MSW; JD/MS Engineering and Policy, Economics
Grading System: 100–65 with a mandatory median of 84–82
Clinical Program Required? No
Clinical Programs Description: Civil Justice, Interdisciplinary Environmental, Employment Law, U.S. Attorney, Capital Punishment, Criminal Justice, Judicial Clerkship, Congressional and Administrative Law Clinic (students can spend their final semester working for a member of Congress, a congressional committee, or an administrative agency in Washington, D.C.)
Legal Writing Course Requirements? Yes
Legal Writing Description: In this year-long course, first-year students learn, through simulated lawsuits, to approach and solve problems as lawyers do and to write clear, concise, and analytical trial briefs and office memoranda. It is taught by 6 full-time faculty. Students meet twice a week in small groups taught by full-time faculty.
Legal Methods Course Requirements? No
Legal Research Course Requirements? Yes
Legal Research Description: Taught in conjunction with the Legal Writing program
Moot Court Requirement? No
Public Interest Law Requirement? No
Academic Journals: *Washington University Law Quarterly, Journal of Law and Policy, Global Studies Law Review*

STUDENT INFORMATION
Enrollment of Law School: 773
% Out of State: 75
% Male/Female: 57/43
% Full Time: 100
% Minority: 21
Average Age of Entering Class: 24

RESEARCH FACILITIES
School-Supported Research Centers: Center for Global Legal Studies, Center for Interdisciplinary Studies

EXPENSES/FINANCIAL AID
Annual Tuition: $27,100
Room and Board (Off Campus): $8,500
Books and Supplies: $1,700
Financial Aid Application Deadline: 3/1
Average Grant: $10,000
Average Loan: $35,000
% of Aid That Is Merit-Based: 100
% Receiving Some Sort of Aid: 75

ADMISSIONS INFORMATION
Application Fee: $60
Regular Application Deadline: 3/1
Regular Notification: 4/15
LSDAS Accepted? Yes
Average GPA: 3.5
Range of GPA: 3.1–3.6
Average LSAT: 162
Range of LSAT: 159–164
Transfer Students Accepted? Yes
Other Schools to Which Students Applied: Boston College, Boston University, Emory University, George Washington University, Georgetown University, Northwestern University, Vanderbilt University
Number of Applications Received: 2,440
Number of Applicants Accepted: 873
Number of Applicants Enrolled: 225

EMPLOYMENT INFORMATION

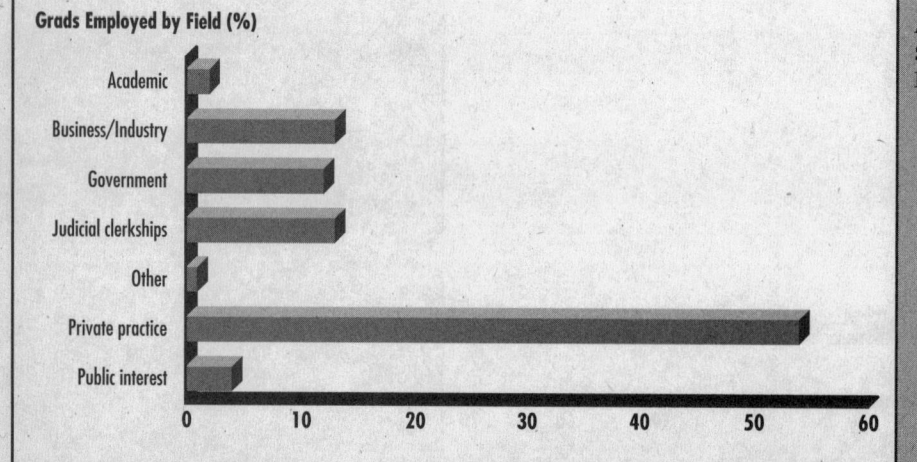

Grads Employed by Field (%)
- Academic: ~1
- Business/Industry: ~13
- Government: ~12
- Judicial clerkships: ~13
- Other: ~2
- Private practice: ~55
- Public interest: ~3

Average Starting Salary: $50,303
State for Bar Exam: MO, IL, CA, NY
Pass Rate for First-Time Bar: 86%

WAYNE STATE UNIVERSITY
Law School

Admissions Contact: Assistant Dean for Recruitment and Admissions, Linda Fowler Sims
471 W. Palmer, Detroit, MI 48202
Admissions Phone: 313-577-3937 • Admissions Fax: 313-993-8129
Admissions E-mail: law.inquire@law.wayne.edu • Web Address: www.law.wayne.edu

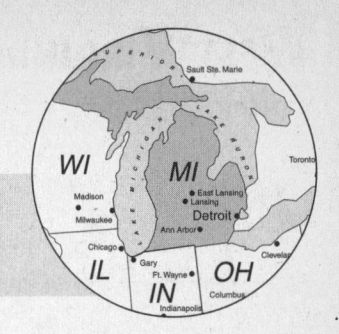

INSTITUTIONAL INFORMATION
Public/Private: Public
Student/Faculty Ratio: 23:1
Total Faculty: 33
% Part Time: 59
% Female: 39
% Minority: 12

PROGRAMS
Academic Specialties: Tax, Labor, Intellectual Property
Advanced Degrees Offered: JD (3 years), LLM (1 year)
Combined Degrees Offered: JD/MBA (4 years), JD/MA (4 years), JD/MADR (4 years)
Grading System: A to E for courses and seminars; Legal Writing is High Pass, Honors, Pass, Low Pass, Fail.
Clinical Program Required? No
Clinical Programs Description: Free Legal Aid Clinic, Commercial Law Clinic, Criminal Appellate Practice, Nonprofit Corporations and Urban Development Law, Civil Rights Litigation Clinic, Disability Law Clinic, Judicial Internship, Civil Law Internship, Criminal Justice Internship, plus numerous simulation courses
Legal Writing Course Requirements? Yes
Legal Writing Description: Covers drafting memos, briefs, contracts, complaints and answers, research methods, and strategy
Legal Methods Course Requirements? No
Legal Research Course Requirements? Yes
Legal Research Description: See Legal Writing.
Moot Court Requirement? Yes
Moot Court Description: At the end of the first-year legal writing course
Public Interest Law Requirement? No
Academic Journals: Law Review, Journal of Law and Society

STUDENT INFORMATION
Enrollment of Law School: 751
% Out of State: 2
% Male/Female: 53/47
% Full Time: 67
% Minority: 19
Average Age of Entering Class: 25

RESEARCH FACILITIES
Research Resources Available: Lexis-Nexis Printing and Database, Westlaw Printing

EXPENSES/FINANCIAL AID
Annual Tuition (Residents/Nonresidents): $7,829/$17,016
Room and Board: $8,970
Books and Supplies: $800
Financial Aid Application Deadline: 3/15
Average Grant: $2,881
Average Loan: $16,511
% Receiving Some Sort of Aid: 80
Average Total Aid Package: $17,943
Average Debt: $45,000

ADMISSIONS INFORMATION
Application Fee: $20
Regular Application Deadline: Rolling
Regular Notification: Rolling
LSDAS Accepted? Yes
Average GPA: 3.3
Range of GPA: 3.1–3.5
Average LSAT: 154
Range of LSAT: 151–157
Transfer Students Accepted? Yes
Other Schools to Which Applicants Applied: Loyola University Chicago, Michigan State University, Thomas M. Cooley Law School, University of Detroit Mercy, University of Michigan
Number of Applications Received: 873
Number of Applicants Accepted: 531
Number of Applicants Enrolled: 250

EMPLOYMENT INFORMATION

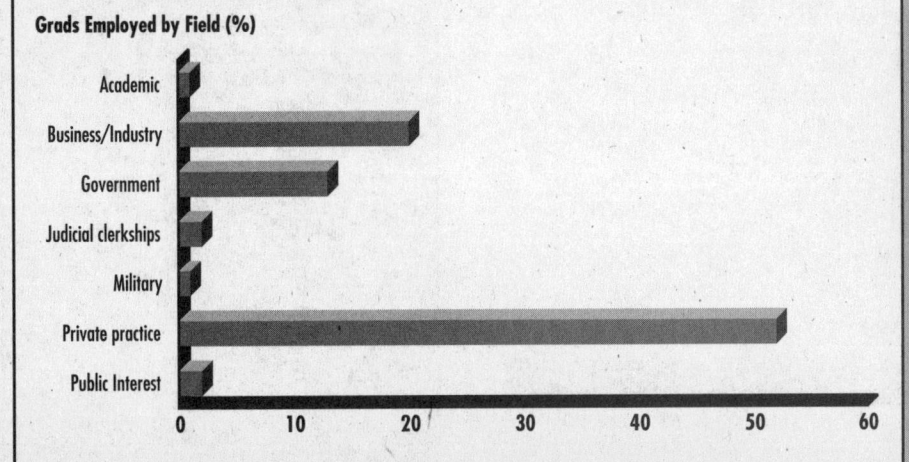

Grads Employed by Field (%)

Field	%
Academic	~1
Business/Industry	~20
Government	~13
Judicial clerkships	~3
Military	~1
Private practice	~52
Public Interest	~2

Rate of Placement: 97%
Average Starting Salary: $58,000
Employers Who Frequently Hire Grads: Leading law firms throughout Michigan; major multinational corporations based in Michigan, including the Big Three U.S. automakers; federal, state and local courts; and governmental agencies and legal service providers
State for Bar Exam: MI
Pass Rate for First-Time Bar: 81%

WEST VIRGINIA UNIVERSITY
College of Law

Admissions Contact: Assistant Dean for Admissions, Janet Armistead
PO Box 6130, Morgantown, WV 26506-6103
Admissions Phone: 304-293-5304 • Admissions Fax: 304-293-6891
Admissions E-mail: lawaply@wvu.edu • Web Address: www.wvu.edu/~law

INSTITUTIONAL INFORMATION
Public/Private: Public
Student/Faculty Ratio: 16:1
Total Faculty: 37
% Part Time: 11
% Female: 11

PROGRAMS
Academic Specialties: The Legal Writing Program, Civil Procedure, Commercial Law, Constitutional Law, Corporation Securities Law, Criminal Law, Environmental Law, Government Services, Human Rights Law, International Law, Labor Law, Legal History, Legal Philosophy, Property, Taxation
Advanced Degrees Offered: JD (3 years)
Combined Degrees Offered: JD/MPA (4 years), JD/MBA (4 years)
Grading System: 4.3 scale
Clinical Program Required? No
Clinical Programs Description: Optional clinical programs help students learn the skills of interviewing, counseling, drafting, litigation planning, negotiation, and trial advocacy. In addition they confront issues of ethics and the professional role and handle cases of violence and social security disability.
Legal Writing Course Requirements? Yes
Legal Writing Description: 1 year
Legal Methods Course Requirements? Yes
Legal Research Course Requirements? No
Moot Court Requirement? No
Public Interest Law Requirement? No

STUDENT INFORMATION
Enrollment of Law School: 446
% Out of State: 18
% Male/Female: 58/42
% Full Time: 98
% Minority: 7
Average Age of Entering Class: 27

EXPENSES/FINANCIAL AID
Annual Tuition (Residents/Nonresidents): $5,296/$12,568
Room and Board (Off Campus): $9,130
Books and Supplies: $853
Average Grant: $4,111
Average Loan: $13,945
% Receiving Some Sort of Aid: 88
Average Total Aid Package: $13,196
Average Debt: $36,373

ADMISSIONS INFORMATION
Application Fee: $50
Regular Application Deadline: 3/1
Regular Notification: Rolling
LSDAS Accepted? Yes
Average GPA: 3.3
Range of GPA: 3.1–3.7
Average LSAT: 154
Range of LSAT: 148–155
Transfer Students Accepted? Yes
Other Admissions Factors Considered: Full file review, all materials are considered
Number of Applications Received: 580
Number of Applicants Accepted: 292
Number of Applicants Enrolled: 152

EMPLOYMENT INFORMATION

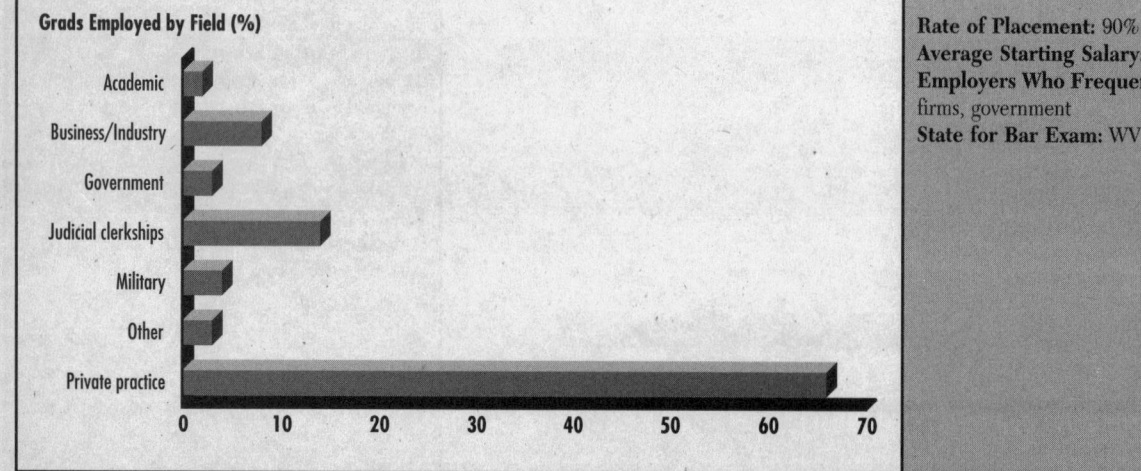

Grads Employed by Field (%)
- Academic
- Business/Industry
- Government
- Judicial clerkships
- Military
- Other
- Private practice

Rate of Placement: 90%
Average Starting Salary: $38,741
Employers Who Frequently Hire Grads: Law firms, government
State for Bar Exam: WV

WESTERN NEW ENGLAND COLLEGE
School of Law

Admissions Contact: Assistant Dean & Director of Admissions, Sherri J. Berendt
1215 Wilbraham Road, Springfield, MA 01119
Admissions Phone: 413-782-1406 • Admissions Fax: 413-796-2067
Admissions E-mail: lawadmis@wnec.edu • Web Address: www.law.wnec.edu

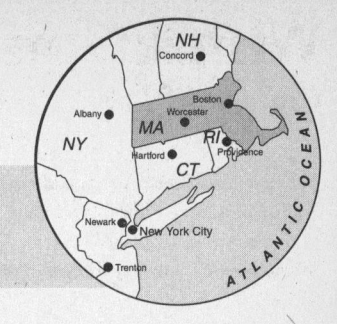

INSTITUTIONAL INFORMATION
Public/Private: Private
Student/Faculty Ratio: 9:1
Total Faculty: 60
% Part Time: 47
% Female: 40
% Minority: 7

PROGRAMS
Academic Specialties: Our faculty teach in a wide variety of legal subjects; electives are offered in almost every area of law a student would wish to investigate. Our clinics in criminal law, civil litigation, consumer protection, and legal services offer additional opportunities for gaining practical experience in these areas.
Combined Degrees Offered: JD/MRP (4 years), JD/MSW (4 years), JD/MBA (4 years)
Grading System: Numerical system, ranging from 55–99. Minimum 70 required for graduation. Pass/Fail available for some courses.
Clinical Program Required? No
Clinical Programs Description: Clinical and simulation courses in a wide variety of areas.
Legal Writing Course Requirements? Yes
Legal Writing Description: Full-year, 2-credit course taken in the first year of law school. Covers legal writing and research and introduction to oral arguments.
Legal Methods Course Requirements? Yes
Legal Methods Description: See Legal Writing.
Legal Research Course Requirements? Yes
Legal Research Description: See Legal Writing.
Moot Court Requirement? No
Public Interest Law Requirement? No
Academic Journals: Western New England Law Review

STUDENT INFORMATION
Enrollment of Law School: 492
% Out of State: 42
% Male/Female: 47/53
% Full Time: 54
% Full Time That Are International: 1
% Minority: 13
Average Age of Entering Class: 27

RESEARCH FACILITIES
Research Resources Available: Wireless technology throughout the building
School-Supported Research Centers: Criminal Law Clinic, affiliated with the Hampden County District Attorney's Office; Discrimination Law Clinic, affiliated with Massachusetts Commission Against Discrimination; Legal Services Clinic, affiliated with Western Massachusetts Legal Services; Consumer Protection Clinic, affiliated with Mayor of Springfield's Office of Consumer Affairs; Colleges of Greater Springfield Consortium; New England Law Libraries Consortium

EXPENSES/FINANCIAL AID
Annual Tuition: $21,866
Room and Board: $9,640
Books and Supplies: $1,155
Average Grant: $8,392
Average Loan: $20,973
% Receiving Some Sort of Aid: 92
Average Total Aid Package: $23,174
Average Debt: $69,013

ADMISSIONS INFORMATION
Application Fee: $45
Regular Application Deadline: Rolling
Regular Notification: Rolling
LSDAS Accepted? Yes
Average GPA: 3.1
Range of GPA: 2.7–3.3
Average LSAT: 151
Range of LSAT: 147–154
Transfer Students Accepted? Yes
Other Schools to Which Applicants Applied: New England School of Law, Quinnipiac University, Roger Williams University, University of Connecticut
Other Admissions Factors Considered: Writing ability as evidenced in personal statement and writing sample on LSAT; background and personal experience that will add to classroom discussions—examples include racial, gender, economic, or physical obstacles
Number of Applications Received: 915
Number of Applicants Accepted: 538
Number of Applicants Enrolled: 154

EMPLOYMENT INFORMATION

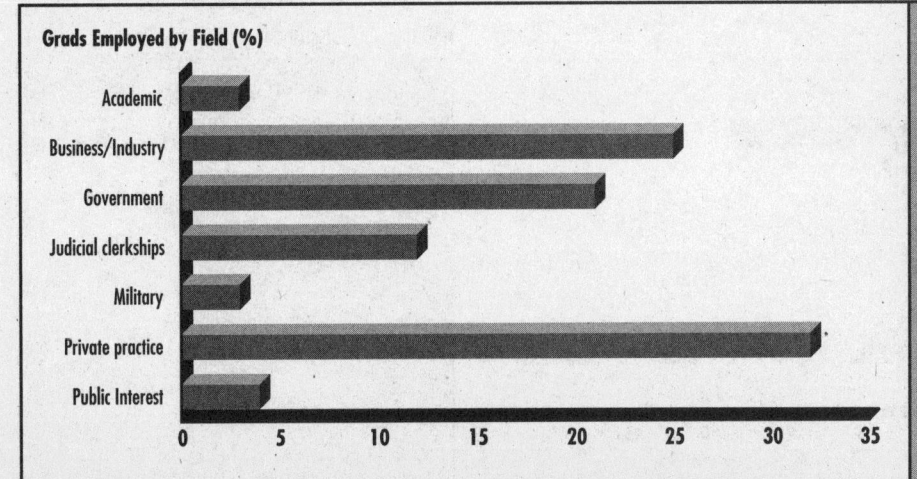

Grads Employed by Field (%)
- Academic: ~1
- Business/Industry: ~25
- Government: ~21
- Judicial clerkships: ~12
- Military: ~1
- Private practice: ~32
- Public Interest: ~4

Rate of Placement: 87%
Average Starting Salary: $50,685
Employers Who Frequently Hire Grads: Law firms (e.g. Bingham Dana; Day, Berry & Howard; Shipman & Goodwin), accounting firms, insurance companies, government agencies
State for Bar Exam: CT, MA, NY, NJ, PA
Pass Rate for First-Time Bar: 71%

WESTERN STATE UNIVERSITY
College of Law

Admissions Contact: Associate Dean of Admission, Paul D. Bauer
1111 North State College Boulevard, Fullerton, CA 92831
Admissions Phone: 714-738-1000 • Admissions Fax: 714-441-1748
Admissions E-mail: adm@wsulaw.edu • Web Address: www.wsulaw.edu

INSTITUTIONAL INFORMATION
Public/Private: Private
Student/Faculty Ratio: 18:1
Total Faculty: 65
% Part Time: 68
% Female: 39
% Minority: 14

PROGRAMS
Academic Specialties: Entrepreneurial Law Center, Professional Skills, Academic Success and Enrichment Program, Criminal Law Practice Center
Advanced Degrees Offered: JD (3 years full time, 4 years part time)
Grading System: 4.0 scale
Clinical Program Required? No
Legal Writing Course Requirements? Yes
Legal Writing Description: Incorporated into Professional Skills I and II and Advocacy courses
Legal Methods Course Requirements? No
Legal Research Course Requirements? Yes
Legal Research Description: Incorporated into Professional Skills I and II and Advocacy courses
Moot Court Requirement? Yes
Moot Court Description: Incorporated into the Advocacy course
Public Interest Law Requirement? No
Academic Journals: *Law Review*

STUDENT INFORMATION
Enrollment of Law School: 157
% Out of State: 17
% Male/Female: 64/36
% Full Time: 64
% Full Time That Are International: 1
% Minority: 31
Average Age of Entering Class: 28

RESEARCH FACILITIES
Research Resources Available: CSU Fullerton

EXPENSES/FINANCIAL AID
Annual Tuition: $22,168
Room and Board (Off Campus): $11,739
Books and Supplies: $810
Financial Aid Application Deadline: 4/14
Average Grant: $6,484
Average Loan: $19,740
% of Aid That Is Merit-Based: 14
% Receiving Some Sort of Aid: 75
Average Total Aid Package: $19,369
Average Debt: $73,000

ADMISSIONS INFORMATION
Application Fee: $50
Regular Application Deadline: Rolling
Regular Notification: Rolling
LSDAS Accepted? Yes
Average GPA: 2.9
Range of GPA: 2.7–3.2
Average LSAT: 147
Range of LSAT: 143–150
Transfer Students Accepted? Yes
Other Schools to Which Students Applied: Chapman University, Pepperdine University, Southwestern University School of Law, Thomas Jefferson School of Law, University of San Diego, Whittier College
Number of Applications Received: 721
Number of Applicants Accepted: 421
Number of Applicants Enrolled: 101

EMPLOYMENT INFORMATION

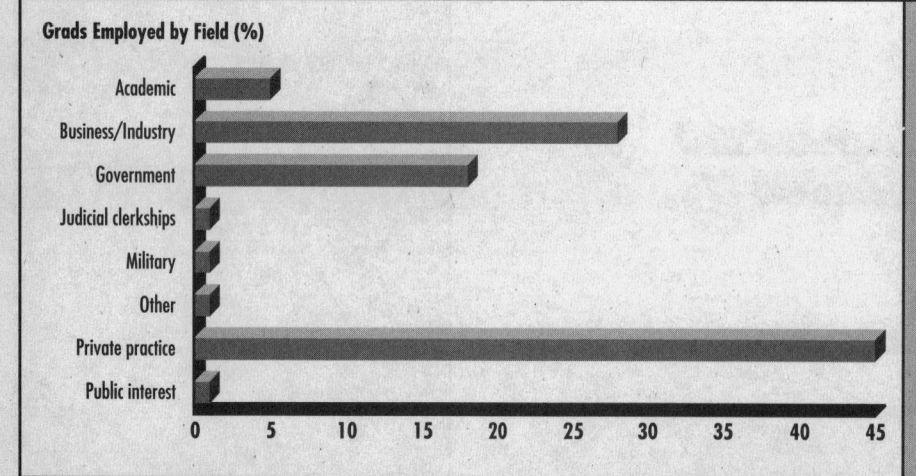

Grads Employed by Field (%)

Field	%
Academic	~3
Business/Industry	~28
Government	~18
Judicial clerkships	~1
Military	~1
Other	~1
Private practice	~45
Public interest	~1

Rate of Placement: 88%
Average Starting Salary: $67,300
Employers Who Frequently Hire Grads: Medium-sized law firms, district attorneys, public defenders, corporations, state governments, federal governments
State for Bar Exam: CA, AZ, TX, OR, NY
Pass Rate for First-Time Bar: 38%

WHITTIER COLLEGE
Law School

Admissions Contact: Director of Admissions, Patricia Abracia
3333 Harbor Boulevard, Costa Mesa, CA 92626
Admissions Phone: 714-444-4141 • Admissions Fax: 714-444-0250
Admissions E-mail: info@law.whittier.edu • Web Address: www.law.whittier.edu

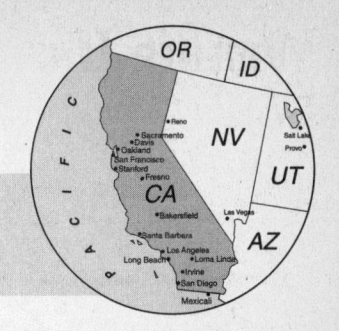

INSTITUTIONAL INFORMATION
Public/Private: Private
Student/Faculty Ratio: 21:1
Total Faculty: 80
% Part Time: 63
% Female: 40
% Minority: 13

PROGRAMS
Academic Specialties: Health Law Symposium, International Law Symposium, Center for Children's Rights, Intellectual Property, International Law
Advanced Degrees Offered: JD (3 years full time, 4 years part time), LLM Foreign Legal Studies (24 credits, 1 year)
Grading System: Letter and numerical system on a 100-point scale; cumulative grade of 77 required for good standing
Clinical Program Required? No
Clinical Program Description: Whittier Law School offers a variety of clinical opportunities for students through an on-campus, live client clinic and off-site externship placements. Up to 10 students per term can enroll in the Children's Rights Clinic. General off-site clinical externships are available to all students who have completed their first year of study. Placements are available throughout Southern California in public interest agencies, governmental offices, and judicial chambers.
Legal Writing Course Requirements? Yes
Legal Writing Description: 5 units of Legal Writing
Legal Methods Course Requirements? No
Legal Research Course Requirements? Yes
Legal Research Description: Part of the 5 units of Legal Writing
Moot Court Requirement? Yes
Moot Court Description: The intramural Moot Court component of the required Legal Skills course is designed to enhance oral advocacy skills. Students pair up to argue against another pair of students before a panel of 3 "judges," who are members of the Moot Court Honors Board. They are given both written and oral feedback on their performance. The Moot Court Honors Board advances student skills in appellate advocacy.
Public Interest Law Requirement? No
Academic Journals: *The Whittier Law Review*

STUDENT INFORMATION
Enrollment of Law School: 712
% Out of State: 25
% Male/Female: 46/54
% Full Time: 60
% Full Time That Are International: 0
% Minority: 43
Average Age of Entering Class: 26

RESEARCH FACILITIES
% of JD Classrooms Wired: 85

EXPENSES/FINANCIAL AID
Annual Tuition: $22,980
Room and Board (Off Campus): $9,325
Books and Supplies: $675
Financial Aid Application Deadline: 4/15
Average Grant: $9,871
Average Loan: $24,406
% of Aid That Is Merit-Based: 97
% Receiving Some Sort of Aid: 90
Average Total Aid Package: $28,500
Average Debt: $76,668
Tuition Per Credit: $766

ADMISSIONS INFORMATION
Application Fee: $50
Regular Application Deadline: Rolling
Regular Notification: Rolling
LSDAS Accepted? Yes
Average GPA: 2.9
Range of GPA: 2.5–3.2
Average LSAT: 148
Range of LSAT: 144–151
Transfer Students Accepted? Yes
Other Schools to Which Students Applied: California Western, Loyola Marymount University, Pepperdine University, Southwestern University School of Law, University of California—Los Angeles, University of San Diego, University of Southern California
Other Admissions Factors Considered: Maturity, capacity for self-discipline, work record, year-to-year progress in college, courses completed, graduate work, participation in student organizations, volunteer work
Number of Applications Received: 1,044
Number of Applicants Accepted: 713
Number of Applicants Enrolled: 206

EMPLOYMENT INFORMATION

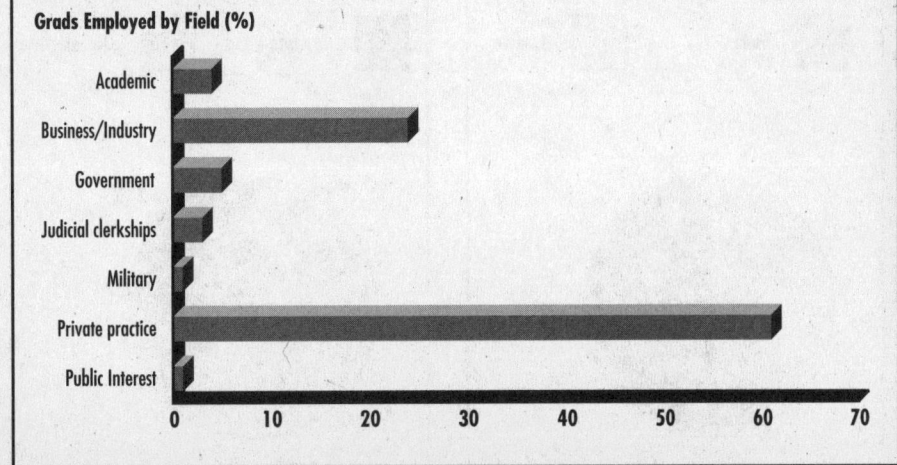

Grads Employed by Field (%):
- Academic: ~1
- Business/Industry: ~25
- Government: ~5
- Judicial clerkships: ~3
- Military: 0
- Private practice: ~62
- Public Interest: ~1

Rate of Placement: 95%
Average Starting Salary: $59,082
State for Bar Exam: CA
Pass Rate for First-Time Bar: 54%

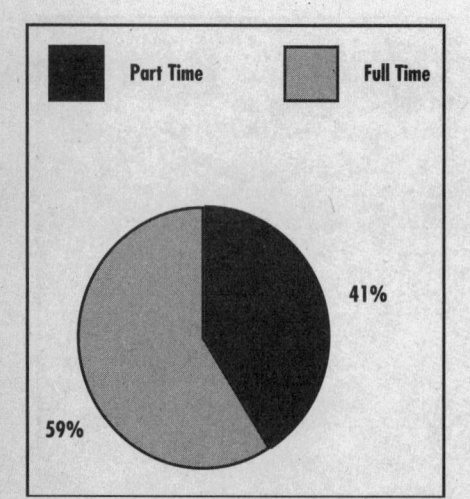

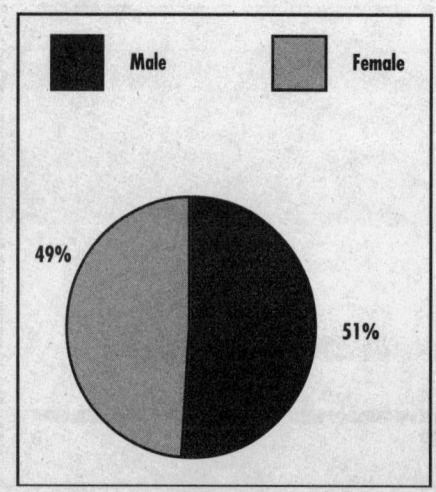

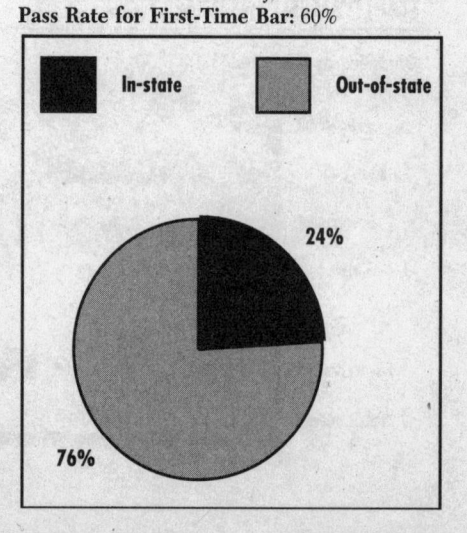

WIDENER UNIVERSITY, DELAWARE
School of Law

Admissions Contact: Assistant Dean for Admissions, Barbara Ayars
PO Box 7474, 4601 Concord Pike, Wilmington, DE 19803
Admissions Phone: 302-477-2162 • Admissions Fax: 302-477-2224
Admissions E-mail: law.admissions@law.widener.edu • Web Address: www.law.widener.edu

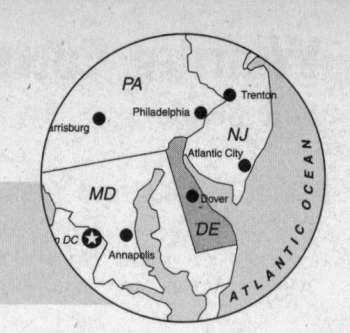

INSTITUTIONAL INFORMATION
Public/Private: Private
Student/Faculty Ratio: 19:1
Total Faculty: 134
% Part Time: 57
% Female: 34
% Minority: 5

PROGRAMS
Academic Specialties: Health Law (Health Law Institute), Corporate Law and Finance, Environmental Law (Environmental Law Clinic), Intellectual Property, Constitutional Law (H. Albert Young Fellowship), International Law, Trial Advocacy (Intensive Trial Advocacy Program), Civil Procedure, Commercial Law, Corporation Securities Law, Criminal Law, Government Services, Human Rights Law, Labor Law, Property, Taxation
Advanced Degrees Offered: LLM Corporate Law and Finance (24 credits), LLM Health Law (24 credits), MJ (30 credits), SJD Health Law (8 credits), DL Health Law (8 credits)
Combined Degrees Offered: JD/PsychD (6 years), JD/MBA (4 years), JD/MMP in conjunction with University of Delaware Graduate College of Marine Studies (4.5 years)
Grading System: A to F (4.0–0.0)
Clinical Program Required? No
Clinical Programs Description: Pennsylvania Civil Law Clinic: Students represent clients in family law and consumer bankruptcy matters. Pennsylvania Criminal Defense Clinic: Students defend clients in criminal matters including capital case prosecutions. Delaware Civil Law Clinic: Students represent clients in domestic violence cases, landlord/tenant disputes, probate issues, divorces, unemployment compensation hearings and related civil litigation matters. Veterans Assistance Program: Students represent disabled veterans and/or their dependents before the Department of Veterans Affairs and Article I and Article III Federal Courts that handle veteran matters. Environmental Law and Natural Resources Clinic: Students represent public interest groups in a variety of environmental matters.
Legal Writing Course Requirements? Yes
Legal Writing Description: 2–3 credit courses taken in the first 3 semesters of law school
Legal Methods Course Requirements? Yes
Legal Methods Description: See Legal Writing.
Legal Research Course Requirements? Yes
Legal Research Description: See Legal Writing.
Moot Court Requirement? No
Public Interest Law Requirement? No
Academic Journals: Delaware Journal of Corporate Law, Widener Law Symposium Journal

STUDENT INFORMATION
Enrollment of Law School: 1,030
% Out of State: 76
% Male/Female: 51/49
% Full Time: 59
% Full Time That Are International: 1
% Minority: 9
Average Age of Entering Class: 25

EXPENSES/FINANCIAL AID
Annual Tuition: $21,200
Room and Board: $7,500
Books and Supplies: $1,000
Financial Aid Application Deadline: 4/15
Average Grant: $8,070
Average Loan: $17,547
% of Aid That Is Merit-Based: 91
% Receiving Some Sort of Aid: 35
Average Total Aid Package: $20,179
Average Debt: $64,567
Tuition Per Credit: $710

ADMISSIONS INFORMATION
Application Fee: $60
Regular Application Deadline: 5/15
Regular Notification: Rolling
LSDAS Accepted? Yes
Average GPA: 3.0
Range of GPA: 2.6–3.4
Average LSAT: 150
Transfer Students Accepted? Yes
Other Schools to Which Students Applied: New England School of Law, Rutgers, Temple, Pennsylvania State, Villanova
Other Admissions Factors Considered: Personal essay, work experience, life experiences, extracurricular activities, letters of recommendation
Number of Applications Received: 1,147
Number of Applicants Accepted: 650
Number of Applicants Enrolled: 197

INTERNATIONAL STUDENTS
TOEFL Required of International Students? Yes
Minimum TOEFL: 220

EMPLOYMENT INFORMATION
Rate of Placement: 87%
Average Starting Salary: $55,762
Employers Who Frequently Hire Grads: Law firms, judges, corporations, government employers
State for Bar Exam: PA, NJ, DE, MD, NY
Pass Rate for First-Time Bar: 60%

WIDENER UNIVERSITY, HARRISBURG
School of Law

Admissions Contact: Assistant Dean of Admissions, Barbara Ayars
PO Box 7474, 4601 Concord Pike, Wilmington, DE 19803
Admissions Phone: 717-541-3903 • Admissions Fax: 717-541-3999
Admissions E-mail: law.admissions@law.widener.edu • Web Address: www.law.widener.edu

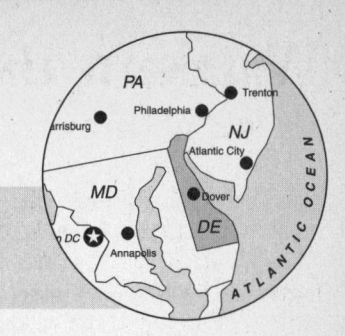

INSTITUTIONAL INFORMATION
Public/Private: Private
Student/Faculty Ratio: 19:1
Total Faculty: 58
% Part Time: 62
% Female: 36
% Minority: 3

PROGRAMS
Academic Specialties: Administrative Law, Constitutional Law, Trial Advocacy, Law and Government, Public Interest Law, Legislation/Legislative Drafting, Commercial Law, Criminal Law, Environmental Law, Government Services, Property, Taxation
Combined Degrees Offered: JD/PsychD (6 years), JD/MBA (4 years), JD/MMP in conjunction with University of Delaware Graduate College of Marine Studies (4.5 years), JD/MS in conjunction with Clarion University (4 years)
Grading System: A to F (4.0–0.0)
Clinical Program Required? No
Clinical Programs Description: Widener offers the Harrisburg Civil Law Clinic, in which students represent clients in various civil litigation areas including domestic relations, truancy, consumer rights, landlord/tenant, and unemployment compensation matters.
Legal Writing Course Requirements? Yes
Legal Writing Description: 2–3 credit courses taken in the first 2 semesters
Legal Methods Course Requirements? Yes
Legal Methods Description: See Legal Writing.
Legal Research Course Requirements? Yes
Legal Research Description: See Legal Writing.
Moot Court Requirement? No
Public Interest Law Requirement? No
Academic Journals: *The Widener Journal of Public Law*

STUDENT INFORMATION
Enrollment of Law School: 387
% Out of State: 24
% Male/Female: 50/50
% Full Time: 61
% Full Time That Are International: 0
% Minority: 7
Average Age of Entering Class: 25

EXPENSES/FINANCIAL AID
Annual Tuition: $21,200
Room and Board (Off Campus): $7,500
Books and Supplies: $1,000
Financial Aid Application Deadline: 4/15
Average Grant: $6,517
Average Loan: $16,644
% of Aid That Is Merit-Based: 88
% Receiving Some Sort of Aid: 36
Average Total Aid Package: $18,741
Average Debt: $71,293
Tuition Per Credit: $710

ADMISSIONS INFORMATION
Application Fee: $60
Regular Application Deadline: 5/15
Regular Notification: Rolling
LSDAS Accepted? Yes
Average GPA: 3.1
Range of GPA: 2.7–3.4
Average LSAT: 147
Range of LSAT: 145–151
Transfer Students Accepted? Yes
Other Schools to Which Students Applied: New England School of Law, Rutgers University, Temple University, The Pennsylvania State University, Villanova University
Other Admissions Factors Considered: Personal essay, work experience, life experiences, extracurricular activities, letters of recommendation
Number of Applications Received: 493
Number of Applicants Accepted: 321
Number of Applicants Enrolled: 103

INTERNATIONAL STUDENTS
TOEFL Required of International Students? Yes
Minimum TOEFL: 220

EMPLOYMENT INFORMATION
Rate of Placement: 84%
Average Starting Salary: $43,495
Employers Who Frequently Hire Grads: Law firms, judges, corporations, government employers
State for Bar Exam: PA
Pass Rate for First-Time Bar: 67%

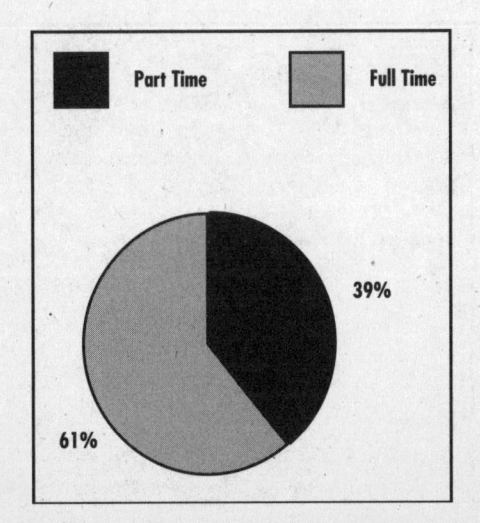

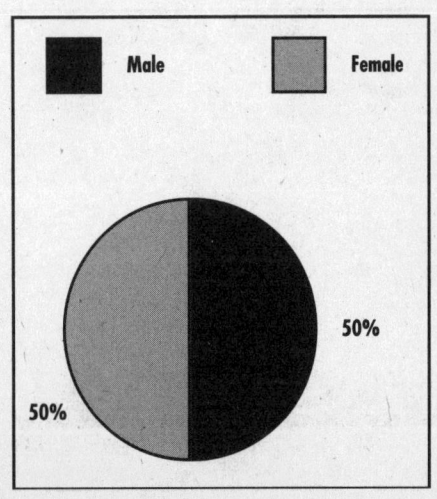

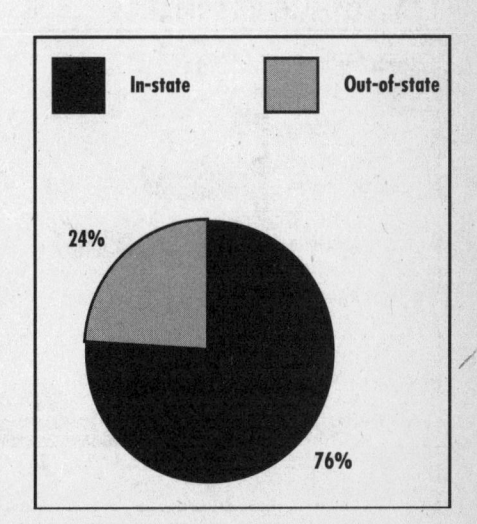

WILLAMETTE UNIVERSITY
College of Law

Admissions Contact: Assistant Dean, Admissions and Communications, Lawrence Seno
245 Winter Street, SE, Salem, OR 97301-3922
Admissions Phone: 503-370-6282 • Admissions Fax: 503-370-6375
Admissions E-mail: law-admission@willamette.edu • Web Address: www.willamette.edu/wucl

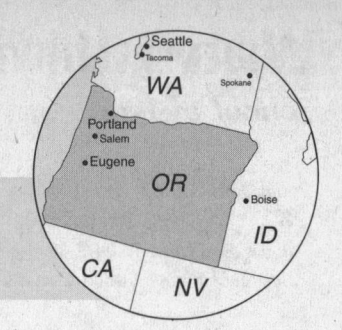

INSTITUTIONAL INFORMATION
Public/Private: Private
Student/Faculty Ratio: 15:1
Total Faculty: 30
% Part Time: 17
% Female: 20
% Minority: 1

PROGRAMS
Academic Specialties: Certificate programs in Dispute Resolution, Law and Government, International Law, and Law and Business
Combined Degrees Offered: JD/MBA with Willamette University Atkinson Graduate School of Management (4 years)
Grading System: A to F
Clinical Program Required? No
Legal Writing Course Requirements? Yes
Legal Methods Course Requirements? Yes
Legal Methods Description: 2 semesters, 2 hours per semester
Legal Research Course Requirements? No
Moot Court Requirement? No
Public Interest Law Requirement? No
Academic Journals: *Willamette Law Review, Willamette Journal of International Law & Dispute Resolution*

STUDENT INFORMATION
Enrollment of Law School: 418
% Out of State: 42
% Male/Female: 52/48
% Full Time: 100
% Full Time That Are International: 3
% Minority: 11
Average Age of Entering Class: 26

RESEARCH FACILITIES
School-Supported Research Centers: Center for Dispute Resolution, Oregon Law Commission

EXPENSES/FINANCIAL AID
Annual Tuition: $20,850
Room and Board: $12,100
Books and Supplies: $1,250
Average Grant: $10,000
Average Loan: $21,133
Average Debt: $60,416
Fees Per Credit: $695

ADMISSIONS INFORMATION
Application Fee: $50
Regular Application Deadline: 4/1
Regular Notification: 4/15
LSDAS Accepted? Yes
Average GPA: 3.2
Range of GPA: 3.0–3.5
Average LSAT: 154
Range of LSAT: 152–157
Transfer Students Accepted? Yes
Other Schools to Which Students Applied: Lewis and Clark College, Seattle University, University of Oregon
Other Admissions Factors Considered: Some additional consideration is given to candidates who have strong ties to Oregon or to the Pacific Northwest and who intend to practice in the state or region.
Number of Applications Received: 742
Number of Applicants Accepted: 445
Number of Applicants Enrolled: 142

INTERNATIONAL STUDENTS
TOEFL Required of International Students? Yes

EMPLOYMENT INFORMATION

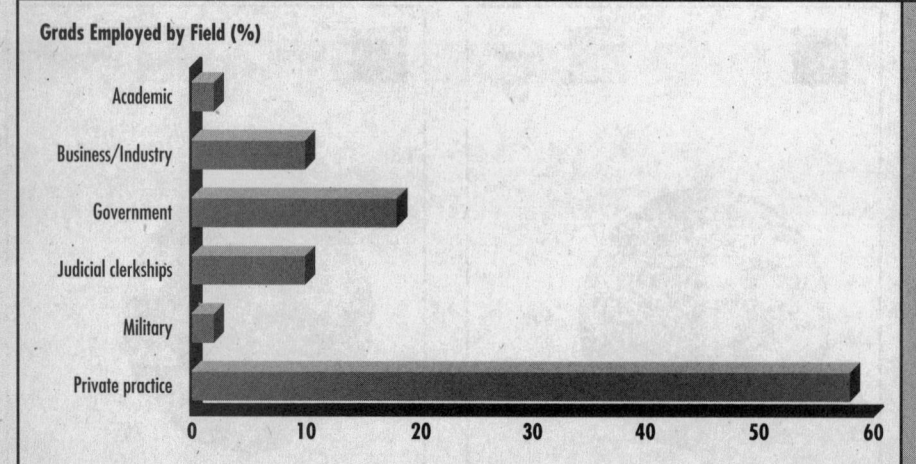

Grads Employed by Field (%):
- Academic: ~2
- Business/Industry: ~10
- Government: ~18
- Judicial clerkships: ~10
- Military: ~2
- Private practice: ~58

Rate of Placement: 78%
Average Starting Salary: $53,354
Employers Who Frequently Hire Grads: Stoel Rives; Marion, Lane, and King counties; Schwabe, Williamson & Wyatt; Ater Wynne; Harrang Long; Miller Nash; Oregon courts
State for Bar Exam: OR
Pass Rate for First-Time Bar: 71%

WILLIAM MITCHELL COLLEGE OF LAW

Admissions Contact: Dean of Students, James H. Brooks
875 Summit Avenue, St. Paul, MN 55105
Admissions Phone: 651-290-6476 • Admissions Fax: 651-290-6414
Admissions E-mail: admissions@wmitchell.edu • Web Address: www.wmitchell.edu

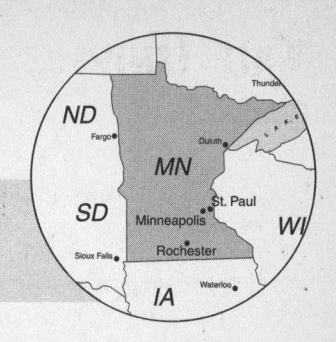

INSTITUTIONAL INFORMATION
Public/Private: Private
Total Faculty: 245
% Part Time: 85
% Female: 38

PROGRAMS
Academic Specialties: Intellectual Property, Business/Commercial, Tort, Tax; lawyering skills and clinic programs
Advanced Degrees Offered: LLM in Taxation (2 years part time)
Grading System: Letter and numerical system on a 4.0 scale
Clinical Program Required? Yes
Clinical Programs Description: Business Law Clinic, Civil Advocacy Clinic, Criminal Appeals Clinic, Immigration Clinic, Legal Assistance to Minnesota Prisoners, Misdemeanor Clinic, Administrative Law Clinic, Attorney General Clinic, Civil and Human Rights Clinic, Court of Appeals Clinic
Legal Methods Course Requirements? Yes
Legal Methods Description: Research, Writing and Reasoning, taught in small groups of approximately 13 students

STUDENT INFORMATION
Enrollment of Law School: 1,019
% Male/Female: 52/48
% Full Time: 51
% Full Time That Are International: 1
% Minority: 10
Average Age of Entering Class: 25

EXPENSES/FINANCIAL AID
Annual Tuition: $19,000
Books and Supplies: $725
Average Grant: $3,846
Average Loan: $17,642
% of Aid That Is Merit-Based: 9
% Receiving Some Sort of Aid: 90
Average Total Aid Package: $19,170
Average Debt: $54,661
Fees Per Credit: $750

ADMISSIONS INFORMATION
Application Fee: $45
Regular Application Deadline: 6/30
Regular Notification: Rolling
LSDAS Accepted? Yes
Average GPA: 3.2
Range of GPA: 2.8–3.5
Average LSAT: 152
Range of LSAT: 148–156
Transfer Students Accepted? Yes
Other Schools to Which Students Applied: University at Albany, Drake University, University of Pennsylvania, Marquette University, University of Minnesota, University of North Dakota, University of Wisconsin
Other Admissions Factors Considered: Motivation, interpersonal skills, work experience, extracurricular activities, community service, overcoming disadvantage
Number of Applications Received: 972
Number of Applicants Accepted: 638
Number of Applicants Enrolled: 352

INTERNATIONAL STUDENTS
TOEFL Required of International Students? Yes

EMPLOYMENT INFORMATION

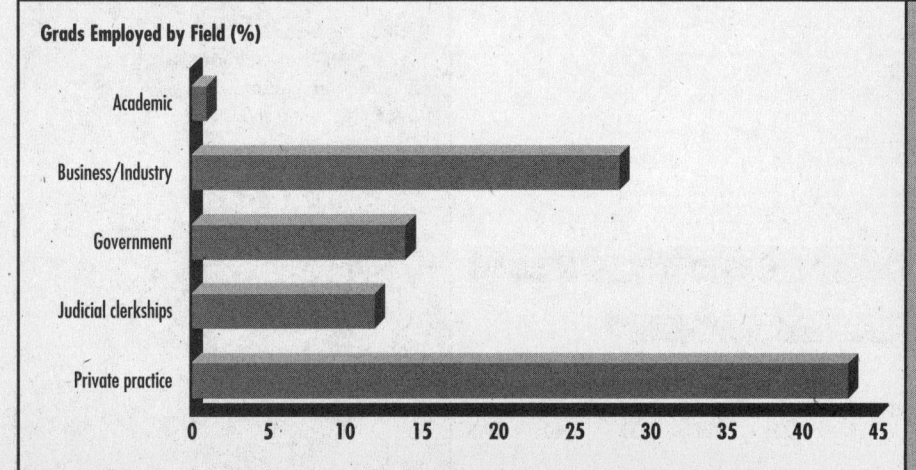

Grads Employed by Field (%)
- Academic
- Business/Industry
- Government
- Judicial clerkships
- Private practice

Rate of Placement: 94%
Average Starting Salary: $52,283
Employers Who Frequently Hire Grads: Briggs & Morgan; Robins, Kaplan, Miller & Ciresi; Gray, Plant, Mooty; The St. Paul Companies; Merchant & Gould
State for Bar Exam: MN
Pass Rate for First-Time Bar: 85%

YALE UNIVERSITY
Law School

Admissions Contact: Director of Admissions, Jean Webb
PO Box 208329, New Haven, CT 06520-8329
Admissions Phone: 203-432-4995
Admissions E-mail: admissions.law@yale.edu • Web Address: www.law.yale.edu

INSTITUTIONAL INFORMATION
Public/Private: Private
Total Faculty: 67
% Female: 24
% Minority: 13

PROGRAMS
Advanced Degrees Offered: JD (3 years), LLM (1 year), MSL (1 year), JSD (up to 5 years)
Combined Degrees Offered: JD/PhD History, JD/PhD Political Science, JD/MS Forestry, JD/MS Sociology, JD/MS Statistics, JD/MBA with Yale School of Management, and others
Grading System: Honors, Pass, Low Pass, Credit, Failure
Clinical Program Required? No
Clinical Programs Description: Clinical opportunities are offered through the Jerome N. Frank Legal Services Organization, which links law students with individuals in need of legal help who cannot afford private attorneys. Faculty-supervised students interview clients, write briefs, prepare witnesses, try cases, negotiate settlements, and argue appeals in state and federal courts, including the U.S. Court of Appeals for the Second Circuit and the Connecticut Supreme Court. There are 8 main projects: Advocacy for Parents and Children, Advocacy for People with Disabilities, Community Legal Services, Housing and Community Development, Immigration, Landlord/Tenant, Legal Assistance, and Prisons. Students also participate in independent projects at two local prosecutors' offices (the New Haven State Attorney and the U.S. Attorney) and at other public service law offices. Other clinics include the Environmental Protection Clinic and the Allard K. Lowenstein International Human Rights Law Clinic. Student-managed programs available to students from their second term include the Capital Defense Project, the Domestic Violence Temporary Restraining Order Project, the Greenhaven Prison Project, Street Law, Thomas Swan Barristers' Union, Morris Tyler Moot Court of Appeals, and numerous reviews and journals.
Legal Writing Course Requirements? No
Legal Methods Course Requirements? No
Legal Research Course Requirements? No
Moot Court Requirement? No
Public Interest Law Requirement? No
Academic Journals: *Yale Law Journal, Yale Journal of International Law, Yale Journal of Law and Feminism, Yale Journal of Law and the Humanities, Yale Journal on Regulation, Yale Human Rights and Development Law Journal, Yale Law and Policy Review*

STUDENT INFORMATION
Enrollment of Law School: 588
% Male/Female: 52/48
% Full Time: 100
% Minority: 30
Average Age of Entering Class: 24

EXPENSES/FINANCIAL AID
Annual Tuition: $29,800
Books and Supplies: $11,840
Financial Aid Application Deadline: 3/15
Average Grant: $9,000
Average Loan: $24,500
% Receiving Some Sort of Aid: 75
Average Debt: $64,900

ADMISSIONS INFORMATION
Application Fee: $55
Regular Application Deadline: 2/15
Regular Notification: Rolling
LSDAS Accepted? Yes
Average GPA: 3.8
Range of GPA: 3.7–3.9
Average LSAT: 171
Range of LSAT: 168–174
Transfer Students Accepted? Yes
Number of Applications Received: 3,315
Number of Applicants Accepted: 290
Number of Applicants Enrolled: 187

INTERNATIONAL STUDENTS
TOEFL Required of International Students? Yes
Minimum TOEFL: 250

EMPLOYMENT INFORMATION

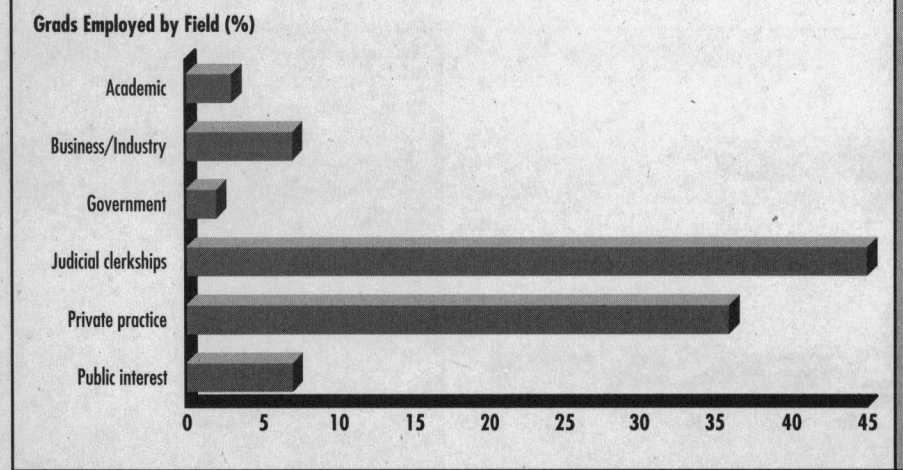

Grads Employed by Field (%)
- Academic: ~2
- Business/Industry: ~5
- Government: ~2
- Judicial clerkships: ~45
- Private practice: ~37
- Public interest: ~7

Rate of Placement: 100%
Average Starting Salary: $76,495
State for Bar Exam: NY
Pass Rate for First-Time Bar: 95%

Yeshiva University
Benjamin N. Cardozo School of Law

Admissions Contact: Assistant Dean for Admissions, Robert L. Schwartz
55 Fifth Avenue, New York, NY 10003
Admissions Phone: 212-790-0274 • Admissions Fax: 212-790-0482
Admissions E-mail: lawinfo@ymail.yu.edu • Web Address: www.cardozo.yu.edu

INSTITUTIONAL INFORMATION
Public/Private: Private
Affiliation: Jewish
Student/Faculty Ratio: 18:1
Total Faculty: 45
% Part Time: 54
% Female: 31
% Minority: 7

PROGRAMS
Academic Specialties: The faculty is particularly deep in Intellectual Property, Corporate Law, Criminal Law and Litigation, and Legal Theory. Other specialties include Civil Procedure, Commercial Law, Constitutional Law, Corporation Securities Law, Human Rights Law, International Law, Legal Philosophy, Property, Taxation, Entertainment Law, and Alternative Dispute Resolution.
Advanced Degrees Offered: JD (3 academic years, 2.5 calendar years, or 2 academic years and 2 summers), LLM Intellectual Property Law and General Studies (1 year full time, up to 3 years part time)
Combined Degrees Offered: JD/MSW (about 4 years), JD/MA (about 4 years)
Grading System: A+ to F; a curve applies to all first-year and large upper-level classes
Clinical Program Required? No
Clinical Programs Description: 15 clinical programs
Legal Writing Course Requirements? Yes
Legal Writing Description: 1 year legal research and writing (fall) and appellate advocacy (spring)
Legal Methods Course Requirements? Yes
Legal Methods Description: 2 credit legal methods course taught during the first half of the fall semester
Legal Research Course Requirements? Yes
Legal Research Description: Advanced Legal Research in second and third years
Moot Court Requirement? No
Public Interest Law Requirement? No
Academic Journals: *Cardozo Law Review, Cardozo Arts and Entertainment Law Journal, Cardozo Women's Law Journal, Cardozo Journal of International and Comparative Law, Cardozo Online Journal of Conflict Resolution*

STUDENT INFORMATION
Enrollment of Law School: 935
% Male/Female: 50/50
% Full Time: 100
% Minority: 20
Average Age of Entering Class: 23

RESEARCH FACILITIES
Research Resources Available: Students may take courses and use the facilities at other divisions of Yeshiva University and at the neighboring New School University. Library has on-site access arrangements with other area academic libraries.
School-Supported Research Centers: Jacob Burns Institute for Advanced Legal Studies; Heyman Center on Corporate Governance; Diener Institute of Jewish Law; Squadron Program in Law, Media, and Society; Jacob Burns Ethics Center; Floersheimer Center for Constitutional Democracy; Kukin Program for Conflict Resolution; Siegel Program in Real Estate Law

EXPENSES/FINANCIAL AID
Annual Tuition: $26,709
Room and Board (Off Campus): $20,727
Books and Supplies: $989
Financial Aid Application Deadline: 4/15
Average Grant: $7,000
Average Loan: $15,000
% of Aid That Is Merit-Based: 40
% Receiving Some Sort of Aid: 82
Average Total Aid Package: $27,500
Average Debt: $80,000
Tuition Per Credit: $1,210

ADMISSIONS INFORMATION
Application Fee: $60
Regular Application Deadline: 4/1
Regular Notification: Rolling
LSDAS Accepted? Yes
Average GPA: 3.4
Range of GPA: 3.1–3.6
Average LSAT: 159
Range of LSAT: 156–160
Transfer Students Accepted? Yes
Other Schools to Which Students Applied: Fordham University, Brooklyn Law School, New York University, New York Law School, George Washington University, Columbia University, Boston University
Number of Applications Received: 2,864
Number of Applicants Accepted: 1,019
Number of Applicants Enrolled: 284

EMPLOYMENT INFORMATION

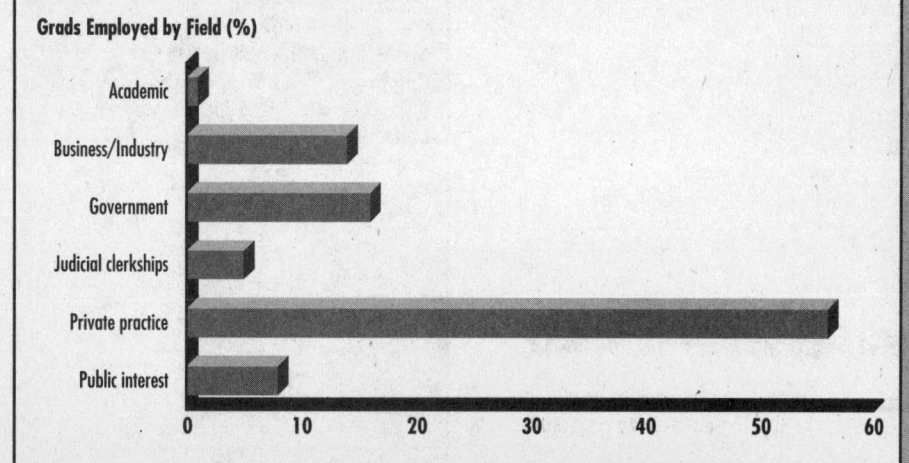

Grads Employed by Field (%)

Field	%
Academic	~1
Business/Industry	~15
Government	~15
Judicial clerkships	~5
Private practice	~57
Public interest	~8

Rate of Placement: 99%
Average Starting Salary: $87,540
Employers Who Frequently Hire Grads: International and national law firms, New York metro area law firms of all sizes, federal and state judges nationwide, district attorney's offices and other state and federal government entities, public interest organizations
State for Bar Exam: NY
Pass Rate for First-Time Bar: 86%

YORK UNIVERSITY
Osgoode Hall Law School

Admissions Contact: Admissions Officer, Louise Resendes
4700 Keele Street, Toronto, ON M3J 1P3 Canada
Admissions Phone: 416-736-5712 • Admissions Fax: 416-736-5618
Admissions E-mail: ozadmit@yorku.ca • Web Address: www.osgoode.yorku.ca

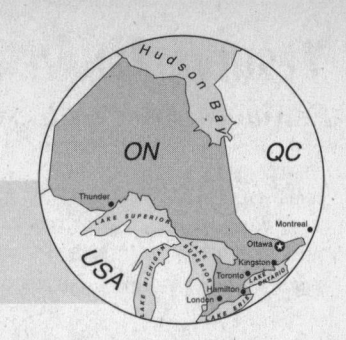

INSTITUTIONAL INFORMATION
Public/Private: Public
Student/Faculty Ratio: 18:1
Total Faculty: 48
% Female: 44

PROGRAMS
Academic Specialties: International Law, Taxation, Litigation
Advanced Degrees Offered: LLM, JD
Combined Degrees Offered: LLB/MBA (4 years), LLB/MES (4 years)
Grading System: A+, A, B+, B, C+, C, D+, D, F, Allowed
Clinical Program Required? No
Clinical Programs Description: Immigration and Refugee, Business, Criminal, Aboriginal, Poverty Law
Legal Writing Course Requirements? Yes
Legal Writing Description: Mandatory year-long course covering case comments, memos, and factum
Legal Methods Course Requirements? Yes
Legal Methods Description: Legal dimensions, 4 times per semester.
Legal Research Course Requirements? Yes
Legal Research Description: Combined with Legal Writing
Moot Court Requirement? Yes
Moot Court Description: First-year program
Public Interest Law Requirement? No
Academic Journals: *Osgoode Hall Law Journal*

STUDENT INFORMATION
Enrollment of Law School: 825
% Male/Female: 48/52
% Full Time: 100
% Minority: 18
Average Age of Entering Class: 25

RESEARCH FACILITIES
School-Supported Research Centers: Centre for Public Law and Policy, Institute for Feminist Legal Studies, Nathanson Centre for the Study of Organized Crime and Corruption

EXPENSES/FINANCIAL AID
Annual Tuition: $8,000
Room and Board (On/Off Campus): $10,000/$7,000
Books and Supplies: $1,300
Financial Aid Application Deadline: 9/2
Average Grant: $4,000
Average Loan: $5,000
% of Aid That Is Merit-Based: 25
% Receiving Some Sort of Aid: 36
Average Total Aid Package: $2,500

ADMISSIONS INFORMATION
Application Fee: $50
Regular Application Deadline: 11/1
Regular Notification: Rolling
LSDAS Accepted? No
Average GPA: 3.7
Range of GPA: 3.3–4.0
Transfer Students Accepted? Yes
Number of Applications Received: 2,054
Number of Applicants Accepted: 665
Number of Applicants Enrolled: 287

INTERNATIONAL STUDENTS
TOEFL Required of International Students? Yes

EMPLOYMENT INFORMATION

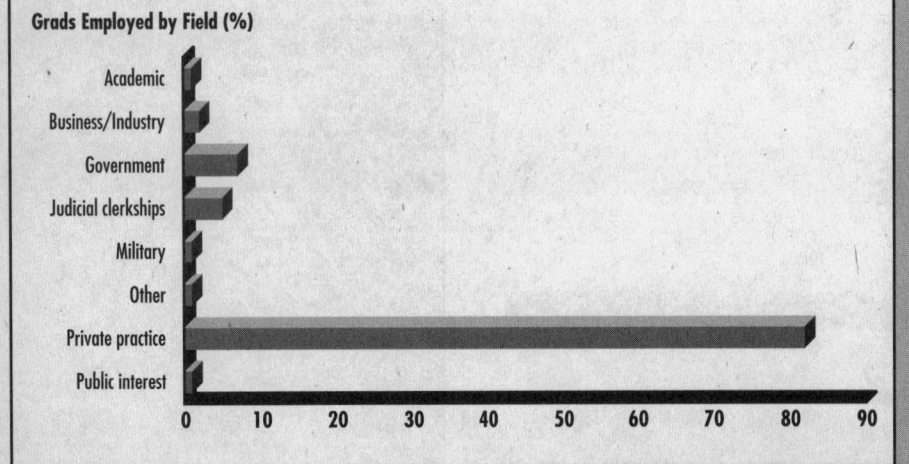

Grads Employed by Field (%)
- Academic
- Business/Industry
- Government
- Judicial clerkships
- Military
- Other
- Private practice
- Public interest

Rate of Placement: 92%
Average Starting Salary: $45,000
Employers Who Frequently Hire Grads: Blake, Cassels & Graydon; Fasken, Martineau, Goodmans
State for Bar Exam: ON
Pass Rate for First-Time Bar: 98%

ADDITIONAL LAW SCHOOL

In this section, you'll find a detailed profile of a law school that is not yet accredited by the ABA, with information about its programs, faculty, facilities, and admissions. The Princeton Review charges a school a small fee to be listed, and the editorial responsibility is solely that of the college.

FLORIDA A&M UNIVERSITY

THE UNIVERSITY AT A GLANCE

Florida A&M University is a comprehensive, public, co-educational and fully accredited land-grant university offering a broad range of instruction, research, and service programs at the undergraduate, graduate, and professional levels. The main campus occupies over 419 acres on the highest of seven hills in the capital city of Tallahassee. The 13 schools and colleges are committed to excellence in instruction, learning, and research, and cover a wide range of academic disciplines and related professional preparation.

Florida A&M University's selection as the 1997 College of the Year by the *Time Magazine/Princeton Review College Guide* was only the crowning achievement among a series of nationally recognized honors. Not only is FAMU the largest single-campus HBCU in terms of enrollment and the number-one grantor of baccalaureate degrees to African Americans, it is one of the country's leading enrollers of National Merit Achievement Scholars. Indeed, FAMU's growing reputation for excellence was recently recognized by Black Enterprise magazine, which named it the Best Public University in America for Black Students.

The College of Law's rich tradition of excellence dates back to its original founding. On December 21, 1949, a division of law was established at the then Florida A&M College and the first class was admitted in 1951. In 1966, the Florida Board of Control (later known as the Board of Regents) withdrew its permission for the institution to admit law students, and two years later, the law school graduated its last class and closed its doors. Between 1954 and 1968, the law school graduated 57 men and women, many of whom have gone on to make significant contributions to the legal profession both within the state and throughout the nation.

The 2000 Florida Legislature unanimously passed legislation establishing a law school at Florida A&M University and on June 14, 2000, Governor Jeb Bush signed the bill into law. The College of Law will admit its first class in fall 2002.

Florida Agricultural and Mechanical University will continue its mission of meeting the educational needs of African Americans and other ethnic minorities, while maintaining its leadership in racial diversity. At the same time, the University seeks students from all racial, ethnic, religious, and national groups, without regard to age, sex, or disability, who have the potential to benefit from a sound education. The University provides for all an atmosphere where excellent teaching and lifelong learning are hallmarks.

OUR ORLANDO LOCATION

Orlando, a racially and culturally diverse community, is considered not only one of the fastest growing metropolitan areas in Florida, but also one of the fastest growing major employment markets in the nation. The Orlando area is projected to be a leader in employment growth through the year 2010. Orlando offers affordable housing, a great climate with mild weather year-round, a reliable public transportation system, and easy access to recreational and cultural activities.

ACADEMIC FACILITY

For the first few years, the Florida A&M University College of Law will be temporarily located in a beautiful ten-story building in downtown Orlando. Because the law school will be located in the heart of downtown Orlando, students will be within walking distance of the courts, the county library, and other government buildings.

Construction of the permanent facility will begin immediately and completion of that new, state-of-the-art facility is scheduled for the 2004–2005 academic year. When the inaugural class begins its third year of law study in the 2004 fall term, the students will attend classes in the newest and one of the most beautiful law schools in the State of Florida.

ACCREDITATION

While the College of Law is committed to becoming one of the major law schools in the State of Florida, in the Southeast, and in this country as well, it is not yet accredited by the American Bar Association. The College of Law will take all steps necessary to pursue ABA approval and accreditation, but makes no representation to any applicant that it will receive that approval prior to the date of graduation of any admitted and enrolled student. Because different states have different rules regarding admission to the bar, students are advised to contact the Board of Bar Examiners in the states in which they intend to practice law to determine the significance of their attendance at an unaccredited law school.

CURRICULUM

The College of Law will offer both a full-time, three-year Day Program and a part-time, four-year Evening Program of study. The Part-Time Evening program is designed for particularly well-qualified and dedicated students who are unable to attend on a full-time basis and want to earn a law degree while working full time. Courses in both programs demand the same standards of performance by students and are taught by full-time faculty members who are assisted by adjunct faculty.

The College of Law's educational program will develop with the addition of dedicated faculty and new courses over the next several years. The law school will offer a rigorous traditional curriculum of required and elective courses that will be complemented by extensive skills training that includes an intensive three-year writing program and a strong clinical program. The College of Law's curriculum is designed to provide students with both the intellectual and practical skills necessary to meet the demands of the modern practice of law by combining theoretical course work with clinical and practical experiences. Through the use of elective courses and leading practitioners as adjunct faculty, students will be introduced to emerging trends and developments in the law.

Community service will be an important facet of our educational program. The Florida A&M University College of Law plans to serve the Orlando community by educating lawyers and future leaders to understand the value of helping those in need. Through pro bono opportunities and a mandatory third-year clinical program, law students will provide pro bono legal services in Orlando while still in law school. In providing the legal services, law students will gain valuable experience and training and at the same time, recognize the need for these services as they start to practice law throughout the state and nation.

Once students have satisfactorily completed the 90 credit hours required for graduation, they earn the Juris Doctorate degree.

FIRST-YEAR CURRICULUM

In their first-year of law study, students will obtain a strong foundation for legal analysis and legal research and writing. That foundation will be provided through an introduction to the following core courses, which are required of all students and which will serve to prepare students for the upper-level curriculum of elective and required courses.

Torts
Civil Procedure
Criminal Law
Criminal Procedure
Legal Bibliography
Legal Methods I and II
Contracts
Property
Professional Responsibility

Full-Time Day program students must successfully complete six semesters or three academic years for their degree requirements. Enrollment in the Day program represents a commitment to the full-time study of law. Under American Bar Association rules, students enrolled as full-time students may not work in excess of 20 hours per week.

The Part-Time Evening program operates year-round. In addition to the fall and spring semesters, two five-week summer sessions are an essential part of the Part-Time Evening Program. Evening program students can complete their degree requirements in four years, consisting of eight semesters and three summers.

The Part-Time Evening Program classes meet between 6:30 P.M. and 10:00 P.M. on Monday, Tuesday, and Thursday evenings. Elective courses open to Day and Evening

College of Law

students may begin at an earlier time. An Evening Program student may enroll in a Day Program course with permission from the Associate Dean for Academic Affairs.

Strong law schools have strong faculty. Over the next several years, the College of Law will build that strong faculty with individuals who are experienced, nationally recognized, and highly regarded in legal education. While they will be respected for their commitment to quality teaching, scholarship, and professional service, they will also be equally committed to the quality of the students' educational and professional growth. Faculty will be accessible to students both inside and outside the classroom, and in professional and social settings, and each student will be assigned a faculty advisor.

The Law Library will provide faculty and students access to primary sources of American law: court reporters, periodicals, microfiche, and online research databases. The Law Library will be an integral part of the Florida A&M University and higher education in Florida and welcomes all members of the Orlando community, the bar, and the judiciary.

ADMISSIONS AND FINANCIAL AID

The College of Law will admit its first class of students in 2002 and will start with a smaller inaugural class of 75 Full-Time Day students and 30 Part-Time Evening students.

The standards for admission in the Full-Time Day and the Part-Time Evening programs are not the same. Greater demands of work and study for Evening Program students necessitate a different emphasis on admissions criteria than in the Day Program. While the entire application file is reviewed, Evening Program admission standards place a greater emphasis on the objective indicators of LSAT scores and undergraduate grade point average than the Day Program.

Applicants have the option of applying to one or both programs at the time of application. Switching between programs after the initial application is made will not be permitted. For admission to the Part-Time Evening program, preference will be given to applicants whose circumstances are such that they can pursue a legal education only on a part-time basis.

The following admission requirements apply to all applicants to the College of Law:

1. All applicants must submit a completed Application for Admission, along with a $20 nonrefundable application fee.
2. All applicants for admission must have a bachelor's degree from an accredited institution of higher education prior to enrollment.
3. All applicants must take the Law School Admission Test (LSAT).
4. All applicants must register for the Law School Data Assembly Service (LSDAS).
5. All applicants are required to submit a personal statement and two letters of recommendation. Rather than submit letters of recommendation with the application, applicants are encouraged to utilize the LSAC letter of recommendation service that is included in the LSDAS registration subscription.

Application files cannot be reviewed until the files are complete. Admissions decisions will be made on a rolling basis after all required materials have been received.

Admission to the College of Law is competitive. Selection for admission is based on a thorough evaluation of all factors in an applicant's file. Because it is presumed that Part-Time Evening Program students will have full-time employment, the College of Law places greater weight on quantifiable achievement predictors for applicants to the Evening Program.

In reviewing the applications of individuals applying for admission to the College of Law, the Admissions Committee will evaluate the following factors:

- The applicant's score on the LSAT
- The applicant's cumulative undergraduate grade point average
- The applicant's writing ability as evidenced by the LSAT writing sample and the personal statement
- The applicant's undergraduate (and graduate) institution
- The applicant's undergraduate (and graduate) major
- The applicant's community or public service
- The applicant's academic honors and other awards
- The applicant's work experience
- The applicant's extracurricular activities
- The applicant's letters of recommendation
- The applicant's character and motivation

TUITION AND FEES

Tuition rates and fees are set annually by the Florida Legislature and the Florida A&M University Board of Trustees and may be changed at any time without advance notice.

For the 2001–2002 academic year, tuition for graduate students at Florida A&M University was $164 per credit hour for Florida residents and $571 per credit hour for nonresidents. In addition, Florida A&M University imposes additional fees on all graduate students.

While subject to change, the following is an estimate of tuition for law students for the 2002–2003 academic year:

For Florida Residents
Full-Time Day (30 Credit Hours): $4,923
Part-Time Evening (22 Credit Hours): $3,610

For Non-Florida Residents
Full-Time Day (30 Credit Hours): $17,139
Part-Time Evening (22 Credit Hours): $12,569

FINANCIAL AID

Florida A&M University offers a comprehensive financial aid program that includes institutional grants and federal loan programs to help eligible students meet the expenses associated with attaining a legal education. These funds are awarded and administered by the University's Office of Financial Aid.

A limited number of scholarships are available to students entering the College of Law. All entering students will be considered automatically for any available scholarships and need not submit a scholarship application. However, for the majority of students, federally sponsored student loans will be the most common type of financial aid received.

All students who wish to apply for federal loans are required to complete either 1) the U.S. Department of Education RENEWAL Free Application for Federal Student Aid, or 2) a standard Free Application for Federal Student Aid (FAFSA) form.

In addition to the federal loan program, there are also private sources for educational loans. The Law Access Loan and the Law Student Loan are loans offered by private lenders to qualified law students. Students must be credit worthy to be eligible.

Applicants who intend to apply for financial aid may contact the University's Financial Aid Office directly at 850-599-3730 for an application and more information and assistance. Applicants are encouraged to begin the financial aid application process early.

For Application and Information, contact:

Florida A&M University College of Law
Admissions Office
PO Box 3113
Orlando, FL 32802-3113
Telephone: 407-254-3268 (FAMU)
Website: www.famu.edu/law

INDEXES

Alphabetical List of Schools

A

Albany Law School	98
American University	99
Arizona State University	100

B

Baylor University	101
Boston College	102
Boston University	103
Brigham Young University	104
Brooklyn Law School	105

C

Cal Northern School of Law	106
California Western	107
Campbell University	108
Capital University	109
Case Western Reserve University	110
Catholic University of America	111
Chapman University	112
City University of New York	113-115
Cleveland State University	116
College of William and Mary	117
Columbia University	118
Cornell University	119
Creighton University	120

D

Dalhousie University	121
DePaul University	122
Drake University	123
Duke University	124
Duquesne University	125

E

Emory University	126
Empire College	127

F

Florida A&M University	304-305
Florida Costal School of Law	128
Florida State University	129
Fordham University	130
Franklin Pierce Law Center	131

G

George Mason University	132
George Washington University	133
Georgetown University	134
Georgia State University	135
Golden Gate University	136
Gonzaga University	137

H

Hamline University	138
Harvard University	139
Hofstra University	140
Howard University	141
Humphreys College	142

I

Illinois Institute of Technology	143
Indiana University—Bloomington	144
Indiana University—Indianapolis	145

J

John F. Kennedy University	146
John Marshall Law School	147

L

Lewis and Clark College	148
Lincoln Law School of Sacramento	149
Louisiana State University	150

Loyola Marymount University	151
Loyola University Chicago	152
Loyola University New Orleans	153

M

Marquette University	154
Mercer University	155
Michigan State University	156
Mississippi College	157
Monterey College of Law	158

N

New College of California	159
New England School of Law	160
New York Law School	161
New York University	162
North Carolina Central University	163
Northeastern University	164
Northern Illinois University	165
Northern Kentucky University	166
Northwestern University	167
Nova Southeastern University	168

O

Ohio Northern University	169
Ohio State University	170
Oklahoma City University	171

P

Pace University	172-174
Pennsylvania State University	175
Pepperdine University	176

Q

Queen's University	177
Quinnipiac University	178

R

Regent University	179
Roger Williams University	180
Rutgers University—Camden	181
Rutgers University—Newark	182

S

St. John's University	183
St. Louis University	184
St. Mary's University	185
St. Thomas University	186
Samford University	187
San Francisco Law School	188
San Joaquin College of Law	189
Santa Barbara College of Law	190
Santa Clara University	191
Seattle University	192
Seton Hall University	193
South Texas College of Law	194
Southern California Institute of Law	195
Southern Illinois University	196
Southern Methodist University	197
Southern University	198
Southwestern University School of Law	199
Stanford University	200
Stetson University	201
Suffolk University	202
Syracuse University	203

T

Temple University	204
Texas Southern University	205
Texas Tech University	206
Texas Wesleyan University	207
Thomas Jefferson School of Law	208
Thomas M. Cooley Law School	209
Touro College	210
Tulane University	211

U

University at Buffalo, State University of New York	212
University of Akron	213
University of Alabama	214
University of Arizona	215
University of Arkansas—Fayetteville	216
University of Arkansas—Little Rock	217
University of Baltimore	218
University of British Columbia	219
University of Calgary	220
University of California, Berkeley	221
University of California, Davis	222
University of California, Hastings	223
University of California, Los Angeles	224
University of Chicago	225
University of Cincinnati	226
University of Colorado	227
University of Connecticut	228
University of Dayton	229
University of Denver	230
University of Detroit Mercy	231
University of Florida	232
University of Georgia	233
University of Hawaii—Manoa	234
University of Houston	235
University of Idaho	236
University of Illinois	237
University of Iowa	238
University of Kansas	239
University of Kentucky	240
University of La Verne	241
University of Louisville	242
University of Maryland	243
University of Memphis	244
University of Miami	245
University of Michigan	246
University of Minnesota	247
University of Mississippi	248
University of Missouri—Columbia	249
University of Missouri—Kansas City	250
University of Montana	251
University of Nebraska—Lincoln	252
University of New Mexico	253
University of North Carolina—Chapel Hill	254
University of North Dakota	255
University of Notre Dame	256
University of Oklahoma	257
University of Pennsylvania	258
University of Pittsburgh	259
University of Richmond	260
University of San Diego	261
University of San Francisco	262
University of South Carolina	263
University of South Dakota	264
University of Southern California	265
University of Southern Maine	266
University of Tennessee	267
University of Texas—Austin	268
University of the District of Columbia	269
University of the Pacific	270
University of Toledo	271
University of Toronto	272
University of Tulsa	273
University of Utah	274
University of Victoria	275
University of Virginia	276
University of Washington	277
University of West Los Angeles	278
University of Windsor	279
University of Wisconsin	280
University of Wyoming	281

V

Valparaiso University	282
Vanderbilt University	283
Ventura College of Law	284
Vermont Law School	285
Villanova University	286

W

Wake Forest University	287
Washburn University	288
Washington and Lee University	289
Washington University	290
Wayne State University	291
West Virginia University	292
Western New England College	293
Western State University	294
Whittier College	295
Widener University, Delaware	296
Widener University, Harrisburg	297
Willamette University	298
William Mitchell College of Law	299

Y

Yale University	300
Yeshiva University	301
York University	302

Law Program Name

Beasley School of Law	204
Benjamin N. Cardozo School of Law	301
Cecil C. Humphreys School of Law	244
Chicago-Kent College of Law	143
Claude W. Pettit College of Law	169
Cleveland-Marshall College of Law	116
Columbus School of Law	111
Cumberland School of Law	187
David A. Clarke School of Law	269
Dedman School of Law	197
Detroit College of Law	156
Dickinson School of Law	175
J. Reuben Clark Law School	104
Jacob D. Fuchsberg Law Center	210
James E. Rogers College of Law	215
Lamar Hall	248
Levin College of Law	232
Louis D. Brandeis School of Law	242
McGeorge School of Law	270
Norman Adrian Wiggins School of Law	108
Northwestern School of Law	148
Osgoode Hall Law School	302
Paul M. Hebert Law Center	150
Ralph R. Papitto School of Law	180
Rutgers School of Law at Camden	181
Rutgers School of Law at Newark	182
Salmon P. Chase College of Law	166
School of Law (Boalt Hall)	221
School of Law at Queens College	113-115
Shepard Broad Law Center	168
SJ Quinney College of Law	274
Thurgood Marshall School of Law	205
Union University	98
Walter F. George School of Law	155
Washington College of Law	99
William H. Bowen School of Law	217
William S. Richardson School of Law	234

LOCATION

USA

Alabama

Samford University	187
University of Alabama	214

Arizona

Arizona State University	100
University of Arizona	215

Arkansas

University of Arkansas—Fayetteville	216
University of Arkansas—Little Rock	217

California

Cal Northern School of Law	106
California Western	107
Chapman University	112
Empire College	127
Golden Gate University	136
Humphreys College	142
John F. Kennedy University	146
Lincoln Law School of Sacramento	149
Loyola Marymount University	151
Monterey College of Law	158
New College of California	159
Pepperdine University	176
San Francisco Law School	188
San Joaquin College of Law	189
Santa Barbara College of Law	190
Santa Clara University	191
Southern California Institute of Law	195
Southwestern University School of Law	199
Stanford University	200
Thomas Jefferson School of Law	208
University of California, Berkeley	221
University of California, Davis	222
University of California, Hastings	223
University of California, Los Angeles	224
University of La Verne	241
University of San Diego	261
University of San Francisco	262
University of Southern California	265
University of the Pacific	270
University of West Los Angeles	278
Ventura College of Law	284
Western State University	294
Whittier College	295

Colorado

University of Colorado	227
University of Denver	230

Connecticut

Quinnipiac University	178
University of Connecticut	228
Yale University	300

Delaware

Widener University, Delaware	296
Widener University, Harrisburg	297

District of Columbia

American University	99
Catholic University of America	111
George Washington University	133
Georgetown University	134
Howard University	141
University of the District of Columbia	269

Florida

Florida Costal School of Law	128
Florida State University	129
Nova Southeastern University	168
St. Thomas University	186
Stetson University	201
University of Florida	232
University of Miami	245

Georgia

Emory University	126
Georgia State University	135
Mercer University	155
University of Georgia	233

Hawaii

University of Hawaii—Manoa	234

Idaho

University of Idaho	236

Illinois

DePaul University	122
Illinois Institute of Technology	143
John Marshall Law School	147
Loyola University Chicago	152
Northern Illinois University	165
Northwestern University	167
Southern Illinois University	196
University of Chicago	225
University of Illinois	237

Indiana

Indiana University—Bloomington	144
Indiana University—Indianapolis	145
University of Notre Dame	256
Valparaiso University	282

Iowa

Drake University	123
University of Iowa	238

Kansas

University of Kansas	239
Washburn University	288

Kentucky

Northern Kentucky University	166
University of Kentucky	240
University of Louisville	242

Louisiana

Louisiana State University	150
Loyola University New Orleans	153
Southern University	198
Tulane University	211

Maine

University of Southern Maine	266

Maryland

University of Baltimore	218
University of Maryland	243

Massachusetts

Boston College	102
Boston University	103
Harvard University	139
New England School of Law	160
Northeastern University	164
Suffolk University	202
Western New England College	293

Michigan

Michigan State University	156
Thomas M. Cooley Law School	209
University of Detroit Mercy	231
University of Michigan	246
Wayne State University	291

Minnesota

Hamline University	138
University of Minnesota	247
William Mitchell College of Law	299

Mississippi

Mississippi College	157
University of Mississippi	248

Missouri

St. Louis University	184
University of Missouri—Columbia	249
University of Missouri—Kansas City	250
Washington University	290

Montana

University of Montana	251

Nebraska

Creighton University	120
University of Nebraska—Lincoln	252

New Hampshire

Franklin Pierce Law Center	131

New Jersey

Rutgers University—Camden	181
Rutgers University—Newark	182
Seton Hall University	193

New Mexico

University of New Mexico	253

New York

Albany Law School	98
Brooklyn Law School	105
City University of New York	113-115
Columbia University	118
Cornell University	119
Fordham University	130
Hofstra University	140
New York Law School	161
New York University	162
Pace University	172-174
St. John's University	183
Syracuse University	203
Touro College	210
University at Buffalo, State University of New York	212
Yeshiva University	301

North Carolina

Campbell University	108
Duke University	124
North Carolina Central University	163
University of North Carolina—Chapel Hill	254
Wake Forest University	287

North Dakota

University of North Dakota	255

Ohio

Capital University	109
Case Western Reserve University	110
Cleveland State University	116

Ohio Northern University	169
Ohio State University	170
University of Akron	213
University of Cincinnati	226
University of Dayton	229
University of Toledo	271

Oklahoma

Oklahoma City University	171
University of Oklahoma	257
University of Tulsa	273

Oregon

Lewis and Clark College	148
Willamette University	298

Pennsylvania

Duquesne University	125
Pennsylvania State University	175
Temple University	204
University of Pennsylvania	258
University of Pittsburgh	259
Villanova University	286

Rhode Island

Roger Williams University	180

South Carolina

University of South Carolina	263

South Dakota

University of South Dakota	264

Tennessee

University of Memphis	244
University of Tennessee	267
Vanderbilt University	283

Texas

Baylor University	101
South Texas College of Law	194
Southern Methodist University	197
St. Mary's University	185
Texas Southern University	205
Texas Tech University	206
Texas Wesleyan University	207
University of Houston	235
University of Texas—Austin	268

Utah

Brigham Young University	104
University of Utah	274

Vermont

Vermont Law School	285

Virginia

College of William and Mary	117
George Mason University	132
Regent University	179
University of Richmond	260
University of Virginia	276
Washington and Lee University	289

Washington

Gonzaga University	137
Seattle University	192
University of Washington	277

West Virginia

West Virginia University	292

Wisconsin

Marquette University	154
University of Wisconsin	280

Wyoming

University of Wyoming	281

CANADA

Dalhousie University	121
Queen's University	177
University of British Columbia	219
University of Calgary	220
University of Toronto	272
University of Victoria	275
University of Windsor	279
York University	302

COST
(IN-STATE TUITION)

Less than $10,000

Arizona State University	100
Brigham Young University	104
Cal Northern School of Law	106
City University of New York	113-115
Cleveland State University	116
Empire College	127
Florida State University	129
George Mason University	132
Georgia State University	135
Humphreys College	142
Indiana University—Bloomington	144
Indiana University—Indianapolis	145
John F. Kennedy University	146
Lincoln Law School of Sacramento	149
Louisiana State University	150
Monterey College of Law	158
North Carolina Central University	163
Northern Illinois University	165
Northern Kentucky University	166
Queen's University	177
San Francisco Law School	188
Southern California Institute of Law	195
Southern Illinois University	196
Southern University	198
Texas Southern University	205
Texas Tech University	206
University at Buffalo, State University of New York	212
University of Akron	213
University of Alabama	214
University of Arizona	215
University of Arkansas—Fayetteville	216
University of Arkansas—Little Rock	217
University of British Columbia	219
University of Calgary	220
University of California, Berkeley	221
University of California, Davis	222
University of California, Los Angeles	224
University of Cincinnati	226
University of Colorado	227
University of Georgia	233
University of Houston	235
University of Idaho	236
University of Illinois	237
University of Iowa	238
University of Kansas	239
University of Kentucky	240
University of Louisville	242
University of Memphis	244
University of Mississippi	248
University of Missouri—Kansas City	250
University of Montana	251
University of Nebraska—Lincoln	252
University of New Mexico	253
University of North Carolina—Chapel Hill	254
University of North Dakota	255
University of Oklahoma	257
University of South Carolina	263
University of South Dakota	264
University of Southern Maine	266
University of Tennessee	267
University of Texas—Austin	268
University of the District of Columbia	269
University of Toledo	271
University of Utah	274
University of Victoria	275
University of Washington	277
University of Windsor	279
University of Wisconsin	280
University of Wyoming	281
Ventura College of Law	284
Washburn University	288
Wayne State University	291
West Virginia University	292
York University	302

$10,000 to $22,000

Baylor University	101
Campbell University	108
Capital University	109
College of William and Mary	117
Creighton University	120
DePaul University	122
Drake University	123
Duquesne University	125
Florida Costal School of Law	128
Franklin Pierce Law Center	131
Gonzaga University	137
Hamline University	138
Howard University	141
John Marshall Law School	147
Marquette University	154
Mercer University	155
Michigan State University	156
Mississippi College	157
New College of California	159
New England School of Law	160
Nova Southeastern University	168
Ohio Northern University	169
Oklahoma City University	171
Pennsylvania State University	175
Regent University	179
Rutgers University—Camden	181
Rutgers University—Newark	182
St. Mary's University	185
Samford University	187
San Joaquin College of Law	189
Seattle University	192
South Texas College of Law	194
Stetson University	201
Temple University	204
Texas Wesleyan University	207
Thomas M. Cooley Law School	209
University of Baltimore	218
University of California, Hastings	223
University of Connecticut	228
University of Dayton	229
University of Denver	230
University of Detroit Mercy	231
University of Maryland	243
University of Minnesota	247
University of Missouri—Columbia	249
University of Pittsburgh	259
University of Richmond	260
University of Toronto	272
University of Tulsa	273
University of Virginia	276
University of West Los Angeles	278
Valparaiso University	282
Villanova University	286
Washington and Lee University	289
Western New England College	293
Widener University, Delaware	296
Widener University, Harrisburg	297
Willamette University	298
William Mitchell College of Law	299

More than $22,000

Albany Law School	98
American University	99
Boston College	102
Boston University	103
Brooklyn Law School	105
California Western	107
Case Western Reserve University	110
Catholic University of America	111
Chapman University	112
Columbia University	118
Cornell University	119
Duke University	124
Emory University	126
Fordham University	130
George Washington University	133
Georgetown University	134
Golden Gate University	136
Harvard University	139
Hofstra University	140
Illinois Institute of Technology	143
Lewis and Clark College	148
Loyola Marymount University	151
Loyola University Chicago	152

Loyola University New Orleans	153
New York Law School	161
New York University	162
Northeastern University	164
Northwestern University	167
Pace University	172-174
Pepperdine University	176
Quinnipiac University	178
Roger Williams University	180
St. John's University	183
St. Louis University	184
St. Thomas University	186
Santa Barbara College of Law	190
Santa Clara University	191
Seton Hall University	193
Southern Methodist University	197
Southwestern University School of Law	199
Stanford University	200
Suffolk University	202
Syracuse University	203
Thomas Jefferson School of Law	208
Touro College	210
Tulane University	211
University of Chicago	225
University of Miami	245
University of Michigan	246
University of Notre Dame	256
University of Pennsylvania	258
University of San Diego	261
University of San Francisco	262
University of Southern California	265
University of the Pacific	270
Vanderbilt University	283
Vermont Law School	285
Wake Forest University	287
Washington University	290
Western State University	294
Whittier College	295
Yale University	300
Yeshiva University	301

Enrollment of Law School

Less than 500 Students

Baylor University	101
Brigham Young University	104
Cal Northern School of Law	106
Campbell University	108
Chapman University	112
City University of New York	113-115
Creighton University	120
Dalhousie University	121
Drake University	123
Empire College	127
Florida Costal School of Law	128
Franklin Pierce Law Center	131
Howard University	141
Humphreys College	142
John F. Kennedy University	146
Lincoln Law School of Sacramento	149
Mercer University	155
Mississippi College	157
Monterey College of Law	158
New College of California	159
North Carolina Central University	163
Northern Illinois University	165
Northern Kentucky University	166
Ohio Northern University	169
Queen's University	177
Quinnipiac University	178
Regent University	179
Roger Williams University	180
St. John's University	183
St. Thomas University	186
San Francisco Law School	188
San Joaquin College of Law	189
Southern California Institute of Law	195
Southern Illinois University	196
Southern University	198
University of Arizona	215
University of Arkansas—Fayetteville	216
University of Arkansas—Little Rock	217
University of Calgary	220
University of Cincinnati	226
University of Colorado	227
University of Dayton	229
University of Detroit Mercy	231
University of Idaho	236
University of Kansas	239
University of Kentucky	240
University of La Verne	241
University of Louisville	242
University of Memphis	244
University of Mississippi	248
University of Missouri—Kansas City	250
University of Montana	251
University of Nebraska—Lincoln	252
University of New Mexico	253
University of North Dakota	255
University of Richmond	260
University of South Dakota	264
University of Southern Maine	266
University of Tennessee	267
University of the District of Columbia	269
University of Toledo	271
University of Utah	274
University of Victoria	275
University of Washington	277
University of West Los Angeles	278
University of Windsor	279
University of Wyoming	281
Valparaiso University	282
Ventura College of Law	284
Wake Forest University	287
Washburn University	288
Washington and Lee University	289
West Virginia University	292
Western State University	294
Widener University, Harrisburg	297
Willamette University	298

500 to 800 Students

Albany Law School	98
Arizona State University	100
California Western	107
Capital University	109
Case Western Reserve University	110
College of William and Mary	117
Cornell University	119
Duke University	124
Duquesne University	125
Emory University	126
Florida State University	129
George Mason University	132
Georgia State University	135
Golden Gate University	136
Gonzaga University	137
Hamline University	138
Indiana University—Bloomington	144
Lewis and Clark College	148
Louisiana State University	150
Loyola University Chicago	152
Loyola University New Orleans	153
Marquette University	154
Michigan State University	156
Northeastern University	164
Northwestern University	167
Ohio State University	170
Oklahoma City University	171
Pace University	172-174
Pennsylvania State University	175
Pepperdine University	176
Rutgers University—Camden	181
Rutgers University—Newark	182
St. Louis University	184
St. Mary's University	185
Samford University	187
Southern Methodist University	197
Stanford University	200
Stetson University	201
Syracuse University	203
Texas Southern University	205
Texas Tech University	206
Thomas Jefferson School of Law	208
Touro College	210
University at Buffalo, State University of New York	212
University of Akron	213
University of Alabama	214
University of British Columbia	219
University of California, Davis	222
University of Chicago	225
University of Connecticut	228
University of Georgia	233
University of Illinois	237
University of Iowa	238
University of Minnesota	247
University of Missouri—Columbia	249
University of North Carolina—Chapel Hill	254
University of Notre Dame	256
University of Oklahoma	257
University of Pennsylvania	258
University of Pittsburgh	259
University of San Francisco	262
University of South Carolina	263
University of Southern California	265
University of Toronto	272
University of Tulsa	273
University of Wisconsin	280
Vanderbilt University	283
Vermont Law School	285
Villanova University	286
Washington University	290
Wayne State University	291
Western New England College	293
Whittier College	295
Yale University	300

More than 800 Students

American University	99
Boston College	102
Boston University	103
Brooklyn Law School	105
Catholic University of America	111
Cleveland State University	116
Columbia University	118
DePaul University	122
Fordham University	130
George Washington University	133
Georgetown University	134
Harvard University	139
Hofstra University	140

Illinois Institute of Technology	143
Indiana University—Indianapolis	145
John Marshall Law School	147
Loyola Marymount University	151
New England School of Law	160
New York Law School	161
New York University	162
Nova Southeastern University	168
Santa Barbara College of Law	190
Santa Clara University	191
Seattle University	192
Seton Hall University	193
South Texas College of Law	194
Southwestern University School of Law	199
Suffolk University	202
Temple University	204
Thomas M. Cooley Law School	209
Tulane University	211
University of Baltimore	218
University of California, Berkeley	221
University of California, Hastings	223
University of California, Los Angeles	224
University of Denver	230
University of Florida	232
University of Houston	235
University of Maryland	243
University of Miami	245
University of Michigan	246
University of San Diego	261
University of Texas—Austin	268
University of the Pacific	270
University of Virginia	276
Widener University, Delaware	296
William Mitchell College of Law	299
Yeshiva University	301
York University	302

Average LSAT

Less than 153

Albany Law School	98
Cal Northern School of Law	106
California Western	107
Capital University	109
City University of New York	113-115
Cleveland State University	116
Creighton University	120
Drake University	123
Florida Costal School of Law	128
Franklin Pierce Law Center	131
Golden Gate University	136
Gonzaga University	137
Hamline University	138
Howard University	141
Humphreys College	142
John Marshall Law School	147
Lincoln Law School of Sacramento	149
Loyola University New Orleans	153
Michigan State University	156
Mississippi College	157
Monterey College of Law	158
New College of California	159
New England School of Law	160
North Carolina Central University	163
Northern Kentucky University	166
Nova Southeastern University	168
Ohio Northern University	169
Oklahoma City University	171
Pace University	172-174
Quinnipiac University	178
Regent University	179
Roger Williams University	180
St. Mary's University	185
St. Thomas University	186
Samford University	187
San Joaquin College of Law	189
South Texas College of Law	194
Southern Illinois University	196
Southern University	198
Stetson University	201
Syracuse University	203
Texas Wesleyan University	207
Thomas Jefferson School of Law	208
Thomas M. Cooley Law School	209
University of Akron	213
University of Arkansas—Fayetteville	216
University of Baltimore	218
University of Dayton	229
University of Detroit Mercy	231
University of Idaho	236
University of North Dakota	255
University of South Dakota	264
University of the District of Columbia	269
University of the Pacific	270
University of Tulsa	273
University of Wyoming	281
Valparaiso University	282
Ventura College of Law	284
Vermont Law School	285
Washburn University	288
Western New England College	293
Western State University	294
Whittier College	295
Widener University, Delaware	296
Widener University, Harrisburg	297
William Mitchell College of Law	299

153 to 156

Arizona State University	100
Campbell University	108
Catholic University of America	111
Chapman University	112
DePaul University	122
Duquesne University	125
Florida State University	129
Georgia State University	135
Hofstra University	140
Illinois Institute of Technology	143
Indiana University—Indianapolis	145
Louisiana State University	150
Marquette University	154
Mercer University	155
New York Law School	161
Northern Illinois University	165
Pennsylvania State University	175
Pepperdine University	176
St. John's University	183
St. Louis University	184
Santa Barbara College of Law	190
Santa Clara University	191
Seattle University	192
Seton Hall University	193
Suffolk University	202
Texas Tech University	206
University at Buffalo, State University of New York	212
University of Arkansas—Little Rock	217
University of Denver	230
University of Florida	232
University of Kansas	239
University of Maryland	243
University of Memphis	244
University of Miami	245
University of Mississippi	248
University of Missouri—Columbia	249
University of Missouri—Kansas City	250
University of Montana	251
University of Nebraska—Lincoln	252
University of New Mexico	253
University of Oklahoma	257
University of Pittsburgh	259
University of San Francisco	262
University of South Carolina	263
University of Southern Maine	266
University of Tennessee	267
University of Toledo	271
Wayne State University	291
West Virginia University	292
Willamette University	298

More than 156

American University	99
Baylor University	101
Boston College	102
Boston University	103
Brigham Young University	104
Brooklyn Law School	105
Case Western Reserve University	110
College of William and Mary	117
Columbia University	118
Cornell University	119
Dalhousie University	121
Duke University	124
Emory University	126
Fordham University	130
George Mason University	132
George Washington University	133
Georgetown University	134
Harvard University	139
Indiana University—Bloomington	144
Lewis and Clark College	148
Loyola Marymount University	151
Loyola University Chicago	152
New York University	162
Northeastern University	164
Northwestern University	167
Ohio State University	170
Queen's University	177
Rutgers University—Camden	181
Rutgers University—Newark	182
Southern Methodist University	197
Stanford University	200
Temple University	204
Tulane University	211
University of Alabama	214
University of Arizona	215
University of British Columbia	219
University of California, Berkeley	221
University of California, Davis	222
University of California, Hastings	223
University of California, Los Angeles	224
University of Chicago	225
University of Cincinnati	226
University of Colorado	227
University of Connecticut	228
University of Georgia	233
University of Houston	235
University of Illinois	237
University of Iowa	238

University of Kentucky	240
University of Louisville	242
University of Michigan	246
University of Minnesota	247
University of North Carolina—Chapel Hill	254
University of Notre Dame	256
University of Pennsylvania	258
University of Richmond	260
University of San Diego	261
University of Southern California	265
University of Texas—Austin	268
University of Toronto	272
University of Utah	274
University of Victoria	275
University of Virginia	276
University of Washington	277
University of Wisconsin	280
Vanderbilt University	283
Villanova University	286
Wake Forest University	287
Washington and Lee University	289
Washington University	290
Yale University	300
Yeshiva University	301

Average Undergrad GPA

3.1 and Lower

Cal Northern School of Law	106
California Western	107
Capital University	109
Chapman University	112
City University of New York	113-115
Cleveland State University	116
Empire College	127
Florida Costal School of Law	128
Golden Gate University	136
Gonzaga University	137
John Marshall Law School	147
Lincoln Law School of Sacramento	149
Loyola University New Orleans	153
Mississippi College	157
Monterey College of Law	158
New College of California	159
North Carolina Central University	163
Northern Illinois University	165
Ohio Northern University	169
Oklahoma City University	171
Pace University	172-174
Quinnipiac University	178
Regent University	179
Roger Williams University	180
St. Mary's University	185
St. Thomas University	186
Samford University	187
San Francisco Law School	188
San Joaquin College of Law	189
South Texas College of Law	194
Southern Illinois University	196
Texas Southern University	205
Thomas Jefferson School of Law	208
Thomas M. Cooley Law School	209
University of Akron	213
University of Dayton	229
University of Denver	230
University of Idaho	236
University of the District of Columbia	269
University of Tulsa	273
Vermont Law School	285
Western State University	294
Widener University, Delaware	296
Widener University, Harrisburg	297

3.2 to 3.3

Albany Law School	98
Arizona State University	100
Campbell University	108
Case Western Reserve University	110
Creighton University	120
Drake University	123
Florida State University	129
George Mason University	132
Georgia State University	135
Hamline University	138
Hofstra University	140
Illinois Institute of Technology	143
Indiana University—Indianapolis	145
Lewis and Clark College	148
Louisiana State University	150
Loyola Marymount University	151
Loyola University Chicago	152
Marquette University	154
Mercer University	155
Northeastern University	164
Northern Kentucky University	166
Rutgers University—Camden	181
St. Louis University	184
Santa Barbara College of Law	190
Santa Clara University	191
Seattle University	192
Stetson University	201
Suffolk University	202
Syracuse University	203
Temple University	204
University at Buffalo, State University of New York	212
University of Alabama	214
University of Arkansas—Fayetteville	216
University of Arkansas—Little Rock	217
University of Connecticut	228
University of Maryland	243
University of Memphis	244
University of Miami	245
University of Missouri—Columbia	249
University of New Mexico	253
University of North Dakota	255
University of Pittsburgh	259
University of Richmond	260
University of San Diego	261
University of San Francisco	262
University of South Dakota	264
University of Toledo	271
University of Wisconsin	280
University of Wyoming	281
Ventura College of Law	284
Willamette University	298
William Mitchell College of Law	299

3.4 and Higher

Boston University	103
Brigham Young University	104
Brooklyn Law School	105
College of William and Mary	117
Columbia University	118
Duke University	124
Emory University	126
George Washington University	133
Georgetown University	134
Indiana University—Bloomington	144
New York University	162
Northwestern University	167
Seton Hall University	193
Southern Methodist University	197
Stanford University	200
Texas Tech University	206
University of British Columbia	219
University of California, Davis	222
University of California, Hastings	223
University of California, Los Angeles	224
University of Colorado	227
University of Florida	232
University of Houston	235
University of Illinois	237
University of Iowa	238
University of Kansas	239
University of Kentucky	240
University of Michigan	246
University of Mississippi	248
University of Nebraska—Lincoln	252
University of Notre Dame	256
University of Oklahoma	257
University of Pennsylvania	258
University of Southern California	265
University of Tennessee	267
University of Texas—Austin	268
University of Toronto	272
University of Utah	274
University of Victoria	275
University of Virginia	276
University of Washington	277
Wake Forest University	287
Washington and Lee University	289
Washington University	290
Yale University	300
Yeshiva University	301
York University	302

Average Starting Salary

Less than $47,000

Campbell University	108
Creighton University	120
Duquesne University	125
Florida Costal School of Law	128
Florida State University	129
Gonzaga University	137
Hamline University	138
John Marshall Law School	147
Lincoln Law School of Sacramento	149
Mississippi College	157
New England School of Law	160
Nova Southeastern University	168
Ohio Northern University	169
Regent University	179
Roger Williams University	180
St. Thomas University	186
San Francisco Law School	188
Seattle University	192
Southern California Institute of Law	195
Southern Illinois University	196
Stetson University	201
Texas Wesleyan University	207
Thomas M. Cooley Law School	209
Touro College	210
University of Arkansas—Little Rock	217
University of Baltimore	218
University of Idaho	236
University of Louisville	242
University of Memphis	244
University of Missouri—Columbia	249
University of Missouri—Kansas City	250
University of Montana	251
University of Nebraska—Lincoln	252
University of New Mexico	253
University of North Dakota	255
University of South Carolina	263
University of South Dakota	264
University of Wyoming	281
Vermont Law School	285
Washburn University	288
West Virginia University	292
Western New England College	293
Widener University, Harrisburg	297
York University	302

$47,000 to $60,000

Albany Law School	98
Baylor University	101
Capital University	109
Cleveland State University	116
DePaul University	122
Drake University	123
Indiana University—Indianapolis	145
Lewis and Clark College	148
Louisiana State University	150
Marquette University	154
Mercer University	155
Northern Kentucky University	166
Ohio State University	170
Oklahoma City University	171
Pennsylvania State University	175
Quinnipiac University	178
Rutgers University—Newark	182
St. Louis University	184
St. Mary's University	185
Samford University	187
Santa Barbara College of Law	190
Suffolk University	202
Texas Tech University	206
Thomas Jefferson School of Law	208
Tulane University	211
University at Buffalo, State University of New York	212
University of Akron	213
University of Alabama	214
University of British Columbia	219
University of Cincinnati	226
University of Dayton	229
University of Denver	230
University of Florida	232
University of Georgia	233
University of Iowa	238
University of Kansas	239
University of Kentucky	240
University of Maryland	243
University of Mississippi	248
University of North Carolina—Chapel Hill	254
University of Oklahoma	257
University of Richmond	260
University of Tennessee	267
University of the District of Columbia	269
University of the Pacific	270
University of Toledo	271
University of Toronto	272
University of Tulsa	273
University of Utah	274
Valparaiso University	282
Wake Forest University	287
Washington University	290
Wayne State University	291
Whittier College	295
Widener University, Delaware	296
Willamette University	298
William Mitchell College of Law	299

More than $60,000

American University	99
Arizona State University	100
Boston University	103
Brigham Young University	104
Brooklyn Law School	105
California Western	107
Case Western Reserve University	110
Catholic University of America	111
Chapman University	112
College of William and Mary	117
Columbia University	118
Cornell University	119
Duke University	124
Emory University	126
Fordham University	130
Franklin Pierce Law Center	131
George Mason University	132
George Washington University	133
Georgetown University	134
Georgia State University	135
Golden Gate University	136
Harvard University	139
Hofstra University	140
Howard University	141
Illinois Institute of Technology	143
Indiana University—Bloomington	144
Loyola Marymount University	151
Loyola University Chicago	152
Michigan State University	156
New York Law School	161
Northeastern University	164
Northwestern University	167
Pace University	172-174
Pepperdine University	176
Rutgers University—Camden	181
St. John's University	183
Santa Clara University	191
Seton Hall University	193
South Texas College of Law	194
Southern Methodist University	197
Stanford University	200
Syracuse University	203
Temple University	204
University of Arizona	215
University of California, Berkeley	221
University of California, Davis	222
University of California, Hastings	223
University of California, Los Angeles	224
University of Chicago	225
University of Colorado	227
University of Connecticut	228
University of Detroit Mercy	231
University of Houston	235
University of Illinois	237
University of Miami	245
University of Michigan	246
University of Minnesota	247

University of Notre Dame	256
University of Pennsylvania	258
University of Pittsburgh	259
University of San Francisco	262
University of Texas—Austin	268
University of Virginia	276
University of Washington	277
University of Wisconsin	280
Vanderbilt University	283
Villanova University	286
Washington and Lee University	289
Western State University	294
Yale University	300
Yeshiva University	301

Pass Rate for First-Time Bar

Less than 75 Percent

American University	99
Cal Northern School of Law	106
Capital University	109
Chapman University	112
City University of New York	113-115
Cleveland State University	116
Duquesne University	125
Golden Gate University	136
Gonzaga University	137
Humphreys College	142
Lincoln Law School of Sacramento	149
Loyola University New Orleans	153
Monterey College of Law	158
New College of California	159
New York Law School	161
Pepperdine University	176
St. Mary's University	185
San Francisco Law School	188
San Joaquin College of Law	189
Santa Barbara College of Law	190
Santa Clara University	191
Southern California Institute of Law	195
Southern University	198
Texas Southern University	205
Texas Wesleyan University	207
Thomas Jefferson School of Law	208
Thomas M. Cooley Law School	209
Touro College	210
University at Buffalo, State University of New York	212
University of Arkansas—Little Rock	217
University of Baltimore	218
University of Detroit Mercy	231
University of San Diego	261
University of San Francisco	262
University of Southern Maine	266
University of the District of Columbia	269
University of the Pacific	270
University of West Los Angeles	278
Ventura College of Law	284
Vermont Law School	285
West Virginia University	292
Western New England College	293
Western State University	294
Whittier College	295
Widener University, Delaware	296
Widener University, Harrisburg	297
Willamette University	298

75 Percent to 89 Percent

Albany Law School	98
Arizona State University	100
Baylor University	101
Brooklyn Law School	105
California Western	107
Case Western Reserve University	110
College of William and Mary	117
Creighton University	120
DePaul University	122
Drake University	123
Empire College	127
Florida State University	129
Fordham University	130
Franklin Pierce Law Center	131
Hamline University	138
Hofstra University	140
Illinois Institute of Technology	143
Indiana University—Indianapolis	145
John Marshall Law School	147
Lewis and Clark College	148
Louisiana State University	150
Loyola Marymount University	151
Michigan State University	156
Mississippi College	157
New England School of Law	160
Northeastern University	164
Northern Illinois University	165
Northern Kentucky University	166
Nova Southeastern University	168
Ohio State University	170
Oklahoma City University	171
Pennsylvania State University	175
Quinnipiac University	178
Rutgers University—Camden	181
Rutgers University—Newark	182
St. John's University	183
St. Louis University	184
St. Thomas University	186
Samford University	187
Seattle University	192
Seton Hall University	193
South Texas College of Law	194
Southern Illinois University	196
Southern Methodist University	197
Stanford University	200
Stetson University	201
Suffolk University	202
Temple University	204
Texas Tech University	206
University of Akron	213
University of Arkansas—Fayetteville	216
University of California, Hastings	223
University of Connecticut	228
University of Dayton	229
University of Denver	230
University of Iowa	238
University of Kansas	239
University of Louisville	242
University of Maryland	243
University of Miami	245
University of Minnesota	247
University of Missouri—Kansas City	250
University of North Carolina—Chapel Hill	254
University of North Dakota	255
University of Notre Dame	256
University of Oklahoma	257
University of Pittsburgh	259
University of South Carolina	263
University of Southern California	265
University of Tennessee	267
University of Toledo	271
University of Tulsa	273
Villanova University	286
Washington University	290
Wayne State University	291
William Mitchell College of Law	299
Yeshiva University	301

90 Percent or More

Boston College	102
Boston University	103
Brigham Young University	104
Campbell University	108
Columbia University	118
Cornell University	119
Duke University	124
Emory University	126
George Washington University	133
Georgetown University	134
Georgia State University	135
Harvard University	139
Indiana University—Bloomington	144
Loyola University Chicago	152
Marquette University	154
Mercer University	155
New York University	162
Northwestern University	167
Tulane University	211
University of Alabama	214
University of Arizona	215
University of British Columbia	219
University of Calgary	220
University of California, Berkeley	221
University of California, Davis	222
University of California, Los Angeles	224
University of Chicago	225
University of Cincinnati	226
University of Colorado	227
University of Florida	232
University of Georgia	233

University of Houston	235
University of Illinois	237
University of Kentucky	240
University of Memphis	244
University of Mississippi	248
University of Missouri—Columbia	249
University of Montana	251
University of Nebraska—Lincoln	252
University of New Mexico	253
University of Pennsylvania	258
University of Richmond	260
University of South Dakota	264
University of Texas—Austin	268
University of Utah	274
University of Virginia	276
University of Washington	277
University of Windsor	279
Vanderbilt University	283
Wake Forest University	287
Washburn University	288
Yale University	300
York University	302

ABOUT THE AUTHOR

Eric Owens has taught courses and worked in various capacities for The Princeton Review since 1994. He attended Cornell College and Loyola University Chicago School of Law. He currently lives in Chicago and is studying (hard) for his bar exam. And with any luck, he'll have passed the bar by the time you read this.

NOTES

NOTES

NOTES

NOTES

NOTES

NOTES

NOTES

NOTES

NOTES

NOTES

NOTES

Understanding the Test

About the LSAT
The best way to prepare for the LSAT is to know as much as possible about the exam. Below is some information to help you prepare.

What is the LSAT and how is it structured?
The Law School Admission Test (LSAT) is a four-hour exam given four times a year. It is comprised of five 35-minute test sections of approximately 25 questions each: Reading Comprehension (1 section), Analytical Reasoning (1 section), Logical Reasoning (2 sections), and an experimental section. You may take the LSAT no more than three times in any two-year span, and the scores remain on your record for five years. Most law schools average multiple LSAT scores, so you will want to get your best possible score the first time.

How is the LSAT scored?
Four of the five multiple-choice sections count towards your final LSAT score. Correct responses count equally, and unlike the SAT, no points are deducted for incorrect or blank responses. Test takers get a final scaled score between 120 and 180. The remaining multiple-choice section is an experimental section used solely to test new questions for future exams. You will not know which section is experimental when you are taking the LSAT. In addition, an essay is given at the end of the exam. This essay is not scored, and is rarely used to evaluate your candidacy by admissions officers.

How important are my LSAT scores?
LSAT scores vary in importance from school to school. However, competitive programs tend to weight your LSAT score more heavily. Be sure to contact the schools to which you are applying in order to determine their attitudes regarding LSAT scores.

How do I register for the LSAT?
This is the easy part, so don't put it off. You can register by mail, by phone, or on the Internet. To register by mail, you will need to request a copy of the Registration and Information Bulletin from Law Services or from your pre-law advisor. To avoid late fees, mail your registration form at least six weeks before the test. By registering early, you are more likely to be assigned your first-choice testing center.

Where can I get more information about the LSAT?
The Princeton Review
800-2Review | www.PrincetonReview.com

Law School Admission Council (LSAC)
215-968-1001 | www.lsac.org

Sample LSAT Questions

Are You Ready?
Try the sample test questions below and see how you do. If you have trouble, we can help. Just call 800-2Review or visit www.PrincetonReview.com.

Logical Reasoning (Arguments):

1. The only dogs in the kennel were retrievers, but they were small retrievers. So the only dogs in the kennel were small dogs.

   Which of the following employs flawed reasoning most similar to the flawed reasoning in the argument above?

   (A) The only flowers in the garden were roses, and they were all pink roses. So all the flowers in the garden were pink.
   (B) All the bushes in the garden were small. The only bushes in the garden were rose and holly. So all the rose bushes in the garden were small.
   (C) All the plants in the garden were flowers. The only flowers in the garden were tall flowers. Thus, the only plants in the garden were tall plants.
   (D) The only fruit tree in the garden was an apple tree, but the apples were not ripe. Thus, none of the fruit growing in the garden was ripe.
   (E) All the hedges in the garden have waxy leaves. All the hedges in the garden also have blue flowers. Thus, hedges with waxy leaves also have blue flowers.

2. Because anyone who opposes animal testing for cosmetics would not purchase this new long-lasting eyeliner, and because anyone who chooses to eat meat does not oppose animal testing for cosmetics, only someone who chooses to eat meat would have even a chance of purchasing this new long-lasting eyeliner.

   The reasoning in the argument is flawed because the argument overlooks the possibility that some people who:

   (A) choose to eat meat do not oppose animal testing for cosmetics.
   (B) choose to eat meat would not purchase this new long-lasting eyeliner.
   (C) do not oppose animal testing for cosmetics would not purchase this new long-lasting eyeliner.
   (D) do not oppose animal testing for cosmetics choose not to eat meat.
   (E) would not purchase this new long-lasting eyeliner choose not to eat meat.

Analytical Reasoning (Games):

Questions 3-4

The ground floor of a college dormitory building features five rooms—numbered 10 through 14 from north to south—side-by-side along a single hallway. The dormitory rooms will house seven participants in a summer band camp: four brass players and three woodwind players. Five of the participants are juniors and two are seniors. The participants must be housed according to the following rules:

No dormitory room contains more than two occupants.
No dormitory room contains both a brass player and a woodwind player.
No junior brass player is housed in a dormitory room immediately beside a dormitory room where a senior woodwind player is housed.

3. Which one of the following must be true?

   (A) At least one junior is housed alone in a room.
   (B) At least one senior is housed alone in a room.
   (C) At least one woodwind player is housed alone in a room.
   (D) At least one woodwind player is a senior.
   (E) At least one brass player is a senior.

4. If room 11 contains at least one junior brass player and room 13 contains two senior woodwind players, which one of the following could be true?

   (A) Room 12 houses two participants in the summer band camp.
   (B) Room 14 houses two participants in the summer band camp.
   (C) Room 10 houses a junior woodwind player.
   (D) Room 11 houses a junior woodwind player.
   (E) Room 14 houses a junior woodwind player.

Correct Answers: 1-c, 2-d, 3-c, 4-e

LSAT Strategies

Below you'll find some general test taking strategies that will help you tackle the LSAT.

Technique #1: Slow Down
Don't try to answer every question on the test. If that's your strategy, you probably won't be spending the amount of time necessary to answer the majority of those questions correctly—which afterall, is the goal! The questions and answers on the LSAT require that you read closely. You need to slow down and do fewer questions with greater accuracy.

Technique #2: Fill In Every Bubble
There is no penalty for guessing on the LSAT, so even if you don't read every question in a section, you'll want to make sure to fill in the rest of the bubbles before time is called. This is such a key concept that you should remember to do it while taking any practice tests, too.

Technique #3: Use the Process of Elimination
Remember, all of the correct answer choices will be in front of you. Naturally, they will be camouflaged by four incorrect answers, some of which will look just as good as, or better than, the credited responses. By using the Process of Elimination, you should look at the answer choices critically, with an eye toward trying to see what's wrong with them. You'll do better on almost any standardized test than if you're trying to find the right answer.

Technique #4: Your Will Is Made of Iron
You'll be nervous on test day, but a little nervousness is okay because it will keep you on your toes, so don't let this psych you out. Remember that when you go into a test, you'll have worked through lots of LSAT problems and you'll be more prepared than many other people in the room. Don't let anything get to you – stay focused on the task at hand.

Technique #5: Practice All the Time, on Real Stuff
Our LSAT courses will give you an abundance of practice materials, including full-length practice exams, recently released exams from LSAC, and explanations to every test question. Don't let more than one, or at most two, days pass without looking at LSAT problems. You'll be extremely prepared for the real LSAT by the time you finish our course, but make sure to keep practicing.

Technique #6: Keep Your Pencil Moving
Don't lose your concentration – if a question is giving you trouble, leave it and come back later if you have time. Don't sit there and obsess about one question if you get stuck – you'll waste valuable time you could've spent on answering three other questions correctly. Keep your pencil moving – mark up the test, cross out answer choices, circle the right answer, underline words in the passages, take notes, anything!

Your LSAT Score

LSAC is emphatic in its recommendation of how an LSAT score is to be interpreted: a score is not an individual number, but rather, it represents a "score band" of plus or minus three points from the reported score. Take a quick look at this table, which correlates percentile rank to scaled score. These numbers vary from year to year, but never by much.

There are two big messages here:

- **Understand** your score and the significance of point-increases as you prepare. For example, a five-point increase can mean a great deal, depending on what you started with.

- **Plan** to prepare for and take the LSAT once, to get your best score, and then get on with life.

Score	% Below	Score	% Below	Score	% Below	Score	% Below	Score	% Below
180	99.90%	168	97.00%	156	71.70%	144	25.50%	132	3.50%
179	99.90%	167	95.90%	155	67.10%	143	22.20%	131	2.90%
178	99.90%	166	94.80%	154	63.30%	142	19.60%	130	2.40%
177	99.90%	165	93.50%	153	59.30%	141	16.90%	129	1.80%
176	99.80%	164	91.90%	152	56.30%	140	14.60%	128	1.50%
175	99.70%	163	90.00%	151	50.00%	139	12.40%	127	1.20%
174	99.50%	162	88.20%	150	47.30%	138	10.60%	126	0.90%
173	99.30%	161	85.70%	149	42.20%	137	9.00%	125	0.80%
172	99.10%	160	83.70%	148	39.30%	136	7.50%	124	0.60%
171	98.70%	159	80.60%	147	35.60%	135	6.30%	123	0.50%
170	98.20%	158	77.40%	146	32.20%	134	5.40%	122	0.40%
169	97.50%	157	74.20%	145	28.40%	133	4.20%	121	0.30%
Mean: 149.9	Standard Deviation: 9.8								0.00%

Courtesy of LSDAS

Our Philosophy

You Are the Focus at The Princeton Review
Our LSAT test preparation programs guarantee results and are designed to accommodate your busy schedule. You decide when, how, and where to prepare.

Put Our Experience to Work for You
We know the test better than anyone else—perhaps even better than LSAC. Our strategies have helped thousands of students maximize their LSAT scores. We offer three test prep programs to help you conquer the LSAT.

ClassSize-8 Classroom Course
Ask anyone who's taken our course: our manuals are the best. They have it all. Plus, you'll take a series of full-length practice tests, so you can monitor your progress and get comfortable with the exam.

Online Courses
Prepare when and where you want with our online courses. Princeton Review *Online* gives you comprehensive, self-paced online test preparation, while *LiveOnline* provides you with the same prep tools, plus real-time instruction and workshops with an expert Princeton Review teacher.

1-2-1 Private Tutoring
If individual attention is what you need to get your best LSAT score, take advantage of The Princeton Review's most personalized, intensive test prep option. Work with a top-notch tutor who will break the material into manageable pieces, move at the optimal pace for you, and focus on areas where you need the most help.

Get the Score You Want
We guarantee you will be completely satisfied with your results. If you are not, we will work with you again at no additional fee for up to one full year. Our guarantee applies to all three of our programs: classroom courses, online courses, and private tutoring.*

*Guarantee applies to tutoring packages of 16 hours or more.

800-2Review | www.PrincetonReview.com

ClassSize-8 Course

Top of the Class
Our premium classroom instruction and powerful online lessons and drills will help you get your best score. Reap the benefits of integrated test prep—only at The Princeton Review.

Small Classes for Maximum Personal Attention
Why waste your time in an overcrowded classroom? At The Princeton Review, there are never more than eight students in an LSAT class. Whenever possible, we group students by ability to help you get the most out of your course. Simply put, personal attention in small classes yields the best results.

Expert Instructors
Our instructors have gone through intensive training to prepare you for the LSAT. They are test-taking experts and masters of Princeton Review LSAT strategy. Not surprisingly, the quality of our instructors is one of the top reasons students recommend our LSAT course to their friends.

Free Extra Help
The Princeton Review is dedicated to helping you achieve your best possible LSAT score. Your instructor is available outside of regularly scheduled class hours to provide extra help, free of charge. Anytime you have difficulty with a particular topic, you can meet with your instructor to work through it.

Online Resources Enhance Classroom Learning
The Princeton Review offers the only LSAT test preparation course with online lessons to support each class session. In our Online Student Center you will find endless ways to practice concepts learned in class, hone your skills in any particularly challenging areas, or prepare for an upcoming class. You will never run out of practice material with our 80 online LSAT modules.

Comprehensive, Up-to-Date Materials & Practice Tests
Our research and development experts work year-round to stay on top of LSAT trends: we make sure that you get the most effective practice and review materials available—all of which are yours to keep forever. You will receive: The Princeton Review's Big Book of LSATs, which contains copies of the 20 most recently released LSATs, a comprehensive course manual and workbook, and four full-length exams taken under actual testing conditions, with a detailed analysis of your performance on each one.

1-2-1 Private Tutoring

The Ultimate in Personalized Attention
There is no substitute for one-on-one instruction. Your *1-2-1* Private Tutoring Program will be customized to meet your individual needs.

Focused Instruction
Our intensive *1-2-1* Private Tutoring Program will focus exclusively on the areas that challenge you the most. There is no way to prepare more effectively for the LSAT. Your tutor will customize the program to ensure that you master each concept and achieve your best score.

Expert Tutors
Our outstanding tutoring staff is comprised of specially selected, rigorously trained LSAT instructors who have performed exceptionally in the classroom. They have scored in the top percentiles on standardized tests and received the highest student evaluations.

Schedules to Meet Your Needs
We know you are busy, and preparing for the LSAT is probably the last thing you want to do in your "spare" time. The Princeton Review *1-2-1* Private Tutoring Program will work around your schedule.

Supplementary Online Lessons and Resources
Your private LSAT instruction is supplemented by lessons in our Online Student Center. They are accessible 24 hours a day, 7 days a week.

Having difficulty juggling deadlines & applications?
The law school admissions process is intricate. Princeton Review *1-2-1* Admissions Consulting will help you choose the law school that is right for you, write admissions essays, update your resume, market yourself as a top candidate, and more.*

* Availability varies by location. Contact your local Princeton Review office regarding scheduling and pricing.

Online Courses

Exceptional Instruction at Your Fingertips
Our online LSAT courses offer the most effective online instruction available. Our lessons are engaging and interactive. You will never just scroll through text or watch video clips.

Online and LiveOnline Courses Tailored to You
Our online lessons adapt to your strengths and weaknesses, so you can make the most of the time that you spend preparing for the LSAT. Work at your own pace through more than 190 multimedia lessons and four diagnostic tests. The lessons are broken down into manageable units, so you can master one concept before moving on to the next. You will also get a set of printed course materials, so you can study even when you are away from a computer. Although the course is designed to take about six weeks to complete, you will have access to all online materials for four months.

The Practice You Need to Get the Scores You Want
The Princeton Review's online LSAT courses contain more practice material than you will probably ever need. But instead of overwhelming you with hours of work, your online course will help you prioritize by giving you practice exercises in the areas you need to focus on. You can even repeat exercises as many times as you want, until you are confident that you know the material.

You Are Never Alone
Questions? Answers are always at your fingertips. Our online courses are equipped with The Princeton Review Online Coach, a person who is available to answer your questions 24 hours a day, 7 days a week. You can also access our Frequently Asked Questions database and our online student discussion groups.

LiveOnline *Course*
Extra features - Our *LiveOnline* Course gives you all of the benefits of our *Online* Course, plus eight sessions that take place in real time over the Internet in a virtual classroom environment. In your workshop of no more than eight students, you can listen via live audio and ask questions as your instructor illustrates concepts using a virtual whiteboard. After class, you can have online discussions with fellow classmates or your instructor.

ExpressOnline *Course*
The Best in Quick Prep – Test date approaching? Looking for a few strategies to help you? The Princeton Review *ExpressOnline* Course is for you. Our multimedia lessons will walk you through basic test-taking strategies to give you the extra edge you need on test day.

The Princeton Review
www.PrincetonReview.com

The Princeton Review Admissions Services

At The Princeton Review, we genuinely care about your academic success, which involves much more than just the SATs and other standardized tests. Admissions Services' PrincetonReview.com is the best online resource available for finding, researching, applying to, and learning how to pay for the right school for you.

No matter what type of program you're applying to—undergrad, graduate, law, business, or medical—you'll find an entire center dedicated to it on PrincetonReview.com, with a main page that acts as a portal sending you directly to all the free information and services you need. When you register, you gain access to even more specific free services tailored to your profile.

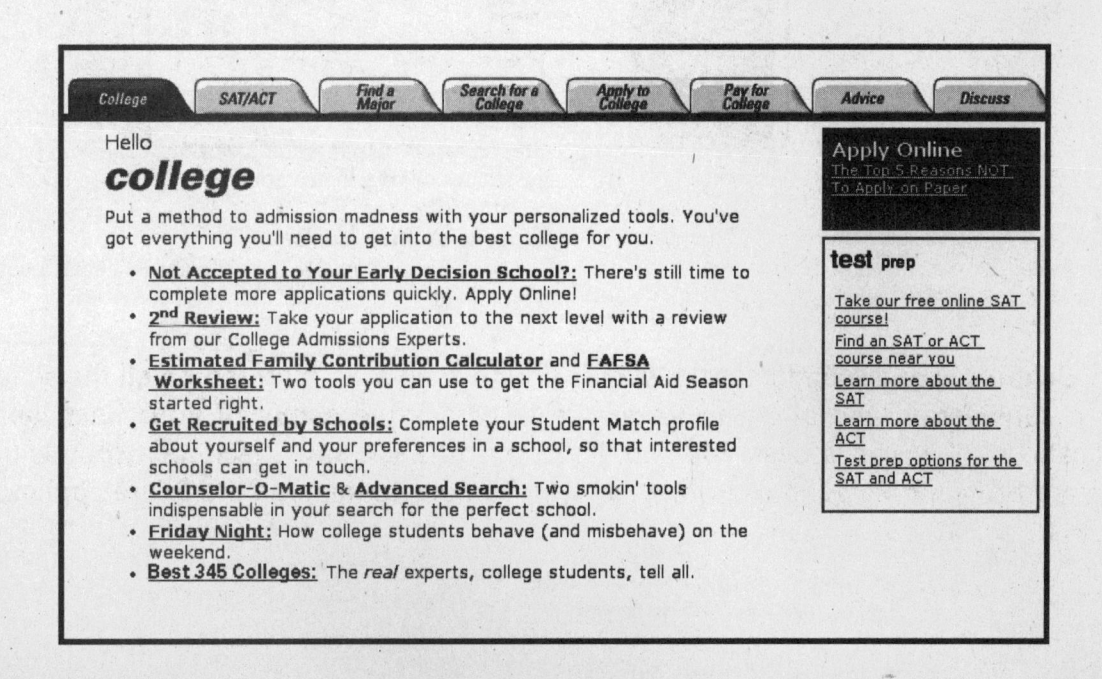

Tabs: College | SAT/ACT | Find a Major | Search for a College | Apply to College | Pay for College | Advice | Discuss

Hello

college

Put a method to admission madness with your personalized tools. You've got everything you'll need to get into the best college for you.

- **Not Accepted to Your Early Decision School?:** There's still time to complete more applications quickly. Apply Online!
- **2nd Review:** Take your application to the next level with a review from our College Admissions Experts.
- **Estimated Family Contribution Calculator** and **FAFSA Worksheet:** Two tools you can use to get the Financial Aid Season started right.
- **Get Recruited by Schools:** Complete your Student Match profile about yourself and your preferences in a school, so that interested schools can get in touch.
- **Counselor-O-Matic** & **Advanced Search:** Two smokin' tools indispensable in your search for the perfect school.
- **Friday Night:** How college students behave (and misbehave) on the weekend.
- **Best 345 Colleges:** The *real* experts, college students, tell all.

Apply Online
The Top 5 Reasons NOT To Apply on Paper

test prep
Take our free online SAT course!
Find an SAT or ACT course near you
Learn more about the SAT
Learn more about the ACT
Test prep options for the SAT and ACT

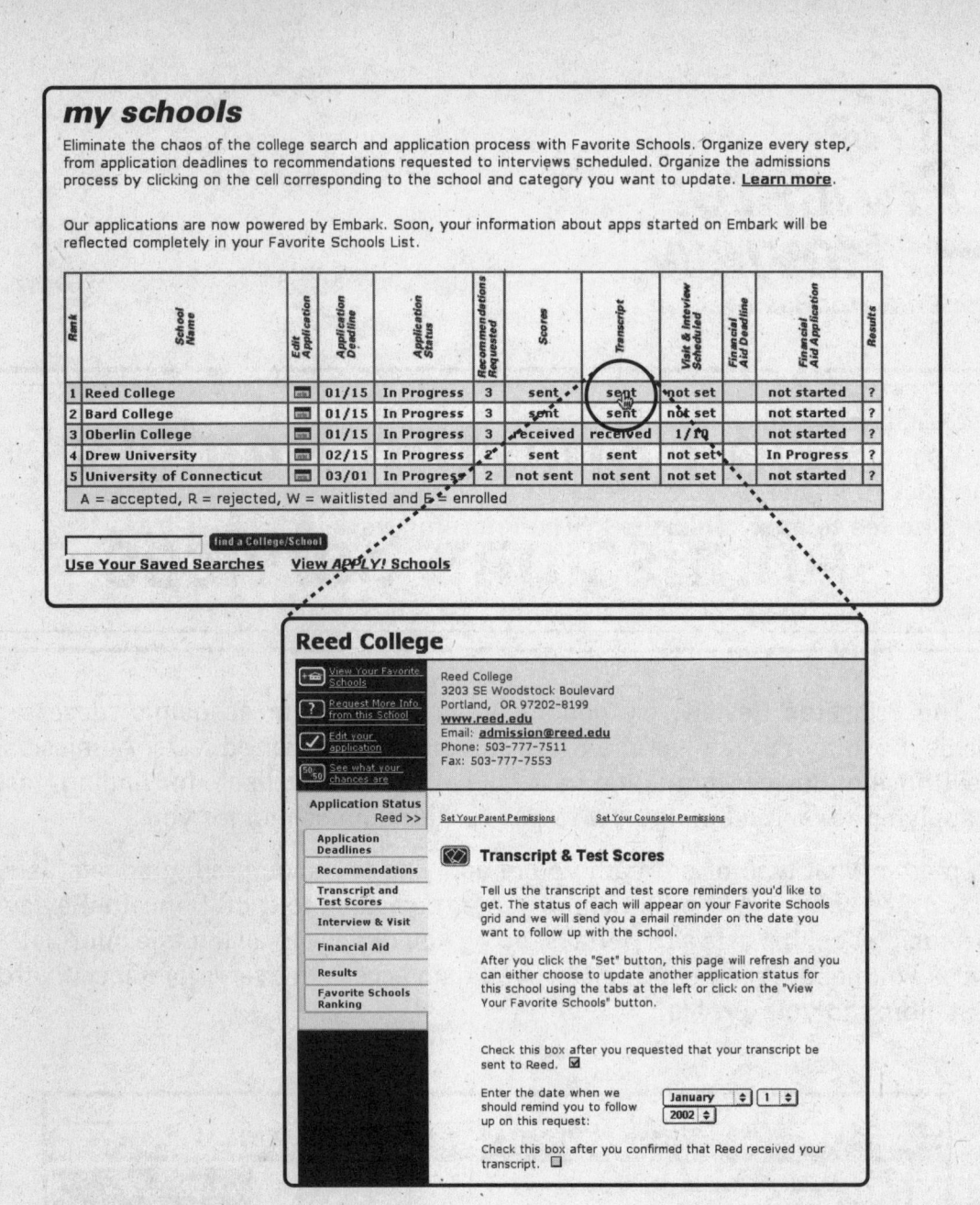

My Schools is one such feature. It allows you to keep a running tab on all the schools you're considering and applying to, as well as track the status of your financial aid applications. You can access your application and each saved school's profile page directly from your My Schools grid, which you can use to manage the entire application process.

ONLINE APPLICATIONS

Applying to college online is faster and easier! Just ask any of the 450,000 students entering college in the fall of 2002 who applied online using our Embark technology. Worried about how the schools you're applying to will feel about electronic applications? The apps that we have on our site are the genuine school applications—and we have more than 700 of them. Every line that you scrawl by hand on a paper application has to be hand-entered by someone at the school's admissions office anyway. Why not save yourself and the school some time and trouble by using the more efficient e-application? Just a few of the perks include not having to fill out basic information more than once for a whole set of applications, being able to stop and save your application at any time and come back to it later, and of course, no need for a postage stamp. **Did we mention that there's no fee to apply online with The Princeton Review? Yes, it's free.**

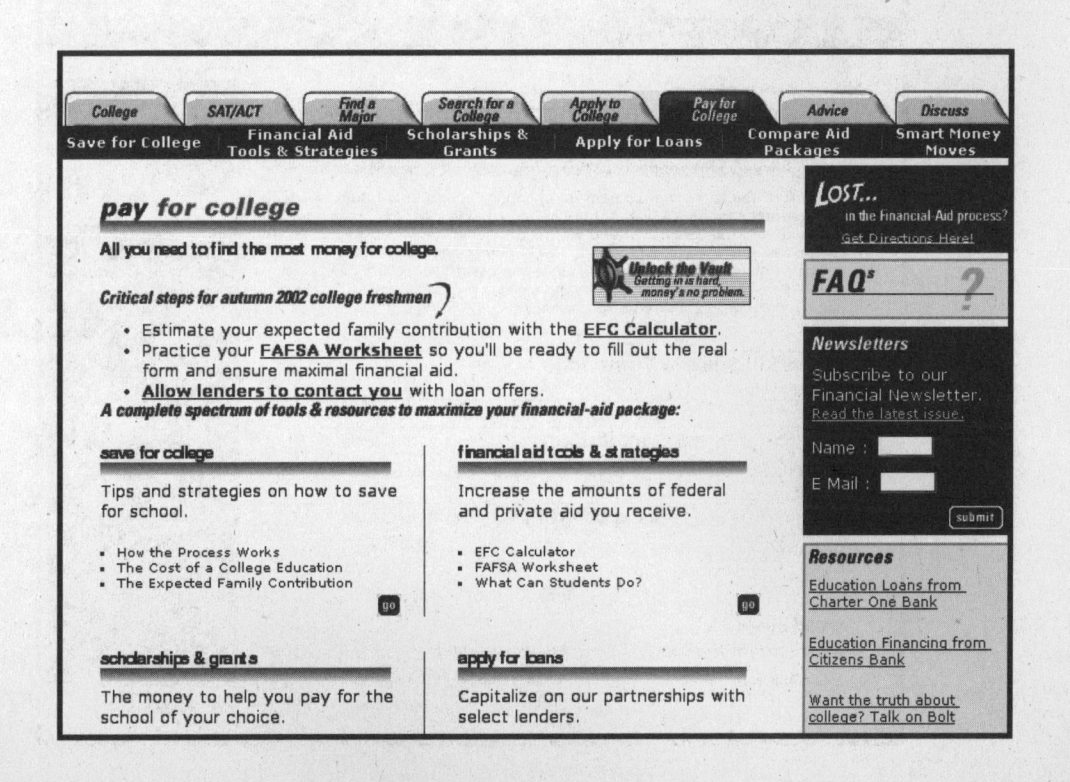

FINANCIAL CENTER

Our revamped Financial Center is a unique resource for parents and students alike. You'll find everything from helpful tips on saving money, tax forms, aid, loans, and scholarships to tools that allow you to compare aid packages and calculate your expected financial contribution. We'll also tell you things you didn't know and were afraid to ask about, such as credit cards, debt, and insurance. For those of you who are completely lost, we can show you the way: we have a straightforward financial timeline telling you exactly what to do and when to do it so you can get the maximum amount of aid.

Two outstanding financial tools you'll find on PrincetonReview.com are the EFC Calculator and the FAFSA Worksheet. **The Need Analysis/Expected Family Contribution Calculator** allows you to calculate your approximate Expected Family Contribution (EFC), which both colleges and the federal government use to determine what they think you and your family should be able to pay for a year's worth of higher education. This is an essential starting point for financial aid, as it helps you understand the federal methodology and gives you a ballpark figure with which you can start the financial aid process.

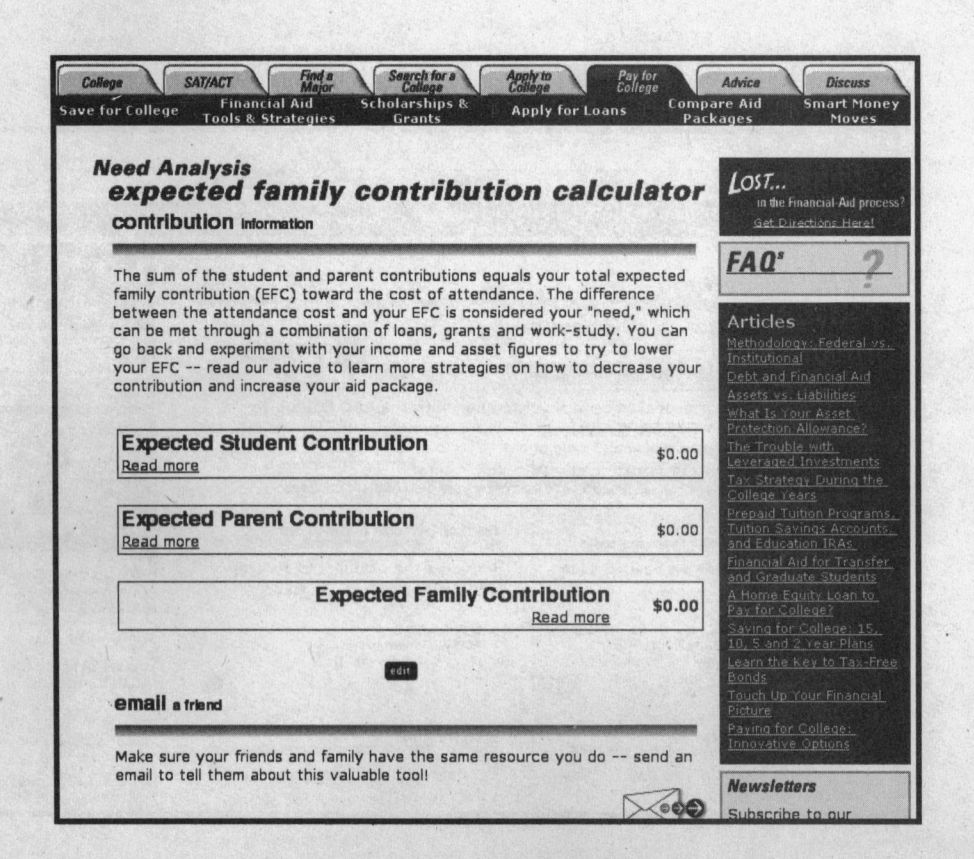

The FAFSA Worksheet is a virtual dress rehearsal for the official FAFSA form. You will *have* to complete the FAFSA if you want any federal financial aid at all. Each question on the worksheet has its own pop-up window with a detailed explanation and tips for entering the response that will benefit you the most.

Note: This worksheet has been known to radically reduce the likelihood that parents and students will suffer from the panic attacks and financial nightmares often attributed to filling out the FAFSA.

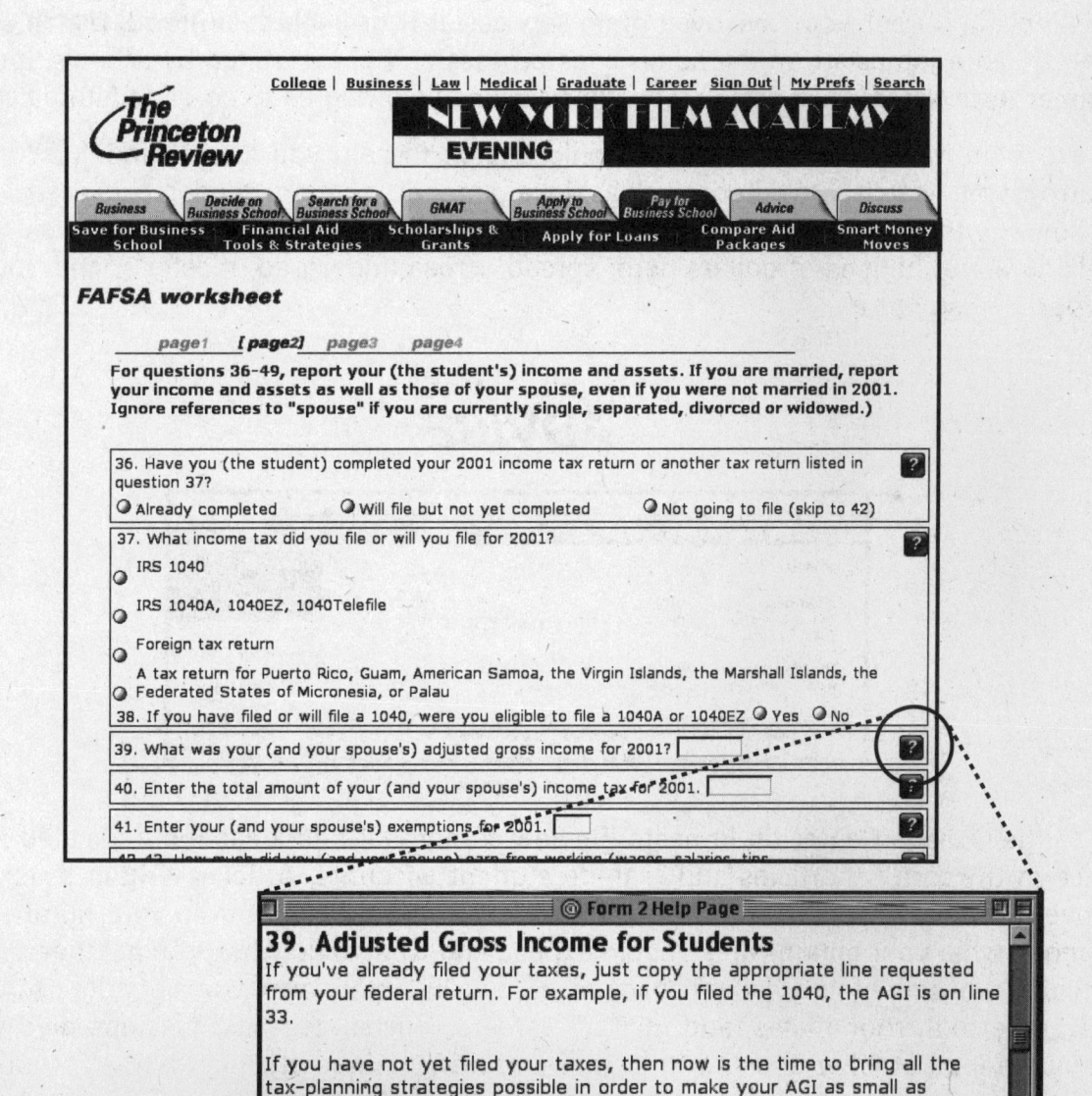

FAFSA worksheet

page1 **[page2]** page3 page4

For questions 36-49, report your (the student's) income and assets. If you are married, report your income and assets as well as those of your spouse, even if you were not married in 2001. Ignore references to "spouse" if you are currently single, separated, divorced or widowed.)

36. Have you (the student) completed your 2001 income tax return or another tax return listed in question 37?
   - Already completed
   - Will file but not yet completed
   - Not going to file (skip to 42)

37. What income tax did you file or will you file for 2001?
   - IRS 1040
   - IRS 1040A, 1040EZ, 1040Telefile
   - Foreign tax return
   - A tax return for Puerto Rico, Guam, American Samoa, the Virgin Islands, the Marshall Islands, the Federated States of Micronesia, or Palau

38. If you have filed or will file a 1040, were you eligible to file a 1040A or 1040EZ? ○ Yes ○ No

39. What was your (and your spouse's) adjusted gross income for 2001? [ ]

40. Enter the total amount of your (and your spouse's) income tax for 2001. [ ]

41. Enter your (and your spouse's) exemptions for 2001. [ ]

@ Form 2 Help Page

39. Adjusted Gross Income for Students

If you've already filed your taxes, just copy the appropriate line requested from your federal return. For example, if you filed the 1040, the AGI is on line 33.

If you have not yet filed your taxes, then now is the time to bring all the tax-planning strategies possible in order to make your AGI as small as possible. If you want to read up on this before you continue, read **A Step-by-Step Guide to the Federal Income Tax Form**. It offers valuable tax tips that can help you increase the amount of aid you can receive.

SEARCHABLE DATABASES

Visitors to PrincetonReview.com can take advantage of our wealth of data by searching for schools, majors, and careers. Each **Major's** profile provides information on curriculum, salaries, careers, and the appropriate high school preparation, as well as colleges that offer it. You can use the feature to search for hundreds of majors, browse an alphabetical list, or search by category. The same thing goes for searching for schools. Our undergrad database alone consists of nearly 2,000 schools, with hundreds more available in the two-year college and career and technical databases. You'll find a detailed profile on almost any school you can think of. **Advanced School Search** helps you find four-year schools based on cost, curriculum, student body, or other categories that might be of primary interest to you.

If you don't mind filling out a bit of information about yourself (don't worry—registration is simple and free), you have even more services at your fingertips: **School Match** allows you to get a jumpstart on the admissions process and get recruited by schools, and the **Career Assessment Quiz** gets you thinking beyond your degree to possible future careers.

We even have an excellent **Scholarship Search** to help you locate funding. You can narrow your search with criteria such as dollar amount, location, gender, club association, ethnicity, athletics, and talent and prospective prizes will appear before your eyes. We're talking about billions of dollars here, spread across undergrad, master's, and doctoral programs, so opt in.

ADVICE

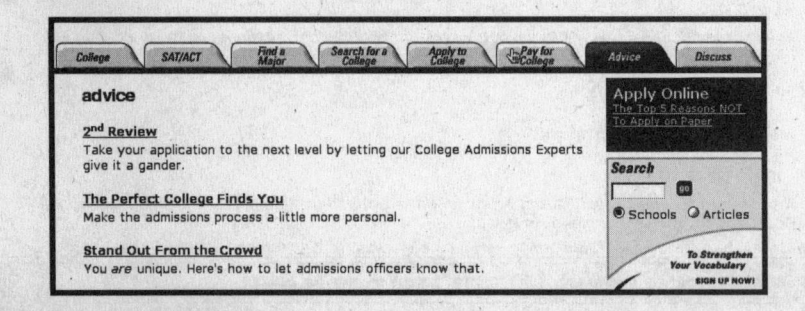

In the **College Center** on PrincetonReview.com you'll find a section dedicated to advice in the form of articles and real-life student accounts. Articles written by experts cover different aspects of each stage of the process: how to get in to your number-one school, what your options are, what to expect, and what to do when you get there. These include tips and info on visiting colleges, essays and interviews, types of admission (EA, ED, deferred), roommates, and military careers. Our student submissions give you a genuine look at what goes on in school and how various students manage work *and* play.

TUFTS UNIVERSITY

BENDETSON HALL, MEDFORD, MA 02155 • ADMISSIONS: 617-627-3170 • FAX: 617-627-3860

CAMPUS LIFE

Quality of Life Rating	87
Type of school	private
Affiliation	none
Environment	suburban

STUDENTS

Total undergrad enrollment	4,869
% male/female	47/53
% from out of state	77
% from public high school	60
% live on campus	80
% in (# of) fraternities	15 (10)
% in (# of) sororities	3 (3)
% African American	7
% Asian	14
% Caucasian	60
% Hispanic	7
% international	7

SURVEY SAYS...
Campus feels safe
Great library
Beautiful campus
Campus easy to get around
Great off-campus food
Student publications are ignored
(Almost) no one listens to college radio
Students are cliquish
(Almost) no one smokes

ACADEMICS

Academic Rating	89
Calendar	semester
Student/faculty ratio	9:1
Profs interesting rating	85
Profs accessible rating	96
% profs teaching UG courses	100
% classes taught by TAs	1
Avg lab size	10-19 students
Avg reg class size	10-19 students

MOST POPULAR MAJORS
international relations
biology
English

STUDENTS SPEAK OUT

Academics

Known for stealing the Ivy wait-list population, Tufts University offers rigorous academics that keep the school's hard-working, career-driven students on their toes. With its small class size, ample funding, and noteworthy professors, Tufts offers a wide variety of solid departments. Of particular renown is the international relations major, which draws in students from all over. Notes one student, "The best part of academics at Tufts are the small classes, the accessible faculty and staff, and the fact that NO classes are taught by TAs." Another opines, "Academically Tufts is impressive. The teachers are always available and ready to help, and if you look well, there are some really interesting classes: History of Reggae, Negotiation and Conflict Resolution, and Yoga." Requirements for first-year students are stiff, and some freshmen are hung up on "pointless requirements," but says one older and wiser student, "As an incoming freshman, it was good to have some idea of what to take. The advising program is excellent." Professors are highly regarded: reports one student, "My professors are incredible! From an astronomy professor who was late to class because he was rushing back from a NASA meeting in Houston to a political science professor who accidentally caught Justice Sandra Day O'Connor with food in her teeth, I have had fantastic and knowledgeable professors throughout my Tufts career. They're all open, honest, and enthusiastic educators with whom it is a pleasure to learn." Administrators "are great.... The president takes a very personal interest in the lives of the students. He is one of three professors leading a community dialogue/class on Leadership for Active Citizenship." On the downside, "Classrooms are ugly at best.... On the outside the buildings are pretty, but our lack of a large endowment has allowed many of them to become somewhat dilapidated on the inside."

Life

Tufts students describe an active campus life, one cram-packed with both class-related activities and extracurriculars. Writes one, "Even though most people are very focused on academics, most find plenty of time to be active in several of our 150-plus diverse activities. We have fantastic volunteer organizations, for example." Agrees another, "School spirit lies primarily in the 150 student activities groups. Within these groups, the most incredible bonds are formed. From the moment I arrived on campus, I joined everything! The daily newspaper, film series, debate team, tutoring, musical theater, etc. There's so much to do, my parents often question when I do my work." Students report that "everyone at this school is either dating someone here or someone at another school. This is far from a 'frat party and hook up' school." As for the Greeks, students explain that "although the fraternities and sororities make up only a fraction of the student body, they are pretty much the center of freshman life on campus. Once you become an upperclassman, though, you realize there is life beyond the Greek system." That life usually takes students into Boston, fortuitously "nearby to offer an outlet for students to live life. A lot of people go to Boston for fun, movies, dinner, and dance clubs." Then it's back to the beautiful campus, secluded in the suburban hills just a short commuter train ride away.

Student Body

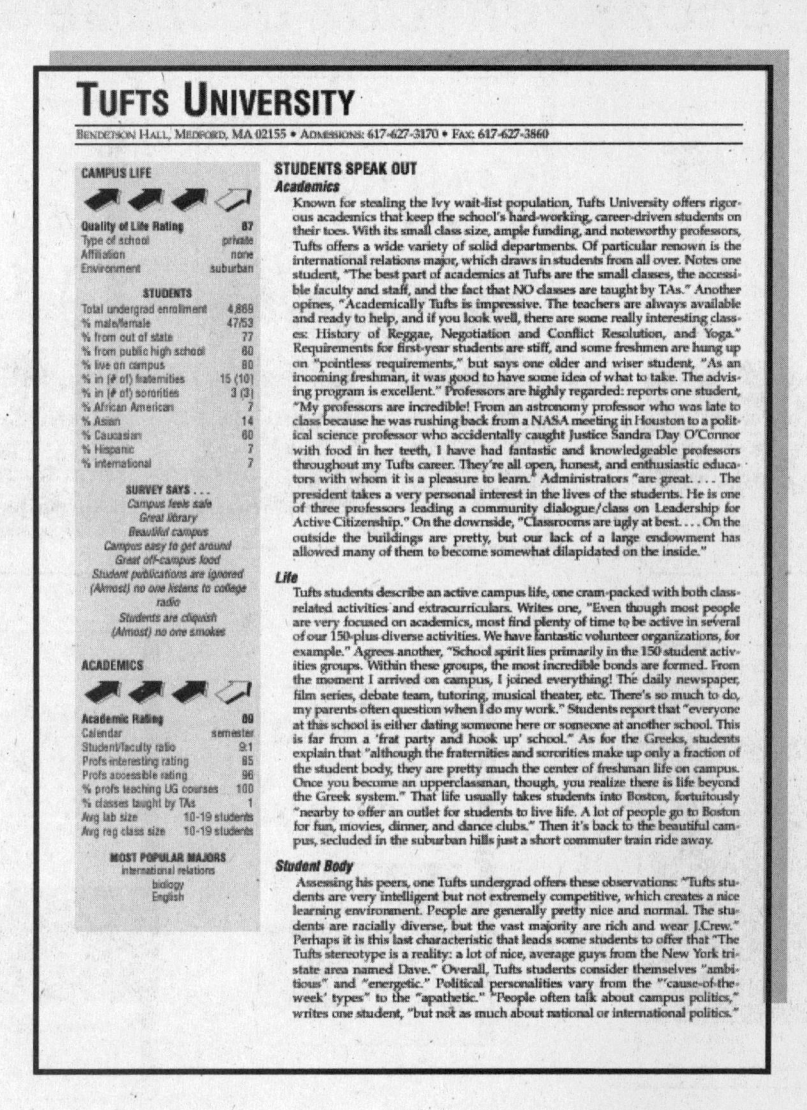

Assessing his peers, one Tufts undergrad offers these observations: "Tufts students are very intelligent but not extremely competitive, which creates a nice learning environment. People are generally pretty nice and normal. The students are racially diverse, but the vast majority are rich and wear J.Crew." Perhaps it is this last characteristic that leads some students to offer that "The Tufts stereotype is a reality: a lot of nice, average guys from the New York tri-state area named Dave." Overall, Tufts students consider themselves "ambitious" and "energetic." Political personalities vary from the "'cause-of-the-week' types" to the "apathetic." "People often talk about campus politics," writes one student, "but not as much about national or international politics."

BOOKS

Admissions Services publishes great data and advice books on undergrad, graduate, and professional schools, as well as careers. As the number-one student advocate in the business, we have the most updated student opinion data on colleges available. Just a few of the college titles we offer are *The Best 345 Colleges*, *The Complete Book of Colleges*, *The K&W Guide to Colleges for Students with Learning Disabilities or Attention Deficit Disorder*, *Visiting College Campuses*, *America's Elite Colleges*, *Paying for College Without Going Broke*, *The Scholarship Advisor*, *The Internship Bible*, and our brand new *Guide to College Majors*. For a complete listing of our available titles, check out our books page at *PrincetonReview.com/college* and click on Bookstore..

MORE BOOKS FOR YOUR COLLEGE SEARCH

Members SAVE More

Join the Student Advantage Membership® Program to save hundreds of dollars a year on food, clothing, travel and more! Members enjoy exclusive, on-going savings at more than 15,000 locations nationwide. Here are just a few:

The Princeton Review
$50 off any GMAT, LSAT, GRE or MCAT course

US AIRWAYS
Member-only discounts and bonus Dividend Miles®

BARNES & NOBLE.com
www.bn.com
Save an additional 5% on new and used textbooks

Liberty Mutual
Save up to $300 or more a year on auto insurance

Plus, receive the **Student Advantage Bonus Savings Book** with over $200 in additional savings from Art.com, Student Advantage Tech Store, Timberland® and more!

HOW TO JOIN...

Go to studentadvantage.com or call 1.877.2JOINSA and use promotion code TPR88P9002.
Get a 1-Year Membership for only $20*!

*Plus $2.50 shipping and handling. Student Advantage® is a registered trademark and product of Student Advantage, Inc.

MORE EXPERT ADVICE FROM THE PRINCETON REVIEW

If you want to give yourself the best chance for getting into the law school of your choice, we can help you get higher test scores, make the most informed choices, and make the most of your experience once you get there. We can also help you make the career move that will let you use your skills and education to their best advantage.

CRACKING THE LSAT
2003 EDITION
0-375-76251-5 $20.00

CRACKING THE LSAT WITH SAMPLE TESTS ON CD-ROM
2003 EDITION
0-375-76252-3 $34.95
MAC AND WINDOWS COMPATIBLE

COMPLETE BOOK OF LAW SCHOOLS
2003 EDITION
0-375-76271-X $22.00

PRE-LAW SCHOOL COMPANION
0-679-77372-X $15.00

LAW SCHOOL COMPANION
0-679-76150-0 $15.00

ALTERNATIVE CAREERS FOR LAWYERS
0-679-77870-5 $15.00

The Princeton Review

Available at Bookstores Everywhere.
www.review.com